D1154616

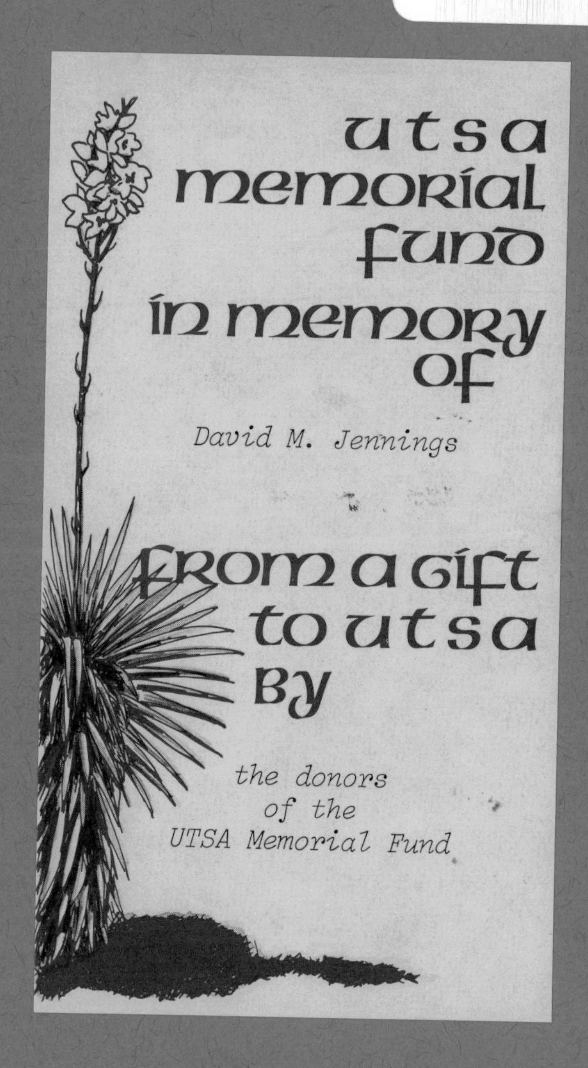
utsa
memorial
fund
in memory
of
David M. Jennings
from a gift
to utsa
by
the donors
of the
UTSA Memorial Fund

Corporations at the Crossroads: Governance and Reform

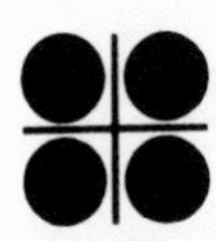

REGULATION OF AMERICAN
BUSINESS AND INDUSTRY SERIES

Goldschmid: Business Disclosure: Government's Need to Know

Edwards: Issues in Financial Regulation

Ginsburg & Abernathy: Government, Technology,
and the Future of the Automobile

DeMott: Corporations at the Crossroads: Governance and Reform

Corporations at the Crossroads: Governance and Reform

---

edited by

DEBORAH A. DeMOTT
Associate Professor, Duke University School of Law

McGRAW-HILL BOOK COMPANY
New York St. Louis San Francisco Auckland Bogotá Düsseldorf Johannesburg London Madrid Mexico Montreal New Delhi Panama Paris São Paulo Singapore Sydney Tokyo Toronto

Library of Congress Cataloging in Publication Data

Main entry under title:

Corporations at the crossroads.

(Regulation of American business and industry series)
Include bibliographical references and index.
1. Corporation law—United States—Addresses, essays, lectures. 2. Disclosure of information (Securities law)—United States—Addresses, essays, lectures. 3. Directors of corporations—Legal status, laws etc.—United States—Addresses, essays, lectures. I. DeMott, Deborah A. II. Series.
KF1414.A2C63 346'.73'066 80-18108

ISBN 0-07-016330-8

1234567890 DODO 7865432109

The editors for this book were Ellen M. Poler and Susan L. Schwartz, the designer was Elliot Epstein, and the production supervisor was Paul A. Malchow. It was set in Palatino by The Heffernan Press Inc.

It was printed and bound by R. R. Donnelly.

Contents

Foreword 1

Deborah A. DeMott

CHAPTER ONE
Thinking Straight About Corporate Law Reform 9

Bayless Manning

CHAPTER TWO
The Cost and Benefits of Government-Required Disclosure: SEC and FTC Requirements 37

AN APPRAISAL, 37
George J. Benston

ECONOMIC ANALYSIS AND ONE PHASE OF UTILITARIANISM, 70
Ted J. Fiflis

CHAPTER THREE
Using Disclosure to Activate the Board of Directors 109

Elliot J. Weiss
Donald E. Schwartz

CHAPTER FOUR
The Impact of the SEC on Corporate Governance 177

A. A. Sommer, Jr.

CHAPTER FIVE
The Role of Corporate Counsel 217

John C. Taylor III

CHAPTER SIX
Federal Corporate Law, Federalism, and the Federal Courts 237

Gordon G. Young

CHAPTER SEVEN
Reweaving the Corporate Veil: Management Structure and the Control of Corporate Information 279

Deborah A. DeMott

CHAPTER EIGHT
Corporate Response to a New Environment 325

THE ENVIRONMENT AND THE DEVELOPMENT OF POLICY
Wm. van Dusen Wishard, 325

ANOTHER VEIW
Richard W. Duesenberg, 351

Index 377

Foreword

Deborah A. DeMott*

Corporations, like death and taxes, may be inevitable incidents in American economic life. Equally as inevitable are periodic efforts to reform corporations in a variety of ways, efforts which have often influenced laws regulating corporate behavior. The focus of the energies of many contemporary reformers of corporations—corporate internal governance structures and decision-making processes—represents the latest phase in a lengthy critical tradition.

In the past fifty years, several distinct patterns of inquiry have been pursued by corporate reformers. One such line of analysis began with Berle's and Means' demonstration that ultimate legal ownership was separate from effective control in large publicly held corporations.[1] Finally persuaded that corporate owners were content to leave managing to professional managers, this school of criticism advocated increased disclosure about corporations to public investors as a means of enhancing the capacity of market mechanisms to check management behavior.

Section 14(a) of the Securities Exchange Act of 1934 also responded to the separation of ownership from control by attempting to create working shareholder democracies—or, at the least, voting republics—through a system of federal proxy regulation. Its underlying theory

* My tasks in editing this book were substantially eased by the capable assistance of Joan M. Ashley. Some of the essays in this book appeared, in different form, in the Summer 1977 issue of *Law and Contemporary Problems*—a journal published by the Duke University School of Law—for which I was special editor. Andrew M. Berlin and J. David Velleman, former senior editorial assistants to the journal, helped with the editing chores in that issue.

1. A. Berle and G. Means, *The Modern Corporation and Private Property* (1932).

postulated that shareholders would be better able to call a corporation's managers to account if they were given certain pieces of information about the corporation's business. In addition, shareholders should know the consequences of decisions which state corporation law requires them to make. These reformers eventually acquired their own critics and skeptics who, asserting the didactic power of economic analysis, analyze the purported benefits of disclosure, quantify its costs, and examine the relevance of the information disclosed to the decisions made by shareholders and investors, or prospective shareholders.

Wholly apart from efforts to increase the accountability of corporate managers through the flow of corporate information to the market and shareholders, much attention has been given to the proper relationship between federal and state regulation of internal corporate decisions. Some critics of corporate theory have been troubled by the conflict in both tone and substance between the constraints imposed on internal corporate functions by state corporation laws and those imposed by the federal securities laws. Outright federal incorporation or minimum federal requirements for state regulation of corporate behavior have been suggested as solutions to this untidy conflict as well as to the substantive deficiencies of promanagement state incorporation laws, perceived by many as insufficiently protective of various shareholder concerns. These proposals pose significant questions about their implications for concerns tangential to federalism, for they challenge the traditional allocation to the states of regulation of internal corporate matters. Indeed, some argue that these proposals are solutions in search of problems, that state corporation laws afford adequate protection to legitimate shareholder interests, and that there have been intimations on the state-court level of a renaissance in the enforcement of managers' fiduciary duties toward the corporation and its minority shareholders.

A separate school of academic criticism has examined the impact of corporate decisions on interests outside the corporation. Its initial concern was whether or not corporations have a duty to behave in socially responsible ways even if that behavior could not be justified as increasing the corporation's profitability. In addition, formal representation within the corporation of constituencies affected by its decisions—labor unions, consumers, environmentalists, racial minorities—was advocated as a means of sensitizing the corporation to the societal implications of its activity. More recently, the focus of this criticism has shifted to an examination of corporations' internal structures and decision-making processes and to an argument that the present internal structures of corporations increase the likelihood of harmful corporate behavior. Related in interest, perhaps, if not in ideology, are those critics who examine and criticize corporations' internal structures with an eye to their effectiveness in controlling management behavior.

The essays in this volume address various aspects of the present legal concern with internal corporate governance. The remainder of this foreword addresses some general issues raised by the corporate governance controversy and summarizes the contribution of each of the essays, describing the points of disagreement among the contributors.

GOVERNING CORPORATE GOVERNANCE

Contemporary concern with internal corporate governance, as Bayless Manning well describes it in his essay, is based upon the notion that corporate management ought to be accountable—to someone or something—external to itself. The popularity of this notion likely explains the growth of interest in the corporation's own governing structure, in how decisions are made within the corporation and in whether the capacity exists to monitor the decision-makers. In theory, of course, this capacity resides in the corporation's board of directors, by law assigned ultimate responsibility for the corporation's activities, but in practice the board's review of operating management may be a ritual without much real content. Further, to some extent the disquiet surrounding corporate governance represents concern about the ends served by private economic power, well beyond any argument that the definition of those ends ought not to be within the unreviewed discretion of corporate management.

Within the general goal of management accountability are subsumed a number of different reasons for attention to corporate governance. If a corporation's management is left wholly to its own devices, unreviewed and unmonitored, it may operate the corporation's business in an inefficient and eventually unprofitable fashion. Further, the opportunity to manage corporate assets in an unreviewable fashion may give rise to a temptation to use them for noncorporate ends, toward the financial aggrandizement of individual managers. Afflicting decisions made by an unaccountable management is the danger that they will be made in a shortsighted and insufficiently deliberate manner and will carry the risk that the world external to the corporation may respond to them in ways unanticipated by the managers.

Public concern with internal corporate governance was piqued by the revelations of the mid-1970's that many American corporations had made secret, and in some instances illegal, payments to candidates for American political office and to representatives—in various capacities—of foreign governments. That the great majority of these payments apparently went undetected by corporations' outside auditors itself cast doubts on the adequacy of the controls and checks on corporate managers, and caused the payments to assume a significance well beyond their lack of economic materiality to the overall size of the corporations' operations. For the sensitive payments incidents made internal corporate governance a topic with political content, and provided the impetus for additional legal regulation of governance procedures. In addition, the consciousness of corporate managers may have been raised—

perhaps permanently, perhaps only fleetingly—to confront the import of public perceptions of the ethical propriety of corporate behavior.

The present legal response to reformers' interest in corporate governance falls into three basic patterns. The first, *increased attention to the composition and operation of corporations' boards of directors*, is reflected in rules and pronouncements of the Securities and Exchange Commission (SEC),[2] in rules of the New York Stock Exchange,[3] and in new provisions in some states' corporation statutes.[4] Increasing the proportion of independent directors on corporations' boards has been forcefully advocated, along with urging greater vigilance by those serving on boards against management abuses. Larger roles for the boards' independent audit and nominating committees have also been proposed. To believe that this pattern of reform will, by itself, accomplish much of merit requires some confidence in the inherent strength of the institutions themselves,—the independent director and board committee—in light of the fallibility of persons who have held comparable positions in the past. Moreover, some of the appeal of these proposals for corporate boards may reside in their apparently self-executing quality as reforms, in the hope that once such devices are put in place, further external intervention in the corporation will be unnecessary. Thus, as instruments of corporate reform or regulation, internal structural changes may be less intrusive than some other alternatives.

The second basic pattern of legal formulations of efforts to improve corporate governance consists of *mandated disclosure of information* about governance-related issues, such as management compensation, the composition and procedures of the board of directors, and the specifics of director selection and resignation. Although disclosing this kind of information may have some impact on the choices made by shareholders and directors, it may serve the additional function of affecting management behavior directly, since managers may find it preferable to eliminate or avoid some practices rather than disclose their existence. This phenomenon makes it difficult to assess the usefulness of the information disclosed, or of the disclosure requirement, to investors and shareholders, because the disclosure mandate produces, along with additional information, the possibility of an aversive change in management behavior. Indeed, if disclosure requirements are effective in reforming corporate governance, their effect may depend as much on the aversive change of practices by management as on the response of shareholders and the market to the information. It is also unclear whether the potential effectiveness of disclosure can be undercut by

---

2. See, e.g., the description in Sommer's article, Chapter 4, *infra*.

3. See, e.g., NYSE Company Manual at p. B.-23 (rule adopted July 16, 1956, requiring outside board members as a condition of new listing).

4. An example is Conn. Gen. Stat. § 33–318(b) (Supp. 1979), requiring specified corporations to have a board audit committee with at least one independent director as a member.

information overload phenomena—by the sheer glut of information made public as a result of legal mandates.

In contrast to these two basic patterns of legal responses to corporate governance, the third pattern of responses specifically identifies the worst potential problems in governance and directly requires *changes in corporate practices.* The most prominent current example, the Foreign Corrupt Practices Act, criminalizes making payments to some officials of foreign governments, for purposes specified in the Act. Further, the Act identifies the lack of adequate internal corporate accounting controls as an especially troublesome obstacle to improving corporate governance and, in an attempt to avoid additional sensitive payments incidents, mandates the development of such controls. It is simply too early to determine the effectiveness of this particular statute, either in eliminating sensitive payments or in improving the general quality of corporate governance.

One difficulty in assessing and then comparing the potential effectiveness of each of those basic patterns of reform is that the real world in which they must be tested, unlike the world of academic theory, is never without a variety of complicating factors that affect the evaluation of legal measures. Thus, to those accustomed to more rigorous—and abstract—analysis, the examination of changes in corporate governance necessarily has a relatively nebulous quality.

CONTRIBUTIONS TO THIS VOLUME

The essays in this volume discuss the virtues and limitations of each of these patterns in the reform of corporate governance and present varying perspectives on related questions about today's legal regulation of corporations. Of course, the strength of such a symposium format is that it affords broad coverage of an area, including the presentation of the inevitable conflicts among the contributors' opinions.

The first essay, "Thinking Straight About Corporate Law Reform" by Bayless Manning, is a description of the widely divergent ends sought by those who advocate corporate reform. These range from simply reducing the potency of private economic power through additional direct government regulation, to adding regulation of specific aspects of corporate behavior that may have adverse societal consequences, to protecting small business enterprises from depredation by large corporations, to improving corporations' treatment of their present and prospective shareholders. Other ends sought are the achievement of more uniformity in the requirements of corporation statutes than occurs at present in state laws, the expansion of the number of constituencies given formal representation on corporations' boards of directors, and the assurance of the accountability of corporate managers. In Manning's view, whatever the inherent merits of these proposals may be, relatively few of them are pertinent to the proper scope of corporate law. He defines that scope as "the internal governing machinery of the incorporated enterprise" and, consequently, concludes that the goals of purported corporate reform ought to be similarly delimited to focus on the process of internal corporate governance.

Two contributions are concerned primarily with reforms centered on the corporation's board of directors, my own essay "Reweaving the Corporate Veil," and that of A. A. Sommer, Jr., "The Impact of the SEC on Corporate Governance." Sommer examines the role of the SEC in reforming corporate governance through defining more deliberately the role of the corporate director. This definition of the director's role has been pursued by the Commission in a variety of ways: through public exhortations to directors to be more vigilant in their stewardship, through settlements in litigation brought by the SEC which change the composition of the defendant's board, and through statements of corporate disclosure obligations which highlight the functions of directors and their independence from the corporation's managers. Further, the Commission urged corporations that had made sensitive or illegal payments to undertake an internal investigation and make public disclosure of the results.

However, any lasting success of the Commission's efforts in changing governance practices and thereby reforming corporate behavior depends, in large part, on the effectiveness of corporate directors. My own essay explores whether it is realistic to assume that independent directors on a corporation's board will, by virtue solely of their independence, necessarily be successful in monitoring the behavior of corporate managers so as to discern inefficient or improper practices. It examines the lack of success of the Emergency Loan Guarantee Board, created to monitor the management of the Lockheed Corporation after it received federal loan guarantees in 1971, in detecting the corporation's extensive involvement in sensitive payments. Further, based on corporations' own reports describing the internal processes which entangled them in sensitive foreign payments and illegal domestic political contributions, there is a description of how corporations make decisions which are internally perceived to be questionable. The essay concludes that one ought not to accept it on faith that corporate reform will be accomplished solely through exhortations to independent directors to be vigilant monitors of management.

Three of the contributions are concerned with the usefulness of mandated corporate disclosure of information. Elliott J. Weiss and Donald E. Schwartz argue in their essay, "Using Disclosure to Activate the Board of Directors," that increasing the required disclosure of information about corporate boards could be a useful vehicle in spurring corporate directors to perform better and encouraging boards to operate more effectively. Weiss's and Schwartz's advocacy is directed toward the SEC in its capacity to make rules governing corporate solicitation of proxies from shareholders; they contrast the SEC's latest revision of its proxy rules with their own proposal for additional disclosure of information about the background and compensation of individual nominees for directorships, about nominating procedures, about the board's organization and the flow of information to its members, about the level of staff assistance to the board, and about the reasons for directors' resignations. Weiss and Schwartz maintain that requiring disclosure of this information would assist investors and shareholders in making decisions and that it would provide occasions for corporations to review the composition and operation of their boards of directors.

Almost completely to the contrary are the assumptions and conclusions of George Benston's article, "An Appraisal," in the chapter, "Costs and Benefits of Government-Required Disclosure." Benston, after comparing the asserted benefits of disclosure required by the SEC and the FTC's line-of-business report program with the various costs of generating and disclosing the information, finds insufficient benefit to justify the costs thereby imposed. Consequently, Benston's approach suggests a posture of skepticism toward increasing required disclosures in the fashion advocated by Weiss and Schwartz, for if these additional disclosure requirements are comparable to present ones, Benston's studies predict, their net benefits will at best be unprepossessing.

However, aspects of Benston's methodology and assumptions are challenged by Ted J. Fiflis in "Economic Analysis as One Phase of Utilitarianism." Fiflis argues that, although Benston contributes much to a clearheaded analysis of disclosure policy, he overstates the costs and understates the benefits of the disclosure statutes administered by the SEC, and relies upon a number of faulty premises. Further, according to Fiflis, the model of economic analysis used by Benston to evaluate the SEC's disclosure efforts is simply too narrow in the universe it reflects. Instead, a broader utilitarian analysis should be used, one that takes into account, among other factors, the effect of disclosure requirements upon society's ability to operate in a perceptibly fair manner.

Discontent with current governance arrangements is reflected as well in proposals that the present pattern of state corporation statutes should be altered through the enactment of federal minimum standards or a federal incorporation statute. Gordon G. Young's essay, "Federal Corporate Law, Federalism, and the Federal Courts," after describing a series of such proposals, analyzes and compares their consequences for the allocation of corporate litigation between the federal and state court systems. Young points out a series of such consequences—for judicial efficiency, for uniformity in statutory interpretation, and ultimately for federalism—not heretofore addressed in the literature.

If corporations' governance structures are substantially altered, no matter what the origin of the changes, the role to be played by corporate counsel needs careful thought, such as that given by John C. Taylor III in his essay, "The Role of Corporate Counsel." If counsel's ultimate responsibility is to the corporation's board of directors, but counsel's primary function is giving advice to members of operating management, maintaining the complete confidence of operating management may be difficult. Taylor considers several different occasions when the task of counseling management or directors is likely to be troublesome.

Perhaps each era's proposals for corporate reform are characteristic of its other social preoccupations. The final two essays in the book examine, from sharply different perspectives, the fit between changes in the legal regulation of corporations and the continuing evolution of American society. William Van Dusen Wishard, in his article in the chapter "Corporate Response to a New Environment," sees substantial shifts in corporate social awareness and concern for human needs as a result of major changes in Americans' attitudes toward the proper functions and the legitimacy of private economic power. Richard Duesenberg, in "Another View" in the same chapter, reviews the philosophical assumptions of the changes in attitude Wishard observes, and argues instead for a perspective based on the enduring tenets of individual self-definition and enterprise.

If any one view emerges from the contents of this book, it is that the present nature of legal regulation of corporations is open to substantial reconsideration and revision. The current temper in reform strategies focuses upon the corporation's internal governance structure as the most likely vehicle for accomplishing changes in corporate behavior. Even if these strategies are overoptimistic in their prediction of prompt success, their implications are too substantial to be ignored.

CHAPTER ONE

Thinking Straight about Corporate Law Reform

Bayless Manning, *Partner, Paul, Weiss, Rifkind, Wharton and Garrison*

"Corporation" has been an inflammatory word in American political history for more than a century. Recently, the embers of controversy about corporations have again been fanned by a number of highly publicized scandals and by calls from a variety of quarters for a new round of corporate law reform. Some strident voices charge that the American corporation and American corporation law are in a condition of crisis that must promptly be met by major changes in the present system of corporate governance and by new state and federal regulation or federal chartering.

The high noise level of these criticisms attracts public attention. But serious discussion of these matters calls for more than noise. We need to identify accurately what it is about existing corporation law that needs reforming, why it needs reform, what reform would best respond to the supposed need, what are the best instruments for achieving the allegedly needed reform, and what would be the costs and negative side effects of such reform. Ultimately, rational public policy debate demands that participants talk about one thing at a time and that if *A* and *B* are different, they not be treated as though they were the same. Those principles are not being followed in today's corporate law reform, as appears in the course of this article. Although I have, along the way, interjected some personal views on some of the issues discussed here, it is not my primary purpose to convert the reader to my own opinions. My hope is to help sort out the complex issues of corporate law reform and contribute analytically to the process of thinking straight about them.

SOME PRELIMINARY COMMENTS ABOUT CORPORATIONS AND CHARTERS

There are a number of reasons why corporations are a natural, even inevitable, source of public irritation and tempting targets for the attention-seeking politician and journalist. The most fundamental reason contains something of a paradox. Precisely because America's corporations have proven to be a remarkably effective social adaptation, we look to them to perform many of the most basic economic functions of the society; and because those functions have generally been well carried out, the American public has very high expectations of performance. As a result, almost any unwelcome economic development or unpleasant business encounter experienced by John Q. Citizen—a rise in insurance rates, a decline in employment, an interruption of electricity, a late aircraft arrival, a malfunctioning appliance, a disappointing wage level, a bankruptcy of a small business, poor service in a hotel—is likely to be laid at the door of some corporation, or "the corporations." Business executives sometimes complain that they are not properly appreciated by the public for the contribution which their companies make to the commonweal; those executives just do not understand that the basic reason the corporations get blamed so much is that they do so much.

A second major contributor to the public's attitudes toward corporations is, simply, ignorance of economic affairs. The nation's educational system does an appallingly poor job of teaching how the nation's economy operates, what business enterprises do, how they do it, what they provide, how they are funded, what their return is, how the return is distributed, and so forth. Unlike the unavoidable factor mentioned first, the lack of public understanding of this field could be, and should be, mitigated by better educational programs.

These two factors, compounded by the sheer economic size and visibility of some enterprises, provide an environment of public attitude that is predisposed against the large enterprise. Against that background, and actively aggravating the situation, is the undeniable fact that business executives as a class are probably about as good and as bad as other classes of human beings and that despite the impressive accomplishments of American corporations and their managers, their history is marred by isolated but regrettably numerous instances of actual fraud, deception, economic bullying, bribery, theft, disregard for employees, personal aggrandizement, distribution of dangerous products, and—the most frequent sin—arrogance and shortsightedness. Whenever such reprehensible conduct is brought to light, it is seen by the public through the magnifying glass of the public's generalized negative attitude toward "the corporations," and a new wave of reform is born.

I have noticed, however, that public attitudes toward the subject of corporations are frequently tinctured by deep-seated suspicions that are unrelated to the actual conduct of business enterprises. Those apprehensions flow from certain vague images of corporations that are, in turn, rooted in conceptual misunderstanding and echoes of medieval history. In the hope of clearing the air of these ghosts, I would like to commence with some rudimentary observations about corporateness and about corporate charters.

Corporations and Corporateness

A corporation is an organizational form. It is a particular legal way of organizing an ongoing operation, as a partnership is a particular legal way of doing so. What incorporation of an enterprise amounts to in substance is that a piece of paper conforming to the corporation act of some state is put on file with the designated state official, certain persons are designated as the board of directors, and if it is a commercial enterprise, certain persons hold an investment interest in the enterprise of a type that is legally designated "shares." Strictly speaking, a corporation is not an economic enterprise; it is a form in which some enterprise is organized. Large enterprises (such as a large auto manufacturer), medium-sized enterprises (such as a fabricator with a single plant hiring 200 employees), and small enterprises (such as a two-man barber shop or even a single practicing physician) that differ in all other respects may have one feature in common: each may be a corporation.[1]

Indeed, the term "corporation" is even more generic than would appear from the last paragraph. All the enterprises instanced there were commercial. But charitable foundations, churches, cemetery associations, consumers' and producers' cooperatives are also usually cast in corporate form. Furthermore, the term "corporation" is not limited to the private sector. Municipalities are corporations; public-private hybrids like Comsat and the Federal National Mortgage Association (Fannie Mae) are incorporated; public enterprises, such as the Tennessee Valley Authority and the Panama Canal Company, are corporations; and even international organizations of sovereign nation-states, like the World Bank, may be incorporated.

From being told that an object is a cube, one can infer nothing about its size, weight, color, smell, or value; from being told that an enterprise is a corporation, one can infer nothing about its scale, character, bargaining power, strategic importance, functioning, or value. Thus, to

---

1. In fact, only a few incorporated enterprises are large. For example, in Connecticut, which in this respect is typical of other states, there were on June 30, 1976, approximately 43,254 domestic corporations active in the state and 6,600 foreign corporations authorized to do business there. As of September 30, 1976, only 221 of these 50,000 companies, or less than one-half of 1 percent, were large enough to be required to file regular reports with the SEC. Telephone conversation with John T. Maloney, Director, Corporations Division, Secretary of the State's Office, Hartford, Connecticut (Dec. 9, 1977).

inveigh against or applaud "corporations" without specifying particular enterprises, or at a minimum a class of enterprises sharing common substantive attributes, is simply to make noise. Most commentators who polemicize against, and politicians who run against, "corporations" have in mind not corporations at all but a particular handful of large-scale commercial enterprises. It may be that the business conduct of some enterprises should be subjected to additional regulation, but it is not because they are corporations. Correspondingly, if one's purpose is to modify the conduct of those enterprises, amendment of state corporation laws, which are of general applicability to all commercial incorporated enterprises, will certainly be misdirected.

The flow of lucid discourse about incorporated enterprises is further muddied by public misunderstanding of the nineteenth-century statement of legal doctrine that a corporation is a "person" or, what is worse, a "fictitious person." The public has always felt, or been taught to feel, that there is something inherently unnatural, spooky, and Frankensteinian about the notion of a fictitious person—to suspect that it is some kind of gimmick by which shady incorporated slickers mulct honest unincorporated yeomen. Well, there have been plenty of thieves and crooks in business enterprises through the ages; but neither their crookedness nor their predatory successes were attributable to the fact that the corporation is said at law to be a fictitious person. To say that a corporation is a fictitious person means nothing more or less than that it is convenient for some purposes to treat the multiplicity of interests in the enterprise as a collectivity—as a single entity. As a matter of legal history, the corporation came to be viewed as a person as soon as the law recognized that "it" could hold title to property and could sue and be sued. The law does the same thing when it groups together millions of people east of the mouth of the Hudson River as a collective entity, New York City, for such indispensable activities as issuing bonds, entering contracts, bringing law suits, and electing officials. New York City is a necessary collective political and legal abstraction of eight million human beings. In the same way, a commercial corporation is a collective legal abstraction grouping together a variety of economic interests in an economic enterprise.[2]

A decision to treat a collectivity of interests as a unit is a matter of administrative convenience and nothing else. Thus, for example, one may view our present corporate tax system as good, bad, or indifferent, but it is meretricious to defend it by arguing that the corporation should

---

2. Readers with a taste for history will be interested to note that the progenitor of the legal concept of the modern corporation was the municipal corporation. The major contributions that the concept of corporateness brought to the law were that title to property held by a collectivity such as the City of London could be continued in spite of the mortality of individual Londoners and mayors and that institutional decisional machinery could be regularized on an ongoing basis in law.

pay a tax because it is a person and equally meretricious to attack it by arguing that the corporation should not have to pay a tax because it is only a fictitious person.

In sum, a corporation is simply an organizational form, a legal carapace that surrounds infinite varieties of enterprises and institutions. That generalized organizational form—not the conduct of the varieties of enterprises that adopt it—is the subject of our corporation laws.

Charters and Chartering

In the long-ago of French and English history, charters for enterprises were granted by monarchs, just as were feudal tenures, titles, and land patents. Such corporate charters often granted economic monopoly rights, either in a line of enterprise or in a geographic area, and vested limited semigovernmental powers in the corporation. From the perspective of the Crown, the technique of royal incorporation was a logical and generally successful adaptation: others invested capital in the enterprise, others invested their energy and careers, others shouldered burdensome administrative chores in remote climes, the nation's commerce and industry were advanced—and the Crown shared in the returns. Necessarily, each charter was hand tailored and unique, especially insofar as it granted monopoly powers. Equally necessarily, the number of such charters was very small.

In the newborn United States of America, it might have been argued with historical consistency that the former charter-granting powers of the Crown were inherently vested in the executive branch of government. But it seems not to have been so argued, and the nation embarked at once upon a system under which corporate charters were granted by state legislatures. This system did not work very well. It soon became evident that legislative bodies were not well equipped to negotiate or draft corporate charters and to enact what were, in effect, private bills. It was inevitable that, in time, special pressures, favoritism, and even overt bribery would be brought to bear on legislators by persons seeking corporate charters—and they were.

But something else more basic and important also occurred. In the burgeoning commerce of the new republic, and especially as the Industrial Revolution came alive, a substantive change occurred in the objectives of those who were seeking charters. The entrepreneur who wanted to build a new toll bridge had to have the permission of the state, and to make the enterprise feasible, he had to have a monopoly for some distance up and down the river; such an entrepreneur needed a charter of the old style, handcrafted to provide that monopoly. The same thing was true, to a slightly lesser extent, of the railroad line. But if the contemplated industrial enterprise was to be a soap factory or a shipyard or a spinning mill, then none of the elements of monopoly or of semigovernmental function was required. With increasing frequency, those who wanted corporate charters simply intended to enter a competitive business arena. They wanted the charter as an administrative mechanism to enable them to attract capital, to provide for continuity of the enterprise, to provide a machinery for decision-making, and (later on) to limit the economic exposure of those who invested their capital as shareholders, as (in a different way) the exposure of those who invested their capital as creditors was limited.

The resultant of these two forces was predictable and constituted sound public policy. It became a key feature of post-Jacksonian populist reform to slay the dragon of legislative favoritism by making corporate charters available to anyone who asked for them. It had become possible to shift to such a generalized system because corporate charters were no longer linked to monopoly grants. The basis was thus laid for the general corporation acts that were swiftly and widely adopted by state legislatures throughout the country beginning in the 1840's. Thereafter responsibility for granting charters (or articles, or certificates, of incorporation, as they came to be called) was transferred from the legislative branch to an administrative officer of the state. It was his or her duty to issue articles of incorporation to any person who requested them and complied with simple prerequisites set forth in the state's general corporation act.

It is simply demagogy for anyone today to proclaim with an air of indignant discovery that state corporation laws do not regulate the economic conduct of enterprises and are easy to comply with. Our corporation acts were expressly designed over a century ago—as the product of a wave of corporate law reform—to make available to everyone the administrative convenience of the corporate form.

In the usual case today, anyone who obtains a certificate of incorporation simply proceeds to go into business. A few lines of economic activity, however, such as public utilities and banks, have long been carved out of the general field of competitive enterprise and brought under direct regulatory control by the government as business affected by the public interest. Analytically, two avenues of organization are possible for a company in a regulated industry. The first route, the old-fashioned way, is to proceed by special charter. In Connecticut, for example, it has remained customary to create new insurance companies through a special statutory chartering process. The alternative for corporate formation in a regulated industry is illustrated by the airlines industry: one may incorporate an airline company in any state under a general corporation act, but the enterprise will not be permitted to enter into the interstate airline business until approval and route awards have been granted by the Civil Aeronautics Board.

The avenue of the special charter is clumsy. It requires a separate procedural framework for each industry and compels the legislature to perform a function that is better performed by an administrative agency. The second approach is more functional, as it leaves to the general corporation act the routine formalities of formation and procedure while remitting to a specialized regulatory agency the substantive regulation appropriate to the industry in question.

It has taken a long time—and is still taking time—for the function of general corporation acts to be widely understood. It is almost enough to make one believe in the existence of a continuing cultural memory to note how readily critics of corporate behavior revert to ancient thought patterns and call for the sovereign to grant corporate charters that will include the special regulations that the reformer holds dear. Advocates of that approach never make clear why such regulations must be built into that vestigial medieval document, the charter. The reasons, I fear, are subconsciously grounded in atavistic images of the corporation as a person, born from the forehead of the sovereign, an invisible, immortal, and dangerous creature—but one that can be genetically restrained by programming it with special DNA instructions at the moment of its birth. Such metaphorical thinking has nothing to commend it.

Congress and state legislatures have commonly imposed curbs on the conduct of incorporated enterprises through general legislation rather than through charter provisions. For generations, administrative agencies have regulated monopoly industries effectively without resort to the antiquarian process of corporate chartering. Meanwhile a century and a half of experience has gone into developing our sophisticated general corporation acts in the states to supersede the machinery of special-charter incorporation. Whether society should impose additional substantive restraints, federal or state, on the behavior of large-scale enterprises is an important subject for public debate; but that debate is simply obscured by introducing the extraneous topic of charters, and, further, in most instances the debate has nothing to do with the subject matter of corporation laws.

SPECIES OF CORPORATE LAW REFORM

As we leave these preliminary observations and turn to the task of sorting out the shotgun charges against modern American corporation law, the key question to ask any reform advocate is: Precisely what is it about today's corporations or corporation law that seems to you so antisocial, dangerous, or unjust? As one reviews the body of published criticism of the modern corporation with this question in mind, no less than nine separate answers, or species of answers, can be identified. The balance of this article is devoted to a review of these nine species. Perhaps there are even more than nine, but nine is quite enough to demonstrate that the complaints about modern large-scale enterprise are not integrated but disparate—are not cumulative but discrete. Scattershot solutions will therefore not do. Each species of criticism must be examined and weighed separately, must stand or fall on its own merits, and if proven must be addressed by remedies hand-tailored to the particular purpose.

Corporate Reform Species I

To one group of critics of large corporate enterprises it seems fundamentally immoral and unwise to permit private-sector companies and those who manage them to make basic decisions about economic production, resource allocation, and investment that are of great importance to everyone in the society. In this view of the matter, the social importance of these financial and economic decisions is so great that they ought to be made by government rather than by private institutions responding to market forces.

The viewpoint of group I critics, of course, represents a fundamental challenge to the basic concept of a free-market economy. If one assumes the validity of this position, what kind of political and legal changes are called for? Obviously, the answer would be that the nation needs some kind of national planning agency; new governmental machinery to mandate price controls, rationing, and ordering of capital investments; and some degree of nationalization. In the light of the experience of dozens of countries over the last fifty years, I find it hard to believe that such a program would inspire much enthusiasm in the United States. But for present purposes the point is that this species of complaints about corporations, and their putative answers, have nothing to do with the field of corporation law. It is an absolute non sequitur to contend that the management of large corporations should not be able to decide whether to reduce steel production and therefore what is needed is federal chartering or reform of state corporation laws. Free-market economy versus socialism is a valid, debatable issue, but it is a wholly independent question that should not be smuggled in under the guise of discussion about corporate reform.

Corporate Reform Species II

In the view of reform advocates of species II, large business enterprises ("the corporations") are inherently rich, immoral, ruthless, and continually engaged in greedy depredations upon the public, such as polluting the environment, cheating consumers, or oversugaring the breakfast cereal. In this perspective, big oil companies invented the energy crisis in order to raise their prices, and increases in interest rates, insurance premiums, and utility bills are attributable to the avarice of banks, insurance companies, and utility companies. It is characteristic of this species to view profit as plunder. Supply and demand are little understood by these critics, and the function of capital investment even less understood. Notably, too, the corporation is not perceived as a collective institution through which revenues are distributed among multiple claimants but as an anthropomorphic creature that grows fat by accumulating profits and wealth for "itself."

As species I is populated by socialists, so species II is the home of the native American populist. He would not eliminate corporations because he sees them as productively efficient, but he believes they are infinitely rich and infinitely malevolent and if left alone in the dark will steal the pennies from the church poor box.

If one holds these views, what direction should one choose for corporate reform? The allegedly deplorable moral character of large enterprises cannot be remedied by tinkering with their internal organization or state corporation laws. What is obviously needed is taxation and economic regulation, more taxation and economic regulation, and still more taxation and economic regulation. In addition, a recurrent impulse is to invoke direct control of pricing, though our experience with that device has hardly been satisfactory. Species II reformers will be found in the forefront of almost any proposal to regulate or tax business enterprises.

Corporate Reform Species III

Members of species III hold a generally high regard for the economic contribution made by American corporate enterprises and a free market, but they nonetheless believe that society must, on an issue-by-issue basis, step in to control particular aspects of corporate conduct and to set the ground rules within which all business enterprises are required to operate. Hardly anyone, I suppose, disagrees with that proposition so generally stated. As new problems arise or are newly perceived in public debate, however, those who belong to species III divide on the question whether new regulation is needed and if so, what kind. When a sufficiently strong case is made to convince a large segment of species III that new substantive controls on business are needed, they join species I and II critics—who are ever ready to increase controls—and another block of restrictive legislation is added to the pile accumulated over the last century.

The 1970's have been a period of intense activity for corporate reform of the species III variety. The nation learned the words ''environment'' and ''ecology'' and a large share of the responsibility for environmental degradation was attributed to large-scale enterprises. Organizations championing the small consumer came to the fore. The flotsam and jetsam that floated to the surface following the sinking of Mr. Nixon included evidence of illegal corporate political contributions on a substantial scale. The Arab oil embargo temporarily dislocated the United States economy and many found it strange that thereafter the profits of some U.S. oil companies rose, even temporarily. Numbers of U.S. enterprises were found to have made questionable payments overseas, and in a few instances, to have bribed foreign officials. The consequence of these events has been a wave of new substantive restraints on enterprises, some enacted by the Congress and state legislatures and others sketched freehand by the courts at the behest of an aggressive bar and self-designated public-interest law firms acting on behalf of real or constructive clients. Federal and state administrative agencies have vied with the legislatures and courts in adding new constraints upon the conduct of commercial enterprises and in requiring increasingly detailed public disclosure of facts and figures about them. The Internal Revenue Service has joined in, using its own special dentist's tools to extract information. Almost without knowing it, we have for some years been living through a period of major corporate reform. Future historians are likely to see the 1970's as ranking in importance with the reform waves that occurred in the first and third decades of this century. Where abuses of corporate conduct have been found, our public institutions have reacted so that such misconduct will not recur or will, at least, be extremely risky for those who perpetrate it.

It may be hoped—though in this I am not wholly optimistic—that the nation's corporate managers and directors will have learned from the experience of recent years that in the long view reprehensible business conduct can only arouse the latent antibusiness animus that is harbored by so many journalists, academics, legislators, and general citizens. If that lesson is not learned, the nation's enterprises will certainly experience a continuing pile-on of government regulations, mandates, and constraints. The ultimate danger is, of course, that at some point the patient will not be able to survive the therapies. At some point, the internal efficiency and flexibility that have made American enterprises such a successful institutional adaptation can be diluted or burdened to a degree where they can no longer function effectively.[3] At that point, the real victims will be not the corporations but the economy of the United States, our citizenry that relies upon that economy, and the interdependent economies of other nations.[4]

---

3. For example, is it clear that American companies operating overseas, already subject to stringent U.S. antitrust and tax laws, will not be put under further competitive disadvantage by new extraterritorial U.S. prohibitions of "expediting payments"? There can be no argument in favor of bribing governmental officials at home or abroad; it is illegal everywhere in the world and cannot be condoned. But expediting payments are endemic to the commercial life of many societies around the world in which U.S. companies must compete against local concerns and large non-U.S. transnational companies. If the Congress and the American people wish to embark upon another campaign of world improvement—a kind of commercial Wilsonianism—that is undoubtedly admirable and one may hope for some success; but it is troubling, and characteristic, that in the debate that attended the enactment of the Foreign Corrupt Practices Act of 1977, Pub. L. No. 95-213 (1977), there was little evidence that the Congress or the public was sensitive to the fact that a balance must be struck between the desire for a better world and the necessity to live in this one. It has also not been an edifying sight to observe the relish with which some American politicians and polemicists have pilloried U.S. business executives whose villainy was that they operated overseas on the principle, When in Rome . . . .

4. In another article, the author has explored this concern in the broader context of the general state of regulation in modern American society. Manning, "Hyperlexis, Our National Disease," 71 Nw. L. Rev. 767 (1977).

The immediate point at hand, however, is that the concerns of corporate critics of the third species relate to substantive behavior of enterprises. Where antisocial behavior is found, the society's response should be to strengthen and rigorously enforce particular substantive laws forbidding it. If one wishes, one may call that social response a variety of corporate reform, but it does not relate to corporation laws or to corporate charters.[5]

Corporate Reform Species IV

As a fourth group of reform-minded critics sees it, large-scale enterprises are monopolists that squeeze out competition and devour small enterprises. This attitude has appealed to Americans for a long time. Out of it have come the Sherman and Clayton Acts and a continuing contest between the major political parties for the honor of being more antitrust. The ideal of the small businessman has a deep-seated attraction that has led to special protective laws like the Robinson-Patman Act and agencies like the Small Business Administration.

It is a fair topic for debate whether existing state and federal antitrust laws are too stringent or not stringent enough and whether they are properly targeted and adequately clear. But there is no real argument about the process through which legislatures and courts should deal with these problems; setting the ground rules for competition is simply one instance of the sort of public policy issues discussed in reference to species III above. The solution to problems of unfair competition does not lie in amendment of corporation laws, and it would not increase the effectiveness of the Sherman Act to require it to be recited in certificates of incorporation.

Corporate Reform Species V

A fifth group of critics of modern American large-scale enterprises are primarily concerned about a completely different group of people: corporate investors. Today's American investorate can hardly be equated with the idle rich. Tens of millions of persons are direct holders of stocks and bonds in this country and perhaps as much as 80 per cent of the adult population are indirect holders or beneficiaries of such investment interests through pension funds, insurance policies, trusts, and mutual funds. In a market economy, the decision whether or not to invest in an enterprise lies with the investor. But in order for him to be able to make decisions intelligently and to invest on a fair and equitable basis, the marketplace must be free and relevant information must be available. Species V critics feel that we have not gone far enough in our

---

5. This point is a bit overstated here for simplicity, and should be read in the context of the discussion on pp. 33–34 *infra*.

securities laws, our accounting rules, our disclosure practices, or our legal doctrines to achieve those conditions.

No informed person would argue that our state and federal securities laws and regulations are at a point of perfection or that modern accounting practices cannot be improved. An atypical fraud like Equity Funding occasionally goes too long before detection; more frequently important information is disclosed to the marketplace later than it ought to have been. These are among proper subjects for attention.

But the fact is that beginning especially with the Securities Acts revisions of 1964 our securities laws have been experiencing continuous and rapid development. Although recent Supreme Court decisions have reflected second thoughts about the virtually unlimited scope of rule 10b-5 liability implied by earlier lower-court decisions, the rate of change in the securities field as a whole has accelerated of late as the SEC has aggressively pressed forward on the issues of competitive commissions rates for brokerage firms, creation of a national securities market, and additional disclosure requirements for reporting companies. At least equally rapid changes have overtaken, or been imposed upon, accounting practices during this period through the work of the Financial Accounting Standards Board, the SEC, and less directly, the courts.

There has been no failure on the part of public agencies to call large incorporated enterprises to task where circumstances indicate that more stringent guidelines should be laid down to protect investors. The existing regulatory system is evolving and responding effectively to new needs as they are perceived. There is every reason to believe it will continue to do so. It is simply not supportable to contend that the deficiencies which group V critics believe they see constitute a crisis that calls for radical reform.

Corporate Reform Species VI

In 1932 it was proclaimed in print (and it apparently came as a shock to academic circles at the time, though it is difficult to reconstruct why) that corporate managements have more to do with corporate business decisions than shareholders and that shareholders usually vote overwhelmingly in favor of management's recommendations.[6] Ever since then, a group of corporate critics—species VI—have been volubly pressing for more participation by common shareholders in corporate affairs, more "shareholder democracy." The concern of these critics is not investors as a whole; it is the subclass of investors who hold common stock.

The shareholder democrats have won some battles over the years. Proxy statements have expanded, even exploded, in size and detail. The

---

6. See A. Berle and G. Means, *The Modern Corporation and Private Property* (rev. ed. 1968).

range of permissible shareholder initiatives for shareholder votes has expanded substantially. The popularity of classified boards of directors has declined and cumulative voting is more widely available. Shareholders today often vote on the choice of company auditors. But what advocates of shareholder democracy have been least successful in doing is arousing the interest of shareholders in their cause. It turns out that shareholders in major enterprises do not buy shares in order to play town-meeting games or in order to give vent to their managerial impulses or to voice their political preferences. They buy their shares as an economic investment; they hold them as long as they continue to believe that the investment is promising, and during that period they are quite willing to follow the leadership of the company management; if they become disenchanted with the prospects of the investment, they sell their shares as rapidly as they can.

Intellectual cousins of the critics discussed later as species VIII, proponents of shareholder democracy adopt as a premise, tacit or express, that a large commercial enterprise is, or ought to be, essentially the same as a political institution. They also adopt two other minor premises: the first is that the only legitimate basis for institutional decision-making is the one-person-one-vote, majoritarian town-meeting model; the second is that the only proper constituency for participating in their imagined corporate town meeting are the persons who hold certificates representing that particular form of investment called common stock. (Members of species VI also run this second principle backwards, asserting that any investment interest that is called common stock should in the nature of things have a voting franchise and therefore nonvoting common stock is immoral.) In this view of the world, common shareholders should have a larger hand in running the affairs of major enterprises, and corporate reform should be pursued in the direction of more shareholder plebiscites, more information distributed to shareholders, and the like—a pattern of reform that is wholly distinct from those described earlier.

As appears later, I believe the axioms of group VI to be unsound, but for present purposes two other observations are more important. The first observation is that as we come to the criticisms of species VI, we are at least getting closer to the subject matter of corporation laws—the internal governing machinery of the incorporated enterprise. The second observation is that not even the most perfervid shareholder democrat would claim that these issues of shareholder participation constitute a national crisis or even make up a significant fraction of the public policy issues that relate to large-scale business enterprises. The American public as a whole has never heard of these questions, and at least 95 percent of those who hold shares in large companies—those who are supposed by the shareholder democrats to be the victims of disenfranchisement—consistently use the franchise they have to vote in favor of management, their supposed depredators. In such circumstances it is difficult to argue that sweeping reform of the existing corporate legal system is called for on the grounds urged by critics of species VI.

Corporate Reform Species VII

Whereas Berle and Means saw the mass of shareholders as victims whose franchise had been usurped, some reform-minded critics of today see the major problem of corporation law as the need to protect minority shareholders from bullying by the majority. As the shareholder democrats of species VI extoll the virtues of majoritarianism, the voices of species VII plead the civil-liberties case of minoritarianism, arguing for the inviolable rights of the individual shareholder, even where all the others have voted against him.

A sophisticated spokesman for this general viewpoint is former SEC Chairman, now professor, William Cary. His arresting phrase "race to the bottom"[7] expresses his concern that each state legislature (especially Delaware's), eager to attract new incorporations in order to collect franchise taxes, is moved to set lower and lower standards of protection for minority shareholders. He feels that the only way to halt this alleged race of permissiveness is to enact a federal statute superseding state laws to set minimum procedural requirements for large enterprises in order to protect shareholders, especially minority shareholders. He does not specify what procedural provisions should be included in such a statute, though he suggests a few as candidates.

Professor Cary has a second criticism of things as they are. He believes that the Delaware courts—the locus of so much important corporate litigation—are insufficiently sensitive to the claims of minority shareholders and insufficiently stringent in setting fiduciary standards for majority shareholders and for corporate directors and managers. Here again, he believes the state courts are engaged in a race of permissiveness. He concludes that a federal minimum-standards law is needed to set a high nationwide fiduciary standard for corporate insiders. He does not say what kinds of provisions he would suggest to achieve this purpose. Concerned about the litigation load that such a federal statute would dump on the federal courts, he suggests tentatively that litigation under the new statute be left with the state courts with certiorari jurisdiction in the Supreme Court to settle conflicting interpretations.

Perhaps Professor Cary in a fundamental sense will prove to be right. In the matter of corporate financial disclosure history affords us one striking instance in which state legislatures failed to act in part because no single state could impose substantially more stringent requirements than others; ultimately the SEC had to be created by the Congress to

---

7. Cary, "Federalism and Corporate Law: Reflections Upon Delaware," 83 Yale L.J. 663, 666 (1974).

raise the national water table of corporate disclosure. Moreover, I think it is probable that regardless of ideological preferences the necessities of an integrated national economy will increasingly induce the federal government to intervene to achieve national uniformity of standards in manufacturing and commerce. Thanks to the wisdom of the Founding Fathers, the United States has avoided Balkanization through internal tariffs, and the problem of conflicting taxes has at least been mitigated. But it is quite likely that we are entering a new era in which the Supreme Court will be called upon repeatedly to invoke federal preemptive power to knock down variations of substantive economic regulation imposed by fifty states in favor of uniform national standards.

Corporate managers will be among those who will most urgently need uniform standards to enable them to produce goods and market them. A day is dawning when the nation's business lobbies will appear in Washington to argue for aggressive federal regulation to preempt the field and relieve them of the impossibility of complying with a multiplicity of state regulations. Similarly, federal legislation on environmental issues offers an example of national standard setting to prevent competing states from using lax codes in an attempt to attract industry.

But despite these generalizations about the changing course of our federal system, it is questionable whether Professor Cary has made out his particular case. To pursue the matter in detail would require another article. But it is interesting to note that none of the provisions he suggests as candidates for inclusion in a federal statute on minimum corporate procedural standards is based on actual instances of corporate misfortune. The nation's antitrust laws, our blue-sky laws, and the Securities Acts of 1933 and 1934 were born out of bitter experience and actual injury. But when one turns to questions of internal corporate procedure, the entire conversation must be conducted in terms of "ought." There is nothing in the sky that informs us that 66⅔ percent is a good number while 51 percent is a bad number for purposes of shareholder voting on mergers. No commentator or scholar ever attempts to establish, nor could it be established, that a higher numerical vote requirement would save incorporated enterprises from unwise mergers (whatever that might mean), even if one were to assume that the prevention of unwise economic transactions is a proper legislative function. Similarly, it cannot be shown empirically that nonvoting common stock is vicious and should be forbidden, while nonvoting (or voting) preferred stock and nonvoting (or voting?) debentures are moral and favored by public policy; to my eye, and that of the marketplace, all three are simply investment variants, useful in appropriate situations. The same is in general true of the other procedural propositions suggested by Professor Cary for inclusion in a federal minimum-standards statute. They proceed from an a priori political image of what the decision-making process of an incorporated macroenterprise "ought" to be. Such oughts (which are based mainly upon the historically familiar[8] plus a classic and healthy American sympathy for the outnumbered) provide material for debates among professionals but do not make a compelling case for a real-world crisis calling for radical reform.

Further, there is considerable doubt about the basic assertion that state legislatures are engaged in a race of permissiveness to attract incorporations. The most recent major corporate law revision in the United States was made by California in 1975. The California legislature did not adopt the Delaware statute, did not strive to outdo Delaware in permissiveness, and in fact increased the level of regulation in some respects. Similarly, the successive modifications of the Model Corporation Act, the predominant corporation act in the country, have not sought to race Delaware to the bottom. Delaware has over several generations made a specialty of incorporation (corporations are among the few things for which there is always plenty of space in a tiny state) and corporate franchise taxes make up a significant part of that state's revenues. But that situation is atypical. For most states, corporate franchise taxes based on local incorporation (unlike the state's corporate income taxes) provide an insignificant percentage of the state's revenues; no matter what corporation laws those states adopt they cannot expect to attract such a flow of new incorporations as to add materially to the state's tax income. From the perspective of tax revenues, states do far better to attract the business operations of enterprises, wherever they may be incorporated. Other states have little tax incentive to engage Delaware in a chase for incorporations.

States should also be further dissuaded from entering into a race with Delaware by the recognition that no matter what statute they pass they can never provide one of the most important assets that Delaware offers, a corpus of sophisticated commercial case law and a judiciary that is educated and literate about business affairs. Professor Cary points out with some asperity that many members of the Delaware judiciary came out of corporate practice. To my mind that is an enormous advantage. Corporate litigation can be a very unsatisfactory experience—whether one is representing or suing management—when the proceeding is before a judge who has spent his practice years in work unrelated to the complex field of contemporary corporation law and when the local case law in business matters is antique and spotty. If Delaware were to repeal its corporation act tomorrow and substitute that of any other state, practitioners with a long view would still continue to incorporate in Delaware because of the experience of the state's administrative officials and judiciary in corporate matters.

As for the claim that Delaware's courts have little compassion for

---

8. In fact, as the author has argued elsewhere, the pattern of shareholder voting rights contained in our corporation laws is based almost entirely on history plus an archaic jurisprudential view of the corporation, with almost no attention paid to the reality of economic transactions. See Manning, "The Shareholder's Appraisal Remedy; an Essay for Frank Coker," 72 Yale L.J. 223 (1962).

minority shareholders and underestimate the importance of high fiduciary standards for corporate management, it must be said that no demonstration to that effect has been made. And no evidence has been adduced to show that shareholders or the treasuries of Delaware companies have been visited by disaster as a result of misbehavior condoned by that state's judges. Then, too, any general legislative statement of corporate fiduciary principles would ultimately have to be applied to real situations by courts; would the fiduciary instincts of Delaware's judges become more acute if such a statement were to be implanted in the U.S. Code?

As I read the history of corporation law over the last twenty years, a stream of securities regulations and law suits against corporate executives, directors, accountants, and lawyers has steadily built up a coral reef of law for the protection of the individual investor and the minority shareholder. In recent years the SEC, the federal courts, the state courts (including Delaware's), and the segment of the bar that specializes in shareholder suits have drawn upon the open-ended due process clause of corporation law—rule 10b-5—to reform what may be called the tort law of corporations as thoroughly as, if not more thoroughly than, it could have been reformed legislatively. The case-by-case process has the advantage that law suits involve real circumstances rather than hypothetical scripts and are addressed to disputes over real economic interests rather than abstract oughts. When in such a case a judge articulates or refines a legal proposition condemning certain conduct by the enterprise or by its managers, directors, or professional advisers, he has the advantage of seeing before him a real rather than imagined example of behavior. Such step-by-step development is not dramatic and does not satisfy the urge of some for publicly spotlighted corporate change. But surely, steadily, and soundly it reforms the law. In the corporate field, that process of continuing reform has been active during the last generation and there is every reason to believe that it will continue.

It is also fair to ask whether it is really necessary or desirable to require that all large corporate structures be the same. There is some variation among state corporation acts, and while Delaware is favored by lawyers selecting a state to incorporate a new enterprise, every state has many enterprises incorporated under its statutes, some of them large. State corporation laws have evolved incrementally over the last 150 years, recently under the magnetic pull of the successive versions of the Model Corporation Act. That healthy evolution would surely be stunted in the future if a single procedural model were set in concrete by federal legislation. Professor Cary's proposal for a federal minimum-standards statute is limited to large-scale enterprises, but if such a statute were in place it would be only a matter of time before its jurisdictional reach was extended to cover a wider spectrum of enterprises. That outcome is made all the more inevitable by the anomalous fact that the problems of minority shareholder protection that mainly concern Professor Cary usually arise not in the context of giant enterprises but in the more entrepreneurial and less professional environment of small and middle-sized companies.

Finally, account must be taken of the dreary fact that any federal minimum-standards statute would be accompanied by some new administrative apparatus, inside the SEC or elsewhere. The public, scholars, and even some government officials are showing increasing alarm and ire at the burgeoning of federal bureaucracy, ever-expanding reporting requirements, and intensified oversight from Washington, D.C. New federal legislative initiatives will undoubtedly be required to deal with problems of national moment, such as energy conservation and urban rehabilitation. But the presumption should be against federal intervention, and the corporate procedural questions that inspire Professor Cary's proposal can hardly be viewed as a national exigency.

In any event, whatever one's views on these matters are, it should be observed that unlike most corporate critics, those of species VII focus squarely upon true questions of corporation law.

Corporate Reform Species VIII

A small group of critics of the American corporation adopts an eighth position that is even more explicitly ideological than that of the corporate democrats. Species VIII takes as an immutable axiom that for all institutions and for all time, the only institutional decisions that are legitimate are those that are arrived at on the basis of a consensus of all persons who have an interest in or are affected by the outcome. Thus, in their view, a board of directors of a corporation should not be allowed to decide to close a plant, since many other people will be affected by that decision. The solution usually proposed by species VIII critics—under the bland name "co-determination"—is that boards of directors should be required by law to include representatives of labor unions. It is pointed out that a variant of this feature has been introduced in Germany and is on its way in Great Britain.

One immediate question raised by this proposal relates to its internal philosophic consistency. If one were truly serious about including on a board of directors representatives of the various parties who have an economic interest in the enterprise, then it would include not only representatives of shareholders and employees but also representatives of lenders, suppliers, customers, contractors, lessors (and lessees), municipalities, states, school districts, charities, the U.S. Treasury, and so on—all of which have a stake in the enterprise's income stream. Would all these groups be enthusiastic to see their interests guarded by labor union representatives?

But assuming that only representatives of unions should be added to the board, which union should it be, especially in the case of a company operating in diversified lines of business and in many parts of the country? Much of the American labor union structure continues to be craft based, unlike the unions in Europe; U.S. unions are more decentralized, and the interests of the local and the national often diverge; and U.S. unions have not historically developed as a centrally disciplined political party. And what of the fact that only a small minority of American workers belong to any union, despite the strong legal protections afforded to union organization?

But the split-board concept is faulty at a more fundamental level. Must special-interest participationism be accepted as a universal axiom to be applied unthinkingly to every form of organized human behavior? Aside from the question of its wider application to other institutions (armies, churches, schools, ship crews, courts, and so on), the core of the question as addressed to commercial enterprises is whether one recognizes and accepts that the commercial corporation—whether small or large—should be first and foremost an organization designed to operate efficiently to produce goods and services for the society, rather than a political organization designed to maximize political expression. To the degree that the managerial and decision-making structure of the incorporated enterprise is altered to resemble a New England town meeting, a Quaker consensus session, an Italian Parliament, or a two-party power negotiation, the capacity of the enterprise to carry out its basic economic function cannot fail to be impeded.

It is undeniable that social controls must be externally imposed on the conduct of large-scale enterprises. Those constraints can be strengthened, added to, or removed by legislatures, public agencies, and courts as circumstances and experience require. Even if particular controls are onerous, misguided, costly, or arbitrarily restrictive, if the modern incorporated enterprise is allowed to compete and have access to capital and resources, it can within remarkably wide limits adjust, adapt, and innovate to do an efficient job of economic production and distribution. But if the internal anatomy of the corporate enterprise is operated upon by an injection of divisive politicization, the predictable result will be to immobilize its decision-making capacity and to drag down the productivity of the U.S. economy to the detriment of all Americans and of other interdependent economies. In the special history of this country, the American labor movement has seen the situation and its own interests exactly right: its principle has been to let the managers make the money—and then do what can be lawfully done to take it away from them. For millennia, mankind has known that it can collect any number of goose eggs over time so long as it does not keep the goose from laying them.

Seen from this perspective, the role of common shareholders as the ultimate constituency of the corporation makes a great deal of sense. Unlike any of the other constituents who tap the income stream of the enterprise—workers, creditors, tax collectors, suppliers, and so on—the common shareholder is playing for the entrepreneurial margin and only the entrepreneurial margin. Nothing so clears the mind and sharpens his taste for efficiency as the recognition that everyone else gets paid ahead of him and that he gets nothing unless there is something left over. No other constituency of the enterprise has the same incentive to achieve a high level of efficiency for the enterprise as a whole, since the economic interest of each other constituency is narrower or has a limiting cap on it or runs directly counter to the interest of the aggregate enterprise in cost control. Shareholders—particularly the professional, sharp-eyed investors with a nervous focus on the bottom line—perform a vital function for the enterprise and for the efficiency of the economy as a whole.

It is the responsibility of the board of directors and management of an enterprise, and it is to the special economic interest of the common shareholders, to attend to the operating efficiency of the enterprise as a whole. No other group has that perspective of the aggregate. To lodge within the board of directors a cell whose commitment is to a single constituency of the enterprise—whether to employees, lenders, consumers, or any other group—rather than to the interest of the aggregate enterprise is a certain way to dilute and in time to destroy the feature of the corporate form that, more than any other, has accounted for its extraordinary economic success.

National politics affords a familiar parallel on this point. The single most difficult problem dogging our federal government emerges directly from its character as a system of pluralistic representation of local geographic, economic, ethnic, and religious interest groups. Such a system must operate by tradeoffs, logrolling, and transient coalitions. In such a setting, the elected representative who would prefer to take the perspective of the interests of the nation as a whole will sometimes find that position to be in conflict with particular narrow interests of his home constituency. In such a situation, to stand for the good of the whole is to court local political suicide, an unwelcome option for most officials. As a result, it is extremely difficult for the President, the only elected official with a nationwide constituency, to persuade members of Congress to take action which the nation as a whole needs but which is unpopular in their home districts. Recent executive-congressional struggles over local dams and a long-term energy program are merely current illustrations of the problem. In national politics, national symbols and patriotism can to some degree be appealed to as a counter to the centrifugal tendencies of parochial interest. Little or no analogous emotional commitment exists within commercial enterprises. Introduction of subconstituency representation into the corporate decisional process would cause it to deteriorate rapidly into logrolling, an attitude of "I've got mine, Jack," and a general disregard for overall efficiency.

It is part of the strength of our present corporate form and a part of the strength of our national economy that corporate managers and directors who are answerable to shareholders can, when all other reasonable means fail, take the unpleasant step of shutting down an uneconomic operation. In the interest of aggregate efficient use of resources, both for the enterprise and the economy as a whole, a plant should be shut down when it cannot be made competitive. Any arrangement that keeps an unprofitable plant operating simply redistributes the loss to others and burdens some other part of the economy. That is not to say, however, that the burden of the shutdown should be callously dumped upon the local employees and the local community. The company should do what it can responsibly do to cushion the event by advance notice, by seeking to introduce new jobs in the locality, by retraining, by transferring personnel to other divisions, and so forth. Even more important, we should long ago have developed better governmental and social techniques for dealing with shutdowns by stimulating new local employment opportunities, by retraining, and by easing occupational transition. That is a function for the society and the government. Economic change is continuous and cannot be halted. The task of the well-managed enterprise is to adapt quickly to, and take advantage of, changes when they occur; it is the task of government to smooth the adjustment. We must develop more effective governmental and social means to distribute the losses of such dislocations. If we do not, companies and their managements will be put under increasing pressure not to take managerial steps that are economically maximizing, and support will increase for changes in the corporate decision-making system that will discourage aggregate efficiency in the interest of avoiding local dislocation.

Corporate critics of group VIII differ from groups VI and VII in their premises, in their perception of the problems, and in their proposed solutions. But they join in centering their focus on the process of corporate governance.

Corporate Reform Species IX

Finally, the ninth group that seeks change in the nation's present corporate system takes as its watchword "management accountability." This group acknowledges the utility and efficiency of the corporate enterprise and wishes to retain and encourage these attributes. But it argues that in any soundly run institution everyone should be accountable to someone else; and that the leader of any institution who is accountable to no one, whose word is law, and who is not in jeopardy of removal from power will in time become arbitrary, arrogant, self-aggrandizing, prodigal, and despotic and will, further, lose contact with reality, isolate himself from unpleasant information, and make increasingly erratic judgments, to the misery of those around him and ultimately to the disaster of the organization which he heads. The fear of group IX critics is that the top officers of large-scale American corporations have achieved, or at least approximated, such a status of nonaccountability and that the situation is both dangerous and morally unacceptable.[9]

---

9. Concern about the issue of accountability of corporate management is, of

In the view of the author, these propositions of human psychology are valid. Indeed, those who agree with this author that the centralized strong-management system of the modern large-scale enterprise is essential to its economic effectiveness must recognize that on the other side of the same coin it is written that: (1) the society should set external legal ground rules for the behavior of enterprises; (2) the society should do what it can to distribute the human costs of economic dislocation; and (3) external and internal forces of accountability must be effectively brought to bear upon corporate managers. The question is whether the existing set of accountability constraints upon corporate management is in fact adequate. That is a key and central subject for public debate.

Corporate chief executives are powerful figures within their enterprises, but not all-powerful. In most large-scale American enterprises substantial forces are at work inhibiting, inspiring, blocking, or mandating particular actions by the chief executive or threatening to eject him from office. The reality of daily life for the chief executive is typically quite different from its portrayal in much of the literature in the field, predominantly written by academics or governmental staff persons with little personal business experience. Former SEC Commissioner Richard B. Smith caught the point well when he said in a recent address that the concept of[10]

> unlimited power of the chief executive comes as something of a surprise to [a] corporate manager, as on a given day, [he is] struggling with—
>
> > capital allocation requests to his board;
> > the meaning of a covenant being pointed to by bank lenders as preventing something he would like the company to do;
> > a strike threat by union negotiators;
> > the next level of standards fixed in environmental statutes that have to be met;
> > a tender offer threat from a well-financed company whose chairman called him last night to tell him that he had picked up 4.9% of the company's stock in the market;
> > increasingly probing questions from his outside directors at last month's board meeting;
> > multiple tax return dates within the next month;
> > auditors filling and overflowing his conference rooms to complete the annual audit;

---

course, not limited to those identified here as group IX. For instance, the recent furor about corporate payments overseas was grounded not only in disapproval of the payments themselves but in shock that some managements had been able to make them without anyone's knowledge and thus seemed to have been accountable to no one. As another example, corporate critics who press to strengthen the processes of shareholder democracy do so on the ground, If shareholders do not hold the management and directors accountable, then who will?

10. Smith, "Federal Corporate Law," p. 10, 11 (unpublished remarks before the Association of the Bar of the City of New York, May 9, 1977).

> a team of outside lawyers and accountants prowling the corridors in the last stages of a sensitive payments investigation;
> he and his subordinates scurrying around for new, or at least less expensive and more assured, energy sources;
> trying to guess the inflationary impact created by the federal government on several long-range decisions he has to make;
> his lawyers telling him about the new law or regulation with which he must now comply;
> financial analysts who have just estimated a downturn in his next quarter's earnings;
> a local zoning body that has ruled against a needed expansion of one of his major plants;
> headhunters seeking to take his two best operating officers;
> an underwriter who is advising him that this is not the time to raise equity capital;
> the comptroller who has just announced a technological break-through that threatens the future sales trend of his most important product . . . .
>
> The list is almost infinite for this person whose power [is said to be absolute].

Mr. Smith's reference to the financial analysts deserves special note. Analysts and financial commentators do not hold the same life-and-death power over managements and enterprises that drama critics often hold over playwrights and plays, but there are similarities in the relationship. A company's earnings per share, stock price, reputation for financial soundness, and growth prospects are to its corporate managers as earned-run averages, batting averages, and coach's evaluations are to baseball players. Financial analysts and commentators, studying a company's reports in scrupulous detail, regularly serve up in public print evaluations of the performance of its executives; professional institutional investors register their evaluations directly by buying or selling or avoiding the company's securities. These clinical outside analyses help inform the company's board of directors, shape the market's estimate of executive performance, and significantly condition the opinion of executive peers, of persons serving on other boards, of directors, and of other professionals. Most corporate executives are acutely sensitive to the estimate of these constituencies and strive mightily to gain their good opinion and avoid their low esteem. That is the essence of accountability. And it is no accident that almost every chief executive of a major company constantly watches the market price of his company's shares, which, with the price/earnings ratio, keeps daily score on the executive's performance.

Unmentioned in Mr. Smith's list is another factor that significantly conditions the executive's power. Seldom can the chief executive of a big company issue orders at whim and expect them to be followed. Large organizations are large organizations whether in the private or public sector. Every successful executive must be acutely mindful of the loyalty networks below; of the capacity of the employees at all levels to block implementation of action which they do not approve; of pervasive bureaucratic conservatism; of the risk of precipitating resignations, transfers of allegiance to competitors, strikes, and general low morale; and of the independence of many employees who are dedicated to high-quality performance and who will refuse to comply with, and perhaps report to authorities or to the press, executive conduct which they find reprehensible. Contrary to popular impression, the successful corporate executive today is far less a despotic battle chieftain than a skilled orchestrator of committees, mediator among warring departments, practicing psychologist, public spokesman, salesman, negotiator, personal charmer, public affairs analyst, long-view thinker, diplomat, and teacher. The job of corporate chief executive requires these skills (in addition to a good business head, a competitive nature, high energy, experience, and a psychological capacity to make close judgments and sleep nights) precisely because there are so many limitations on his power and because there are so many constituencies that must be dealt with successfully if the enterprise is to prosper. Not often are all these attributes found in one person. When such persons come along and are identified through performance, they are inevitably in great demand, as star performers in other fields are in great demand, and the marketplace runs their compensation up to high figures.

There seems to be a time lag between reality and the accepted image of the unremovability of the corporate executive. Of late hardly a day passes on which the financial pages do not report the sudden departure of high executives from major companies. Managements do get fired these days, and not infrequently. Sometimes chief executives are displaced at the initiative of the directors, or some of them; occasionally an inside executive coup is successful; in some cases a critical financial press plus the weight of unhappy shareholders, individual or institutional, can bring down the roof. The circumstances surrounding these downfalls are not usually publicized, and they are most often explained as the result of "personal plans" or "personality differences" or "policy differences." But the outcome is the same. The corporate executive's seat is not nearly as secure as it once was. When to this insecurity is added the ever-present risk of outside takeover and management succession by boarding party, the executives may be forgiven for finding irony in allusions to their omnipotence and lifetime tenure.

Finally, the image of the all-powerful corporate executive developed in a day when corporate disclosure requirements were much weaker than they are today. Over the past fifteen years the SEC, the courts, the stock exchanges, and the auditors have, step by step, raised the water table of disclosure for large-scale enterprises. Recent revelations of illegal or questionable corporate payments overseas were all the more shocking because the payments had not been detected by the auditors. Though the magnitude of these transactions was not material compared to the scale of the assets and operations of the enterprises, the malodorous character of the payments led to a demand for disclosure, just as the special character of executive compensation and insider transactions has led to special rules of disclosure. The aftermath of the publicity surrounding questionable payments has inspired new disclosure requirements and new criminal sanctions; thus one more step, based on experience, has been taken to make executive behavior and enterprise conduct accountable to the scrutiny of the public eye.

The issue of executive accountability is thus not whether executive accountability is essential—it is—or whether some processes of accountability are functioning—they are—but whether those processes are working well enough, whether they can be improved so that they work significantly better, and whether additional machinery is needed.

Reflection on the content of the concept of accountability reveals that it contains several quite different components, each of them important and each perhaps calling for special processes of monitoring, reporting, review, or check and balance. Consider the following corporate situations which raise four different aspects of the problem of accountability:

(1) A company's officers improperly line their own pockets with assets of the company or its shareholders by self-dealing contracts at unfair prices, by paying themselves undeserved compensation, by trading in the company's stock on inside information, or the like.

(2) In a misguided but unselfish effort to advance the interests of the company, its officers lead the company to violate the law, to infringe standards of decent business practice, or to behave in a socially irresponsible manner.

(3) Through laziness or incompetence, the company's officers operate the enterprise inefficiently and let it go to pot financially.

(4) The board of directors of the company fails to exercise due care to keep itself informed about the company's affairs; or fails to exercise due care to prevent management's cheating, illegal conduct, poor profit performance, or reprehensible social behavior; or fails to exercise due care to see to it that appropriate timely disclosure about the company's affairs is made to the public, the market, and the appropriate authorities.

To enact laws against these different categories of blameworthy corporate and managerial behavior is helpful, but not in itself enough. Prosecution can catch only a few evildoers, and it also has the disadvantage of coming after the fact. The criminal sanction is also clearly inappropriate to deal with simply managerial inefficiency. What is needed is a set of built-in institutional arrangements that on a daily, ongoing basis prevent, or at least contain within tolerable limits, undesirable conduct or ineffective performance by corporate managers, directors, and their companies. To achieve that result while retaining the important advantages of our strong-management corporate system requires several conditions, some of which are external to the corporate enterprise, and some of which are internal to it.

Requisite conditions external to the corporation are: an effective

SEC; honest and exacting public accountants; a competent and skeptical corps of financial analysts and commentators; and a body of rigorous legal doctrine invocable in shareholders' suits by an able corporate plaintiffs' bar. What are the facts? The SEC has been consistently vigorous and activist. The profession of independent accounting (with a little prodding help from others) has of late been experiencing, and is still experiencing, a major evolution toward more scrupulous procedures and greater independence from corporate management. The financial press and analysts have become increasingly sophisticated and gimlet eyed in recent years. The plaintiffs' bar is alive and well, and shareholder litigation flourishes, despite some recently demonstrated indispositions by the Supreme Court to continue to expand the reach of class actions and rule 10b-5. So far, so good.

The other two requisites of management accountability are internal to the corporate structure. They are a board of directors that is not controlled by management and a flow of reliable information. Those two elements are essential. *If the strong-executive model of corporate governance is to be maintained, it must be accompanied by a flow of solid and honest data sufficient to permit management's stewardship to be evaluated in all respects, and that flow must go (in the first instance) to a board of directors made up of members who are able and willing to evaluate management's performance objectively from the perspective of the interests of the enterprise as a whole.* Contained in that single sentence, it seems to me, is the crux of current policy questions about corporate reform.

In these two matters, as in almost all areas discussed here, reform has in fact been underway all around us over the last few years. The concept of the outside board on which a majority of the members are not current or former company officers has been steadily growing in acceptance and today is a feature of most publicly held companies. With increasing frequency nominating committees of the board, charged with the selection of nominees to be presented to the shareholders (and nearly always elected), are coming to be controlled by outside directors, as they should be. Audit committees have come to be required of companies listed on the stock exchanges, and it is increasingly accepted that such committees should be predominantly composed of outside directors. Increasingly it is becoming standard practice that the controller, the independent auditor of an enterprise (and the internal auditor, where there is one) should have a direct channel of access to the board's audit committee.[11] Rigorous new guidelines for directors, developed by the American Bar Association, will soon be promulgated.

Though this situation is markedly better than it was even a decade ago, there is still room for improvement, and a good many questions

---

11. A statistical review of procedural changes in recent years appears in The Conference Board, *The Board of Directors: Perspectives and Practices in Nine Countries* (1977). See also The Role and Composition of the Board of Directors of the Large Publicly Owned Corporation (Statement of the Business Roundtable, Jan. 1978).

merit study, argument, and experimentation. What else can be done to assure that outside directors are truly independent and serious about their responsibility as directors? Should they be paid more to increase their commitment of time and energy to the enterprise? Or would an increase in their income from the enterprise tend to put them in liege to the management? Should the board of directors or committees of the board be provided with their own staff resources? And if so, of what kind and how? How useful is the device of the nonofficer chairman of the board, a familiar arrangement in nonprofit corporations? High corporate executive compensation is a red flag to many persons, often taken as proof that the management is unaccountable to anyone and pays itself whatever it wants; what procedures can be installed to guarantee that executive compensation levels are genuinely the product of bargaining and market supply and demand? Are existing incentives and disincentives for service on boards of directors and for effective performance by board members in proper balance? What can be done to assure the integrity and availability of the independent reporting channel of the outside and inside auditor to the audit committee? What additional information about the company's affairs, if any, should be made public and in what detail? What should be the jurisdiction of an audit committee? i.e., where is a line to be drawn (if at all) between inquiry into accounting matters and inquiry into the general quality of management's performance? Is the state of the remedy of shareholders' suits too restricted or too inviting to the irresponsible plaintiff's lawyer? Can any practical and administrable scheme be devised to broaden participation in the process for nominating directors? How can boards of directors be encouraged to do a better job of monitoring the economic efficiency as well as the morals of management, and to remove chief executives who do not perform effectively?

Despite the importance of these and many questions like them, the immediate need today is to disseminate to all large-scale enterprises the management accountability practices that are being employed at present by the most forward-looking companies. To bring about that spread of better practices may ultimately call for an orchestration of state corporation law, judicial doctrine, stock exchange regulations, informal standard setting by the associations of professional corporate advisers, and SEC and state administrative action.

CONCLUSION

A capacity for independent critical judgment by boards of directors and an adequate information flow—these should be the two key objectives of corporate reform for the present and near future. This task has not just been discovered. Nor does it arise from a crisis that has suddenly overtaken us. The job at hand is to make an extremely complex and diverse process work reliably every day in hundreds of enterprises throughout the nation. Our record for corporate reform has been remarkably good for the last thirty-five years and notably effective for the last ten years. That reform has been brought about by incremental modifications, by experience, and by changes in attitudes. So far, it has also been achieved without suffocating the corporate goose. We should continue to move forward along that line. There is every reason to believe that we can and will do so if we focus clearly on the real problems that call for reform, if we acknowledge the primacy of the economic function of corporate enterprises, and if we keep firmly in view not only the problems of our corporate system but the benefits that the society as a whole reaps from its efficient operation.

CHAPTER TWO

The Costs and Benefits of Government-Required Disclosure: SEC and FTC Requirements

AN APPRAISAL

George J. Benston, *Professor, Graduate School of Management and Center for Research in Government Policy and Business, University of Rochester*

Supreme Court Justice Brandeis' metaphorical argument "Sunlight is said to be the best of disinfectants; electric light the most efficient policeman" is regarded by many as a truism.[1] The Securities Act of 1933 (characterized as a disclosure statute) and the Securities Exchange Act of 1934 are based on this assumption.[2] President Roosevelt opted for disclosure rather than attempt to establish as federal statute the merit regulation of securities sales that had been enacted in the blue-sky laws adopted in about half the states. As he put it in his message to Congress supporting the 1933 Act:[3]

> There is, however, an obligation upon us to insist that every issue of new securities to be sold in interstate commerce shall be accompanied by full publicity and information, and that no essentially important element attending the issue shall be concealed from the buying public.
>
> This proposal adds to the ancient rule of caveat emptor, the further doctrine, "Let the seller also beware." It puts the burden of telling the whole truth on the seller. It should give impetus to honest dealing in securities and thereby bring back public confidence.

The 1934 Act, though not explicitly called a disclosure statute, has evolved into the more demanding of the two Acts. As amended, it requires annual disclosure of a large amount of financial data, more limited quarterly statements, monthly reports of "significant" events,

1. L. Brandeis, *Other People's Money*, p. 62 (1933).
2. Securities Act of 1933, 15 U.S.C. §§ 77a–77aa (1970); Securities Exchange Act of 1934, 15 U.S.C. §§ 78a–78jj (1970).
3. 77 Cong. Rec. 937 (1933).

proxy information, and so forth. The event and form of disclosure required has expanded greatly in the past several years to include product-line data, compensating balance arrangements for loans, and most recently the replacement costs of large corporations' fixed assets. There is every reason to believe that more rather than less specific disclosure of data will be required as a consequence of the review of disclosure policies recently completed.[4]

The disclosure requirements for most corporations (all those with more than 500 shareholders or $1 million in assets) are based in large measure on the assumption that investors would be insufficiently served were the laws and regulations not in place and administered by the Securities and Exchange Commission. In brief, the benefits which are assumed to flow from these requirements are: less fraud on investors, better administration of the reporting corporations, more equitable and efficient capital markets, and a more efficient allocation of resources in the economy. In addition, it is claimed that government officials require the data made public by corporations to improve the administration of their offices and their management of the economy.

This latter presumed benefit is one of the major motivating forces behind other enacted and proposed legislation that requires public disclosure by private enterprises. In particular, many regulated industries have long had to report detailed data on their operations to supervisory commissions. Railroads report to the Interstate Commerce Commission, utilities to public service commissions, insurance companies to state agencies, banks to federal and state agencies, and so on. There are two predominant reasons for this type of reporting requirement. One is that the companies enjoy a natural or government-created monopoly, and hence their operations, management, revenues, costs, assets, liabilities, and financing must be revealed to the agencies charged with their regulation. The other is that financial institutions, such as banks and insurance companies, are guardians of the public's funds and hence must be scrutinized by the public's servants.

The New Deal promulgated another reason for requiring that private companies report to government. While the public and the government officials generally believed that the "invisible hand" of the profit-oriented decisions by business persons and consumers resulted in the optimal allocation of resources (except in natural or government-franchised monopolies), there was little reason for government to gather and use private financial data other than for tax collection. But once this view was replaced with the belief that private enterprise was not working well and that government officials should manage the economy, extensive reporting of data on business and other operations was considered necessary. Furthermore, the concern that the economy

---

4. See *Report of the Advisory Comm. on Corporate Disclosure to the Securities and Exchange Commission*, printed for the House Comm. on Interstate and Foreign Commerce, 95th Cong., 1st Sess. (Comm. Print 1977) [hereinafter cited as *Report*].

was characterized more by oligopolies which administered prices than by competing enterprises led to a demand by government agencies such as the Federal Trade Commission for detailed data on market and industry shipments, sales, advertising, profits, investments, and so forth.

Finally, the recent revelations of corporate misbehavior, particularly with respect to illegal domestic political contributions and questionable overseas payments, have increased demands that the operations of larger corporations be subject to greater public scrutiny.[5] These demands are but continuations of a movement prevalent at least since the 1930's to require private enterprises to disclose their financial and other data to government agencies and to the public.

In light of what appears to be a strong public preference for more rather than less disclosure, it might seem foolish to question whether the costs of required corporate disclosure exceed the benefits. Few people can recall a time when the SEC did not exist, and therefore few may even be able to imagine a situation in which corporations would not have to file S-1's when they sell stock and periodically file 10K's, 10Q's, 8K's, etc. Government officials, such as those who attempt to manage the energy situation, must bemoan the paucity of data that are reported to them, rather than the reverse. The FTC, in particular, is attempting to implement a massive data collection effort. Its line-of-business report program would require some 440 of the largest manufacturing corporations to report very detailed financial data annually, disaggregated into standard industrial code (SIC) classifications.[6] While such a data collection program may have been considered overwhelmingly expensive in the past, the development of high-speed computers has made it relatively inexpensive for a government agency to store and process large amounts of data. Thus a past restraint on government data collection no longer exists.

But this is also a time when traditional beliefs are being questioned. Perhaps it is no more ridiculous to ask whether more required financial disclosure is better than less than it is to ask whether a woman's place is always in the home, or whether smoke pouring out of factory chimneys necessarily is a sign of progress and prosperity.

I must emphasize at the outset that my concern is with *required* financial disclosure. As I demonstrate below, corporations published financial statements long before the SEC existed. We can presume that this disclosure met the cost-benefit criterion, since it was made volun-

---

5. See, e.g., Staff of Subcomm. on Oversight and Investigations of House Comm. on Interstate and Foreign Commerce, 94th Cong., 2d Sess., *Report on SEC Voluntary Compliance Program on Corporate Disclosure*, pp. 1–15 (Comm. Print 1976).

6. See *Agriculture-Environmental and Consumer Protection Appropriations for 1975: Hearings Before Subcomm. on Agriculture-Environmental and Consumer Protection of the House Comm. on Appropriations, Part 9*, 93rd Cong., 2d Sess., pp. 601–51 (1974) [hereinafter cited as *Hearings*].

tarily. A corporation could sell shares without disclosing much, and many did so; but others provided information apparently because they believed that the benefits from, say, enhanced interest from investors exceeded the cost to them of preparing and distributing the data and of having their competitors learn about their operations. Audits were conducted by C.P.A.'s, annual reports were voluntarily issued, new developments were announced, and so forth before 1934. The question at issue, then, is not whether disclosure as such is a good thing, but whether the benefits of government-mandated disclosure exceed its costs and which persons (e.g., consumers, investors, or government officials) obtain the benefits and assume the costs. To keep the discussion within reasonable bounds, I have limited this paper to the reporting requirements of the SEC and the FTC. Each provides a good example of two aspects of government-mandated disclosure.

THE COSTS OF MANDATED DISCLOSURE

The Direct Costs

SEC REPORTS

Not all of the costs of record keeping, auditing, and report preparation are due to mandated disclosure. Corporations keep many records that aid in the management of their enterprises. As was mentioned above, most larger publicly owned corporations were audited by C.P.A.'s before the SEC in effect imposed this requirement.[7] Furthermore, almost all corporations whose shares were traded on stock exchanges (and hence, until 1964, the only ones subject to the periodic reporting requirements of the Securities Exchange Act of 1934) published annual financial statements.[8] Therefore, the direct costs of meeting the requirements imposed by laws and government agencies should include only the expenses that otherwise would not have been incurred.

These additional expenses are considerable for several reasons. First, the amount of detailed data required is considerably greater than corporations would have recorded and reported voluntarily. SEC forms, for example, call for information on compensating balances, detailed schedules of asset amounts, accumulated depreciation and expense amounts, pension costs and provisions, location of plants, and other data that probably would not have been published otherwise. A recent example is the current requirement that large companies report the

---

7. In 1926, 82 percent of the companies whose shares were traded on the New York Stock Exchange (NYSE) were audited by C.P.A.'s. By 1934 the percentage had increased to 94 percent. Benston, "The Value of the SEC's Accounting Disclosure Requirements," 44 Accounting Rev. 515, 519 (1969).

8. At least since 1926 all NYSE-traded corporations issued balance sheets and income statements. Id.

replacement costs of their fixed assets.[9] Few, if any, corporations have made those estimates. My conversations with a number of comptrollers indicate that the cost of obtaining these data are considerable, even under the SEC's proposed safe-harbor provision, which would limit the liability of the companies for presenting estimates.

Second, some specific reports probably would not be prepared and disseminated were it not for the SEC's requirements. One example is audited quarterly reports. While many companies voluntarily prepared quarterly reports, it is doubtful that many would incur the expense of having them certified if the SEC did not require auditors to attest to these data in the annual report. Another example is the requirement that annual reports be sent to shareholders with proxy requests and that 10K reports be made available to the public. Except for companies whose shares are listed on the major stock exchanges, it also is doubtful that many firms would file monthly or more frequent reports of changes in control, the acquisition or disposition of a significant amount of assets, material legal proceedings, and so forth, as required in form 8K.

Therefore, the costs to companies not previously subject to the SEC's reporting requirements probably are not trivial. Unfortunately, I know of no studies of the amount of these costs. One gets only occasional newspaper reports of the additional costs incurred by companies newly subject to SEC regulations and of the effort by some smaller companies to reduce their number of shareholders to free themselves from this burden. I have been unable to verify these data.

In general, though, once a corporation has adapted its records to the SEC's requirements, the additional direct cost of filling in the periodic report forms may not be very great, though it may exceed the benefits thereof. However, the relative burden on smaller corporations is most likely much greater and may be quite onerous.

The direct cost of filing a registration statement (such as the S-1) for a securities issue represents a burden that otherwise might not have been incurred, for several reasons. Companies contemplating their first security issue must gather and record a wealth of data, such as detailed descriptions of the business, its development during the past five years, and future activities to be undertaken; information about the directors and promoters over the past five years; audited and certified profit-and-loss, funds, and retained-earnings statements for the past three years; and a summary of earnings for the past five years with a textual analysis thereof. A consequence of these requirements is that prospectuses usually run to fifty or more pages (measuring 7½ by 9 inches). In addition, when the SEC requires data that are not recorded in a corporation's records, the cost of obtaining the numbers can be considerable. One example is the requirement that companies going public for the first time file three years' profit-and-loss statements certified by an

---

9. SEC Accounting Series Release No. 190 (March 23, 1976), 5 Fed. Sec. L. Rep. (CCH) ¶ 72,212; SEC Accounting Series Release No. 203 (Dec. 9, 1976), 5 Fed. Sec. L. Rep. (CCH) ¶ 72,225.

independent auditor, which means that at least three years' inventories have to have been audited. Nonregistered companies which had not employed independent auditors over that time period for that purpose would suffer the cost of delay. It is not sufficient that they simply disclose that past inventories have not been audited.

The SEC's regulations also require corporations to incur additional auditing, reporting, and printing costs that are higher than for ordinary reporting. An important determinant of these higher costs is the increased legal liability of accountants and others for SEC reports. Independent auditors have been sued successfully for audit failures and reporting errors. Furthermore, it is not unusual for them to be sued when companies go bankrupt or suffer serious reverses.[10] The cost to them of such suits is not only the monetary awards imposed and the legal cost of defense, but the cost of damage to their reputations as honest, competent professionals. Hence they must take all suits seriously, whether justified or not. Therefore, the independent auditors must conduct a more extensive, more careful audit and check the effect of post-audit, prefiling events when the figures are to be used in an SEC report. The expense of these procedures obviously is reflected in higher audit fees.

Legal costs and printing fees are higher for SEC reports (particularly new-issues filings) than for others because of legal liability, as just discussed. In addition, since corporate managements and directors also are liable for misstatements and errors in the reports, they cannot passively rely on their hired experts. Therefore, an additional cost is the time and effort of management that could be otherwise employed. Since many, if not most, of these costs do not vary with the dollar amount of the securities issue, the reporting burden falls heavily on smaller companies that plan to raise less money with an issue than their larger competitors do.

FTC'S LINE-OF-BUSINESS REPORT PROGRAM

The direct costs of government-mandated disclosure such as the proposed FTC line-of-business (LB) report may be even greater than the costs of reporting to the SEC. Unlike most of the SEC's required reports, the FTC's reports are not consistent with the usual record keeping and reporting system maintained by any business. Because the FTC wants to use the data to determine whether profits earned by industries (originally they were concerned with markets) are "excessive" and to test hypotheses about the relationship of market structure to performance, it requires corporations to aggregate their data into predeter-

---

10. Robert Kellogg has found that investments in firms that are sued generally were earning risk-adjusted negative returns before the suits and that discovery of actionable violations of the federal Securities Acts appears to be associated with abnormally poor firm performance. R. Kellogg, An Empirical Study of Disclosure Error Civil Lawsuits Under the Federal Securities Laws (dissertation in progress, University of Rochester).

mined categories. These categories follow industries defined by standard industrial codes (SIC). For example, FTC category 31.02 consists of SIC's 313 (footwear, except rubber) and 314 (boot and shoe cut stock and findings); the category includes bindings, bows, buckles, heel lifts, laces, soles, house slippers, men's, women's, infants', and babies' footwear, including dress, casual, and work shoes, boots, and sandals.[11] Revenues, the cost of operating revenue, traceable and nontraceable media advertising, other selling expenses, general administrative expenses, payrolls, depreciation, and assets must be reported for each defined FTC (SIC) code. Unlike the SEC and the Financial Accounting Standards Board (FASB) line-of-business regulations, the FTC regulations do not permit respondents to report these data according to the product and production groups that the management ordinarily uses. Consequently, the data processing costs can be very large.

The extent of these costs is in dispute, but we at least have some estimates. In discussing the 1973 version of its current forms, the FTC said that twenty-five companies estimated annual compliance costs that range from $5,000 to $1,800,000, with a median value of $56,000.[12] The FTC staff then used a series of very questionable adjustments to reduce the estimated median cost of complying with the newer, somewhat more simplified report form to $24,000 per company.[13] The initial setup costs of the program were between $10,000 and $20,000 per firm, according to the FTC's submission to the General Accounting Office (GAO), which is charged with approving the form.[14] These figures were based on data submitted by twenty-five companies for the earlier (1973) form. Their estimates range from $75,000 to $2,000,000, with a mean value of $548,000. The FTC reduced this amount to between $10,000 and $20,000 by another series of questionable adjustments. Though a detailed analysis is not useful here (and may be found elsewhere[15]), it may

---

11. *Hearings*, *supra* note 6, at p. 631; Office of Management and Budget, *Standard Industrial Classification Manual*, pp. 133–34 (1972).

12. 1974 Form LB Revision 7, Bureau of Economics Staff Memorandum (July 1, 1975).

13. The questionable adjustments include the following: (1) use of a median value as a sufficient statistic to describe a range of values between $50,000 and $1,800,000; (2) arbitrary reduction of the median value by a third; (3) conversion of costs to a cost per line of business when there is no conceptual or empirical relationship between the number of lines and compliance costs; and (4) multiplication of the computed cost per line of business by the estimated number of lines of the average company (a number that was arbitrarily adjusted downward). A detailed analysis of the procedures used may be found in G. Benston, "The Cost of Complying with a Government Data Collection Program: The FTC's Line-of-Business Report" (unpublished paper on file with author, 1977).

14. "Cost to Firms of LB Programs" (memorandum from Keith B. Anderson and William F. Long, Economists, Federal Trade Commission, to James M. Folsom, Acting Director, Bureau of Economics, May 8, 1974).

15. Benston, *supra* note 13.

be instructive to point out one particularly dubious procedure followed by the FTC staff. To estimate the effect on costs of reducing some reporting requirements, the staff telephoned six companies and asked someone (not identified) to estimate the percentage by which the company's previous estimate could be reduced if the requirements were changed. The average percentage reduction in cost is reported to be 82 percent. This may seem to be a rather large reduction. In fact, examination of the underlying data reveals that this average is computed from the following percentage reductions of each of the six companies: 30, 73, 77, 86, 99, 99. Thus two companies are reported to have said that the proposed changes would reduce their cost of compliance by 99 percent. It does not seem reasonable (to me, at least) that they could produce the form for only 1 percent of their previous estimates because of some not very extensive, or at least not radical, changes in the reporting requirements.

The most recent cost estimates submitted by the FTC are derived from a telephone survey of some officials of seventeen companies who had completed the form. The seventeen companies were chosen from among the thirty companies with the largest number of manufacturing lines of business making sales of over $10 million. In telephone conversations (apparently not detailed studies) conducted in May and June 1977, the company officials estimated compliance costs of between $2,100 and $100,000, with a mean amount of $28,640.

Many of the companies which would be required to submit line-of-business data to the FTC dispute its estimates of the cost of compliance. Of the 440 companies served with demands to complete the forms, some 170 have filed motions to quash. These noncomplying companies have brought suit in federal court to have the program discontinued. The deliberation in the United States District Court for the District of Columbia before Judge Thomas A. Flannery in June 1977 was restricted to the costs of the program. Judge Flannery requested that five corporations submit affidavits detailing the costs they expected. Table 2-1 gives the costs listed in those affidavits.

These companies base their much higher estimates on the fact that their present data recording and processing systems are not congruent with the FTC's prescribed definitions of lines of business. Hence they would have to record all of their basic data, rewrite computer programs, and restructure reports to provide the data required by the FTC. Furthermore, they disagree with the Commission's procedure of estimating compliance cost for a company on the assumption that there is a positive, reasonably meaningful relationship between the number of lines of business and compliance cost. In addition to the fact that the available data show no such relationship (the correlation is not significant),[16] the companies who are suing to stop the program contend that the cost of compliance is due primarily to the amount of divergence between a company's accounting system and the FTC's reporting re-

16. See G. Benston, *supra* note 13.

TABLE 2-1 Estimated Costs of Compliance with the FTC Line-of-Business Report Program

E.I. duPont de Nemours and Company:[a]			
Manual efforts to get data for 1974 and 1975/76 Form LB			$1,000,000 to $1,500,000
Initial additional investment in new computer programs			1,000,000 to 1,500,000
Annual costs thereafter			100,000 to 200,000
Eaton Corporation:[b]			
1974 report:			
Direct payroll costs (including fringe benefits)	401,811		
Overhead	100,452	502,263	
following years (direct costs, no overhead)		286,843	
Hobart Corporation:[c]			
Estimate made in 1975 (initial costs; current costs should be higher)			1,000,000 to 3,000,000
Annual maintenance costs		500,000 plus	
Goodyear Tire and Rubber Company:[d]			
Direct costs		150,000	
W.R. Grace and Company:[e]			
Estimate made in 1974		500,000	

[a] Affidavit of Howard L. Siers, Assistant Comptroller, filed May 5, 1977.

[b] Affidavit of F. C. Roberts, Vice President and Controller, filed May 5, 1977.

[c] Affidavit of Harland L. Mischler, Vice President and Controller, filed May 5, 1977.

[d] Affidavit of G. A. Sampson, Vice President and Controller, filed May 5, 1977.

[e] Affidavit of John F. Spellman, Vice President and Controller, filed May 5, 1977.

Source: *In re* FTC Line of Business Report Litigation, 432 F. Supp. 274 (D.D.C. 1977).

quirements. The affidavits filed give fairly detailed numbers and descriptions of procedures in support of this contention and of estimates presented.

The FTC counters that the companies are refusing to take advantage of the instructions that permit "well-informed estimates."[17] Rather, they say, the companies insist on basing their reports on data that meet the requirements of generally accepted accounting principles (GAAP). Furthermore, the Commission does not ask that the respondents restructure their data processing systems. The companies can provide the demanded data, the Commission claims, primarily by adjusting already existing reports to the requirements of form LB.

17. Affidavit of William F. Long (director of the LB report program), and testimony at evidentiary hearings before the Honorable Thomas A. Flannery, United States District Judge, United States District Court for the District of Columbia, June 17, 1977, *in re* FTC Line of Business Report Litigation, Misc. No. 76-0127 (D.D.C. 1977).

However, the companies see themselves in an adversary relationship with the FTC. This view is based on the fact that a primary purpose of the LB report is the gathering of data that will be used to direct antitrust investigations. Though the Commission insists that individual company data will not be used for this purpose, many companies do not believe they can rely on this assurance, considering the FTC's adversary role. In addition, many companies do not believe that the data they report will or can be kept confidential, since their file copies are subject to subpoena. Therefore, they may be revealing data that will be useful to competitors or for private law suits. Consequently, they cannot be casual or rely on well-informed estimates to report specific numbers.

The Indirect Costs

The major indirect cost of government-mandated reports of accounting data follows from the adversary nature of mandated disclosure. This is the opportunity cost of having data reported that are correct with respect to the regulations but misleading for the purposes of the report's user (type II error). Another opportunity cost is incurred when data that would be useful to users cannot be reported because the government regulations forbid this reporting or because the risk of an adversary action is too great (type I error).

A possible example of the first (type II error) cost is the immediate write-off of goodwill that the SEC insisted on until recently.[18] Another possible example is the SEC's insistence (again, until recently) that only historically determined numbers be used, which meant that assets could not be shown at more than their original costs, even where the original costs were demonstrably and significantly less than market values.[19] (The qualifier "possible" is inserted because it is not known whether these reporting requirements actually misled investors.) The FTC's insistence that companies aggregate their operating data into lines of business that do not reflect markets or other natural groupings of products is another instance of the mandated reporting of potentially misleading data. For example, the FTC may report a high profit rate on sales or assets for the industry (or market) listed as "footwear, except rubber; boot and shoe cut stock and findings . . . ," FTC code 31.02. Assuming that the profit rate reported measures the economic rate of profit (which it most likely does not), the high rate could be due to a

---

18. "There was a period, for example, when the SEC was conducting something in the nature of a campaign to eliminate goodwill from all balance sheets filed with it." L. Rappaport, *SEC Accounting Practice and Procedure* 7.10 (3d ed. 1972).

19. "I was on the SEC staff at the time [late 1930's], and involved in the decision, when after some years of case-by-case decision, the SEC became firm on the point that historical cost was the required basis of accounting." Kripke, "A Search for Meaningful Securities Disclosure Policy," 31 Bus. Law. 293, 295 (1975).

very high rate on women's dress shoes that offsets a low rate on men's dress shoes or women's casual shoes, or a multitude of other combinations. If potential entrants to the industry take the numbers seriously, they are very likely to make bad decisions. Similarly, should a shoe manufacturer compare his or her financial results to the numbers the FTC publishes, the manufacturer is likely to be misled.

An example of the second (type I) cost is the SEC's prohibition on the publication of "soft" data, such as the estimated value of natural resources, patents, or land.[20] Forecasts, for example, cannot be presented in prospectuses. Until recently, the SEC's adherence to historical-cost-based numbers discouraged, if not prohibited, the presentation of current-market- or price-level-adjusted reports.

It is understandable that government-mandated reporting would result in the agencies' requiring adherence to relatively rigid rules or in the respondents' deciding to report only objectively determined data. The agencies have to process a large amount of data. Generally it is not administratively feasible for them to determine whether a company is "correct" (in some sense) when it uses a subjectively derived estimate of value. Hence, the SEC prohibited the use of appraised values for assets, particularly those appraisals of unmined natural resources, such as coal, silver, and oil, that are difficult, if not impossible, to check.[21] Similarly, the value of intangibles often cannot be measured accurately. Therefore, it is not surprising to find agencies such as the SEC refusing to accept subjectively determined numbers. If they accept such numbers, they run the risk of permitting dishonest managements to publish deliberately misleading data, the cost of which will be borne by the government agency as well as the public. However, where the agency only permits the publication of objectively determined, though not useful, data, neither the agency nor the companies filing the reports are likely to be criticized, particularly when the procedures used have been endorsed by a respected professional body, such as the American Institute of Certified Public Accountants (AICPA) or FASB. Only the public, if they are not fully aware of the data's limitations, will bear the cost.

One consequence of the SEC's past insistence on conservative, historical-cost-based numbers seems to be that some corporations avoid offering debt securities to the public. From 1900 to 1934, only about 3 percent of all corporate debt securities were directly placed, but from 1935 to 1965 46 percent were directly placed.[22] While there no

---

20. See Schneider, "Nits, Grits, and Soft Information in SEC Filings," 121 U. Pa. L. Rev. 254–305 (1972). The prohibition is being reconsidered, see text accompanying note 4 *supra*.

21. See analysis of reasons for adverse decisions on accounting in registrations under the Securities Act of 1933 in Benston, "The Effectiveness and Effects of the SEC's Accounting Disclosure Requirements," in *Economic Policy and the Regulation of Corporate Securities*, p. 23, at pp. 56–58 (H. Manne ed. 1969).

22. A. Cohan, *Yields on Corporate Debt Directly Placed*, p. 1 (1967).

doubt are many reasons for the change (such as the growth of life insurance companies who tend to invest directly in corporate debt securites), it appears that a major factor was the restrictions imposed by the SEC on information that could be publicized for public security sales. I tested this hypothesis in the following manner. The eight industries for which (since 1953) the SEC publishes data on private and public debt issues were ranked by several professional accountants according to the negative bias imposed by the SEC's accounting rules. (Agreement among these professionals was complete.) Rankings then were made of the ratio of debt directly placed to the total amount floated in each year 1953 through 1966 by each industry. Despite the fact that other institutional factors support direct debt placement by some industries (such as railroads) or require the sale of securities by competitive bidding (as is the case with public utilities), the rankings are almost perfectly correlated with direct debt placement—the greater the bias imposed by SEC, the greater the percentage of debt directly placed.[23]

The factors which motivate agencies such as the FTC to require reporting of essentially useless or potentially misleading data are somewhat different from those that motivate the risk-reducing actions of the SEC. An agency such as the FTC wants information reported in predetermined, uniform aggregates and categories to reduce the cost to them of analyzing data from individual companies. Ease of data handling and mechanical analysis triumph over meaningfulness and accuracy. The alternative probably would require a very large staff that would exceed the FTC's budget and its ability to attract a sufficient number of competent researchers. The consequence of this administrative cost saving is the imposition of the cost of meaningless and potentially misleading data on unwary or careless users.

Thus the direct costs of government-mandated financial reporting borne by corporations (and hence by equity holders, consumers, and taxpayers) include the direct costs of recording, processing, auditing, printing, and reporting the data required. These costs are increased by corporate fear that the data reported may be used to support law suits, antitrust litigation, and other adversary actions against them. An additional consequence of this fear is the reporting of data by procedures that are supported by authorities even when the numbers are not reflective of the events they are supposed to reflect. The agencies also tend to want data that are easy and safe to administer. Consequently, the data reported are of limited value to those who would use them as a basis for economic decisions.

Nevertheless, though their value is limited, the data may not be totally useless. I turn, therefore, to a consideration of the benefits that might be derived from the data reported to the SEC and the FTC.

---

23. Benston, *supra* note 21, at pp. 67–75.

THE BENEFITS OF GOVERNMENT-MANDATED FINANCIAL DISCLOSURE

SEC Required Disclosure

The Federal Securities Acts were passed to correct presumed wrongs and to improve the operations of the securities markets in particular and of the economy in general. Seven benefits have been or might be claimed for the corporate disclosure sections of the Acts.[24] The first four pertain to the fairness of securities investments. Though the concept of fairness is difficult to define operationally, it seems clear that it is a strong reason for the passage and extension of the Acts. The last three benefits are claimed in the belief that the data which corporations could be required to disclose in financial reports are useful for investment decisions. Consequently, the Acts are thought to reduce the cost of investing and improve the allocation of resources in the economy. The following seven benefits are delineated:

(1) Reduction of fraud on investors who might be misled by financial statements that were intended to mislead them;

(2) Reduction or elimination of possibly inadvertent misrepresentation in financial statements that affect investors' allocation of funds;

(3) Reduction or elimination of security price manipulation that is made possible or enhanced by inadequate disclosure of financial information;

(4) Enhanced fairness to noninsiders through the publication of information that otherwise would be available only to insiders;

(5) Greater availability of information that otherwise would not be published, not because managements or insiders would attempt to cheat noninsiders but because the benefits of the information could not be garnered fully by the shareholders of corporations, even though the information would be beneficial to investors in general;

(6) Greater efficiency in making securities investments, as a result of the publication of information that meets known and relatively unambiguous standards of accuracy, reliability, and meaning, that is published in standard format, and that otherwise would not have been available; and

(7) Enhanced public confidence in the securities market because the information disclosed can be trusted, while voluntarily supplied information cannot.

Little, if any, evidence supports the belief that these possible benefits have been achieved. Nor is there much, if any, evidence that is consistent with the claim that the Acts addressed a real problem. Furthermore,

---

24. These benefits were delineated by me from readings and conversations. To be fair to the proponents of SEC-required disclosure, I tried to err towards specifying more rather than fewer benefits.

reason does not support the belief that the benefits claimed can be achieved or are indeed benefits. Since I have analyzed these (and other) reasons for required disclosure at some length in *Corporate Financial Disclosure in the UK and the USA*,[25] the following discussion is not as extensive as it could be. Chapter 4 of that book can be consulted for the references that support the assertions made here. The conceptual bases are discussed first, followed by a review of the evidence.

CONCEPTUAL BASES FOR SEC-REQUIRED DISCLOSURE

Fraud, Manipulation, and Unfairness. The first group of claims—prevention or reduction of fraud, misrepresentation, and other manipulations or unfairness—are derived from two basic assumptions. One is that the financial-statement data would be and can be used to mislead investors; the other is that government regulation of financial disclosure would be effective in preventing this misuse.

It is reasonable to believe that perpetrators of frauds would be willing to use falsified or misleadingly presented financial data to effect their ends. It also seems likely that promoters, managers, and insiders would prefer to hide improprieties or inept performance by preventing disclosure of data that would betray these activities. They also might want to delay or otherwise manage the disclosure of good performance or fortunate occurrences until they were able to secure shares in the enterprise at a less-than-equilibrium price. Thus it seems clear that financial statements might be used in attempts to defraud or mislead investors.

Whether financial statements would have the desired effect is another question. Since it is obvious that improper financial statements may be used to deceive, it also is obvious that investors will rather quickly become aware of the dangers they face in relying on the statements. This is why certified public accountants exist. They are independent experts whose stock-in-trade is an integrity that is rarely compromised. Should they permit their certification of financial statements to be purchased, they risk losing their most valuable asset: their value to clients as certifiers of financial reports.[26]

A second source of protection for the public is the reputation of the investment bankers who market securities. Their role was described well by Arthur Dewing in the 1934 edition of his comprehensive work *The Financial Policy of Corporations*.[27]

> Probably 99 out of 100 prospective investors in the securities of a new company have neither the training, inclination, nor the will to carry on any independent investigation of their own, no matter how much information

---

25. G. Benston, *Corporate Financial Disclosure in the UK and the USA* (1976).

26. For a more complete exposition see Benston, "Accountants' Integrity and Financial Reporting," 43 Financial Executive 10–14 (1975).

27. A. Dewing, *The Financial Policy of Corporations*, pp. 1018–19 (3d rev. ed. 1934).

> is put at their disposal. In the last analysis, it is the authority of the investment banker that inspires confidence in the new enterprise and not the investor's reliance on his own powers of analysis. And the investor knows, moreover, that the banker has spent far more time in investigating all the ramifications of the undertaking than he is likely to spend; and he knows that the banker's reputation is bound up in the success or failure of the undertaking.

Thus there is reason to believe that the security underwriter's and public accountant's reputations would afford investors protection from fraudulent or misleading financial statements in the absence of government disclosure regulations.

However, it can be argued that C.P.A.'s and investment bankers can be compromised by those from whom they receive fees: being human, they may succumb to greed. Government regulation may play a role in requiring the publication of inside dealings and potential conflicts of interest, in ensuring the independence of C.P.A.'s and investment bankers, and in prosecuting those who violate their fiduciary responsibilities.

With respect to the question of fairness, it should be noted that in general, it is not conceptually possible for government disclosure regulations to make security investment fair for all in the sense that all investors have equal access to all information. Even if corporations are required to announce everything to the press, someone must obtain the information first. The chain of transmission includes those who prepared the release, typed it, delivered it, read it before setting it in type, read the galleys, and read the newspaper. Furthermore, some people are more capable of using information than others. Therefore, as is discussed further below, a program of government-mandated disclosure is perhaps more likely to be unfair to shareholders than not. Small shareholders and investors in particular are not likely to benefit, since they probably would not be early in the chain of receivers of the information or have the ability or resources to exploit it efficiently. Whether outright fraud and misrepresentation were a serious problem before passage of the Securities Acts and whether the SEC has eliminated or at least reduced such occurrences are empirical questions that are discussed below.

Efficiency of Investment and Allocation of Resources. The second group of claims for the benefits of mandated disclosure—improved efficiency of investment and allocation of resources—are derived from the assumption that published financial information is useful for investment decision-making. In the case of government-mandated disclosure, this assumption has the following corollaries: (1) the specific disclosures that companies would tend to withhold and the government would require them to disclose are useful; (2) the government (or its delegates, e.g., the FASB) can know which financial numbers are relevant to investment decisions; (3) the disclosures can be sufficiently timely to be of value to the investor.

With respect to the first corollary, it is argued that companies suppress useful information about their operations solely because they cannot restrict this information to their shareholders. To understand this argument—and its errors—it is important to note that more information is not always better if it requires resources to produce, distribute, and use. As is true of all goods, there is an optimal quantity that is determined by the cost of the information and its value: the optimal quantity is that amount for which the marginal cost is no greater than the marginal value. Information will be produced by corporations when they have a comparative advantage, when the costs to them are less than the costs to others, *ceteris paribus*.

If corporations could give their shareholders an exclusive property right in information, they would produce all information which costs the shareholders no more than it benefits them.[28] This information may even include data about other corporations that would benefit other investors, since the shareholders could sell any information they did not use themselves. In fact, similar reasoning holds in the absence of an exclusive property right in information so long as the shareholders' access to the information is superior to others'. In this situation, the price of the shares will reflect the value to investors of receiving information about the corporation, since receipt of this information will save investors the cost of obtaining it otherwise; hence the shares will be more valuable by the amount saved. The information will still repay the shareholders for the expenses it occasioned on their account, even though their right in it is not absolute.

Nevertheless, the impossibility of granting shareholders an exclusive property right in information does have one effect on the information economy. Corporations who act in their shareholders' interest will not produce and publish information that on balance will benefit other investors at shareholders' expense. Corollary (1) above is based on the argument that this information, which would be withheld in the absence of disclosure requirements, would be of general value if disclosed. But let us see what the value of that information would be.

A requirement that this information be published will harm shareholders, not only by the advantage that the information affords other investors, but also by imposing the cost of the information on shareholders. Shareholders might benefit from required disclosure if there were sufficiently large economies of scale in the production and use of information that are not specific to individual corporations. In this event, the required disclosure by all corporations would provide information that, in total, is of greater value than its cost of production. All investors would benefit, and it is possible that the benefits accruing to the shareholders from information published by other companies would exceed the costs they bear of publishing the information about

28. For a complete analysis, see F. Milne and R. Watts, "Corporate Information: A Public or a Private Good" (unpublished manuscript, University of Rochester, August 1977).

their own. If sufficient economies of scale do not exist, however, the disclosure requirement will harm shareholders and benefit only other investors.

One counterargument to this is that information is a public good in the sense that its consumption by one person does not reduce its value to another. (Another example is the receipt of a television signal.) But this is true only when prices are in equilibrium. Gonedes, Dopuch, and Penman, for example, say that if the information[29]

> provides a completely reliable signal pertaining to the true value of an asset's relative risk . . . [it can be used to assess] the equilibrium return on the asset. But the same signal can be used by any other agent who wishes to assess the equilibrium expected return on the asset.

When a share price is out of equilibrium, one person's use of information drives the price towards equilibrium, thereby reducing and ultimately eliminating the value of the information. Hence required disclosure would benefit some persons at the expense of others in this respect as well.

Another argument for the value of required disclosure is that the information disclosed is less costly for investors to use than are voluntarily disclosed numbers. One reason is that the numbers are produced under standards that are known to users. Another reason is that the data are presented in standard formats and are centrally available. This reasoning, however, leads to some questions. What reason is there to believe that C.P.A.-audited data are not reliable and that data produced pursuant to the SEC's historical-cost bias and standards determined by the regulatory rather than the market process are likely to be more useful to investors? And why is it a government function to standardize data or require that corporations produce standardized data?

Finally, the value of disclosed information is affected by the physical problem of transmission described in the previous section. Some shareholders or investors—whoever gets the information first—will trade on it, to the possible detriment of someone who has not yet received it.

Thus, if required fiancial disclosure is useful, it is useful (a) to the investors who receive the information first; (b) only to investors who are not shareholders, unless there are sufficiently great economies of scale in producing the information; or (c) only when the price is out of equilibrium, and then only to some investors. Aside from questions of equity, a determination of whether society as a whole benefits depends on whether the total cost of required disclosure exceeds the total benefits. This determination depends, in part, on whether required disclosure is likely to produce information or simply data, a distinction discussed below.

---

29. Gonedes, Dopuch, and Penman, "Disclosure Rules, Information-Production and Capital Market Equilibrium: The Case of Forecast Disclosure Rules," 15 J. Accounting Research 89, 96 (1976).

This brings us to the second corollary listed above, which states that the government (or its delegates) can know which information is relevant to financial decisions. The theory on which this proposition is based is not as well articulated as one would like. A reasonably good stock-valuation model has yet to be constructed. Economists, accountants, analysts, and others differ considerably on specifically what information is useful for investment decisions. While most people would accept the definition of assets and liabilities as the present value of expected cash flows, it is generally recognized that determination of the relevant cash flows and discount rates is essentially subjective and perhaps impossible. The arguments revolve around which variables and which models are the best proxies for the desired numbers. Therefore, it is questionable whether the employees of the SEC are more likely to determine the relevant data that should be disclosed than are others, particularly those who are investing their own resources. (In this regard, it is useful to note that the SEC has almost consistently opposed cash flow accounting, even though it is consistent with the present-value model, assuming that past cash flows are useful for estimating future cash flows.)[30]

Finally, let us consider the third corollary listed above: If the numbers produced are not distributed with sufficient dispatch to investors, their information content may be learned from other sources. Hence the numbers disclosed will be data, not information, since their receipt will not affect people's expectations. While this essentially is an unresolved empirical question, it seems clear that numbers produced pursuant to government regulations that make the issuer liable to penalties should the reports violate the regulations are likely to be less timely than numbers produced voluntarily. In fact, the SEC has consistently opted for accuracy and conformance with regulations over speed of transmission, particularly with respect to security registration statements.

Though, in my opinion, the weight of the theory does not support the belief that required disclosure is likely to result in benefits gross of costs, the empirical evidence should be considered. The evidence relevant to each of the seven presumed benefits is discussed in turn.

THE EVIDENCE ON SEC-REQUIRED DISCLOSURE

Fraud in Financial Statements. There is almost no evidence to support the assertion that the financial statements of publicly traded companies were fraudulently or misleadingly prepared in the years prior to the passage of the Securities Acts.[31] The U.S. Senate hearings that preceded passage of the 1934 Act cite only a few instances of fraudulent financial statements.[32] There were very few cases before 1934 that charged ac-

30. SEC Accounting Series Rel. No. 142 (Mar. 15, 1973), 5 Fed. Sec. L. Rep. (CCH) ¶ 72,164.

31. See G. Benston, *supra* note 25 § 4.2.2 for references.

32. See Senate Comm. on Banking and Currency, Stock Exchange Practices, S. Rep. No. 1455, 73d Cong., 2d Sess. (1934).

countants or companies with fraudulent or grossly negligent financial statements.[33] This lack of cases, however, may have been due to the difficulty of suing certified public accountants because of the prevailing rule of privity. This rule maintained that only the person for whom the statements were directly prepared (usually the company) could sue, unless the auditor had made a reckless misstatement or insincere expression of opinion. The Securities Acts altered that situation, making it incumbent on the accountant to demonstrate that he was free from negligence or fraud inasmuch as, after reasonable investigation, he believed the statements certified were true. Nevertheless, there were few actions against accountants until the 1960's, which is consistent with the belief that there was no pent-up desire to sue public accountants that was suppressed by the difficulty of maintaining a suit.

There is evidence that many prospectuses contained little financial data before passage of the Securities Act of 1933. Though I do not know of a study of the facts, the literature is replete with assertions to this effect.[34] Other than self-evidently outrageous puffery that implied a promise of great wealth, I know of no evidence of fraudulent financial data in prospectuses. It seems likely, however, that some fraud must have occurred.

However, it also is clear that fraud in financial statements has not been eliminated as a consequence of the Securities Acts. Indeed, such instances as *Equity Funding*,[35] *Home-Stake Investment*,[36] *Yale Express*,[37] *H. L. Green*,[38] and *National Student Marketing*[39] eclipse the cases of the pre-SEC period. From current evidence, it almost seems as if it is now easier to defraud some investors, possibly because the existence of the SEC lulls them into believing that fraud is a problem of the past.

Misrepresentation in Financial Statements. Misrepresentation—reporting the results of income and operations, assets and liabilities, so as to hide or obscure bad performance or give the illusion of good performance—is thought by many to be a more serious problem than fraud. The misrepresentation may be accomplished by choosing among alternative acceptable accounting procedures (e.g., using the pooling rather than

---

33. See, e.g., Ultramares Corp. v. Touche, Niven & Co., 255 N.Y. 170, 174 N.E. 441 (1931).

34. See, e.g., Friend "The SEC and the Economic Performance of Securities Markets," in *Economic Policy and the Regulation of Corporate Securities* (H. Manne ed. 1969).

35. *In re* Equity Funding Corp. of Am. Sec. Litigation, 416 F. Supp. 161 (C.D. Cal. 1976).

36. Geo. H. McFadden & Bros. v. Home-Stake Production Co., 295 F. Supp. 587 (N.D. Okla. 1968).

37. Fischer v. Kletz, 266 F. Supp. 180 (S.D.N.Y. 1967).

38. H.L. Green Co. v. Childree, 185 F. Supp. 95 (S.D.N.Y. 1960).

39. SEC v. Nat'l Student Marketing Corp., 402 F. Supp. 641 (D.D.C. 1975).

purchase method to account for an acquisition), by changing accounting methods (e.g., shifting from first-in-first out (FIFO) to last-in-first-out (LIFO) inventory accounting), by recording revenue or expenses when convenient (e.g., choosing which asset to sell when similar assets were recorded at different historical costs or capitalizing rather than expensing research and development costs), or by deciding which figure to report as earnings per share (e.g., charging extraordinary expenses to retained earnings or not clearly disclosing the number of common shares that might be issued pursuant to options). Government control over the alternatives that can be used by a corporation for reporting its financial situation is said to be a means of reducing the extent to which such manipulations can occur.

First, the available evidence does not support the claim that manipulations of reported accounting data are successful in fooling investors.[40] Numerous studies have been conducted that attempt to measure the effect on stock prices of changes in earnings per share that result from changes in accounting procedures. Among the changes studied are shifts from FIFO to LIFO inventory accounting, from accelerated to straight-line depreciation, from statutory to GAAP-determined earnings of life insurance companies, and from historical to price-level-adjusted earnings. Other studies have measured the effect on share price of one method of accounting rather than another. These studies include flow-through versus deferral accounting for income taxes where tax and book depreciation differ, pooling versus purchase accounting for acquisitions, and full-cost versus write-off accounting of oil and gas exploration costs. The findings of these studies are not consistent with the belief that share prices are affected by differences in accounting procedures alone. Hence, while a requirement that one method or another be used by most companies in an industry might result in less criticism of regulators and accountants, the evidence indicates that it would not benefit investors.

To the contrary, if published accounting statements provide investors with information, a movement towards uniform accounting is likely to reduce the value of that information. This would occur when a particular accounting procedure that provides a meaningful measurement for one firm produces a misleading measurement for another. For example, whether straight-line or accelerated depreciation describes the decline in present value of an asset depends on the pattern of its expected net cash flows. Another example is the requirement that research and development expenses be written off. The correctness of this procedure depends on the expected economic life of the research output. Since regulatory agencies (and accountants fearful of law suits) prefer to minimize risk and criticism should the future turn out to be worse than expected, they tend to require conservative, uniform procedures that are likely to result in the publication of misleading financial statements.

---

40. See G. Benston, *supra* note 25, § 4.2.3 for citations.

Security Price Manipulation. It is alleged by the SEC that security price manipulation in the late 1920's and early 1930's[41]

> resulted in a situation in which no one could be sure that market prices for securities bore any reasonable relation to intrinsic values or reflected the impersonal forces of supply and demand . . . . One of the principal contributing factors to the success of the manipulator was the inability of investors and their advisors to obtain reliable financial and other information upon which to evaluate securities.

The SEC refers to the manipulation of the shares of over one hundred companies listed on the New York Stock Exchange. I obtained the names of these companies.[42] All had financial statements published in *Moody's Investors Service* for at least two years before their securities were allegedly manipulated. All provided investors with balance sheets and income statements that were audited by C.P.A.'s. The only major items not reported were sales and cost of goods sold. However, the percentage of companies which did not publish these data (in 1929, for example, 39 percent did not reveal sales and 50 percent did not disclose cost of goods sold) was smaller in this group than among other NYSE-listed companies whose stock presumably was not manipulated. Thus periodic financial disclosure seems to have had little to do with stock price manipulation.

Fairness to Noninsiders. An operational definition of fairness to a noninsider might be that when he purchases or sells shares, the price paid or received should reflect all of the information known to insiders about the company. Thus the price would reflect the intrinsic value of the company, in the sense that while it might not be correct in the light of subsequent events, the probability that this error will be in the investor's favor is equal to the probability that it will be to his loss. Thus the market would be a fair game for the noninside investor.

Of course it is not possible to measure whether the market price of shares reflects all the information that anyone knows about a corporation. In addition, it is not physically possible for all investors to receive all information simultaneously and evaluate it with equal effectiveness. However, it has been shown that if all known information were impounded in share prices, successive price changes would be independent, appearing to follow a random walk.[43] Thus one can measure

41. Securities and Exchange Commission, *A 25-Year Summary of the Activities of the Securities and Exchange Commission*, pp. xi–xvi (1959).

42. Benston, "Required Disclosure and the Stock Market: An Evaluation of the Securities Exchange Act of 1934," 63 Am. Econ. Rev. 132, 136 (Mar. 1973). See also Friend and Westerfield, "Required Disclosure and the Stock Market: Comment, 65 Am. Econ. Rev. 467 (1975); Benston, "Required Disclosure and the Stock Market: Rejoinder," 65 Am. Econ. Rev. 473 (1973).

43. See G. Benston, *supra* note 25, § 4.2.5 for citation to works referred to in this section.

fairness by the statistical properties of past share prices; for if the changes were independent, the data would be consistent with the hypothesis that the market was a fair game. (However, this test would not prove the hypothesis.)

Numerous studies of United States share price behavior have been conducted with share price data before and after passage of the Securities Acts, with prices of shares traded on registered exchanges and over the counter, and with daily, weekly, and monthly changes. European stock market data have also been studied. Almost all of these studies report that share price changes are independently distributed. These data indicate, at least, that the Securities Acts have had no measurable effect on the independence of successive share price changes, and that the market was and is in this sense a fair game without this type of legislation.

Nevertheless, it seems likely that there is and was some unfair trading by insiders. Someone must get information before someone else, and the first person is likely to attempt to benefit from his knowledge. However, there is no evidence of which I am aware that shows that the extent of fairness to noninsiders was a serious problem before the Securities Acts were enacted or is any different as a consequence of the financial-disclosure provisions of the legislation.

Availability of Information That Otherwise Would Not Be Published. A primary benefit that the Securities Acts are presumed to achieve is the availability to investors of information that enables them to make informed decisions. Granting that information is beneficial for investment decisions, the efficacy of SEC-required disclosure (gross of costs) is based on the following assumptions, as stated in the discussion of the concepts involved: that the information produced would not have been otherwise forthcoming, and that it is indeed information.

There is some empirical evidence that speaks to the assumptions. First, as is indicated above, a considerable amount of financial data were published before passage of the Securities Acts. Most corporations whose shares were traded on the major exchanges produced the standard audited financial statements.[44] Though it is said that prospectuses accompanying new securities issues did not provide much information, no study of the extent or adequacy of the information presented has been made, to my knowledge.

Second, there is evidence that the numbers produced pursuant to the SEC's regulations are not information. The major financial item that was not disclosed by a significant number of corporations prior to passage of the 1934 Act is sales. Thirty-eight percent of the NYSE-listed corporations did not disclose this number. A statistical test of the meaningfulness of the required disclosure of sales was made by analyzing the behavior of share prices of the corporations that formally disclosed this

---

44. See *id.* § 4.2.6 for citations to works referred to but not footnoted in this section.

number for the first time.[45] I hypothesized that if the required disclosure of sales provided investors with information, the share prices of the affected corporations would differ significantly from the predisclosure magnitudes and variances, with other factors that affect share prices accounted for. The share price behavior of other corporations (62 percent) that had disclosed sales before 1934 served as a control sample. The statistics showed no significant difference between the pre- and post-SEC period or between the samples that did and did not disclose sales prior to the SEC disclosure requirement. Thus investors appear either to have learned about sales from other sources or to have found the numbers of no measurable (or at least measured) value.

Another test of the market's reaction to SEC-mandated disclosure was conducted by Daniel W. Collins, who was concerned with the post-1970 SEC requirement that corporations publish data by product line.[46] Since the SEC required that these data be published for prior years, Collins was able to calculate the value of the retrospective data had they been available to investors. For this purpose, he developed and tested share pricing strategies that depend on knowledge of product-line data and compared these to strategies using consolidated data only. Collins found that investors would have made significantly greater returns before commissions, etc., in 1968 and 1969 but not in 1970 had they had this information. Horwitz and Kolodny also examined the usefulness of required product-line disclosure by examining its effect on the share prices and market measures-of-risk of companies which reported segment-income data for the first time in 1971, using a sample of companies that did not as a control. They conclude, "[Our] results provide no evidence in support of the universally accepted contention that the SEC required disclosure furnished investors with valuable information."[47]

Finally, there is evidence that by the time financial reports are released to the public, their information content is known. Numerous studies have shown that the publication of annual statements is not accompanied by significant share price changes, which indicates that the data contained therein were known and previously discounted, that the statements do not contain information, or that the research was faulty.[48] Since other research indicates a greater volume of trading in the period when earnings results are announced, it would seem that the financial statements are not totally ignored.[49] This somewhat conflicting

---

45. Benston, *supra* note 42.

46. Collins, "SEC Product-Line Reporting and Market Efficiency," 2 J. Financial Econ. 125 (1975).

47. Horwitz and Kolodny, "Line of Business Reporting and Security Prices: An Analysis of an SEC Disclosure Rule," 8 Bell J. of Econ. 234, 237 (1977).

48. See G. Benston, *supra* note 25, § 4.2.6 for references.

49. *Id.*

finding was replicated in a recent, as yet unpublished study that speaks directly to the question of the effect of SEC-mandated disclosure. Paul Griffin studied the impact of 1975–76 sensitive-foreign-payments disclosures.[50] He found a significant increase in transactions in the weeks before and after foreign-payments disclosure. The value of the corporations' shares, though, showed but a small temporary decline: prices reverted to their normal levels within two weeks.

Efficiency in Security Investment and in the Allocation of Resources. There is little direct evidence on the effect of required disclosure on the efficiency with which securities markets operate. I do not know of any measurements of the cost of securities analysis and choice that permits a comparision of the pre- and post-SEC periods. Nevertheless, it is generally believed that the SEC's prospectus regulations result in considerably higher costs than had previously been incurred. Not only are auditing, legal, and printing costs higher, but also the delay that underwriters and corporations must endure while waiting for clearance by the SEC can be very costly. It may be that investors benefit from these expenditures by getting better information that enables them to make more effective decisions. However, even friendly critics of the SEC demur; for example, Homer Kripke says:[51]

> I have reluctantly come to the conclusion that the Securities Act of 1933 is not operating as it should and that the prospectus has become a routine, meaningless document which does not serve its purpose. Trying to keep from going entirely academic on the ivory shelf by maintaining my contacts with the practicing bar, I have reached the conclusion that most lawyers agree with me, and think of the registration process as simply a useless, but lucrative bit of paperwork.

It would seem that the costs outweigh the benefits.

Indirect evidence also may be brought to bear on this question. First, as discussed above, the findings that share price changes were independently distributed before the Securities Acts and in countries that do not regulate disclosure as does the United States are consistent with the hypothesis that government-mandated disclosure is irrelevant to the efficient impounding of information within share prices. Other evidence on the immediate effect of SEC-mandated disclosure is also generally consistent with this conclusion. Second, the specific financial information currently published by such financial serves as Moody's Manuals and Standard and Poors has changed very little from that published before 1934. If investors wanted the data that are made available in the 10K's, one would expect these services to provide them.

---

50. P. Griffin, "Disclosure Policy and the Securities Market: The Impact of the 1975–76 Sensitive Foreign Payment Disclosures" (unpublished manuscript, Stanford University, Graduate School of Business, November 1976).

51. Kripke, "The Myth of the Informed Layman," 28 Bus. Law. 631 (1973).

Also, few shareholders have requested 10K's, even when they have been offered at no charge.[52]

It is difficult to determine whether the Securities Acts have enhanced or hindered the efficient allocation of resources in the economy. I do not believe that a detailed study is required to show that investors still make investment decisions that turn out to be disastrous. Sudden and long-run stock market declines have characterized the post-SEC period at least as much as the pre-SEC years. If anything, it would appear that the higher costs of floating new securities, particularly for small companies, may have hindered the efficient allocation of resources in the economy. Even if some shareholders have been saved from making bad investments, others have been prevented from making good ones.

Public Confidence in the Securities Market. The evidence on this presumed benefit also is mostly indirect. The amount of new securities issues in proportion to capital formation was much lower after the Securities Acts were enacted than before.[53] The use of private placements instead of public sales of securities also increased dramatically after 1933. The post-SEC period is also characterized by the growing importance of mutual funds and other institutional investors. This evidence is inconsistent with the belief that the Securities Acts enhanced public confidence in the securities markets.

Additionally, it is not clear why greater individual investment in equity securities is a good thing. As recent experience once more shows, equity investments entail risk. Many people might be better advised to invest their savings through financial intermediaries. Why, then, is it a government function to support a particular form of saving?

The FTC's Line-of-Business Report Program[54]

The FTC claims that the data collected pursuant to its LB program will yield benefits to government, economicst, business, labor, investors, and consumers. The specific benefits expected are said to include the following, gleaned from the statements of purpose produced by the FTC:[55]

(1) The government's antitrust enforcement activities will be more

52. "Shareholders Exhibit Lack of Interest in 10-K Data, 138 J. Accountancy 21 (Nov. 1974).

53. See G. Benston, *supra* note 25, § 4.2.8 for citations to works referred to.

54. For a more detailed analysis see Benston, "The Federal Trade Commission's Line of Business Program: A Benefit-Cost Analysis," in *Government Informational Needs and Business Disclosure* (H. Goldschmid ed. 1979).

55. These are from the Federal Trade Commission, *Annual Line of Business Report Statement of Purpose* (1973); *Bureau of Economics Staff Report,* Federal Trade Commission Line of Business Reporting Program (1974); and Federal Trade Commission, *Supporting Statement, FTC Form LB 1974 Survey Version* (1975).

efficient, since the LB rate-of-profit and other data will provide improved guides for investigations.

(2) Macroeconomic policy will be supported by the improved quality of data used in the government's efforts to control inflation and unemployment.

(3) Resources will be allocated more efficiently because investors will get data that will point out the industries in which demand is inadequately satisfied and, as a consequence, profits will be particularly high. Stock analysts and investors will also learn more about the performance of individual corporations; this will in turn force managers to use the resources at their command more efficiently.

(4) Economic studies of industry performance will be improved considerably, particularly those that seek to measure the interrelationship among market structure, research and development costs, marketing expenditures, and profits.

(5) Business will benefit by having data that can be used to evaluate performance and pinpoint new opportunities at low cost. Buyers will be able to use the LB data to form judgments concerning the appropriateness of price/cost margins and profit rates.

(6) Labor will benefit because the LB data will facilitate comparisons among industries of labor's share of the pie.

(7) Investment analysts and investors will be able to use the LB reports to evaluate the prospects for particular industries.

(8) Consumers will benefit from the improvement in the markets for goods, services, and capital.

These expectations are based on three key assumptions. First, the LB categories defined by the FTC are presumed to be meaningful aggregates for the purposes delineated above. Second, the data collected are presumed to provide economically meaningful measures of profits per dollar of sales and assets. The third assumption, similar to the SEC's, is that the data that would be collected are not otherwise available to the market. Since the FTC, at the suggestion of the court of appeals, postponed the compliance deadline to give the court time to consider the case, the analysis must be limited to a consideration of the conceptual basis for the program.[56] However, in this instance this analysis should be sufficient.

LB CATEGORIES AND THE DEFINITION OF MARKETS

Most of the benefits claimed for the LB report program depend on the data's being aggregated into meaningfully defined markets. For example, the antitrust laws refer to illegal collusion among producers of a

---

56. *In re* FTC Line of Business Report Litigation, 5 Trade Reg. Rep. (CCH) ¶ 62,152 (D.C. Cir.), *affirming* 432 F. Supp. 291 (D.D.C. 1977), *cert. denied*, 99 S. Ct. 362 (1978).

specific product or group of products. Investment decisions similarly require data on markets—groups of products that are substitutes in use. Economic studies and, to some extent, macroeconomics intelligence may use industry rather than market data for some purposes, but the industries defined should include only goods that are substitutes in production. Furthermore, for the data to be useful for purchasing agents, labor leaders, or businesspersons, the numbers should relate to the specific products with which they are concerned. If the LB categories are broad aggregates of products, potential users will not be able to determine the source of a high or low rate of return.

When one examines the FTC-defined categories which are based on standard industrial codes, it is clear that the aggregates cannot be useful for any of the purposes delineated. First, the SIC categories were designed primarily to reflect production rather than consumption groupings. Thus copper roof gutters are in one category and plastic gutters are in another. That is why Betty Bock, Director of Antitrust Research for the Conference Board, says: "[A] detailed analysis of the LB categories made up of single 4-digit SIC codes would be likely to show that few, if any, could be directly correlated with markets whose boundaries are not open to serious debate."[57] Since half of the FTC's codes are even broader (being aggregates of SIC four-digit codes), she concludes:[58]

> I have come to believe that published data for the LB categories could cause the Commission and all other users to make errors so serious that, if the Commission were to proceed with the program, such users would be well advised to behave as if the data did not exist.

Second, the categories are too broad to be useful for most of the delineated purposes. For example, consider one of the more meaningful categories, FTC code 20.07, frozen specialities. Say an antitrust agency official believes that the market for frozen waffles is monopolized, or a potential manufacturer considers entering the field, or an investor or manager wants to compare the performance of his company with the industry. How can the relevant information be determined when FTC code 20.07 includes data from other frozen products such as baked foods, dinners, pies, pizza, soups, and spaghetti and meat balls? A high (or low) rate of profit for FTC code 20.07 may be due to a high (or low) rate on some of these products combined with a low (or high) profit rate on frozen waffles.

Third, the FTC categories, defined as they are, are contaminated. Because corporations do not keep their records according to FTC codes, they must group the data. To reduce somewhat the otherwise very high reporting burden, the FTC permits respondents to combine data derived from given cost or profit centers (or other established units) that

---

57. Affidavit of Betty Bock with Respect to Proposed 1974 FTC Form LB Before Federal Trade Commission, Statement in Behalf of Aluminum Co. of America, et al., p. 8 (May 15, 1975).

58. *Id.*, at pp. 9–10.

belong in different FTC codes, and report all the numbers as if they were due to a single FTC code if revenue properly belonging to that code is at least 85 percent of the total. The costs related to the buried FTC codes can be any percentage of the total. An analysis by Dr. Bock indicates that over one-quarter of the FTC categories are likely to be contaminated with respect to revenues (overstated, understated, or both) by more than 15 percent, and almost half by more than 10 percent.[59] No one (including the FTC) will be able to estimate the degree of cost contamination from the data reported. In addition, FTC rules that permit vertically integrated companies to combine data from several FTC codes additionally contaminate the reported categories and eliminate reporting of the categories thus combined. Therefore, even if the FTC defines meaningful aggregates, the data reported would not reflect what they purport to reflect.

THE MEANINGFULNESS OF LB DATA

Assuming that an FTC line-of-business category represents some meaningful aggregation of data, such as a market, we must next consider whether the data reported represent meaningful measures of profits and rates of return. Most of the benefits expected from the program depend on these measurements. Unfortunately, it is doubtful that this requirement is met because of unsolved and essentially unsolvable problems of intracompany transfers, allocations of common and joint expenses and assets, and the general lack of coherence between accounting numbers and economic values.

Intracompany Transfers. Intracompany transfers are a problem because many, perhaps most, companies do not price them at market prices. For a variety of reasons (control, nonavailability of data, cost-center rather than profit-center organization, tradition, and so on) they use other values, such as actual or standard direct or total cost, and negotiated prices. The FTC recognizes the effect of these practices in its 1973 *Statement of Purpose*, as follows: "Given the needs of the FTC, it appears that the use of market prices is appropriate. The use of any alternative procedure would distort the measurement of relative profitability."[60] They illustrate how a 10 percent difference between market and non-market transfer prices can distort a rate of return on sales or assets by 21 to 30 percent. Nevertheless, the FTC permits companies to use whatever method they choose when reporting transfer prices, because they learned that the companies could convert their data to market prices

---

59. Bock, "Line of Business Reporting: A Quest for a Snark?," 12 Conference Board Rec. 10, 18 (Nov. 1975).

60. Federal Trade Commission, *Annual Line of Business Report Program, Statement of Purpose* 11 (1973).

only at a very high cost, if at all. Thus the reported data will be distorted by unknown amounts.

Allocations of Joint and Common Cost. Even more of a problem than transfers, these allocations are particularly troublesome for the corporations that are the subjects of the FTC's program, since an important reason for the existence of multiproduct companies is the efficiency of joint and common production and distribution. That is why multiproduct companies are not just simple aggregates of single-product companies, as are mutual funds or holding companies. Many (perhaps most) companies do not allocate to operating divisions such expenses as central office operation, research and development, and marketing and warehousing. Many more do not allocate divisional expenses to product lines (as the companies define them) or to products. The procedures for making many of these allocations are necessarily arbitrary, since there is no conceptually correct way to allocate a cost to an individual activity if the cost is jointly determined by several activities. Where costs are common to several activities, there usually is no practical way to determine the amounts that would have resulted had only one of the activities been undertaken. Without this knowledge, allocations are not useful for most economic decisions and are likely to provide misleading data. The problem is particularly serious for the FTC line-of-business report, because almost no company is organized according to the FTC's line-of-business categories. Hence the amount of expenses and assets that must be allocated arbitrarily can be considerable.

The FTC recognizes the problem but nevertheless insists that all expenses (other than interest and income taxes) and all assets be assigned and allocated to one or another designated line of business. The magnitude of the distortions due to arbitrary allocations can be estimated from data presented in a study by Mautz and Skousen.[61] In their survey of 255 companies, they find the average ratio of noninventoried common costs to sales is 0.078, while the average ratio of net income to sales is 0.063. Thus differences in allocating these costs can have a considerable effect on reported net profits. The magnitudes of these effects can be determined from Mautz and Skousen's analysis of the effect of alternative acceptable methods of allocating common costs on the product-line net profits of six companies. A comparison of the net profits per line that a company would report by using its preferred method (designated P^*) compared to the net profits it would report using an alternative (designated P) was made by expressing P/P^* in percentage terms. This calculation was made for a total of thirty lines of business on which the six companies reported. In one case, the alternative method reported net profits that were only 3 percent of the profits reported by the preferred method; in another, the alternative yielded

61. Mautz and Skousen, "Common Cost Allocation in Diversified Companies," 36 Financial Executive 15–17, 19–25 (June 1968).

843 percent of the preferred-method profits. Between those two extreme, the other ratios were scattered as follows: two others fell below 5 percent, four fell between 6 percent and 10 percent, nine between 11 percent and 20 percent, four between 21 percent and 40 percent, two between 41 percent and 60 percent, one between 61 percent and 80 percent, and six in addition to the high of 843 percent were over 140 percent.[62] Thus the method of cost allocation can exert a great influence on the net profits reported. The effect of different allocation methods is likely to be even greater for the FTC data, since they specify many more lines and since their categories do not generally conform to the lines determined by the companies. Furthermore, alternative methods for allocating assets may (and will) be employed. As a consequence, the variance in the profit rate on assets (a key number) will be even greater.

The Lack of Coherence Between Accounting Numbers and Economic Values. Expenses should reflect the opportunity costs of earning the revenue reported. Assets should be valued at the cost of replacing their productive potential. As is well known, accounting numbers often provide poor measures of these values. Therefore, unless the magnitudes of the divergence between economic values and the numbers reported is relatively small or can be adjusted, the LB figures will be misleading or meaningless for the purposes of the program.

Two of the variables on which the FTC apparently intends to concentrate, advertising and research and development, are particularly affected by accounting. Accountants charge virtually all expenditures on these items (and other expenditures for intangibles) to current expenses, even though they recognize that many of the expenditures have future value, i.e., are assets. Therefore, companies who once engaged in large amounts of advertising and research that presently are generating sales and profits will report misleadingly high rates of return on assets. Another source of divergence between economic values and accounting numbers is the historical-cost method that, until recently, the SEC insisted upon. Clearly, the practice of not adjusting assets and liabilities for changes in the purchasing power of the dollar and for changes in supply and demand distorts many figures. For example, older companies that purchased fixed assets in the past will show lower-valued assets, lower depreciation, and hence higher profits and higher rates of return on assets than will newer companies, *ceteris paribus*. Consider also the case of a mining company which purchased coal property many years ago. With the greatly increased demand for coal, it will show a high rate of profit, since its depletion charge is based on the original cost of the mine. The profit, though, is due primarily to the company's having purchased the mine at what turned out to be an advantageous time. Antitrust law enforcement officials and potential entrants would not be able to distinguish a profit made from monopoly

---

62. See Benston, *supra* note 54, at Table 7 for details.

or monopsony practice from one due to a fortunate purchase and historical-cost-based accounting.

The total effect of the problems briefly described above can be considerable. For example, a 5 percent overstatement or understatement of costs can change an actual profit rate on sales or assets from 15 percent to either 19 or 10 percent. A 10 percent overstatement or understatement of costs changes the "true" 15 percent rate to either 24 or 7 percent.[63] These differences in the rates of return would swamp the numbers that distinguish a monopolistic from a competitive industry or a good from a bad investment.

CONCLUSION: TOTAL COSTS AND BENEFITS

I believe that the weight of the arguments and data rather strongly supports the conclusion that the costs to society of government-required disclosure exceed the benefits that may be derived therefrom. This conclusion is particularly strong for the FTC's line-of-business report program. The cost to the corporations which would be required to report the data are high and the benefits are nonexistent at best and probably negative. The costs of the SEC-mandated disclosure are not as high, since the SEC generally permits corporations to follow their usual record keeping formats. Unlike the FTC's line-of-business program, it may have some positive benefits, on balance. Even so, these benefits do not seem to offset the costs.

It is clear that government-mandated corporate financial disclosure programs are being extended rather than reduced. The committee established to consider changes in the SEC's disclosure regulations[64] has primarily recommended extensions of disclosure, though it has not recommended all that was proposed to it. The FTC's efforts to require large corporations to complete its forms are unrelenting, despite vigorous protests against its program. A question that should be considered, therefore, is: Why is government-required disclosure supported, despite its faults and costs? One answer to this question, I believe, can be found in the answer to another question: Who benefits from government-mandated disclosure? Another answer may be found in an analysis of the public's belief in the necessity for government regulation.

One group of beneficiaries of government-mandated disclosure obviously consists of the government agencies and agents who administer the laws and use the data. Let me concede, at the outset, that many government employees are honest, hard working, and public spirited. Therefore, they naturally come to believe that the laws and regulations they administer are necessary, or at least desirable, for the efficient and

---

63. See *id.* at Table 11 for a greater range of examples and for the formula on which these numbers are based.

64. See *Report*, *supra* note 4.

equitable functioning of that part of society whose welfare is their charge. As they go about their jobs, they come to see that some scoundrels avoid the intent of the laws and regulations, or they find that the data they have are inadequate to answer some question. Hence they ask for improved and more extensive disclosure. But it is not conceptually possible for the disclosure ever to be adequate. As is discussed very briefly above, accounting numbers generally are poor measures of economic values and almost any system of accounting measurement can be misused by miscreants. Nevertheless, more data are demanded of corporations because more is almost always better than less to those who do not have to pay the cost of production.

A second group of beneficiaries consists of those people outside of government who use the data but who also, like the regulators, do not have to pay for it. SEC data are used by many (not all) securities analysts and by firms who process the data for sale to the public. It is not surprising, therefore, to find analysts among those who are most insistent on extending disclosure. For example, the Fixed Income Analysts Society has proposed to the SEC Advisory Committee on Corporate Disclosure that corporations be required to "send annual and quarterly reports to holders of registered corporate bonds, . . . disclose in annual and quarterly reports . . . information facilitating protection against defaults on payments of interest and of safety and market value of principal," and so forth.[65] Their proposal seems curious, since these requirements could be written into the bond indenture agreements. One wonders, therefore, why bondholders have not asked for these data before, unless they had determined that the cost of the information (which they would pay for in reduced interest) was not worth the benefit. Analysts, however, work in the after-issue market. The required data would cost them nothing.

Accountants and lawyers are other groups that benefit from the disclosure required by the SEC. Both groups of professionals are in the business of selling their expertise, and the more extensive the regulations (up to a point), the greater the demand for their services. However, the benefits to them of greater disclosure are offset, in part, by the costs of greater legal liability and regulatory constraints. These costs have been imposed more on accountants than on lawyers (thus far at least). Perhaps that is one reason why the accountants have not been as supportive of extended SEC regulations as might have been expected.

Economists who specialize in industrial organization are an important group that hopes to benefit from the FTC's line-of-business data. These economists conduct studies of the relationships among market structure and profits, research and development expenditures, market-

---

65. Fixed Income Analysts Society, Committee on Corporate Disclosure, *Corporate Disclosure to Bond Investors and Analysts: A Report to the Securities and Exchange Commission and to the SEC's Advisory Committee on Corporate Disclosure*, pp. 3–4 (1977).

ing, and so on. The movement of corporations towards conglomerate form has deprived them of data on what they have been willing to describe as markets. Therefore, they look towards the FTC's line-of-business data as a plentiful source of grist for their mill. Since they neither have to pay the very high costs of producing these data nor even submit a grant application for the required financing, their interest is not surprising.

Finally, it is important to note that the public generally either (1) is unaware that the costs of required corporate disclosure are paid, ultimately, by consumers in the form of higher prices for goods and services and higher taxes; (2) overestimates the benefits and/or underestimates the costs; or (3) believes that the benefits outweigh the costs. The first factor is understandable. The costs of required disclosures are small relative to other costs of production. Therefore, even a doubling of disclosure costs that is reflected in prices probably would not be noticed by consumers, particularly in a period when inflation is so great and so variable. The second factor is also easily explained. The benefits from required disclosure are extolled by government officials, brokers, and analysts. Few voices are heard to the contrary. (Corporations do a very poor job in directing public attention to the effects of even more costly government programs.) The third factor, I believe, stems from a general feeling that the markets for goods, services, and capital essentially are not competitive and are plagued with shady dealings or worse. Furthermore, the economy is thought to be in need of control and regulation. These feelings may be residues from the experience of the Great Depression, when what was generally thought to be a competitive, free-enterprise, uncontrolled, and well-functioning economy apparently failed. From that time, increasing attention was paid to critics of the economy. The old beliefs were overthrown, generally with as little evidence as had supported their previous acceptance. But since the Second World War, a considerable body of analysis and empirical research has given us reason to question the assumption that the market economy had failed in the 1920's and early 1930's. Furthermore, forty years of experience with government regulation has provided evidence that its promise is not often achieved. If evidence is effective in altering beliefs, we have reason to hope for a change in the public's attitude towards the relative benefits of regulated versus unregulated enterprise.

ECONOMIC ANALYSIS AS ONE PHASE OF UTILITARIANISM

Ted J. Fiflis,* *Professor of Law, University of Colorado*

George Benston would dismiss the SEC and its staff as useless, and repeal the securities laws, or large portions of them, because they cost more than they are worth. Radical though these measures may seem, that alone is no reason for rejecting his views. After all, if Benston has perceived that the emperor, rather than wearing an invisible cloak, is as naked as the day that he was born, the rest of us should recognize that we have been deceived into accepting current disclosure policy only because of our fear that we should otherwise appear to be fools.[1]

Interestingly, leaders of the securities bar and the accounting profession have begun to fear that Benston and his allies may well have seen through a mere imaginary cloak of disclosure policy to the naked truth. The SEC Advisory Committee on Corporate Disclosure opened its report by stating that the central issue of securities law disclosure policy is "whether there are presently economic and public policy justifications for the existence of a disclosure system that . . . is characterized by a strong mandatory dimension regulated by a federal agency."[2]

---

* I wish to acknowledge the assistance of my colleagues Professors Clifford H. Calhoun and Stephen F. Williams, in addition to that of Professors Richard C. Posner and Homer Kripke, each of whose helpful comments and willingness to educate me have been extremely valuable. They, of course, are not responsible for the views expressed, and, indeed, disagree with many of my statements and conclusions.

1. Compare H. C. Andersen, *The Emperor's New Clothes* (1837).

2. *Report of the Advisory Committee on Corporate Disclosure to the Securities and Exchange Commission*, printed for the House Comm. on Interstate and Foreign Commerce, 95th Cong., 1st Sess., p. V (Comm. Print 1977) [hereinafter cited as

The Advisory Committee identified the pertinent question as whether *some* mandatory disclosure is justified, thereby stating the issue precisely as Benston does,[3] although the Committee reached the opposite conclusion: that some mandatory system is desirable. Unfortunately, once the Committee reached that conclusion, it was unable, like all who have tried before, to answer the next logical question: How much and what kind of mandatory disclosure is optimal under a cost-benefit analysis?[4] Nevertheless, as will appear, I believe the Committee's answer to the first question is correct, at least for the time being, and that it took the right road toward the answer to the second question, also at least for the time being. This article examines Benston's analysis of the first question and in so doing, perhaps clarifies the framework of reference for beginning analysis of the second one.

Ever since the first wild beast realized that trickery might facilitate the acquisition of a good meal, there has been a potential for fraud and unfairness which has often been realized. In the United States, as the complexities of modern corporate finance made it unconscionably easy for exploiters of their fellow human beings to bilk them of millions of dollars by the sale and purchase of something called a "security,"[5]

Report], abstracted in [1977–1978 Transfer Binder] Fed. Sec. L. Rep. (CCH) ¶ 81,357.

The Committee made abundantly clear its concern that the economic analysts may be right by enjoining the Commission to stay alert to further developments in economic research. At Report xlix, the Committee stated: "In concluding that radical change is not now desirable, the Committee would reiterate its belief that the Commission should observe closely developments in economic theory and should modify its policies to reflect such developments when they have achieved a tenability sufficient to sustain policy."

Accountants also have recognized the threat to the institution of published financial statements posed by some advocates of the efficient market hypothesis. See, e.g., Financial Accounting Standards Board, *Tentative Conclusions on Objectives of Financial Statements*, pp. 40–41 (1976).

3. Benston, "An Appraisal," at pp. 39–40 in this volume.

4. For a statement that the Committee has so failed, see Kripke, "Where Are We on Securities Disclosure After the Advisory Committee Report?" 2 J. Acctg. Auditing & Fin. 4 (1978). The Chairman of the Advisory Committee points out that a cost-benefit analysis is but one element, albeit an important one, in determining how much disclosure should be mandated, and that the Committee tackled several other elements of the question. Sommer, "Foreword to Survey: Report of the Advisory Committee on Corporate Disclosure to the Securities and Exchange Commission," 26 U.C.L.A.L. Rev. 48, 50 (1978).

5. "Securities" as defined in the federal securities laws are a narrower class than what the economist designates securities. The economist includes in the term any income-earning asset. See W. Sharpe, *Portfolio Theory and Capital Markets*, p. 19 (1970), defining "security" as a "decision affecting the future."

The narrower definition of the securities laws presumably was selected because legislatures sought to reverse the rule of caveat emptor only for securi-

sufficient voices were raised in indignant calls for change to cause first the states, and then, a few years later, the federal government, to adopt the present securities laws.[6] Congress and the President did not like what they saw in corporate finance and reacted with the 1933 and 1934 Acts[7] and, subsequently, further legislation.[8] However, at the time of those Acts, there was merely a crudely determined legislative belief that somehow market forces were not operating satisfactorily, accompanied by only a vague consideration of the relative advantages and disadvantages of the securities law disclosure system which was adopted.

Later writers have analyzed these crude legislative determinations in an effort to supply us with a rational economic basis for a mandatory disclosure system. They have argued that the free market will not operate to provide an efficient[9] disclosure system because of externalities.[10] For example, it is forcefully maintained that if a company publishes information specific to the particular firm, the benefits will accrue in part, at least, to nonshareholders while the firm (and, it is said, therefore its shareholders) will bear the entire cost.[11] Hence a

---

ties which were so intangible and abstract as to be uniquely different from such securities as investment chattels and real estate, for which the law of caveat emptor was deemed more appropriate. Consumerism is extending the list of items no longer governed by the concept of caveat emptor.

6. For a history of the state and federal securities laws, see L. Loss, *Securities Regulation*, vol. 1, chapter 1 (2d ed. 1961).

7. Securities Act of 1933, 15 U.S.C. §§ 77a–77aa (1976); Securities Exchange Act of 1934, 15 U.S.C. § 78a–78jj (1976) [hereinafter cited as "1933 Act" and "1934 Act" respectively].

8. Public Utility Holding Company Act of 1935, 15 U.S.C. §§ 79a–79z (1976); Trust Indenture Act of 1939, 15 U.S.C. § 77aaa–77bbb (1976); Investment Company Act of 1940, 15 U.S.C. §§ 80a-1 to -52 (1976); Investment Advisers Act of 1940, 15 U.S.C. §§ 80b-1 to -21 (1976).

9. Efficiency means that point at which maximum net economic benefits will be obtained as measured by voluntary market transactions; i.e., the point at which there is the greatest difference between the economic benefits of a system and its costs; put otherwise, that point at which the size of the economic pie (net benefits) is largest; in short, wealth maximization.

10. "Externalities" include costs as well as benefits. External costs are those incurred by persons other than those who benefit from the transaction. External benefits are the benefits obtained without cost to the beneficiary.

11. See Benston, "An Appraisal," at pp. 51–52 in this volume. I am not satisfied that it has been established that shareholders bear these costs. Employees, consumers and taxing bodies may bear some or all, and perhaps, in fact, investors bear them so that there are no net externalities. But the burden of establishing lack of externalities would seem to be on the proponent of such a view.

portion of the benefits of disclosure are conferred on nonshareholders without payment by them of proportional costs. Economists, who base their dismal science on economic self-interest expressed in voluntary market transactions, therefore conclude that the market will induce less than the optimal amount of disclosure.

In addition, the rationalizers of mandatory disclosure assert, with sufficient reason, that the structure of the public corporation is such that there are two additional powerful economic disincentives to voluntary disclosure. The first of these is the securities trading advantage corporate insiders may obtain by nondisclosure for themselves and those they tip. The second is management's incentive to conceal poor performance for a variety of ends.[12] Thus if a cost-effective system of disclosure in a free maket cannot be attained for these reasons, *some* governmental regulation is posited as necessary. This seems to be the generally held belief today justifying mandatory disclosure. Benston argues that this belief is incorrect primarily because, in his assessment, there are no benefits net of costs to be obtained from governmentally mandated disclosure.

THE BATTLE LINES

For many years, lawmakers failed to recognize the possibility that at some point (perhaps even the beginning point) the disadvantages of regulation might exceed the advantages. Thus, for example, on the lazy Thursday afternoon when the Securities and Exchange Commission (SEC) adopted rule 10b-5, thereby substantially extending securities law disclosure, the unanalytical approach to disclosure law was epitomized in the reasoning of one Commission member, who stated, "Well we're against fraud, aren't we," indicating little awareness of the possible disadvantages of additional government regulation.[13]

Since then, economists such as Benston have provided a great service by articulating vividly the concept of economizing—making the most of resources by analyzing costs and benefits in order to achieve maximum wealth.

---

12. See *Report, supra* note 2, at pp. 625–40 for a fuller explanation by Professor Beaver. As explained under the heading "Conceptual Bases for SEC-Required Disclosure" below, one complicating feature with any such analysis of the costs and benefits of disclosure is that a substitute for, or at least a complement of, mandated disclosure may be the liability for misrepresentation in damages, criminal penalties, or equitable relief.

13. See SEC Securities Exchange Act Release No. 34-3230 (1942); and remarks of Milton Freeman in "Proceedings, Conference on Codification of Federal Securities Laws," 22 Bus. Law. 921–22 (1967) where this folklore of rule 10b-5 is memorialized.

The initiator of the economic inquiry into securities regulation was George Stigler who, in his famous 1964 article,[14] attacked the Special Study of the Securities Markets[15] for its failure to take into account the economic impact of its recommendations. His startling conclusion was that the 1933 Act disclosure, instigated at Brandeis' suggestion, is not worth the effort required to make it.[16] Although Stigler's article has been challenged for its nearly inexcusable weaknesses,[17] his major purpose, raising the consciousness of securities lawmakers concerning the utility of economic analysis,[18] has been achieved through his efforts and those of numerous others, including Benston. The latest manifestation of the success in making legislators conscious of the costs of government intervention in general is a bill entitled the Reform of Regulation Act of 1979, which has as its purpose requiring regulatory agencies to make a cost-benefit analysis for proposed regulations prior to adoption.[19]

Further, Benston, in a well-known paper,[20] developed findings that no net economic benefit has been gained from the disclosure provisions of the 1934 Securities Exchange Act, and much of that writing is drawn upon in his present article.[21] Similarly, in his current piece, Benston concludes that the costs of government-mandated disclosure exceed its benefits. Although he deals with both securities law disclosure and the FTC's new line-of-business disclosure requirements, my comments here are limited to the former.

In any evaluation of Benston's arguments, the placement of the burden of proof will be crucial because of the lack of conclusive evidence by which to validate his position. By *burden of proof* I mean the dual burdens of producing evidence and persuading the

---

14. Stigler, "Public Regulation of the Securities Markets," 37 J. Bus. 117 (1964).

15. *Report of the Special Study of the Securities Markets of the Securities and Exchange Commission*, 88th Cong., 1st Sess., House Doc. 95 (1963).

16. L. Brandeis, *Other People's Money*, p. 62 (1933).

17. Some of which Stigler himself immediately admitted. See Stigler, "Comment," 37 J. Bus. 414 (1964).

18. *Id.*

19. S. 262, 96th Cong., 1st Sess. (1979). In addition, note that President Carter in Executive Order No. 12044, 43 Fed. Reg. 12,661 (1978) issued instructions directing government agencies, inter alia, to consider the burdens imposed by regulations. However, independent regulatory agencies such as the SEC are not affected by this order.

20. Benston, "Required Disclosure and the Stock Market: An Evaluation of the Securities Exchange Act of 1934," 63 Am. Econ. Rev. 132 (1973).

21. For a concurrent criticism of Benston's 1973 paper, see Friend and Westerfield, "Required Disclosure and the Stock Market: Comment," 65 Am. Econ. Rev. 467 (1973), rebutted in Benston, "Required Disclosure and the Stock Market: Rejoinder," 65 Am. Econ. Rev. 473 (1973).

reader. If the burden is on Benston, I believe he has not met it; however, if it is on the supporters of the status quo, they would possibly be hard put to meet it. Given the existence of mandated disclosure, the great upheaval which would result from scrapping it, the intuitive bases for the existing system, and the available evidence in support of it, the burdens of going forward with the evidence and of persuasion should be on Benston. Of course, others may argue that the current public mood, antagonistic toward regulation, and fed by astute politicians, shifts the burden to the champions of the extant system. They could add, more persuasively, that my allocation of the burden of proof creates a ratchet effect: once enacted, proponents of repeal have the burden of proof, so that enactment establishes its own safeguard against repeal. They might instead urge a sunset review, with the burden on the proponent of legislation to justify it after a period of years. This seems wrong in the absence of more evidence that nihilism in disclosure policy would not be disruptive. Moreover, few proponents of deregulation argue for totally eliminating mandatory securities law disclosure—Benston is still a member of a tiny minority.

In addition, although Benston's writing are valuable as consciousness-raising efforts, they illustrate the limited utility of economic analysis. As a more satisfactory alternative, I propose that a more complete model, along twentieth century utilitarian lines and not confined merely to economics, should be used, to bring out all the factors appropriate for consideration in determining disclosure policy. By use of the term *twentieth century utilitarianism*, I seek to signal the reader that I do not endorse use of the coarse, mean-spirited, and mechanical utilitarianism of Jeremy Bentham, which lends itself so easily to being a straw man for antiutilitarian critics.[22]

My view of twentieth century utilitarianism, roughly stated, is that it tests the goodness or badness of laws by taking account of all their consequences in furthering the ultimate fulfillment of humankind. Henry Hart and Albert Sacks say it best in suggesting that "the social problem has been broadly described as that of 'establishing, maintaining and perfecting the conditions necessary for community life to perform its role in the complete development of man.' "[23] Then, in eloquent

---

22. Perhaps there is more than a straw man here. At least one modern legal philosopher continues to take Bentham's details quite seriously. J. J. C. Smart, "An Outline of a System of Utilitarian Ethics," in J. J. C. Smart and B. Williams, *Utilitarianism: For and Against* (1967). And see Barry, "Book Review," 88 Yale L.J. 629 (1979) describing the current waning of utilitarianism in philosophical writings, not in lawyers' work. See, e.g., Posner, "Utilitarianism, Economics, and Legal Theory," 8 J. Leg. Stud. 103 (1979).

23. H. Hart and A. Sacks, *The Legal Process: Basic Problems in Making and Application of Law*, pp. 110–113 (Tent. ed. 1958), quoting from Snee, "Leviathan at the Bar of Justice," in *Government Under Law*, p. 47, at p. 52 (1955).

manner, they explain their view of the fundamental objectives of any institutional system of laws. They summarize it in this way:

> . . . the underlying imperative of group life: to avoid the disintegration of social order and the consequent destruction of the existing benefits of group living.
>
> . . . the great desideratum: to maximize the total satisfactions of valid human wants, and keep on maximizing them, by making a steadily more effective use of the resources of group living—the primary and overriding goal of positive social effort.
>
> . . . the pragmatic necessity of a currently fair division.[24]

---

24. *Id.* So described, this twentieth century utilitariansim is a far cry from Posner's depiction of a hedonistic, sadistic utilitarianism which he first resurrects from the philosophical graveyard and then redestroys in his recent article, see Posner, *supra* note 22. To illustrate, although some utilitarian writers once took into account the benefits to animals from their (the animals') senses of pleasure and pain, the modern view, except for J. J. C. Smart, *supra* note 22, leaves no room for any but human wants (which may, however, take animal welfare into account). See H. Hart and A. Sacks, in the text accompanying this note. Yet Posner in his article repeatedly seeks to prove the disutility of utilitarianism by beating dead horses (or sheep) to make his points. Thus he notes the so-called "boundary problem" of utilitarianism—its uncertainty of domain—and states, "In utilitarian morality, a driver who swerved to avoid two sheep and deliberately killed a child could not be considered a bad man, since his action may have increased the amount of happiness in the world." Posner, *supra* note 22, at 112. This suggests the sheep's happiness exceeded the pain of the child and his relatives, friends, and acquaintances. This is not what modern utilitarians believe, as Posner apparently concedes in his paragraph which follows the above.

But worse yet, a little later he admits that he and other economic analysts would preserve sheep over humans so long as there are enough of the sheep being saved—100,000 in his example. *Id.* at 133. The ostensible difference between his two illustrations is that the nineteenth century utilitarian would consider the feelings of the sheep while the modern wealth maximizer considers only what the collective society of humans will pay for the sheep as compared to what they will not pay for a safeguard against the danger to the life of some human. This *calculus pencunium*, although abhorrent when articulated, Posner correctly justifies as in accord with modern ethical values. The modern utilitarian would probably reach the same conclusion, but both he and the economic analyst would desire that the market be informed about the price of the sheep as including human lives, although the economic analyst would weigh the costs of information. Government intervention would be necessary to cause the information to be provided.

This note simply suggests that Posner's article raises a straw man utilitarianism and discredits it; but that obviously does not discredit modern utilitarianism. Later we shall, in passing, consider whether the implicit position that economic analysis is superior to twentieth century utilitarianism is adequately established. See "A Twentieth-Century Utilitarian Approach" *infra*, at pp. 104–108.

This is not merely the brilliantly articulated view of two legal philosophers. It is a description of the way modern American lawmaking currently functions,[25] although all lawyers may not consciously be aware of it. My own further views will appear in the course of this article, but the basic theme is that economic analysis supplies only part of the data which must be taken into account in determining the utility of laws—sometimes a large part and sometimes a very small one, but almost never all—and it totally ignores the extremely important problem of equity among the members of society. To state my case more strongly: economic analysis is to modern utilitarianism what analyses of environmental consequences, psychological consequences, esthetic consequences and all other consequences are—part, but not all of that which must be considered; taken as the only consideration, economic analysis will often yield wrong results. Economics can supply but one segment of the necessary data. In the end, despite the promises of the champions of economic analysis, there is no easy arithmetical answer to the question of what is an optimal disclosure policy.[26]

THE DUAL ASPECTS OF THE SEC DISCLOSURE SYSTEM, AND THE PYGMALION SYNDROME

The Dual Nature of the Securities Law Disclosure System

Before Benston's specific findings are reviewed, two matters must be explained. First, it must be noted that there are two complementary systems for regulating securities law disclosure—the antifraud provisions and the reporting requirements.[27] The antifraud provisions, with their private and public sanctions for certain omissions and misrepresentations, ranging from sanctions against an issuer for nonnegligent misrepresentations in a registration statement,[28] through negligence,[29]

---

25. "It should be noticed that the suggestion is not that these are fully understood objectives of every society, much less of every member of them. What are here in question are the objectives of social effort which correspond with the conditions of social existence, whether people understand them or not." H. Hart and A. Sacks, *supra* note 23, at 114.

26. Chairman Williams of the SEC, in a speech at the Columbia University/McGraw-Hill Lectures in Business and Society, October, 1978, entitled "Egalitarianism and Market Systems," also apparently evidenced concern for the incompleteness of economic analysis as a sufficient ethical governor of disclosure policy, despite his great respect for free markets. See Sec. Reg. & L. Rep. (BNA) No. 473 at A-11 (Oct. 11, 1978) for a report of that speech.

27. *Report, supra* note 2, at p. 624; R. Posner, *Economic Analysis of Law*, pp. 271–72 (2d ed. 1977).

28. Section 11 of the Securities Act of 1933, 15 U.S.C. § 77k (1976).

29. *Id.* §§ 11, 12(2), 15 U.S.C. §§ 77k, 77l(2) (1976).

to misrepresentations with scienter,[30] arguably could constitute the exclusive system for securities disclosure. Courts could fashion rules which would extend the duty of affirmative disclosure by issuers,[31] having already established substantial rules against insiders, tippees, and certain others who trade on the basis of nonpublic information,[32] as well as rules against misrepresentations to the market and in securities transactions.[33]

In the context of consumer fraud regulation, it has been suggested that privately enforced common law actions could make a more efficient disclosure system than do the reporting provisions of the Federal Trade Commission Act.[34] The securities laws' antifraud provisions, with their provisions for SEC enforcement as well as private enforcement, could be even more powerful since the SEC would prosecute many actions which private parties might not find it feasible to pursue. Indeed, it is not unrealistic to contemplate a scheme in which private and SEC enforcement of the antifraud provisions would be the first line of defense, with the SEC's other administrative powers deployed as a backup force. On the other hand, the antifraud provisions are probably essential to a disclosure system: liability could not be imposed for failure to properly report without a proscription against false or otherwise misleading reports.[35]

Since experience shows that the imaginations of acquisitive people make it impossible to codify the law of fraud efficiently, the effectiveness of the antifraud provisions is dependent upon a thoughtful structuring of fraud liability by the courts.[36] In recent years the United States

---

30. For example, rule 10b-5, 17 C.F.R. 240.10b-5 (1978); Ernst & Ernst v. Hochfelder, 425 U.S. 185 (1976); Section 18 of the Securities Exchange Act, 15 U.S.C. § 78r (1976).

31. There is probably already a crude duty of affirmative disclosure for publicly held companies, whether or not reporting to the SEC. Cf. Financial Industrial Fund, Inc. v. McDonnell Douglas Corp., 474 F.2d 514 (10th Cir.), *cert. denied*, 414 U.S. 874 (1973); cited approvingly in Goldberg v. Meridor, 567 F.2d 209, 221 n. 10 (2d Cir. 1977), *cert. denied*, 434 U.S. 1069 (1978).

32. E.g., SEC v. Texas Gulf Sulphur Co., 401 F.2d 833 (2d Cir. 1968), *cert. denied*, 404 U.S. 1005 (1971); Shapiro v. Merrill Lynch, Pierce, Fenner & Smith, Inc., 495 F.2d 228 (2d Cir. 1978); SEC v. Bausch & Lomb, Inc., 565 F.2d 8 (2d Cir. 1977); United States v. Chiarella, 588 F.2d 1358 (2d Cir. 1978), *petition for cert. filed*, 47 U.S.L.W. 3529 (U.S. Feb. 13, 1979) (No. 78-1202).

33. Heit v. Weitzen, 402 F.2d 909 (2d Cir. 1968), *cert. denied*, 395 U.S. 903 (1969); Mitchell v. Texas Gulf Sulphur Co., 446 F.2d 90 (10th Cir. 1971), *cert. denied*, 404 U.S. 1004 (1971).

34. R. Posner, *supra* note 27, at p. 272.

35. State law of fraud or reporting could also be relied upon.

36. But see Blackstone, "A Roadmap for Disclosure vs. A Blueprint for Fraud," 26 U.C.L.A.L. Rev. 74 (1978).

Supreme Court has substantially refashioned the federal law of fraud, reacting to the explosion of federal securities litigation but without any apparent vision of social utility other than the notion that the less federal litigation, the better.[37] I suspect a strong case could be made for the view that insufficient concern has been shown by the Court for the features of the federal system and interstate and international commerce which should make this area one of primary federal judicial concern.[38] The result of the Supreme Court's decisions has been the placement of

---

37. This view is straightforwardly articulated in Blue Chip Stamps v. Manor Drug Stores, 421 U.S. 723, 739–49 (1975), but less candidly implemented in several other opinions of the Court, including United Housing Foundation, Inc. v. Forman, 421 U.S. 837 (1975); Ernst & Ernst v. Hochfelder, 425 U.S. 185 (1976); Piper v. Chris-Craft Industries, Inc., 430 U.S. 1976 (1977); Santa Fe Industries, Inc. v. Green, 430 U.S. 462 (1977); Int'l Bro. of Teamsters v. Daniel, 99 S. Ct. 790 (1979).

38. The reaction to the Supreme Court's recent braking of fraud law development has been several calls for increased federal regulation of corporate activity, including requiring federal chartering of certain corporations.

This is no place to detail my views on what should be the federal law of fraud in the securities area but a few points may suffice to indicate what is meant in the text. In my view, the courts (as well as Congress) should perceive and observe at least the following objectives: (1) Regardless of the content of the substantive law, it appears that for large companies, which do business in several states, procedural obstacles to suing them and their affiliates under the securities laws in a single suit should be minimized. Directors or officers of large firms have a lesser claim of inconvenience or prejudice from being sued elsewhere than in their personal domiciles than do automobile drivers or other individual defendants. Thus rules of federal court jurisdiction, especially pendent jurisdiction, service of process and venue should be liberally construed or applied for claims against large firms and their affiliates, regardless of the substantive law, merely as an efficiency measure. (2) For the sake of the same efficiency, class actions (whether on behalf of a plaintiff class or against a class as defendants) should be facilitated. (3) Concerning the substantive law, it would seem that General Motors should not be subjected to fifty-one different sets of disclosure or tender offer rules in the United States. A single law should regulate. The reasons for a single federal law have nothing to do with any desire on my part to increase government regulation. Rather, it seems that a national interest exists in the securities markets for the securities of large businesses and it is absurd to have the corporate law sections of the respective bar associations of Delaware or Nevada (or two or three of their members) fix national policy for the national securities markets. For that matter in several states, the general counsels of certain large companies have drafted laws, e.g., tender offer legislation, which were then rubber-stamped by an agreeable state legislature. (4) Note that I am not here espousing a federal corporations code. It is merely a national securities law that I endorse—but one which covers all interests of securities investors, including their interest in honest management. (5) Finally, federal courts, recognizing that fraud and fiduciary obligations of necessity are best administered by courts not legislatures, should treat general fraud legislation of Congress more hospitably than has the current Supreme Court.

greater pressure on the other aspect of securities law disclosure, regulation of reporting.[39]

Benston does not make clear the dual aspects of the securities law disclosure system and the dynamic nature of each subsystem. In addition, he seems to limit his attack to the reporting system and is apparently willing to allow the antifraud rules to exist in some form. This is troublesome because, as I have suggested, the antifraud provisions could be expanded to take over the whole disclosure task, and it is not clear what Benston would do with the antifraud rules if the reporting requirements were eliminated.

A Cautionary Note—the Pygmalion Syndrome[40]

The "real world" is the universe of all facts. Often, problems may be better solved or understood by constructing a model of only the relevant segment of the universe and further simplifying it by eliminating many of the characteristics which are irrelevant or immaterial to the problem at hand.

At the risk of sticking too closely to the real-world terminology, an example may be helpful using the models of the earth called maps. We draw maps, which condense the earth's surface and eliminate most of its configurations, to enable us to do such things as plan an unfamiliar trip from one point on that surface to another. But there are all sorts of maps. Most of us know that a straight line drawn between the points designated for Chicago and London on a flat Mercator projection map (a map having straight-line parallels and meridians intersecting at right angles) will not be the shortest distance on the earth's surface. To determine the shortest distance we would use a globular projection of the earth's surface, draw a great circle passing through London and Chicago and select the shorter of the two arcs of this circle to plot the shortest distance. Now if we transpose the great circle route to our Mercator projection, we will find the shortest distance between Chicago and London is an arc that first curves northward from Chicago over Newfoundland and then bends toward the south to London—not a

---

39. For example, Congress has responded with the Foreign Corrupt Practices Act of 1977, Pub. L. No. 95-213, 91 Stat. 1494 (1977), not a reporting act in itself but a prophylactic measure to make reports more accurate and reliable. See also Block and Schwarzfeld, "Corporate Mismanagement and Breach of Fiduciary Duty After Santa Fe v. Green," 2 Corp. L. Rev. 91 (1979).

40. Although the explanation in this section is my own, it is the concept of a physicist writing on the general and special theories of relativity. H. Synge, *Talking About Relativity*, pp. 16–27 (1970). After I understood Synge's explanation of the Pygmalion syndrome, it appeared so obvious that I began to feel he and I were naive in believing that not everyone was already aware of it. However, since then I have come to see that in fact the Pygmalion syndrome is as rife among those concerned with economic analysis as Synge found it rife among physicists.

straight line. Hence, these two models show that if we wish to solve the problem of the shortest distance over the earth's surface, drawing a straight line between the two points on the flat map model would yield the wrong answer.

This is a simple point to make. Models of the real world, by simplifying it, may give great leverage to the human brain in solving real-world problems. But most importantly, one must be constantly aware of dealing with a model with limited utility, and sometimes wrong results will be obtained which are not sufficiently absurd to be recognized as possibly wrong. And in a few cases, undue respect for a model may even cause one to yield to patently absurd results just because one does not understand the limitations of models.[41]

Synge called the failure to keep in mind that a model is not the real world the "Pygmalion syndrome,"[42] named for the symptoms of the mythical sculptor who, having carved a virgin from marble, saw it come to life in his mind's eye and became infatuated with her. Such infatuation is a common one for model builders and users. The trick is to avoid the Pygmalion syndrome,[43] while respecting the utility of models of the real world for the leverage they provide in solving real-world problems.[44]

SOME PRELIMINARY OBSERVATIONS ON WEAKNESSES OF A COST-BENEFIT MODEL OF THE SEC MANDATORY DISCLOSURE SYSTEM

Benston has developed an economic model of disclosure policy which may profitably be examined in light of these two preliminary points—the dual aspects of securities law disclosure, and the Pygmalion syndrome. With these in mind, we perceive that there are several obvious

---

41. As an illustration, I note what I hope is an apocryphal story. A recent recipient of a Ph.D. from the University of Chicago has asserted that anyone who wishes to do so should be allowed to detonate an atomic bomb so long as he or she is willing and able to pay the costs. Bus. Week, Nov. 21, 1977, at p. 100. The suggestion of this presumably fictional fellow illustrates a misunderstanding, perhaps not entirely his fault, of George Stigler's statement that "the issue is precisely that of the use of 'scientific method' *versus* 'common sense'." Stigler, "Comment," 37 J. Bus. 414, 416 (1964) (emphasis added).

42. H. Synge, *supra* note 40, at p. 18.

43. Cf. then-Judge Cardozo in Berkey v. Third Ave. Ry. Co., 244 N.Y. 84, 94, 155 N.E. 58, 61 (1926): "Metaphors in law are to be narrowly watched, for starting as devices to liberate thought, they end often by enslaving it."

44. The character of models as abstractions of the real world also causes a misunderstanding of an opposite nature—causing many to reject models as not comporting with the real world. See M. Friedman, "The Methodology of Positive Economics," in *Essays in Positive Economics*, p. 3 (1953) explaining this error, referred to in R. Posner, *supra* note 27, at p. 13.

difficulties facing one who seeks to construct an economic model of the securities law disclosure system from within that universe for the purpose of making a cost-benefit analysis of the system:

(1) Given the existence of externalities in corporate disclosure, economic efficiency probably cannot be attained merely by operation of market forces, as we have seen, and once the government undertakes to regulate, there is no longer a free market and hence no market-determined price for the governmentally imposed benefits and costs. Consequently they must be hypothetically appraised in a largely subjective fashion, counter to the basic tenet of efficiency which fixes values based on willingness to pay.

(2) Not all advantages and disadvantages of disclosure are measurable, i.e., quantifiable, as economic costs or economic benefits, the only factors which the economic model takes into consideration.

(3) Some societal values have nothing to do with the quantity of net benefits but are concerned with the distribution of costs and benefits among individuals, or equity. Even if it is considered more desirable to decrease the size of the economic pie and give more nearly equal slices to all individuals, the economic model is useless, except to tell us the cost of a given increment of "equality."[45]

(4) This universe is dynamic, not static, and it is not perfectly predictable.

(5) The disclosure system underlying the model is also dynamic and its future is therefore not predictable with accuracy. Although economic models need not be static, Benston's is.

Each of these difficulties is evidenced in Benston's analysis, which does not succeed in overcoming them.

Efficiency in the Presence of Government Regulation

Given the lack of an actual market when the government intervenes, how can the analyst measure costs and benefits?[46] To eliminate this

---

45. Willingness to pay, the basis of the efficiency and value concepts, is a function of many things, including the distribution of income and wealth. Were income and wealth distributed differently, the pattern of demands might also be different and efficiency would require a different deployment of our economic resources. Since economics yields no answer to the question whether the existing distribution of income and wealth is good or bad, just or unjust—neither does it yield an answer to the ultimate question whether an efficient allocation of resources would be good, just or otherwise socially or ethically desirable.

R. Posner, *supra* note 27, at p. 10. And see Posner, *supra* note 22, at p. 135.

46. See R. Posner, *supra* note 27, at p. 11, where he suggests there is no need to throw in the towel at this point, saying a

possible approach is to try to *guess* whether, if a voluntary transaction had

problem, Benston has chosen, among several possible surrogates for the market, the following mechanism: if he finds a zero or trivial value for benefits purportedly established by government regulation of disclosure, he assumes there is no need to appraise the value of the costs if he, in addition, finds costs are nontrivial. We shall examine his findings to this effect in detail *infra* under the heading "The Benston Argument."

Measurability

When one attempts to make a cost-benefit analysis, one is constructing a model of the real world which presumes that all costs and benefits of the system underlying the model may be measured, i.e., quantified, at least approximately. Otherwise there would be no utility in comparing costs and benefits.[47] But a model which insists on quantification faces the difficulty that not all things in the real world are measurable. To carry the economic pie metaphor to an extreme, economics tells us nothing of how to improve the flavor, appearance, or texture of the pie—only its size.[48]

Anyone familiar with accounting for business entities, for example, is well aware that even the measurement of simple economic units is highly speculative. And when one gets to valuing such things as public confidence in the securities markets, the social costs of fraud, and the like, one is in a very subjective realm.[49] For a further example, persons sensitive to the attitude of distrust prevalent in this country during and after the Watergate period may perceive some benefit toward preserv-

---

> been feasible, it would have occurred. If, for example, the question were whether clean water was more valuable as an input into paper production than into boating, we might try to determine, *using whatever quantitative or other data might be available* to help us, whether *in a world of zero transaction costs* the paper industry would purchase from boaters as a class the right to use the water in question.

(Emphasis added). This emphasizes my point that hypothetical appraisals are highly subjective.

47. This point may be simply illustrated. It is not enough, for example, to view benefits as "plusses" and costs as "minuses"; each item must be first valued and the members of each class aggregated and the aggregates then compared. For example, if a study finds two "plusses" for a particular system and one "minus," the plusses may have values of 2 and 3 and the minus a value of 10. Where quantification is not possible, the analysis founders and must import judgments of value which may not be generally agreed upon.

48. But see Williams, "Subjectivity, Expression, and Privacy: Problems of Aesthetic Regulation," 62 Minn. L. Rev. 1 (1977).

49. I am not unaware that some purport to have been able to value even a human life, at so many dollars. See, e.g., Thaler and Rosen, "The Value of Saving a Life: Evidence from the Labor Market," in *Household Production and Consumption*, p. 265, pp. 286–98 (N. Terleckyj ed. 1975).

ing the social organization in the provision of assurance that the law, at least in the abstract, if not in effect, compels full and fair disclosure. Perhaps virtue is its own reward in this sense—but it is not measurable. In the securities law area, a pretense of ability to measure all things by the supporters of economic analysis is endemic. We shall see that Benston, recognizing these difficulties of measurement, nevertheless was not able to overcome them.

I must hasten to point out that those who evaluate nonquantifiable matters are not using economic analysis, whose main pride is in eschewing subjective evaluations in favor of the market's evaluations (except in what they call hypothetical markets). Rather the person who takes into account nonmeasurables (as well as the equities, as described under the next heading) is using some form of utilitarian analysis—a quite different model for determining desirability of laws.[50]

Dividing the Economic Pie

Another problem with economic analysis, concerned as it is with measurements of relative costs and benefits, is that it cannot tell us how the economic pie should be divided among the individuals in our society. For example, in the disclosure context, who among analysts, shareholders, potential shareholders, managers, brokers, and so on should pay what portion of the costs of disclosure?

Benston recognizes this problem as a noneconomic issue for he poses its empirical counterpart as the other half of the issue he is addressing in his paper. He states: "The question at issue, then, is not whether disclosure as such is a good thing, but whether the benefits of government-mandated disclosure exceed its costs *and which persons (e.g., consumers, investors, or government officials) obtain the benefits and assume the costs*."[51] (Emphasis is mine.)

However, he never seems to cope satisfactorily with this last half of the problem except to intimate from time to time that the just result is

---

50. See text accompanying and following note 22 *supra*, and text accompanying note 145 *infra*. However, a fundamental point of Posner's article, note 22 *supra*, is this: The economist who is willing to guess freely enough could try to put a price tag on the value of social cohesion or what have you. The neglect of nonmeasurable values is not entailed by economic analysis but is simply an unfortunate by-product of wanting to minimize the element of guesswork. Posner would say, however, that because utilitarians begin with a concept—satisfaction of wants—that is even more vague than value, they are, as the text suggests, less reluctant to make guesses about the weight to be assigned various nonmeasurable aspects. Although I see this as a source of strength, Posner would note that it fairly invites expansive government regulation because it is so easy to conjure up plausible nonmeasurables to throw in the balance on the side of regulation. Posner doubtless would regard this as dangerous in its implications for the permissible scope of government regulation.

51. Benston, "An Appraisal," at p. 40 in this volume (emphasis added).

that only those who pay the costs should get the benefits. This could be an appropriate result, but it requires an articulated defense since it is not a universally accepted view and is inconsistent with societal acceptance of public welfare.

Unpredictability of the Future of the Universe

In addition, some of the factual premises underlying Benston's analysis are unreliable. Benston's model assumes that the remainder of the now extant universe is the context for testing and does not allow for realistically expectable changes in that remainder. For example, in considering the question of comparative costs and benefits of mandated disclosure, he assumes the then current Financial Accounting Standards Board (FASB) pronouncements to be part of the universe of facts[52] and finds the incremental costs of additional disclosure mandated by the SEC to be a certain amount.[53] But if the model were instead to include potential increases in FASB disclosure requirements, incremental costs of SEC requirements would be reduced as FASB requirements were increased. Since change is more likely to occur than is no change, the FASB pronouncements will likely change in the future. But in which direction? Toward more disclosure (resulting in lesser incremental costs for SEC disclosure) or toward less disclosure (resulting in greater incremental costs for SEC disclosure)? And how much more or less? Since a model assuming no change in FASB disclosure requirements, a positive change, or a negative change, most likely will not comport with what actually occurs,[54] the result of using any model may not be correct

---

52. I note that Benston on occasion suggests that the FASB pronouncements are induced or vitalized by the SEC and therefore he may be saying they are not external to the SEC's mandatory disclosure system. See, e.g., *id.*, p. 51 (referring to the FASB as the SEC's "delegate"). But I do not believe that in fact he takes this position. Nor should he, because it is arguable that an FASB would exist even without the SEC. The major basis for that argument is that at least some firms believe that accounting disclosure audited by independent accountants is of value to the firm, and Benston apparently agrees. See *id.*, p. 40. And it appears likely that the profession would seek to set some uniform standards through a central agency even without government regulation.

However, the opposite view is that the accounting profession's development of uniform accounting principles and standards could not exist without the SEC umbrella. Kripke, "Nature of Competition in the Accounting Profession: A Legal View" (unpublished paper prepared for delivery to U.C.L.A. Graduate School of Management, Invitational Conference on Regulation and the Accounting Profession, May 24–25, 1979). Kripke even suggests that present professional standards-setting may violate the antitrust laws. *Id.*

53. See Benston, "An Appraisal," at pp. 40–41 in this volume.

54. The model attempting to predict the future is likely to be inaccurate since the amount of the change is not likely to be accurately predicted even if the direction of change is constant and is correctly predicted.

because of changes in the remainder of the universe. This undercuts the effect of findings of the model used since even if those findings are against the existing system, they are not against *any and all* systems of government intervention.

Similarly, assuming that Benston distinguishes between the two branches of the securities law disclosure system, the antifraud provisions and the mandatory reporting and disclosure provisions, and that he is concerned in his article only with the latter,[55] his model does not contemplate changes in the judicial and legislative regulation of fraud. Since the antifraud rules will change from time to time, the incremental costs and benefits of the reporting system will also change inversely.

Dynamism of the Mandatory Disclosure System

Further, in anything as intricate and complex as the SEC's mandatory disclosure system, how can the model builder know how that system will change? It clearly is not appropriate to assume that the SEC's mandatory disclosure system is immutable. It is quite dynamic. If that is so, how can a particular model of it be apt for all future changes in the mandatory disclosure system so as to answer the question of whether any mandatory disclosure system is desirable? For example, in determining the costs of the SEC's system, Benston cites as one cost the prohibition of certain "soft" information causing readers of SEC reports to be misled.[56] But even as he was writing, the SEC was changing its view on soft information disclosure, albeit haltingly.[57] Hence Benston's

---

A related problem is caused by interaction of the subject of the model with the remainder of the universe. For example, the SEC's mandated replacement cost data is part of Benston's model. Of course he could not take into account the FASB's recent proposal regarding disclosure of consumer price index-adjusted or current cost data because it postdated his articles. Financial Accounting Standards Board, *Financial Reporting and Changing Prices* (Exposure Draft 1978). But the relevant question is whether the FASB would have moved as it did without the SEC's action. And will the SEC now alter its requirements as FASB Chairman Kirk suggests? See *New York Times*, Jan. 11, 1979, at p. D5, col. 1. And how does a model builder accurately anticipate all these things? This last is a rhetorical question.

55. It is not entirely clear whether Benston is confining his article to the mandatory disclosure features of the securities laws or also includes the antifraud provisions. In either case, his model suffers because if it excludes the antifraud provisions, as I believe it does, as stated in the text, it fails to take prospective changes in that part of the universe into account. Similarly if his model includes the antifraud provisions, it fails to take into account prospective changes in the system which underlies the model; see the discussion *infra* under "Dynamism of the Mandatory Disclosure System."

56. Benston, "An Appraisal," at pp. 46–47 in this volume.

57. Securities Act Release Nos. 5992, 5993, [1978 Transfer Binder] Fed. Sec. L. Rep. (CCH) ¶¶ 81,754, 81,756 (1978). See Fiflis, "Soft Information: The SEC's Former Exogenous Zone," 26 U.C.L.A.L. Rev. 95 (1978).

model failed to take this potential change into account, yielding a wrong "cost."

It is probable no one could avoid these problems because it is doubtful that a feasible model could be built to take them into account. If it could, still other problems could be found. That is unavoidable, since no model can accurately predict and duplicate a dynamic real world, complete with all future changes.[58] If the model builders did replicate the real world, they would no longer have a simple model facilitating thought but would instead have a copy of the universe leaving them to view its complexities and attempt to solve problems with all those obfuscatory facts in mind.[59] This, of course, is why any sensible person knows that problem solving through building and analyzing economic or other kinds of models must be taken with at least a grain of salt to avoid the Pygmalion syndrome.[60] Some, emphasizing the shortcomings of models, would say, forget the model and the salt, and use judgment or common sense and experience in solving the problem.[61] I, for one, am willing to look at the results of the models as one set of data, except when the models are apparently mere hobbyhorses,[62] in which case I prefer not to go for the ride. Benston's model is not of that nature.

Having said all this, am I convinced by Benston's case that the costs of mandatory disclosure exceed the benefits? My answer is no.

THE BENSTON ARGUMENT

More specifically, what can be said of Benston's argument that the costs of mandated disclosure exceed the benefits?

---

58. The great volatility of those areas of the real world with which lawyers and other social scientists deal is one reason why they have not utilized model-building techniques as frequently as have the physical scientists, who deal with a relatively static portion of the universe. By the time a lawyer builds and studies a model of some societal system, more likely than not substantial unpredicted changes will have occurred. The physicist, on the other hand, deals with matters that substantially change only over eons if at all.

59. One advantage of recognizing the difference between theoretical models and the real world is that as other techniques for extending the human mind (such as computer technology) develop, we may be able to construct and use more complex models, more realistically simulating real-world conditions. In fact, one may envision the ultimate "model" of the real world which incorporates every feature of the real world and which can be used to experimentally solve real-world problems without real-world consequences. So far only computer technology holds hope for building such complex models.

60. Note, for example, that Posner routinely tests his conclusions by reference to common sense as he perceives it. See, e.g., Posner, *supra* note 22, at 122–25, 131–36.

61. See notes 41 and 44 *supra*.

62. See note 41 *supra*.

The Direct Costs of SEC Reports

Benston first concedes that the costs of mandated disclosure include only the incremental costs over what would have been incurred by voluntary disclosure. Here appears the first defect in his model.

Since he assumes a static system of voluntary disclosure in order to measure the incremental costs, he necessarily ignores the fact that the universe in which the mandatory disclosure system operates is dynamic, not static. Thus it is clear that the costs of disclosure beyond SEC mandates are frequently changed—hence the incremental costs of SEC disclosures must also change inversely. For example, in 1976 the SEC mandated footnote disclosure of certain replacement cost data,[63] clearly imposing an incremental cost of SEC requirements. But recently the FASB proposed disclosure of consumer price-indexed (or fair value) data,[64] and it has been suggested by the chairman of the FASB that this may prompt elimination of the SEC-mandated replacement cost information.[65] To be most accurate in measuring incremental costs of mandated disclosure, Benston's model should perfectly predict all changes in the universe having to do with voluntary disclosure, an impossible task.[66]

At any rate, Benston concedes that he "know[s] of no studies of the amount of these [direct] costs" and is forced to conclude only that they are probably not trivial.[67] This is manifestly of limited value to a cost-benefit analysis since quantification of costs is necessary to determine whether costs exceed benefits unless the costs are nontrivial and benefits are zero or so obviously trivial as to not match the nontrivial costs.[68]

Recognizing this, Benston resorts to the very demanding alternative of attempting to demonstrate that benefits are probably trivial. We shall shortly examine his findings to determine whether he has succeeded on that score.

---

63. SEC Accounting Series Release No. 190, 5 Fed. Sec. L. Rep. (CCH) ¶ 72,212 (1976).

64. Financial Accounting Standards Board, *Financial Reporting and Changing Prices* (Exposure Draft 1978).

65. See note 54 *supra*.

66. Benston seems to vacillate as to whether he regards the FASB requirements as part of the voluntary disclosure system or part of the SEC-mandated system. See note 52 *supra*.

In either case, he must defend his view. Even if he regards the FASB as an arm of the SEC, it is reasonable to argue that the FASB strives for disclosure to give audited financial statements maximum value, and that the FASB would so behave even without an SEC. In any event the point in the text is merely illustrative.

67. Benston, "An Appraisal," at p. 41 in this volume.

68. See text accompanying and following note 52 *supra*.

Indirect Costs

But first, a brief reference to his determination of indirect costs shows similar weakness in this part of his cost-benefit equation. In noting what he calls "type II errors"[69]—mandated disclosure which is more harmful than beneficial because it is misleading—he notes several examples such as the SEC's required reporting of historical cost. Of course, here too he is required by empirical evidence to concede that it is probable that no one is fooled by historical cost figures.[70] However, his analysis at this point ignores the fact that the SEC disclosure system on which his static model is built is in fact dynamic. Indeed the SEC is rapidly moving away from limiting disclosures to historical cost.[71]

Benston also suggests a second class of so-called type I errors consisting of prohibitions by the SEC against disclosure of certain useful data such as various types of soft information (e.g. earnings forecasts). This point illustrates another failure of Benston's model to account for the dynamism of the mandated disclosure system. As he was writing, the SEC was in the very process of deciding to encourage disclosure of earnings forecasts.[72]

Indeed, this same power to regulate disclosures which the SEC used restrictively to limit disclosure to historical cost and other "hard" data, may prove useful when used affirmatively, for example, to compel fair-value accounting. Accounting practitioners, by and large, oppose any but historical cost accounting, partly because of the subjectivity of appraisals of fair value but also in large measure because of the fear of destroying their own credibility and incurring potential liability. With-

---

69. I am informed that "type II" errors is a term used in statistics meaning acceptance of a false hypothesis. A "type I" error means rejecting a correct hypothesis.

70. Cf. Boulding, "Economics and Accounting: The Uncongenial Twins," in *Studies in Modern Accounting Theory*, at pp. 44, 55 (W. Baxter and S. Davidson eds. 1962):

> A known untruth is much better than a lie, and provided that the accounting rituals are well known and understood, accounting may be untrue but it is not lies; it does not deceive because we know that it does not tell the truth, and we are able to make our own adjustment in each individual case, using the results of the accountant as evidence rather than as definitive information.

71. Witness SEC Accounting Series Release No. 190, *supra* note 63 (replacement cost); Securities Act Release Nos. 5992, 5993, *supra* note 57 (projections); as well as SEC Accounting Series Release No. 253, 5 Fed. Sec. L. Rep. (CCH) ¶ 72,275 (1978) (reserve recognition accounting proposals for oil and gas companies).

72. See Benston, "An Appraisal," at p. 46 in this volume, and note 57 *supra*. In fact even before Benston's article, the Commission would have permitted such disclosure. See Securities Act Release No. 5699, [1975–76 Transfer Binder] Fed. Sec. L. Rep. (CCH) ¶ 80,461 (1976).

out SEC prodding, requiring replacement cost disclosure,[73] I doubt that the FASB's current proposal for alternative disclosure of price-indexed or fair value data would have been made. In fact, its implementation may still require an SEC order.

In the end, nevertheless, Benston is forced to conclude only that the indirect as well as the direct costs of mandated disclosure are probably not trivial, but he does not give their measure. As already noted, this compels him to determine whether benefits are trivial, since only if they are can it be concluded that costs probably outweigh benefits.

The Benefits of Government-Mandated Disclosure—Examination of the Conceptual Basis

Benston cites seven claimed benefits of mandated securities law disclosure, divided into two main categories which he calls, "Fraud, Manipulation, and Unfairness" and "Efficiency of Investment and Allocation of Resources."[74] Before proceeding to the empirical evidence, he examines the logic of the system to determine whether the benefits are likely to accrue.

He points out that the first group—"Fraud, Manipulation, and Unfairness"—rests on the mistaken beliefs that investors can be misled by accounting data and that government regulation can prevent it. However, in asserting (perhaps correctly) that investors will not rely on the accounting data alone but will look to the auditors and underwriters to protect them, he is forced to make another significant concession—that government regulation may play a role in "requiring the publication of inside dealings and potential conflicts of interest, *in ensuring the independence of C.P.A.'s and investment bankers*, and in prosecuting those who violate their fiduciary responsibilities."[75] (Emphasis is mine.) It seems that he thus concedes at least one nontrivial benefit of regulation—ensuring the independence of the two professions which are investors' guardians. Moreover, this power, which the Commission has frequently exercised, to enforce better procedures to assure beneficial disclosure is a substantial and effective one. For example, the Commission has been instrumental in imposing greater duties to investigate and disclose on auditors,[76] and underwriters[77] as well as outside directors.[78]

---

73. SEC Accounting Series Release No. 190, *supra* note 63.

74. Benston, "An Appraisal," at pp. 48–49 in this volume.

75. *Id.*, at p. 50 (emphasis added).

76. E.g., Accounting Series Release No. 19, 5 Fed. Sec. L. Rep. (CCH) ¶ 72,020 (1940) (re McKesson & Robbins). And see Fiflis, "Current Problems of Accountants' Responsibilities to Third Parties," 28 Vand. L. Rev. 31, 52–58, 93–102, 128–44 (1975).

77. In the Matter of Walston & Co., Securities Exchange Act Release No. 8165 [1966–67 Transfer Binder] Fed. Sec. L. Rep. (CCH) ¶ 77,474 (1967).

Perhaps a related benefit is the probability that preparers of regulated disclosure documents are more likely to pay due professional care, knowing of the regulations, than they would without regulation. Moreover, is it not likely that more companies publish audited statements because that is required of 1934 Act registrants? Most of the 10,000-odd SEC registrants do not have stock exchange listings and might never issue audited statements were they not required for SEC filing.

At this point the defense of *some* government regulation could rest since Benston has failed to show that no nontrivial benefit accrues. But there is more.

Still dealing with the first group of benefits involving fraud, he states that even with governmentally mandated disclosure, equal access to information by all investors is not possible, since someone, such as the printer for the corporation's press releases, will always be first to obtain the information and hence be in a position to trade advantageously. Here Benston fails to address the fact that the other aspect of the disclosure system, the antifraud provisions, may apply to those persons whom the courts find to be in a status requiring imposition of a duty not to trade, thereby, for example, minimizing the printer's opportunity.[79]

Moreover, inside trading or trading by the person who first receives information is not a problem which can be properly addressed by the efficiency criterion; in fact, it has been suggested that insider trading promotes efficiency in the securities markets.[80] Rather insider trading is one of those problems which deals with dividing up the economic pie—should insiders profit at the expense of outsiders? Benston apparently disagrees with those who support insider trading as an aid to efficiency, stating the view that insider trading is undesirable because unfair.[81] But it is incorrect to term this unfairness an economic "cost" to be subtracted from benefits since it is a costless transfer from one person to another. Further, as previously stated, it may be minimized by appropriate tailoring of the antifraud rules.

Benston's more compelling arguments deal with the second group of benefits—those having to do with "Efficiency of Investment and Allo-

---

78. E.g., Securities and Exchange Commission, Report of Investigation in the Matter of National Telephone Co., Inc. [1977–78 Transfer Binder] Fed. Sec. L. Rep. (CCH) ¶ 81,410 (1978).

79. Cf., e.g., United States v. Chiarella, 588 F.2d 1358 (2d Cir. 1978), *petition for cert. filed*, 47 U.S.L.W. 3529 (U.S. Feb. 13, 1979) (No. 78-1202) (a case of first impression involving a financial printer's employee who may be distinguishable from a news printer).

80. E.g., Wu, "An Economist Looks at Section 16 of the Securities Exchange Act of 1934," 68 Colum. L. Rev. 260 (1968). However, one would expect increased deception and nondisclosure if insider trading were permitted by law. However, Posner rejects the belief that insider trading furthers market efficiency. See R. Posner, *supra* note 27, at p. 308.

81. Benston, "An Appraisal," at pp. 57–58 in this volume.

cation of Resources."[82] He states that these are "derived from the assumption that published financial information is useful for investment decision-making" and three corollary assumptions that:

(1) specific mandated disclosures are useful;

(2) government can know what information is useful; and

(3) the disclosures can be timely, i.e., not have been previously impounded in securities prices.

As to the first corollary, he states that the probability that the benefits of corporate disclosures accrue to nonshareholders indeed does result in suppression of data by managements, but that the data is of little value anyway.[83] The basis for this evaluation is remarkable. He first states that disclosure would "harm" existing shareholders because they must bear the costs without equivalent benefits. But again I must protest that this point does not show costs in excess of benefits. Rather it shows costs in excess of benefits to existing shareholders—no proof of inefficiency, but only inequity—an issue not reached by the efficiency criterion. Benston admits that this "inequity" exists only when share prices are not in equilibrium. Although he proceeds to find other "inequities," in the end he ultimately concludes what he must, that: "Aside from questions of equity, a determination of whether society as a whole benefits depends on whether the total cost of required disclosure exceeds the total benefits. This determination depends, in part, on whether required disclosure is likely to produce information or simply data, a distinction discussed below."[84]

Hence, the net effect of this passage is that we still do not know whether there is a net benefit from mandated disclosure. In addition, Benston must go beyond cost-benefit analysis in addressing how the costs of disclosure ought to be allocated, thus furthering the case for a utilitarian analysis. Moreover, his findings on the equities are not convincing unless one holds Benston's apparent view that everyone should pay for his own lunch—a view that is defensible, but certainly not unanimously held in our world, rife as it is with externalities, justified on grounds of public welfare.

As to the second corollary assumption that government can know what information is useful, he simply states that the criterion of what is useful information is: What will help investors to predict and appropriately to discount future cash flows? This is a task which is "essentially subjective and perhaps impossible" for government as well as everyone else.[85]

82. *Id.* at p. 51.

83. *Id.* at pp. 52–53.

84. *Id.* at p. 53.

85. *Id.* at pp. 53–54.

This is a powerful point. However, it may be argued that the SEC is more likely than are private parties to require unbiased disclosure. Further, the Commission may and often has required several alternative items of disclosure, at least some of which may be helpful in ascertaining properly discounted future cash flow.[86] In addition, securities analysts seem to demand mandated disclosures[87] and apparently are willing to incur opportunity costs by spending their time studying the information disclosed. For a proponent of free markets to imply that this demand should be ignored is at least bad form.

As to the third corollary assumption—that mandated disclosure can be timely—he again makes a concession; namely, that it is an as-yet-unanswered empirical question whether the mechanics of disclosure favor some investors who have earlier access to information releases.[88] However, he then adds that "it seems clear that numbers produced pursuant to government regulations that make the issuer liable to penalties should the reports violate the regulations are likely to be less timely than numbers produced voluntarily."[89]

Although I agree with this conclusion, it has been forcefully pointed out that management's knowledge that the day of reckoning must come when an SEC report will be filed imposes a disciplining effect on the earlier informal disclosures which helps assure their integrity.[90] It has also been suggested that the SEC reports will provide much more detail.[91] It may be added that the filed document is often extremely useful for a plaintiff in prosecuting an antifraud action—the other, complementary aspect of the dual disclosure system.

Further, the view that SEC disclosures are not timely is based on the efficient market theory and studies tending to substantiate it.[92] That theory suggests that since the market incorporates in securities prices all public data almost immediately, later SEC documents can add nothing. But these studies have been confined to the most efficient of markets—the New York Stock Exchange,[93] many of whose securities are

---

86. See its release on reserve recognition accounting for oil and gas firms, SEC Accounting Series Release No. 253, *supra* note 71.

87. See Benston, "An Appraisal," at p. 68 n. 65 in this volume.

88. *Id.* at p. 54.

89. *Id.*

90. Sommer, "Financial Reporting and the Stock Market: The Other Side," Fin. Exec. Mag., May 1974, at pp. 36, 38; *Report, supra* note 2, at p. xlvi.

91. *Id.*

92. Cf. *Report, supra* note 2, at xix.

93. Cf. J. Lorie and M. Hamilton, *The Stock Market, Theories and Evidence*, ch. 4 (1973). If SEC disclosure does not affect NYSE prices, that may be thought to be a basis for eliminating SEC reporting requirements for NYSE-listed firms. Indeed, state securities laws frequently exempt blue-sky registration of offer-

closely scrutinized by financial analysts (unlike most other securities).[94] For less efficient markets, it may be that studies not yet made will find information content in SEC numbers.

In sum, Benston concludes that at least in theory it is unlikely that the benefits of mandatory disclosure will exceed the costs.[95] To this point, however, in my view he has certainly not carried the burden of persuasion.

The Empirical Evidence

The theoretical work of accountants and economists in recent years concerning the utility of disclosure of firm-specific data in both accounting reports and SEC documents has spawned a host of empirical studies testing various hypotheses. Benston, who has been involved in this research himself, proceeds in his article to consider the empirical evidence as it concerns each of the seven claimed benefits of disclosure, and ultimately finds "some positive benefits, on balance [but] [e]ven so, these benefits do not seem to offset the costs."[96] This is somewhat confusing since, as seen above, he has not succeeded in measuring the costs, and similarly fails to measure the benefits. Therefore it is difficult to see how he is able to compare them, except perhaps by a subjective intuition, not a very scientific or very persuasive approach. Nevertheless, we may examine this conclusion for reasonableness.

FRAUD IN FINANCIAL STATEMENTS

He describes this claimed benefit as involving "intentional"[97] as well as negligent misrepresentation,[98] and asserts that "[t]here is almost no evidence to support the assertion that the financial statements of publicly traded companies were fraudulently or misleadingly prepared in the years prior to the passage of the Securities Acts."[99] If that is so, his point is that there can be no benefit from eliminating a nonexistent evil. Ignoring the question of who now has the burden of producing evidence of the lack of pre-1933 fraud, he goes on to admit that the lack of litigation may have been due to the prevailing rule of the *Ultramares*

---

ings by such companies. However, we cannot know whether elimination of SEC-mandated reporting and other SEC regulation of stock exchanges would result in debilitation of this market.

94. *Report, supra* note 2, at pp. 39–42.

95. Benston, "An Appraisal," at p. 47 in this volume.

96. *Id.* at p. 67.

97. *Id.* at p. 49.

98. *Id.* at p. 54.

99. *Id.*

case, requiring privity to impose liability on a defendant for negligent misrepresentation.[100] Then, as if it were a complete answer, he suggests that since the 1933 Act dispensed with privity for negligence (although only for misrepresentations in effective registration statements) and there was no rash of post-1933 cases, there was "no pent-up desire to sue public accountants," intimating that somehow therefore there was little pre-1933 Act misrepresentation.[101]

Clearly, the lack of cases before and after 1933 may have been due to factors other than an uncoerced lack of misrepresentations. These other causes could include, for example, the heavy transaction costs involved in bringing and prosecuting suits. After 1933, plaintiffs' excessive unrealized fears of the effects of the section 11(e) provision authorizing award of attorneys' fees as costs could have limited suits for some time after 1933.[102] There is also the possibility that the 1933 Act may well have succeeded in minimizing both negligent and intentional misrepresentations in SEC documents and elsewhere, thereby minimizing suits—the very point which Benston seeks to negate.

In any event, Benston concedes that "[i]t seems likely that some fraud may have occurred" before 1933, but then, he asserts, "it also is clear that fraud in financial statements has not been eliminated as a consequence of the Securities Acts" and, without an iota of authority, that "it almost seems as if it is now easier to defraud some investors, possibly because the existence of the SEC lulls them into believing that fraud is a problem of the past."[103] This conclusion, as we have noted, that there is a zero benefit in the diminution of misrepresentation, is essential to Benston's argument, but he clearly does not succeed in proving the point since he does not show that there is now as much fraud as there would have been without the securities laws. What is more, he cannot make this showing since the universe of facts has now changed so substantially that without actual experimentation by repeal of the securities laws (and even then devising a reliable test would be difficult), there is no way of knowing how much misrepresentation would exist today in the absence of those laws.[104]

Since the burden of going forward with the evidence, if not the burden of persuasion, is on the party suggesting elimination of the securities laws reporting requirements, we again could stop here. But instead, we may also note that experience suggests that many frauds

---

100. Ultramares Corp. v. Touche, Niven & Co., 255 N.Y. 170, 174 N.E. 441 (1931).

101. Benston, "An Appraisal," at pp. 54–55 in this volume.

102. 15 U.S.C. § 77k(e) (1976).

103. Benston, "An Appraisal," at p. 55 in this volume.

104. See R. Frost, "The Road Not Taken," in *The Poetry of Robert Frost*, p. 105 (Latham ed. 1969), the title of which also brings to mind the phrase, "what ne'er was, nor is, nor e'er shall be," A. Pope, "An Essay on Criticism," line 254. Such questions seem best left to poets who speculate sublimely.

now probably never get off the ground because of the obstacle of required disclosure and the greater care paid by underwriters, auditors, and other potential defendants.[105]

There are other potential fraud-minimizing benefits of SEC requirements. Securities law practitioners are aware of the general "house cleaning" that goes on when a first public offering is contemplated.[106] Thus inventories are frequently undervalued by closely held companies to minimize income taxes, but, when it comes time to "go public" these same inventories are more accurately presented in the financial statement.[107]

In addition, the antiseptic effects of disclosure on violations of state law fiduciary duties soon may become more evident. Although the Supreme Court has limited rule 10b-5 to misrepresentations and manipulations,[108] it left open the possibility that these could include nondisclosures of fiduciary breaches which if disclosed would induce shareholder action under state law.[109]

MISREPRESENTATION IN FINANCIAL STATEMENTS

Here Benston has in mind the claimed benefit of SEC regulation through elimination of "managed income" practices. Such practices include selecting or changing accounting principles to produce management-favored financial statements, such as switching from FIFO to LIFO in a period of rising prices to diminish apparent earnings in order to discourage wage demands.[110] Benston would also include such devices as manipulating income by choosing between two similar assets to sell when the firm has a lower recorded cost for one than it has for

---

105. For example, see the reference to the Penn Central debenture offering which was cancelled when disclosure was insisted upon by one attorney, in Sommer, *supra* note 90, at p. 38. Every securities lawyer knows of other such cases from personal experience.

106. *Id.*

107. See T. Fiflis and H. Kripke, *Accounting for Business Lawyers*, p. 62 (2d ed. 1977).

108. Santa Fe Industries, Inc. v. Green, 430 U.S. 462 (1977).

109. *Id.* at 474, n. 14. Cf. Goldberg v. Meridor, 567 F.2d 209 (2d Cir. 1977), *cert. denied*, 434 U.S. 1069 (1978). But see Wright v. Heizer Corp., 560 F.2d 236 (7th Cir. 1977), *cert. denied*, 434 U.S. 1066 (1978); Goldberger v. Baker, 442 F. Supp. 659 (S.D.N.Y. 1971); Valenti v. Pepsico, [1978 Transfer Binder] Fed. Sec. L. Rep. (CCH) ¶ 96,496 at 93,858–59 (D. Del. 1978); and Note, 91 Harv. L. Rev. 1874 (1978).

110. FIFO refers to the first-in-first-out method of costing inventory by assuming that inventory consists of the latest goods received. In a period of rising prices for inventory items, this will maximize the recorded carrying value of inventory, and hence of earnings. See T. Fiflis and H. Kripke, *supra* note 107, at p. 216, for further explanation. LIFO refers to last-in–first-out, resulting in costing of inventory as if earlier purchased items remain in inventory.

the other, or manipulating earnings and earnings-per-share by bypassing or not bypassing the income statement.[111]

Benston first argues that there is no benefit to be obtained from eliminating managed income because, in any event, investors are not fooled by these accounting tricks. Although he makes a powerful point, noting the very substantial empirical evidence,[112] there are several problems with the use of that evidence. Basically, the studies deal with rather easy-to-perceive accounting manipulations, such as shifts from FIFO to LIFO, from accelerated to straight-line depreciation,[113] and from historical to price-level-adjusted earnings and the like. In addition, the studies cover the use of one accounting method rather than another, e.g., "flow-through" of income tax savings rather than "normalization" when tax and financial accounting depreciation methods differ,[114] pooling instead of purchase accounting for mergers and acquisitions,[115] and "full costing" for oil and gas producers instead of "successful efforts" accounting.[116]

In each of these cases, there is sufficient disclosure in the notes to the financial statements of the method chosen, or, in the case of change of method, the effects of the change, that any sophisticated analyst can appropriately assess the matter if only after additional investigation. This footnote disclosure is at least in part the result of the securities laws, including the requirement of *United States v. Simon* that regardless of the use of generally accepted accounting principles (GAAP), additional information must be disclosed if GAAP otherwise would be misleading.[117] Further, the SEC staff frequently imposes pressure to prevent such accounting manipulations. Since efficient markets impound all available information, including footnotes, we need not be

---

111. Bypassing the income statement, now largely eliminated as an option by FASB Statement No. 16 (1977), means not including some expense or revenue item in earnings on the ground that it is extraordinary and would distort the trend of earnings shown by consecutive income statements. See T. Fiflis and H. Kripke, *supra* note 107, at chapter XV.

112. Benston, "An Appraisal," at p. 56 in this volume.

113. Which, because the change generally reduces the charge to depreciation expense, thereby increases reported earnings.

114. See T. Fiflis and H. Kripke, *supra* note 107, at pp. 524–30.

115. See *id.* at pp. 605–18.

116. See *id.* at pp. 255–57.

117. 425 F.2d 796 (2d. Cir. 1969), *cert. denied,* 397 U.S. 1006 (1970). See Fiflis, "Current Problems of Accountants' Responsibilities to Third Parties," 28 Vand. L. Rev. 31, 67–80 (1975) for an analysis of the implications of *Simon*. This concept always has been the law—it was not newly invented in *Simon*. See, e.g., Kaiser-Frazer Corp. v. Otis & Co., 195 F.2d 838, 844 (2d Cir.), *cert. denied,* 344 U.S. 856 (1952); and *In re* Associated Gas & Elec. Co., 11 S.E.C. 975, 1058–59 (1942).

surprised by the results of the empirical studies showing that now investors are not fooled by managed income.

What Benston instead must show, which he does not, is that in the absence of the securities acts, investors similarly would not be fooled. The fact is that these studies do not test the value of SEC-mandated disclosure in avoiding this class of misrepresentations since they do not determine whether the footnote disclosures mentioned above would be made in the absence of SEC requirements.

Benston next argues that elimination of managed income is no benefit at all because uniformity of accounting means rigidity,[118] which is "likely" to reduce the value of the information because it prevents needed flexibility in giving an accurate picture of financial facts.[119] How this comports with his first point, that investors are not fooled by accounting choices, is not apparent. Nor is it apparent that any misleading effects of rigidity would not be removed by supplemental disclosures in footnotes or elsewhere, as required by *United States v. Simon*.

I conclude that Benston has failed to carry his burden of proof on this second suggested benefit of SEC disclosure.

SECURITY PRICE MANIPULATION

In an article published in 1973, Benston purported to show that there was information available for some companies whose shares were manipulated before 1934, and that therefore SEC-mandated information would do nothing to diminish manipulation.[120] Given the intuitive appeal of the opposite position—that ignorance facilitates manipulation and disclosure minimizes ignorance—it is not with great ease that one accepts Benston's conclusions. His hypothesis seems to have been that if information was available before the manipulations, lack of information was not the cause of the manipulations. However, that information

---

118. See Uniformity in Financial Accounting, 30 Law and Contemp. Prob. 621 (1965) for a symposium devoted to the issue of uniformity versus flexibility.

119. One example is the intimation, in Benston, "An Appraisal," at p. 56 in this volume, that flexibility in choice of depreciation accounting methods is desirable because the choice of straight-line or accelerated depreciation may depend on which better describes the decline in present value of an asset and the pattern of expected cash flows. This is an unfortunate example since the selection of one or the other method of depreciation in practice is arbitrary and is seldom based on even a rough effort to make it comport with expected cash flow. Although there is a rational theory of depreciation relating to the expected cash flow, see W. Baxter, *Depreciation*, p. 31 (1971), it has not been observed in practice. Moreover, the systematic charge of depreciation in conformity with a geometrically charted curve on a graph (as is required) is unlikely to bear any more than a most superficial resemblance to cash flow expectations.

120. Benston, "Required Disclosure and the Stock Market: An Evaluation of the Securities Exchange Act of 1934," 63 Am. Econ. Rev. 132, 136 (1973).

was the simple balance sheet and income statement reprinted in Moody's in the 1920's and early 1930's. How do we know whether that data was as extensive as that required by the SEC in 10K's, 10Q's and 8K's, or the section 16(a) reports of changes in holdings by officers, directors and 10 percent shareholders, or the affirmative disclosures required under rules 144[121] and 10b-5? We are not told how extensive the Moody's reports were before 1934 but they probably did not include as much data as current SEC documents, and perhaps did not even include footnotes to the financial statements. Further, Benston did not test for accuracy of the pre-1934 information in the Moody's statements. If it was inaccurate, it probably is not comparable with present SEC-mandated disclosure.

In sum, if manipulations occurred before 1934 although Moody's financials were then available, there is no logical reason to believe that the current more extensive, more accurate SEC-mandated disclosure would not be more effective to avoid manipulation. Nevertheless, Benston's study was probably correct to the extent that it finds that disclosure in periodic reports like 10K's is not likely to deter manipulations in the classic sense of stock pools, market corners and the like. Former Commissioner Sommer has pointed out that the antifraud provisions and *not* the periodic reporting provisions are designed to inhibit manipulation.[122] In addition, deterrence of securities professionals, who are likely to be involved in manipulations, by proceedings affecting licensing is similarly an important SEC function.[123] I find here another failure to disprove a substantial benefit from SEC-mandated disclosure.

FAIRNESS TO NONINSIDERS

As we have noted, insider trading and whether or not it is unfair have little to do with maximizing net economic benefits; securities pricing

---

121. 17 C.F.R. 230.144 (1978) (dealing with resales by certain existing security holders).

122. Sommer, *supra* note 90. See also the Domestic and Foreign Investment Improved Disclosure Act of 1977, amending § 13(d) of the 1934 Act and adding subsections 13(g) and (h); Rule 144 concerning resales of securities and reports thereof (17 C.F.R. 230.144) (1978); 1934 Act §§ 9b, 10b, 16(b); 15 U.S.C. §§ 78i, 78j(b), 78p(b) (1976). Cf. Ernst & Ernst v. Hochfelder, 425 U.S. 185, 199 (1976), and Santa Fe Industries, Inc. v. Green, 430 U.S. 462 (1977) (discussing technical manipulations).

123. See, e.g., rule 252(d) (17 C.F.R. 230.252(d) (1978) (disqualifying underwriters and others from participating in "Reg. A" offerings when they have previously been involved in certain wrongdoing); § 15(c) of the 1934 Act, 15 U.S.C. § 78o(c) (1976) (outlawing manipulations by broker-dealers) and § 21 thereof, 15 U.S.C. § 78(u) (1976) (providing for SEC investigations, injunction actions and criminal references).

would probably be more efficient if such trading were allowed.[124] Rather, the unfairness of insider trading is a matter of dividing the economic pie, or doing equity; the issue is whether insiders should be allowed to take insider trading profits at the expense of outsiders, or should instead be prohibited from doing so. For this reason a cost-benefit analysis seems inappropriate.

Benston approaches this question by assigning a value to elimination of insider trading; however, he then finds that SEC reporting has no substantial impact on such trading. Further, he argues that various studies indicate that the market impounds all information known to insiders but that, nevertheless, it seems likely that there was before 1934, and is now, unfair trading by insiders.[125]

In fact not all the empirical studies agree that the market does impound insiders' information. Some purport to have found what Benston suspects and what securities lawyers know—that some insiders do trade and make an unfair profit from insider trading.[126]

Nevertheless, his principal argument is that securities laws have done little to diminish insider trading, a point he purports to substantiate by finding no evidence to the contrary. Once again, however, Benston has simply failed to assume his burden of proof by failing to demonstrate that SEC-mandated disclosure has not had some impact on insider trading. Nevertheless, in the absence of evidence, we examine the logical possibility that insider trading is less with mandatory reporting under the securities laws than it would have been without.

We will continue to assume that Benston is excluding the antifraud rules from his evaluation of the mandatory reporting provisions. Therefore we should not consider whether rule 10b-5 might have diminished unfair insider trading because that is an antifraud rule which Benston may not wish to abolish. However, section 16(a) of the 1934 Act[127] is a *reporting* provision which requires certain insiders (directors, officers and 10 percent shareholders) of issuers of SEC-registered securities to file an initial report of holdings and monthly reports of changes in holdings. Since the information in these reports is widely available (for example, it is published in newspaper financial pages) and since insiders are liable to the corporation for profits from sales and purchases within six months under section (b), and potentially liable under rule 10b-5, as well, if profits from either the purchase or sale were obtained

---

124. See note 80 *supra*. Professor Manne has put forth the thesis that insider profits are an appropriate form of incentive for insiders. H. Manne, *Insider Trading and the Stock Market* (1966).

125. Benston, "An Appraisal," at p. 58 in this volume.

126. Niederhofer and Osborne, "Market Making and Reversal on the Stock Exchange," 61 J. Am. Stat. Assoc. 897 (1966); Lorie and Niederhofer, "Predictive and Statistical Properties of Insider Trading," 11 J. L. & Econ. 35 (1968).

127. 15 U.S.C. § 78p (1976).

while in possession of material inside information,[128] one would expect at least a few of these insiders to limit their unfair trading. Since this limitation is nearly free of costs, the benefit is likely to exceed costs. That being so, the burden of proof of an opposite result should be on the proponent of repeal of this mandatory disclosure provision.

If Benston objects that his quarrel is with neither section 16 nor rule 10b-5, but only with mandatory disclosures in periodic reports (and proxy materials?), one can still cite anecdotal evidence of insiders being discouraged from trading because of their awareness that information will ultimately have to be disclosed which an investor, on hindsight, may perceive as having been inside information which was probably known by the insider.[129] If this is so, as it must be, again one seeking to eliminate SEC-mandated reporting of insider trading should be required to assume and discharge the burden of proof that mandated reporting does not diminish insider trading—something which Benston has not done.

AVAILABILITY OF INFORMATION THAT OTHERWISE WOULD NOT BE PUBLISHED

Here two questions are posed as relevant:

(1) Would the information have been forthcoming without mandatory rules?

(2) Even if not, is the mandated information useful?

Interestingly, on this point Benston states there is evidence, but comes to no conclusion as to the information content of SEC-mandated disclosure. He cannot, since the empirical studies to date are in conflict. Both the Griffin[130] and Collins[131] studies cited and described show that there may be at least some usefulness to certain SEC-mandated disclosures, although there are conflicting findings of others.

In addition, two studies have found possible deficiencies in the

---

128. *In re* Sterling Drug, Inc., Securities Exchange Act Release No. 14675, [1978 Transfer Binder] Fed. Sec. L. Rep. (CCH) ¶ 81,570 (the trade need not be motivated by the inside information); SEC v. Texas Gulf Sulphur Co., 401 F.2d 833 (2d Cir. 1968), *cert. denied*, 404 U.S. 1005 (1971).

129. If the SEC makes stick its announced view in *Sterling Drug, supra* note 129, that an insider is liable when he is in possession of inside information regardless of whether he actually misused it, the prophylactic effect of the knowledge of subsequent disclosure will become very effective.

130. Griffin, "Disclosure Policy and the Securities Market: The Impact of the 1975–76 Sensitive Foreign Payment Disclosures" (unpublished manuscript, Stanford U. Grad. Sch. of Bus., Nov. 1976). (I have not read this paper.)

131. Collins, "SEC Product-Line Reporting and Market Efficiency," 2 J. Fin. Econ. 125 (1975).

methodology Benston employed in his own 1973 study which he here describes and in which he found the periodic reports under the 1934 Act to be useless. Thus Gonedes and Dopuch noted that numerous factors not taken into account by Benston, other than the impotence of the 1934 Act, could explain his results.[132] Deakin[133] also reviewed Benston's tests and found them inadequate to test for effects of the 1934 Act, finding some effect of the securities laws, quite to the contrary of Stigler and Benston.

Moreover, there may be another utility to SEC filings: the previously noted "disciplining effect" from the knowledge held by corporate managers and their advisers, when they issue press releases and other reports not mandated by the SEC that the day of reckoning will come shortly thereafter when they must file SEC reports either confirming or denying the prior publication.[134] This is a benefit derived from mandatory reporting which would otherwise be unavailable.

EFFICIENCY IN SECURITY INVESTMENT AND IN THE ALLOCATION OF RESOURCES

On this question, whether there is greater efficiency in making security investments as a result of SEC reporting, Benston admits there is no study measuring the costs of securities analysis and choice before and after 1933. Nonetheless he cites the widely held belief that 1933 Act registration statements are more costly than beneficial in this respect, referring to Homer Kripke's opinion, with which I am inclined to agree.[135] However, Benston does not address the value of 1934 Act reports, on which the popular view is quite to the contrary.[136]

His asserted "indirect evidence" that the securities laws have not promoted efficiency in the allocation of investments seems to be unpersuasive.[137] And opposed to his view is the fact that investment analysts,

---

132. Gonedes and Dopuch, "Capital Market Equilibrium, Information, Production, and Selecting Accounting Techniques: Theoretical Framework and Review of Empirical Work," Studies of Financial Accounting Objectives § 8 (Supp. to J. Acctg. Research 1974).

133. Deakin, "Accounting Reports, Policy Interventions and the Behavior of Securities Returns," 51 Acctg. Rev. 590 (1976).

134. See *Report, supra* note 2, at xlvi, and text at note 90 *supra*.

135. Kripke, "The Myth of the Informed Layman," 28 Bus. Law. 631 (1973).

136. Since first spelled out in Milton Cohen's article, " 'Truth in Securities' Revisited," 79 Harv. L. Rev. 1340 (1966), the concept of integrated disclosure has been implemented in numerous SEC rules to encourage more and better 1934 Act reporting while deemphasizing 1933 Act registration. See, e.g., SEC Rules 137, 139, 174, 434 and 15c2–8, 17 C.F.R. 230.137, –.139, –.174, –.434 and 17 C.F.R. 240.15c2–8 (1978), respectively.

137. For example, his suggestion that if investors wanted more information,

according to the recent SEC Disclosure Policy Study, consider the information they obtain to be of some value.[138] I recognize the fact that since analysts do not pay for this information, their craving does not establish that there is a net benefit. However, it does show a presumably positive value (more than zero), since if it were of zero value, they would not be interested in it. Since Benston imposes on himself the burden of proving zero value, this evidence contradicts his thesis. Again Benston seems to have failed in carrying his burden of coming forward with evidence, let alone in meeting the burden of persuasion at least with respect to 1934 Act disclosures.

PUBLIC CONFIDENCE IN THE SECURITIES MARKETS

The final claimed benefit of mandatory disclosure, enhancing public confidence in the securities markets, was one of the major purposes of the securities legislation.[139] It is a major basis as well for the recent flurry of legislative concern for increased disclosure regarding municipal securities,[140] indicating that it is still widely believed that disclosure maintains confidence in the market.

Benston again finds no direct evidence one way or the other but purports to find indirect evidence of diminished confidence from the drop in the proportion of new issues to capital formation after 1933, increased use of private placements and the growth of institutional investors.[141] However, each of these can be explained by causes other than a decrease in public confidence in the markets. For example, fewer public offerings may be due to the higher transaction costs caused by the securities laws, rather than by lesser public confidence. Perhaps, more persuasively, the great growth in institutional investors better explains this phenomenon; the institutional investors with their economies of scale can study an issue on behalf of numerous smaller investors, spreading the cost among all their clients, at the same cost each smaller investor would otherwise have had to incur separately. Indeed if there were no confidence in the markets one would hypothesize that we would find less investment in the institutional investors, with inves-

---

Moody's would include it (see Benston, "An Appraisal," at p. 60 n. 52 in this volume) fails to note that sophisticated analysts go far beyond Moody's, which is more suitable for amateurs.

138. *Report, supra* note 2, at pp. 50–93. Further, see Benston's own citation at p. 68 n. 65 in this volume.

139. See President Roosevelt's message to the Congress supporting the bill for the 1933 Act, 77 Cong. Rec. 937 (1933).

140. Securities and Exchange Commission, "Final Report in the Matter of Transactions in the Securities of the City of New York," 16 SEC Docket 952 (Feb. 20, 1979).

141. Benston, "An Appraisal," at p. 61 in this volume.

tors putting more money into alternatives such as real estate. Further, Benston's conclusion is also inconsistent with his earlier statement in his discussion of the first benefit—diminished fraud—that investors are possibly lulled into believing that fraud is a problem of the past because of SEC reporting.[142]

Finally, he suggests that encouraging individual investment in the securities markets as opposed to investment through intermediaries may not be an appropriate goal of government policy after all.[143] Others may go further and urge that the government ought not to encourage investment in securities any more than it encourages investment in phonograph records, and much may be said for this view. In any event, the burden of going forward with evidence has not been met.

A TWENTIETH CENTURY UTILITARIAN APPROACH

Benston's economic model provides some useful insights but I believe that it alone is not enough. Apparently conceding that he has not shown zero or trivial benefits from SEC disclosure, he admits mandated securities law disclosure "may have some positive benefits" but he then retreats to the position that on balance "these benefits do not seem to offset the costs."[144] However, this latter position is unsubstantiated because he has not succeeded in providing evidence of the relative measurements of each of the costs and benefits which would enable an objective comparison.

Nonetheless, my arguments take nothing away from the great benefit bestowed by the demands of Benston and others for a critical economic assessment of securities law disclosure. Nor can it be said that this response disposes of the matter. Although my own intuitive belief is that we do have too much regulation in the securities markets, I do not believe that this proposition has been established nor am I prepared to specify which regulations must go. Further study is essential and may prove fruitful.

However, in making this further study I believe it to be unwise to limit the analysis to a strict economic model since I would expect any economic analysis to be incomplete as well as inconclusive, as I find the Benston article to be. Rather, I recommend a utilitarian analysis.[145]

Fortunately, when considering legislative rules, as here, we need not get embroiled in the perennial debate of legal philosophers over the question of how judges should resolve cases at common law when there are no unambiguous rules to follow and whether a utilitarian approach

---

142. *Id.* at p. 55.

143. *Id.* at p. 61.

144. *Id.* at p. 67.

145. We are cautioned to note that utilitarianism is different from economic analysis. R. Posner, *supra* note 27, at p. 12; Posner, *supra* note 22, at pp. 103–107.

is appropriate in such cases.[146] Rather, it is generally agreed that legislative policies may encompass every factor considered appropriately relevant to the subject of the proposed legislation.

The question posed here is: Are only the factors of economic analysis appropriately relevant to a determination of federal securities law disclosure, or should a broader utilitarian analysis be made?

The approach typically used by legislators in this country in considering legislative proposals for the past 200 years, usually without conscious articulation, has been a utilitarian one addressed to the question, What will be the consequences of the proposed legislation to society? In more recent decades, the system has become refined, as described by Henry Hart and Albert Sacks in their somewhat cryptic summary at the outset of this article.[147] Whether they know it or not, legislators have come to ask of proposed legislation whether it is good or bad according to the consequences it will have in furthering valid human wants by utilizing available resources, always having in mind the "underlying imperative" of preserving the social order and the "pragmatic necessity of a currently fair division" of resources.[148]

Although it may seem self-evident that the broader considerations of twentieth century utilitarianism, taking into account all the factors which tend to affect valid human wants and equity among individuals, would be better than the narrower consideration of the effects of the legislation on aggregate wealth, this view has been persuasively challenged, at least with respect to judicial lawmaking, by Richard Posner, in an article entitled, "Utilitarianism, Economics, and Legal Theory."[149] I believe the challenge was not intended to exclude legislation although that is not clear. In any event, only a few aspects of Posner's discussion are relevant to testing the goodness or badness of securities disclosure legislation and they may be briefly answered here.

The superiority of economic analysis in Posner's view comes down to the belief that production for others is preferable to fulfillment of individual wants[150]—the Puritan ethic. But on review of the Posner article it seems that also underlying it is an extremely high valuation of three features for ethical systems:

(1) definiteness;

(2) mechanical feasibility;

(3) propensity to avoid government intervention.

In Posner's view, apparently, a system which is certain, and yields

146. See, e.g., Jurisprudence Symposium, 11 Ga. L. Rev. 969–1424 (1977).

147. See text accompanying and following note 22 *supra*.

148. See H. Hart and A. Sacks, *supra* note 23.

149. Posner, *supra* note 22, at pp. 122–27.

150. See *id.* at p. 104.

relatively clear results, especially results which exclude governmental intervention, is to be highly valued.

Of course, an ethical system which is narrow, taking into account only limited factors, and which calls for government intervention only in a narrow range of cases—i.e., when the market does not maximize wealth—will always be more definite and easier to apply and will less often call for intervention. Hence, one who holds these values high will prefer economic analysis.

But let us consider the question on Posner's own ground. After acknowledging that an ethical theory cannot be validated, he sets forth criteria for judging whether an ethical system may be rejected,[151] testing his nineteenth century utilitarianism and economic analysis against them, and comes down in favor of economic analysis. The criteria for rejection which he posits are three:

> First, that the theory fails to meet certain basic formal criteria of adequacy, such as logical consistency, completeness, definiteness, and the like;
>
> Second, that the theory yields precepts sharply contrary to widely shared ethical intuitions—precepts such as that murder is in general a good thing or that a sheep is normally entitled to as much consideration as a man; or
>
> Third, that a society which adopted the theory would not survive in competition with societies following competing theories.[152]

He then applies only the first two of the criteria and, without rejecting nineteenth century utilitarianism, finds economic analysis to better meet the criteria. Testing twentieth century utilitarianism as it applies to legislation instead of judge-made law, what result accrues?

At the risk of deviating too greatly from the subject of this paper and the further risk of an inadequate treatment of the Posner paper, I will nevertheless suggest that Posner's case for preferring economic analysis over a modern utilitarian analysis is far from conclusive in the area of legislation concerning corporate disclosure.

Criterion One: Formal Adequacy in Terms of Logical Consistency, Completeness, Definiteness, and the Like

Given Posner's own admission that a priori it would seem that "an ethical theory premised on one preference—the desire for wealth—must be inferior to an ethical theory which takes account of the whole set of preferences,"[153] he has not met the burden of persuasion this reasoning places upon him. This seems especially clear in light of his further concession that people are not purely wealth maximizers but have other

---

151. *Id.* at p. 110.

152. *Id.* at pp. 110–11.

153. *Id.* at p. 122.

preferences as well[154]—preferences that only utilitarianism takes into account completely.

This being so, even Posner would probably concede that, in the abstract, utilitarianism would be superior as more complete. Nonetheless his position presumably is, in fact, that no one is sufficiently skilled to be able infallibly to measure all utilitarian benefits and disadvantages and that it is better to let the marketplace vote with its money for preferences.

But, even if it were agreed that wealth maximization should be the sole objective, modern markets do not always, or even very often, work perfectly, and the economic analyst is frequently called upon to do what the utilitarian must do—hypothetically measure costs and benefits. Because of externalities in the corporate disclosure area, this is precisely what Benston was forced to do and, as I suggest, without success. Thus economic analysis, perhaps in a large number of cases, and certainly in corporate disclosure, is indefinite, just as is a utilitarian analysis.

However, Posner argues that measuring economic costs in a hypothetical market is less difficult than measuring pleasure and pain in the utilitarian's sense.[155] I agree. But is it better to be precisely wrong than approximately correct? We saw earlier that Mercator projections also work for many purposes; they are especially easy to construct and use since they are flat. But they sometimes yield wrong results, as when a straight line drawn on one of them does not give the shortest distance between two points.[156]

As to Posner's "perils of instrumentalism," by which he means the danger that an ethical system will be operated on the doctrine that ends justify means, he finds utilitarianism will more often call for government intervention. Posner, perhaps correctly, finds this an evil per se. But he also concedes that when the market does not operate efficiently as when there are large externalities, intervention is justified even under economic analysis. We have seen that externalities are conceded to exist in the area of securities law disclosures. If they are "large," neither economic analysis nor utilitarianism would reject intervention here.

Criterion Two: Congruence with Widely Shared Ethical Intuitions

Moreover, economic analysis of securities law disclosure, as we have seen, provides no guidance in terms of equality among participants. For example, it cannot tell us whether insider trading is good or bad in allocating wealth as between insiders and outsiders. On the other hand,

---

154. *Id.*

155. *Id.* at p. 130.

156. See text at note 40 *supra.*

utilitarianism displays its superiority by explicitly taking equality into account.

Further, the whole basis of securities law disclosure is a concern for openness and honesty, one of the most highly regarded of our widely shared ethical intuitions. Utilitarianism, therefore, would value it as a collective pleasure, whereas economic analysis would be neutral, unless it is shown that honesty increases collective wealth. Given the opposite thesis of some economists that market efficiency is enhanced by insider trading[157] (and hence wealth is maximized), it appears that economic analysis would yield results opposed to honesty.

Hence, by Posner's own criteria, his ethical system based on wealth maximization falls short compared to modern utilitarianism in assessing securities law disclosure policy.

CONCLUSION

For these reasons, I suggest that in fixing securities law disclosure policy, Congress and the SEC should continue to apply a utilitarian analysis, as they always have and as the Advisory Committee on Corporate Disclosure urged in its Report,[158] taking the results of economic analysis as but one part of the data. That analysis, performed by Benston, appears not to have established that costs of SEC-mandated disclosure exceed the benefits.

---

157. See note 80 *supra*.

158. See *Report*, *supra* note 2.

CHAPTER THREE

Using Disclosure to Activate the Board of Directors

Elliott J. Weiss * *Associate Professor of Law, Benjamin N. Cardozo School of Law, Yeshiva University*
Donald E. Schwartz* *Professor of Law, Georgetown University Law Center*

The theme of this article can be stated simply: in order to improve the manner in which boards of directors function and to ensure that important information about boards is made available to investors, the Securities and Exchange Commission should require reporting companies to disclose considerably more information about their boards of directors.

There are three concerns which underlie this proposal. First, ineffective performance by many corporate boards leads to below optimal corporate efficiency. Second, information about boards of directors that is potentially important to investment decisions is not now available to the public. Third, the paucity of meaningful information that is available about boards serves to undermine the operation of a system of fair corporate suffrage.

This article is divided into two parts. The first sets forth our reasons for believing the SEC should require disclosure of additional information about the boards of all reporting companies. It includes discussion of:

(1) the background of the disclosure provisions of the Securities Exchange Act of 1934, which makes clear that the SEC can properly mandate disclosure for the purpose of influencing corporate conduct where the information to be disclosed is important to decisions to be made by investors;

(2) the relevance of a properly functioning board to the efficient operation of corporations in a free-market economy as well as to the integrity of the disclosure process administered by the SEC;

* The authors were fortunate in having the research and editorial assistance of Gerard L. Hawkins, a third year student at Georgetown University Law Center. Professor Weiss expresses appreciation to the Ford Foundation for its financial support to him over the period during which he prepared this article.

(3) the importance of information about boards to individuals and institutions that make investment, disinvestment, and corporate suffrage decisions;

(4) the advantages of using disclosure rather than either ad hoc enforcement or mandatory requirements to influence constructively the functioning of corporate boards of directors;

(5) the recent SEC efforts that improve the quality of disclosure about boards.

The second part of this article describes the elements of our proposed disclosure system—a system that focuses on the processes by which boards operate. We describe our proposals as a model and compare it with current requirements for disclosure of information about individual nominees for election as directors, the procedures and criteria used by boards to select nominees, the organization and activities of boards, and the reason for all resignations of directors.

Our proposal is limited; it may be viewed by some as too limited when evaluated in terms of our concerns. We recognize that improving disclosure about corporate procedures cannot ensure an improvement in corporate conduct, particularly since altering the procedures themselves cannot give that assurance. However, there are many instances in which a legal system cannot assure a desired outcome but is limited to creating an environment in which that outcome is more likely.[1] In the case of boards of directors, directors cannot be made to perform responsibly simply by being told they must do so, and the threat of liability has failed to accomplish desired results. The time has come, we believe, to attempt to stimulate constructive change by relying on disclosure.

THE CASE FOR A DISCLOSURE APPROACH

Legislative History and Background

An examination of the background of the federal securities laws makes it clear that Congress was aware of the power of disclosure when it passed those laws in the midst of the Great Depression. More specifically, Congress anticipated that the disclosures to be required by the SEC would influence investors' views about the importance of certain information and would encourage or discourage certain kinds of corporate conduct.

The Commission used its disclosure authority for these purposes and, in general, SEC disclosure requirements seemingly calculated to influence corporate conduct were challenged only when it appeared unlikely that the data to be disclosed should or would be considered important by investors.

---

1. See C. Schultze, *Public Use of Private Interests* (1977).

LEGISLATIVE HISTORY

The formal legislative documents pertaining to the securities laws indicate that Congress anticipated that disclosure would influence the activities of corporate directors, but do not make clear how Congress thought that process would work. The House Interstate and Foreign Commerce Committee, in its report on the Securities Act of 1933, stated,[2]

> Honesty, care, and competence are the demands of trusteeship. These demands are made by the bill on the directors of the issuer. . . . If it be said that the impositon of such responsibility upon these persons will be to alter corporate organization and corporate practice in this country, such a result is only what your committee expects . . . . Directors should assume the responsibility of directing and if their manifold activities make real directing impossible, they should be held responsible to the unsuspecting public for their neglect.

In adopting the 1934 Act Congress stated that its objective in the regulation of proxy solicitation[3] was "fair corporate suffrage."[4] The House report did not elaborate on what was meant by that term, but did go on to discuss the existing obstacles to that objective. The concern was that insiders would have little difficulty retaining their control "without an adequate disclosure of their interest and without an adequate explanation of the management policies they intend to pursue.[5] There was inadequate disclosure of the reasons for the solicitation of proxies and the use to which they would be put. The Senate report also noted that stockholders should be enlightened about the financial condition of the corporation and about "major questions of policy, which are decided at stockholders' meetings."[6]

LITERATURE OF THE DAY

While the legislative documents do not make clear how Congress believed disclosure would lead to fair corporate suffrage, a review of the literature of the day provides important insights into the expectations of the policymakers who fashioned the securities laws. Those policymakers clearly understood the manner in which the SEC would influence the behavior of corporations by use of its disclosure authority.

The framers of the securities laws were aware that attaining shareholder democracy, in the political sense of that term, was not a realistic

---

2. H.R. Rep. No. 85, 73d Cong., 1st Sess. 5 (1933).

3. Sec. Exch. Act of 1934, § 14, 48 Stat. 895 (codified at 15 U.S.C. § 78n (1970)).

4. H.R. Rep. No. 1383, 73d Cong., 2d Sess. 13–14 (1934).

5. *Id.*

6. S. Rep. No. 1455, 73d Cong., 2d Sess. 77 (1934).

objective. Professors Adolf A. Berle and Gardiner Means, the former a powerful member of the New Deal Brain Trust, in their classic work *The Modern Corporation and Private Property*, had demonstrated that control of the large corporation had become separated from its ownership.[7] Berle and Means recognized that two approaches might be utilized to influence directors' conduct: stricter application of fiduciary principles and expanded disclosure requirements.[8]

Professor William Z. Ripley, whom Berle and Means acknowledged as the pioneer in their field, [9] had emphasized earlier the merits of disclosure.[10] He made it clear, however, that while disclosure would influence corporate behavior, it was unlikely to do so through an upsurge in shareholder activism:[11]

> No one believes that a great enterprise can be operated by town meeting. It never has been done successfully; nor will it ever be . . . . Nor is it true that the primary purpose of publicity, the sharing of full information with owners, is to enable these shareholders to obtrude themselves obsequiously upon their own managements.

Rather, Ripley noted, information about the corporation, its board, and its operations would have an impact because a select group of sophisticated investors would understand the information, would act on it, and also would translate it into terms meaningful to the mass of investors and disseminate the information to them.[12] Thus, the work of Ripley,

---

7. A. Berle and G. Means, *The Modern Corporation and Private Property*, chapters IV and V (1932).

8. Berle had written earlier that corporate powers of control were held in a fiduciary capacity and that the law must be used to constrain directors and managers in their exercise of corporate power. See Berle, "Corporate Powers as Powers in Trust," 44 Harv. L. Rev. 1049 (1931).

9. A. Berle and G. Means, *supra* note 7, at p. ix.

10. He wrote that "[s]tockholders are entitled to adequate information, and the state and general public have a right to the same privilege." W. Ripley, *Main Street and Wall Street*, p. 165 (1926).

11. *Id.* at pp. 168–69.

12. *Id.* The observation anticipates by many years the proponents of the efficient-market theory. See Fama, "Efficient Capital Markets: A Review of Theory and Empirical Work," 25 J. Finance 383 (1970). It is also consistent with the views of somewhat stronger believers in the efficacy of full disclosure that the principal value of disclosure is for the experts who distill the information and make it available to non-experts. Kripke, "The Myth of the Informed Layman," 28 Bus. L. 631 (1973).

Perhaps Ripley's most farsighted suggestion, however, was one he partially attributed to Berle: to create a permanent agency to be more representative of the shareholders' interest. "Such a body, either created out of hand or else evolved from present boards of directors, might be expressly empowered in the

and Berle and Means, taken together, made clear that disclosure would promote corporate democracy not by stimulating ordinary shareholders to attend annual meetings and cast informed votes but through much more indirect and sophisticated mechanisms.[13]

The work of other scholars and commentators over the same period made clear that the SEC by requiring disclosure could be expected to influence both corporate conduct and investors' assessments of that conduct. The seminal observation in this regard was made by Louis D. Brandeis, who extolled the virtue of disclosure as a regulator in the classic statement, "Sunlight is the best disinfectant; electric light the best policeman."[14] Professor Allison Anderson, in her study of the securities laws, states that the decision by the Roosevelt administration and Congress to rely heavily on disclosure—rather than attempt direct substantive regulation of corporate conduct—reflected the influence of Brandeis' observation.[15]

That this was so, and that the SEC was expected to decide what corporate activities were in need of policing and to use disclosure to police them, are evidenced by the contemporary writing of two other scholars, both of whom were important in the Roosevelt administration and both of whom were subsequently named to the Supreme Court. After the adoption of the Securities Act in 1933, Professor Felix Frankfurter stated:

> The Securities Act may well exercise indirect but important influence . . . upon corporate managers. . . . By compelling full publicity of 'every essentially important element attending the issue of new securities' so that the public may have an opportunity to understand what it buys, the Act seeks to promote standards of competence and candor in dealing with the public. . . .There is a shrinking quality to such transactions; to force knowledge of them into the open is largely to restrain their happening. Many practices

---

charter to assume certain responsibilities and to perform certain functions by way of check-up, so to speak. Its primary function would have to do with adequate publicity through independent audit." W. Ripley, *supra* note 10, at p. 133. He saw little prospect of this with boards of directors as then constituted. *Id.* at 139.

13. The complementary views of Ripley, Berle, Means and other scholars were reflected in the substance of the federal securities laws adopted in 1933 and 1934. Knauss, "A Reappraisal of the Role of Disclosure," 62 Mich. L. Rev. 607, 613–15 (1964).

14. L. Brandeis, *Other People's Money,* p. 62 (1933). Brandeis had long since been appointed to the Supreme Court when the securities laws were passed, but the influence of his ideas was as strong as if he had been a member of Roosevelt's Brain Trust. See L. Loss, *Securities Regulation* vol. 1, p. 123 (2d ed. 1961).

15. Anderson, "The Disclosure Process in Federal Securities Regulation: A Brief Review," 25 Hastings L.Q. 311, 318, 330 (1974). Anderson also notes that the choice of disclosure rather than direct regulation to achieve substantive goals was partly motivated by political considerations. *Id.* at 331.

safely pursued in private lose their justification in public. Thus social standards newly defined gradually establish themselves as new business habits.

Similarly, Professor William O. Douglas observed that[17]

> [p]ublicity alone can accomplish much—not publicity in the sense of a registration in some dusty file in Washington or in some state capitol, but publicity in the sense of direct and unequivocal statement in the periodical reports to stockholders. . . . That simple expedient will go far as a corrective of conditions which have been constantly recurring in our corporate history. Its prophylactic effects will equal in importance any other single measure which can be adopted.

Thus it seems clear Congress fully understood the power of disclosure and the manner in which the SEC would influence corporate conduct by requiring disclosure.[18]

SUBSEQUENT DEVELOPMENTS

The view that disclosure is to be used by the SEC as a regulatory tool has gained widespread support. In the Disclosure Policy Study—known as the Wheat Report—the SEC's philosophy of disclosure was set forth as follows:[19]

---

16. Frankfurter, "The Federal Securities Act: II," Fortune, Aug. 1933, p. 53, at p. 55.

17. Douglas, "Directors Who Do Not Direct," 47 Harv. L. Rev. 1305, 1323–24 (1934).

18. At the same time Congress probably did not intend direct regulation to affect internal corporate changes. The Conference Report to the 1934 Act contained the following statement:

> The House bill does not contain a provision corresponding to that contained in subsection (d) of Section 13 of the Senate amendment providing that nothing in this title shall be construed as authorizing the Commission to interfere with the management of the affairs of an issuer." This provision is omitted from the substitute as unnecessary, since it is not believed that the bill is open to misconstruction in this respect.

H.R. Rep. No. 1838, 73d Cong., 2d Sess., accompanying H.R. 9323, at p. 36 (1934).

19. Disclosure Policy Study (Wheat Report) 10 (1969). The deterrent capacity and objective of disclosure has been recognized by the courts. In Laurenzano v. Einbinder, 264 F. Supp. 356 (E.D.N.Y. 1968), a court refused to dismiss a complaint for lack of a causal relationship between an allegedly misleading proxy statement and injury to the plaintiff where the defendants owned sufficient shares to approve the transaction without obtaining any proxies. The court observed that it could not be said that the defendants would have used their power in the same way if they were required to make full disclosure of the facts. In Mills v. Electric Auto Lite, 396 U.S. 375 (1970), the Supreme Court

The emphasis on disclosure rests on two considerations. One relates to the proper function of the Federal government in investment matters. Apart from the prevention of fraud and manipulation, the draftsmen of the '33 and '34 Acts viewed that responsibility as being primarily one of seeing to it that investors and speculators had access to enough information to enable them to arrive at their own rational decisions. The other, less direct consideration rests on the belief that appropriate publicity tends to deter questionable practices and to elevate standards of business conduct.

Where SEC disclosure requirements or proposed requirements have been the subject of controversy, the dispute usually has focused not on whether disclosure can properly be used as a regulator but on whether the information to be disclosed is material to decisions of legitimate concern to the Commission—those involving purchase, sale, and voting of securities.[20] The Commission has declined to use disclosure to pursue social objectives, such as environmental protection, where it has not viewed the information involved to be of particular importance to investors.[21] And while in some cases the SEC has not made clear the

---

found a causal connection between a misrepresentation in a proxy statement and injury to stockholders based solely on a finding that the misrepresentation was material. Defendants owned more than a majority of the stock but still needed to solicit proxies to gain the requisite votes. Although the reasoning of Justice Harlan proceeds along the same path as Judge Dooling in *Laurenzano,* the Court did not have to, and did not, embrace *Laurenzano* and overrule cases to the contrary. 396 U.S. at 385 n.7.

20. The use of disclosure as a tool to elevate corporate standards is a legitimate concern of the SEC. William L. Cary, former Chairman of the SEC, advocated the use of disclosure for this purpose. See Cary, "Corporate Standards and Legal Rules," 50 Cal. L. Rev. 408, 411 (1962) ("In other words, disclosure restrains because of sensitivity to public reaction, caution about response to the 'dissident' shareholder, and the possibility of legal action.") The SEC confirmed this view in its response to the report of the Advisory Committee on Corporate Disclosure. SEC Securities Act Release No. 33-5906 (Feb. 15, 1978), [Current] Fed. Sec. L. Rep. (CCH) ¶ 81,505, at 80,047–48.

21. Scholars have urged the Commission to use its disclosure powers to pursue social objectives, such as environmental protection. See, e.g., Schoenbaum, "The Relationship Between Corporate Disclosure and Corporate Responsibility," 40 Fordham L. Rev. 565 (1972); Branson, "Progress in the Art of Social Accounting and Other Arguments for Disclosure on Corporate Social Responsibility," 29 Vand. L. Rev. 529 (1976); Sonde and Pitt, "Utilizing the Federal Securities Laws to "Clear the Air! Clean the Sky! Wash the Wind!," 16 How. L.J. 831 (1971).

The Commission has been wary about using disclosure for such purposes, however, and has somewhat casually refused to adopt rules in the environmental protection area. Judge Richey, however, ordered the Commission to hold hearings or make more careful findings in this area. See Natural Resources Defense Council v. SEC, 389 F. Supp. 689 (D.D.C. 1974). After lengthy hearings, the Commission proposed modest rules, 40 Fed. Reg. 51,656 (1975), which it

primary purpose for which disclosure has been required,[22] in others it has made clear that disclosure is being required primarily to influence corporate behavior.[23] When it has used disclosure to promote these regulatory objectives, as in the recent instances where it required disclosure of illegal and questionable payments by corporations, controversy has centered on whether the information was of concern to investors.[24]

We do not conclude from this background that the SEC should adopt disclosure rules that have no potential for informing investors. But the Commission should not shrink from adopting disclosure rules for the explicit purpose of influencing corporate conduct where that conduct is of legitimate concern to the Commission and where the information to be disclosed is relevant to decision-making by investors.[25]

---

modified still further in the final version. 41 Fed. Reg. 21,632 (1976). On appeal, Judge Richey held that the Commission's refusal to adopt rules was arbitrary and capricious and remanded the matter for further consideration. Natural Resources Defense Counsel v. SEC, 432 F. Supp. 1190 (D.D.C. 1977). An appeal has been taken by the Commission.

22. A concern for the public interest is too broad to sustain the Commission's interest. See NAACP v. FPC, 425 U.S. 662 (1976).

23. Examples of this are disclosure requirements concerning transactions between management and a corporation, see items 11(a) (promoter's transactions), 17 (remuneration of officers and directors), and 20 (transactions between management and the registrant) of form S-1 and item 7 of regulation 14A; disclosure intended to discourage illegal corporate political contributions and other questionable payments, see proposed rule 13b-2 of the Securities Exchange Act of 1934, SEC Securities Exchange Act Release No. 34-13185, 11 SEC Docket No. 8, at 1505 (Jan. 19, 1977) and Release No. 33-5466, 3 SEC Docket No. 18, at 647 (March 8, 1974) (disclosure of illegal political contributions); and disclosure designed to strengthen the position of public accountants in relation to corporate managements, see item 4, form 8K (change of certifying accountants), SEC Accounting Series Release No. 165, [1977] Fed. Sec. L. Rep. (CCH) ¶ 72,189.

24. Commissioners have expressed recognition that one of the main accomplishments of the so-called management fraud programs directed against illegal or questionable payments has been to influence corporate conduct. See "Truth or Consequences," (address by John Evans, SEC Commissioner, before Securities Cooperative Enforcement Conference, Denver, Colo., May 15, 1975), at p. 12; "Disclosure and Corporate Management," (address by Ray Garrett, Chairman of the SEC, before the Wharton Graduate Business School Club and Harvard Business School Club, New York, N.Y., April 14, 1975); "Address" (by Roderick Hills, Chairman of the SEC, before the *New York Law Journal*, New York, N.Y. (June 30, 1976)), at p. 11; See also Stevenson, "The SEC and the New Disclosure," 62 Cornell L. Rev. 50, 92 (1976).

25. This view is consistent with the recommendations of the SEC Advisory Committee on Corporate Disclosure. See Digest of Report, 427 Sec. Reg. & L. Rep. (BNA) E-1 and separate statement of Elliott J. Weiss, E-14. (Mr. Weiss was a member of the Advisory Committee.)

The Need to Strengthen Boards of Directors

We turn next to the question whether the SEC should use disclosure for the regulatory purpose of improving the performance of boards of directors of registered companies. This inquiry raises three subsidiary questions: Is there a constructive role in a corporation that can best be played by a board of directors? Can we determine what kinds of boards are capable of playing that role? Are boards now failing to play that role? We conclude that the answer to all three questions is yes, thereby establishing a policy basis for SEC regulatory intervention to strengthen boards of directors.

THE IMPORTANCE OF THE BOARD

We start with the premise that the principal underlying purpose of the securities laws was and is to strengthen the basic institutions of the American capitalist economic system. Publicly held corporations, probably the most important of those institutions, are strengthened if they operate more efficiently and if those who control them are viewed as doing so legitimately.

Some would argue that market forces and state corporate laws assure the efficiency of corporations and provide them with legitimacy, so that no intervention by the federal government is required.[26] We dispute those contentions.

Despite the existence of a number of market devices that theoretically promote efficiency, market forces do not adequately control the conduct of corporations. Two principal market regulators are in operation: the capital market, where investors function, and the product market, where consumers function. In the first investors may eliminate inefficiency by causing a change in the control of a corporation or denying it needed capital; in the second inefficiency may be eliminated by business failure. Both reactions are extreme, and both suffer from the defect that substantial slack is tolerated before inefficiency is corrected.

The mechanisms available in the capital market to change corporate control—the takeover bid and the proxy contest—are costly to mount and uncertain of success, especially if management's incompetence is

---

26. The view that market forces adequately control the conduct of the corporation is largely premised on the belief that the corporation is a profit maximizer or a profit "satisfier." See Alchian, "The Basis of Some Recent Advances in the Theory of Management of the Firm," 14 J. Indus. Econ. 30 (Nov. 1965), reprinted in The Economics of Legal Relationships 487 (H. Manne ed. 1975); Peterson, "Corporate Control and Capitalism," Q.J. Econ., Feb. 1965, at 1. See Note, "Decision-making Models and the Control of Corporate Crime," 85 Yale L.J. 1019, 1101 (1976). Substantial doubt about profit maximization as the motivating force behind corporate action is expressed in J. Galbraith, *The New Industrial State* 166–78 (1967).

less than total.[27] In many cases the disciplinary effect of investors' decisions to withhold capital is minimal because the firms can meet their needs with internally generated funds.[28] Investors also experience great difficulty in using a less drastic remedy—imposing personal liability on management for its failings—because of the broad protection furnished to management by the business-judgment rule.

In the product market the ultimate penalty of insolvency is reserved for the most inefficient firms and imposed only after an extended period of inefficiency. To the extent that an inefficient firm enjoys a monopoly it can escape the control of the product market. Finally, because of the complexity of the corporate structure and the fact that corporate activity is carried out by lower level managers, the signals of the product market may not be transmitted to the senior managers who have the power and responsibility to react to such stimuli.[29] Since the market does not provide an automatic assurance that corporate goals will be pursued, we conclude that there is a need for organizational strategies directed towards that objective.

One potential role for a board of directors is as a disciplinary force within a corporation. A board, given its legal authority within the firm and its potential access to information and resources, can ride herd on management more effectively than any of the market devices, all of which are external to the firm.

A second potential role for a board is to ensure that management is pursuing a coherent business strategy that is in tune with the corporation's external as well as internal environment. Corporations are made up of people who plan and deal with problems "in the context of an organization chart, a system of measurement and information and a system of managerial reward and punishment that primarily reflects the short-run needs of day-to-day operations."[30] This emphasis on short-term results often leads to biases in planning and decision-making that are quite harmful to a company.[31] The possibility of such biases is

---

27. Moreover, in recent years the takeover bid has been used more to acquire well-managed companies whose stock is viewed as undervalued. See Metz, "Babcock and Wilcox: A Battle that Shook Wall Street Notions," N.Y. Times, Sept. 19, 1977, at p. 57.

28. Berle, "Modern Functions of the Corporate System," 62 Colum. L. Rev. 433, 440 (1962). Following a great rise in the dollar value of securities offered by issuers to the public in the 1960's during the so-called hot issue days, the amount of securities offered by issuers to the public since 1969 has been relatively stable. See [1976] SEC Ann. Rep. 42, at 199.

29. C. Stone, *Where the Law Ends,* p. 201 (1975); P. Drucker, *Management: Tasks, Responsibilities, Practices,* p. 623 (1974).

30. Bower, "On the Amoral Organization," in *The Corporate Society,* p. 178, at p. 195 (R. Marris ed. 1974).

31. *Id.*

increased in most large corporations by their divisional organization, which leads to evaluation of managers on the basis of short-run economic and technical results[32] and to the common modern practice of frequently rotating executives to different jobs, which often increases the importance attached to short-run results.[33]

In addition, management's tendency to measure performance on the basis of short-term, objective standards often leads a firm to ignore the social impact of its operations, which is often difficult to measure. Environmental pollution most readily comes to mind. The corporate decision-maker's interest in achieving results that best promote his or her personal goals under the existing reward system often causes the corporation to generate more harmful pollution in order to reduce measurable costs and increase measurable profits.[34] Thus, as to this facet of corporate performance, market-oriented behavior is counterproductive, encouraging conduct which damages society as a whole. Economist Robin Marris has observed that industrial societies "are increasingly affected by 'externalities' . . . to such an extent that 'competitive' or market-type systems of socio-economic organization can no longer even approximately tend to optimize social welfare."[35] A board can play an important leadership role in developing and measuring implementation of organizational strategies that will enable a corporation to deal more effectively and responsibly with these problems.[36]

Some might argue that corporate chief executive officers (CEO) should be charged with the task of coordinating and controlling the activities of senior and middle managers to promote the best interests of their firms and that board intervention is not necessary. But frequently the chief executive does not play that role. Studies have found that most CEO's of large firms tend to emphasize short-term goals that "they are single-mindedly, almost slavishly, committed to achieving. . . ."[37] Thus, it is the board that must counteract this inclination; it best can serve as a "potent force in moderating the management's understandable internal interest in day-to-day achievement."[38]

---

32. R. Ackerman, *The Social Challenge to Business* (1975). This leads to the phenomenon described as "subgoal pursuit." O. Williamson, *Corporate Control and Business Behavior: An Inquiry into the Effects of Organization Form on Enterprise Behavior*, pp. 47–52 (1970). See C. Stone, *supra* note 29, at 46; cf. M. Maccoby, *The Gamesman* 241–42 (1977).

33. See Bower, *supra* note 30.

34. *Id.*

35. Marris, "Conclusion," in R. Marris, *supra* note 30.

36. See Andrews, "Can the Best Corporation be Made Moral?," 51 Harv. Bus. Rev., May–June 1973, at 57–64.

37. Argyris, "The CEO's Behavior: Key to Organizational Development," 51 Harv. Bus. Rev., March–April 1973, at 55, 57.

38. Andrews, *supra* note 36.

A board also can function to reduce the likelihood of unnecessary errors by a corporation. Economist Kenneth J. Arrow, a Nobel laureate, defines errors as unnecessary "when the information [to deal with a problem] is available somewhere in the organization but not available to or not used by the authority [i.e., management]."[39] Unnecessary error arises from[40]

> overload of the information and decision-making capacity of the authority. . . . [Moreover, the] efficiency loss due to informational overload is increased by the tendency in that situation [for management] to filter information in accordance with . . . [its] preconceptions. It is easier [for management] to understand and accept information congruent with the previous beliefs than to overcome cognitive dissonance.

To deal with these problems, which are common to all large organizations, Arrow states, some agency of "responsibility" capable of correcting errors must be created. However, the agency of responsibility should not so limit the discretion of the authority or become so involved in operating decisions that it destroys "the genuine values of authority."[41] Within the corporate context a boardlike entity clearly is best suited to serving the responsibility functions described by Arrow.

Finally, a board can serve to provide legitimacy to a corporation, particularly if it demonstrates that it in fact imposes accountability on management. The problem of corporate legitimacy has been discussed in many contexts, but perhaps never so cogently as by Professor Edward S. Mason in his introduction to *The Corporation in Modern Society*:[42]

> [W]e are all aware that we live not only in a corporate society but a society of large corporations. The management—that is, the control—of these corporations is in the hands of, at most, a few thousand men. Who selected these men, if not to rule over us, at least to exercise vast authority, and to whom are they responsible? The answer to the first question is quite clearly: they selected themselves. The answer to the second is, at best, nebulous. This, in a nutshell, constitutes the problem of legitimacy.

A ROLE FOR THE BOARD

Having described functions that can best—or only—be performed by a board of directors does not answer the second of our questions: What kind of board can in fact perform those functions? This question is far from unimportant; one can trace more than forty years of scholarly

---

39. K. Arrow, *The Limits of Organization* 74 (1974).

40. *Id.* at 74–5.

41. *Id.* at 79.

42. *The Corporation in Modern Society*, p. 5 (E. Mason ed. 1959).

writing expressing confusion about the proper role of a board and describing the failure of boards to perform various important functions, but not addressing the question of what sort of board could perform them.[43]

But now the situation has changed. A consensus has developed in recent years in support of one model for boards that if adopted could perform the functions we have urged.[44] The model is of a board with a majority of part-time directors who are completely independent of management.[45] The principal function of this board is not the tradi-

---

43. Typical of this body of literature is the observation by Peter Drucker that "In reality the board as conceived by the lawmaker is at best a tired fiction. It is perhaps not too much to say that it has become a shadow king. In most of the large companies, it has in effect been deposed and its place taken by executive management." P. Drucker, *The Practice of Management*, p. 178 (1954); see also R. Gordon, *Business Leadership in the Large Corporation*, pp. 143–45 (1945).

Naturally, there were numerous proposals for change of the board. Some suggested that the membership be redrawn to include representatives of various constituencies, such as employees, consumers, or social activists, see Interview with Ralph Nader, N.Y. Times, Jan. 24, 1971, § 3, at p. 9, col. 2; others suggested the employment of professional directors, see Townsend, "Let's Install Public Directors," Bus. & Soc'y Rev. Spring 1972, at 69, a suggestion that had been advanced earlier by Justice Douglas when he was chairman of the SEC, see W. Douglas, *Democracy and Finance*, 52–3 (1940); others asked boards to professionalize themselves by creating special staffs for outside directors, see Goldberg, "Debate on Outside Directors," N.Y. Times, Oct. 20, 1972, § 3, at p. 1, col. 3. See generally The Conference Board, *The Board of Directors: New Challenges, New Directions* (1972) [hereinafter cited as *Conference Board 1972 Report*].

44. One can argue, quite convincingly, that until recently the Commission should have declined to impose disclosure requirements relating to boards because neither it nor anyone else had a clear idea of what constituted a properly functioning board of directors. When Congress adopted the securities laws it tacitly adopted the governance scheme of the corporation statutes which provided that "The business of every corporation . . . shall be managed by a Board of Directors . . . ." Gen. Corp. L. of Del., § 9 (Ch. 65, 1935 Code). Little attention was paid in the 1930's to what that statutory mandate meant and practically no consideration was given to the board as an institution. See Weinberg "A Corporation Director Looks at His Job," 27 Harv. Bus. Rev. 585, 587 (1949). The statutory mandates were apparently relics from the time the prototype corporation was family owned and directors, executives, and principal stockholders were the same. See Douglas, "Directors Who Do Not Direct," 47 Harv. L. Rev. 1305 (1934).

The position that no one has a clear idea of what constitutes a properly functioning board of directors is untenable today. See notes 43–51 *infra* and accompanying text.

45. Most observers agree that the board should be composed predominantly of persons who are independent of management. See generally C. Brown, *Putting the Corporate Board to Work* (1976) (major theme is independence of the board).

tional one of managing the business of the corporation but the more modest, but indispensible, one of monitoring management's performance.[46]

The monitoring function of the board was first stressed by Professor Melvin Aron Eisenberg:[47]

> A corporate organ comprised in significant part of nonexecutives can rarely either manage the corporation's business or make business policy. . . . There is, however, one cluster of critical functions which such an organ is optimally suited to perform: selecting, monitoring, and removing the members of the chief executive's office. It therefore follows that the primary objective of the legal rules governing the structure of corporate management should be to ensure effective performance of that cluster of functions—if possible, without precluding the board from playing additional roles if it so chooses.

Professor Eisenberg concluded that the "major effect of according the policymaking function central importance, therefore, has been to divert legal and corporate institutions from implementing a function that is both critical and achievable: monitoring."[48] He also stressed that for monitoring to be effective, a majority of a board should be independent of management.

The concept of the monitoring board has received support from many quarters. The Model Business Corporation Act and several state statutes have been amended to provide that "the business and affairs of a corporation shall be managed *under the direction* of, a board of directors . . . ."[49] The draftsman of the model act explained in the official comment:[50]

> Many commentators have recently voiced concern that [the language requiring that the business be managed *by* the board of directors] may be interpreted to mean that the directors must become involved in the detailed administration of the corporation's affairs. Before the advent of the so-

---

Movement in this direction has occurred as most boards are now composed of mainly nonemployees. See J. Bacon, *Corporate Directorship Practices: Membership and Committees of the Board*, p. 3 (1973). A later study confirms the trend and forecasts its continuation. See Heidrick & Struggles, Inc., *The Changing Board: Profile of the Board of Directors* (1977).

46. The board's independence and its monitoring function are closely related: indeed, a board will not succeed in monitoring unless it is independent.

47. Eisenberg, "Legal Models of Management Structure in the Modern Corporation: Officers, Directors and Accountants," 63 Calif. L. Rev. 375, 402–3 (1975).

48. *Id.* at 438.

49. E.g., ABA-ALI Model Bus. Corp. Act § 35 (Supp. 1977).

50. ABA Comm. on Corp. Laws, "Changes in the Model Business Corporation Act," 30 Bus. Law. 501, 504–5 (1975).

called "outside" director, it was not unreasonable to expect the board to be actively involved in the corporation's business; however, with the development of board participation by individuals not otherwise actively involved with the corporation, any such expectation can no longer be viewed to be reasonable. Indeed, such involvement is clearly neither practical nor feasible insofar as today's complex corporation, other than perhaps the closely-held corporation, is concerned . . . . To adapt to current corporate life the revision provides that the business and affairs of a corporation shall be managed *under the direction* of a board of directors.

A special subcommittee of the American Bar Associations's Committee on Corporate Laws, which issued a *Corporate Director's Guidebook* in November, 1976, [51] interpreted the Model Business Corporation Act as placing responsibility on directors to establish basic corporate objectives, to select senior executives, to ensure the recruitment of competent managers, and to monitor the performance of the enterprise and its managers.[52] The subcommittee also recommended that a majority of a board be persons independent of management in order to ensure the integrity of the monitoring function.[53]

Professors Noyes E. Leech and Robert H. Mundheim, in an extensive study of outside directors' responsibilities, agreed that monitoring was the central role for outside directors and suggested that statutory requirements for mutual fund directors provide a model.[54] In enacting the Investment Company Act of 1940[55] Congress decided that stock-

---

51. Subcomm. on Functions & Responsibilities of Directors of the A.B.A. Comm. on Corporate Laws, Section of Corporation, Banking & Business Law, "Corporate Director's Guidebook," 32 Bus. Law. 5 (1975) [hereinafter cited as Corporate Director's Guidebook].

52. *Id.* at 20.

53. *Id.* at 33–35. Another ABA group, The Committee on Corporate Law Departments (composed entirely of inside corporate counsel) has attacked almost every major recommendation of the subcommittee. "Report of the Committee on Corporate Law Departments On Corporate Directors Guidebook," 32 Bus. Law. 1841 (1977) [hereinafter cited as Guidebook Report]. They contend that the recommendations are not required by law and they conflict with sound policy, at least as a universal model. Insofar as the Law Department Committee opposes recommendations favoring a majority of independent directors, and audit and nominating committees composed only of independent directors, it seems to be fighting a distinctly rear-guard resistance against a developing trend. The Law Department Committee does correctly point out that the Guidebook is not an official ABA statement and, true to its title, it is a guidebook, not a model statute. Following these comments, the guidebook was amended in certain minor respects and republished as an approved document of the section of Corporation, Banking and Business Law, and endorsed by the American Society of Corporate Secretaries. 33 Bus. Law. 1595 (1978).

54. Leech and Mundheim, "The Outside Director of the Publicly Held Corporation," 31 Bus. Law. 1799, 1804 (1976).

55. Conflicts of interest were inherent in the mutual fund industry when Congress

holders could be protected by independent directors who would monitor the relationship between a fund and its management.[56]

The courts have given emphasis to these objectives. Management has been held to have violated its fiduciary duty to stockholders by not informing disinterested directors of an opportunity to reduce advisory fees.[57] The decision of independent directors concerning an advisory contract and management fee has been accorded the benefits of the business-judgment rule, but only when it was a fully informed exercise of judgment.[58] Independent directors may not escape liability just because they relied on opinions of counsel if that reliance appears to be unjustified under all the circumstances.[59]

While the analogy between the boards of mutual funds and those of other publicly held companies cannot be drawn too closely,[60] the

---

adopted the Act. Funds were managed by outside companies that contracted with the fund, acting through its board of directors, to provide investment advisory services. The selection of the investment advisor and the determination of the fee were self-dealing transactions that could neglect the stockholders' interests.

56. Nutt, "A Study of Mutual Fund Independent Directors," 120 U. Pa. L. Rev. 179, 182–3 (1971). The Act sought to achieve these objectives by requiring that at least forty percent of the board consist of persons who are neither officers nor employees of the fund and who are "unaffiliated" with its investment advisors. Investment Co. Act of 1940, § 10(a) (codified at 15 U.S.C. § 80a-10(a) (1970)). The SEC concluded in its 1966 mutual fund report, however, that unaffiliated directors, particularly as defined in the statute, had failed to provide the necessary protection for stockholders. The Congressional solution was to substitute the broader notion of "interested person" for the narrower definition of "affiliated persons." "Interested person" is defined in the statute so as to exclude from the category of independent directors more than just officers, directors, 5-percent stockholders, and controlling persons. Those persons are defined as affiliated and, consequently, interested. But, "interested" also includes their close relatives, lawyers for the fund, broker-dealers, and persons whom the Commission shall have determined to be interested by reason of having had a material business or professional relationship with the fund and certain other persons. Section 2(a)(19) defines "interested person" and the concept is carried into §§ 10(a) and 15(c) of the Act.

57. Moses v. Burgin, 445 F.2d 369 (1st Cir.), *cert. denied*, 404 U.S. 994 (1971); Fogel v. Chestnutt, 533 F.2d 731 (2d Cir. 1975), *cert. denied*, 429 U.S. 824 (1976).

58. Tannenbaum v. Zeller, 552 F.2d 402 (2d Cir. 1977).

59. Papilsky v. Berndt, [1976–77 Transfer Binder] Fed. Sec. L. Rep. (CCH) ¶ 95,627 (S.D.N.Y. 1976).

60. This is because there is little else except monitoring that is appropriate or necessary for outside directors of a mutual fund. Directors of most mutual funds have little to do, as the fund is generally externally managed. Conflicts of interest between management and stockholders almost invariably exist, requiring special attention by outside directors. The business of the fund is not complex and many of the fund's activities are regulated by statute. See generally

mutual fund experience demonstrates an acceptance of the monitoring function by independent directors. Moreover, judicial experience under the Investment Company Act indicates that the courts are able to work with the concept of a monitoring board.

The SEC, too, has demonstrated its support for the concept of the independent monitoring board, though the Commission has demonstrated less concern for the contribution a board might make to the efficiency of management than for the way in which such a board can enhance corporate compliance with the reporting and disclosure requirements of the federal securities laws.[61]

Roderick M. Hills, while SEC chairman, noted that these are important roles to be played by a monitoring board. He said:[62]

> Management is too often complacent, self-perpetuating, and unresponsible. When reported profits decline to such an extent as to threaten the serenity of their well paid isolation, some managers are tempted to change the accounting, the figures or the morals of their company in order to present a more pleasing profit picture.

Effective, responsive, and responsible boards of directors will operate to prevent management from going this route, he continued, while boards that are "missing . . . a truly independent character that has the practical capacity to monitor and to change management" will not.

Chairman Hills and other members of the SEC have stressed that by ensuring the integrity of corporate reports, the board can provide valuable protection for investors.[63] The Commission, as a body, em-

---

Mundheim, "Some Thoughts on the Duties and Responsibilities of Unaffiliated Directors of Mutual Funds," 115 U. Pa. L. Rev. 1058 (1967).

61. The SEC's recent expression of interest dates from the bankruptcy of the Penn Central Co. and was followed by a more general interest in the role of directors. See Staff of the SEC, The Financial Collapse of the Penn Central Company, Report to the Special Subcomm. on Investigations of the House Comm. on Interstate and Foreign Commerce, 92d Cong., 2d Sess. 152 (Subcomm. Print 1972) (SEC staff finds Penn Central board failed "to effectively monitor management"); Address of G. Bradford Cook, Chairman of the SEC, reprinted as Speech on Director's Responsibilities, [1973 Transfer Binder] Fed. Sec. L. Rep. (CCH) ¶ 79,301 (announces preparation of SEC guidelines on the responsibilities of corporate directors); What the SEC Expects of Corporate Directors, Address by Ray Garrett, Jr., Chairman of the SEC, before the Arthur D. Little Corporate Directors Conference, Wash., D.C. (Dec. 17, 1974) (SEC abandons preparation of guidelines due to inability to specify directors' responsibilities in every possible situation; in a common-law approach, SEC urges director to "do his duty").

62. *Corporate Rights and Responsibilities: Hearings before the Senate Comm. on Commerce*, 94th Cong., 2d Sess. 301–07 (1976) [hereinafter cited as *Senate Hearings*] (remarks of Roderick M. Hills).

63. An independent board is likely to view ensuring the accuracy of corporate

phasized this in its *Report of Investigation in the Matter of Stirling Homex Corporation Relating to the Activities of the Directors of Stirling Homex Corporation,*[64] where it took to task two outside directors of Stirling Homex for failing to discover that management had been deceiving both them and the investing public.[65]

However, probably the most important assertion of the SEC's views about the importance of boards has been in enforcement proceedings brought by the Commission.[66] In a wide variety of cases ranging from conventional failures to furnish adequate information to the more celebrated incidents of illegal political contributions and foreign payoffs, the Commission has perceived that the best remedy to a problem lay in providing for a more effective board.[67]

---

financial reports and other disclosure documents as one of its principal obligations. See Gould v. American-Hawaiian S.S. Co. 535 F.2d 761 (3rd Cir. 1976); Escott v. Barchris Construction Corp., 283 F. Supp. 643 (S.D.N.Y. 1968).

64. SEC Securities Exchange Act Release No. 11516, [1975–76 Transfer Binder] Fed. Sec. L. Rep. (CCH) ¶ 80,219.

65. The board of Stirling Homex was a particularly passive one. The Commission noted that only seven meetings were held over two years, most of which were perfunctory and several of which were conducted by telephone; that the only committee was an executive committee composed entirely of inside directors, and that no written agenda or memorandums were furnished to assist the board in its functions.

The Commission concluded that the two outside directors "did not provide the shareholders with any significant protection in fact, nor did their presence on the Board have the impact upon the company's operations which shareholders and others might reasonably have expected." *Id.*

66. The Commission has no power to impose substantive changes in the makeup or operations of the boards of registered corporations. Although the Commission has attempted to make limited changes in registrants' boards by seeking ancillary relief in judicial proceedings, its power in this regard has not been tested judicially. See Comment, "Equitable Remedies in SEC Enforcement Actions," 123 U. Pa. L. Rev. 1188 (1975); Comment, "Court-Appointed Directors: Ancillary Relief in Federal Securities Law Enforcement Actions," 64 Geo. L.J. 737 (1976).

67. In its report to the Senate Banking, Housing and Urban Affairs Committee, the Commission observed that "corporate accountability can be strengthened by making the role of the board of directors more meaningful . . . ." Commenting on the remedies that had been obtained in the cases, the SEC found "the thoroughness and vigor with which these [audit] committees have conducted their investigations demonstrates the importance of enhancing the role of the board of directors, establishing entirely independent audit committees as permanent, rather than extraordinary, corporate organs and encouraging the Board to rely on independent counsel." Securities and Exchange Commission, *Report on Questionable and Illegal Payments and Practices,* submitted to the Senate Banking, Housing and Urban Affairs Comm., 94th Cong., 2d Sess., p. 68 (May 12, 1976); see also Subcomm. on Oversight and Investigations, House Interstate

The most important of these actions, in our view, was *SEC v. Mattel, Inc.*,[68] which involved the filing of false financial statements. The SEC negotiated a consent decree whereby, in effect, it caused a sweeping change in the management of the company. The company agreed to name a majority of unaffiliated directors satisfactory to the SEC, to maintain an executive committee with a majority of unaffiliated directors, to create a financial controls and audit committee and a litigation and claims committee consisting mainly or wholly of unaffiliated directors, and to have special counsel designated by a majority of the new directors.[69]

This was a deep intrusion into corporate governance, with vast potential significance.[70] The significance of *Mattel* does not revolve about whether the relief was justified or even whether such sweeping ancillary relief was authorized. It revolves about the SEC's judgment that the way to deal with a problem in the management of a corporation was to create an independent monitoring board, even if this meant that the usual legal procedures under state law for selecting directors were swept aside. Since *Mattel* the SEC has continued to seek similar remedies for numerous other kinds of management dysfunction[71] both to

---

and Foreign Commerce Comm., 95th Cong., 2d Sess., *Federal Regulation and Regulatory Reform*, pp. 34–35 (Comm. print 1976). Private litigation in questionable payment cases has reflected this perception. See, e.g., Gilbar v. Keeler, 75 Civ. Action No. 611-EAC (C.D. Cal. 1975) (settlement required majority of "independent outside directors" on the board, its audit committee, and its nominating committee through amendment of bylaws); see also Springer v. Jones, 74 Civ. Action No. 1455-F (C.D. Cal. 1975).

68. [1974–75 Transfer Binder] Fed. Sec. L. Rep. (CCH) ¶ 94,754 (D.D.C. 1974).

69. See also SEC v. VTR, Inc., [1966] SEC Ann. Rep. 32, at 116–17 (S.D.N.Y. 1965) (though SEC sought appointment of receiver, court directs controlling group to elect four independent directors to a five-member board to supervise filing of accurate reports); SEC v. Coastal States Gas Corp., SEC Litigation Release No. 6054 (S.D. Tex.), 2 SEC Docket No. 13, at 451 (Sept. 25, 1973); SEC v. Westgate-California Corp., SEC Litigation Release No. 6142 (S.D. Cal. 1973), 3 SEC Docket No. 1, at 30.

70. Malley, "Far-Reaching Equitable Remedies Under The Securities Acts and the Growth of Federal Corporate Law," 17 Wm. & Mary L. Rev. 47 (1975); Ruder, "Current Problems in Corporate Disclosure," 30 Bus. Law. 1081, 1084 (1975).

71. SEC v. Allied Chemical Corp., 77 Civ. Action No. 0373 (D.D.C. 1977) (company agreed to investigate environmental risk and to take appropriate action based on that investigation); SEC v. Ormand Industries, Inc., 77 Civ. Action No. 0790 (D.D.C. 1977) (settlement required company to appoint three additional directors satisfactory to the SEC, who were unaffiliated with the company and who would remain on the board for three years); SEC v. General Tire & Rubber Co., 76 Civ. Action No. 0799 (D.D.C. 1976) (company agreed to create a special review committee consisting of five outside directors, with special counsel, to conduct an investigation into unlawful political activities and related matters); SEC v. Sanitas Corp., 75 Civ. Action No. 0520 (D.D.C. 1975) (settlement re-

correct noncompliance with the law and to reform the structure of the subject companies' board of directors.[72]

An enhanced role for directors, particularly independent directors, has received a great deal of attention in recent years. The Business Roundtable has urged the desirability of a board composed of a majority of nonmanagement directors that has certain and specific responsibilities and that is assisted by a minimum number of active committees.[73] The Fifty-fourth American Assembly of Columbia University made detailed recommendations concerning the composition of the board and its responsibilities.[74] Notwithstanding all this attention, however, Peter Drucker has observed that "the responsibilities of a board of directors as a whole is a subject that receives too little attention in most companies."[75]

The emergence of the audit committee of the board of directors exemplifies the growth of the board's role as a monitor. As already noted, the SEC has made use of audit committees in its settlements of illegal or questionable payment cases. Roderick Hills, when he was chairman of the SEC, wrote to the chairman of the board of the New York Stock Exchange to suggest that the Exchange amend its rules to require listed companies to have audit committees. The Exchange responded by requiring audit committees comprised solely of directors

---

quired the company to maintain audit and legal committees, each composed of outside directors, and each with broad powers). See Wall St. J., Aug. 22, 1977, at p. 8, col. 1 (settlement with Zale Corp. requires extensive board reform). The Commission spelled out in particular detail the functions it required a newly created independent audit committee to perform in SEC v. Killearn Properties, Inc. (N.D. Fla. 1977), 421 Sec. L. Rep. D-2 (BNA), Sept. 28, 1977.

These enforcement actions represent important substantive intrusions into corporate affairs. See generally Note, "Bribes, Kickbacks, and Political Contributions in Foreign Countries—the Nature and Scope of the Securities and Exchange Commission's Power to Regulate and Control American Corporate Behavior," 1976 Wisc. L. Rev. 1231, 1261. But cf. Santa Fe Indus., Inc. v. Green, 430 U.S. 462 (1977).

72. Two SEC enforcement attorneys have written that by employing ancillary remedies "the Commission acts as an effective catalyst for corporate reform to a far greater extent than would be possible solely by the use of its own budgetary and manpower resources." Herlihy and Levine, "Corporate Crisis: The Overseas Payment Problem," 8 Law & Pol. in Int'l Bus. 547, 581 (1976).

For a civil suit in which the SEC attempted to impose its concept of directors' obligations, see SEC v. Penn Central Co., [1973–74 Transfer Binder] Fed. Sec. L. Rep. (CCH) ¶ 94,527 (E.D. Pa. 1974); Note, "Penn Central: A Case Study of Outside Director Responsibility Under the Federal Securities Laws," 45 U. Mo. K.C. L. Rev. 394 (1977). See also SEC v. Shiell, [current] Fed. Sec. L. Rep. (CCH) ¶ 96,190 (N.D. Fla. 1977).

73. "Statement of Business Roundtable," 33 Bus. Law. 283 (1978).

74. *Corporate Governance in America,* 54th American Assembly (1978).

75. P. Drucker, "The Real Duties of a Director," Wall St. J., June 1, 1978, at p. 20.

"independent of management and free from any relationship that in the opinion of the board would interfere with the exercise of independent judgement."[76]

The audit committee in particular, but the board as a whole as well, undoubtedly has new responsibilities as a result of the Foreign Corrupt Practices Act of 1977. Section 102 of that Act requires companies subject to the Act, among other things, to "devise and maintain a system of internal accounting controls sufficient to provide reasonable assurances" that certain specified objectives, relating to books and records and preservation of assets, are met. The Senate Report made clear that "the establishment and maintenance of a system of internal control and accurate books and records are fundamental responsibilities of management."[77] While the statute will probably place its heaviest burdens on the auditors, there is clearly a role for the board of directors to monitor management's compliance and to review the existing control system.[78]

The monitoring board envisioned by Eisenberg, by the ABA subcommittee, by Leech and Mundheim, and by the SEC, we believe, has the potential to fulfill each of the important board functions described above.[79] Clearly, with its emphasis on monitoring, it would be able to play the disciplinary role. Removed from day-to-day management and from pressures for short-term results, it would be in a better position than management to question whether short-run performance was congruent with long-range corporate goals. Similarly, because the board would be subject to less intense and exhaustive pressures than management, it would be well situated to assist management in dealing with some of the problems of information overload identified by Professor Arrow. Finally, at least to the extent that the board demonstrated its independence from management and its commitment to hold management accountable, the monitoring board could substantially enhance the legitimacy of the corporation.

ARE BOARDS FAILING TO ACT AS INDEPENDENT MONITORS?

We come, then, to our third subsidiary question: Are boards failing to act as independent, effective monitors of management's performance?

---

76. Rule 499, N.Y.S.E. Co. Manual, at A29–30. The state of Connecticut amended its corporate statute in 1977 to require a corporation with at least 100 stockholders to have an audit committee with at least 1 independent director, unless it is subject to a similar federal or stock exchange requirement. Conn. Gen. Stat. § 33-318(b) (Supp. 1979).

77. S. Rep. 114, 95th Cong., 1st Sess., to accompany S. 305, at 4 (1977).

78. See Touche Ross & Co., *The New Management Imperative*, p. 9 (1978); Price Waterhouse & Co., *A Discussion of Management and Director's Responsibilities for Monitoring Compliance with Control Systems under the Foreign Corrupt Practices Act* (1978).

79. See notes 30–42 *supra* and accompanying text.

We believe many corporate boards are not performing in the desired fashion.

As we will point out below, relatively few data exist about what boards actually do, so any conclusion on this point must be somewhat impressionistic. But our conclusion is supported by one of the most thorough field investigations of boards of directors, which was completed by Professor Myles Mace in 1971. In a book provocatively titled *Directors: Myth and Reality*,[80] Professor Mace described a situation in which most directors serve as passive, friendly advisors to management but rarely ask penetrating questions or attempt to evaluate management's performance critically. In recent testimony before the SEC, Professor Mace indicated that he does not believe the situation has changed dramatically since he completed his study.[81]

Professor Mace's conclusion is supported by other data and other observers. In many recent cases involving so-called unusual corporate payments, for example, it has been clear that the boards of directors of the companies that made those payments were completely unaware of the questionable means being used to facilitate a large portion of the companies' business.[82] Surveys conducted by management consulting firms and by the Conference Board indicate that there is a remarkable diversity in how boards conceive of their roles and carry out their functions, with some substantial proportion of all boards operating rather ineffectively.

Thus, in our view, there is no doubt but that there is a widespread failure of boards to function as independent monitors of management performance. Constructive intervention by the SEC could lead to a marked improvement in the effectiveness of many corporations' boards of directors.

We recognize, of course, that significant changes have occurred in the composition, structure and functions of boards of directors in recent years. The studies cited[83] show a much larger proportion of independent directors comprising boards, and a majority of public companies having audit committees. The latter development, of course, has become a foregone conclusion as a result of the New York Stock Exchange rule,[84] but the development undoubtedly affects even those companies that are not listed on the New York Stock Exchange. The statistics alone do not tell the entire story, however, and other studies continue to show a marked variance in actual practice among companies that appear to be

---

80. M. Mace, *Directors: Myth and Reality* (1971).

81. *SEC Hearings on Corporate Suffrage*, Washington, D.C., (Sept. 30, 1977) (statement of M. L. Mace).

82. Securities and Exchange Commission, *Report, supra* note 67, at pp. 93–112.

83. See Smith, "The Boardroom Is Becoming a Different Place," Fortune, May 8, 1978, at p. 151.

84. See note 76 *supra*.

doing the same thing. The inadequacies of the board of directors may not be as pronounced as they once were but there is still cause for concern.

The Importance of Information About Boards

As we noted above, it is generally agreed that before the SEC can adopt disclosure requirements designed to influence corporate conduct it must determine that the information to be disclosed is of material importance to investors.[85] Disclosure requirements intended to promote more effective boards of directors will cause corporations to reveal information that should allow investors to determine what role a board plays within a corporation. That information, in our view, is material to both investment and corporate suffrage decision-making.

INVESTMENT DECISIONS

Information about the operations of a board is important to investors because the effectiveness of the board of directors can be an important element in an assessment of the quality of management of a corporation, and quality of management is a key element in investment decisions.[86] Courts have held that the "question of the integrity of management gives materiality" to information about illegal payments, even where there was little economic significance to the payments in question, and no self enrichment by management.[87]

The Commission acknowledged this point explicitly in *Matter of Franchard Corporation,*[88] where it stated:[89]

---

85. In making that determination, though, the Commission can use its expertise to decide what information should be important to investors, as well as reviewing what information investors say is important to them. See SEC Advisory Comm. on Corporate Disclosure, *Report to the Securities and Exchange Commission,* submitted to the House Comm. on Interstate and Foreign Commerce, 95th Cong., 1st Sess., chapter VIII (Comm. Print 1977).

86. A recent survey of individual investors' use of information, conducted by the SEC, found that information about the quality of a company's management was rated "extremely useful" by more respondents (54 percent) than any data except the future economic outlook of the industry of which the company is a part. (Only 50 percent rated financial-statement information extremely useful). Yet information about the quality of management was said to be inaccessible by more respondents than was any other information, with one-third of all those who thought it moderately or very useful characterizing it as inaccessible. SEC Advisory Committee on Corporate Disclosure, *supra* note 76, "Survey of Individual Investor Opinion," Questions 3(a) and (b).

87. SEC v. Jos. Schlitz Brewing Co., 452 F. Supp. 824, 830 (E.D. Wis. 1978).

88. 42 S.E.C. 163 (1964) (Commission rejects staff recommendation that disclosure be found defective because it failed to mention inadequacy of board of direc-

> Evaluation of the quality of management—to whatever extent it is possible—is an essential ingredient of informed investment decision. A need so important cannot be ignored, and in a variety of ways the disclosure requirements of the Securities Act furnish factual information to fill this need.

However, at the time of *Franchard* and today the disclosure requirements of the Securities Act and the Exchange Act did not and do not provide investors with nearly enough information to assess the performance of individual directors or the role played by the board within a corporation.

VOTING DECISIONS

Information that will allow shareholders to assess the performance of individual directors and of the board as a group is also material to shareholders' voting decision. In fact, it seems likely that the SEC, by its failure to require more meaningful disclosure about boards of directors, has undermined the concept of fair corporate suffrage that the 1934 Act was designed to promote.

The contribution corporate suffrage (in the sense described by Professor Ripley) can make to the efficient operation of a corporation, and the manner in which the SEC's inadequate disclosure requirements have undermined corporate suffrage, are best understood through the work of Professor Albert O. Hirschman, an economist. In *Exit, Voice and Loyalty*[90] Professor Hirschman points out that when an organization is operating at less than peak efficiency (as almost all large organizations do), some combination of "exit"—selling one's stock—and "voice"—attempting to influence the organization's conduct—probably will lead to the greatest possible increase in efficiency. However, Professor Hirschman states, people's willingness to rely on voice depends heavily on their estimates of the prospects for success, and[91]

> while exit requires nothing but a clearcut either-or decision, voice is essentially an *art* constantly evolving in new directions. This situation makes for an important bias in favor of exit when both options are present: customer-members [or stockholders] will ordinarily base their decisions on *past* experience with the cost and effectiveness of voice even though the possible *discovery* of lower cost and greater effectiveness is of the very essence of voice. The presence of the exit alternative can therefore tend to *atrophy the development of the art of voice.*

---

tors' performance; rejection due to Commission view that such finding would require determination of board's adequacy under state law; decision does not deny investors' interest in obtaining information about board).

89. *Id.* at 169–71.

90. A. Hirschman, *Exit, Voice, and Loyalty* (1970).

91. *Id.* at p. 43 (emphasis in original).

This analysis demonstrates not only why the "Wall Street rule" (vote with management or sell) is a popular choice for investors but also why it is unsatisfactory.[92] Professor Hirschman's argument supports the notion that voice, that is, stockholder participation, is necessary to the health of a corporation. Exit is a blunt instrument; voice is needed for finely tuned attempts to deal with defects in an organization.

Professor Hirschman's analysis also indicates how the effectiveness of voice is enhanced by an improved disclosure process. Disclosure will lower the costs of attempting to use voice. Since a stockholder in a corporation rarely stands to obtain enough direct benefits from attempts to improve corporate governance to make the endeavor profitable to him, costs are a matter of great concern.[93] If one makes them low enough, in absolute terms, by ensuring that adequate information is readily available to interested shareholders, reliance on voice—or increased shareholder attention to corporate governance—is likely to increase.[94]

Finally, Professor Hirschman's work makes clear why SEC intervention is needed to facilitate corporate suffrage. Hirschman notes that the management of an organization will try to direct its critics to the pressure mechanism to which it is less sensitive, because "the short-run interest of management in organizations is to increase its own freedom of movement . . . .[95] In the case of large corporations, management usually is not as sensitive to stock sales by disenchanted stockholders as it is to activism on the part of those stockholders. Conse-

---

92. In light of Hirschman's analysis of why voice tends to fall into desuetude, it is not surprising that investors in general are not clamoring for changes in the proxy rules to allow for more shareholder participation in corporate affairs. The SEC Advisory Committee on Corporate Disclosure, which surveyed both institutional and individual investors, found little active demand for proxy rule changes. SEC Advisory Committee on Corporate Disclosure, *Final Report,* chapter XXIV, at pp. 27–30 (draft 1977).

93. This is a classic positive externality situation—one in which not enough of a social good (here, improved corporate performance) is produced because no individual who can produce the good can capture more than a small share of the benefits from his action. See A. Alchian and W. Allen, *Exchange and Production: Theory in Use,* pp. 249–50 (1969).

94. The experience of institutional investors who used the services of the Investor Responsibility Research Center (IRRC) is illustrative. The cost to each institution of learning enough about social issues affecting portfolio corporations was high enough to deter them from dealing with those issues. But when IRRC began to make that information available at a much lower cost to each institution, many of them found that the cost of becoming an active shareholder was low enough to warrant pursuing that course of action. See Schwartz and Weiss, "An Assessment of the SEC Shareholder Proposal Rule," 65 Geo. L.J. 635, 648 (1977).

95. See A. Hirschman, *supra* note 90, at p. 123.

quently, management will encourage use of exit and intervention by some third party will be necessary to encourage a better balance between the use of exit and of voice.

The Case for a Disclosure Approach

While the SEC has relied heavily on the concept of the monitoring board in its enforcement program, at least until recently it made little use of its disclosure authority either to encourage the development of independent monitoring boards or to elicit information about boards that is of considerable importance to investors. We have outlined above the reasons why the Commission should seek to attain both of these objectives. We elaborate here our reasons for believing that disclosure is particularly well suited to achieving these goals. It is time, however, to move from the pathological remedy of enforcement proceedings to the prescriptive treatment of improved disclosure.

CURRENT DISCLOSURE REQUIREMENTS

The initial proxy rules, adopted in 1935,[96] called for no information about boards or candidates for election as directors. In 1938, the Commission adopted regulation 14A, the present designation of the proxy rules, requiring information to be sent to stockholders in a proxy statement.[97] The facts required about directors were sparse: the number of shares in the corporation owned by each director, the relationship of any director with the firm's underwriter, and the identity of any person or body which had nominated a candidate for election to the board.

In the ensuing years, despite periodic revisions of the proxy rules, little additional information was elicited about boards or individual directors.[98] More information about remuneration of directors, their transactions with the issuer, and their prior experience was demanded, but most of the data sought was rudimentary and related primarily to conflict of interest.

---

96. SEC Securities Exchange Act Release No. 34-378 (Sept. 24, 1935).

97. SEC Securities Exchange Act Release No. 34-1823 (Aug. 11, 1938).

98. Subject to limitations of the First Amendment, which extend to some aspects of commercial speech, see Virginia State Bd. of Pharmacy v. Virginia Citizens Consumer Council, 425 U.S. 748 (1976), the Commission's authority to adopt rules under 14(a) is quite broad. It is not even limited to ensuring full disclosure. L. Loss, *Securities Regulation,* vol. 2, p. 868 (2d ed. 1961). When the stockholder proposal rule was adopted in 1942, the reaction on the part of a few members of Congress was so hostile that it provoked the introductions of bills to suspend their effectiveness. Hearings were held, but no action resulted. *Hearings on H.R. 1493, H.R. 1821, and H.R. 2019 before the House Comm. on Interstate and Foreign Commerce*, 87th Cong., 1st Sess. (1943) [hereinafter cited as *House Hearings*].

More recently, the Commission has begun to strengthen its disclosure requirements for boards. It first proposed some modest changes in November 1976[99], and in April 1977 undertook the first broad reexamination of the proxy rules since 1942.[100] The Commission thereby joined others in believing it ripe to explore the workings of corporate governance. The Commission's action appears to have been stimulated in part by controversy about its shareholder proposal rule,[101] concern over the adequacy of the mechanisms to achieve managerial accountability, and in part by the work of its Advisory Committee on Corporate Disclosure. The Advisory Committee recommended that the SEC adopt "a package of disclosure requirements that, taken as a whole, will strengthen the ability of boards of directors to operate as independent effective monitors of management performance and will provide investors with a reasonable understanding of the organization and role of the board of any given issuer."[102]

The Commission followed the unusual procedure of conducting four hearings around the country in order to obtain a wide range of opinions on the issues set out in the April 1977 release, as more specifically restated in August 1977.[103] More than 300 persons and organizations appeared in person or submitted comments.[104] The Commission followed this with proposals for new disclosures along the following lines:[105]

(1) Identify directors and nominees as "management," "affiliated non-management" or "independent," as defined in the rules. The Commis-

99. SEC Securities Exchange Act Release No. 34-12946 [1976–77 Transfer Binder] Fed. Sec. L. Rep. (CCH) ¶ 80,783 (Nov. 2, 1976).

100. SEC Securities Exchange Act, Release No. 34-13482, 12 SEC Docket No. 2, at p. 239 (April 28, 1977).

101. See Schwartz and Weiss, *supra* note 94. The SEC first advanced the stockholder proposal rule in 1942. *House Hearings, supra* note 98, at pp. 34–36. Providing stockholders with access to proxy statements for nomination of directors has received some scholarly support. Caplin, "Shareholder Nominations of Directors: A Program for Fair Corporate Suffrage," 39 Va. L. Rev. 141 (1953); Eisenberg, "Access to the Corporate Proxy Machinery," 83 Harv. L. Rev. 1489 (1970); Note, "A Proposal for the Designation of Shareholder Nominees for Director in the Corporate Proxy Statement," 74 Colum. L. Rev. 1139 (1974).

102. Minutes of meeting of SEC Advisory Committee on Corporate Disclosure (May 7–8, 1977). The recommendation was adopted by a vote of 8 to 7.

103. SEC Securities Exchange Act, Release No. 34-13901 (Aug. 29, 1977), 42 Fed. Reg. 44860 (Sept. 7, 1977).

104. Hearings were held in Washington, Los Angeles, Chicago, and New York, and a record of about 10,000 pages was compiled. The staff prepared a 125-page summary of comments that is available to the public.

105. SEC Securities Exchange Act Release No. 34-14970 (July 18, 1978), 43 Fed. Reg. 31945 (July 24, 1978).

sion proposed that certain family, business, creditor or professional relationships would deprive a director or nominee of "independence."

(2) Disclose whether the company has standing audit, nominating, and compensation committees of its board, and disclose whenever the functions of those committees are other than the "customary functions" as described in the rule. Whether the nominating committee will consider candidates submitted by stockholders should also be disclosed.

(3) Disclosure of the name of any director who attended fewer than 75 percent of board or commmittee meetings since the last annual meeting.

(4) Whenever a director resigns or declines to stand for reelection due to a disagreement relating to the company's operations, policies and practices, the company must disclose, with an explanation, those facts. The director can set forth his version of the facts in a separate letter.

(5) The settlement terms of contests for the election of directors, including costs to the company.

(6) Disclosure by specified parent companies of institutional investors and broker-dealers, investment advisers, and investment companies of their policies and procedures on the voting of shares held by them, including whether and how beneficial owners are consulted on voting, and procedures for considering—and the voting record for—contested matters.

The Commission received almost 600 letters of comment on its proposals, a record response. The principal specific criticism was of the proposal to label directors, but in general many opposed the proposals on grounds that this constituted an unauthorized intrusion into corporate governance.[106] The Commission took up the proposals at an open meeting on November 15, 1978,[107] at which four of the five commissioners were present; Commissioner Pollack, who might have been expected to be a strong supporter of the changes, was absent on long-standing Commission business. Some of the original disclosure requirements were eliminated or modified, but in adopting important amendments to the disclosure rules the Commission accepted the basic premises about the role of the board and the role of disclosure that we have set out in this article. The rules as adopted include the following:[108]

---

106. Opening Statement of Harold M. Williams, Chairman of the SEC at the Commission's consideration of the rule-making proposals, announced in Release No. 34-14970 (Nov. 15, 1978); "SEC Corporate Governance Proposals: An Update," (address by Commissioner John R. Evans, Santa Barbara, California, November 3, 1978).

107. 479 Sec. Reg. & L. Rep. A5 (BNA) (Nov. 22, 1978); 5 News for Investors 213 (IRRC) (Dec. 1978).

108. SEC Securities Exchange Act Release No. 34-15384 (Dec. 6, 1978).

(1) As to the composition of the board, the Commission eliminated director labeling. However, the proxy statement must describe certain significant economic and personal relationships with the issuer. The existence of certain supplier, customer, creditor or professional relationships must be disclosed. Moreover, the Commission noted that issuers should exercise caution in voluntarily characterizing directors or candidates as independent.

(2) As to committee structure, the proxy statement must disclose the existence or nonexistence of standing audit, nominating and compensation committees, the membership of any such committee, and a brief description of the functions actually performed. This eliminated the negative disclosure about the "customary" functions.

(3) The number of meetings of the board and the audit, nominating, and compensation committees must be disclosed.

(4) Whether a director has attended fewer than 75 percent of the aggregate number of meetings of the board and of the committees on which he serves must be disclosed.

(5) If a director who has resigned or refuses to stand for reelection because of a disagreement about operations, policies, or practices so requests, a statement of the resignation or refusal and a summary of the director's description of the disagreement shall be filed with the Commission on Form 8K and described in the proxy statement. The company may set forth its version of the disagreement. The key change is that disclosure must be triggered by the retiring director's request.

(6) The settlement terms of an election contest, as originally proposed, must be disclosed.

(7) As to the compensation of directors, the proxy statement must disclose any standards arrangement by which directors are compensated, including amounts paid for committee participation or special assignments, or the amount of remuneration paid pursuant to arrangements other than the standard one.[109]

---

109. This requirement was announced in a separate release that dealt with the broader subject of management remuneration disclosure requirements. SEC Securities Act Release No. 33-6003 (Dec. 4, 1978).

The Commission withdrew the proposal for disclosure of institutional voting because it recognized that the requirement as framed was not material to the persons to whom it was made. SEC Securities Exchange Act Release No. 34-15385 (Dec. 6, 1978). That is, there may be great significance in the facts that were required to be disclosed, but they would not appear so to the holders of the institutional parent's stock who would receive the disclosure documents. We find that conclusion consistent with our view that Commission should limit disclosure requirements to instances where it relates to conduct of legitimate concern to the Commission and "where the information to be disclosed is relevant to decisionmaking by investors." See note 25 *supra* and accompanying text.

We believe it is both desirable and appropriate for the Commission to use its disclosure authority for the purpose of strengthening the boards of reporting companies. The Commission expressly recognized the significance of a strong, independent board in its governance inquiry, and of the use of disclosure to help achieve it. We think the Commission has made a respectable beginning towards that goal. We think it should go further towards the model we describe *infra* under the heading "A Model Disclosure System."

Disclosure as a means to encourage change is preferable to the obvious alternative—establishment of substantive rules governing the composition and organization of boards of directors.[110] In light of the amount of experimentation and change occurring in corporate boards at this time, it would seem inadvisable, at least under the prevailing federal system where most substantive power over corporate affairs rests with state law, to lock all corporations into one pattern of organization.[111]

A major benefit of a disclosure approach to regulation is that it allows for a diversity of responses. New disclosure requirements relating to boards of directors should be designed to force all corporations to think through how their boards should be constituted and what roles they should play, but there is no reason to believe that all corporations will arrive at the same answers to these questions. To be sure, corporations will feel pressure to arrive at answers that they can justify in their public statements, and in many instances that pressure will cause change. But at the same time many corporations will find in their particular circumstances reasons to deviate from the model suggested by the disclosure system. Consequently, a desirable diversity of board practices should

---

110. The Commission probably would have to obtain new legislative authority in order to enforce such standards. Cf. Santa Fe Industries v. Green, 430 U.S. 462 (1977). However, there is some Congressional support for having the SEC set substantive standards. In 1976, the investigations Subcommittee of the House Commerce Committee issued a report calling on the SEC to issue rules to assure that (a) a director of a publicly owned corporation receives compensation and independent staff sufficient to perform responsibly his board duties; (b) a majority of the board is independent of senior management and operating executives and from any other conflicts of interests; (c) the board reviews and approves the corporation's code of business conduct and system of internal controls; (d) the board's auditing committee has available to it independent expert advisors; and (e) the board has the authority to hire and fire the independent accountant, legal counsel, the general counsel, and senior operating executives. House Committee on Interstate and Foreign Commerce, 94th Cong., 2d Sess., *supra* note 67, at p. 52.

111. See *Senate Hearings, supra* note 62, at p. 221 (remarks of Professor Mundheim) (legislation, which is difficult to rescind, is inappropriate at a time of experimentation); *Guidebook Report, supra* note 53, at p. 1843 (variety of corporate governance practices is desirable).

result. Even those urging more sweeping corporate reform[112] must admit that this is a sound first step.[113]

A MODEL DISCLOSURE SYSTEM

It is not a simple task to formulate disclosure requirements that will promote independent monitoring boards by providing shareholders and investors with information of substantial value. No small number of facts will demonstrate that a corporation has an independent monitoring board.[114] Indeed, many aspects of a board's role—particularly its relationship with senior management—cannot be quantified. As the SEC recently learned, opponents of change will direct their fire at individual components of a disclosure system which, taken separately, may not appear worth fighting over, but which, when pieced together, unearth significant data.

However, as is now widely recognized, the difficulty of quantifying information should not preclude an SEC requirement that it be disclosed.[115] Rather, disclosure requirements should be judged by their

---

112. Schwartz, "A Case for Federal Chartering of Corporations," 31 Bus. Law. 1125 (1976).

113. Disclosure was described as an alternate regulatory device in the report of the American Bar Association's Commission on Law and the Economy, *Federal Regulation: Roads to Reform,* p. 60 (1978). Its principal virtue was seen as reducing the cost of mistakes.

114. The converse is not necessarily true. If a corporation's board is made up largely or entirely of inside directors who hold small amounts of stock in the corporation, it would be reasonable to infer that the board is not likely to serve as an effective independent monitor of management's performance. See M. Mace, *Directors: Myth and Reality,* chapter 6 (1971); J. Bacon and J. Brown, *Corporate Directorship Practices: Role, Selection, and Legal Status of the Board,* p. 67 (1975). Similarly, while information that a board has certain characteristics will not demonstrate dispositively that it is functioning effectively, disclosure that certain characteristics are lacking will give rise to the inference that the board is not playing an effective role. For an amusing, but realistic, illustration of how a CEO can foster the appearance that he has an effective board while actually emasculating the board, see Lauenstein, "Preserving the Impotence of the Board," 55 Harv. Bus. Rev., July–Aug. 1977, at 36.

115. The debate in this area has focused largely on disclosure of information relating to projections of earnings and business plans. See, e.g., Schneider, "Nits, Grits and Soft Information in SEC Filings," 121 U. Pa. L. Rev. 254 (1972); Kripke, "The SEC, the Accountants, Some Myths and Some Realities," 45 N.Y.U.L. Rev. 1151 (1970). The SEC's Advisory Committee on Corporate Disclosure has urged the Commission to amend its rules to facilitate disclosure of considerably more "soft" information, which the Committee has found often is of prime interest to investors. See Memorandum from Mary E. T. Beach, Staff Director, to members of the Advisory Committee on Corporate Disclosure, Exhibits E–J (May 26, 1977) (on file with the authors) [hereinafter cited as Beach Memo].

potential benefits and costs.[116] The benefits of effective boards have been discussed; the promotion of such boards by means of disclosure requirements could bring a number of added benefits:

(1) Shareholders and investors would better understand whether a corporation has an active, independent monitoring board, which bears on their investment decisions.

(2) Shareholders and investors would have a sound basis for comparing the activities and organization of different corporations' boards and for the use of "voice" to stimulate change where it seems desirable.

(3) Shareholders could better assess individual candidates in board elections. They could also better analyze specific board recommendations on which they are asked to vote.

(4) Probably most important, all corporations subject to these disclosure requirements would feel pressure to develop effective monitoring boards.

In our view, the Commission can attain these benefits through new disclosure requirements by drawing on the extensive recent literature on the elements of board effectiveness.[117] At the same time, we recognize the constraints on any SEC effort to mandate new disclosures about registrants' boards.

One such constraint is the need for confidentiality in boardroom deliberations. These deliberations must be confidential if a board is to discuss business freely and affect it significantly. Confidentiality will be particularly important in a board's relationship with its CEO, which may be delicate while the board is first asserting itself but which is crucial to the board's ultimate effectiveness.[118] A chief executive unaccustomed to supervision may resist the board's attempt to monitor him and may withold information the board needs.[119] Placing such a board

---

116. Beach Memo, *supra* note 115, Exhibit C.

117. The leading works are Eisenberg, *supra* note 47; Leech and Mundheim, *supra* note 54; "Corporate Director's Guidebook," *supra* note 51; and C. Brown, *supra* note 45.

118. Development of a board that effectively monitors management's performance does not imply either board interference with management or the development of an adversary relationship between the board and management. "[A]ll that the monitoring function implies is a willingness to be vigilant and questioning in an effort to determine what is in the best interests of the corporation." Leech and Mundheim, *supra* note 54, at 1805.

119. Robert Haack, former president of the New York Stock Exchange and now a professional director, has commented that "if you, as a chief executive officer, knew about 80% more than your average director—and in most cases it's 90%—it's very easy—not by any cupidity or any deviousness, but by sheer emphasis or de-emphasis of a point—to persuade a board to your point of view." "Corporate Boards of Directors: A Time for Change?" (transcript, Inves-

in a fishbowl may encourage directors' traditional preference for passivity and the CEO's attempts to retain autonomy.[120]

Another constraint lies in the purpose of disclosure, which is to provide information pertinent to decisions necessarily made by shareholders—investment and voting decisions.[121] The disclosure system should not encourage shareholders to range beyond their appropriate sphere and begin to second-guess specific business judgments made by a corporation's board or management. Thus, disclosure requirements should focus on organization and procedures of corporate boards rather than the substance of their decisions.

In addition, disclosure requirements should not drown shareholders in a sea of minutiae. As a committee of the American Bar Association recently noted, requiring more disclosure in proxy materials can be "a matter of diminishing returns. It is not only that the marginally useful disclosure items will not be read, but they obscure and detract from those that are useful."[122] As courts have recognized, "less is more."[123] Disclosure requirements should therefore be limited to crucial items. If the disclosure system is successful, it will encourage shareholders to interest themselves in corporate governance and thus to seek out the additional details.[124]

A final constraint is that the Commission should require the disclosure of meanigful information rather than empty jargon. Because some significant information about boards is difficult to quantify, corporations may tend to respond to disclosure requirements with "boilerplate"—formula statements that convey little useful information and are drafted primarily to avoid liability for misrepresentation. The Commission can discourage this in public and private; corporations

tor Responsibility Research Center Conference, May 31–June 1, 1974) at p. 70 [hereinafter cited as IRRC Transcript].

120. See Investor Responsibility Research Center, Inc., "Shareholders, the Board of Directors and Corporate Governance: Occidental Petroleum Corp.," Analysis No. 3, Supp. No. 5, at 3-45, 3-49 (1975) (statement of Paul C. Hebner, vice-president, secretary, and board member of Occidental Petroleum Corp.) (board discussions productive only if confidential).

121. SEC Securities Act Release No. 5627, 8 SEC Docket No. 2, at 20, 41 (Oct. 14, 1975).

122. Letter from Kenneth J. Bialkin, Chairman, Committee on Federal Regulation of Securities, American Bar Association, to George A. Fitzsimmons, Secretary, SEC (Dec. 14, 1976) (SEC Public File No. 57-658).

123. Great Western United Corp. v. Kidwell, 577 F.2d 1256, 1280 (5th Cir. 1978), *rev'd on other grounds sub nom* Leroy v. Great Western United Corp., 47 U.S.L.W. 4844 (U.S. June 26, 1979).

124. Shareholders wishing to suggest changes in board procedures would probably be able to put their proposals in a form that could be voted on by all shareholders, using the procedure set out in rule 14a-8 of the Securities Exchange Act of 1934. For a discussion of how shareholders can make use of those procedures, see Schwartz & Weiss, *supra* note 94, at 635.

and their counsel are not oblivious to this kind of exhortation.[125] Furthermore, the factors that have led to past reliance on boilerplate may not be present in our proposal. In the past the SEC distrusted subjective information and conditioned its respondents to provide "hard" data and standard descriptions, no matter how little value they contained.[126] Recently the Commission has modified this distrust and has required or encouraged the disclosure of certain kinds of "soft" information.[127]

---

125. Several factors lie behind our judgment that the prognosis for a constructive corporate response to the proposed disclosure requirements is good. The corporate community is under widespread attack in the United States, and many of its critics focus on the lack of an independent board as one of the factors that undermines the institutional legitimacy of the large, publicly held corporation. See R. Nader, M. Green, and J. Seligman, *Constitutionalizing The Corporation: The Case for Federal Chartering of Giant Corporations* (1976). The business community is concerned by these attacks. One sign of that concern is the symposium that the Business Roundtable, an association of large corporations, recently sponsored concerning corporate boards. D. Ruder, *The Role and Composition of the Board of Directors of a Large Publicly Held Corporation* (1977) (report on a symposium of business school deans and others held at the Harvard Business School, May 12–14, 1977 [hereinafter cited as Harvard Symposium]). See also The Business Roundtable, *The Role and Composition of the Board of Directors of the Large Publicly Owned Corporation* (1978).

As Robert M. Estes, former general counsel of General Electric Co., has pointed out, businessmen must build on the differences in the role and responsibilities of the CEO and the directors of a corporation if they "hope to avoid governmental imposition of measures of accountability having a high disaster potential for the viability of the institution." Estes, "The Case for Counsel to Outside Directors," 54 Harv. Bus. Rev., July–Aug. 1976, at 125, 127. The proposed rules, we believe, will provide concerned corporations and boards with a framework within which to highlight steps they have taken to enhance the legitimacy of the board and of our current system of corporate governance. Participants in The Business Roundtable's symposium noted that by demonstrating the board's independence and its ability to provide meaningful scrutiny of corporate internal affairs, some of the criticism of corporate operations may be met. Harvard Symposium, *supra* at 16.

126. See Schneider, *supra* note 115; Kripke, "A Search For a Meaningful Securities Disclosure Policy," 31 Bus. Law. 293 (1975). Among the sections of the registration statement that have been most susceptible to meaningless disclosures are the description of business (item 9 of Form S-1), particularly the part dealing with a description of competition, and the description of litigation (item 12 of Form S-1). The Commission attempted to cure that defect when it amended the guides for preparing a registration statement in 1972. See "New Approaches to Disclosure in Registered Security Offerings," 28 Bus. Law. 505, 522 (1973) (remarks of Warren Grienenberger). See also 160 Sec. Reg. & L. Rep. (BNA) A-3 (1972) (remarks of former SEC Chairman William Casey).

127. The Commission has revised rule 14(a)-9, 17 C.F.R. § 240, 14(a)-9 (1977), to delete its prohibition on dividend projections. See SEC Securities Act Release No. 5699, 9 SEC Docket No. 10, at 471 (Apr. 23, 1976); Gerstle v. Gamble-Skogmo, Inc., 478 F.2d 1281 (2d Cir. 1973). SEC Securities Act Release No. 35-5992, [1978 Transfer

Despite the difficulty the SEC has in ensuring the accuracy and adequacy of these data, the results of these efforts have been moderately encouraging.[128]

Fear of civil liability under the SEC's antifraud rules has also encouraged vacuous disclosure in the past. By requiring disclosure of the process and not the substance of decisions, we would abate such fears. It should not require excessive care for corporations to avoid misstatements about board processes. Moreover, in uncontested elections the lack of a causal relationship between misstatements and potential harm would remove virtually all threat of money damages.[129] The threat of an injunction would remain, but it alone is not likely to lead to timid responses to our proposed disclosure requirements.[130]

Proposed Disclosure Requirements

Set out below is proposed language for a set of SEC disclosure requirements relating to elections of directors. While each requirement is designed to reveal information of particular significance, the individual requirements are not designed to be evaluated in isolation. Rather it is our intent that they be judged on whether they will contribute meaningful pieces to a mosiac that, taken as a whole, will provide shareholders and investors with a reasonable picture of the role the board of directors is playing within a corporation.

We propose that proxy statements issued prior to shareholders' meetings at which directors are to be elected be required to disclose:

(1) Information about individual nominees
   a. Identification of each nominee (and each other person whose term of office as a director will continue after the election meeting) as a management, affiliated nonmanagement, or unaffiliated nonmanagement director and for each affiliated nonmanagement director, a state-

Binder] Fed. Sec. L. Rep. (CCH) ¶ 81,756 (Nov. 7, 1978) (adopting new guidelines for disclosure of projections).

128. The diversity of corporate responses to the requirements of Guide 22, which requires a management discussion and analysis of the summary of operations, illustrates this point very well. See H. Goodman and L. Lorensen, *Illustrations of the Summary of Operations and Related Management Discussion and Analysis* (1975); SEC Advisory Committee on Corporate Disclosure, Minutes of Meeting of Feb. 7–8, 1977, at p. 5 (on file with the authors).

129. Sisters of the Precious Blood Inc. v. Bristol-Myers Co., 431 F. Supp. 385 (S.D.N.Y. 1977); Lewis v. Elam, [1977–1978 Transfer Binder] Fed. Sec. L. Rep. (CCH) ¶ 96,013 (S.D.N.Y. 1977); Levy v. Johnson, [1976–77 Transfer Binder] Fed. Sec. L. Rep. (CCH) ¶ 95,899 (S.D.N.Y. 1977); cf. Mills v. Electric Auto Lite Co., 552 F.2d 1239 (7th Cir. 1977); *In re* Tenneco Securities Litigation, 449 F. Supp. 528 (S.D. Tex. 1978); Limmer v. General Tel. & Elec. Corp. [1977–78 Transfer Binder] Fed. Sec. L. Rep. (CCH) ¶ 96,111 (S.D.N.Y. 1977).

130. Rafal v. Geneen, [1972] Fed. Sec. L. Rep. (CCH) ¶ 93,505 (E.D. Pa.).

ment of the significant relationship with management that has caused the nominee to be classified as affiliated.
b. The amount of director's fees paid to each nonmanagement director during the previous fiscal year, including separate statements of annual fees, meeting attendance fees, committee membership fees, and committee meeting attendance fees.
c. A tabulation of the number of board and committee meetings held during the previous fiscal year, the total amount of time the board and each committee was in session, and for each board member, the number of board and committee meetings he attended and the total amount of time he spent at board meetings and at meetings of each committee of which he was a member.
d. A list of all other registrants on whose board each nominee serves.

(2) Information about nominating procedures
a. A brief description of the procedures used to select new nominees for election as directors and to determine whether to renominate sitting directors.
b. A brief description of the criteria used to select new nominees for election as directors and to determine whether to renominate sitting directors.
c. A statement whether the registrant's proxy materials have been reviewed and approved by the board of directors (or a committee of the board) prior to their distribution to stockholders and whether the board of directors (or a committee of the board) must specifically authorize or approve all expenditures in connection with management's proxy solicitation.

(3) Information about the organization and activities of the board
a. A brief description of the authority and responsibilities of each standing committee of the board, including information about the frequency with which and the procedure by which each committee reports to the full board and the procedures used for selecting the members of each committee.
b. A statement:
i. Whether board members regularly receive an agenda at least forty-eight hours in advance of meetings of the board and of committees of which they are members, including all documentary materials they need to consider matters proposed by management for approval at the meeting; and
ii. Whether the board or any committee took action on any matters during the previous fiscal year without benefit of such advance information and, if the matters involved material transactions, what the transactions were and what actions the board took.
c. A brief description of the procedures and objective criteria, if any, used by the board to monitor or evaluate the performance of management during the previous fiscal year.
d. A description of any staff assistance furnished to the directors.

(4) Information about resignation of directors
a. A list of all directors who have resigned since the last annual meeting or are not standing for reelection, and a brief statement of the reason why each resigned or is not standing for reelection. The statement either

should describe any factors in the operations of the corporation or the organization of activities of its board of directors that bore a significant relationship to the director's decision to resign or not stand for reelection, or should note that there were no such factors.
b. A statement that each retiring director has reviewed and approved as accurate the statement described above, or a description of such factors prepared by each retiring director (which management, in its discretion, may limit to 300 words).

Explanation of Proposed Requirements

INFORMATION ABOUT NOMINEES

Directors are elected as individuals, not as a group.[131] Information about individual nominees may be relevant to shareholders' decisions to vote for or against them. It can also contribute significantly to shareholders' and investors' understanding of the role the board and each of its committees plays within a corporation. Through 1978, the SEC required registrants to furnish a limited amount of basic data about nominees and directors. Late in that year, however, the Commission amended its regulations to require disclosure of considerably more information about nominees and directors.[132] The new disclosure requirements are similar in many respects to those we propose. However, they fall short of our model in several significant areas. The specifics of these requirements, as well as our reason for proposing that they be modified, are as follows.

Affiliations. Probably the most important information about each nominee and director concerns the relationship with the management of the corporation.[133] Such information is widely regarded as highly

---

131. In the 1976 proxy statement of Mobil Oil Corp. stockholders were furnished an opportunity to indicate from which candidates, if any, stockholders wanted to withhold proxies. The fact that directors are individually elected is at the heart of the suggestion that stockholders have the opportunity to include their nominees in the corporation's proxy statement. See Note, "A Proposal for the Designation of Shareholder Nominees for Director in the Corporate Proxy Statement," 74 Colum. L. Rev. 1139 (1974).

132. See SEC Securities Exchange Act Release No. 34-15384, [1978 Transfer Binder] Fed. Sec. L. Rep. (CCH) ¶ 81,766 (Dec. 6, 1978); SEC Securities Act Release No. 33-6003, [1978 Transfer Binder] Fed. Sec. L. Rep. (CCH) ¶ 81,765 (Dec. 4, 1978). Both releases are effective for fiscal years ending after Dec. 25, 1978. Many of the disclosures required in these releases were proposed in an earlier version of this article. See E. Weiss and D. Schwartz, "Using Disclosure to Activate the Board of Directors," 41 L. & Contemp. Prob. 63, 91–95 (Summ. 1977).

133. The classification terms we suggest are drawn from the Corporate Directors Guidebook, *supra* note 51, at 31. The Guidebook notes that "the terms 'affiliate'

relevant to assessing the probable independence of individual directors from management, and thus of the board.

Many believe that directors who are officers or employees of a corporation cannot be expected to monitor management,[134] though some would argue that this is not always the case.[135]

Opinion is also divided about whether nonemployees who have professional, business, or familial relationships with the management of a corporation—such as outside counsel, investment bankers, commercial bankers, or officers of major suppliers or customers—can be counted on to use their position on a board primarily to promote the interests of shareholders. The leading commentators argue that a relationship of this kind may cause a director to defer to management or to use his or her position on the board to promote personal interests even when they conflict with the interests of the corporation.[136] Another view, advanced most often by persons who are associated with the

---

and 'affiliated directors' have special meanings, not applicable here, for purposes of the federal securities laws." We attach the same caveat to our use of those terms.

We envision a proxy statement in which the directors in each of the three categories are listed under the appropriate heading, to present most clearly how the board is divided among those groupings.

Use of labels is required elsewhere under the federal securities laws, perhaps most notably in the requirement that "high risk factors" be prominently identified as such in registration statements. See SEC Securities Act Release No. 33-4936 (Dec. 9, 1968).

134. See Eisenberg, *supra* note 47, at 404–409, "SEC's Williams Calls for Independent Boards, Warns of Federal Intervention into Governance," No. 437 Sec. Reg. & L. Rep. (BNA) A-22 (Jan. 25, 1978); sources cited in note 114 *supra.* A professional director has commented that "it's difficult to generate any wild enthusiasm among the inside board members over challenging a proposal which has just been advanced by the man who pays your salary." Investor Responsibility Research Center, Inc., *Changes in the Corporate Board Room: What Should be Done? Who Should Do It?* 35 (1974) [hereinafter cited as IRRC Report] (quoting John A. Patton).

135. One argument sometimes advanced is that employee-directors can be very effective if their principal economic stake in the company is as shareholders, rather than as employees. Investor Responsibility Research Center, Inc., Corporations and the Political Process: Ashland Oil Co., Analysis No. 1, Supp. No. 5, at 1-68 (1975) (quoting Orin E. Atkins, CEO of Ashland Oil Co.).

On the other hand, some of the arguments for electing insiders to the board partake of a certain Alice-in-Wonderland character. For example, Bacon and Brown cite one CEO who argued that a chief executive's tendency to misrepresent the company's performance, though not inhibited by one insider on the board, would be inhibited by two. J. Bacon and J. Brown, *supra* note 114, at pp. 64–65.

136. See Eisenberg, *supra* note 47, at 405–406; Leech and Mundheim, *supra* note 54, at 1830–31; M. Mace, *supra* note 114, at pp. 199–203.

management of corporations they serve as directors, is that persons with business or professional relationships with a corporation are particularly knowledgeable about the affairs of the corporation, and the board should not be denied the benefits of their expertise.[137]

Of course, requiring disclosure of a director's economic and familial relationships with a corporation and its management will not enable shareholders to determine whether the director possesses varrious intangible personal attributes (such as strength of character and maturity of judgment) which are likely to be the ultimate determinants of his ability to serve effectively. But these intangibles cannot be measured or defined, for purposes of disclosure, while economic and familial relationships can be both measured and defined. Moreover, the existence of such relationships is likely to be significant to shareholders' "consideration of the fact and appearance of the director's independence and other qualifications for corporate office."[138]

In our view, communication to shareholders concerning the makeup of a corporation's board would be facilitated by requiring corporations to categorize their directors as "management," "affiliated nonmanagement," and "unaffiliated nonmanagement." These terms are relatively neutral, but they also serve to signal that significant distinctions may exist between different groups of outside directors.

As the Fifty-Second American Assembly stated when it recommended that at least a majority of a board of directors be outside directors, "family ties, business or other professional arrangements may not disqualify one from serving as a director, but such an individual cannot be held out as an 'outside director' and the appropriate public documents should so indicate."[139] Requiring the identification of such persons as affiliated directors and identifying their exact affiliation will not remove them from the boards of corporations, though it may create a pressure on boards to reduce their number.[140]

---

137. See IRRC Report, *supra* note 134, at 52–54; J. Bacon and J. Brown, *supra* note 114, at pp. 45–47; Guidebook Report, *supra* note 53, at 1850.

138. H. Williams, Chairman, SEC, "Opening Statement at the Commission's Consideration of Rulemaking Proposals Concerning Shareholders Communications, Shareholders Participation in the Corporate Electoral Process and Corporate Governance Generally," p. 6 (Nov. 15, 1978).

139. The Ethics of Corporate Conduct, Report of the Fifty-Second American Assembly, Harriman, N.Y., 5 (April 14–17, 1977). The New York Stock Exchange, by way of comparison, abandoned its effort to identify which directors are outside directors for purposes of its requirement that all listed companies have audit committees made up of nonmanagement directors. It left to companies' boards the decision as to which directors are "independent of management and free from any relationship that . . . would interfere with the exercise of independent judgment as a committee member," while providing them with some nonbinding guidance concerning factors to be considered in making that determination. New York Stock Exchange, Audit Committee Policy (Jan. 6, 1977).

140. It is difficult to determine, from available data, what proportion of the persons

The SEC, when it proposed changes in its disclosure requirements relating to corporate boards, tentatively embraced the concept of requiring categorization of directors. However, the Commission proposed that nonmanagement directors with no significant affiliations with a corporation be called "independent,"[141]—a much more value-laden term than the one we propose—and this proposal evoked a heated negative response. Numerous commentators objected that use of this terminology created an inference that other directors were viewed by the Commission as incapable of making independent judgments.[142] The Commission denied that this was its intent but, faced with overwhelming opposition to this proposal and lacking a record on the basis of which it could evaluate the merits of alternative terminology, the Commission withdrew its proposal and substituted a requirement that corporations include in their proxy statements "a brief description, in tabular form to the extent possible, of any of certain significant economic and personal relationships which exist between the directors and the issuer."[143]

As to what constitute significant relationships that must be disclosed, we have only one significant quarrel with the standards adopted by the SEC, which represent a modest modification of long-standing requirements set out in Item 6 of Schedule 14A.[144] The Commission

---

now serving as nonmanagement directors of corporations would be classified as affiliated. Korn/Ferry International found that in 1976, companies had "one or more of the following individuals" (who might be classified as affiliated directors) on their boards:

Senior Executive (other companies)	85.5%
Commercial Banker	48.6%
Attorney (provides legal services to the company)	33.3%
Investment Bankers	30.9%

Korn/Ferry International Board of Directors: Fourth Annual Study 8-9 (Feb. 1977) [hereinafter cited as Korn/Ferry Survey].

141. SEC Securities Exchange Act Release No. 34-14970 [1978 Transfer Binder] Fed. Sec. L. Rep. (CCH) ¶ 81,645 (July 18, 1978).

142. See H. Williams, *supra* note 138, at p. 5; J. Evans, "SEC Corporate Governance Proposals: An Update," Address to Am. Soc. of Corp. Secys., Santa Barbara, Ca. (Nov. 3, 1978); SEC Securities Exchange Act Release No. 34-15384 at 12-13, [1978 Transfer Binder] Fed. Sec. L. Rep. (CCH) ¶ 81,766 at 81,089 (Dec. 6, 1978).

143. The Commission also cautioned corporations not to label their directors in a manner that might be misleading, such as describing as "independent" directors with significant business relationships with a corporation. See SEC Securities Exchange Act Release No. 34-15384 [1978 Transfer Binder] Fed. Sec. L. Rep. (CCH) ¶ 81,766 (Dec. 6, 1978).

144. *Id.* Perhaps most significantly, the SEC now requires disclosure whenever a director is associated with a law firm or investment banker which has performed any services for the corporation in the last two years or which the issuer proposes to have perform services in the next year.

should also have required disclosure where directors are involved in reciprocal directorship relationships—that is, where X is an officer or employee of one corporation and a director of a second corporation, and Y is an officer or employee of the second corporation and a director of the first. How these relationships arise, and how they are apt to warp a director's judgment, have been succinctly described by Marvin Chandler, former CEO of the Northern Illinois Gas Company:[145]

> When A serves on B's board, A gets to know B and views him as a fine executive, a compatible person, and an ideal director for A's company. . . .
> It is asking too much of A to pull no punches in his director's role at B's company, when he knows that B in turn is appraising his (A's) performance. It becomes almost like, "You set my salary this week and I'll set your salary next week."

We are not aware of any survey data concerning reciprocal directorship relationships, but anecdotal evidence suggests they are fairly common. More importantly, we believe that a director will have a significantly greater propensity to be influenced by a reciprocal relationship than by the fact that he is a nonmanagement director of two corporations, one of which derives slightly more than one percent of its income from sales to the other. Yet the latter relationship, and others of similar importance, must now be disclosed.

Compensation. The amount of compensation paid to directors, and the basis on which it is paid, may be significant indicators of the seriousness with which management views the board of directors and the seriousness with which the directors take their responsibilities. As Roderick M. Hills, then chairman of the SEC, remarked, "Compensation for directors of too many large corporations is set at a figure which makes it apparent that no real work is expected."[146] Similarly, Ralph M. Lewis, editor of the *Harvard Business Review*, has noted that "if a high level of activity is expected of an outside director, he should be well paid. . . . [O]utside directors are human, and they tend to view as important those activities for which they are well paid, even if the actual money is inconsequential to them."[147]

While the disclosure that directors are paid a pittance may indicate they are not expected to do much, it does not necessarily follow that

---

145. Chandler, "It's Time to Clean Up the Boardroom," 53 Harv. Bus. Rev., Sept.-Oct. 1975, at 73.

146. Senate Hearings, *supra* note 62, at p. 301 (statement of Roderick M. Hills).

147. Lewis, "Choosing and Using Outside Directors," 52 Harv. Bus. Rev., July-Aug. 1974, at 70, 72. See also Harvard Symposium, *supra* note 125, at 7.
Recent surveys indicate corporate directors are paid fees within a wide range, and on the basis of several different compensation arrangements. See Korn/Ferry Survey, *supra* note 140, at pp. 11–16; Heidrick & Struggles, Inc., *supra* note 45; J. Bacon, *Corporate Directorship Practices: Compensation* (1975).

directors who are well paid can be assumed to be playing an active and effective role. But substantial fees are one indication that a corporation takes its directors seriously.[148]

The SEC recently adopted regulations requiring corporations to disclose their standard arrangements for compensating directors for their services, including specific disclosure of amounts payable for service on board committees and for special assignments undertaken by directors.[149]

Attendance. It seems self-evident that whether a director regularly attends board and committee meetings is relevant to an evaluation of his or her performance.[150] Indeed, the companies that responded to a recent survey of boards of directors ranked attendance at board meetings as the second most important factor in evaluating directors' performance, with 77 percent of the respondents listing it as significant.[151] Thus a strong case exists that such information should be disclosed to the public.[152]

The SEC has determined that corporations should disclose whether any incumbent director failed to attend 75 percent of aggregate number of meetings of the board and of board committees on which he sits.[153] This requirement is useful, but it does not go far enough. Requiring data on the frequency and duration of board and committee meetings,

---

148. Texas Instruments pays fees to its outside directors based in part on the amount of time they devote to company business, and one commentator has suggested that corporations should generally adopt this practice. Mace, "Designing a Plan for the Ideal Board," 54 Harv. Bus. Rev., Nov.–Dec. 1976, at 20, 36. [hereinafter cited as Mace, Ideal Board].

General Motors Corp., in the proxy statement for its 1977 annual meeting, described in some detail its compensation plan for directors. General Motors Corp. proxy statement dated May 20, 1977. However, it only published the exact amounts paid to the two outside directors who received more than $40,000 in 1976—the threshhold above which compensation must be reported. See item 7 of regulation 14A.

149. SEC Securities Act Release No. 33-6003, [1978 Transfer Binder] Fed. Sec. L. Rep. (CCH) ¶ 81,765, at 81,084 (Item 4(C)) (Dec. 4, 1978).

150. "[I]t is expected that a non-management director will devote substantial time to the affairs of the corporation. . . ." Corporate Director's Guidebook, *supra* note 51, at p. 33.

151. Heidrick & Struggles, Inc., *supra* note 45, at p. 12.

152. In the *Stirling Homex* release, *supra* note 64, the Commission noted somewhat disparagingly that the board had met only seven times in two years.

153. Securities Exchange Act Release No. 34-15384, [1978 Transfer Binder] Fed. Sec. L. Rep. (CCH) ¶ 81,766 (Dec. 6, 1978). The Commission has not defined attendance. Presumably any form of director participation in a meeting that qualifies as attendance under state law will count toward the 75 percent threshhold set by the SEC. See section 141(i), Del. Gen. Corp. Law, 8 Del. Code Ann. (1975).

as we propose, would facilitate comparisons among boards and board committees of different corporations.[154] In addition, it would provide stockholders with an opportunity to determine whether committees have devoted adequate time to their responsibilities. It also would restrain exaggerations about the responsibility that a company may claim the board has exercised.[155] For example, there is evidence that in the last few years many audit committees substantially increased the time they devoted to reviewing companies' internal controls and financial reports.[156] Shareholders and investors should be provided with a sound basis for determining whether this trend has occurred at a corporation, or whether the audit committee is merely "spending two to four hours a year in cut-and-dried settions with a perfunctory look at the figures and the situations raised by the independent auditor's management letter," a level of performance that one professional director has stated "is not my idea of . . . the proper discharge of the responsibilities associated with service on an audit committee."[157]

Other Directorships. To do a conscientious job a director must be able to devote a substantial amount of time to the affairs of a corporation. Information about other directorships, particularly when combined with information about a director's principal occupation and attendance at board meetings, should provide shareholders with an indication of whether the director is overextended. The SEC now requires that this information be disclosed.[158]

---

154. For example, one author describes a board with fifteen members, "some of whom spend relatively little time on company problems," and an executive committee made up of the CEO and four outside directors which plays quite an active role in overseeing the affairs of the company and meets much more frequently than does the full board. See Lewis, *supra* note 147, at 77; Korn/Ferry, *supra* note 140, at p. 19. The proposed disclosure requirement would provide shareholders with significant indications that a board was so organized.

Korn/Ferry found directors spent an average of 102.5 hours in 1976 on board business, including board and committee meetings and "expected homework."

155. Since the minutes of board and committee meetings usually state the time meetings began and ended and the times directors present for less than the full meeting arrived or left, compiling this data would not be very burdensome. Moreover, the existence of the minutes would serve as a safeguard against puffing of a director's attendance figures.

156. See Mace, "From the Boardroom," 53 Harv. Bus. Rev., Sept.–Oct. 1975, at 18, 170–171.

157. Barr, "The Role of the Professional Director," 54 Harv. Bus. Rev., May–June 1976, at 18, 24. On the relationship between time commitments and the effectiveness of the audit committee, see generally Lovdal, "Making the Audit Committee Work," 55 Harv. Bus. Rev., March–April 1977, at 108.

158. Some argue, though, that requiring disclosure of other directorships would not serve this purpose. The chairman of a large insurance company stated that he

There is a clear nexus between the process by which directors are selected and the likelihood that directors will serve as independent monitors of management's performance. Similarly, the process of selection may have a large bearing on the diversity of a board. The selection process is likely to influence both the kinds of people chosen as directors and the manner in which these people, once chosen, will serve on the board. The salient point to remember is that nomination as a management candidate is tantamount to election.

In most publicly held corporations, the CEO selects the nonmanagement candidates for election to the board. A recent survey of directorship practices found that the "initial decisionmaker in approving board prospects" was the chief executive officer in 46.5 percent of the corporations responding, the board as a whole in 24.9 percent of the companies, the board's executive committee in 15.5 percent, a board nominating committee in 8.2 percent, the inside directors in 2.9 percent, and others in 2.0 percent.[159]

In selecting outside directors, the CEO faces a conflict of interest. He has a personal interest in avoiding candidates with the characteristics that make effective, independent members of the board. According to one authority:[160]

---

and most other outside directors are already seriously overcommitted. Consequently, he said, reducing the number of boards on which he serves would not really allow him to devote much more time to those on which he continued to serve. IRRC Report, *supra* note 134, at pp. 39–40.

159. Heidrick & Struggles, Inc., *supra* note 45, at p. 8. See also J. Bacon and J. Brown, *supra* note 114, at p. 28 (similar conclusions from discussions with CEO's and directors).

160. Lewis, *supra* note 147, at 71. See also Leech & Mundheim, *supra* note 54, at 1826; Cole, "New Attention on the Corporate Director," N.Y. Times, Apr. 29, 1977, § D, at p. 1.

One authority on boards suggests the following as typical of the way one CEO would invite another to join his board:

> George, we have a vacancy on our board, and I would be pleased if you would agree to join us. You know most of our current board memebers. You are as busy as everyone else but we meet only once a quarter at lunch, and meetings rarely take more than two hours. You have to eat somewhere and we hope you will accept. I won't burden you with a lot of homework. In fact we don't send out any material prior to meetings. Your point of view as a corporate CEO, a proven generalist, would be most helpful to me.

Mace, "Attracting New Directors," 54 Harv. Bus. Rev., Sept.-Oct. 1976, at 46, 48.

It is interesting to note that Heidrick and Struggles found 44.5 percent of the chairmen surveyed listed the reputation of their company as the most persuasive appeal for attracting directors and 38.4 percent listed the opportunity to contribute. "In contrast two-thirds of recently elected outside directors sur-

The typical CEO picks his outside directors with two things in mind:

> (1) He wants someone with whom he can feel comfortable. He needs no surprises. He feels he has enough problems running his business. The old friend, whose reactions he knows well, with whom he can discuss confidential issues, is a prime candidate. If the CEO moves outside the group he knows personally, the candidate is rigorously investigated, the major questions being "Is he solid?" and "Is he sympathetic?"
>
> (2) At the same time, the CEO wants someone who will lend prestige to his board.

Similarly a professional director found that in the replies of 160 CEO's to a poll that he conducted about professional directors "there was an undercurrent . . . that could be paraphrased, 'We wish to God that we did not have any outside directors, but especially no professional directors.' "[161] The author commented that this view appeared to reflect the desire of the managements of many large corporations to reinstate the autocratic management styles used by those companies' founders. "[I]t is only natural," he said, "that many managements today must look back with a certain nostalgia to the days of the founder and the inside board."[162]

The directors selected by a CEO are not likely to bite the hand that picked them. Most of these directors will be chief or senior executives of other business corporations, members of the peer group of the CEO. They usually are busy people, they sense that the CEO is not interested in having an active board, and they behave passively.[163] Robert M. Estes, former general counsel of General Electric Company, has perceptively noted that the reason "why it's so difficult to arouse outside directors as a class" is that most outside directors are executives of other corporations. The "primary reactions" of such an executive to suggestions that boards be more active, Mr. Estes stated, "will tend to be controlled by his primary role. In terms of the theory and practice of corporate boards, his instinctive concern is the board where he carries the ultimate personal responsibility for the success of the enterprise," not the boards on which he sits as a nonmanagement director.[164]

The disinclination of outside directors selected by the CEO to be assertive is reinforced by the social ethic which dominates most boards'

---

veyed the Heidrick and Struggles in another study report that the opportunity to contribute was the reason they joined boards. Only one fourth were motivated primarily by company reputation." Heidrick & Struggles, *supra* note 45, at p. 8.

161. Barr, *supra* note 157, at 19.

162. *Id.* at 20. See also Groobey, "Making the Board of Direcors More Effective," 16 Cal. Management Rev., Spring 1974, at 25, 27.

163. IRRC Transcript, *supra* note 119, at p. 12–14 (remarks of Myles L. Mace).

164. Estes, *supra* note 125, at p. 127.

operations. A nonmanagement director of several corporations remarked to one of the authors:[165]

> Being invited to sit on a board is just like being invited to join an exclusive private club. In that atmosphere, I wouldn't think of asking the man in charge of [a] division of [the] corporation why his rate of return is half that of the industry average. It just isn't done.

Moreover, the pressures that constrain directors from asking penetrating questions about the performance of division managers operate even more forcefully when it is the chief executive's performance that a board is evaluating. Indeed, as Professor Mace has described, a board made up of directors selected by the CEO is likely to remove him from office only when his "performance becomes so bad that even his mother thinks he has to leave. . . ."[166]

Finally, a nonmanagement director who is inclined to assert himself may hesitate if the chief executive officer retains effective control over the nomination of directors for reelection. A director's "independence may be jeopardized if the board member's compensation is materially important to him and if the management or chief executive officer has (or appears to have) the dominant voice in the renomination of incumbent members."[167] This problem may be even more acute for the director who depends on management for the maintenance of a material professional or business relationship which might be terminated, together with the director's membership on the board, if the director behaves in a fashion that management decides is too independent.[168] In sum, if the CEO controls the proxy process, that control will tend to reinforce "his economic and psychological dominance" of board members whom he has selected personally.[169] It aggravates the situation that outside directors often are chosen exclusively from the business com-

---

165. Clarence Randall, former chairman of Inland Steel, similarly acknowledged businessmen's belief "that criticism from outside is to be expected, *but that it should never come from within the lodge itself*" (Emphasis added.) C. Randall, *The Folklore of Management* (1959) *quoted in* C. Brown, *supra* note 45, at p. xxvi. See also Groobey, *supra* note 162, at 28–29; Lasker v. Burks, 567 F.2d 1208, 1212 (2d Cir.), *rev'd on other grounds*, 99 S.Ct. 1831 (1979) ("It is asking too much of human nature to expect that the disinterested director will view with necessary objectivity the actions of colleagues in a situation where an adverse decision would be likely to result in considerable expense and liability for the individuals concerned.")

166. IRRC Transcript, *supra* note 119, at p. 9 (remarks of Myles L. Mace). See also McColough, "The Corporation and its Obligations," 53 Harv. Bus. Rev., May–June 1975, at 127, 131–132.

167. Leech and Mundheim, *supra* note 54, at 1830.

168. *Id.*

169. Eisenberg, *supra* note 47, at 408.

munity, which furnishes too narrow a base from which to choose the entire board.[170]

Short of making revolutionary changes in the corporate governance system,[171] the best alternative to having directors selected by the CEO is to assign the task of selecting and renominating directors to a nominating committee made up of unaffiliated nonmanagement directors.[172] The *Corporate Director's Guidebook* states that a nominating committee so constituted "is potentially the most significant channel for improved corporate governance, since over a period of time it can have a marked impact on the composition of the board of directors and the manner in which management succession is effected."[173]

Professor Leech and Mundheim also assign a crucial role to the nominating committee. They state:[174]

> An important step in creating an environment conducive to an independent attitude on the part of outside directors is selection of outside directors by a nominating committee composed wholly of outside directors. Although the nominating committee should consult with the chief executive officer about possible board candidates, the committee should not feel bound to adopt management's slate of candidates.

The existence of a nominating committee made up of outside directors is not apt to result in dramatic changes in the membership of a

---

170. See note 178 *infra*.

171. Such as having stockholders use the proxy materials to solicit support for their nominees. We do not rule out the wisdom of such changes; we simply do not deal with them in this article.

172. General Motors Corp., among others, has such a nominating committee. See Leech and Mundheim, *supra* note 54, at 1807.

173. Corporate Director's Guidebook, *supra* note 51, at 35.

174. Leech and Mundheim, *supra* note 54, at 1830. See also C. Brown, *supra* note 45, at pp. 48–49; Eisenberg, *supra* note 47, at 407–408; Transcript, Conference on Federal Chartering of Corporations, American Enterprise Institute, Wash., D.C., pp. 128–29 (June 21, 1976) (remarks of Roderick M. Hills, then Chairman of the SEC); cf. Mace, "John J. McCloy on Corporate Payoffs," 54 Harv. Bus. Rev., July-Aug. 1976, at 14, 159 quoting McCloy:

> Professional managers have had too much authority in selecting directors and in determining what their functions are. The selection of new members of the board should not be the prerogative solely of the management. The outside board members already in place should more actively participate in the selection. . . .

The American Assembly recommended establishment of nominating committees with a majority of outside directors "to search for qualified candidates of diverse background for submission to the full board as possible nominees to the board." The Ethics of Corporate Conduct, *supra* note 139, at p. 5.

board, but it is likely to increase the director's feeling of loyalty to the board rather than to the CEO. Over time both the new selection process and the resultant feelings of independence are likely to become institutionalized.[175]

The requirements we propose for disclosure about the nominating process aim not only to inform shareholders but to influence the electoral process as well. The latter objective is justified by the SEC's interest in enhancing board independence, which depends upon the selection process.[176] Disclosure is especially well suited to effect change in this area. Many chief executives are notorious for their consistent claims of obeisance to the interests of their stockholders and the dictates of their boards. Rather than admit publicly that they monitor their own monitors, they are likely to surrender some of their control over nominations.[177] Disclosure should also affect shareholder participation. With information about nominating procedures and criteria, shareholders will be better equipped to discuss prospective candidates with management or the board.[178]

Procedures. The disclosure of procedures used to select nominees would include a description of who—the CEO, a nominating committee, the full board, or others—is responsible for recommending board prospects; what processes are used to identify and screen prospects; whether the CEO has a right to veto new candidates or nominees for reelection; and whether the board, or any committee of the board, regularly solicits or reviews shareholders' recommendations on changes in board membership.[179] A corporation should also be required to

---

175. IRRC Report, *supra* note 134, at 22.

176. This point has been made by Professor Alfred Conard, who has argued that directors' liability should be premised principally on their failure "to remove incompetent directors, or . . . to call for investigation of symptoms of malfunction." See Conard, "A Behavioral Analysis of Directors' Liability for Negligence," 1972 Duke L.J. 893, 917.

177. See Harvard Symposium, *supra* note 125, at p. 14.

178. For example, when a shareholder group tried to question the chairman of General Motors Corp. about the reasons why two new directors had been added to GM's board, it received responses that added little to its understanding of why those persons had been chosen. See Schwartz, "The Public Interest Proxy Contest: Reflections on Campaign GM," 69 Mich. L. Rev. 419, 477–78 (1971).

179. The Corporate Director's Guidebook says that a procedure allowing shareholders to make suggestions to a nominating committee will be "a more effective and workable method of affording access to the nominating process to individual shareholders than a direct 'right' of nomination in the corporation's proxy materials." Corporate Director's Guidebook, *supra* note 51, at 35. The SEC does not require disclosure of nominating procedures generally. However, it now requires registrants to disclose whether they have nominating committees, what functions those committees perform, whether a nominating committee

notify shareholders if these procedures have not been followed with respect to any nominee.[180]

Criteria. The disclosure of criteria for selection of nominees should identify the traits that the person or persons responsible for nominations look for in all candidates and formulas that may be used in order to obtain a desired balance on the board.[181] For example, a recent survey found seven considerations were listed by at least 10 percent of the respondent companies as relevant to their selection of new directors.[182] Some corporations clearly prefer a board made up primarily of CEO's of other companies;[183] in those cases that criterion would be

---

will consider nominees recommended by shareholders and, if so, what procedures shareholders should follow to recommend nominees. SEC Securities Exchange Act Release No. 15,384 [1978 Transfer Binder] Fed. Sec. L. Rep. (CCH) ¶ 81,766 (Dec. 6, 1978).

180. The notification requirement should promote independence among the directors by making arbitrary action against them more difficult to pursue. See C. Brown, *supra* note 45, at p. 84; Leech and Mundheim, *supra* note 54, at 1831.

181. See Heller, "The Board of Directors: Legalistic Anachronism or Vital Force," 14 Cal. Management Rev., Spring 1972, at 24, 28:

> What steps should a company take to make sure that the proper people are serving on its board of directors? Specific criteria should be developed and tailored to the needs of the individual company. . . .
>
> Once the specific criteria for a company's board members have been developed and agreed upon, the present composition of the board should be analyzed and evaluated. A program must then be developed to recruit to fill identified needs and to develop a strategy for retiring board members whose future contributions are likely to be limited.

182. The factors and the percentages of companies that considered them in selecting directors were:

Probable ability to contribute	98.6%
Stature	52.6%
Functional area represented	45.5%
Experience as directors	35.4%
Time availability	26.9%
Stock ownership	12.3%
Geographic area represented	10.0%

Heidrick & Struggles, *supra* note 45, at p. 9. See also J. Bacon, *supra* note 45, at pp. 40–47.

183. See Barr, *supra* note 157, at 19, commenting on this phenomenon. Another atypical director of several major corporations notes that "an individual who spends his or her life solely in the pursuit of greater corporate efficiency and maximizing the profits of the stockholder is somewhat removed from the day-to-day ferment of political life." Harris, "New Constitutencies for the Board," in Conference Board 1972 Report, *supra* note 43. See also Harvard Symposium, *supra* note 125, at p. 8; Mace, Ideal Board, *supra* note 148, at 30.

mentioned. Similarly, if a corporation had a policy limiting the number of CEO's on its board, a policy barring all affiliated persons from being directors, a policy limiting the number of management directors, or a policy requiring that a certain proportion of the board be made up of unaffiliated nonmanagement directors, these policies would be disclosed. Armed with this information, shareholders would be in a much better position to suggest nominees to management and to evaluate whether new nominees were qualified in terms of the announced criteria.[184] If they disagreed with the corporation's criteria, they would be in a position to make more informed and sophisticated suggestions for altering them.

Requiring disclosure of the criteria for renomination of directors would let stockholders know if a board had some standards or process for evaluating directors' performance. While some of the criteria disclosed, such as the quality of a director's suggestions, might be relatively meaningless, others—such as attendance at board and committee meetings, time devoted to reviewing the company's operations, or specified ages or circumstances for retirement—would be moderately significant to an evaluation of the board's operations and the manner in which it actually applied these criteria to nomination for reelection. The

---

184. A few companies have volunteered information about how they select directors by examining that information; we can gain some insight into what information registrants might make available pursuant to the proposed disclosure requirement and how that information might be used by investors.

The criteria used by Northern Illinois Gas Co. for evaluating a potential nonmanagement director appear in Chandler, *supra* note 145, at 76. A description of the criteria and process used to select nonemployee directors of Exxon Corp. and how they performed in one instance appears in 2 IRRC News for Investors 100–01 (May 1975). General Motors, in its proxy statement for its 1975 annual meeting, included a discussion of the basis on which it selected directors. As a part of its director selection process, Pullman, Inc., reportedly uses a matrix to analyze the skills needed to perform directorship duties and the skills possessed by its current directors. See Mace, *supra* note 160, at 54.

While a corporation probably would use the same language from year to year to describe its criteria—unless those criteria change—these statements would not be meaningless formulae. Rather they would provide a basis for shareholders to use voice to bring about changes in the criteria. See notes 90 to 95 *supra* and related text.

By publishing the criteria used to select directors, a corporation also would better inform shareholders when it was undertaking major shifts in the makeup of its board. That rarely is done now. For an example, in the early 1970's Xerox Corp. shifted from a board made up largely of Rochester, N.Y.-based businessmen to one made up of prominent academics and international businessmen, but did not provide shareholders with an explicit statement that it was making such a shift or an explanation as to why it was being made. See Investor Responsibility Research Center, Inc., Shareholder Nomination of Candidates for Director: Xerox Corp., Analysis No. 7, Supp. No. 2 (April 30, 1973).

publication of such criteria might also make it easier for the board to rid itself of deadwood without undue embarrassment.

Proxy Review. There is no specific legal requirement that the board of directors review a corporation's proxy materials, and we are not suggesting that the SEC impose such a requirement. However, if our other recommendations are adopted, much of a registrant's proxy statements will be devoted to the selection of directors and the organization and operations of the board. It would then be desirable for the SEC to require that shareholders at least be informed whether the board itself had reviewed the proxy materials before they were published.

Finally, requiring disclosure of the manner in which the board exercises control over proxy solicitation expenses will complete the picture of who controls the corporation's participation in the election process. Control of the purse strings is an important part of that process, and information should be made available about how closely the board or any of its committees supervises expenditures for proxy solicitations.

INFORMATION ABOUT BOARD ORGANIZATION AND ACTIVITIES

Requiring disclosure of how a board is organized and how it has functioned can both influence the board's performance and generate information of considerable importance to shareholders. Information about the organization and activities of directors is highly relevant to board elections, since the vast majority of candidates for election as directors are standing for reelection. Data about the performance of those candidates and the boards on which they have served are likely to be highly relevant to shareholders' voting decisions in cases where there is any choice, as well as relevant to nominations.

It is in the area of board activities, however, that the constraints of confidentiality, of limiting disclosure requirements to matters of legitimate interest to shareholders, and of keeping disclosure within manageable limits all are likely to be most vexing.

In our view, the best approach to balancing these conflicting interests is to be selective in developing disclosure requirements relating to the activities of a board, and to focus those requirements on the processes through which the board operates rather than on the substance of the board's deliberations or decisions. Specifically, the disclosure requirements should focus on the board's committee system, on the flow of information to the board, and on the process by which the board monitors management's performance. Related to these matters is the amount of staff assistance furnished to the board.

The SEC has taken little action in this area, perhaps as a consequence of the difficulties it perceives may bedevil any effort to develop meaningful and appropriate disclosure standards. But without disclosure about a board's organization and activities, shareholders will have a critically incomplete picture of the role the board has played, and can be expected to play, within a corporation. Consequently, we hope that the SEC, in the subsequent stages of its review of corporate governance issues, will devote considerable effort to fleshing out disclosure requirements in this area.

Committees. Boards are coming to rely more heavily on committees as a means of carrying out their responsibilities,[185] and that trend is likely to accelerate if a recent amendment to the American Bar Association's Model Business Corporation Act is adopted widely as part of state corporation laws. The amendment allows a director to rely on information and reports presented by a board committee on which he does not serve if he reasonably believes that the committee deserves his confidence.[186]

Information about what committees a board has, what their authority and responsibilities are, how they report to the full board, and how committee members are selected can be vital to any appraisal of the role that board plays.[187]

Moreover, the information about a board's committee system will be complemented by the proposed disclosures about directors' affiliations with management and the frequency and length of committee meetings. Viewed together, this information should help shareholders and other interested persons to understand the contribution of each committee and its members to the activities of the board.

The SEC, when it amended its disclosure rules, required corporations to disclose whether or not they have standing audit, nominating and compensation committees. If they do, they are further required to name committee members, state the number of committee meetings

---

185. See IRRC Report, *supra* note 134, at pp. 15–16 for a description of the committee system developed by the board of General Electric Co.; and *id*. at 42–44 for a discussion of the pros and cons of increasing use of committees. See Leech and Mundheim, *supra* note 54, at 1807–09 for a description of the committee system developed by the board of General Motors Corp. See also Harvard Symposium, *supra* note 125, at p. 10; under a recently adopted New York Stock Exchange Rule, by June 30, 1978, all listed companies must have audit committees comprised solely of independent, nonmanagement directors. New York Stock Exchange, *supra* note 139.

186. ABA-ALI Model Bus. Corp. Act § 35 (Supp. 1977). See also the comment of the ABA Committee on Corporate Laws on this portion of its amendment to the Act in ABA Comm. on Corporate Laws, *supra* note 50.

187. Few data are available about these apects of board practice. It is interesting to note, though, that the Corporate Director's Guidebook, *supra* note 51, at 27, says a "director is entitled to receive a copy of minutes of all meetings of the full board and each board committee (whether or not he is a member)." Yet only 35.6 percent of the companies responding to recent survey said they provided directors, prior to board meetings, with summaries of action taken by board committees subsequent to the last board meeting. Heidrick & Struggles, Inc., *supra* note 45, at 10.

held during the previous fiscal year and describe briefly the functions performed by each of these committees.[188]

This new regulation clearly goes a long way toward providing shareholders with important data about board committees that previously was not available for many corporations. However, it is significantly defective in that it does not require that similar data be made available about all board committees including, in particular, a board's executive committee. Some boards have executive committees that meet much more frequently than the full board, that are authorized to exercise all the powers of the full board except those reserved to the board by statute, that do not report regularly or in any detail to the full board, and that are made up wholly or primarily of management directors selected by the CEO. Other corporations have executive committees that meet infrequently, that limit themselves to matters of relatively minor importance, that require formal board approval, that report all their actions to the full board, and that are made up mostly of nonmanagement directors who are selected by the board as a whole.[189] In appraising a board of directors' role, it could be critically important to know whether the board has an executive committee, and if so, which of these two models it most resembles. The same might be said of other committees, such as finance and public policy committees, though the considerations of greatest importance with regard to any one committee may depend on the committee and the makeup of the board as a whole.

Information Systems. Information is the lifeblood of a board's activities. Without an adequate flow of accurate information, it is close to impossible for a board to play any meaningful role within a corporation.[190] A

---

188. *Id.* In promulgating this requirement, the Commission abandoned an earlier proposal that would have listed customary functions of each of these committees and required corporations to state which of those functions, if any, their committees did not perform. Release 14970. The Commission recognized that corporations' practices in this area vary considerably and consequently moved from a negative to an affirmative disclosure approach. SEC Securities Exchange Act Release No. 15,384, [1978 Transfer Binder] Fed. Sec. L. Rep. (CCH) ¶ 81,766 (Dec. 6, 1978).

See J. Bacon and J. Brown, *supra* note 114 at pp. 117–140 for a discussion of the different roles played in different corporations by audit, compensation, finance, nominating, social responsibility, contributions, and other board committees. For a useful illustration of a framework within which a "well-functioning compensation committee might perform," see Leech and Mundheim, *supra* note 54, at 1823–24.

189. The range of practices corporations follow with respect to the organization, authority, and membership of their executive committees is outlined in J. Bacon, *supra* note 45, at pp. 64–68, and J. Bacon and J. Brown, *supra* note 114, at pp. 105–117.

190. See Corporate Director's Guidebook, *supra* note 51, at 16; The Business Roundtable, *supra* note 125, at pp. 15–16. See also Heller, *supra* note 181, at 26: "To

board needs information for two purposes. One is monitoring management's performance, and the other is passing on specific transactions or policy recommendations.

The SEC has an interest in assuring that registrants' boards receive the information they need to meet their obligations under the securities laws, and investors have an interest in knowing whether the board had access to all information it felt it needed.[191] However, defining thorough standards of general application for what is an adequate flow of information is not feasible, and requiring disclosure of all information that is transmitted to a board is probably neither practicable nor desirable.[192] Thus, fashioning a disclosure requirement relating to the flow of information to the board presents a formidable problem.

Our recommendation concerning information flows recognizes these problems, and is intended to achieve only a limited objective: to deter the board from serving as a rubber stamp for management's recommendations, and to assist shareholders in determining whether the board is acting in that fashion.[193] If, for example, a board regularly approves the consummation of major transactions on the basis of information first presented to it at board meetings, we believe the inference can fairly be drawn that the board exercises very little independent judgment in reviewing management's recommendations.[194]

---

make board meetings as effective as possible, each board member should receive an advance information package and should have at least three or four days to study this material before he is asked to act on it at the meeting."

191. In its Report of Investigation Concerning Stirling Homex Corp., the Commission placed great stress on the fact that "There existed no internal system by which they [the outside directors] were regularly provided with significant information concerning corporate affairs. . . ." SEC Securities Exchange Act Release No. 11516, *supra* note 64, at ¶ 85,462.

192. See Mace, "Management Information Systems for Directors," 53 Harv. Bus. Rev., Nov.-Dec. 1975, at 14, 17 (corporate practice in informing directors varies). For more specific information on the variety of corporate practices in this area, see J. Bacon and J. Brown, *supra* note 114, at pp. 89–98; Heidrick & Struggles, Inc., *supra* note 45, at p. 10.

193. Professor Mace reports:

> I recently learned of companies which follow the practice of not mailing out anything prior to meetings and requiring that any company information provided at the meeting be turned in prior to leaving the boardroom. The explanation was that directors could not be trusted to observe the confidentiality of sensitive inside information.

Mace, Ideal Board, *supra* note 148, at 198.

194. See "The Board: It's Obsolete Unless Overhauled," Special Report, Bus. Week, May 22, 1971, at pp. 50, 55 (Quoting Robert E. Brooker, chairman of the executive committee of Marcor, Inc.: "If you're going to have an effective outside board, it must be briefed in advance. It's unfair to ask directors to make decisions only from board discussions.")

The basic disclosure called for is whether the board regularly receives at least two days in advance of board and committee meetings what it considers to be adequate information about matters management suggests it address at those meetings. If the board regularly receives such information, it would be able to note that fact. (Of course disclosure that the board received information does not guarantee that it then made an independent judgment on the basis of that information. But it at least increases the chance.) However, if there were times when the board authorized or approved material transactions without advance information, we believe shareholders should be informed of those facts. Our guess is that in most such instances the board also would choose to explain to shareholders why it believed taking such action without advance information had been in the shareholders' best interest, even though such explanations would not be required.[195]

Monitoring Systems. Given the importance of the board's monitoring role, it is essential that the disclosure system both encourage boards to play such a role and provide shareholders with the basis for understanding whether and how the board is doing so.[196] As Peter Drucker has stated:[197]

> The first task of a functioning board is to insist that company management design adequate yardsticks of performance for itself. . . . [T]op management should be expected by a functioning board to spell out its expectations and to be judged, a few years later, by results as measured against these expectations.

A requirement that registrants disclose the procedures and criteria used by their boards of directors to monitor management's performance should go a long way toward attaining this goal. First, to the extent that the disclosure requirement causes a board to think through and articulate its monitoring process, it will make a major contribution to the institutionalization of that process within the corporation. More than two-thirds of the corporations responding to one recent survey reported that they did not have a formal management audit procedure for directors to follow.[198] Yet as Professors Leech and Mundheim point out:[199]

---

195. For example, a board might feel impelled to take a major action without advance information because the corporation faced an unexpected crisis, such as an unexpected tender offer to which management wants to react very quickly. See Wall St. J., June 13, 1977, at p. 4, col. 1 (Avis board decides not to accept competing tender offer for Avis stock).

196. Eisenberg, *supra* note 47, at 402–403.

197. P. Drucker, "The Real Duties of a Director," Wall St. J., June 1, 1978, at p. 20.

198. Korn/Ferry Survey, *supra* note 140, at p. 18.

199. Leech and Mundheim, *supra* note 54, at 1827.

It is not enough to encourage the chief executive to want to have a board which does an effective monitoring job. The only effective instrument for change is the institutionalization of processes that make it mandatory for the chief executive to account to a strong board.

Once the principal components of the monitoring system have been published, a board would be under considerable pressure to use the system and to explain its actions toward management in terms of the criteria it had announced. For example, if one element of a corporation's evaluation system was to "evaluate the performance of the CEO and division presidents quarterly, based on comparisons with the performance of competitors, when appropriate competitive information is available,"[200] the board would probably feel compelled to question the performance of a lagging division, and either to change the management of that division or to explain to shareholders why the division was having problems and what the board or management intended to do about them.

Secondly, the description of the procedures used, when combined with information about directors' affiliations and about time devoted to board activities, would provide investors with a good indication of the independence of the monitors and of the amount of time they are devoting to this task. It also would enable investors to know whether a board, or the responsible committee of the board, regularly used the services of persons outside the corporation's management—such as management consultants—to assist it in developing a monitoring system or data to be used in evaluating management's performance.

Finally, publication of the criteria used to evaluate management's performance should provide investors with valuable insights into the corporation's future performance. It is well documented that corporate officials generally are very responsive to the criteria used to rate their performance.[201] Thus, investors would better understand and predict management's behavior if they knew that a corporation's board evaluated management on any of the following criteria: quarterly, annual, or five-year goals; increases in sales, net income, or return on assets employed or shareholders' equity; development of new products; diversification or consolidation; management of pension fund contributions and assets; or responsiveness to social pressures or government programs.[202] Moreover, while corporations, corporate officials, or re-

---

200. This was one of the responsibilities of the board set out in a model charter for the board of directors. Mace, Ideal Board, *supra* note 148, at 21.

201. See, e.g., R. Ackerman, *supra* note 32.

202. For a recent illustration of how management evaluation systems influence corporate performance, see Wall St. J., June 1, 1977, at p. 1, col. 6 (in many corporations evaluation systems stressing return on investment have operated to deter needed investment in new capital equipment).

Information about a board's evaluation system also will aid interested parties

searchers have listed all of these criteria as components of their evaluation systems,[203] several of them are inconsistent with others, and many of them could not sensibly be used together in the unique circumstances presented by individual companies. As a consequence, it seems unlikely that corporations would respond to this requirement with standardized language ("boilerplate"), and to the extent that they do, shareholders and investment analysts are likely to subject their boards and managements to vigorous criticism for failing to develop a consistent set of goals in terms of which the corporation's performance can be evaluated.[204]

Staff Assistance. The lack of institutionalized staff assistance caused Arthur J. Goldberg to resign from the board of directors of TWA.[205] Justice Goldberg advocated the creation of a staff of professionals who would serve the outside directors of the corporation, thereby enhancing their independence. There was much adverse comment on the proposal,[206] but most of the criticism was focused on Goldberg's proposal that the staff be independent from the company.

---

in determining whether the board sees its primary responsibility to be preventing financial disasters or driving management to outperform its competitors. See Clendenin, "Company Presidents Look at the Board of Directors," 14 Cal. Management Rev., Spring 1972, at 60.

203. See Mace, Ideal Board, *supra* note 148, at 21–22 (listing numerous factors to be used in evaluating management); IRRC Transcript, *supra* note 119, at p. 55 (remarks of Louis V. Cabot, describing evaluation of CEO against a set of five-year goals); Bauer, Cauthorn & Warner, "Auditing the Management Process for Social Performance," Bus. & Soc'y Rev., Fall, 1975, at 39 (suggesting a "process audit" of management responsiveness to social pressures); Berkshire Hathaway Corp., 1976 Annual Report to the Stockholder (letter from chairman of the board Warren E. Buffet stating that rate of return on shareholder's equity is "a much more significant yardstick of economic performance" than total operating earnings); P. Drucker, *supra* note 197 (listing several factors). Cf. "RCA's New Vista: The Bottom Line," Bus. Week, July 4, 1977, at p. 38 (noting a shift in RCA Corp.'s strategy away from promoting technological innovation in favor of increasing short-term earnings, which RCA's annual report "subtly underscores" by featuring a cover picture of a Hertz Corp. airport bus, rather than the traditional picture of some aspect of RCA Corp. technology).

204. If a board can demonstrate that it acts as an independent monitor of management's performance, management, too, would benefit in that proof of board review would effectively insulate management's decisions from judicial second-guessing, if those decisions are challenged by shareholders. See Leech and Mundheim, *supra* note 54, at 1805.

205. Goldberg, *supra* note 43.

206. See Blough, "The Outside Director at Work on the Board," 28 Record of N.Y.C.B.A. 202 (1973); Smith, "The Goldberg Dilemma: Directorships," Wall St. J., Feb. 7, 1973, at p. 14, col. 3; Eisenberg, *supra* note 47, at 390. But see Schwartz, "A Plan to Save the Board," 28 Record of N.Y.C.B.A. 279 (1973).

The desirability of providing staff assistance has gained significant support. General Motors furnishes its board committees with considerable employee assistance, although no one is assigned to assist the board on a permanent basis.[207] When asked at an annual meeting what kind of staff assistance GM's Public Policy Committee received, Chairman James Roche responded, "They have access to all the staffs in General Motors for whatever purpose they may require."[208] Robert Estes, former general counsel of General Electric Company, has urged the assignment of counsel to the outside directors, since so much of what properly concerns them involves legal issues.[209]

It does seem clear that the judgments directors are required to make involve complex matters on a wide range of subjects. No busy director, not even the most versatile, can give proper attention to all these matters without some assistance. He can obtain it on his own, or he can follow the lead of other, more knowledgeable colleagues on the board, but both of these methods seem chancy. Alternatively, the corporation can provide staff assistance. What is done in this regard seems to us to bear on the professionalism and performance of the outside directors, the board, and the corporation.

The information to be provided should cover not only the existence of a staff available to service the board, but also whether the board has a regular budget to cover the costs of special consultants and advisors. The existence of such a budget makes it much more likely that a board will seek outside help whenever a need for it is perceived. A board that must specifically request budgetary authority to hire consultants, on the other hand, is apt to view such actions as extraordinary and resort to it only in extreme circumstances.[210]

INFORMATION ABOUT DIRECTORS' RESIGNATIONS[211]

Explanation of the Proposal. Finally, we have proposed that the Commission impose on registrants new disclosure requirements relating to

---

207. Leech and Mundheim, *supra* note 54, at 1808.

208. Transcript of Annual Meeting of GM Stockholders, May 21, 1971, at p. 281 (on file with the authors).

209. Estes, *supra* note 125. See also IRRC Report, *supra* note 134, at p. 42.

210. This conclusion emerged from discussions at the ALI-ABA Regional Symposium on the Structure and Governance of Corporations, Buck Hill Falls, Pa. (May 4–5, 1978). Mr. Weiss was a rapporteur at the symposium.

211. The proposed requirement would apply to resignations, retirements, situations where a director chooses not to stand for reelection, and situations where the persons in control of the registrant's proxy materials do not nominate a director for reelection. Registrants also should be required to file the information required by this section in a Form 8K since the information may be material to ongoing investment decision-making. Cf. SEC Accounting Series Release No. 165 [1977] Fed. Sec. L. Rep. (CCH) ¶ 72,187 (Dec. 20, 1974), requiring increased

directors' resignation and retirement. Registrants would be required to list all directors who have left the board since the last annual meeting or are not standing for reelection, and to state the reasons why each of them has taken such action.

These disclosure requirements would differ from the others we have proposed in that each of the other requirements was to some degree oriented toward affecting a director's or a board's conduct in a particular way. Here the purpose of our proposed requirement is not to encourage or discourage directors to resign, and we do not believe there is any sound basis for predicting that it would have either of those effects.

Moreover, the other disclosure requirements we have proposed are designed to assist shareholders in understanding whether and how individual directors and the board are meeting their legal responsibilities. No analogous legal standard relevant to the proposed disclosure requirements governs resignations. Specifically, it is well established that directors are free to resign for any reason they choose,[212] so long as they do not resign to secure some private pecuniary gain[213] or as part of a plan to transfer control of the corporation to persons who they have reason to believe will manage the corporation in a manner that is adverse to the interests of the shareholders.[214]

However, although the proposed requirements do not aim to influence directors' decisions to resign, we believe they would serve two important purposes. First, they would strengthen the independence of the board by strengthening the position of directors within the corporation. Second, they would ensure that potentially significant information about a corporation or its board is made available to investors.

The SEC has recognized for some years, in the case of registrants' independent public accountants, that required disclosure about the circumstances under which a registrant has changed accountants can enhance the independence of accountants. In late 1971 the SEC instituted a requirement that companies report a change in the auditors who certified their most recent financial statements.[215] In late 1974 the Commission amended and strengthened that requirement.[216] After not-

---

disclosure in Form 8K relating to registrants' changes of independent public accountants.

212. "A director or other officer of a corporation may resign at any time and thereby cease to be an officer. . . ." W. Fletcher, 2 *Cyclopedia of the Law of Private Corporations,* § 345 (1969).

213. *Id.* § 348; Essex Universal Corp. v. Yates, 305 F.2d 572 (2d Cir. 1962).

214. Gerdes v. Reynolds, 28 N.Y.S.2d 622 (Sup. Ct. 1941).

215. Item 12, Form 8K was adopted in SEC Securities Exchange Act Release No. 9344, [1971–72 Transfer Binder] Fed. Sec. L. Rep. (CCH) ¶ 78,304 (Sept. 27, 1971) (now renumbered as item 4).

216. SEC Accounting Series Release No. 165, [1977] Fed. Sec. L. Rep. (CCH) ¶ 72,189 (Dec. 20, 1974).

ing that "[o]ne of the underpinnings of the Commission's administration of the disclosure requirements of the federal securities laws is its reliance on the reports of independent public accountants on the financial statements of registrants," the Commission stated that "to enhance the accountant's independence," registrants should be required to report the resignation or dismissal of their principal accountants and the details of any "significant disagreement" between registrants and their accountants during the past two years.[217] This requirement was intended to deter registrants from dismissing their accountants because they did not like the accountants' proposed treatment of some matter or the accountants' stated intent to qualify their opinion. It also was intended to notify investors of the existence of a dispute where it had led a registrant to change accountants.[218]

A nonmanagement director of a corporation who attempts to exercise independent judgment is in a position similar to that of the independent public accountant—that is, the director is weak because his activities primarily benefit persons other than management (i.e., the shareholders) and because he must obtain the support of a majority of the board.[219] Management, which may control the proxy process or command the loyalities of a majority of the board, has little stake in allowing or encouraging the director to pursue activities that it views as prejudicial to its interests. One approach to strengthening the director's position is to provide him with a new base of power by ensuring that his point of view will be provided to investors. A disclosure requirement in this area should discourage a corporation's management from denying directors' legitimate demands or from pressuring a director or the board as a whole to behave in an inappropriate fashion.[220] It gives

---

217. *Id.*

218. For a discussion of the requirement, see Hawes, "Stockholder Appointment of Independent Auditors: A Proposal," 74 Colum. L. Rev. 1 (1974); Hawes, "Changing Auditors," 7 Rev. Sec. Reg. 935 (1974).

219. For an enlightening analysis of the dynamics of the auditor-management relationship, see Nichols and Price, "The Auditor-Firm Conflict: An Analysis Using Concepts of Exchange Theory," 51 Accounting Rev. 375 (1976).

220. Nichols and Price state that one approach to increasing the power of the auditor is to increase "the ability of a replaced auditor to cause sanctions to be imposed on the firm resulting from unjustified replacement." *Id.* at 344. They cite the SEC rules governing replacement of auditors as an example of this approach. They conclude, though, that these procedures will have variable success. *Id.* at 345. Similarly, the existence of the proposed disclosure requirements will not ensure that directors will assert their independence.

Nichols and Price suggest two other ways to influence the balance of power between auditors and firms, both of which also are suggestive of steps that might be taken to strengthen the position of directors. The first would be to increase the expected cost to the auditor of taking inappropriate actions, for example by providing "greater specification of auditing and accounting standards." *Id.* Simi-

bite to a director's conscience-driven threat to resign unless certain reforms are instituted or certain disclosures made.

The proposed disclosure requirement will also ensure that shareholders are informed when one or more of the persons they have elected as directors are leaving a board because they have serious misgivings about the activities or organization of the corporation or its board. The social ethic that now discourages controversy even within the boardroom creates a barrier that, in general, assures that all but the most independent directors will decline to go public about the concerns that have caused them to leave a corporate board.[221] The director who is uncomfortable about his position is more likely to resign quietly or to decline to stand for reelection. Yet it seems clear that the concerns that lead a director to resign may be of considerable interest to shareholders and to those considering purchasing the stock of the corporation.

The resignation of Robert Odell from the board of the Penn Central Company illustrates dramatically the problems our proposed requirement would alleviate.[222] Odell resigned in 1970 when his inquiry into Penn Central's involvement with Great Southwest Corporation was frustrated by both management and fellow directors.[223] Odell's inquiry would have uncovered Penn Central's massive real estate losses and its manipulation of Great Southwest to conceal them,[224] but his

---

larly, directors' behavior might be influenced by making more clear the legal responsibilities of directors. The second would be to change "the structure of the auditor-firm contractual relationship" by shifting away from management the responsibility for selecting auditors. *Id.* As we discussed above, similar changes relating to the selection of directors appear quite promising. See notes 173–175 *supra,* and accompanying text.

221. We can recall only two instances in which nonmanagement directors announced publicly that they had resigned from a corporate board because of concern about corporate or board activities. One was Arthur J. Goldberg's resignation from the board of TWA because he thought outside directors should be provided with their own staffs and with better access to information about major corporate decisions. Goldberg, *supra* note 43. The other involved Norton Simon's decision to resign from the board of Burlington Northern. The company circulated to its shareholders a statement written by Simon setting out his disagreements with the business strategy Burlington Northern was pursuing. Burlington Northern, Inc., Report on Fourth Annual Meeting (held May 10, 1973). Apparently, Simon also brought his concerns about the accounting practices being used by Burlington Northern to the attention of the enforcement staff of the SEC, which after investigation, brought an enforcement action against the company. See also "Burlington Northern Accepts SEC Order Involving Disclosure," Wall St. J., April 29, 1977, at p. 16, col. 3.

222. This incident is described in considerable detail in Staff of the SEC, *supra* note 61.

223. "The other directors paid little attention to the whole matter, particularly because Odell was 'solving' the problem for them by leaving." *Id.* at p. 170.

224. For details of Penn Central's involvement with Great Southwest Corp., see *id.* at pp. 121–150.

misgivings—though clearly expressed to management and board—were not related to the shareholders until after Penn Central had declared bankruptcy. Our proposed requirement would have discouraged the management from bringing Odell to the point of resignation; or once he resigned, his reasons would have been explained publicly.[225]

Framing the Requirement. A key issue in drafting the proposed disclosure requirement concerning directors' resignations is that registrants should feel compelled to report the factors affecting resignations of directors that are likely to be of legitimate interest to shareholders. The SEC faced a similar issue when it drafted its regulations about registrants' relationships with their auditors. In that case the Commission decided not to require a registrant to disclose the reason for every change of auditors, largely because many changes are made because of disagreements about auditor's fees, and the Commission concluded registrants should not be required to explain their decisions in those situations.[226] Eventually, the SEC decided to require detailed disclosure only if during the two years prior to change of accountants, there had been a disagreement between the registrant and its accountant about a matter which, had the disagreement not been resolved in favor of the accountant, would have resulted in the accountant qualifying his opinion.[227]

The standard adopted by the SEC to define when detailed disclosure is required in the case of a change of accountants has given rise to a number of interpretive problems,[228] yet it probably is more precise than any standard that might be developed to define which reasons for a

---

225. We do not intend to suggest that any of these consequences would have prevented the collapse of the Penn Central, but they might have helped to limit some of the damage done by management's deception, including the almost disastrous impact on financial markets of the company's seemingly sudden collapse. *Id.* at pp. viii–x.

See also the letter of another director, Louis Cabot, to the chairman of Penn Central, *id.* at pp. 164–65 (expresses concern about the relationship between Penn Central's management and board).

226. See Bedingfield and Loeb, "Auditor Changes—An Examination," 137 J. Accountancy 66, 67–68 (1974).

227. SEC Accounting Series Release No. 165, 5 Fed. Sec. L. Rep. (CCH) ¶ 72,187 (Dec. 20, 1974). The Commission proposed to amend its rules to require that the reason for an auditor's resignation be made public in all cases. SEC Securities Act Release No. 5868 [1977–1978 Transfer Binder] Fed. Sec. L. Rep. (CCH) ¶ 81,305 (Sept. 26, 1977), but later withdrew the proposal. SEC Securities Act Release No. 5934, 5 Fed. Sec. L. Rep. (CCH) ¶ 72,269 (May 26, 1978). It suggested that the information be disclosed on a voluntary basis. At the same time it cautioned companies and accountants not to read the requirement narrowly.

228. These problems are discussed in Kay, "Disagreements Under Accounting Series Release No. 165," 142 J. Accountancy 75 (1976) and Weiss, "Disclosure Surrounding a Change in Auditors: Accounting Series Release 165," 45 CPA J. 11 (1975).

director's decision to leave a board are likely to be of interest to shareholders. Consequently, patterning the disclosure requirements here on the approach the SEC has followed with respect to changes of accountants does not appear to be an available course.

A better approach, we believe, would be to require a statement of the reasons why each director has left the board and, if factors involving the operations of the corporation or the organization or activities of its board of directors bore no significant relationship to the director's decision to leave, to require an affirmative statement to that effect. Requiring an explanation of all resignations should not cause any severe problems, as it is difficult to see how anybody would be discomforted by a disclosure that a director resigned "for personal reasons" or "due to the press of other commitments"—the factors that probably motivate most resignations.[229] At the same time, requiring a statement that no factors of a kind likely to be of interest to investors bore a significant relationship to the director's decision should maximize the pressure on registrants to disclose any such factors, since making a false or misleading statement in this regard could give rise to liability under the antifraud provisions of the securities laws.

Thus, if a director resigns because of a dispute over corporate strategy, because of concerns that the board is not receiving adequate information about the corporation, because he disagrees with the system used by the board to evaluate management's performance, because he feels the board tries to involve itself too deeply in the details of managing the corporation's business, or for other comparable reasons, the registrant would include a statement to that effect in its proxy statement. Moreover, to further safeguard the integrity of the process, registrants would be required to provide a director who has left the board with a draft of the statement explaining his action, and either to report that the director does not dispute the statement or to circulate to shareholders a statement prepared by the director setting forth his point of view.

Potential Problems. There are three problems which, we believe, some might suggest will be caused by requiring disclosure about directors'

---

229. These explanations probably could legitimately cover those situations where a director has been fired because he has not made a sufficient contribution to the board. Heidrick and Struggles asked the companies it surveyed if they had ever fired a director and received the following responses:

None ever fired	63.6%
Resignation requested	19.2%
Not renominated	12.5%
Asked not to run again	10.1%
Size of board reduced	2.7%
Other	0.3%

Heidrick & Struggles, Inc., *supra* note 45, at p. 12.

resignations. One is that corporate managements, fearful of what might have to be disclosed, will withhold important information from boards to prevent controversy. Second is that because of concern about these disclosure requirements, competent people will decline to serve on boards. Third, there is the risk that the power given directors will be abused. In our view, none of these concerns has merit.

As we pointed out above, information is the lifeblood of a board's operations. The absence of an adequate flow of information, perhaps more than any other factor, is likely to lead directors to resign.[230] Moreover, to the extent that directors are becoming more concerned about meeting their responsibilities under state corporation laws and the federal securities laws, they are apt to insist on receiving more information from management. Given these factors, we do not give credence to the argument that managements will be able to withhold important information from their boards of directors.

Similarly, we do not believe these disclosure requirements will make it more difficult for registrants to find competent nonmanagement directors. The argument that the supply of directors will dry up is made virtually every time any action is proposed to increase directors' obligations.[231] Curiously, this argument is made in response to a proposal that will not so much increase the responsibilities of outside directors as increase their power. The best answer to it is that people should not accept positions that involve substantial responsibilities to others, such as corporate directorships, unless they are willing to make the effort required to acquit themselves of those responsibilities.[232] Surely we should not endeavor to maintain a system in which the directors are little more than figureheads. A second response, applicable to this situation, is that if this and other changes are made in the institutional framework to provide directors with an opportunity to play a more constructive role, more competent people are likely to demonstrate an interest in becoming directors.[233] Thus, instead of drying up the sup-

---

230. The Corporate Director's Guidebook, *supra* note 51, at 22, mentions only one situation in which a director "in all likelihood should consider resigning." It is when "he believes that adequate information is not being provided . . . and is unsuccessful in his efforts to remedy that situation . . ."

231. See, e.g., Estes, "Outside Directors: More Vulnerable Than Ever," 51 Harv. Bus. Rev., Jan.–Feb. 1973, at 107.

232. See Address by SEC Chairman Ray Garrett, Jr., *supra* note 61.

233. See C. Brown, *supra* note 45, at p. 90:

> [I]t is no doubt true that, if the attractiveness of board membership were enhanced, many highly competent people would seriously consider second careers as professional directors after early retirement from a variety of first career experiences. . . .
>
> The possibility of a second career, involving a release from routine activities, the prospect of living with intellectually exhilarating challenges, and

ply, the proposed change is likely to increase it and to contribute in another, indirect fashion to the revitalization of registrants' boards of directors.

Finally, there is the fear that misguided directors will carry their threat to resign to a point where management must yield or face needless embarrassment. Not every minority director will be as right as Odell. No doubt management could describe instances where outside directors were eased out quietly because of incompetence and where the tale was best left untold. We are convinced that the risk must be incurred, especially since management can counter foolishness with its version of the facts. As with our other recommendations which incur the risk of abuse, we think the potential gain outweighs the costs.

The Commission's New Rule. The Commission initially proposed to require disclosure on Form 8K and in the proxy statement whenever a director resigned or declined to stand for reelection because of a disagreement "on any matter relating to the registrant's operations, policies or practices." The departing director would have the opportunity to put in his own statement, if he acted promptly.

This corresponded closely to our proposal. It limited disclosure to those events where we believe detailed disclosure is necessary, although it would not require the type of disclaiming disclosure we have suggested. The difference is not too great, although there may be liability consequences. That is, if a company fails to file a report of resignation where it is required, because the disagreement was over policy, its silence will make whatever report is filed deficient. It might not cause liability under section 18 of the Securities Exchange Act, however, because of plaintiff's need to establish reliance. Reliance on silence is not easy to prove. Indeed, reliance on a nonreport—the 8K would not even be filed where the registrant claims that the resignation was for personal reasons—would be impossible under section 18. An affirmative statement that is inaccurate would more likely lead to liability, though the difference is inconsequential if liability can be based on rules 10b-5 or 14a-9.[234]

The Commission departed from its proposal in the final release, and weakened the requirement. Its initial view was that disclosure should be triggered by the event, not the affirmative action of the departing director because of the likelihood that social pressures would produce

---

an opportunity to share in constructive leadership, would serve as a powerful magnet to attract experienced and talented people and, in time, enlarge the pool of those eligible for board positions in the future.

234. Whether courts will continue to allow suits under these rules, based on implied private rights of action, an endangered species, for conduct that is subject to liability under § 18, is open to some doubt. See Ernst & Ernst v. Hochfelder, 425 U.S. 185, 211, n.31 (1976); Kulchok v. Government Employees Insurance Co., [1977–1978 Transfer Binder] Fed. Sec. L. Rep. (CCH) ¶ 96,002 (D.D.C. 1977).

silence. Without contradicting its earlier premise, the Commission now requires disclosure only if the departing director initiates it. The Commission noted the opposition of some commentators to the original proposal on grounds that it would cause divisiveness on the board and increase the difficulty of attracting and retaining directors with divergent viewpoints, but the Commission never indicated whether it agreed with those comments. The Commission maintained its position that disclosure of resignations "*would* provide useful information to investors in assessing the quality of management, consistent with the increasing emphasis on the monitoring function of corporate boards." (Emphasis added).[235]

Our judgment is that the Commision's initial proposal was better calculated than the final one to provide the desired information. While the existence of an SEC regulation requiring that the reasons for a director's resignation may increase directors' willingness to ask that resignation statements be filed, it is not likely to reverse the social ethic that now leads most dissident directors to act like old soldiers and just fade away.[236]

Experience with the new rule may prove us wrong, but monitoring the effect of the rule will not be easy. Resignations will not be flagged for the SEC, and determining why directors resigned will involve follow-up by the Commission staff. More likely than not, the rule will do little more than contribute to what Professor Eisenberg calls the "quack-cure problem."[237]

CONCLUSION

We have proposed what we regard as a constructive step towards improving corporate governance and corporate and management accountability. We perceive improved governance and accountability to be widely shared objectives that are essential to the preservation and strengthening of our economic system.

Many forces must contribute to the attainment of these objectives. Voluntary initiatives by corporate management are an important part. So are legal mandates. Amond the instrumentalities of law that must contribute to the solution is the SEC—not to take on the entire problem

---

235. SEC Securities Exchange Act Release No. 34-15384, [1978 Transfer Binder] Fed. Sec. L. Rep. (CCH) ¶ 81,766, at 81,096.

236. See note 221 *supra* and accompanying text. We recognize that at times such subtle changes can be effective, see text accompanying note 210 *supra*, but we do not believe the proposed rule is likely to have a significant impact here, given the strength of the social ethic against which it operates.

237. He uses this term to describe the effect of a rule that purports to deal with a problem and its effectiveness in practice, which lulls shareholders, legislators, and the public into thinking that a problem has been dealt with, but where the solution is an illusion. Eisenberg, *supra* note 47, at 384.

but to operate within its historical sphere of requiring disclosure of information material to stockholders and investors. The SEC is an appropriate agency to involve itself in this process because it has acquired great knowledge about corporate management and accountability through its other activities, and because it enjoys high respect from business and the public. We have limited ourselves to discussing the disclosure function, not because we think it is the whole story, but because we think it is a good place to begin.

Improvement in disclosure has begun. The SEC has scheduled further steps, as outlined in its reports and in speeches by Commissioners. At the same time, it must keep a close eye on what it has already done. The Commission must monitor corporate disclosures and corporate dysfunctions, and try to relate the two.

Harold Williams, chairman of the SEC, has said that we are approaching the middle of a long play entitled "Federal Legislation on Corporate Accountability—subtitle: Federal Regulation of the Corporate Decision-making Process." He sees the business community vigorously resisting federal intervention until it is overwhelmed in the end—a third act of the drama that he seeks to rewrite. We believe a serious and long overdue inquiry into the governance of corporations is now in process. Reform in one shape or another is probably inevitable, although we do not think it will necessarily come into the form of a detailed federal regulatory statute. The fact is, those who are engaged in this process are not just reading the drama, they are writing it, and there is still time for revision. We suggest that by starting with a disclosure approach, strengthened in the manner we have suggested, the final production will look and sound better.

CHAPTER 4

The Impact of the SEC on Corporate Governance

A. A. Sommer, Jr.* *Partner, Wilmer, Cutler & Pickering; Commissioner of the Securities and Exchange Commission, 1973–1976*

While the role of corporations in American society has been an occasion of recurring debate in this country for many years, the debate has quickened again, with perhaps unprecedented intensity, in the last half decade. Many circumstances have renewed this controversy. There is the continuing concern with the accountability of institutions that control so much of the nation's wealth.[1] The consumer and civil rights movements have compelled examination of the extent to which American corporations are inattentive to environmental, safety, equal employment, and other challenges and have created demands for measures to heighten corporate sensitivity to these concerns.[2]

No single incident or group of incidents, however, has done as much to intensify these discussions as the revelations following the 1972

---

* The author gratefully acknowledges the splendid assistance of Abigail Shaine, Fern Fisher, Kent T. Anderson, and Michael T. Wiles, all of whom were summer associates at Jones, Day, Reavis & Pogue.

1. R. Nader, M. Green, and J. Seligman, *Taming the Giant Corporation* (1976).

   Justice Douglas noted in his dissent from the Supreme Court's dismissal of SEC v. Medical Committee for Human Rights, 404 U.S. 403, 409 (1972): "The modern super-corporations, of which Dow is one, wield immense, virtually unchecked power. Some say that they are 'private governments,' whose decisions affect the lives of us all" (footnotes omitted).

2. See Medical Committee for Human Rights v. SEC, 432 F.2d 659 (D.C. Cir.), *cert.granted,*401 U.S. 973 (1970) *appeal dismissed,* 404 U.S. 403 (1972); Natural Resource Defense Council, Inc. *v.* SEC, 389 F. Supp. 689 (D. D.C. 1974), and 432 F. Supp. 1190 (D. D.C. 1977); Note, "Disclosure of Payments to Foreign Government Officials Under the Securities Acts," 89 Harv. L. Rev. 1848, 1863–64 (1976).

presidential election that numerous major American corporations, in what seemed to be clear defiance of the law, contributed to the campaign of a presidential candidate and in some cases had made repeated illegal political contributions in the past,[3] that these payments had often been falsified on the books and records of the corporations;[4] that many corporations had also engaged in other questionable conduct at home and abroad;[5] and that in many instances top management was aware of the misconduct and often masterminded it.[6]

Most of the ventilation of these matters stemmed from the energetic and imaginative work of the enforcement staff of the Securities and Exchange Commission.[7]

Many questions have been asked as a consequence of these disclosures. Among the most probing and basic have been those related to the governance of the American corporation: Is there an inherent structural defect in the corporation that permits such misconduct? Is there need for a reconstruction of the governing structure of the corporation to avoid recurrences of these events? Is there a willingness and ability to reform within the corporate community? Is there a need finally for federal incorporation law?

These events have occasioned congressional hearings and numerous legislative proposals,[8] as well as regulatory initiatives;[9] and the end is not in sight.

---

3. See Securities and Exchange Commission, *Report on Questionable and Illegal Corporate Payments and Practices* (submitted to the Senate Banking, Housing, and Urban Affairs Comm.) (May 12, 1976) exhibits A & B [hereinafter cited as *Report*].

4. See *Hearings on the Activities of American Multinat'l Corps. Abroad Before the Subcomm. on Int'l Econ. Policy of the House Comm. on Int'l Relations*, 94th Cong., 1st Sess. 36–37 (1975) [hereinafter cited as *Hearings*]; *Report, supra* note 3, at 41–42.

5. See *Hearings, supra* note 4, at pp. 36–37; *Report, supra* note 3.

6. See *Report, supra* note 3, at p. 41.

7. See generally *Report, supra* note 3; cases cited notes 71–76, *infra*.

8. In December 1977 Congress adopted and the President signed P.L. 95-213, which directly prohibits United States businesses from, among other things, making any payments, promises of payment, or authorizations of payment of anything of value to any foreign official, political party, candidate for office, or intermediary for the purpose of inducing such individual or party (1) to use his or its influence with a foreign government or instrumentality or (2) to fail to perform his or its official functions, to assist in the obtaining or retaining of business or to influence legislation or regulations. This extremely broad language might in some instances prohibit even so-called facilitating payments (although it would appear that such an interpretation of the bill would be outside the intendment of those who drafted the statute). Willful violations of these prohibitions subject the violator to criminal prosecution and substantial penalties.

Perhaps of prime importance, however, has been the acceleration of tendencies which had been emerging slowly and hesitantly for the Securities and Exchange Commission to move increasingly into matters of corporate governance and corporate structure, notwithstanding an apparently narrow mandate only to fashion and enforce a disclosure system for publicly held American business corporations. The description of this Commission activity—its development and its tendencies—is the purpose of this article.

HISTORICAL BACKGROUND

Historically, the internal governance of private corporations has been the province of state government under our federal system. During the colonial period corporations—then always organized for special, limited, quasi-public purposes—were created by royal grants.[10] When the colonies achieved independence, though no specific constitutional provision reserved to the states the right to create corporations, the states assumed that power.[11] In the early days of the republic, as before, corporations were organized to perform socially needful and significant tasks: to build and operate roads, waterways, railroad, flour mills, and so on.[12] Only in the first third of the nineteenth century did the notion become common that corporations organized for less publicly necessary purposes should be granted privileges accorded earlier corporations.[13] Gradually the powers and attendant privileges of corporations were expanded. While at first the requirement continued that a corporation be organized for specific purposes defined by the legislature which

---

In addition to these prohibitions the legislation requires issuers subject to SEC filing requirements to maintain adequate books and records and systems of internal control sufficient to provide specified assurances.

9. See SEC Exchange Act Release No. 13185 (Jan. 19, 1977), [Current] Fed. Sec. L. Rep. (CCH) ¶ 80,896; SEC Securities Act Release No. 5466 (Mar. 8, 1974), [1974–1975 Transfer Binder] Fed. Sec. L. Rep. (CCH) ¶ 79, 679; Letter from SEC Commissioner R. Hills to Hon. J. E. Moss (May 21, 1976), [1976] Sec. Reg. & L. Rep. (BNA) No. 354 (May 26, 1976); SEC Securities Act Release No. 10673 (Mar. 8, 1974).

10. J. Hurst, *The Legitimacy of the Business Corporation,* pp. 3–7 (1970).

11. See generally A. Berle, Jr., *Historical Inheritance of American Corporations,* p. 189 (1950); Williston, "History of the Law of Business Corporations Before 1800," 2 Harv. L. Rev. 105, 149, 165–66 (1888).

12. J. Hurst, *supra* note 10, at p. 17; R. Nader, M. Green, and J. Seligman, *supra* note 1, at 34; Conard, "An Overview of the Laws of Corporation," 71 Mich. L. Rev. 623, 632–33 (1973)

13. J. Hurst, *supra* note 10, at pp. 18, 21; R. Nader, M. Green, and J. Seligman, *supra* note 1, at p. 34.

granted the charter, later the grant of the charter became less a matter of legislative discretion and more one of ministerial power.[14]

Gradually general laws of incorporation became prevalent in the states.[15] These laws determined, in effect, the basic structure of any corporation which was organized under their provisions. If a group banded together under the umbrella of these laws and followed the ritual prescribed, then certain consequences followed: the shareholders had specified rights and limitations on their liabilities; the directors had specified rights and responsibilities; certain matters that were peculiar to the corporation might be dealt with in the charter or bylaws; and some of the basic relationships within the corporation might be changed by following prescribed procedures. Toward the end of the nineteenth century, the potentials of this approach to corporation law became apparent, and first New Jersey, then Delaware and other states, began the process, often derided,[16] of minimizing the opportunities for shareholders to participate in corporate affairs and maximizing the latitude of management to order them.

During the 1920's, the nation experienced an explosive expansion of corporate activity. While this yielded demonstrable economic benefits and a seemingly high measure of prosperity, the subsequent description of attendant abuses after the 1929 stock market debacle displayed numerous instances of abuse by corporate officials of the power accorded them under state statutes.[17] Federal laws of incorporation or licensing that would succeed or supplement state legislation, which had been proposed time and again since the earliest days of the republic by conservatives and liberals alike, were urged as means of eliminating the abuses unveiled during congressional hearings.[18]

---

14. J. Hurst, *supra* note 10, at pp. 46, 56–57.

15. *Id.*

16. R. Nader, M. Green, and J. Seligman, *supra* note 1, at pp. 51–63; Cary, "Federalism and Corporate Law: Reflections upon Delaware," 83 Yale L.J. 663 (1974); *see* Liggett Co. *v.*Lee, 288 U.S. 517,557–67 (1933) (Brandeis, J., dissenting); Note, "Federal Chartering of Corporations—a Proposal," 61 Geo. L.J. 89 (1975).

17. Senate Committee on Banking and Currency, *Stock Exchange Practices*, S. Rep. No. 1455, 73d Cong., 2d Sess. 55–68 (1933).

18. James Madison twice proposed to the Constitutional Convention that Congress be given power to charter corporations. The Convention defeated his motions in the belief that federal incorporation was unnecessary and would be conducive to the development of monopolies. J. Madison, *Notes of Debates of the Federal Convention* 638 (W. Norton & Co. ed. 1966). Reformers urged federal licensing of corporations as a solution to abuses of power by business trusts in the late 1800's, but Congress passed the federal antitrust laws instead. Watkins, "Federalization of Corporations," 13 Tenn. L. Rev. 89, 92 (1935). Presidents Theodore Roosevelt and Taft each favored federal incorporation, the latter President proposing optional federal incorporation in a special message to Congress on January 7, 1910. Watkins, *supra* at 93. One commentator writes that

Notwithstanding the sorry record played in the hearings and notwithstanding strong urgings, Congress rejected the idea that the federal government should directly legislate rules for the governance and organization of corporations and instead adopted a limited approach designed to introduce larger measures of integrity, not into corporate governance, but rather into the corporate securities distribution and trading processes.

Thus, Congress adopted the Securities Act of 1933,[19] which related principally to the distribution of securities by those who issued them and those who controlled the issuers; and the Securities Exchange Act of 1934,[20] which was a potpourri of restraints on the conduct of insiders and trading markets, mandates for continuous disclosure, and regulation of the proxy-soliciting process used by listed corporations.

The principal thrust of these statutes was disclosure—disclosure which would permit investors to make informed investment decisions and permit shareholders to exercise their rights effectively and intelligently. Congress appeared to eschew the use of disclosure as a regulatory mechanism, that is, the use of disclosure to modify corporate conduct. This is repeatedly affirmed in the legislative history of the Acts.[21]

However, the aphorism underlying the legislation was the familiar one uttered by Brandeis in 1914: "Sunlight is said to be the best of

---

between 1905 and 1909 thirteen bills which authorized federal incorporation or licensing were introduced in Congress. Note, "Federal Chartering of Corporations: Constitutional Challenges," 61 Geo. L.J. 123, 126 (1972). Such proposals surfaced again in the 1930's, most notably in the *Federal Trade Commission Report on Utility Corporations*, S. Doc. No. 92, 73d Cong., 1st Sess. pt. 69-A (1934). That report contains an exhaustive review of the history of federal licensing or chartering proposals. Additional proposals (sponsored primarily by the New York Stock Exchange) surfaced in the Senate hearings, *Stock Exchange Practices: Hearings on S. Res. 84 (72d Cong.) and S. Res. 56 & 57 (73d Cong.) Before the Senate Banking and Currency Committee*, 73d Cong., 2s Sess. 6637, 6583–84, 6678, 6939 (1932). Senators O'Mahoney and Borah continued to introduce federal licensing legislation through the remainder of the 1930's. Reuschlein, "Federalization—Design for Corporate Reform in a National Economy," 91 U. Pa. L. Rev. 91, 106-07 (1942). See generally L. Loss, *Securities Regulation* 107–11 (1961); *Federal Trade Commission Report on Utility Corporations, supra.*

19. 15 U.S.C. §§ 77–77aa (1970).

20. 15 U.S.C. §§.78a–78hh-1 (1970).

21. S. Rep. 792, 73d Cong., 2d Sess. 10 (1934):

> The principal objection against the provisions for corporate reporting is that they constitute a veiled attempt to invest a governmental commission with the power to interfere in the management of corporations. The Committee has no such intention, and feels that the bill furnishes no justification for such an interpretation. To make this point abundantly clear, section 13(d) specifically provides that nothing in the act shall be construed to authorize interference with the management of corporate affairs.

disinfectants; the electric light the most efficient policeman."[22] This statement implies strongly that disclosure was a means of inducing right conduct, of cleansing society of misconduct, of causing would-be miscreants to forego undesirable conduct for fear of exposure.

While the dominant theme in the legislative history of the 1933 and 1934 Acts was indeed disclosure to assist intelligent investment and meaningful participation in the corporate suffrage process, still there may be discerned glimpses of the purposes implied in Brandeis' comment. For instance, the House committee that considered the 1934 Act said in its report:[23]

> The Committee is aware that these requirements are not air-tight and that the unscrupulous insider may still, within the law, use inside information for his own advantage. It is hoped, however, that the publicity features of the bill will tend to bring these practices into disrepute and encourage the voluntary maintenance of proper fiduciary standards by those in control of large corporate enterprises whose securities are registered on the public exchanges.

Great expectations were entertained for "corporate democracy."[24] The belief was strong that if shareholders were given the opportunity to participate meaningfully and with possession of full information in the determination of issues that were required by state law to be presented to them, *e.g.*, election of directors, adoption of plans of merger, and the like, corporate conduct might be molded to a more responsible pattern. Thus, the 1934 Act gave the newborn SEC very broad power to regulate the solicitation of proxies.[25]

In contrast to the approach adopted in the 1933 and 1934 Acts, in 1940 Congress chose to direct in a substantive manner the governance of investment companies, though even here the touch was light and occasional, and there continued to be heavy emphasis on disclosure. The Investment Company Act of 1940[26] established that no more than 60 percent of the board of an investment company could be "affiliated" persons, and it defined with some particularity those who fitted into that category.[27] Similarly, the 1940 Act provided that certain specified

---

22. L. Brandeis, *Other People's Money*, p. 62 (Harper Torchbook ed. 1967).

23. H. R. Rep. No. 1383, 73d Cong., 2d Sess. 13 (1934).

24. See H. R. Rep. No. 1383, 73d Cong. 2d Sess. 5, 13 (1934) ("Fair corporate suffrage is an important right that should attach to every equity security bought on a public exchange.") cf. SEC v. Transamerican Corp., 163 F.2d 511, 518 (3d Cir. 1947) (in enacting the Securities Exchange Act of 1934 "[i]t was the intent of Congress to require fair opportunity for the operation of corporate suffrage."), *cert. denied*, 332 U.S. 847 (1948); J. Hurst, *supra* note 10, at p. 97.

25. 15 U.S.C. § 78n (1970).

26. Investment Company Act of 1940, 15 U.S.C. §§ 80a-1–80a-52 (1970).

27. 15 U.S.C. §§ 80a-10 (1940).

matters had to be approved by shareholders,[28] that indemnification of directors could be made only in specified circumstances,[29] that directors had to conform to certain standards of conduct,[30] and so on. This contrasted sharply with the statutory standards of the 1933 and 1934 Acts, which avoided entirely the temptation to shape the relationships among management, directors, and shareholders and the internal structures of corporations.

In the Public Utility Holding Company Act of 1935,[31] too, Congress touched lightly on the problem of corporate governance by limiting the affiliations of directors (subject to SEC rule-making) and regulating certain other narrow corporate governance matters.[32]

Through most of its history the Commission has heeded the general thrust of the legislative history which led to its creation, and regarded its mandate as one of disclosure for investor and shareholder use, not disclosure for the purpose of altering the conduct of corporate management. True, Schedule A of the 1933 Act[33] required (subject to modification by the Commission) the disclosure of compensation paid certain officers and directors and the details of certain transactions between the corporation and management. It may well be argued that these disclosure requirements would condition and have conditioned management conduct; every lawyer who has represented a publicly held corporation has seen an affiliate transaction aborted because of the necessities of disclosure. Still, these requirements appear to have been designed principally to assist investors and shareholders in making suffrage and investment decisions. Thus, the relative indifference of the Commission to the problems of corporate governance seemingly dictated by the 1933 and 1934 Acts continued relatively unabated until the early 1970's.

THE EMERGENCE OF SEC CONCERN WITH CORPORATE GOVERNANCE

During the first part of the decade the issues of corporate governance and corporate responsibility became a subject of far wider concern, largely under the flogging of public interest representatives.[34] Special-

---

28. 15 U.S.C. §§ 80a-13(a), 80a-15(a) (1970).

29. 15 U.S.C. §§ 80a-17(h) (1970).

30. 15 U.S.C. §§ 80a-35 (1970).

31. Public Utility Holding Company Act of 1935, 15 U.S.C. § 79–79z-6 (1970).

32. 15 U.S.C. § 79g(c) (1970).

33. 15 U.S.C. § 77aa (1970).

34. See M. Mace, *Directors: Myth and Reality* (1971); C. Stone, *Where the Law Ends* (1975); Eisenberg, "Legal Models of Management Structure in the Modern Corporation: Officers, Directors and Accountants" 63 Calif. L. Rev. 375 (1975);

ized publications such as *Business and Society* gave considerable prominence to such issues. The celebrated contretemps of former Justice Arthur Goldberg, in which he, as a TWA board member, insisted upon having a separate staff, fired further discussion of the role of directors and the limitations on their utility.[35] Such events moved the discussion out of academic journals, onto the business pages of the *New York Times* and into the *Wall Street Journal*.

The Commission responded to these forces, and during the early seventies deeper Commission concern with corporate governance became apparent. It has become increasingly clear that the Commission is no longer content with its traditional role of abstention from interference with corporate governance and is restlessly seeking to affect the manner in which corporations are governed, the relationships between their managements and shareholders, the constitution of their boards of directors, and the manner in which the various parts of the corporate community conduct themselves and relate to each other.

The 1933 and 1934 Acts contain few references to directors. This is surprising in view of the fact that prior to 1933 there had been recurring expressions of concern over the manner in which boards were functioning. For instance, in 1926 the Michigan Supreme Court said:[36]

> It is the habit in these days for certain well-to-do men with influence in their respective communities to accept positions on boards of directors of corporations as honorary directors, and then never render any service except to sign on the dotted line, vote as requested by the one in charge and afterwards to cash their directors' checks for attending the meeting. They give no judgment upon questions of business policy, and make no investigation of the real financial condition of the company. It is this kind of service by directors that helps to extract such a tremendous annual toll out of the public who happen to own industrial securities. The law requires a different kind of service of them.

During the course of the hearings in the House and the Senate which led to the 1933 and 1934 Acts, there were repeated references to boards which had failed to perform their duties.[37] In 1933, after the enactment

---

Eisenberg, "The Legal Role of Shareholders and Management in Modern Corporate Decisionmaking," 57 Calif. L. Rev. 1 (1969); Proceedings, The Airlie House Symposium, "An In-Depth Analysis of the Federal and States Roles in Regulating Corporate Management," 31 Bus. Law. 863 (1976); Roth, "Supervision of Corporate Management," 51 N.C.L. Rev. 1369 (1973).

35. "The Goldberg Variation," Newsweek, Oct. 30, 1972, at p. 88; New York Times, Oct. 29, 1972, § 3, at p. 1.

36. Chapple v. Jacobson, 234 Mich. 558, 208 N.W. 754 (1926).

37. Stock Exchange Practices, Letter from Counsel for the Committee on Banking and Currency, pursuant to S. Res. 84, 73d Cong., 1st Sess. 7–35 (1933); Senate Committee on Banking and Currency, *Stock Exchange Practices*, S. Rep. No. 1455, 73d Cong., 2d Sess. 55–68 (1933).

of the 1933 Act but before the enactment of the 1934 Act, then Professor William O. Douglas remarked in an article, *Directors Who Do Not Direct,* that[38]

> A popular theme in recent years has been that "Directors should assume the responsibility of directing and if their manifold activities make real directing impossible, they should be held responsible to the unsuspecting public for their neglect." . . .
>
> In other words, the criticism has been symptomatic of indignation and disapproval of many different abuses and malpractices disclosed in recent years . . . .

This dissatisfaction with directors found explicit expression in the basic statutes only twice: in the 1933 Act directors as such became liable for material omissions and material misstatements in registration statements filed with respect to the distribution of securities unless they could establish that after reasonable investigation they had reason to believe and did believe that the registration statement suffered from no material misstatement or omission;[39] under the 1934 Act directors had a liability to repay profits realized in short-term trading.[40]

All other responsibilities and liabilities of directors found under those Acts have stemmed either from strictures that applied equally to everyone or as a consequence of a director's being deemed a "controlling person."[41] For instance, directors might have liability if they directly participate in a violation of section 12(1) of the 1933 Act[42] or engage in manipulative activity contrary to section 9 of the 1934 Act.[43] Though not explicitly stated in the statutes, it has been generally accepted that in some circumstances directors might have liability as aiders and abettors of the offenses of others,[44] as conspirators,[45] or in

---

38. Douglas, "Directors Who Do Not Direct," 47 Harv. L. Rev. 1305, 1305–06 (1934).

39. Sections 11(a)(2) and 11(b)(3)(A) of the Securities Act of 1933, 15 U.S.C. §§ 77k(a)(2) and 77k(b)(3)(A) (1970).

40. Section 16(b) of the Securities Exchange Act of 1934, 15 U.S.C. § 78p(b) (1970).

41. 15 U.S.C. § 77o (1970); 15 U.S.C. § 78t (1970).

42. 15 U.S.C. § 77*l*(1) (1970).

43. 15 U.S.C. § 78i (1970).

44. 18 U.S.C. § 2 (1970):

> § 2. Principals.
>
> (a) Whoever commits an offense against the United States or aids, abets, counsels, commands, induces or procures its commission, is punishable as a principal.
>
> (b) Whoever willfully caused an act to be done which if directly performed by him or another would be an offense against the United States, is punishable as a principal.

some other secondary role.[46] As mentioned, they might be liable as controlling persons; both the 1933 Act and the 1934 Act contain sections creating liability for controlling persons who could not establish one of the statutorily afforded defenses.[47]

Before the 1970's the only occasion on which the Commission commented as a body upon the application of the securities laws to the responsibility of directors was *In the Matter of Franchard Corporation,*[48] and even then it commented only obliquely. In that administrative proceeding the staff urged the Commission to determine that the respondent's registration statements were deficient because, among other reasons, they failed to disclose that the directors had virtually abdicated their responsibility to the principal officer and shareholder of the company. The Commission said that the issue was "whether the prospectuses were deficient in not disclosing that the directors, in overseeing the operations of the company, failed to exercise the degree of diligence which the Division believes was required of them under the circumstances in the context of the day-to-day operations of the company."[49] Significantly, the charge was not that there had been a violation of the securities laws by the failures of the directors to exercise their responsibilities properly; the assertions of the staff clearly related to deficiencies of disclosure. The Commission concluded, "We find no deficiencies in this area."[50]

In its decision the Commission adopted a conservative (at least by today's standards) stance and emphasized that the directors' respon-

---

See generally Ruder, "Multiple Defendants in Securities Law Fraud Cases: Aiding and Abetting, Conspiracy, In Pari Delecto, Indemnification, and Attribution," 120 U. Pa. L. Rev. 597 (1972).

45. 18 U.S.C. § 371 (1970):

> § 371. Conspiracy to commit offense or to defraud United States.
>
> If two or more persons conspire either to commit any offense against the United States, or to defraud the United States, or any agency thereof in any manner or for any purpose, and one or more of such persons do any act to effect the object of the conspiracy, each shall be fined not more than $10,000 or imprisoned not more than five years, or both.
>
> If, however, the offense, the commission of which is the object of the conspiracy, is a misdemeanor only, the punishment for such conspiracy shall not exceed the maximum punishment provided for such misdemeanor.

See generally Ruder, *supra* note 44.

46. See L. Loss, *Securities Regulation* 1476, 1992 (1961), and cases cited therein.

47. Section 15 of the Securities Act of 1933, 15 U.S.C. § 77o (1970). Section 20 of the Securities Exchange Act of 1934, 15 U.S.C. § 78t (1970).

48. 42 S.E.C. 163 (1964).

49. *Id.* at 175.

50. *Id.* at 176.

sibilities were set by state law. It said, "The [Securities] Act [of 1933] does not purport, however, to define federal standards of directors' responsibility in the ordinary operations of business enterprises and nowhere empowers us to formulate administratively such regulatory standards."[51]

It could be argued, of course, that the staff was not asking for a formulation of regulatory standards but simply a determination that there had been a deficiency of disclosure. The Commission apparently felt that a decision with respect to the sufficiency of disclosure would necessarily have involved them in a substantive determination of matters that lay within the province of state law. The Commission has not, of course, allowed the problems of making such determinations to deter it in its administration of rule 14a-8 pertaining to shareholder proposals.[52]

It is an interesting speculation whether the Commission would today adopt such a sweeping statement of the limitations on its power; at a minimum one might expect that the Commission would suggest that a failure of directors to exercise their responsibilities under the securities laws is an appropriate matter for disclosure. As suggested in the Commission's release with respect to the outside directors of National Student Marketing Corporation,[53] drawing the line between the general responsibilities of directors and their responsibilities under the securities laws is not easy, and the distinction is not one the Commission is now overly fastidious in drawing.

However, consistent with its approach in the *Franchard* case, the Commission has never established an explicit rule with respect to the conduct of directors in any formal fashion. The closest it came to this was an effort, following a speech by Chairman G. Bradford Cook in 1973, to establish guidelines for the conduct of directors in securities matters. In his speech, Chairman Cook said:[54]

> The Commission feels a sense of obligation to the courts, to public investors, to the securities bar and to those persons whose activities may place them within the strictures of the federal securities laws, to enunciate the broad standards these Acts impose. I believe the players have a right to know what the rules of the game are.

---

51. *Id.*

52. 17 C.F.R. § 240.14a-8 (1977). One of the bases upon which management may omit a proposal from its proxy statement (relying often upon an expression of opinion from the staff of the Commission as to the propriety of its so doing) is "if the proposal as submitted is, under the laws of the issuer's domicile, not a proper subject for action by security holders."

53. SEC Exchange Act Release No. 11516, [1975–1976 Transfer Binder] Fed. Sec. L. Rep. (CCH) ¶ 80,219.

54. The Director's Dilemma, Address before the Southern Methodist University School of Business Administration, SEC News Release, April 6, 1973, at p. 4. See [1973] Sec. Reg. & L. Rep. (BNA) No. 197: A-7 (April 11, 1973).

Subsequently Chairman Ray Garrett, Jr., reaffirmed Chairman Cook's commitment to develop guidelines. However, he later acknowledged the difficulty of developing such guidelines and stated the project had been abandoned.[55] During the interim, members of the Chairman's staff had made a diligent effort to develop such guidelines and had even gone so far as to draft proposals. Among the difficulties encountered was the fact that the Commission's authority at its broadest extended only to matters concerning securities transactions. It would have been difficult to articulate guidelines that avoided the charge of Commission intrusion into matters of state law, that meshed appropriately with state requirements, and that provided any guidance superior to that already furnished by general articulations of directors' duties.

Policy by Commissioner Statement ("Jawboning")

Notwithstanding this aborted effort to state an official Commission position on directors' responsibilities in securities matters, individual Commissioners have repeatedly expressed their personal opinions with regard to directors' responsibilities. These, for the most part, have had the mark of consistency. In short, while the Commission itself has not spoken as a body, individual Commissioners have articulated what appear to be the generally accepted conceptions of the Commission with respect to directoral conduct. In the 1973 speech mentioned above, Chairman Cook described the responsibility of directors in securities matters in this way:[56]

> [D]irectors are fiduciaries and have an affirmative responsibility to act fairly and honestly to seek to assure that their corporations do the same. They owe this responsibility not only to their own shareholders but to all public investors who buy, sell or hold their company's securities. . . .
>
> . . . I believe the federal securities laws require that all directors avoid negligence in the performance of their responsibilities. Now I recognize that negligence is a vague enough term which has filled the casebooks with thousands of decisions. But perhaps I can focus a bit more precisely on this. Essentially, a director is negligent if he knows, or should have known, of actions or potential actions that could violate the securities law. The concern here is with the conduct and not whether it actually is known to be a violation of the law. The courts do not require proof that an accused director knew the precise scope of the law. What is required to be shown is that the director knew, or should have known, of conduct which later is held to be in violation of the federal securities laws. . . .

---

55. Corporate Directors and the Federal Securities Laws, Address before the Thirteenth Annual Corporate Counsel Institute, Northwestern University School of Law, SEC News Release, Oct. 3, 1974, at pp. 4–5. See [1974] Sec. Reg. & L. Rep. (BNA) No. 272: A-11 (Oct. 9, 1974). See also A Commission Dilemma, Address before the Conference Board, SEC News Release (May 7, 1974).

56. The Director's Dilemma, *supra* note 54, at pp. 7–8.

. . . All directors have a duty to act on wrongdoing of which they are, or should be, aware—even when they do not carry responsibility for that particular area. As holders of a public trust, directors who learn of any fraudulent conduct must insure that appropriate steps are taken to prevent or rectify violations. This is particularly crucial in the securities field, where most violations and their impacts are long enough enduring. The knowledge or indication of fraudulent corporate actions puts a clear obligation on all directors to insure that corrective action is taken. . . .

. . . When outside directors are asked to vote on critical issues, they should be able to determine whether they have enough information upon which to base an intelligent and informed vote. I do not think the federal securities laws will tolerate outside directors meeting anything less than this burden, completely and fully. Outside directors who choose to gamble by approving action without sufficient basis for doing so may find the cost to be very high. As in all areas of professional responsibility, a great deal of trust must be placed in the integrity and conscientiousness of all those people who assume the position of corporate directors. And the existence of civil liability is a deterrent to a cavalier disregard of these obligations. . . .

. . . Outside directors should resist all attempts to pressure them into approving complex decisions in the absence of adequate time for preparation and full understanding. This includes insisting on ample time to digest and understand vital documents. I recognize that it would be far easier if outside directors could rely upon other members of the board of directors or corporate employees to read and summarize these materials for them, but I believe that a director's basic responsibility requires that he read these materials. Although directors cannot delegate their responsibility to direct, I do believe they should have access to reliable experts who can help them decipher some of the highly technical jargon contained in corporate releases and filings. . . .

In Chairman Cook's remarks the distinction between misconduct under the federal securities laws and misconduct under the general standards relating to director conduct is obscured; much of what he appears to consider violative of the securities laws is simply violation of the director's general duty of care.

During the following four years, Chairman Garrett and other Commissioners addressed these questions on numerous occasions. All of their statements emphasized the high measure of responsibility borne by directors when their corporations engage in securities transactions, and might well be read as stating a general standard of conduct. For instance, Commissioner Loomis said in 1975:[57]

The Congress quite clearly was dissatisfied with the way boards of directors operated in the 20's and imposed responsibilities and liabilities upon

---

57. Director Responsibility—A Government View, Remarks at Loyola College, Baltimore, Md., SEC News Release, April 8, 1975, at p. 14. See [1975] Sec. Reg. & L. Rep. (BNA) No. 298: A-29 (April 16, 1975).

directors as one means of protecting investors and advancing the public interest. Any developments which improve the effectiveness and status of directors should serve that end. While the idea that directors should serve as watchdogs for the stockholders can be, and often is, overdone, nevertheless vigilant and independent directors, functioning effectively, can be an important safeguard.

Similarly, Chairman Garrett on several occasions addressed this problem and stated:[58]

> In determining whether a director has been diligent and conscientious in performing his responsibilities, I think it important to look at such factors as whether he regularly attended board meetings, whether he sought and obtained information from management with respect to important corporate transactions, and carefully considered the information he receives, whether he was an active participant in board meetings and raised questions with the management, as well, of course, as the time he spent in discharging his duties.

Earlier Chairman Garrett had suggested that the Commission's activities with respect to the directors might be seen as an extension of the Commission's historic franchise, but Garrett wept no tears at the prospect:[59]

> It is true that, in order to find authority in ourselves to proceed, and jurisdiction under Rule 10b-5 or cognate provisions of the laws that we administer, there must be a fraudulent or deceptive element or failure of disclosure of material information. It is also true that in some cases the gravamen of the complaint lies in the substantive evil of the conduct involved and not in the failure to disclose this to investors. In this sense, we may be going beyond enforcement of disclosure and engaged in efforts to encourage right conduct among corporate directors. If this is the case, I make no apology for it. Except for specific, limited types of misbehavior, there is no other agency, state or federal, with responsibility or authority over the activities of our publicly-owned corporations, and while plaintiffs and their attorneys in class actions on the whole do more than we do in this area, we think there is need for official federal action.

Similarly, the writer, while a Commissioner of the SEC, stated:[60]

> A skepticism, an alertness to the possibility of wrongdoing on the part of corporate officers, should be the stock in trade of every director. This is not to suggest that there is a need of hostility, that directors cannot wine and

---

58. A Commission Dilemma, *supra* note 55, at p. 22.

59. Corporate Directors and the Federal Securities Laws, *supra* note 55, at pp. 4–5.

60. Directors and the Federal Securities Laws, Address by A. A. Sommer, Jr., before the Colorado Association of Corporate Counsel, Denver, Colo., [1974] Sec. Reg. & L. Rep. (BNA) No. 241: F-1, F-5 (Feb. 1974).

dine with the officers of the corporation, that the good fellowship that characterizes many boards cannot be maintained. But it does mean that if a man assumes a responsibility to the public which a board member does then he must realize that his client, if you will, is not management but the public shareholders and the public market place.

Under the leadership of Chairman Harold M. Williams the members of the Commission have become even more pointed and specific in their comments on corporate governance and corporate accountability. Chairman Williams particularly has, since becoming Chairman, been systematically elaborating his ideas with respect to governance. Initially at Arden House in April 1977,[61] then twice at meetings in San Diego early in 1978,[62] he has outlined his conception of the ideal board: it would consist entirely of independent directors with the exception of the chief executive officer who would not be chairman of the board. Again in San Diego in 1979 he elaborated means he felt would increase the effectiveness of boards;[63] and in between these speeches he has spoken repeatedly on this theme, always emphasizing the necessity for initiative in the private sector if greater governmental intervention is to be avoided.

Chairman Williams has not been alone among presently sitting Commissioners in urging corporate responsibility. He has been joined in this cry by Commissioners Roberta A. Karmel and Philip A. Loomis.[64] Recent pronouncements of the Commissioners have a continuity with past declarations. There has been in these remarks greater specificity than in the past, as, for instance, more comment on the role of audit committees and other mechanisms for effectuating responsible corporate governance.

Policy by Litigation and Settlement

The Commission has not limited itself to words. The greatest impact the Commission has had on corporate conduct and corporate governance has been the byproduct of its use of its powers over the disclosure obligations of corporations.

The potential of disclosure to shape corporate conduct is most clearly seen in the disclosures that have resulted from the Commission's activities with respect to political contributions and sensitive overseas and domestic payments. Throughout the development of these disclo-

---

61. Corporate Ethics, Address by Harold M. Williams, American Assembly, Columbia University (April 16, 1977).

62. [1977] Sec. Reg. & L. Rep. (BNA) No. 437: A-22 (Jan. 25, 1978).

63. *Corporate Accountability: One Year Later,* Sixth Annual Securities Regulation Institute, San Diego, CA. (Jan. 18, 1979).

64. See note 62 *supra,* at A-12.

sures the Commission and its staff have contended that the purpose of the program was simply to inform investors and shareholders,[65] while critics have contended the Commission's activity was an unwarranted and unauthorized extension into areas of substantive law.[66] Regardless of the motives for the Commission's activities, the fact is that these endeavors have unquestionably affected the manner in which American corporations are conducting and governing their affairs.

This has been occurring in several ways. First, the Commission has, in settling litigation involving political contributions and sensitive payments, developed imaginative approaches to remedies.

At one time the Commission typically sought only conventional injunctive relief. However, in recent years it has increasingly tried to expand the remedies sought in an effort to make more meaningful the relief resulting from civil court proceedings, a response perhaps to the criticism that the typical result of its civil proceedings has been only a slap on the wrist. Thus, in some cases the Commission has sought and secured the appointment of a receiver,[67] the rescission of transactions,[68] the disgorgement of ill-gotten gains,[69] and other remedies.

---

65. *Hearings, supra* note 4, at 36 (prepared statement of Commissioner Loomis); see SEC Securities Act Release No. 5466 (Mar. 8, 1974), [1974–1975 Transfer Binder] Fed. Sec. L. Rep. (CCH) ¶ 79,699.

66. See Freeman, "The Legality of the SEC's Management Fraud Program," 31 Bus. Law. 1295 (1976); Note "Disclosure of Payments to Foreign Government Officials Under the Securities Act," 89 Harv. L. Rev. 1848, 1861, 1863, 1969–70 (1976); Note, "Foreign Bribes and the Securities Acts Disclosure Requirements," 74 Mich. L. Rev. 1222, 1241–42 (1976). But see Stevenson, "The SEC and Foreign Bribery," 32 Bus. Law. 53 (1976).

67. Investment Company Act of 1940, § 42(e), 15 U.S.C. § 80a-41(e):

> In any proceeding under this subsection to enforce compliance with section 80a-7 of this title [relating to proscribed transactions], the court as a court of equity may, to the extent it deems necessary or appropriate, take exclusive jurisdiction and possession of the investment company or companies involved and the books, records and assets thereof, wherever located; and the court shall have jurisdiction to appoint a trustee, who with the approval of the court shall have jurisdiction to appoint a trustee, who with the approval of the court shall have power to dispose of any or all of such assets, subject to such terms and conditions as the court may prescribe.

Pursuant to this authority, the Commission has successfully sought the appointment of receivers for investment companies in:

> (1) SEC v. Fifth Ave. Coach Lines, Inc., 289 F. Supp. 3 (S.D.N.Y. 1968), *aff'd* 435 F.2d 510 (2d Cir. 1970).
>
> (2) SEC v. Fiscal Fund, 48 F. Supp. 712 (D. Del. 1943).
>
> (3) SEC v. Keller Corp., 323 F.2d 397 (7th Cir. 1963).

The Court in *Keller* also expressed its belief that the district court possessed inherent power to appoint a receiver, independent of the specific statutory authorization in § 42, upon a showing of violations of the fraud provisions of § 17(a) of the Securities Act, 15 U.S.C. § 77q(a) (1970), and the registration provisions of the Investment Company Act:

> The district court was vested with inherent equitable power to appoint a trustee-receiver under the facts of this case. The prima facie showing of fraud and mismanagement, absent insolvency, is enough to call into play the equitable powers of the court. It is hardly conceivable that the trial court should have permitted those who were enjoined from fraudulent misconduct to continue in control of Keller's affairs for the benefit of those shown to have been defrauded. In such cases the appointment of a trustee-receiver becomes a necessary implementation of injunctive relief."

323 F.2d at 403.

(4) SEC v. S & P Nat'l Corp., 360 F.2d 741 (2d Cir. 1966).

The SEC has also successfully sought appointment or receivers in the absence of explicit statutory authorization in cases of egregious violations of the antifraud provisions of the 1933 and the 1934 Acts.

(1) SEC v. Bowler, 427 F.2d 190 (4th Cir. 1970):
Defendants resist strongly the appointment of a receiver on the ground that the defendant corporations were not insolvent. The short answer is that the authorities cited do not limit the appointment of a receiver to cases where insolvency is shown. Rather, a receiver is permissible and appropriate where necessary to protect the public interest and where it is obvious, as here, that those who have inflicted serious detriment in the past must be ousted.

427 F.2d at 198.

(2) SEC v. Manor Nursing Centers, Inc., 458 F.2d 1082 (2d Cir. 1972):
Once the equity jurisdiction of the district court has been properly invoked by a showing of a securities law violation, the court possesses the necessary power to fashion an appropriate remedy. Thus, while neither the 1933 nor the 1934 Acts specifically authorize the ancillary relief granted in this case, '[i]t is for the federal courts to adjust their remedies so as to grant the necessary relief where federally secured rights are invaded.'

J.I. Case Co. v. Borak, 377 U.S. 426, 433 (1964), 458 F.2d at 1103.

(3) SEC v. Charles Plohn & Co., 433 F.2d 376 (2d Cir. 1970).

68. SEC v. American Agronomics Corp., SEC Litigation Release No. 5667 (N.D. Ohio 1972); SEC v. Rassco Rural & Suburban Settlement Co., SEC Litigation Release No. 4157 (S.D.N.Y. 1969); SEC v. Codition Corp., SEC Litigation Release No., 3799 (S.D.N.Y. 1967).

69. SEC v. Manor Nursing Centers, Inc., 458 F.2d 182 (2d Cir. 1972):

> Clearly the provision requiring the disgorging of proceeds received in connection with the Manor offering was a proper exercise of the district court's equity powers. The effective enforcement of the federal securities

In recent years, the most noteworthy use of novel remedies has been in the area of corporate governance and accountability. This practice commenced prior to 1973[70] (the first emergence of the problem of political and sensitive payments), but has flourished most fully in the context of those problems.

Historically most of the Commission's cases have been concluded with settlements, for which it has been criticized. As a consequence, it is unclear whether a court, in the context of a contested case, would conclude that it could or should grant the sort of relief which the Commission has repeatedly secured through settlements. In at least one injunctive case, in which the Commission sought an ouster of the chief executive officer of a real estate investment trust, the District Court for the Eastern District of Virginia rebuffed the Commission and said:[71]

> The relief asked for by the SEC would require the Court to replace the Chief Executive of ART and appoint new trustees without providing the protection of continuous supervision of this Court. Even if the power existed, it would seem unwise under these facts to replace an incumbent President, appoint additional trustees to serve on the Board, and oversee the operation of the Trust. Such expansive authority should not be exercised except in the most extreme cases.
>
> The relief sought here by the SEC, the appointment of trustees and removal of the President, infringe on activities traditionally controlled by the states.

> laws requires that the SEC be able to make violations unprofitable. The deterrent effect of an SEC enforcement action would be greatly undermined if securities law violators were not required to disgorge illicit profits.

(The court of appeals remanded the case for a proper determination of the amount defendants were required to refund, holding defendants were not required to refund profits made while utilizing the proceeds of fraudulent action.) SEC v. Golconda Mining Co., [1969–1970 Transfer Binder] Fed. Sec. L. Rep. (CCH) ¶ 92,504 (S.D.N.Y. Oct. 30, 1969); SEC v. Shapiro, 494 F.2d 1301 (2d Cir. 1974); SEC v. VTR, Inc., SEC Litigation Release No. 3311 (S.D.N.Y. 1965), [1964–1966 Transfer Binder] Fed. Sec. L. Rep. (CCH) ¶ 91,618; SEC v. Skogit Valley Telephone Co., SEC Litigation Release Nos. 3390, 3393, & 3482 (W.D. Wash. 1965–66); SEC v. Parvin Dohrmann Co., SEC Litigation Release No. 4848 (S.D.N.Y. 1970); SEC v. Frigitemp Corp., No. 73-596 (D.D.C. March 28, 1973).

70. SEC v. VTR, Inc., SEC Litigation Release No. 3311 (S.D.N.Y. 1965):

> In lieu of appointing a receiver, the court directed the controlling group to cause the election of four independent directors [of a five-man board] designated by the court to supervise the filing of proper annual reports and proxy statements with the Commission and to supervise a determination of the exact amount misappropriated.

32 SEC Ann. Rep. 116–17 [1966]; SEC v. Tilco, Inc., [1971–1972 Transfer Binder] Fed. Sec. L. Rep. (CCH) ¶ 93,240 (D.D.C. 1971).

71. SEC v. American Realty Trust, 429 F. Supp. 1148, 1177–78 (E.D. Va. 1977), *rev'd on other grounds*, [1978 Transfer Binder] Fed. Sec. L. Rep. (CCH) ¶ 96,605 (4th Cir. 1978).

The federal securities laws are at best a limited federal corporate law and the SEC and federal courts are "bound to respect the limits which are inherent in a statutory scheme aimed at ensuring disclosure in the sale of securities and not the substantive regulation of business itself." *Equitable Remedies in SEC Actions,* 123 U. Pa. L. Rev., 1188, 1216 (1976). Except in the most egregious cases, courts should not interfere with corporate democracy. Those circumstances are not present in the instant action.

The Court of Appeals for the Fourth Circuit reversed the District Court and remanded the matter for further proceedings.[72] While it is not explicit, presumably the Court of Appeals intended for the District Court to reconsider the remedies in the light of the reversal.

It is through the medium of settlements of these proceedings that the Commission has made its most motable inroads into corporate governance and accountability. And it is the implications of these settlements that will endure and influence corporations long after the issues of political and sensitive payments have ceased to claim newspaper space.

Basically the Commission's settlements involving governance and accountability may be grouped in this way:

(1) settlements which require the appointment of additional outside directors;[73]

(2) settlements in which specific responsibilities, sometimes of an ad hoc nature, sometimes of a continuing nature, are imposed on an existing board;[74]

(3) settlements which require the appointment of an audit and/or other committee given special responsibilities;[75]

---

72. [1978 Transfer Binder] Fed. Sec. L. Rep. (CCH) ¶ 96,605 (4th Cir. 1978).

73. SEC v. Canadian Javelin, SEC Litigation Release No. 6441 (S.D.N.Y. 1974), 4 SEC Docket No. 17, at 620 (June 30, 1974); SEC v. Mattel, Inc., SEC Litigation Release Nos. 6531 & 6532 (D.D.C. 1974), 5 SEC Docket No. 8, at 241 (Oct. 16, 1974).

74. SEC v. Emersons Ltd., SEC Litigation Release No. 7392 (D.D.C. 1976), 9 SEC Docket No. 12, at 667 (May 25, 1976); SEC v. Foremost-McKesson, Inc., SEC Litigation Release No. 7479 (D.D.C. 1976), 9 SEC Docket No. 20, at 1074 (July 21, 1976); SEC v. Brad Ragan, Inc., SEC Litigation Release No. 7681 (W.D.N.C. 1976), 11 SEC Docket No. 1, at 1113 (Dec. 14, 1976); SEC v. General Telephone and Electronics Corp., SEC Litigation Release No. 7760 (D.D.C. 1977), 11 SEC Docket No. 16, at 1662 (Feb. 15, 1977).

75. SEC v. Canadian Javelin, SEC Litigation Release No. 6441 (S.D.N.Y. 1974), 4 SEC Docket No. 17, at 620 (June 30, 1974); SEC v. Mattel, Inc., SEC Litigation Release Nos. 6531 & 6532 (D.D.C. 1974), 5 SEC Docket No. 8, at 241 (Oct. 16, 1974); SEC v. American Ship Building Co., SEC Litigation Release No. 6534 (D.D.C. 1974), 5 SEC Docket No. 8, at 242 (Oct. 16, 1974); SEC v. Minnesota Mining & Mfg. Co., SEC Litigation Release No. 6711 (D. Minn. 1975), 6 SEC Docket No. 6, at 272 (Feb. 18, 1975); SEC v. Gulf Oil Corp., SEC Litigation Release No. 6780 (D.D.C. 1975), 6 SEC Docket No. 11, at 465 (March 25, 1975);

(4) settlements which require the appointment of a special counsel to conduct an investigation into certain practices;[76] and

(5) the appointment of a special auditor to assist in the work of special counsel.[77]

A review of these cases indicates that some settlements have combined different components. For example, the *Canadian Javelin* settlement provided that 40 percent of its directors be outside, independent directors approved by the Commission; that an outside counsel approved by the SEC be named to take responsibility for reviewing the dissemination of all information to the public and for securing compliance with securities laws by Javelin; that Javelin designate a public-information officer; and that Javelin establish a standing committee a majority of which would be independent outside directors. The settlement further stipulated that the special outside counsel could not be

---

SEC v. Missouri Public Service Co., SEC Litigation Release No. 7299 (W.D. Mo. 1976), 9 SEC Docket No. 2, at 9117 (March 16, 1976); SEC v. General Tire & Rubber Co., SEC Litigation Release No. 7386 (D.D.C. 1976), 9 SEC Docket No. 12, at 667 (May 25, 1976); SEC v. Firestone Tire & Rubber Co., SEC Litigation Release No. 7443 (D.D.C. 1976), 9 SEC Docket No. 17, at 920 (May 30, 1976); SEC v. Chicago Milwaukee Corp., SEC Litigation Release No. 7472 (D.D.C. 1976), 9 SEC Docket No. 19, at 1008 (July 19, 1976); SEC v. J. Ray McDermott & Co., SEC Litigation Release No. 7603 (D.D.C. 1976), 10 SEC Docket No. 13, at 687 (Oct. 19, 1976); SEC v. Diversified Industries, Inc., SEC Litigation Release No. 7650 (D.D.C. 1976), 10 SEC Docket No. 19, at 980 (Oct. 30, 1976); SEC v. Brad Ragan, Inc., SEC Litigation Release No. 7681 (W.D.N.C. 1976), 11 SEC Docket No. 1, at 1113 (Dec. 14, 1976); SEC v. Uniroyal Inc., SEC Litigation Release No. 7759 (D.D.C. 1977), 11 SEC Docket No. 9, at 1581 (Feb. 8, 1977); SEC v. General Telephone & Electronics Corp., SEC Litigation Release No. 7760 (D.D.C. 1977), 11 SEC Docket No. 10, at 1662 (Feb. 15, 1977); SEC v. Anheuser-Busch, Inc., SEC Litigation Release No. 7930 (D.D.C. 1977), 12 SEC Docket No. 6, at 502 (June 7, 1977).

76. SEC v. Canadian Javelin, SEC Litigation Release No. 6441 (S.D.N.Y. 1974), 4 SEC Docket No. 17, at 620 (June 30, 1974); SEC v. Mattel, Inc., SEC Litigation Release Nos. 6531 & 6532 (D.D.C. 1974), 5 SEC Docket No. 8, at 241 (Oct. 16, 1974); SEC v. General Tire & Rubber Co., SEC Litigation Release No. 7386 (D.D.C. 1974), 9 SEC Docket No. 12, at 664 (May 25, 1976); SEC v. Emersons Ltd., SEC Litigation Release No. 7392 (D.D.C. 1976), 9 SEC Docket No. 12, at 667 (May 25, 1976); SEC v. Brad Ragan, Inc., SEC Litigation Release No. 7681 (W.D.N.C. 1976), 11 SEC Docket No. 1, at 1113 (Dec. 14, 1976); SEC v. Ormand Inds., Inc., SEC Litigation Release No. 7910 (D.D.C. 1977), 12 SEC Docket No. 4, at 415 (May 29, 1977).

77. SEC v. Mattel, Inc., SEC Litigation Release Nos. 6531 & 6532 (D.D.C. 1974), 5 SEC Docket No. 8, at 241, 242 (Oct. 16, 1974); SEC v. Brad Ragan, Inc., SEC Litigation Release No. 7681 (W.D.N.C. 1976), 11 SEC Docket No. 1, at 1113 (Dec. 14, 1976).

removed without prior notification of the Commission.[78] In another case, after the Commission was informed that Mattel, Inc. filed financial statements which overstated its profits and understated its costs, a settlement was reached which stipulated that the majority of Mattel's board of directors would be SEC- and court-approved unaffiliated directors, that the new unaffiliated directors could appoint a special counsel, and that the special counsel could appoint a special auditor to be approved by Mattel, the Commission, and the court in order to audit the financial statements of Mattel.[79] Emersons Ltd.'s difficulties with false financial statements and illegal payments from liquor, wine, and beer producers resulted in the requirement that Emersons appoint three approved independent directors and additional independent directors as replacements for any present board members who cease to serve as directors until independent directors constitute a majority of Emersons' board of directors.[80] This particular part of the settlement may be distinguished from the *Mattel* settlement in that the number of independent directors would increase gradually.[81] The *Emersons* settlement also provided for the appointment of a special counsel and a special committee comprised of the independent directors, who would review financial reporting, releases, and communications to the public, accounting policies, and the selection of auditors.[82]

Other SEC settlements have affected corporate governance and conduct in a variety of ways. In the *Foremost-McKesson* settlement the SEC required only that the existing board assume some additional responsibilities. These responsibilities included the completion of an investigation into various matters, the submission of a written report, and the maintenance by the board of a policy prohibiting any cash payment or rendering of merchandise in violation of laws or regulations, or the payment of anything of value which is material in nature, directly or indirectly to any foreign governmental official or entity.[83] The General Tire and Rubber Company was required to establish a special review

---

78. SEC v. Canadian Javelin, SEC Litigation Release No. 6441 (S.D.N.Y. 1974), 4 SEC Docket No. 17, at 620 (June 30, 1974).

79. SEC v. Mattel, Inc., SEC Litigation Release Nos. 6531 & 6532 (D.D.C. 1974), 5 SEC Docket No. 8, at 241 (Oct. 16, 1974).

80. SEC v. Emersons Ltd., SEC Litigation Release No. 7392 (D.D.C. 1976), 9 SEC Docket No. 12, at 667 (May 25, 1976).

81. Compare SEC v. Emersons Ltd., SEC Litigation Release No. 7392 (D.D.C. 1976), 9 SEC Docket No. 12, at 668 (May 25, 1976) with SEC v. Mattel, Inc., SEC Litigation Release Nos. 6531 & 6532 (D.D.C. 1974), 5 SEC Docket No. 8, at 241 (Oct. 16, 1974).

82. SEC v. Emersons Ltd., SEC Litigation Release No. 7392 (D.D.C. 1976), 9 SEC Docket No. 12, at 668 (May 25, 1976).

83. SEC v. Foremost-McKesson, Inc., SEC Litigation Release No. 7479 (D.D.C. 1976), 9 SEC Docket No. 20, at 1074 (July 21, 1976).

committee to conduct an extensive investigation with the help of a special counsel.[84] Again in the *Missouri Public Service Company* settlement, a special review committee was required to investigate unlawful contributions.[85] The major requirement in the *Anheuser-Busch, Inc.*, settlement was the appointment of a review person by the company's auditing committee, with the approval of the Commission, to review the adequacy of the auditing committee's investigation and the disclosure based thereon.[86] The *GTE* settlement stipulated that GTE's board of directors would adhere to guidelines adopted by GTE with respect to payments by GTE to any official or employee of any private customer or government or to any official or employee of any entity owned or controlled by any government when those payments are unlawful under the laws of the United States or such foreign country. Any change in the guidelines must be filed with the Commission.[87]

In a settlement[88] little noticed until Chairman Harold Williams referred to it in his testimony before the Senate Subcommittee on Reports, Accounting and Management in June 1977, the Commission caused the court to set forth with particularity its notions of what the duties of an audit committee should be. While the settlement, of course, is binding only upon the defendants, it does provide significant insights into the Commission's conception of audit committees' duties in general. The court order referred to three "special duties" of the audit committee:[89]

(1) Review the engagement of the independent auditors, including their compensation, the scope and extent of their review of the company's financial statement, and the audit procedures they will utilize;

(2) Review with the company's independent accountants and chief financial officer (as well as other appropriate personnel) the general policies and procedures used by the company with respect to internal auditing, accounting, and financial controls;

(3) Review releases by the company to the media, shareholders, and the public which concern financial matters.

Under each of these three areas the order specifies with considerable

---

84. SEC v. General Tire & Rubber Co., SEC Litigation Release No. 7386 (D.D.C. 1974), 9 SEC Docket No. 12, at 664 (May 25, 1976).

85. SEC v. Missouri Public Service Co., SEC Litigation Release No. 7299 (W.D. Mo. 1976), 9 SEC Docket No. 2, at 114 (March 16, 1976).

86. SEC v. Anheuser-Busch, Inc., SEC Litigation Release No. 7930 (D.D.C. 1977), 12 SEC Docket No. 6, at 502 (June 7, 1977).

87. SEC v. General Telephone and Electronics Corp., SEC Litigation Release No. 7760 (D.D.C. 1977), 11 SEC Docket No. 10, at 1662 (Feb. 15, 1977).

88. SEC v. Killearn Properties, Inc., [1977] Sec. Reg. & L. Rep. (BNA) No. 421: D-2, 3 (Sept. 28, 1977).

89. *Id.*

particularity the actions which the audit committee must take in carrying out its responsibilities.[90]

The above is by no means a complete delineation of the cases in which the Commission in negotiating settlements has secured relief which has affected the structure of corporate governance and the manner in which authority is exercised within the corporation; a member of the Commission staff has informally stated to the writer that he counts some sixty cases in which the settlements have affected corporate governance. These cases and others not discussed display a remarkable variety of judicially mandated techniques and practices to deal with corporate wrongdoing through modifications of corporate practices and structures. These judicial orders and others similar to them, of course, constitute direct intervention in corporate structure and corporate governance. The orders are binding upon the corporations under penalty of contempt of court and appear to be binding in perpetuity. Thus, in effect, the charters of these affected corporations are amended and the requirements of state corporation laws, which generally require only that a corporation have a board of directors and do not specify any particulars (e.g., the number of inside versus outside directors) other than the minimum number of directors, are significantly and permanently supplemented by federal court decree.

The decrees in these cases obviously are only binding on the parties to the case; nonetheless the emergence of these patterns in numerous cases has drawn considerable attention to the various role players in the corporate process. While it is difficult to trace such corporate reforms as the introduction of larger numbers of outside directors, the institution of audit committees, and the like directly to these settlements, the publicity accorded such settlements has certainly in some measure conditioned the minds of corporate leaders to accept these trends and to enhance them. This is evident in many of the discussions of these problems which frequently allude to the settlements.[91]

Policy by Coaxing

A second, perhaps even more far-reaching example, of the manner in which corporate conduct has been conditioned by the disclosures arising out of Watergate is found in the Commission's so-called voluntary disclosure program.

---

90. The *Killearn* settlement appeared to provide the pattern for the Commission's delineation of its conception of an audit committee's responsibilities contained in its corporate governance proposals. This delineation was eliminated from the disclosure requirements finally adopted. See text accompanying notes 113–117 *infra*.

91. See Comment, "Court Appointed Directors," 64 Geo. L.J. 737 (1976); see generally "Northrop's Punishment for Campaign Giving," Bus. Week, Feb. 24, 1975, at p. 60.

On July 17, 1975, the Commission, speaking through Commissioner Philip A. Loomis, Jr., who testified before the Subcommittee on International Economic Policy of the House of Representatives International Relations Committee, proposed that corporations which suspected that they might have engaged in questionable conduct undertake an internal investigation and then publicly report the results of it.[92] Commissioner Loomis stated:[93]

> With respect to past activities, we propose to publish a summary of the cases which we have already brought, together with a description of other situations of a similar nature which have come to our attention, and accompany this by a suggestion that other companies who, upon reviewing their own affairs, conclude that they may have a similar problem might proceed somewhat as follows:
>
> First, make a careful investigation of the facts, similar, I might add, to those that have been made by the companies we have had the problem with, under the auspices of persons not involved in the activities in question, such as their independent directors.
>
> If this investigation discloses that a problem does in fact exist, the board of directors of the company should consider in consultation with their professional advisers what types of disclosures seem to be called for.
>
> Such companies would probably find it advisable to discuss the matter with our staff prior to filing any documents with us. Companies often do that where they have a somewhat novel problem.
>
> In order to consider the adequacy of the proposed disclosure, our staff would need to be fully informed as to the facts.
>
> While our enforcement activity in this area will continue, we are going forward, the foregoing procedures could lessen the need for enforcement action in particular cases, especially where the Commission is informed in advance that a company which is not now under investigation proposed to proceed in this manner.

How many corporations have satisfied all the conditions of the voluntary program is uncertain, but at the date of this writing about four hundred corporations have made public disclosure of questionable or illegal activity at home or abroad.

The Commission has never adopted any rules incorporating the voluntary disclosure program. The only official elaboration has been in the Commission's May 12, 1976, report to the Senate Banking, Housing and Urban Affairs Committee and in statements by Commissioners and staff.[94]

To qualify for the uncertain benefits of the voluntary disclosure

---

92. *Hearings, supra* note 4, at pp. 63–64.

93. *Id.*

94. *Report, supra* note 3, at 6–13.

program (these were asserted to be a reduction in the likelihood of a Commission proceeding against the errant corporation and its officers)[95] a corporation, as noted, would have to undertake to cease the practices described.

No one has suggested that the Commission has the power to proscribe these activities, although it has often negotiated settlements that included undertakings and injunctions that prohibited substantive misconduct as well as the failure to disclose it.[96] But by holding out the conditional promise of immunity from Commission proceedings, the Commission has succeeded in causing innumerable companies to undertake to desist from courses of conduct some of which at least were not clearly illegal.

By its failure to articulate standards for disclosure concerning sensitive payments and related matters (except to the extent that standards may be said to be stated in its May 12, 1976, report), the Commission has created in the corporate community and among corporate advisors profound uncertainty concerning the kinds of conduct that are subject to the SEC reporting requirements.[97] Partly as a consequence of this uncertainty, a very large proportion of the publicly held companies in the United States (and there are some ten thousand subject to the 1934 Act reporting requirements) have engaged in some internal soul-searching, and many of those which have not made disclosures have nonetheless determined to forego the types of conduct that have been the subject of suits brought by the Commission, if for no other reason than to create equities which might forestall an injunction in the event the SEC discovered the nondisclosure and brought an action. (While much is made of the number of companies that have made disclosures, it should not be overlooked that there are over nine thousand companies reporting to the Commission that have not made any disclosures.) And it is not unlikely, though it may not be acknowledged, that the increased presence of outsiders on boards of directors and the organization of audit committees have often flowed from these behavioral decisions.

The impact of these disclosures upon the behavior of corporate America would appear to exceed by far the impact on investors. Most studies that have been done (though none claim to be conclusive or of definitive depth) would indicate that disclosures of improper activity abroad or at home have not had a lasting effect on either the prices or

---

95. *Id.* at p. 8 n.7.

96. E.g., SEC v. Northrop Corp., No. 75-0536 (D.D.C., filed April 18, 1975); SEC v. Phillips Petroleum Co., No. 75-0308 (D.D.C. Mar. 6, 1975).

97. Lowenfels, "Questionable Corporate Payments and the Federal Securities Laws," 51 N.Y.U. L. Rev. 23 (1976); Note, "Disclosure of Corporate Payments and Practices: Conduct Regulation Through the Federal Securities Laws," 43 Brooklyn L. Rev. 681 (1977).

volume of trading of a company's securities.[98] Anecdotal evidence of the relative indifference of shareholders to confessions of corporate misconduct is common: at the first United Brands stockholder meeting following the tragic suicide of Eli Black and the disclosure of United Brands' bribes in a Central American country to forestall a substantial levy on bananas, shareholders present were far more interested in conventional matters—earnings prospects, for instance—than in the relatively recent scandal involving their company.[99] Similarly, shareholders at other meetings have shown little concern with the morality of their officers. At Northrop Corporation, the governing structure of which was substantially reorganized as a consequence of shareholder litigation, the restructured board, including a majority of outsiders agreeable to the plaintiff in the action, restored the principal author of the corporation's misconduct to all of his offices because they concluded his talents were essentially irreplaceable.[100]

Ephemeral as the consequences of the disclosures may be to investors and shareholders, the consequences in the structure and governance of these corporations, both those making disclosures and those not, remain and bid fair to become a permanent part of the corporate landscape.

Policy by Statutory Transference

Another subtle source of influence on corporate governance derives from the Investment Company Act of 1940.[101] As remarked above, this Act more than any other statute administered by the Commission addresses questions of corporate governance explicitly. It may be suggested that in some measure the attitude of the Commission and the staff with regard to such matters in general is determined by concepts of directoral responsibility which have developed under the 1940 Act. Less as a consequence of Commission activity than of private litigation, the responsibilities of investment company directors under the 1940 Act have been increasingly delineated. While most of the cases involve situations that are unique to investment companies—transfer of investment-advisor contracts, the desirability of using different arrangements for executing securities transactions, the fairness of man-

---

98. See Note, "Disclosure of Payments to Foreign Government Officials Under the Securities Acts," 89 Harv. L. Rev. 1848, 1855 n.45 (1976); Griffin, "Disclosure Policy and the Securities Markets: The Impact of the 1975–76 Sensitive Payment Disclosure" (submitted to the SEC Advisory Committee on Corporate Disclosure) (Dec. 1976).

99. New York Times, August 19, 1974, at pp. 45, 51.

100. Wall Street Journal, Jan. 17, 1975, at p. 1; *Id.* Jan. 18, 1975, at p. 14.

101. Investment Company Act of 1940, 15 U.S.C. §§ 80a-1–80a-52 (1970).

agement fees—the courts have nonetheless been steadily stating principles that may have a much broader relevance.[102]

The evolution of concepts originating in the 1940 Act into concepts broadly applicable to corporations in general is, of course, difficult to document; as a matter of fact, in its *Tannenbaum* brief the Commission explicitly disavowed any intent to state standards that had applicability beyond the 1940 Act.[103] However, discussions with staff members and examination of evolving attitudes indicate that the standards stated in that brief, as an example, indeed bear close similarity to the Commission's and the staff's convictions concerning the responsibility of all outside directors:[104]

> Specifically, the decision of the board of directors of this investment company—to forego capture of excess brokerable commissions—should be dispositive *if* this Court satisfies itself that—
>
> (1) in so deciding, the independent directors were truly independent of domination by or undue influence of the advisor;
>
> (2) the independent directors were completely informed, and fully aware, of the available alternative; and
>
> (3) the decision reached was a reasonable business judgment made after a thorough review of all relevant factors by the independent members of the board.

While the footnote following this portion of the brief disavows any intention to apply these standards to non-investment-company directors, it is nonetheless difficult to derive these standards solely from the 1940 Act. They resemble closely statements made by Commission and staff members concerning their conceptions of the responsibilities of all directors, especially outside directors, under the securities laws in general.[105]

In *Lasker v. Burks*[106] the Court of Appeals for the Second Circuit, reversing the District Court, refused to dismiss a derivative action brought by shareholders of an investment company against its investment adviser and others on the basis of the defendants' assertion that the "disinterested" directors had, in the exercise of business judgment, determined the maintenance of the suit was adverse to the interests of the investment company. The Court expressly stated its decision was

---

102. See, e.g., Moses v. Burgin, 445 F.2d 369 (1st Cir. 1971); Tannenbaum v. Zeller, 399 F. Supp. 945 (S.D.N.Y. 1975); Fogel v. Chestnutt, 533 F.2d 731 (2d Cir. 1975); Papilsky v. Berndt, 466 F.2d 251 (2d Cir.), *cert. denied*, 409 U.S. 1077 (1972); Rosenfeld v. Black, 445 F.2d 1337 (2d Cir. 1971).

103. Brief of the Securities and Exchange Commission (*amicus curiae*) at 20 n.24. Tannenbaum v. Zeller, 399 F. Supp. 945 (S.D.N.Y. 1975).

104. *Id.* at 20.

105. See generally, The Director's Dilemma, *supra* note 54; A Commission Dilemma, *supra* note 55.

106. [1977–1978 Transfer Binder] Fed. Sec. L. Rep. (CCH) ¶ 96,282 (2d Cir. 1978).

strictly within the context of the Investment Company Act and should not be construed as indicative of the position it would take in a case involving a non–investment-company entity. The Supreme Court has granted the petition for certiorari.[107] Not withstanding the Court of Appeals' effort to limit applicability of its opinion to investment companies, the Supreme Court may well speak to the broader question.[108]

Policy by Rule-Making—Direct and Indirect

The Commission has moved cautiously toward the imposition-by-rule of substantive standards in the area of corporate governance. Two examples of this have been the release proposing rules in connection with "going private" transactions and the release announcing hearings on changes in the proxy rules.

In its initial release with respect to going private,[109] the Commission proposed alternative rules. Both of these proposed rules, in addition to requiring extensive disclosure (no one appears to dispute that the Commission has power to compel disclosure under section 13(e) of the 1934 Act), contained substantive provisions: e.g., a requirement that a "fair price" be determined in a specified way; provisions similar to those contained in section 14(d) of the 1934 Act pertaining to third-party tender offers with respect to withdrawal of deposited shares; requirement of a "take out" period for shareholders who did not accept the offer; and a requirement that there be a valid business purpose for the transaction. In addition to these proposals, the Commission asked specifically for comment on other substantive questions such as a possible requirement that controlling interests vote their shares in proportion to the votes of other shareholders or perhaps with the majority.[110]

---

107. 47 U.S.L.W. 3077 (U.S. Aug. 15, 1978) (No. 77-1724). (Editor's note: The Supreme Court reversed and remanded, holding that state law is determinative of the scope of independent directors' authority to the extent consistent with the Investment Company Act, and that that Act does not absolutely prohibit director termination of nonfrivolous actions. 99 S. Ct. 1831 (1979).

108. In other cases not involving investment companies, courts have dismissed shareholders' suits on the basis of determinations by "independent directors" that the claims should not be pursued. See Abbey v. Control Data Corp., 460 F. Supp. 1242 (D. Minn. 1978); Gall v. Exxon Corp., 418 F. Supp. 508 (S.D.N.Y. 1976); cf. Maldonado v. Flynn, [1979] Sec. Reg. & L. Rep. (BNA) No. 497: I-1 (2d Cir., April 4, 1979) (recognizes validity of disinterested directors' amendment of stock option plan).

109. SEC Securities Act Release No. 5567 (Feb. 6, 1975), 6 SEC Docket No. 7, at 250 (Feb. 25, 1975).

110. The argument of those who assert that the Commission was not given power to regulate substantive matters under section 13(e) is well stated in the comment of the Committee on Federal Regulation of Securities, ABA Section of Corporation, Banking, and Business Law (submitted in response to the proposed rule making) (July 18, 1975).

On November 17, 1977, the Commission published for comment revised proposed rules concerning going-private transactions. While the revised rules depart in many ways from the earlier proposals, they would most significantly require that the transaction be fair, and would specify procedures and indicia which would tend to assure fairness.[111]

In 1977, again purporting to use its powers over disclosure, the Commission issued two releases announcing proceedings looking toward the amendment of the proxy rules. The releases suggested several areas for consideration; many of these bore in one measure or another upon questions of corporate governance. For instance, the Commission solicited comment on whether shareholders should have access to management's proxy-soliciting material for the purpose of making nominations for election to the board of directors; whether in conflict situations affiliates or other persons should be required to vote their shares in accordance with the majority or in proportion to the votes of the shareholders not having a conflict; whether the Commission should recommend legislation providing for federal incorporation or federally established minimum standards for officers' and directors' conduct; whether institutions should be required before voting shares they hold to solicit the views of persons having an economic interest in the shares.[112]

In a similar vein the Commission's Advisory Committee on Corporate Disclosure recommended that[113]

> The Commission should develop a package of disclosure requirements that, taken as a whole, will strengthen the ability of boards of directors to operate as independent, effective monitors of management performance and that will provide investors with a reasonable understanding of the organization and role of the board of any given issuer.

In some measure in response to the recommendation of the Advisory Committee (Chairman Williams, prior to his appointment to the Commission, was a member of the Advisory Committee and of the Subcommittee of that group concerned with disclosure and corporate governance), the Commission held hearings in four cities and received extensive testimony and written submissions on corporate governance matters.[114] After the hearings the Commission proposed a series of

111. SEC Securities Act Release No. 5884, [Current] Fed. Sec. L. Rep. (CCH) ¶ 81,366 (Nov. 17, 1977).

112. SEC Securities Exchange Act Release No. 13482 (Apr. 28, 1977), 12 SEC Docket No. 2, at 239 (May 10, 1977); SEC Securities Exchange Act Release No. 13901 (Aug. 29, 1977), 20 SEC Docket No. 20, at 1630 (Sept. 12, 1977).

113. SEC Advisory Committee on Corporate Disclosure, *Final Report* (November 3, 1977).

114. SEC Securities Exchange Act Release Nos. 13482, 13901 and 14970 [1977–1978 Transfer Binder] Fed. Sec. L. Rep. (CCH) ¶¶ 81,130, 81,296 (1977) and [1978 Transfer Binder] Fed. Sec. L. Rep. (CCH) ¶ 81,645 (1978).

rules designed to furnish additional information concerning the constitution of boards of directors of SEC-reporting companies and the manner in which they functioned.[115] Among the proposed requirements were these: that each director and nominee for director be designated as either management, affiliated nonmanagement, or independent according to standards proposed which would result in many outside counsel, investment and commercial bankers, and customers and suppliers being denied the label "independent"; that an issuer state whether it had audit and nominating committees along with their members; and that the issuer state whether these committees failed to perform any of the duties specified in the release as appropriate for them.

These proposals elicited the largest amount of comment ever received in response to a Commission proposal. The response was overwhelmingly negative, with particular criticism directed at the labeling proposal.[116] In response to this avalanche the Commission modified its proposals in a number of particulars, most notably by eliminating the labeling requirement.[117]

While these new disclosure requirements were clearly promulgated with conventional justification, the utility of the information to shareholders and investors, lurking in them is the Commission hope and expectation that they will lead to substantive changes in the institutions and processes of corporate governance: more, and more effective, nominating, compensation, and audit committees; reduction in the proportion of directors with significant economic ties to the issuer; and greater diligence and meeting attendance by directors.[118]

Another example of proposed rule-making that appears to represent a broadened perception by the Commission of its power in governance

---

115. SEC Securities Exchange Act Release No. 14970, *supra* note 114.

116. SEC Securities Exchange Act Release No. 15384 [1978 Transfer Binder] Fed. Sec. L. Rep. (CCH) ¶ 81,766 (1978).

117. *Id.*

118.

> The legislative history of the federal securities laws reflects a recognition that disclosure, by providing corporate owners with meaningful information about the way in which their corporations are managed, may promote the accountability of corporate management. Thus, while the federal securities laws generally embody a disclosure approach, it has long been recognized that disclosure may have beneficial effects on corporate behavior. Accordingly, although the Commission's objective in adopting these rules is to provide additional information relevant to an informed voting decision, it recognizes that disclosure may, depending on determinations made by a company's management, directors and shareholders, influence corporate conduct.

Id. at 81,088 (footnotes omitted).

matters, and which had potentially significant consequences for corporate governance, was SEC Exchange Act Release No. 13185. In 1976, as a consequence of the disclosures with respect to sensitive payments, including disclosure that these had generally been accompanied by financial record falsification, a number of legislative proposals were introduced in Congress to deal with the problem. The proposals that gained the strongest support were contained in S. 3664. These provided in substance that United States businesses would be prohibited from, among other things, making payments to any foreign official, political party, candidate for office, or intermediary for the purpose of inducing some individual or party to influence a foreign government, its legislation, or regulations or fail to perform official functions or assist in obtaining or retaining business. More important perhaps, this legislation provided that it would constitute a violation of law if a company failed to maintain proper internal controls or failed to maintain proper books and records, or if anyone misrepresented information to an auditor or falsified the records of the corporation.

These latter provisions were incorporated in the bill at the behest of the Commission, which had suggested in its May 12, 1976 report to the Senate Banking, Housing and Urban Affairs Committee[119] that, since experience suggested that improper payments were almost invariably accompanied by accounting distortions, the only legislative action necessary to deal with the problem was legislation addressed to accounting matters.

This legislation passed the Senate on September 15, 1976, by a vote of 88 to 0 and it was confidently expected to pass the House by a wide margin. However, a combination of circumstances prevented the House Rules Committee from voting on the proposal, and thus it died with the Ninety-Fourth Congress.[120]

Shortly thereafter, however, the Commission proposed to adopt, virtually verbatim, the accounting portions of the aborted legislation under its traditional rule-making power. Thus in SEC Exchange Act Release No. 13185 it proposed rules that would require issuers registered under section 12 of the Exchange Act or required to file periodic reports under section 15(d) of that Act to[121]

> (1) maintain books and records which accurately reflect the transactions and dispositions of assets of the issuer;
>
> (2) maintain a system of internal accounting controls which would provide reasonable assurance that:

---

119. See note 3 *supra*.

120. The bill was, however, reintroduced by Senator Proxmire in the ninety-fifth session of Congress (S. 305, 95th Cong., 1st Sess. (1977)) and was adopted and signed in December 1977.

121. SEC Securities Exchange Act Release No. 13185 (Jan. 19, 1977), [Current] Fed. Sec. L. Rep. (CCH) ¶ 80,896, 42 Fed. Reg. 4854 (1977).

(a) transactions are executed in accordance with management's general or specific authorization;

(b) transactions are recorded as necessary (a) to permit preparation of financial statements in conformity with generally accepted accounting principles or any other criteria applicable to such statements and (b) to maintain accountability for assets;

(c) access to assets is permitted only in accordance with management's authorization; and

(d) the recorded accountability for assets is compared with the existing assets at reasonable intervals and appropriate action is taken with respect to any differences.

The proposal would also have prohibited:
(a) falsification of an issuer's accounting records; and
(b) false or misleading statements to accountants by directors, officers, or shareholders of an issuer.

In December 1977 Congress adopted and the President signed Public Law 95-213 (generally known as the Foreign Corrupt Practices Act, even though it is not confined either to foreign matters or practices which have generally been regarded as "corrupt practices"), which included the prohibitions against foreign payments and some of the accounting provisions—with some modifications—but omitted the prohibitions against falsification of records and misrepresentation to accountants. Early in 1979, the Commission adopted rules incorporating the provisions omitted from the statute.[122]

The enactment by Congress of a requirement that corporations maintain systems of internal controls obviated the adoption of a rule to this effect by the Commission. However, the fact that the Commission seriously considered such a rule is clear evidence of its willingness to extend its reach over corporate governance by the rule-making route.

In other instances the Commission has also manifested an intention to make rules that affect deeply the processes of corporate governance and corporate accountability. Having indicated in Securities Exchange Act Release No. 13185 the primacy it accords satisfactory internal controls, the Commission's intention, as expressed by Chairman Williams, is to propose a rule which would require management to make an annual public statement of its assessment of the corporation's internal controls.[123] Further, it has been suggested that the auditors should similarly state their assessment.[124] Obviously such a proposal is fraught with problems, not the least of which stems from the fact that since

---

122. SEC Securities Exchange Act Release No. 15570 [Current] Fed. Sec. L. Rep. (CCH) ¶ 81,959 (Feb. 15, 1979).

123. [1978] Sec. Reg. & L. Rep. (BNA) No. 458: D-3 (June 21, 1978).

124. *Id.*

enactment of the Foreign Corrupt Practices Act, failure to maintain adequate internal controls may have been a criminal offense.

Further, largely at the behest of the Commission, the American Institute of Certified Public Accountants undertook consideration of whether it should in some measure seek to mandate, either by defining "independence" or modifying accepted conceptions of "generally accepted auditing standards," the creation of audit committees by auditor clients.[125] While that effort was pending, the Commission, in its first annual report on the accounting profession to Congress, stated that if the profession's effort came to naught, then the Commission might undertake to effect such a mandate; it had previously received the opinion of its General Counsel that it had the power to make such a rule.[126] The Institute declined to adopt any requirement in this area and at the time of writing the Commission has not indicated whether it will undertake an initiative in this area.

However, it may well be that the issue has been largely foreclosed by other events. As indicated below, the New York Stock Exchange now requires all companies there listed to have audit committees. The National Association of Securities Dealers is considering such a mandate, as is the American Stock Exchange (although the Chairman of the Amex has stated the belief that such a mandate may not be practicable for companies of the sort listed on his exchange);[127] in the eyes of some, the Foreign Corrupt Practices Act has in effect mandated the organization of audit committees.[128]

Ironically, the increasing Commission presence in the area of corporate structure and governance occurs at a time when the Supreme Court has been delineating the limits of the federal securities laws more narrowly than at any time in their history. It has sharply rejected efforts to expand the definition of "security,"[129] the ability of rule 10b-5 plaintiffs to recover,[130] the availability of relief under the tender-offer provisions of the 1934 Act to defeated tender offerors,[131] the standing of someone who is neither a purchaser nor seller to maintain an action

---

125. AICPA, The Commission on Auditors' Responsibilities, *Report, Conclusions, and Recommendations* p. 106.

126. Memorandum, Harvey L. Pitt to Chairman Williams (March 2, 1978), reprinted in [1978] Sec. Reg. & L. Rep. (BNA) No. 444: I-1 (March 15, 1978).

127. Address of Arthur Levitt, Jr., to the Sixth Annual Securities Regulation Institute, San Diego, Cal. (Jan. 17, 1979).

128. See, e.g., Borowski, "The SEC and the Audit Committee," in Practicing Law Institute Handbook, *The Emergence of the Corporate Audit Committee*, p. 201 (1978).

129. United Housing Foundation, Inc. v. Forman, 421 U.S. 837 (1975).

130. Ernst & Ernst v. Hochfelder, 425 U.S. 185 (1976.

131. Piper v. Chris-Craft Industries, Inc., 430 U.S. 1976 (1977).

under rule 10b-5,[132] and the applicability of rule 10b-5 to breaches of fiduciary duty by those having control of corporations.[133] However, the clearest rejection of the effort to stretch the federal reach into areas traditionally regarded as those of state government was stated in *Cort v. Ash*:[134]

> Corporations are creatures of state law, and investors commit their funds to corporate directors on the understanding that, except where federal law expressly requires certain responsibilities of directors with respect to stockholders, state law will govern the internal affairs of the corporation . . . .
>
> . . . *[B]*ecause implication of a federal right of damages on behalf of a corporation under § 610 would intrude into an area traditionally committed to state law without aiding the main purpose of § 610, we reverse.

However, several circumstances suggest that successful challenge of the Commission's initiatives in these matters may not be forthcoming. For one thing, the peculiar dynamics of securities regulation minimize the likelihood of such a challenge. Issuers seeking proxy statement clearance have not the time to contest the Commission's demand for additional information or text modification, and it is unlikely that an issuer would find it prudent or feasible to contest, for instance, a Commission requirement with respect to proposals to amend a corporation's bylaws to provide for shareholder nominations. Similarly, a company seeking to go private would probably find compliance with the Commission's mandates a less costly, more reliable, and more expeditious process than prolonged litigation. Securities transactions and proxy solicitations are time limited: events do not generally permit a long delay. Furthermore, while the Supreme Court has curtailed significantly the applications of the federal securities laws,[135] the Commission's rule-making power has not been limited; hence an assault upon action taken under the Commission's broad rule-making power would have an uncertain outcome. Finally, while one may read the Supreme Court decisions as indicating a strong tendency to limit the implication of remedies, there is nothing in recent Supreme Court history to justify the conclusion that the Court felt similarly inclined to deal narrowly with agency rule-making powers.

The Commission has intervened in corporate governance in other, somewhat subtler, ways. In 1976, SEC Chairman Roderick M. Hills wrote William M. Batten, chairman of the New York Stock Exchange, urging that the exchange amend its listing agreement to require each

---

132. Blue Chip Stamps v. Manor Drug Stores, 421 U.S. 723 (1975).

133. Santa Fe Industries, Inc. v. Green, 430 U.S. 462 (1977).

134. Cort v. Ash, 422 U.S. 66, 84-85 (1975).

135. See cases cited in notes 129–133 *supra*.

listed company to have an audit committee made up predominantly if not exclusively of outside directors.[136] The New York Stock Exchange responded affirmatively to this and on March 9, 1977,[137] adopted an amendment that required domestic companies already listed on the exchange to comply by June 30, 1978, and those listing for the first time to comply before listing. The proposal required that[138]

> Each domestic company with common stock listed on the NYSE, as a condition of listing and continued listing of its securities on the NYSE, shall establish no later than June 30, 1978, and maintain thereafter an audit committee comprised solely of directors independent of management and free from any relationships that, in the opinion of its Board of Directors, would interfere with the exercise of independent judgment as a committee member.

Policy by Pronouncement

In cases and reports on investigations involving outside directors the Commission has with considerable particularity set forth its conception of the responsibilities of directors; again it should be emphasized that these have occurred in the context of settlements and do not represent judicial conclusions concerning directors' responsibilities.

In *Report of Investigation in the Matter of Stirling Homex Corporation Relating to Activities of the Directors of Stirling Homex Corporation*[139] the Commission criticized sharply the failures of two outside directors. While recognizing that the outside directors were deceived by the management of Stirling Homex, the Commission faulted them on several scores:[140]

> In the Commission's opinion, they did not obtain a sufficiently firm grasp of the company's accounting practices and other aspects of the company's business related thereto to enable them to make an informed judgment of its more important affairs or the abilities and integrity of its officers. Kheel and Castellucci relied upon the fact that Stirling Homex's independent accountants had accepted these accounting practices as being in conformity with generally accepted accounting principles. While this reliance was understandable, it resulted in their making no significant effort to analyze or familiarize themselves generally with these accounting practices . . . and

---

136. See *Report, supra* note 3, Exhibit D.

137. See SEC Exchange Act Release No. 13346 (Mar. 9, 1977), 11 SEC Docket No. 15, at 1945 (March 22, 1977), for a discussion of this matter.

138. SEC Exchange Act Release No. 13245, (Feb. 4, 1977), 11 SEC Docket No. 11, at 1072 (Feb. 21, 1977), 42 Fed. Reg. 8737 (1977).

139. [1975-1976 Transfer Binder] Fed. Sec. L. Rep (CCH ¶ 80,219, at 85,462–63 (July 16, 1975).

140. *Id.*

their susceptibility to abuse. While they periodically asked general and conclusory questions, they frequently obtained only superficial answers which they accepted without further inquiry.

While the Commission recognizes the difficulties which may confront outside directors, particularly in a situation such as this, where management as part of a fraudulent course of conduct to deceive the public was not willing either to take the outside directors into their confidence or to keep them even reasonably well informed, this case illustrates a situation where these directors, in the opinion of the Commission, did not provide the shareholders with any significant protection in fact, nor did their presence on the Board have the impact upon the company's operations which shareholders and others might reasonably have expected.

Similarly in *SEC v. Shiell,*[141] the Commission alleged that the outside directors did not exercise sufficient care with respect to the affairs of the corporation and did not go beyond officers' statements in ascertaining the state of the business.[142]

The minutes and agendas of the Board of Directors meetings starting in 1973 reflect that the directors had in effect relinquished substantial control over the president. The directors, as outside directors, relied upon the president as their sole source for all information regarding the activities and operations of the company. The minutes do not reflect that any other officers of the company were present at the meetings nor did the directors require any other officer to report to them regarding the activities of the company to any significant extent. The testimony of the directors indicates that they did not deem it necessary to have other officers present at meetings for they believed (by accepting the president's report at face value) that they were getting accurate and complete information from the president. Additionally, they felt that questioning other officers about the company's activities or in fact requiring other officers to report to them independently of the president would 'constitute an intrusion into the functions of management.' Even when the directors visited the company offices from time to time, and encountered other key officers, there were few discussions regarding the company's activities.

In a similar vein, in its report to the Congress with respect to its study of the Penn Central collapse, the Commission staff dwelt at length on the failures of the directors of Penn Central to come to grips with the worsening situation of the corporation. The staff summarized this failure in these words:[143]

---

141. [1976] Sec. Reg. & L. Rep. (BNA) No. 383: A-8 (Dec. 22, 1976).

142. *Id.* at A-10.

143. Staff of the Securities and Exchange Commission, *The Financial Collapse of the Penn Central Company* p. 153 (1972) (submitted to the Special Committee on Investigations).

> The Board failed in two principal ways. It failed to establish procedures, including a flow of adequate financial information, to permit the board to understand what was happening and to enable it to exercise some control over the conduct of the senior officers. Secondly, the board failed to respond to specific warnings about the true condition of the company and about the questionable conduct of the most important officers. As a result, the investors were deprived of adequate and accurate information about the condition of the company.

The Commission followed this report with the filing of a complaint naming, among others, three outside directors of Penn Central as defendants. In the fourth cause of action of the complaint these directors (all of whom had long service on the board of the company and one of its predecessors, and all of whom had backgrounds indicating familiarity with financial matters) were charged with knowing or having reason to know that securities were being sold without disclosure of adverse information concerning Penn Central.[144]

As a part of the Commissions's settlement of a complaint against Gould Inc. and two of its officers for alleged violations of the securities laws (one of the violations involved nondisclosure of a transaction in which the company and some of its officers were involved, although they were not dealing with each other), the Commission issued a report of investigation under section 21(a) of the 1934 Act describing the allegedly wrongful transactions and stating its opinion with respect to the responsibility of directors when confronted with such transations:[145]

> With regard to the review of the board of directors of management involvement in a transaction affecting the company, the Commission is of the opinion that in such instances, the board should carefully ascertain all the relevant facts to determine whether the transaction is in all ways fair to the company and to assure that it has been fully disclosed to shareholders as required by the federal securities laws. In ascertaining facts, the board should not rely solely on information from interested management but should also seek information from independent non-interested sources when available.

CONCLUSION

Several significant aspects of these activities of the Commission with respect to corporate governance deserve comment. First, the Commission has affected corporate governance. The increasing number of outside directors on boards, the explosive growth in the number of audit committees, the adoption of codes of conduct by many companies, the eschewing of previously accepted business practices by multinational

144. SEC v. Penn Central Co., [1973-1974 Transfer Binder] Fed Sec. L. Rep. (CCH) ¶ 94,527, *complaint filed* (E.D. Pa. May 2, 1974).

145. [Current] Fed. Sec. L. Rep. (CCH ¶ 96,077, at 91,863 (D.D.C. June 9, 1977).

corporations—these and many more developments have had their strongest impetus from the activities of the Commission.

Second, the Commission's impact on corporate governance has been accomplished with surprisingly few formal actions by the Commission either in the realm of rule-making or in enforcement actions specifically aimed at directors. As noted, the most direct effort to provide standards for director conduct—the effort to articulate guidelines—aborted. The number of actual suits filed by the Commission against outside directors because of their conduct as such is only two, and in one, *SEC v. Shiell,*[146] the relationship of the directors to the company was significantly different from the conventional relationship of outside directors to a publicly held corporation: they had been among the founders, were clearly the controlling persons and in general there was an atypical intimacy of involvement.

Third, the Commission has incontestably concluded that to administer the securities laws effectively it is necessary to address the problem of corporate governance. With the exception of its sponsorship of section 1 of S. 305, it has not sought additional power from Congress. Rather it has been through resourceful use of jawboning by Commission and staff members, skillful expansion of its enforcement powers (including imaginative settlement proposals and provisions), and artful use of its powers to accelerate the effectiveness of registration statements and release proxy-soliciting materials, that the Commission has enormously changed the structure and governance of American corporations.

This paper passes no judgment on either the power of the Commission to do as it has done (though full disclosure compels admission that the writer participated in many of the actions which have promoted these tendencies) or the propriety of its actions. Critics of both the tendencies in general and the particular deeds have not been wanting.[147] These critics are undoubtedly dismayed by signs that under the chairmanship of Harold M. Williams, a veteran of both the business and the academic worlds, the effort of the Commission to influence corporate governance will not only continue but accelerate. In an address shortly after his accession to the chairmanship of the Commission, he said:[148]

> It is my ideal . . . that a board consist of the chief executive and outside directors. Standards need to be set for what is expected of an outside

---

146. [1976] Sec. Reg. & L. Rep. (BNA) No. 383: A-8 (Dec. 22, 1976).

147. See Freeman, "The Legality of the SEC's Management Fraud Program," 31 Bus. Law. 1295 (1976); Note, "Disclosure of Corporate Payments and Practices: Conduct Regulation Through the Federal Securities Laws," 43 Brooklyn L. Rev. 681 (1977).

148. Note 61 *supra*.

director in terms of behavior and performance. I would also urge that the chairman of the board not be the chief executive officer.

What it means is that the large corporation has ceased to be private property—even though theoretically owned by its shareholders. It is now a quasi-public institution. If it is such a quasi-public institution, then the self-perpetuating oligarchy that constitutes management does not have the same rights it once had.

This is not the language of a person who will lead the Commission in a retreat from its forward position in the field of corporate governance.

Moreover, repeatedly since becoming Chairman, Mr. Williams has addressed problems of corporate governance and accountability, and possible solutions. It may reasonably be said that this has been the dominant theme of his chairmanship so far.

This article has not discussed the manner in which the Commission is affecting corporate governance by its increased oversight of the accounting profession[149] and its increased concern with the role of corporate counsel in the corporate structure.[150] The Commission appears to see an insistence upon the expansion of the responsibilities of these professionals as a means of furthering management responsibility and conformity to acceptable standards of conduct; it may be that this will prove to be the most potent weapon in the Commission's arsenal.

---

149. To assure Congress of its ongoing concern with accounting profession, the Commission on the occasion of the Metcalf hearings promised to submit an annual report to Congress on the accounting profession. *Accounting and Auditing Practices and Procedures: Hearings Before the Subcomm. on Reports, Accounting and Management of the Senate Comm. on Governmental Affairs,* 95th Cong., 1st Sess. 1761 (1977). On July 1, 1978 it submitted the first such report.

150. Symptomatic of this concern was the speech of Chairman Williams at the annual luncheon of the Section of Corporation, Banking and Business Law of the American Bar Association on August 8, 1978. 34 Bus. Law 7 (1978).

CHAPTER FIVE

The Role of Corporate Counsel

John C. Taylor III *Partner, Paul, Weiss, Rifkind, Wharton & Garrison*

The initial issue in the debate over proposed changes in corporate governance is whether existing corporate structures can serve as an adequate frame for making corporations responsible managers of business activity. Almost everyone pressing for corporate reform today begins from the premise that the traditional pattern of public company governance, in which a small group of corporate officers is the sole initiator and executive of corporate policy, has proved itself inadequate in making our major corporations responsive to changing public attitudes and the changing demands of our society.[1] Those who oppose structural change acknowledge past failures but put the blame on the manner in which individuals have administered affairs within the structure, absolving the structures from fault. They claim that the present system, having been alerted to its past failures, can perform better in the future. Whether it can do so is the critical issue in the debate.

The same events which thrust upon the corporate manager the immediate need to improve performance of his role are making that role infinitely more complex and difficult to perform. It is becoming increasingly clear that the long-range future of corporate business entities is in significant part dependent upon management's ability to anticipate and to deal with changing and developing public ethics and mores. In addition to conforming his marketing practices to the intricacies of the

---

1. See, e.g., R. Nader, M. Green, and J. Seligman, *Taming the Giant Corporation* (1976); Cary, "Federalism and Corporate Law: Reflections Upon Delaware," 83 Yale L.J. 663 (1974).

This article appeared in the *Rutgers Law Review* as part of a symposium on corporate governance which appears in Volume 32.

Robinson-Patman Act[2] and the as-yet-undefined strictures of the Foreign Corrupt Practices Act,[3] the manager must anticipate where political pressure and stockholder action will take the law over the next few years with respect to issues such as investment in South Africa, improvement of the environment, and employment and retirement practices. Failure to do so, and to respond effectively, will build additional pressures for structured change similar to those that grew out of Watergate, Koreagate, improper foreign payments, and freezeouts of public shareholders. The virtual certainty that the areas of public- and consumer-responsive regulation will continue to expand[4] forces the manager to turn increasingly to those who can assist him in anticipating and reacting to new regulatory problems.

At the same time, judicial and legislative reaction to the conduct of corporate managements in such transactions as "going private" mergers and tender offers has considerably complicated the legal environment in which managements must deal with their own shareholders, and those of other companies.[5]

The result of these developments is a serious need for more effective performance by corporate counsel. All of these emerging areas of management responsibility, as well as all of the events which gave rise to the initial demands for change in governance structure, involve serious legal, as well as moral, issues. They are surrounded by legislative and regulatory requirements and activity. Appropriate response requires anticipation of what courts, legislatures, and government regulators are

---

2. 15 U.S.C. §§ 13-13b, 21a (1976).

3. 15 U.S.C. §§ 78m(b), 78dd-1, 78dd-2, 78ff (1976).

4. Despite a growing pressure from a vocal group of academics urging a reduction of government regulation, see, e.g., Green and Nader, "Economic Regulation v. Competition: Uncle Sam the Monopoly Man," 82 Yale L.J. 871 (1973); Volner, "Getting the Horse Before the Cart: Identifying the Causes of Failure of the Regulatory Commissions," 5 Hofstra L. Rev. 285 (1977); Winter, "Economic Regulation vs. Competition: Ralph Nader and Creeping Capitalism," 82 Yale L.J. 890 (1973) and some concrete steps toward deregulation in specific areas, such as the Airline Deregulation Act of 1978, Pub. L. 95-504, 92 Stat. 1705, and relaxation of restrictive laws regulating the activities of both commercial and savings banks, government regulation is increasingly pervasive. The Equal Credit Opportunity Act, 15 U.S.C. §§ 1691–1691f (1976), the Fair Credit Reporting Act, 15 U.S.C. § 1681, the Antitrust Improvements Act of 1976, 15 U.S.C. § 18A (1976), the President's Wage-Price Program, Exec. Order No. 12092, 43 Fed. Reg. 51375 (1798), and the creation of the Department of Energy, Department of Energy Organization Act, Pub. L. 95-91, 91 Stat. 565 (codified in scattered sections of 3, 5, 7, 15, and 42 U.S.C.), all demonstrate that our society's response to problems, more often than not, is to increase government controls.

5. See Santa Fe Industries, Inc. v. Green, 430 U.S. 462 (1977); Williams Act, 15 U.S.C. §§ 78 M (d)(e)(f) (1976); Singer v. Magnavox Co., 380 A.2d 969 (Del. 1977); Brudney & Chirelstein, "A Restatement of Corporate Freezeouts," 87 Yale L.J. 1354 (1978).

likely to do in the future as well as interpretation of their existing mandates. The professional training and experience of corporate lawyers qualifies them as essential advisers in these areas.

But, like the corporate manager, the corporate lawyer is finding his role increasingly harder to identify, much less to fulfill. As recent developments have dramatically increased the opportunity for counsel to make a significant and constructive contribution to corporate decision-making, the role of counsel has grown, without an understanding by management or counsel of the scope or limitations of counsel's proper role. As a result, corporate counsel finds himself with only a vague definition of his responsibility and uncertain lines of communication to corporate decision-makers.

Before counsel can effectively assist his client, he and his client must properly define and understand his role. Whether they can do so can be critical in determining whether existing corporate structures will survive intact or undergo radical surgery.

This time of uncertainty for corporate counsel unhappily corresponds with a period of change and uncertainty in other areas of corporate governance and control, which further complicates the identification of counsel's proper relationship to the other players on the corporate stage. Boards of directors are playing larger and more significant roles, in some cases initiating as well as acting as final arbiter of significant corporate policy changes; audit committees and nominating committees are flexing their muscles, with significant impact on the governance of some of our major corporations; and stockholder initiatives, although rarely drawing more than 5 or 6 percent of corporate votes, are having a significant impact on corporate governance.[6] Counsel can no longer limit himself to head to head consultation with the Chief Executive Officer and conclude that he has discharged his function in advising his corporate client.

The last ten years have seen a dramatic change in the respective roles of in-house and outside corporate counsel that has resulted in consider-

---

6. During the 1979 proxy season shareholders have proposed resolutions involving social questions to more than 100 public corporations. VI News for Investors 22, 48–51 (Investor Responsibility Research Center Inc. 1979). These resolutions may have an effect on the corporation despite a lack of shareholder support. See, e.g., V *id.* at 76 (resolution requesting board of directors to take whatever steps are necessary to provide for nomination of a qualified woman for election to the board withdrawn in view of company assurances that an active search for such a candidate was being made); VI *id.* at 54 (resolution requesting corporation to adopt a policy that neither it nor its subsidiaries will make or renew any contracts or agreements to sell, lease or service its computers or their components to the South African government withdrawn after company issued a statement that it would not "inject new investment capital into South Africa under present social conditions" and formalizing "a policy for South Africa directing [the corporation's] employees against knowingly selling equipment for use for oppressive purposes.").

able confusion as to the respective roles of inside and outside counsel and, in many cases, jealousy and conflict between the two.[7] Corporate house counsel departments are no longer groups of lawyers responsible for day-to-day or narrowly specialized legal activity and corporate housekeeping. Indeed, many in-house corporate legal departments are now the equal of outside counsel in ability and scope of operation.[8] Lines of communication between outside counsel and upper-level management are clouded and tangled and, in many cases, neither inside nor outside attorneys are sure of the dimensions of their responsibilities. Too often the result is what one might expect when authority is not clearly assigned—each narrowly performs what is asked and neither takes an initiative in areas of future planning and anticipation of future problems.

Counsel can choose from among many views of what their role should be. At one extreme is the belief that counsel should be neither seen nor heard but should merely create a written record implementing management's decisions and issue legal opinions on matters about which he is consulted. In the opposite direction lies a position, which has been at least implied by certain representatives of the Securities and Exchange Commission, that lawyers are legally obligated to obtain detailed information about management action and to inform the public and the Commission promptly if any of those actions might be improper or illegal.[9] Between these extremes there is an array of opinion on the subject of what counsel's role ought to be.[10] Unfortunately, none results from a careful analysis considering events over the past ten years

---

7. This article does not attempt to differentiate between functions properly discharged by inside counsel and those properly assigned to outside counsel. That allocation of functions must necessarily differ from corporation to corporation. Except where the context clearly indicates that remarks below are relevant only to outside counsel, everything contained in this article applies equally to the activities of inside and outside counsel.

8. A recent study indicates that almost one-third of companies with annual sales of over $2 billion have in-house legal staffs consisting of more than forty-five attorneys. More than half of such companies employed more than twenty-five attorneys. A. T. Kearny, Inc., *The Corporate Legal Function* § B7 (1978). Legal departments in almost 75 percent of such companies had budgets in excess of $1 million. *Id.* § B4.

9. This position has been hinted at by former SEC Commissioner A. A. Sommer, see Sommer, "Emerging Responsibilities of the Securities Lawyer," N.Y.L.J., Jan. 30, 1974, at 1, col. 1, and has been publicly adopted by Director of Enforcement Stanley Sporkin.

10. See, e.g., Cohen, Wheat & Henderson, "Professional Responsibility—The Corporate Bar," 4 Inst. Sec. Reg. 181 (1973); Shipman, "The Need for SEC Rules to Govern the Duties and Civil Liabilities of Attorneys Under the Federal Securities Statutes," 34 Ohio St. L.J. 231 (1973); Sonde, "The Responsibility of Professionals Under the Federal Securities Laws—Some Observations," 68 NW.U.L. Rev. 1 (1973).

and few, if any, have been tested by exposure to public debate. Given the growing visibility of lawyers on the corporate scene, it is surprising that the lawyer's role has been so neglected by participants in the governance debate while the roles of stockholders, directors, officers, public interest groups, government agencies, legislators, and state and federal courts have been discussed at length.

This article is not an attempt to detail all of the functions properly performed by corporate counsel nor is it intended to be a definitive legal description of the obligations of, or restrictions on, counsel. It is an attempt to point out a few important areas where counsel can and should contribute constructively to corporate governance and to discuss briefly, in the practical context of day-to-day corporate operations, some of the obstacles which have prevented counsel from performing adequately and how those obstacles can be surmounted.

Any definition of counsel's role should not depart from the basic premise that, to use military parlance, counsel performs a staff function, not a line or command function. Counsel does not play an executive role in corporate governance. Counsel's impact on corporate decisions is always through influence that counsel exerts on decisions and actions of some third party who wields corporate power. The first step in defining counsel's role in corporate governance is therefore to identify the persons who make the decisions on which counsel should properly have an impact.

The locus of decision-making power in the modern corporation has been well explored. Two groups, the directors and the shareholders, are, at least formally, the holders of corporate decision-making power.[11] There is, of course, a third group, which counsel certainly cannot neglect and which has traditionally been the only group to be counselled by corporate lawyers: the management itself.[12] Executive officers, boards of directors, and shareholders all have a significant stake in the well-being of the corporate enterprise, all have some impact on corporate decision-making, and counsel has professional responsibility to each of them. In addition, today's corporate counsel cannot, in the face of regulatory attitudes toward the role of the lawyer[13] and the recent pronouncements of some of our federal courts,[14] ignore the claims of

---

11. Under state corporation statutes, directors are responsible generally for the day-to-day operation of the entity, e.g., 8 Del. Code tit. 8, § 141(a) (1974); N.Y. Business Corporation Law § 701 (McKinney 1963), while organic making is reserved to the shareholders. E.g., Del. Code tit. 8, §§ 251(c); 271(a); 275 (1974) (b); N.Y. Business Corporation Law §§ 903, 909, 1001 (McKinney 1963).

12. The meaning of the term "management" is also undergoing change. It is used here in its traditional sense to designate the principal executives of the corporation and does not include the directors as it often does in today's usage.

13. See note 9 *supra*.

14. See SEC v. National Student Marketing Corp., 457 F. Supp. 682, 713 (D.D.C. 1978).

regulatory agencies that counsel, in certain circumstances, has a legal obligation to them as representatives of the public. The question faced by counsel is how to deal with each of these four groups.

THE LEGAL DEFINITION OF THE ROLE OF CORPORATE COUNSEL

In traditional lawyerly fashion, we must examine first what the law currently says about the lawyer's legal responsibility to each. What do the statutes, the canons, and the cases spell out as those obligations?

The ABA's Code of Professional Responsibility is less than helpful in the lawyer's search for guidance as to his responsibilities to various elements of the corporate family. Its only direct consideration of the problem is in Ethical Consideration 5-18,[15] which states the truism that counsel to a corporation owes his allegiance to the entity, rather than to any particular group—a statement which Gertrude Stein might paraphrase as "Your client is your client is your client." In 1940, the Committee on Professional Ethics of the American Bar Association issued an opinion which, for the first time, gave official endorsement to the concept that counsel owes ultimate responsibility to the board of directors.[16] The concept embodied by this opinion found virtually unanimous acceptance among lawyers because it is consistent with a basic principle of corporate law, embodied in the corporate statutes of almost every jurisdiction, that the board of directors has responsibility and authority to manage the corporation's business.[17] It made counsel responsible to the persons who were authorized to make decisions and to take action on behalf of the client corporation. The opinion was considered by many to fix firmly the situs of corporate counsel's loyalty and, not surprisingly, there seems to have been relatively little further discussion of the subject until recently.

The issue was reopened in a series of cases testing the extent to which corporate management and directors can assert the attorney-client privilege in the face of a suit brought by plaintiffs to whom they owe fiduciary obligations. The lead case is *Garner v. Wolfinbarger,*[18]

---

15. A lawyer employed or retained by a corporation or similar entity owes his allegiance to the entity and not to a stockholder, director, officer, employee, representative, or other person connected with the entity. In advising the entity, a lawyer should keep paramount its interests and his professional judgment should not be influenced by the personal desires of any person or organization.

ABA Code of Professional Responsibility, Ethical Consideration 5-18 (1977).

16. ABA Comm. on Professional Ethics, Opinions, No. 202 (1940).

17. See note 11 *supra*.

18. Garner v. Wolfinbarger, 430 F.2d 1093 (5th Cir. 1970), *cert. denied,* 401 U.S. 977 (1971).

where the corporation sought to invoke the attorney-client privilege to deny the plaintiff shareholders access to legal advice previously received by the board of directors in connection with an allegedly fraudulent sale of the corporation's stock to the plaintiffs. Denying the availability of the privilege, the court rejected the "entity-is-your-client" theory by noting that "[c]onceptualistic phrases describing the corporation as an entity separate from its stockholders" were not "useful tools of analysis."[19] Nor was the court convinced by the policy argument, pressed by the American Bar Association as *amicus curiae,* that the benefits of disclosure were outweighed by the harm done to the attorney-client relationship.[20] The court ruled that although the "privilege still has viability for the corporate client," protection of the corporation, its stockholders and the public requires that "the privilege be subject to the right of the stockholders to show cause why it should not be invoked in the particular instance."[21]

By refusing to adopt a per se rule that the corporation, acting through its board of directors, could invoke the privilege to prevent disclosure to the corporation's shareholders, *Garner* suggests that shareholders cannot be treated as unrelated outsiders with respect to advice given by counsel. "When all is said and done management is not managing for itself."[22] This suggestion has been reinforced as *Garner* has been followed and expanded.[23] However, *Garner* and its progeny have been

---

19. 430 F.2d at 1101.

20. *Id.* at 1102.

21. *Id.* at 1103–04. The court remanded the case to the district court for a determination of whether there was good cause, under the facts of the case, for not invoking the privilege and listed some factors to be considered by the district court in making this determination. *Id.*

22. *Id.* at 1101.

23. *Garner* has withstood the test of time and has been followed and expanded. In Bailey v. Meister Brau, Inc., 55 F.R.D. 211 (N.D. Ill. 1972), a case arising out of Meister Brau, Inc.'s purchase of the James H. Black Company, the court permitted the plaintiff, a shareholder of Black, to discover conversations between a Meister Brau director who was also a director of Black, and Meister Brau's counsel concerning Meister Brau's acquisition of the Black Company. The court rejected the defendant's attempt to distinguish *Garner* by arguing that the director was acting as a Meister Brau rather than a Black director. 55 F.R.D. at 214 ("a fiduciary cannot turn his responsibilities on and off like a faucet. . . ."). *Garner* was followed in Valente v. Pepsico, Inc., 68 F.R.D. 361 (D. Del. 1975), where a shareholder of a subsidiary corporation sought to prevent the parent corporation from asserting the attorney-client privilege concerning communications between the parent corporation and its counsel. The court noted that the communicants were directors of either the parent or the subsidiary or both and, therefore, owed fiduciary obligations to the subsidiary and its minority shareholders. The court further noted that "fiduciaries owe obligations to their beneficiaries to go about their duties without obscuring the reasons from the

read to suggest the far broader proposition that corporate counsel has an attorney-client relationship directly with shareholders, and this suggestion, in turn, has led some commentators to the conclusion that counsel has an affirmative duty to reveal information to stockholders.[24]

If the cases are read carefully, it is clear that they do not stand for such broad propositions. Each case involved an attempted assertion of the attorney-client privilege to withhold information from stockholders who were litigating parties adverse in interest to the directors or the management. The question before the courts certainly was not whether counsel had an obligation to reveal information to shareholders or debentureholders. The question was merely whether discovery by those adverse litigants could be thwarted by a corporate exercise of the attorney-client privilege.

These cases do not address even the intermediate question of whether counsel could voluntarily have made the information available to the plaintiffs without violating professional obligations. The definition of information that the Code of Professional Responsibility requires an attorney to keep confidential is far broader than the definition of material which is subject to a proper claim of attorney-client privilege by the client.[25] The *Garner* line of cases does no more than rule on the privilege question. Those cases do not hold, or even imply, that counsel had an affirmative obligation to convey information to the plaintiffs. With the one exception discussed below,[26] there appears to be no existing statutory or case law which requires, or permits, disclosure by counsel to shareholders of confidential information in circumstances that would not permit similar disclosure to parties unrelated to the corporation.

---

legitimate interest of the beneficiaries." 68 F.R.D. at 370. See also Broad v. Rockwell Int'l Corp. [1977–1978 Transfer Binder] Fed. Sec. L. Rep. (CCH) ¶ 95,894 (N.D. Tex. 1977) (extending *Garner* to apply where plaintiffs are debenture-holders); *in re* Transocean Tender Offer Securities Litigation, 78 F.R.D. 692 (N.D. Ill. 1978) (communications between a corporate agent and corporate counsel may not be privileged in the face of a lawsuit brought by someone who stands in a fiduciary relation with the corporate agent who communicates with counsel).

In re Colocotronis Tanker Securities Litigation, 449 F. Supp. 828 (S.D.N.Y. 1978), refused to extend *Garner* to cover the situation where several plaintiff banks, who had entered into participation agreements on a tanker financing deal, sought to hurdle the attorney-client privilege asserted by the lead bank. The court's rationale was that the contracts represented arm's-length agreements between relatively sophisticated financial institutions and did not establish fiduciary relationships.

24. "Lawyer's Responsibilities and Liabilities Under the Securities Laws," 11 Colum. J.L. Soc. Prob. 99, 122–27 (1974) (remarks of Alan B. Levinson).

25. *ABA Code of Professional Responsibility, Ethical Consideration* 4-4, *Disciplinary Rule* 4-101(A) (1977).

26. See text accompanying notes 30–36 *infra*.

Nor, as a policy matter, should the line of cases be extended to require such disclosure. Given today's reality that disclosure to shareholders of any public corporation is disclosure to the world at large, the policy reasons for requiring professionals to protect confidential information from third parties also mandate that such information not be disclosed to shareholders. Clearly there are times when counsel has an obligation to make disclosure to the shareholders of the client corporation; but these are cases when the client has committed fraud or a crime and are in substance the same cases in which counsel has an obligation to make disclosure to government or law enforcement officials or to the other party to a transaction.[27] That obligation exists whether the client is a corporation or an individual.

The *National Student Marketing* case[28] represents a clear exception. It holds on the facts there presented that counsel not only *could* reveal to shareholders facts which traditionally would be classified as confidential information which counsel has a responsibility not to disseminate to persons other than his client,[29] but that counsel *had a professional obligation to do so* and was derelict in permitting a transaction to close without having done so.[30] In so holding, *National Student Marketing* constitutes an exception to the general rule that counsel owes his professional obligation to the board of directors.[31]

The rationale of the holding is, however, totally consistent with the rationale of the rule to which it creates an exception. The significant

---

27. See *ABA Code of Professional Responsibility, Disciplinary Rules* 4-101(c); 7-102(B) (1977).

I do not address the widely discussed dilemma of the lawyer who is faced with the immediate issuance of a 10K at the time he discovers his client engaged in massive price-fixing violations on which the statute of limitations will run within the next six months. While the current state of the law, and certainly the attitude of the staff of the Securities and Exchange Commission, would give any lawyer serious pause before he recommended that disclosure not be made, query whether counsel should be obligated, in order to protect strangers to the corporation who might otherwise purchase shares of the corporation, to make disclosures which could have a serious adverse impact on the corporation and its current shareholders—that is, on all persons who could conceivably be deemed to be the client at the time of disclosure.

28. SEC v. National Student Marketing Corp., 457 F. Supp. 682 (D.D.C. 1978).

29. See *ABA Code of Professional Responsibility, Disciplinary Rule* 4-101(A) (1977) (information gained in the professional relationship that the client has requested be held inviolate or the disclosure of which would be embarrassing or would be likely to be detrimental to the client).

30. "In view of the obvious materiality of the information, especially to attorneys learned in securities law, the attorneys' responsibilities to their corporate client required them to take steps to ensure that the information would be disclosed to the shareholders." 457 F. Supp. at 713.

31. See text accompanying notes 15 and 16 *supra*.

characteristic of the *National Student Marketing* fact situation which distinguishes it from the fact situations in *Garner* and its progeny is that the corporate action in *National Student Marketing* required, as a matter of law, the affirmative approval of the stockholders of the corporation.[32] It was action outside the scope of the authority legally delegated to the board of directors. The principle that counsel owes his professional obligation to the body charged with responsibility for corporate decision-making led in that case not to the board of directors but to the stockholders. The *National Student Marketing* holding thus was not inconsistent with the ABA's 1940 opinion;[33] it was an extension of that opinion.

Many of the cases in the *Garner* line are recent; the lines are certainly not fully drawn. But the cases to date are consistent with the rule that counsel, as a matter of law, owes his professional obligation, including his obligation to preserve confidentiality, to the board of directors of the corporation except in those instances where the stockholders rather than the directors are the legally designated decisionmakers for the corporation.[34]

DEFINING CORPORATE COUNSEL'S ROLE IN PRACTICE

Unfortunately, most discussions of corporate counsel's role are limited to discussion of counsel's legal responsibilities. Those discussions, while necessary to establish a framework within which counsel must operate, tend to obscure rather than to help define the appropriate role for counsel who wants to make a constructive contribution to his client's decision-making. Legalistic discussion tends to cast counsel in the role of police officer or watchdog. With rare exceptions counsel's proper role is one of assistance and counsel rather than of monitoring and supervision.

The practical problems of defining counsel's role are determining whom counsel ought to advise, on what matters, and from what perspective. Unless management, counsel, and the board of directors can reach a satisfactory understanding on those issues, counsel will be unable to render maximum service to the corporation.

Our attempt to chart an appropriate role for counsel runs immediately into a serious dilemma. We have already seen that, conson-

---

32. 457 F. Supp. at 690–91. Shareholder approval of the National Student Marketing Corporation/Interstate National Corporation merger was required under the laws of the District of Columbia, 29 D.C. Code Ann. §§ 927c, 927g, and Nevada, Nev. Rev. Stat. §§ 78.470, 485.

33. See note 16 *supra*.

34. The considerations may be quite different in the case of closely held corporations. Perhaps the responsibilities of counsel should also be different, particularly in corporations with constituent documents which reserve to shareholders substantial portions of authority normally alloted to directors.

ant with the notion that the authority to make most business decisions rests with the board of directors, counsel's ultimate responsibility is to the board.[35] At the same time, despite growing activity by many boards of directors, the great majority of corporate decisions on which counsel can have a significant impact are made by management, either without reference to the board or with board approval based upon recommendations made by management and on supporting information and reasoning supplied by management. Furthermore, counsel cannot have an impact on corporate decisions unless he is consulted with respect to them and given adequate facts on which to base his advice. Opportunity to consult, and access to factual information are controlled by management and, as a practical matter, will not be supplied by management unless counsel has management's complete confidence and is viewed by management as being of substantial assistance to the decision-making process. The necessity of establishing and maintaining the total confidence of management is, therefore, a critical factor in defining a proper role for corporate counsel.

Balancing that element with the proper discharge of his obligation to the board of directors is one of counsel's most difficult tasks. Counsel must so conduct himself that management will freely confide in him knowing that counsel's ultimate obligation is not to management but to the board.

This dilemma is not insoluble. Management has, by and large, come to realize that cooperation with counsel is in its self-interest. Most managements, contrary to what many advocates of corporate reform seem to believe, want to operate legally, fairly and in a manner consistent with the public interest. The "public be damned" attitude of corporate management is becoming rarer and rarer for many reasons, not the least important of which is a pragmatic realization by upper-level corporate managers that, in the wake of *Gulf Oil*[36] and *Lockheed,*[37] action of questionable legality may well cost them their jobs. Managers of public corporations are coming more and more to realize, with the growth in number and competence of independent public directors, audit committees, and other director groups, most of whom are intensely conscious of their legal accountability, that their conduct of

---

35. See text accompanying notes 15 and 16 *supra*.

36. A Special Review Committee headed by John J. McCloy revealed that the Gulf Oil Corporation had made approximately $12.3 million in illegal or questionable payments both in the United States and abroad. N.Y. Times, Dec. 31, 1975, at p. 1, col. 1. These revelations led to the resignations of Gulf's chief executive officer and several other top level executives. *Id.*, Jan 14, 1976, at p. 1, col. 2.

37. Within weeks of the issuing of the report of the committee investigating Gulf Oil, see note 36 *supra,* the chairman and vice-chairman of Lockheed Aircraft Corporation resigned amid disclosures that Lockheed had paid millions of dollars in overseas bribes to promote the sale of its aircraft. N.Y. Times, Feb. 14, 1976, at p. 1, col. 5.

corporate affairs will be monitored and subjected to scrutiny, much of it with the 20-20 vision of hindsight. Managers are increasingly anxious not to be second-guessed and therefore seek to anticipate problems rather than to struggle with them after they arise.

Management's and counsel's legal obligations to the board are not dissimilar. If counsel establishes the proper working relationship with management, his advice as to discharge of those obligations should be welcomed.

Counselling Management

To establish that relationship and therefore to contribute effectively to management decision-making, counsel should conduct himself when counseling management as if management were his individual client. In accordance with this governing principle, counsel should start with the presumption that information which comes to his attention in the course of his employment, including what is said by management, should be revealed by him to no one except management. Despite his overriding legal obligation to the directors, counsel must avoid revealing such information even to the board of directors except in the most extreme circumstances. Like it or not, as a practical matter, whenever counsel causes matters to be brought to the board's attention without first having persuaded management that consultation with the board is appropriate, the attorney reduces the likelihood that management will confide in him in the future and, therefore, lessens his future effectiveness.

To say that counsel ought to treat management as if it were an individual client, does not, of course, mean that the corporate client does not generate problems unique to the corporate form. There are at least three areas in which a lawyer counsels his corporate client which are not involved in other types of representation, and all relate significantly to issues of corporate governance.

The first concerns the lawyer's traditional obligation to be familiar with and to advise his client with respect to the vast array of statutory, regulatory, and judicial rules that increasingly circumscribe the activities of public corporations.[38] The attorney is trained to analyze and to understand the often obscure language of this body of law and to relate it to the activities of each particular client. The meaning and effect of the provisions of the Robinson-Patman Act are, like the uses of tobacco, not always obvious at first glance. The provisions of the Foreign Corrupt Practices Act indicate that they soon may come to rival those of the Robinson-Patman Act in creating confusion. It is impossible for management, responsible for the day-to-day operations of an active and complex business, to remain current with rapidly proliferating and increasingly complex statutes or their regulatory and judicial

---

38. See note 2 *supra*.

interpretation; but management must be advised of their application to the corporation's business if the corporation is to conform to publicly acceptable standards of conduct and to avoid costly violations of law. Advice of counsel concerning compliance with existing law in areas such as antitrust, environmental law, and employment practices can have a significant impact on corporate activity and can avoid corporate activity which, because it is viewed by the public as unacceptable, leads to demands for change in the corporate structure.[39] This area of legal contribution is traditional and well understood.

An important and necessary extension of this area, although not often recognized or accepted by either counsel or executives, may be the area where counsel can play his most constructive role in making existing corporate structures responsive to the demands being placed on them. Changes in public morality, and federal and state legislation reflecting such changes, have repeatedly required corporations to take expensive and painful action to correct or modify a status quo created by corporate action that appeared to be legal at the time it was taken, but which appears to be no longer acceptable in light of regulatory hindsight or tenable in the face of changed public morality. Two obvious recent examples are mandated affirmative action to correct past discrimination against blacks, other minorities, and women, and legislatively required action to correct plant conditions which are deemed destructive to the environment or hazardous to health or safety. Action required by public attitudes toward corporate investment in South Africa may prove to be another.

While no one could have predicted all of these recent changes in public attitude any more than one can now predict similar developments which are sure to occur during the remainder of the century, farsighted corporate action at the time such issues began to surface would have done much to avoid the dislocation and expense later incurred by many of our major corporations and would have done even more to protect the public image of corporate management, perhaps avoiding the current demands for change in corporate structure. It is difficult for a corporate executive, concentrating on the operation of one or two discrete business enterprises, to anticipate problems of such a broad nature. The lawyer, like the professional outside director, deals with numerous business enterprises in many fields and often has a better perspective from which to anticipate such problems. The lawyer, in addition, has access in his daily professional literature to information, such as reports of legislative hearings and public statements by administrators, which should serve to provide early warnings of such developments.

It can be argued that a lawyer who, in 1950, counseled a corporate client to examine its employment and promotion practices in order to

---

39. See Manning, "Thinking Straight About Corporate Law Reform," 41 Law & Contemp. Prob. 3, 11–12, 27–28 (1977).

take steps to eliminate racial discrimination or who, in 1970, advised his client that it should conduct a study aimed at locating and terminating bribes being paid by overseas employees would have done so at the risk of an annoyed client and no constructive results. Perhaps. But the attitude of corporate executives toward such advice has changed dramatically during the last few years, and a number of corporate executives now express the view, at least in private, that these are the kinds of matters for which counsel should take responsibility.

The second area of counseling, unique to the representation of corporate management, is the domain of public-disclosure policy. Although the need for legal supervision of the preparation of technical legal documents such as SEC reports, proxy material, and registration statements is generally acknowledged, many public companies have no significant legal input when issuing press releases—even those announcing quarterly earnings—or when making statements to securities analysts and other members of the public. Public disclosure may be viewed as peripheral to corporate governance, but it is an important element of shareholder participation in that process, and failure of corporate managements to make what the public views as adequate, fair, and timely public disclosure has been a significant factor in the rising tide of anticorporate opinion.[40]

The lawyer is the member of the corporate community charged with knowledge of the statutory, regulatory, and judicial requirements for minimum disclosure. He also has, in most cases, the broadest experience of those on the corporate stage in considering what is appropriate and proper disclosure of various types of corporate news. Unlike most managers, he deals with the problem for numerous corporations and is likely to have faced other problems similar to problems faced by his client at any given time. Concepts such as materiality cut broadly across all types of business activities. Whether a pending litigation, a default on a contract or a fluctuation in currency exchange rates ought to be discussed in a disclosure document are not issues that are peculiar to any one industry or line of business.[41] Management and the directors are entitled to considerable discretion in determining the form and content of disclosure, but counsel should play a significant role in identifying areas of possible disclosure and in giving advice with respect to the judgment decisions to be made.

The third, and perhaps most important, area in which the lawyer counsels management is management's interaction with the board of directors. An increasing sensitivity of directors to their legal obligations as managers of the corporation and the growing number of outside

---

40. *Id.* at 13–15.

41. The standards embodied in the Supreme Court's definition of materiality, see TSC Industries, Inc. v. Northway, Inc., 426 U.S. 438, 449 (1976), are the type of concepts that law students are forced to wrestle with from the first weeks of law school.

nonmanagement directors are rapidly eliminating the rubber-stamp board. Boards are demanding more information as backup for decisions they are asked to make or endorse, in many cases postponing action which management is anxious to execute promptly, when the directors do not feel that adequate background has been provided. Chief executives are aware that directors are taking their responsibilities more seriously, that directors expect management to act within the limits of its authority and to report important action to the board and that failure of management to satisfy these expectations may well result in disciplinary action by the board or at least a reduction of the board's confidence and a consequent shortening of its leash on management. Chief executives are, at the same time, coming to realize that, if properly informed and consulted, their boards can be of substantial help in managing the corporation and, on a more pragmatic level, that the better informed the board, the less likelihood that the board will second-guess management at a later date.

In this context, the manner in which management communicates with the board and the decisions management makes as to when it will seek board approval are critical to the manner in which corporations will be governed. Counsel's experience with a variety of corporations and the manner in which various executives communicate with their boards, combined with the attention which corporate counsel necessarily gives to pronouncements of administrative bodies and the courts as to what information is relevant in corporate decision-making, should enable counsel to assist executives in preparing appropriate and complete presentations to the board. Counsel is less involved in day-to-day corporate operations and can take a more detached and objective view in deciding when consultation with or approval by the board is appropriate. Facilitating the flow of appropriate information between the board and the chief executive can and should be one of counsel's most important roles.

In these three areas of counseling, the question often arises as to the propriety of counsel's expressing his opinions or volunteering advice which is based on other than legal considerations. Some managers strongly object to such advice as being outside the lawyer's province, and relations between management and counsel can become particularly strained when counsel expresses reservations about a proposed course of action on grounds that it appears unfair, unwise, or immoral, although not in violation of any law.

Fortunately, for reasons mentioned earlier,[42] managers are coming to welcome such advice—or at least to accept its propriety. Where management objects to such advice, however, counsel may be professionally obligated to give it anyway, hopefully with consummate tact, and to bear the brunt of the executive's displeasure. The Code of Professional Responsibility admonishes the lawyer to bring the "full-

---

42. See pp. 229–30 *supra*.

ness of his experience" to his representation and indicates that the lawyer's advice "need not be confined to purely legal considerations."[43] Indeed, the Code indicates that it is desirable that the lawyer point out factors leading to action that is morally just.[44] By informing himself about developing public, legislative, and regulatory attitudes which may affect the future activities of his corporate client rather than limiting himself to the present state of the law itself, counsel is not only equipping himself to influence corporate decisions to the benefit of his client but is carrying out to the fullest extent the goals of the Code of Professional Responsibility.

Counseling the Directors

Given the day-to-day relationship between corporate counsel and management, what is the proper relationship between the lawyer and the directors, to whom counsel owes his ultimate professional responsibility? A few principles should govern.

The basic principle, which affects all aspects of the professional relationship, is that board members should always have direct and free access to corporate counsel. That access has traditionally been an anathema to corporate executives, but counsel clearly cannot properly discharge his role unless direct communication with the directors exists.[45] Only through direct contact with the directors can counsel familiarize himself with the attitudes and interests of the board so as to enable him to aid the chief executive in structuring communications to and relationships with the board. Only by direct contact with counsel can board members develop the kind of confidence in counsel which will make them receptive to his advice and comfortable in relying on it. In addition, directors sometimes require legal advice on matters which are not appropriate for discussion with management, such as legally

---

43. *ABA Code of Professional Responsibility, Ethical Consideration* 7-8.

44. "In assisting his client to reach a proper decision, it is often desirable for a lawyer to point out those factors which may lead to a decision that is morally just as well as legally permissible." *Id.*

45. There may be occasions when there is need for the corporate director to have outside advice. The director should be assured that, in appropriate circumstances, he (alone or together with fellow directors) has a direct channel of communication with the enterprise's principal advisors, including its auditors, its regular corporate counsel and, when such a relationship exists, its investment banking advisors and its executive compensation counselors. Further, there may be occasions when an outside advisor should be specially retained to assist the board or a committee in connection with a particular matter. The need for outside advice should be infrequent, arising most often in the unusual or corporate crisis situation.

ABA, Committee on Corporate Laws, Section of Corporation, Banking and Business Law, *Corporate Director's Guidebook*, 33 Bus. L. 1595, 1611 (1978).

permissible structures for executive compensation or discharge of an executive from the position he currently holds. Finally, directors often require legal advice that can be adequately provided only by direct discussion with counsel. The directors are entitled to such advice, and cannot discharge their legal obligations without it.[46] The Audit Committee, in particular, given the role in which it is now being cast and the importance which is being placed on its activities, is entitled to direct advice of lawyers.[47]

An alternative to a direct relationship with the corporation's counsel is to provide separate counsel for the board of directors itself, a position advocated by Arthur Goldberg.[48] That alternative would enormously increase legal costs because of the need to educate two sets of counsel with respect to any matter under discussion and is likely to decrease the reliability of counsel's advice because special counsel is unlikely to acquire as broad or as deep an understanding of the corporation's problems as counsel who is working with the management on a day-to-day basis.

Given the corporate manager's traditional suspicion of direct relationships between counsel and the directors, counsel must toe a very narrow line in order to acquire and preserve the confidence of both

---

46. *Id.* at 1611, 1618. Some recent well-publicized events which undoubtedly raised questions in the minds of directors which required direct face to face legal advice were the reemployment by Columbia Pictures Industries, Inc. of an executive officer who had been accused (and later pleaded no contest to charges) of embezzling corporate funds, Fortune, Aug. 28, 1978 at 38; the rejection by McGraw-Hill directors of the American Express offer at a very substantial premium over market, Wall St. J., Jan. 16, 1979 at p. 5, col. 1, and Feb. 1, 1979, at p. 2, col. 2; and, the consideration by the directors of American Express of the effect on their proposed tender for McGraw-Hill stock of the presence of a senior American Express officer on the McGraw-Hill board and executive committee, *id.*, Feb. 2, 1979 at p. 12, col. 3.

47. The basic concept of the Audit Committee is that it should operate independently of the corporation's executive officers, and one of its principal functions is to be responsible for insuring that the internal and external audit functions are conducted in such a manner as to create the maximum possible checks and balances against improper executive or employee action. Advice to the board of directors, must, therefore, be direct and not given through the executive officers themselves. That point was brought home forcefully by the many investigations of potentially improper foreign and domestic payments which were conducted under the direct supervision of Audit Committees and which, in many cases, involved not only difficult questions of the legal propriety of various corporate actions but also legal definition of the rights which a corporation might have against one or more executives or employees and the related question of whether the corporation was obligated to enforce its rights of recovery against such executives or employees, regardless of the effect such enforcement might have on the welfare of the corporation itself.

48. Goldberg, "Debate on Outside Directors," N.Y. Times, Oct. 20, 1972, § 3, at p. 1, col. 3.

management and directors. Yet if counsel is able to achieve the confidence of both, he can play an important role in establishing proper communication between the two, thereby improving the trust and working relationship between management and the board.

In walking that line, it is critical for counsel to reduce the need for direct communication with the directors to a minimum and to avoid bypassing the normal channels of communication from management to the board. He must always attempt to have his advice with respect to all important matters passed to the board through the chief executive officer and other normal management channels. In particular, it is important that, except for the extermely rare instances where a director may have good reason for not wanting the chief executive officer to be aware of the subject of his direct consultation with counsel,[49] counsel should keep management informed, on a current basis, of discussions he has had with directors and of advice he has given to any director. Counsel should make it clear in any consultation with the directors that he will so inform the management unless instructed by the director or directors not to do so.

A corollary of this rule of direct access is that whenever asked for advice by a director or by the board,[50] counsel is obligated to give advice just as he would give it to any other client. This corollary becomes important when the advice asked for by the board or by an individual director may lead to board action contrary to that recommended by management. The corollary becomes critical where counsel's advice has previously been given to management but management has found the advice not to be determinative of its ultimate recommendation to the board. Counsel can, to a considerable degree, avoid conflicts with management in such situations by urging management to include in its presentation of any matter to the board any legal advice which management has received which might be relevant to consideration of the issue by the board.

A third basic rule for counseling directors is that counsel should not attempt to substitute his judgment for that of the chief executive officer. The board of directors has selected the chief executive officer to manage the day-to-day operation of the business. When counsel has advised management with respect to matters brought to his attention, but management chooses not to follow counsel's advice, counsel generally is

---

49. See notes 45-47 *supra* and accompanying text.

50. There is a danger that an individual director, particularly a dissident director, will ask counsel for advice on questions which are not germane to issues properly before the board or to the board's responsibilities. Such situations create dificult problems for counsel. They should be resolved ultimately by the board's exerting control over such a member or by appropriate instructions from the board to counsel with respect to such requests. An arrangement under which counsel responds to directors only when requested to do so by majority board action is an undesirable alternative.

entitled to respect that decision and has no obligation to inform the board that he disagrees with the decisions or recommendations of management. He should not volunteer to the board the advice he has previously given to the management—so long as the decision on which he differs with the management is a matter of judgment and not a matter of legality. In those instances of judgment, the lawyer is in a position similar to that of a vice-president in charge of marketing or a plant manager. The chief executive has responsibility and authority for judgment calls in the legal area as well as in all other areas of corporate management. Counsel who volunteers a contrary position is likely to interfere with proper corporate decision-making and surely will impair his relationship with both management and directors.

If the action recommended by counsel is legally required or is necessary to prevent violation of law, and the advice is disregarded, counsel is obligated to demand that the chief executive report counsel's advice to the board, and if the chief executive refuses to do so, to advise the directors himself.[51] Such situations would arise where management intends to take action which, in the opinion of counsel, cannot be legally taken without board approval, where management intends to take or has taken action which is illegal or constitutes a fraud or crime or where counsel believes that action being recommended by management would subject the corporation or the directors to material legal liability, and the directors have not been adequately informed of that risk. Happily, such circumstances seldom arise. When they do, counsel's obligation is absolute despite the fact that such action may render it impossible for him to operate effectively with that management thereafter.

Expanding demands for corporations to act as public-spirited citizens as well as producers of dividends, reflected in proliferating government regulation as well as in stockholder and consumer pressures, have focused the spotlight on individual failures of corporate performance. If those failures continue in the face of public examination and criticism, those who today claim that the current legal structures of corporate governance are inadequate and must be changed by fiat will be proven correct and basic changes will be made in the way our corporations are governed. The burden of proof is rapidly shifting to those who resist structural change. Corporate counsel have contributed considerably to the past derelictions, by omission if not by commission, and now have an obligation, and an opportunity, to play an important role in putting the corporate house in order.

---

51. Counsel should be careful to warn corporate employees, particularly middle and lower level managers, that counsel acts as counsel to the corporation, not as counsel to the individual employees. Such warnings are necessary to avoid an assumption by the employee that his communications are privileged and cannot be revealed without the employee's rather than the corporation's consent.

CHAPTER SIX

Federal Corporate Law, Federalism, and the Federal Courts

Gordon G. Young,* *Associate Professor of Law, Syracuse University College of Law*

INTRODUCTION

During this decade there has been a resurgence in the movement for more federal regulation of the internal affairs of the nation's most powerful corporations.[1] The proposals, described below, to effect such a change raise questions ranging from basic issues of federalism to mechanical jurisdictional problems. For example, Professor Cary's proposal to create federal fiduciary standards for the managers of such corporations, to confer mandatory and exclusive jurisdiction over cases involving such standards upon state courts, and to subject such courts to review by lower federal courts,[2] involves a relationship between state courts and the federal government arguably unprecedented in our 200 years under the Constitution. An example of a more mundane problem

* The author wishes to thank Charles F. Corcoran, a third-year law student, for his unusually able assistance.

1. See, e.g., Miller, "At Odds Over Corporate Governance," N.Y. Times, December 24, 1978, § 3 (Business and Finance), at 1, col. 3; R. Nader, M. Green, and J. Seligman, *Taming the Giant Corporation* (1976) [hereinafter cited as R. Nader]; Cary, "Federalism and Corporate Law: Reflections Upon Delaware, 83 Yale L.J. 663 (1974); Henning, "Federalism and Corporate Law: The Chaos Inherent in the Cary Proposal," 3 Sec. Reg. L.J. 362 (1976); Kaplan, "Foreign Corporations and Local Corporate Policy," 21 Vand. L. Rev. 433 (1968); Note, "Federal Chartering of Corporations: A Proposal," 61 Geo. L.J. 89 (1972); *Corporate Rights and Responsibilities: Hearings Before the Senate Committee on Commerce*, 94th Cong., 2d Sess. at 57 (1976) [hereinafter cited as *Hearings*] (Statement of A. A. Sommer).

   For a sampling of earlier consideration of federal incorporation see R. Nader, *supra* at 65–71, and authorities cited in Kaplan, *supra* at 480–81 n. 127.
2. Cary, *supra* note 1, at 700–05.

is the possibility that exclusive federal chartering—another proposed, less likely, and more drastic form of federalization of corporate law—might well result in the abolition of a large amount of diversity jurisdiction.[3] For those primarily interested in the quality of corporate justice, even nonconstitutional jurisdictional questions have a subtle but vital importance. An argument can be made, for example, that in order to insure the highest quality of justice under new federal corporate law,[4] suits under some of its provisions should be cognizable exclusively in the federal courts.[5] These and other issues of federalism connected with federal corporate law proposals are the subject of this article.

My interests run both to the study of federalism and to that of corporation law. What follows immediately in this introduction is, first, a description of the current state-law dominated system of regulating the internal affairs[6] of national corporations and, second, a sketch of current proposals for increasing the regulatory role of the federal government.

Current Regulation

Federal deference to state regulation characterizes the current system of regulating the internal affairs of corporations with substantial interstate connections. By "internal affairs" is meant those matters concerning domestic corporations which states typically purport to govern by their business corporation laws.[7] While such laws vary in content from state to state, they all deal primarily with various relationships among shareholders, directors, and officers and to a lesser extent with the relationship of such groups to third parties, particularly creditors. With the exception of matters concerning the internal affairs of a very few corporations, such as national banking associations which hold federal charters,[8] the federal government has not chosen to make law governing the internal affairs of private business corporations, no matter how extensive their connections with interstate commerce.

---

3. See discussion at pp. 271–74 *infra.*

4. To be distinguished from the federal corporate law currently existing under the federal securities law, but recently circumscribed by the Supreme Court. See note 101 *infra*, and accompanying text.

5. See discussion at pp. 259–69 *infra.*

6. By "law governing internal affairs," I mean the law which determines the rights and duties of officers, directors, and shareholders *inter sese*. Restatement (Second) of Conflict of Laws §§ 301–13 (1971) observe the distinction between laws governing the relationship of a corporation to the external world and the law governing its internal affairs. See *id.* § 313 Comments a & b. Compare *id.* § 301 with §§ 302–10.

7. See note 6 *supra* and accompanying text.

8. 12 U.S.C. §§ 21–24 (1976).

The concept that a person is subject to full in personam jurisdiction only in a state where he is present or domiciled ultimately leads to tension with the original conception of a corporation as a person located only in the state that issued its corporate charter.[9] As long as corporations were, for the most part, active only in the commerce of their chartering states,[10] the tension was more theoretical than real. With the advent of numerous corporations active in interstate commerce, their national nature was sensed by the courts, if not clearly understood. Unlike natural persons, such corporations not only could be, but were, "present" in several places at the same time.[11] Where such presence was substantial, courts found additional forums with full in personam jurisdiction.[12]

Conceptually, matters might have proceeded differently. A corporation's substantial presence in two or more states might have been made an operative fact triggering a federal scheme of internal affairs regulation. No such choice was made and, as a result, at least theoretical choice-of-law questions arose. Two or more state forums having general in personam jurisdiction over any corporation had, as an apparent consequence, shared power to render judgments affecting its internal affairs. What limitations of reasonableness, and even of constitutional law, are there upon the choices of law such forums may make in deciding matters of the internal affairs of a corporation?

The limitations imposed by reasonableness involve the needs for planning and for coherence.[13] Corporate shareholders, officers, and directors need to know in advance of certain actions what laws will govern such matters as whether preemptive rights exist, what is an appropriate record date for dividends, and whether shares can be voted cumulatively.[14] The need for coherence is distinct from the need for certainty. Even were it to be predictable in advance, the application of differing substantive laws to parts of certain transactions often would be undesirable. For example, the application of one state's cumulative voting rule and another's straight voting rule to different shareholders

---

9. See E. Dodd, *American Business Corporations* 51 (1954).

10. *Id.* at 179.

11. See International Shoe Co. v. Washington, 326 U.S. 310 (1945). The concept of multiple presence developed slowly. See R. Field & B. Kaplan, *Materials for a Basic Course in Civil Procedure* 677–79 (1973); E. Dodd, *supra* note 9, at 51, 174–78.

12. International Shoe Co. v. Washington, 326 U.S. 310 (1945).

13. See note 15 *infra* and accompanying text.

14. For an example of a provision creating preemptive rights see N.Y. Bus. Corp. Law § 622 (McKinney 1963). For an example of a provision defining appropriate record dates see id. § 604 (McKinney 1963). For an example of a provision permitting cumulative voting see *id.* § 618 (McKinney 1963).

voting in the same corporate election of directors would lead to results undesirable under any theory.

Such potential conflict-of-laws problems have rarely caused difficulty. Courts which take jurisdiction of suits involving the internal affairs of a corporation incorporated in another state have sensed the need for certainty and coherence in the choice of such law and have used the bright-line solution of applying the law of the state of incorporation.[15] The exceptions are, for the most part, predictable and include suits involving the internal affairs of pseudoforeign corporations and other suits where the needs for certainty and coherence pale next to the forum's interest in applying its own corporate law.[16] Earlier in this century the Supreme Court occasionally invalidated, on constitutional grounds, a choice of law made by a state court; but there has never been a Supreme Court case invalidating a state's choice of the law to govern

---

15. For the proposition that most American courts have followed this bright-line solution see Kaplan, *supra* note 1, at 440. Restatement (Second) of Conflict of Laws generally accepts such a rule (§ 302(1) & (2)) arguing for it as follows in Comment c:

> *Rationale*. Application of the local law of the state of incorporation will usually be supported by those choice-of-law factors favoring the needs of the interstate and international systems, certainty, predictability and uniformity of result, protection of the justified expectations of the parties and ease in the application of the law to be applied. Usually, application of this law will also be supported by the factor looking toward implementation of the relevant policies of the state with the dominant interest in the decision of the particular issue.
>
> Uniform treatment of directors, officers and shareholders is an important objective which can only be attained by having the rights and liabilities of those persons with respect to the corporation governed by a single law. To the extent that they think about the matter, these persons would usually expect that their rights and duties with respect to the corporation would be determined by the local law of the state of incorporation. This state is also easy to identify, and thus the value of ease of application is attained when the local law of this state is applied.
>
> In addition, many matters involving a corporation cannot practicably be determined differently in different states. Examples of such matters, most of which have already been mentioned in Comment a, include steps taken in the course of the original incorporation, the election or appointment of directors and officers, the adoption of by-laws, the issuance of corporate shares (see Comment f), the holding of directors' and shareholders' meetings, methods of voting including any requirement for cumulative voting, the declaration and payment of dividend and other distributions, charter amendments, mergers, consolidations, and reorganizations, the reclassification of shares and the purchase and redemption by the corporation of outstanding shares of its own stock.

But see Kaplan, *supra* note 1, at 476.

16. Restatement (Second) of Conflict of Laws at § 302, Comment g. See also Western Airlines v. Sobieski, 12 Cal. Rptr. 719 (Cal. App. 1961).

the internal affairs of a classical business corporation.[17] The absence of such a case may be attributable to state courts' faithfully employing the "law of the state of incorporation" conflicts rule. Had state courts not behaved so reasonably in choosing to apply to the internal affairs of a corporation the law of its chartering state, there would have been numerous serious challenges. Had the ability of shareholders, officers, and directors of interstate corporations to plan their actions in light of a certain and coherent set of rules ever been seriously jeopardized, interstate commerce in turn would have been severely harmed and the federal government would have had two options: The first would have been to federalize the substantive law dealing with the internal affairs of such corporations; the second would have been to mandate, as a matter of federal constitutional law, a choice of law system similar to the one the states have, in fact, voluntarily created.

The lack of a federal corporate law to govern the internal affairs of interstate corporations—at least the largest of them—seems a result of the evolution of this country's commerce. In the early days of the republic, corporations were largely intrastate enterprises.[18] Slowly more corporations became truly interstate in operations. Because there never was a dramatic beginning of an age of interstate corporations, state regulatory schemes continued to govern them. As we have seen, the states have used the old models with ingenuity, developing their own unofficial federalism by means of parallel choice-of-law rules.[19]

Of course, we cannot conclude that the regulation of activities which developed gradually should be changed simply because the regulation would be different if the activities had developed all at once. A system designed for the regulation of corporations conceptually linked to particular states has been adjusted to permit a reasonably intelligent accommodation to the change in the nature of corporations. The devel-

---

17. An example of the Supreme Court's invalidation of a state's choice of law is Home Ins. Co. v. Dick, 281 U.S. 397 (1930). See generally R. J. Weintraub, *Commentary on the Conflict of Laws,* Chapter 9 (1971). The theory of the cases invalidating states' choices of law has been predicated upon the due process or full faith and credit clauses, but not upon the commerce clause.

While the Supreme Court has never invalidated a state's choice of law to govern the internal affairs of a classical business corporation, it has done something quite similar in the context of fraternal benevolent associations. In four cases decided between 1915 and 1948, the Supreme Court invalidated a state's refusal to apply to the internal affairs of such associations the law of their respective jurisdictions of organization or incorporation. Order of United Commercial Travelers of America v. Wolfe, 331 U.S. 586 (1947); Sovereign Camp of the Woodmen of the World v. Bolin, 305 U.S. 66 (1938); Modern Woodmen of America v. Mixer, 267 U.S. 544 (1925); Supreme Council of the Royal Arcanum v. Green, 237 U.S. 531 (1915). There is at least some doubt as to the continued viability of such cases, see R. J. Weintraub, *supra* this note, at 410.

18. E. Dodd, *supra* note 9, at 179.

19. See note 15 *supra* and accompanying text.

opment of the prevailing choice-of-law rule described above is evidence of that.

Recent Proposals for More Federal Corporate Law

The current impetus for more federal corporate law has come entirely from those who feel that the current state-oriented system of regulating truly national corporations—those with substantial interstate operations and a nationwide shareholder constituency—is perverse.[20] The focus of the critics is not primarily upon the abstract abdication of federal responsibility inherent in the current state-oriented system, but rather upon how poorly the states have discharged their responsibility. Weak state substantive laws are seen as no accident. The current system is perverse not merely because it permits the states to regulate national corporations but also because it contains built-in incentives for the states to regulate in a way designed to ignore the interests of small investors.

Under the current system, except in unusual circumstances, the law of the state under which a corporation has been incorporated governs the relations *inter sese* of stockholders, directors, and officers.[21] There are no federal limitations determining in what state a business may incorporate; indeed a business may incorporate in a state where it has no connections of any sort.[22] While there are limitations upon the taxes which may be charged by a state where a corporation is not chartered,[23] a state is free to charge a corporation large annual fees for the privilege of holding a corporate charter and the concomitant benefit of having that state's laws rule its internal affairs.[24] Critics of the current system of regulation claim that those who control national corporations shop for corporate law favorable to them and that this, for the most part, means shopping for internal rules which benefit controlling interests by reduc-

---

20. See, e.g., R. Nader, *supra* note 1, at 43–61, 246; Cary, *supra* note 1, at 663–92; Kaplan, *supra* note 1, at 437, 476–81; *Hearings, supra* note 1, at 57–58 (Statement of A. A. Sommer), 241–46 (Statement of H. Goldschmid), 333 (Statement of D. Vagts).

21. Kaplan, *supra* note 1, at 440. See Restatement (Second) of Conflict of Laws §§ 301–13 (1971).

22. See Kaplan, *supra* note 1, at 435 n.4 and accompanying text.

23. See, e.g., Cudahy Packing Co. v. Hinkle, 278 U.S. 460 (1928) (striking down a state's annual tax upon foreign corporations based upon their authorized capital stock). Taxes on foreign corporations must generally be apportioned to the amount of business done within the taxing state. General Motors Corp. v. Washington, 377 U.S. 436, 439–42 (1963), *reh. den.*, 379 U.S. 875 (1964).

24. See Del. Code Ann. tit. 8, §§ 501, 503 (1975 & Supp. 1978) providing that only domestic corporations pay an annual franchise tax based upon authorized capital stock.

ing the rights of small investors and others.[25] The rest of the tale, according to the critics, is that the sellers of corporate law are only too pleased to accommodate the buyers by continuously improving their product to make it competitively promanagement.[26] The competition among states to make their corporate laws attractive to the management has been described by a distinguished scholar of corporation law as "the race to the bottom."[27]

The common element of the proposed alternatives to the current system is a concern for the welfare of noncontrolling shareholders.[28] Some proponents of a larger federal role in the governance of national corporations would go further, extending corporate legal protection to employees, creditors, and society at large,[29] classes of persons who are the beneficiaries of few rights under current state business corporation law.[30] While the areas of substantive difference among the proponents' regulatory schemes suggest an infinite number of possible legislative packages, the structural differences suggest two models: (1) retention of the current system with some new federal regulation superimposed[31] or (2) exclusive federal chartering and comprehensive regulation of the internal affairs of national corporations.[32]

The proponents of more federal regulation agree that the most likely objects of such new laws are this nation's largest, most powerful corporations.[33] References made below to "national corporations" are to this

---

25. See R. Nader, *supra* note 1, at 663–70.

26. R. Nader, *supra* note 1, at 54–61; Cary, *supra* note 1, at 668–92.

27. Cary, *supra* note 1, at 705.

28. R. Nader, *supra* note 1, at 75–118, 254; Cary, *supra* note 1, at 902; Henning, *supra* note 1, at 362–67; Kaplan, *supra* note 1, at 478–80; Note, *supra* note 1, at 113–21; *Hearings, supra* note 1, at 58 (Statement of A. A. Sommer).

29. R. Nader, *supra* note 1, at 181–236, 245, 253–54.

30. See, e.g., Del. Code Ann. tit. 8 (Supp. 1971); N.Y. Bus. Corp. Law (McKinney 1963); *Hearings, supra* note 1, at 57 (Statement of A. A. Sommer).

31. The main substantive features of Cary's proposal are presented in note 57 *infra*. Nader's proposal is also one of joint state-federal regulation. R. Nader, *supra* note 1, at 239–40. Indeed, while Nader proposes federal chartering, he proposes that state chartering be retained as well. *Id.* at 239–40.

32. See proposal of A. A. Sommer, note 59 *infra*.

33. Cary proposes that his scheme of partial federal regulation apply to all corporations having more than $1 million in assets and 300 shareholders, noting that such a scope would parallel the American Law Institute's proposed Federal Securities Code. Cary, *supra* note 1, at 701. This selective test seems to be the product of practical political considerations since Cary states clearly that it might be preferable to apply his mode of regulation to "all public companies engaged in or affecting interstate commerce." *Id.* at 702–03.

Other proponents seem satisfied with a fairly selective test for the selection of corporations to be federally regulated. They propose: R. Nader, *supra* note 1,

nation's wealthiest corporations whether defined with reference to *Fortune*'s annual listing or by some other similar definition.[34]

This article does not deal with the question of whether state laws regulating national corporations are so inadequate substantively as to warrant federal intervention. That task has been performed admirably by others. Instead, this article deals with matters of jurisdiction and federalism which should be considered by any legislator who has preliminarily decided that some federal intervention is justified by the substantive inadequacy of state regulation.

"Jurisdiction of State and Federal Courts under a New Federal Corporate Law" *infra* deals with a host of jurisdictional issues which would be raised by various proposals for more federal regulation. Because, for the most part, both the partial-regulation model and the total-federal-preemption model discussed above raise the same issues to different degrees, they will be discussed together except where context indicates separate discussion. "Federal Corporate Law: Problems of Judicial Efficiency Arising from the Fit Between Federal and State Law," the concluding portion of this article, deals briefly with problems of federalism which should to some extent influence the precise scope of any federal regulation proposed to remedy the inadequacy of state law.

JURISDICTION OF STATE AND FEDERAL COURTS UNDER A NEW FEDERAL CORPORATE LAW

Federalization and the Caseloads of the Lower Federal Courts Under Existing Jurisdictional Grants

In order to consider the potential effect of a new federal corporate law for national corporations upon the caseloads of the lower federal courts, it is useful to discuss separately those effects attributable to federalization alone and those attributable to the difference between the substantive content of such a law and that of current state law. To isolate the former effects we must assume, with respect to whatever federal law we are discussing, that its content is identical to that of the state law it supplants. It would seem natural to suppose that the mere federaliza-

---

at 240–41 (sales of $250 million or 10,000 employees during any of the previous three years); Henning, *supra* note 1, at 370–71 ("the top 200 to 500 corporations" using criteria similar to those defining size for purposes of earlier wage and price control regulations); Note, *supra* note 1, at 98–99 (New York Stock Exchange listing test: $14 million in assets and more than 3000 shareholders). A. A. Sommer would have Congress completely preempt state law including the state chartering process with respect to corporations having more than 500 shareholders and $1 million in assets. See his testimony before a Senate committee quoted in note 59 *infra*.

34. It would include all corporations chosen by criteria described as "fairly selective" in note 33 *supra*.

tion of any aspect of corporate regulation would have the effect of increasing the caseload of the lower federal courts by an amount equal to the litigation which would have been previously maintained under the identical state standard. To make a more precise guess about the effect of any particular scheme of federalization upon the jurisdiction of the lower federal courts, more analysis is necessary. This is true because some claims arising under current state corporation laws are presently cognizable in the federal courts.

First, notwithstanding recent limitations, many state-law claims continue to be maintainable in federal court as pendent to federal securities laws claims which arise from identical or overlapping facts.[35]

Second, many suits arising under state business corporation laws are maintainable in federal court pursuant to the diversity-of-citizenship jurisdictional grant.[36] This is particularly true of derivative suits brought on behalf of a national corporation against management or controlling shareholders for breach of fiduciary responsibilities.[37] Such

---

35. For examples of state-law claims heard by federal courts because they were pendent to claims under the securities laws see Klaus v. Hi-Sheer Corp., 528 F.2d 225, 231 (9th Cir. 1975); Kasner v. H. Hentz & Co., 475 F.2d 119, 120 (5th Cir. 1973), *cert. denied,* 414 U.S. 823 (1973); Vanderboom v. Sexton, 422 F.2d 1233, 1241–42 (8th Cir. 1970), *cert. denied,* 400 U.S. 852 (1970); Strahan v. Pedroni, 387 F.2d 730, 731 (5th Cir. 1967); Ellis v. Carter, 291 F.2d 270, 275 (9th Cir. 1961). My conclusion that the Supreme Court has recently narrowed the possibility of such pendent jurisdiction is based upon the following analysis. First, while a doubtful federal cause of action asserted by plaintiff is sufficient to make available pendent jurisdiction over a related state-law claim even though plaintiff's view of federal law is ultimately rejected (see United Mine Workers v. Gibbs, 383 U.S. 715, 728 (1966); Bell v. Hood, 327 U.S. 678, 685 (1946) (Stone, C. J., dissenting)), a clearly insubstantial one is not sufficient (Warrington Sewer Co. v. Tracy, 463 F.2d 771 (3d Cir. 1972); Williams v. United States, 405 F.2d 951 (9th Cir. 1969)). Included as insubstantial federal causes of action are those clearly foreclosed by previous decisions of the Supreme Court or otherwise wholly without merit. Levering & G. Co. v. Morrin, 289 U.S. 103, 105 (1933). Second, after Blue Chip Stamps v. Manor Drug Stores, 421 U.S. 723 (1975) a larger number of securities law cases are clearly foreclosed by previous decision of the Supreme Court. See discussion note 101 *infra* and accompanying text.

36. 28 U.S.C. § 1332 (1976). For examples of state-law derivative suits maintained in federal courts pursuant to diversity jurisdiction see Niesz v. Gorsuch, 295 F.2d 909 (9th Cir. 1961); Topik v. Catalyst Research Corp., 339 F. Supp. 1102 (D.C. Md. 1972); Irwin v. West End Development Co., 342 F. Supp. 687 (D.C. Colo. 1972); Dowd v. Front Range Mines, Inc., 242 F. Supp. 591 (D.C. Colo. 1965); Himmelblau v. Haist, 195 F. Supp. 356 (S.D.N.Y. 1961); Weinstock v. Kallet, 11 F.R.D. 270 (S.D.N.Y. 1951).

37. Sullivan, "The Federal Courts as an Effective Forum in Shareholders' Derivative Actions," 22 La. L. Rev. 580, 603 (1962). The amount-in-controversy test applies solely to the interest of the corporation. Fed. R. Civ. P. 23.1. See Koster v. American Lumbermens' Mut. Cas. Co., 330 U.S. 518 (1947) (decided under predecessor rule 23(b)); rule 23.1 did not change the substance of rule 23(b) and

suits are extremely unlikely to be brought at all if the corporation does not have a substantial chance of recovering or saving more than $10,000.[38] If the corporation has a financial interest of more than $10,000 in such litigation, a federal district court has subject-matter jurisdiction to hear a derivative suit brought by any shareholder with diverse citizenship, regardless of the extent of his shareholding.[39] Similarly, the significant subject-matter jurisdictional barriers to a defendant's removal of a derivative suit are (1) the nondiversity of the parties[40] or (2) the fact that one of the defendants has been sued in his own domicile.[41] As a consequence, it is primarily the citizenship pattern of parties which will eliminate the possibility of federal diversity jurisdiction for either plaintiffs or defendants in derivative suits. Federalization of the laws defining the fiduciary responsibilities of management and controlling shareholders to national corporations will increase the caseload of the lower federal courts by the number of cases in which a party to a derivative suit which could be maintained in state court prefers a federal forum but cannot demonstrate the requisite diversity of citizenship.[42]

---

under the current rule the jurisdictional amount requirement is satisfied if there is a substantial claim that the corporation has suftered damage in excess of $10,000. C. Wright, *Law of Federal Courts* 358, 360–61 (3d ed. 1976).

38. Sullivan, *supra* note 37, at 596.

39. 28 U.S.C. § 1332 (1976). Its requirement of diverse citizenship is met only if the citizenship of each party defendant is diverse from that of each party plaintiff. Strawbridge v. Curtiss, 7 U.S. (3 Cranch) 267 (1806). For purposes of determining the existence *vel non* of diversity, only the citizenship of the representative plaintiff shareholder is considered. See Snyder v. Harris, 394 U.S. 332, 340 (1969); Winegar v. First Nat'l Bank, 267 F. Supp. 79 (M.D. Fla. 1967). It is possible however that more stringent federal procedural requirements—as to the need for demands upon shareholders and as to the need for plaintiffs' stock ownership at the time of the wrong alleged—might also screen out of federal court some derivative suits maintainable in state court even though the requirements of diverse citizenship and jurisdictional amount are satisfied. See C. Wright, *supra* note 37, at 358–60, concerning the unsettled applicability of such federal rules to diversity-based derivative suits.

40. See discussion note 39 *supra*.

41. 28 U.S.C. § 1441(b) (1976) forbids removal of such an action. Barrier (2) discussed in text above is in a sense a special case of barrier (1).

42. Of course beyond establishing diversity jurisdiction, a party seeking a federal forum must find one which (i) has proper venue and (ii) can reach all practically necessary parties with process. The difficulties of finding such a forum are described in the next paragraph of this note. Note, however, that unless an unusually generous service-of-process and/or venue provision were to accompany federal regulation of national corporations, the combined venue-process difficulties in derivative suits brought under federal law would be at least as great as those currently besetting plaintiffs in diversity derivative suits. 28

While only the requirement of diverse citizenship currently screens derivative suits out of the federal courts, as a result of Supreme Court decisions defining the relationship of Federal Rule of Civil Procedure 23 to jurisdictional amount requirements, individual shareholder suits will face the additional and formidable hurdle of the amount-in-controversy requirements.[43] In order to maintain an individual suit, a plaintiff must demonstrate a personal financial interest of more than $10,000 in the litigation.[44] Additionally, a diversity-based class action is possible only if every class member has more than a $10,000 personal interest in the outcome of the litigation.[45]

To the extent that either the citizenship requirement or the jurisdictional amount requirement currently screens suits to vindicate individual rights under state corporate law, the federalization of such rights by means of a statute supplanting state law would open the district courts to them. While the general grant of jurisdiction over suits arising under the laws of the United States is itself limited by a $10,000 amount

---

U.S.C. § 1391(a), (c) (1976) are more generous in providing venue for diversity cases than for federal-question cases and Fed. R. Civ. P. 4(d)(7), (f) do not distinguish between the two sorts of cases in defining the process-reach of federal district courts. Note, however, that the effect of the nationwide service-of-process provision which is likely to accompany any new federal corporate regulatory program (see Cary, *supra* note 1, at 702) would completely eliminate the obstacles described in the next paragraph and greatly alleviate some of the inconvenience which currently exists even when there is a forum with venue which can reach all necessary parties.

Currently 28 U.S.C §§ 1391(a), (c) and 1401 (1976), in effect, specify four proper venues of derivative suits brought pursuant to diversity jurisdiction. They are the judicial districts where (i) all plaintiffs reside, (ii) all defendants (including the corporate defendant) reside, (iii) the claim arose, or (iv) the corporation might have sued the same defendants. See 7A C. Wright and A. Miller, *Federal Practice and Procedure* § 1825 (1972). In at least some cases there will be no federal court which both (i) has proper venue and (ii) can reach all practically necessary parties with process. There are severe limitations upon the process-reach of any federal district court in diversity cases. Fed. R. Civ. P. 4(f) limits such reach to the territorial limits of the state in which the district court sits and, in some instances, beyond, as far as within 100 miles of the place where the action is commenced. Additionally, rule 4(d)(7) provides for service in any manner sufficient under state law, giving the court the benefit of any valid state long-arm statute. See C. Wright, *supra* note 37, at 306–07. It is surprising, however, how few states subject nonresident officers and directors of domestic corporations to in personam jurisdiction for any breach of fiduciary responsibility. The statutes existing as of 1968 are collected in G. Hornstein, *Corporation Law and Practice* § 714 n. 53 (1959 & 1968 Supp.).

43. Zahn v. International Paper Co., 414 U.S. 291 (1973); Snyder v. Harris, 394 U.S. 332 (1969).

44. 394 U.S. at 337.

45. 414 U.S. at 301.

requirement,[46] suits to enforce duties created by federal corporate law would be cognizable without regard to the amount in controversy by virtue of 28 U.S.C. section 1337. Section 1337 confers upon federal district courts jurisdiction over suits arising under any act of Congress regulating interstate commerce.[47] As section 1337 has been interpreted, it confers jurisdiction over any suit to enforce a duty created by an act of Congress if such act is grounded to some substantial extent upon Congress' power under the commerce clause.[48] Were Congress to regulate national corporations' internal affairs in a fairly comprehensive manner but to make no special provision concerning jurisdiction,[49] a great many suits to vindicate small individual claims would become subject to original federal jurisdiction.[50] Because the recent Supreme

---

46. 28 U.S.C. § 1331 (1976).

47. The full text of that statute reads:

> The district courts shall have original jurisdiction of any civil action or proceeding arising under any Act of Congress regulating commerce or protecting trade and commerce against restraints and monopolies.

48. Wenningham v. HUD, 512 F.2d 617, 621 (5th Cir. 1975). See also Leonardis v. Local 282 Pension Trust Fund, 391 F. Supp. 554 (E.D.N.Y. 1975) (suit charging violation of 1974 Employee Retirement Income Security Act); Citizens for Clean Air, Inc. v. Corps of Engineers, 349 F. Supp. 696 (S.D.N.Y. 1972).

49. Congress could impose an amount-in-controversy requirement; it has almost complete power to limit the jurisdiction of the lower federal courts. Sheldon v. Sill, 49 U.S. (8 How.) 441 (1850). There may be, however, some limitations. See Eisenberg, *infra* note 81; Hart, "The Power of Congress to Limit the Jurisdiction of the Lower Courts: An Exercise in Dialectic," 66 Harv. L. Rev. 1362 (1953). For possible limits more germane to the topic of this article see discussion at note 77 *infra* and accompanying text.

50. Any cause of action arising directly or fairly inferable from an act of Congress itself conferring rights upon shareholders would be maintained in federal court without respect to dollar amount. See Garrett v. Time-D.C., Inc., 502 F.2d 627 (9th Cir. 1974); Murphy v. Colonial Federal Savings and Loan Ass'n, 388 F.2d 609 (2d Cir. 1967). Under exclusive federal regulation, even causes of action to enforce rights arising from optional charter provisions might well be found to be fairly inferable from the structure of a federal business corporation law of the enabling variety. Cf. Murphy v. Colonial Federal Savings and Loan, 388 F.2d 609 (2d Cir. 1967), which appears to recognize the proposition that the rights of shareholders of national corporations are to be determined by a federal common law (at 612 n.2) and that a claim under such law is a sufficient predicate of federal jurisdiction under § 1337 (at 614–15). Query whether, in the context of exclusively federally chartered and regulated corporations, a shareholder agreement external to the corporate charter would arise under a federal common law dealing with such contracts. This possibility seems at least somewhat doubtful in light of Justice Rehnquist's opinion for the Court in Miree v. DeKalb County, 433 U.S. 25 (1977). But see Chief Justice Burger's concurring opinion. *Id.* at 34.

Court cases narrowing federal class action jurisdiction relied upon the jurisdictional amount requirements,[51] these cases would impose no limitations upon class actions brought to vindicate federal rights of classes of shareholders of national corporations.

Given the current record keeping system of the federal district courts,[52] it is impossible, without reading the pleadings in several hundred cases, to guess the extent to which federal jurisdiction is presently both available and employed with respect to claims arising under current state corporate law. It is clear that the inevitable large increase in lower federal court caseloads due to federalization of duties running to the corporation should be discounted somewhat to account for what must be an appreciable amount of currently available diversity jurisdiction.[53] It is also clear that the increase in federal district court caseloads attributable to the federalization of duties running to individual shareholders could be great and should be discounted substantially less because diversity jurisdiction is currently less frequently available in such actions.

While the increase in the caseloads of the federal courts resulting solely from a shift to a federal regulating authority might well be dramatic, the accompanying change in the substance of the regulation would also cause a significant increase.[54] Laws which create new duties enforceable by private damage actions result in increased judicial burdens. Our experience with civil damage actions under rule 10b-5 is a prime indication that a dramatic increase is to be expected.[55]

In the section which follows, this article deals with possible congressional response to such an increase.

---

51. See notes 43 and 44 *supra* and accompanying text.

52. Director of the Administrative Office of the United States Courts, *Annual Report 1976* presents separate caseload figures for the category "stockholder suits and partnership dissolution." Such figures, however, include only suits predicated upon contract theory. *Id.* 293. The number of such suits commenced in 1975 and 1976 respectively are zero and one. *Id.* A call to the office of the Clerk for the United States District Court for the Southern District of New York confirms that all derivative suits are not reflected in such figures.

53. See Sullivan, *supra* note 37, at 603.

54. As noted in footnote 7 *supra* and accompanying text, those who advocate more federal regulation of national corporations do so because of a perceived need for a major change in the substance of the law that governs the internal affairs of national corporations.

55. While I know of no study of the volume of litigation under rule 10b-5, the 246 pages of annotations to § 10 of the Securities Exchange Act appearing in 15 U.S.C.A. § 78j and 1977 pocket part offer ample testimony to its great magnitude. While some cases appearing in such annotations involve only section 10a of the Securities Exchange Act, the vast preponderance arise under section 10b and subsidiary rule 10b-5.

GENERAL CONSIDERATIONS

The analysis presented above assumes a congressional substantive program without its own tailor-made jurisdictional provisions. What would be the best way for Congress to allocate possibly increased jurisdiction under federal corporate law in light of (1) the need for sound judicial development of any such body of law, (2) the familiar strident complaints about the already onerous federal court workloads, and (3) the interests of the states? I will start with Cary's proposal to deal with pressures against increased federal caseloads by creating exclusive state-court jurisdiction over cases arising under new federal corporate laws.[56] After concluding that such exclusive jurisdiction would be unwise, I will discuss the remaining legislative choices: concurrent state-federal jurisdiction or exclusive federal jurisdiction. Cary's minimum-standards proposal is a good example of what the substance of a partial federal regulatory scheme might be. His description of its substantive features is quoted in the footnote hereto.[57] The discussion which follows below is, however, equally applicable to problems of allocation of jurisdiction under schemes of more comprehensive regulation like that proposed by Nader[58] or to problems of federal chartering and complete federal preemption like that proposed by A. A. Sommer.[59]

---

56. See Cary, *supra* note 1, at 704–05.

57. The proposal is to continue allowing companies to incorporate in the jurisdiction of their choosing but to remove much of the incentive to organize in Delaware or its rival states. Such companies, nevertheless, must be subject to the jurisdiction of the federal courts under certain general standards. To illustrate, some of the major provisions of such a federal statute might include (1) federal fiduciary standards with respect to directors and officers and controlling shareholders; (2) an "interested directors" provision prescribing fairness as a prerequisite to any transaction; (3) a requirement of certain uniform provisions to be incorporated in the certificate of incorporation: for example, authority to amend by-laws, initiate corporate action or draw up the agenda of shareholders' meetings shall not be vested exclusively in management; (4) a more frequent requirement of shareholder approval of corporate transactions, with limits placed upon the number of shares authorized at any one time; (5) abolition of nonvoting shares; (6) the scope of indemnification of directors specifically prescribed and made exclusive; (7) adoption of a long-arm provision comparable to § 27 of the Securities Exchange Act to apply to all transactions within the corporate structure involving shareholders, directors, and officers.

The foregoing suggestions do not pretend to offer a complete model for a minimum standards act. Indeed it can scarcely be expected that even these would survive political pressure unscathed.

Cary, *supra* note 1, at 702 (footnotes omitted).

58. R. Nader, *supra* note 1.

59. In recent hearings before the United States Senate Committee on Commerce the following exchange occurred between Senator John A. Durkin of New Hamp-

Exclusive State-Court Jurisdiction. Near the end of his proposal for the partial federal regulation of national corporations, Cary states:[60]

> Concern over the growth of federal litigation is a separate issue. If this is a matter of crucial importance, and if the grant of concurrent jurisdiction would be futile because plaintiffs typically would sue in the federal courts, then I would propose that the federal standards written into corporation law be subject initially to state court interpretation, with some form of certiorari jurisdiction on the part of the courts of appeal to achieve uni-

---

shire and A. A. Sommer, formerly a member of the Securities and Exchange Commission:

> *Senator Durkin:* I gather that you would favor a more restrictive Federal law.
>
> *Mr. Sommer:* Yes.
>
> In the remainder of my prepared statement, which I omitted because of time considerations, I state there is a lot to be said for a Federal corporation law that would be of an "enabling" sort, similar to those that exist in States, and I would hope that one of the more enlightened States would be the model for it.
>
> There is a desirability in a uniform set of standards to be developed through statutory law and in cases concerning the relationships between managers, directors, and shareholders. I feel that burdening that sort of statute with a number of regulatory provisions that would apply only to large corporations is not sound policy. I think those regulatory provisions, such as concern for environment, concern for labor, concern for equal employment, should be dealt with across the board and be binding upon all businesses and all corporations. I think they should be dealt with separately from the question of what is the desirable configuration for corporate law.
>
> *Senator Durkin:* The corporate law, to allow for pollution, but allow the criminal law dealing with bribery—
>
> *Mr. Sommer:* Deal with them separately but reasonably, as has been done in most cases.
>
> I think mixing those matters with corporation law which is designed to deal with the relationship between managers, directors, and shareholders and the procedural matters of how to hold meetings and that sort of thing, is undesirable.
>
> *Senator Durkin:* Would you recommend preempting State law?
>
> *Mr. Sommer:* With regard to a corporation that would be subject to Federal corporation law, yes. I think some sort of cut should be made. In other words, corporations of only a certain size would be required to incorporate under Federal law. As you probably know, at the present time, the corporations that have more than 500 shareholders and $1 million of assets are required to file a periodic report with the SEC.
>
> A similar kind of discrimination, I think, would be appropriate with regard to Federal corporation law.

Hearings, supra note 1, at 57.

60. Cary, *supra* note 1, at 704–05.

formity. If necessary, there could be a special corporate court to handle such cases.

Cary is not proposing exclusive state jurisdiction as an essential or even desirable part of his scheme of substantive regulation.[61] He is, however, proposing it as a possible way of making more federal corporate regulation attractive to those seriously concerned about increasing the caseload of the lower federal courts.[62] It is because such a solution is likely to appeal to those so concerned and because it seems so unprecedented and unwise that several arguments against it will be presented.

I assume from Cary's use of the phrases "subject initially to state court interpretation" and "ced[ing jurisdiction] to the state courts subject only to review [by the United States courts of appeals] for purposes of establishing uniform standards,"[63] that under his scheme federal courts would not be open to hear claims under federal corporate law. There are other interpretations of Cary's proposal, equally unprecedented and perhaps unworkable, but these are devoid of serious problems of federalism. For example, the federal courts might be closed off to claims under federal corporate law only in states where the legislatures agreed (perhaps in exchange for federal compensation) that their courts would shoulder the entire burden of deciding cases under federal corporate law.

As I understand Cary's proposal, however, exclusive jurisdiction would be imposed upon the state courts by federal legislation. Whether such jurisdiction is unprecedented or not depends upon how one reads the precedents. Prior to 1875 the lower federal courts had no general federal-question jurisdiction;[64] during this period most of the legal

---

61. Indeed at one point Cary seems to suggest that, in the absence of resistance from those concerned about lower-federal-court caseloads, the lower federal courts would have a significant role to play. Compare Cary, *supra* note 1, at 702, 1st sentence, 2d full paragraph with the quotation from Cary's article presented immediately above in the text of this article. The precise meaning of the former is, however, not completely clear.

62. See, e.g., H. Friendly, *Federal Jurisdiction: A General View* 15–33 (1973).

63. Cary, *supra* note 1, at 705.

64. 13 C. Wright, A. Miller & E. Cooper, *Federal Practice and Procedure* § 3503 at 9 (1975). This statement must be qualified: for a period of slightly over a year beginning in February 1801 and ending in March 1802, the United States circuit courts (courts having both original and appellate jurisdiction) possessed trial jurisdiction over "all cases in law or equity arising under the Constitution and laws of the United States, and treaties made [thereunder] . . ." Act of February 13, 1801, 2 Stat. 89. The repealing legislation was Act of March 8, 1802, 2 Stat. 132. The legislation restoring such federal-question jurisdiction was Act of March 3, 1875, 18 Stat. 470. Currently federal district courts have such jurisdiction pursuant to 28 U.S.C. 1331 (1970).

claims which arose under the few extant federal regulatory schemes were heard exclusively by the state courts.[65] Moreover, state courts are currently the only courts open to hear some cases arising under the Constitution and laws of the United States involving an amount in controversy of no more than $10,000.[66] Federal district courts are generally closed to such cases and presumably state courts have an obligation to hear them. On several occasions the Supreme Court has required unwilling state courts to hear federal claims because the state courts' refusals to do so were not based upon "valid excuses."[67] Valid excuses include an application of traditional forum non conveniens[68] doctrine and perhaps the inability of state courts to hear similar cases arising under state law.[69] Emphatically excluded from the category of valid excuses is a refusal to entertain a federal cause of action solely because the underlying claim is based on federal law.[70]

It is not hard to read these precedents, taken together, as establishing the power of Congress to force state courts to assume jurisdiction not shared by federal courts over all suits arising under a federal regulatory program. For example, in 1958 the Supreme Court of New Mexico reached a similar view of Congress' power.[71] Citing the United States Supreme Court cases referred to in the preceding paragraph, it de-

---

65. See, e.g., Lapham v. Almy, 95 Mass. 301 (1866); United States v. Smith, 4 N.J.L. (1 South) 38 (1818).

66. 28 U.S.C. § 1331(a) (1976), the basic course of federal district court jurisdiction over federal-question cases reads as follows:

> The district courts shall have original jurisdiction of all civil actions wherein the matter in controversy exceeds the sum or value of $10,000, exclusive of interest and costs, and arises under the Constitution, laws, or treaties of the United States except that no such sum or value shall be required in any such action brought against the United States, any agency, thereof, or any officer or employee thereof in his official capacity.

With the exception stated in the last portion of § 1331(a) and unless some other more specialized federal-question statute is available (see note 47 *supra*), a case arising under the Constitution, laws, or treaties of the United States but involving $10,000 or less in controversy generally can be brought only in the state courts. Under 28 U.S.C. § 1441(a), (b) (1976) a defendant can remove to federal court a federal-question case brought in state court only if the plaintiff could have maintained the action in federal court originally.

67. Testa v. Katt, 330 U.S. 386 (1947); McKnett v. St. Louis & S.F. Ry., 292 U.S. 230 (1934); Mondou v. New York, N.H. & H.R.R., 223 U.S. 1 (1912).

68. Douglas v. New York, N.H. & H.R.R., 279 U.S. 377, 387–88 (1929). See also Testa v. Katt, 330 U.S. 386 (1947) (dictum).

69. Testa v. Katt, 330 U.S. 386, 394 (1947) (dictum).

70. *Id.*; McKnett v. St. Louis & S.F. Ry., 292 U.S. 230, 233–34 (1934).

71. Bourguet v. Atchison, T. & S.F. Ry., 65 N.M. 200, 204–06, 334 P.2d 1107, 1110–11 (1958).

clared[72] the following statute of that state, passed in 1947, violative of the United States Constitution:[73]

> Jurisdiction of courts to enforce federal law restricted. No court of the state of New Mexico shall have jurisdiction of, or enter any order or decree of any character in any action instituted in the courts of this state, seeking to enforce, directly or indirectly, any federal statute, or rule or regulation . . . where the Congress of the United States has curtailed, withdrawn, or denied the district courts of the United States the right to enforce such statutes, rules or regulations aforesaid.

The New Mexico statute is evidence of the potential for friction in the federal government's abuse of its partnership with state government. However, it probably does go too far in asserting states' rights.[74] If it is

---

72. *Id.* (alternative holding). In the proceedings below in *Bourguet,* a state trial court dismissed a case against the railroad brought under the Federal Employers' Liability Act (FELA). Its dismissal was based upon the statute quoted in the text accompanying note 73 *infra*. The defendant's argument was that the jurisdiction of federal district courts over FELA cases was restricted within the meaning of the New Mexico statute. Despite the fact that plaintiffs were given an option to bring damage suits in FELA cases to federal courts, defendants asserted that an absolute prohibition upon removal by defendants constituted a restriction within the meaning of the New Mexico statute. In a state-ground holding the court rejected such an interpretation of the New Mexico statute, 65 N.M. at 201–03, 334 P.2d at 1108–09. Note the court had to determine whether Congress has "curtailed withdrawn or denied jurisdiction," but because those are the words of the New Mexico statute, the question is whether Congress has done so within the meaning of that law. *Id.* In the alternative holding the court decides that the statute, applied to exclude New Mexico courts, would violate the supremacy clause of the United States Constitution. 65 N.M. at 206, 334 P.2d at 1111. The court's rationale would seem to apply to the exclusion of any federally created civil action, if not to all federally created actions.

The preceding description of *Bourguet* was presented for purposes of completeness. For purposes of this article, the fact of primary interest is that the state legislature bridled at perceived federal abuse.

73. N.M. Stat. Ann. § 16-1-7 (1953).

74. The legislative history of § 16-1-7 is instructive. Chapter 43 of Laws 1947 had a preliminary first section which read:

> The legislature of the state of New Mexico hereby finds that: (a) The Congress of the United States has heretofore authorized, and may hereafter authorize, by congressional act, the courts of the several states to entertain jurisdiction of and enforce causes of action created by or arising from federal statutes, or by rules or regulations of federal regulating bodies or agencies, and
>
> (b) The Congress has no power to require the state courts of the several states to take cognizance of such actions, and
>
> (c) The Congress has from time to time, and may hereafter, withdraw

valid, state courts are not obliged to hear those federal-question cases with amounts in controversy of $10,000 or less which now cannot be maintained in federal court. A plausible constitutional argument can however be made that the current division of labor under the $10,000 jurisdictional amount requirement and Cary's jurisdictional proposal are significantly different. Whether or not the argument ultimately succeeds as a constitutional argument, it strongly suggests the lack of wisdom of an exclusive state jurisdiction scheme. This argument follows in the next several paragraphs.

All of the Supreme Court cases reversing as error state refusals to hear federally created causes of action involved causes of action of a kind which were concurrently cognizable in the federal courts.[75] Those suits under federal law which now can be heard exclusively in state

---

> from the courts of the United States jurisdiction to enforce such statutes or rules or regulations aforesaid or to entertain actions for such purpose or to enter judgments or decrees based thereupon, and
>
> (d) In such event actions to enforce such statutes or rules or regulations aforesaid, or rights or obligations arising therefrom may hereafter be instituted in the courts of this state, burdening and taxing such courts, and placing upon the courts and people of the state the burden and expense of enforcing such federal statutes, rules or regulations, or settling disputes arising therefrom.
>
> *Title of Act.*
>
> An act relating to the jurisdiction of the state courts of New Mexico to enforce certain federal statutes, rules and regulations under certain circumstances, and declaring an emergency.—Laws 1947, ch. 43.
>
> *Emergency Clause.*
>
> Section 3 of ch. 43, Laws 1947 declared an emergency and provided that the act should take effect upon its passage and approval. Approved March 8, 1947

Compiler's notes to § 16-1-7, 4 N.M. Stat. Ann. 5 (1953).

75. The three cases in which such reversals occurred are listed in note 67 *supra* and are discussed in the next paragraphs of this note.

McKnett v. St. Louis & S.F. Ry., 292 U.S. 230 (1934), and Mondou v. New York, N.H. & H.R.R., 223 U.S. 1 (1912), arose under the same version of the Federal Employers' Liability Act (FELA), 34 Stat. 232 (1906), *as amended by* 35 Stat. 65 (1908) and 36 Stat. 291 (1910) (current version at 45 U.S.C. §§ 51, 54, 56, 60). A reading of such legislative history indicates (i) that private damage suits under the FELA were made explicitly concurrently cognizable in state and federal courts by the 1910 amendments and (ii) that no amount-in-controversy requirement ever existed.

Testa v. Katt, 330 U.S. 386 (1947), arose under the Emergency Price Control Act of 1942, (EPCA), 56 Stat. 23 (1942) *as amended by* 56 Stat. 767 (1942), 57 Stat. 566 (1943), 58 Stat. 633 (1944), 59 Stat. 306–09 (1945), and 60 Stat. 664 (1946) (repealed 1947). A reading of such legislative history indicates that during the existence of the EPCA, private damage suits thereunder were concurrently cognizable in state or federal court without regard to dollar amount.

court all involve causes of action which can be brought in federal court as long as more than $10,000 is in controversy.[76] This pattern results in the federal government's sharing with the states some of the judicial costs of each variety of legal action permitted by each of its substantive programs, and consequently, also results in a practical restraint upon irresponsible (not cost justified) substantive laws. Recent cases and scholarly commentary suggest that the Supreme Court may be recognizing a state sovereignty resistant to at least some otherwise permissible federal regulation under the commerce clause.[77] It has been argued that a congressional attempt to override the valid-excuse doctrine described above might fail as an unconstitutional intrusion upon state sovereignty.[78] Perhaps making the states bear all of the judicial costs of federal substantive programs is another such intrusion.

---

76. Where jurisdiction is shared on a concurrent basis, the rights of plaintiffs and defendants are not invariably symmetrical. For example, suits under the Securities Act of 1933 can be brought at plaintiff's option in federal court regardless of the amount in controversy. If a plaintiff chooses instead to sue in state court in a case where federal jurisdiction could be based only upon the presence of the Securities Act claim, the defendant has no removal action. 15 U.S.C. § 77(v) (1976). The suits in *McKnett* and *Mondou* (see discussion in note 75 *supra*) were identical in this respect to suits under the Securities Act, because suits against interstate railroads were not (and are not) removable. Act of April 5, 1910, c. 143, 36 Stat. 291 (current version 28 U.S.C. § 1445 (1970)). Under this pattern, despite the restrictions upon removal, the federal courts do share with the state courts the expenses of hearing causes of action under any portion of the Securities Act.

77. In National League of Cities v. Usery, 426 U.S. 833 (1976), the Court found unconstitutional that portion of the 1974 amendments to the Fair Labor Standards Act which applied the minimum wage laws to state and municipal public employees. The Court stated:

> This Court has never doubted that there are limits upon the power of Congress to override state sovereignty, even when exercising its otherwise plenary powers to tax or to regulate commerce which are conferred by Art. I of the Constitution.

426 U.S. at 842.

> The Amendment (10th) expressly declares the constitutional policy that Congress may not exercise power in a fashion that impairs the States' integrity or their ability to function effectively in a federal system.

Id. at 843 (quoting Fry v. United States, 421 U.S. 542, 547 n.7 (1975)). See also New York v. United States, 326 U.S. 572 (1946) (dictum) (rejects proposition that federal government could tax the states except to the extent that they carry on business as would private employers); Redish & Muench, "Adjudication of Federal Causes of Action in State Court," 75 Mich. L. Rev. 311, 340–59 (1976).

78. *Id.* Redish and Muench suggest that National League of Cities v. Usery, 426 U.S. 833 (1976), forms the basis of an at least plausible argument that Congress would

There is strong evidence that at the time the Constitution was framed, it was understood that the creation of lower federal courts was entirely at the option of Congress[79] and that to the extent such courts were not available, state courts were obliged to hear claims under federal law.[80] Indeed, as mentioned above, lower federal courts were not generally available to hear such claims until 1875. In a recent article Theodore Eisenberg[81] argues that even if lower federal courts were optional in 1789, changed circumstances result in their being constitutionally required today.[82] His argument is that in the early days of the republic, the concept of Congress' power to dispense with lower federal courts was not at war with the concept of the federal judiciary as envisioned by the framers.[83] He argues that today, given the inability of the Supreme Court to decide finally all questions of federal law raised in state courts, those two concepts are at odds.[84] The constitutional argument against mandatory exclusive state jurisdiction over federal causes of action is structurally similar to Eisenberg's.[85] Prior to the great

---

intrude on state sovereignty if it were to attempt to override the valid-excuse doctrines which permit states to refuse to entertain federal causes of action. *Id.* at 348–49, 358–59. The circumstances discussed by Redish and Muench as possibly appropriate for state refusals involve nondiscriminatory application of state rules of jurisdiction, venue, and forum non conveniens. My argument is similar but not identical. It is that mandatory exclusive state jurisdiction over federal causes of action is plausibly another circumstance in which a state refusal to hear a federal cause of action would be justified as protective of its sovereignty.

79. See M. Farrand, *The Framing of The Constitution of the United States* 79–80 (1913); Warren, "New Light on the History of the Federal Judiciary Act of 1789," 37 Harv. L. Rev. 49, 65–66 (1923).

80. See Note, "State Enforcement of Federally Created Rights, 73 Harv. L. Rev. 1551, 1552 (1960).

81. Eisenberg, "Congressional Authority to Restrict Lower Federal Court Jurisdiction," 83 Yale L.J. 498 (1974).

82. Without conceding that lower federal courts were ever dispensable, Eisenberg argues that, in light of the current circumstances of the national judiciary, abolition of the lower federal courts would violate an essential aspect of the framers' constitutional plan. *Id.* at 504–14.

83. *Id.* at 504, particularly n.38 and accompanying text.

84. *Id.*

85. *Id.* Of course, under any scheme of exclusive state-court trial jurisdiction over a system of federal causes of action, some costs of judicial administration—the costs of deciding some appeals—would be borne by federal courts. My argument is premised on the probability that the costs of administering justice at the appellate level over a system of federal causes of action would be relatively insignificant when compared with such costs at the trial-court level. Note also that in cases where federal appellate courts had reviewed issues of federal corporate law decided by state courts, the states presumably would have incurred costs themselves at the appellate level.

expansion in federal legislative power under the commerce clause,[86] the concepts of state sovereignty and of unlimited congressional power to use state courts as federal forums were not incompatible. As the notion that the federal government is one of limited powers has become less meaningful since the creation of the Interstate Commerce Commission (ICC) in 1887, there has developed a real potential for conflict.[87] There seems to be no good reason to challenge the system of concurrent jurisdiction over federal-question cases with which we have lived successfully for over a century. On the other hand, can a departure from that system be justified if it permits the federal government to use the state courts alone for the administration of any federal law? The establishment of such a pattern seems not only a symbolic blow to state sovereignty, but also an irresistible invitation to its own replication as a means of reducing the federal costs of future federal programs.

Under prevailing circumstances it seems at least unfortunate, if not unconstitutional, for the federal government to begin to insulate itself from the judicial costs of its regulation and impose them entirely upon the courts of the states. The New Mexico statute described above and never repealed by the state legislature is tangible proof of the potential for state-federal friction inherent in an exclusive state jurisdiction scheme.[88]

The remaining choice between some form of shared state-federal jurisdiction and exclusive federal jurisdiction over cases under a new federal corporate law is the subject of the next subsection.

---

86. "Large scale regulatory action by Congress began with the Interstate Commerce Act in 1887 and the Sherman Anti-Trust Law in 1890. . . ." G. Gunther & W. Dowling, *Constitutional Law* 240 (8th ed. 1965).

87. *Id.* See also R. Cushman, *The Independent Regulatory Commissions* 19 (1972).

88. The arguments against mandatory exclusive state jurisdiction presented above are all grounded upon the concept of state sovereignty. Arguments made in the next section that exclusive federal jurisdiction may be a desirable way of dealing with cases arising under certain portions of new federal corporate regulation are, a fortiori, arguments against exclusive state jurisdiction over such cases.

Beyond this, even with respect to cases over which exclusive federal jurisdiction is not needed because there will be little reviewable lawmaking (see notes 105–08 *infra* and accompanying text) a removal option is necessary to protect plaintiffs against the promanagement biases described by Cary. Cary, *supra* note 1, at 670–92. Cary concludes such biases would abate greatly were state courts to apply federal law. *Id.* at 705. I am not sure the promanagement bias he ascribes to Delaware judges is the product of legislative pressures as much as of lifelong perspectives. In any event, as long as the states continue to charter and provide significant forums for the settlement of intracorporate disputes of domestic corporations, management engaged in charter-state shopping would undoubtedly prefer states whose judges read federal law through properly corrected lenses. A liberal removal provision would dispense with these problems; exclusive state jurisdiction would create them.

Choice Between Shared State-Federal and Exclusive Federal Jurisdiction. Exclusive state-court jurisdiction over causes of action arising under a new federal corporate law having been rejected as unsound, what is the most desirable alternative? As has been noted, Congress can permit[89] and even require[90] state-court jurisdiction over federal causes of action, at least in cases where that jurisdiction is shared with the federal courts on some reasonable basis. Additionally, Congress can confer jurisdiction exclusively upon the federal courts, as it has previously done in the case of suits under certain federal statutes.[91] In the usual case where no express jurisdictional limitation is provided for a federal cause of action, it is treated as cognizable in both the federal and the state courts.[92] In unusual circumstances, such a cause of action will be found, by virtue of its "nature," to be excluded from state-court cognizance.[93] How should a legislator contemplating federal regulation of national corporations decide between the concurrent and exclusive federal modes of jurisdiction?

Benefits of Exclusive Federal Jurisdiction. A recent article by Redish and Muench offers guidance to courts which are asked to decide, in the absence of an express provision dealing with jurisdiction, whether suits under a particular federal cause of action are to be treated as exclusively within the jurisdiction of the federal courts.[94] As an alternative to the traditional legislative-historical approach, the article suggests that courts engage in "creative judicial lawmaking,"[95] and it further suggests several factors bearing on the wisdom of a finding of exclusivity.[96] A creative judicial lawmaker and his responsible congressional counterpart should be concerned with many of the same problems in choosing a jurisdictional mode. Consequently, the authors' analysis is helpful to our inquiry from a legislator's perspective.

A major factor favoring exclusivity cited by Redish and Muench is that the substantive law in question, in the absence of exclusive federal jurisdiction, would be interpreted without uniformity among the states.[97]

---

89. Claflin v. Houseman, 93 U.S. 130, 136 (1876).

90. See note 67 *supra* and accompanying text.

91. The Moses Taylor, 71 U.S. (4 Wall.) 411 (1866). See, e.g., 28 U.S.C. § 1338 (1976), conferring upon lower federal courts exclusive jurisdiction over suits arising under the patent laws.

92. Claflin v. Houseman, 93 U.S. 130, 136 (1876); Redish & Muench, *supra* note 77, at 312–25 (1976).

93. 93 U.S. at 136; Redish & Muench, *supra* note 77, at 313–25.

94. Redish & Muench, *supra* note 77, at 311–40.

95. *Id.* at 329–40.

96. *Id.*

97. *Id.* at 331–33.

In dealing with this factor, that of the possibility of disuniformity, the authors conclude:

> The most significant factor in this inquiry is the nature of the federal statute creating the particular cause of action. In other words, a court should determine whether the federal statute is likely to provide the judiciary wide latitude in developing federal rights, or whether the cause of action is sufficiently detailed in its scope and clear as to its purpose that the likelihood of future judicial gloss is comparatively limited. . . .
>
> . . . [T]o the extent that a statutory right depends upon judicial development for its content, the danger of legal chaos will vary directly with the number of courts independently interpreting the right. In light of the fact that an overworked Supreme Court is capable of providing a uniform practice for only a fraction of the numerous issues of federal law that arise each year, the danger of divergent judicial interpretations must be taken seriously.
>
> Such divergence is likely to be harmful for several reasons. First, to the extent that varying or contrary interpretations are given in different areas of the nation, the nationally unifying force of federal law is undermined, and the post-Civil War development of federal supremacy over local interests is weakened. Second, the arbitrariness of the enjoyment of federal rights that this divergence would produce presents a significant moral problem. . . . Finally, in many cases the proliferation of judicial interpretations of a federal right will unduly undermine the predictability in enforcement of that right, thereby interfering with the often significant planning of primary commercial, social, or personal conduct and decision-making.
>
> Where, on the other hand, a federal statute is comparatively clear in its directives, the danger of varying or contrary judicial interpretations is presumably reduced, even if the number of courts interpreting the right is substantial.[98]

Any federal regulation of national corporations, whether it follows the Cary model of partial regulation or the comprehensive federal chartering model, might well contain vague standards defining the responsibility of management (and possibly controlling shareholders) to the general body of shareholders. It is the vagueness of such standards which, in at least some respects, renders them useful: they are an invitation to courts to deal creatively with a host of situations not foreseeable in advance. An example of such a process of judicial lawmaking is the use made of rule 10b-5[99] by the lower federal courts prior to *Blue Chip*

---

98. *Id.*

99. Securities and Exchange Commission rule 10b-5, 17 C.F.R. § 240.10b-5 (1978), was promulgated by the Commission pursuant to section 10b of the Securities Exchange Act of 1934, 15 U.S.C. § 78j(b) (1976). It reads as follows:

> It shall be unlawful for any person, directly or indirectly, by the use of any

Stamps v. Manor Drug Stores.[100] In that case the Supreme Court severely limited what had been described as the creation of a general federal law of fiduciary responsibility.[101]

Some of the new federal corporation law envisioned by Sommer, Cary, and others could involve an invitation from Congress to some courts for those courts to engage in a process similar to the pre-*Blue Chip Stamps* process described above.[102] It might seem then that any

---

means or instrumentality of interstate commerce, or of the mails or of any facility of any national securities exchange,

(a) To employ any device, scheme, or artifice to defraud,

(b) To make any untrue statement of a material fact or to omit to state a material fact necessary in order to make the statements made, in the light of the circumstances under which they were made, not misleading, or

(c) To engage in any act, practice, or course of business which operates or would operate as a fraud or deceit upon any person,

in connection with the purchase or sale of any security.

100. 421 U.S. 723 (1975).

101. For the proposition that the development of such a federal corporate law was recognized see, e.g., Fleischer, "Federal Corporation Law: An Assessment," 78 Harv. L. Rev. 1146 (1965); Lowenfels, "The Demise of the Birnbaum Doctrine: A New Era for Rule 10b-5," 54 Va. L. Rev. 268 (1968); Note, "Standing Under Rule 10b-5 After Blue Chip Stamps," 75 Mich. L. Rev. 413, 414 (1976).

Birnbaum v. Newport Steel Corp., 98 F. Supp. 506 (S.D.N.Y. 1951), *aff'd,* 193 F.2d 461 (2d Cir. 1952), *cert. denied,* 343 U.S. 956 (1952), restricted the application of rule 10b-5 to transactions involving a purchase or sale of securities. For a discussion of the erosion and occasional rejection of the *Birnbaum* rule prior to *Blue Chip Stamps,* see Lowenfels, *supra* this note, and Note, *supra* this note, at 427 n.94. For a discussion of the Supreme Court's endorsement of a stringent but still imprecisely defined purchaser-seller rule in *Blue Chip Stamps,* see Note, *supra* this note, at 427–44. The Note's author suggests that *Blue Chip Stamps* may be consistent with at least some of the prior erosion of the purchaser-seller rule and may be truly significant only as a limitation upon future erosion. *Id.* at 429.

102. In a 1974 speech, A. A. Sommer recognized that the benefits of at least some vagueness in fiduciary standards could well be worth the resulting uncertainty costs:

> I spoke of Rule 10b-5 being both fortunate and unfortunate. I think it is unfortunate that we have, because of the circumstances that I mentioned, been impelled to load so much on this Rule, which after all was admittedly adopted in haste, expressed with bewildering and sometimes even angering breadth and generality, and which is only 115 words long. Responsible commentators have suggested that it is wholly inappropriate for the Commission and the courts to try to draw through some alchemy out of those few words a whole code of conduct for the legal profession, the accounting profession, directors, corporate officers, insiders of all types, financial analysts and a host of other people. It would perhaps indeed be better if through the debative process by which legislation is developed greater particularity had become a part of this endeavor and perhaps it

vaguely worded federal fiduciary standard should be interpreted only by the federal courts. In fact more analysis is necessary.

Redish and Muench's argument turns upon the superiority of exclusive federal jurisdiction as a unifier of federal law. Their explanation of such superiority is as follows:[103]

> It is true, of course, that even a finding of exclusive federal jurisdiction will not insure uniformity of interpretation. Nevertheless, the likelihood of varying interpretations of federal law, both in terms of degree and occurrence, is substantially reduced when only federal courts are making the interpretations. Since there are only eleven courts of appeals which, though not bound by decisions of other circuits, generally give them significant weight, and since a common basis for the Supreme Court's decision to grant certiorari is the existence of a conflict among the circuits, the danger of proliferation is considerably reduced.

Such an argument seems convincing,[104] but it is relevant only to the

---

> would have been better if there had been at some point in time a more comprehensive realization of what was being done, rather than a piecemeal, case-by-case manner of achievement that has characterized the growth of the Rule 10b-5 concept. While such an ordered structural development has much to commend it, I think there would also be within that severe disadvantage: inflexibility. Social commentators have repeatedly warned that the pace of change in our life is steadily accelerating and that our institutions, our psyches and even our bodies must develop a capacity to change more quickly. The corporate world is not immune to this rapidly accelerating pace of change and it is extremely important that the means of social control of this terribly important part of our national economic life be flexible and relatively swift reaction. Through Rule 10b-5 I think we have accomplished a great deal of that flexibility and the ability to adapt that is so necessary.
>
> The price that is paid for such flexibility and adaptability of course, is the inability to have a photographic rendition of the state of law at any given moment which is fixed, clear, delineated, sharply focused and reliable.

Address by A. A. Sommer, American Bar Association 97th Annual Meeting (August 14, 1974), reprinted in *Hearings, supra* note 1, at 72–73.

In other settings Mr. Sommer has indicated his view that it is better to deal with the responsibilities of management of national corporations more directly by means of federal fiduciary standards than by means of adapting laws designed principally to deal with trading abuses. *Hearings, supra* note 1, at 65–66 (written statement prepared for submission at hearing). See also *id.* at 58. Presumably general federal fiduciary standards would also need to be somewhat flexible.

103. Redish & Muench, *supra* note 77, at 332 n.88.

104. It should be noted that there is possibly an alternative method for unifying the law which would not rely upon exclusive federal jurisdiction. The United States courts of appeals could be given appellate jurisdiction over cases decided by state courts involving claims under federal corporate law. Cary proposes such

extent that a vague standard invites judicial lawmaking in trial courts which is reviewable by appellate courts and, consequently, is capable of being unified by such courts. It is important not to assume that the vagueness of any fiduciary standard will result in a large and constant amount of precedent-making throughout its existence. Assume the following familiar rule is part of a scheme of federal regulation:

> A director shall perform his duties as a director . . . in good faith and with that degree of care which an ordinarily prudent person in a like position would use under similar circumstances.[105]

Would this rule result in a great deal of lawmaking? There would be initial questions about whether the standard resembled more an ordinary- or a gross-negligence model. Once it is determined whether the standard of care for corporate management is to resemble current lenient standards under state law[106] or a more exacting standard, even

---

review as an adjunct to his scheme of exclusive state-court jurisdiction, presumably because he too perceives a need for law unification which Supreme Court review can no longer fulfill. Cary, *supra* note 1, at 704–05. To the extent such review is considered compatible with our federalism, it would work as well to mitigate uniformity problems generated by concurrent state-federal jurisdiction over a body of cases.

It is tempting to look for constitutional infirmities of such a review system since, with the possible but distinguishable exception of federal habeas corpus jurisdiction over the cases of state prisoners, nothing resembling lower-federal-court review of state-court cases has existed in our federal system. The few judges and scholars who have considered such review in the abstract, however, conclude it is constitutional. See Stolz, "Federal Review of State Court Decisions of Federal Questions: The Need for Additional Appellate Capacity," 64 Cal. L. Rev. 943, 945–48 (1976). While possibly constitutional, such a system of review would be an extraordinarily controversial means of assuring uniformity. This article proceeds upon the assumption that such a system is unlikely.

105. N.Y. Bus. Corp. Law § 717(b) (McKinney 1963). The transactions which such a corporation may avoid on the ground of unfairness are those which involve an interested director and which have not been insulated from such a power of avoidance by means of the approval of a disinterested majority of fully informed directors or by means of shareholder approval.

106. The search for cases in which directors of industrial corporations have been held liable in derivative suits for negligence uncomplicated by self-dealing is a search for a very small number of needles in a very large haystack. Few are the cases in which the stockholders do not allege conflict of interest, still fewer those among them which achieve even such partial success as denial of the defendants' motion to dismiss the complaint. Still, it cannot be denied that there is a small number of relatively recent cases which do seem to lend a modicum of substance to the fears of directors of industrial or mercantile corporations that they may be stuck for what they like to call "mere" or "honest" negligence. My own collection, based on

some additional real lawmaking might occur. For example, courts would determine whether certain familiar recurrent omissions—e.g., missing directors' meetings—constitute per se violations of the standard. Perhaps in light of the need for uniformity, the fact that this much lawmaking would result argues in favor of exclusive federal jurisdiction. It seems likely, however, that most decisions applying such a law will be analogous to decisions generally requiring a determination of whether particular conduct was negligent; they will involve the application of its vague standard of care to situations which are sui generis and therefore not of great precedential effect.[107] Another example of a vague standard not having a great capacity to generate hard legal precedents is that of a provision which permits a corporation to avoid certain transactions to which it is a party and in which one of its directors has an interest unless it is demonstrated affirmatively that the transaction is fair and reasonable.[108] The rules as to what is a sufficient interest to trigger the statute's application can be made reasonably clear and therefore could be the subject of relatively little reviewable judicial lawmaking. Decisions about the fairness and reasonableness of various transactions would, for the most part, involve sui generis and unreviewable determination of mixed questions of law and fact.

On the other hand, if, for example, Congress were to write a regulation requiring that management and controlling shareholders of a cor-

---

> extensive (although not exhaustive) investigation, includes four such specimens.

Bishop, "Sitting Ducks and Decoy Ducks: New Trends in the Indemnification of Corporate Directors and Officers," 77 Yale L.J. 1078, 1099 (1968). See also Cary, *supra* note 1, at 683–84; Address by A. A. Sommer, *supra* note 102, reprinted in *Hearings, supra* note 1, at 61, 75–76.

107. In describing the relationship between the fact-finding and the law-declaring processes in negligence actions, Professor Francis Bohlen stated:

> The jury has no power to declare the law, using that term in the sense above stated.
>
> But since it is impossible to anticipate the innumerable combinations of circumstances which may arise, it is impossible for the law to formulate in advance definite standards by which the propriety of conduct under every conceivable set of circumstances may be judged. It can at best announce broad general principles, which give the materials and general directions for the construction of the standard to be applied in each specific case.

Bohlen, "Mixed Questions of Law and Fact," 72 U. Pa. L. Rev. 111, 113 (1925). See also Address by A. A. Sommer, *supra* note 102, reprinted in *Hearings, supra* note 1, at 76–77, suggesting that, while traditional notions of degrees of fault seem obsolete, fiduciary standards for management must be based upon the *Gestalt* of the relationship between the parties. Sommer does however suggest that fiduciary standards be made at least somewhat more specific. *Id.*

108. See, e.g., N.Y. Bus. Corp. Law § 713 (McKinney Supp. 1977).

poration deal fairly with those holding noncontrolling equity interests, years of true judicial lawmaking would ensue.[109] Perhaps this is an argument for Congress to attempt clearer and more specific standards which would provide fairer notice to those subject to new duties.[110]

The primary thrust of this analysis is that when Congress considers allocation of jurisdiction with respect to any statutory scheme, it should hear expert testimony on the type of adjudication that each significant position is likely to spawn. If after such careful consideration, Congress concludes that the flexibility of a standard vague as to persons or activities aimed at is worth the uncertainty generated, it should then seriously consider exclusive federal jurisdiction for suits brought under such standard.[111] The greater the possibility that reviewable lawmaking will be done by the courts, the greater the uniformity benefits of exclusive federal jurisdiction.

Costs of Exclusive Federal Jurisdiction. Assuming a provision of federal corporate law is likely to result in a great deal of judicial lawmaking and is a candidate for exclusive federal jurisdiction, what are the costs against which the benefits of uniformity are to be weighed?

Jurisdiction of suits under the Securities Exchange Act of 1934 is exclusively federal.[112] There are suggestions that this exclusive jurisdiction under the Securities Exchange Act has caused serious problems of efficiency, particularly in the area of proxy regulation. Citing Professor Loss' discussion of such difficulties, the current tentative draft of the American Law Institute's Federal Securities Code opts in favor of concurrent state-federal jurisdiction over most suits under its provisions which are of the sort currently arising under the Securities Exchange Act.[113] The most severe difficulty cited by Loss and presumably troubling those drafting the Securities Code is the possibility that in the context of a particular case, no court, state or federal, could grant relief with respect to all of a plaintiff's claims arising out of one set of factual transactions.[114] At the time Loss wrote, it was possible for state and

---

109. See Kaplan, "Fiduciary Responsibility in the Management of the Corporation," 31 Bus. Law. 883, 907–10 (1976).

110. See R. Nader, *supra* note 1, at 104.

111. A. A. Sommer describes the tradeoff nicely. See note 102 *supra*.

112. 15 U.S.C. § 78aa (1976).

113. ALI, *Study of the Division of Jurisdiction Between State and Federal Courts* 183–84 (1969).

114. Loss, "The SEC Proxy Rules and State Law," 73 Harv. L. Rev. 1249 (1960). Two major sorts of difficulties are described by Loss. The first is the difficulty that any court, state or federal, will often have in determining the relationship between the state and federal laws that together govern the process of shareholder voting (both as to directors and on referenda) with respect to the affairs of national corporations. Such problems of fit between federal and state laws are

federal claims to arise out of a common nucleus of fact and yet, in some circumstances, for a federal court to consider itself without power to hear the state-law claims on a pendent jurisdiction theory. As a result, a plaintiff might need to bring two actions to assert all of his rights arising from one set of facts.[115] Additionally, even if a federal court had pendent jurisdiction over all of a plaintiff's state-law causes of action, multiple suits could result from the inability of that court to grant remedies provided for by state law which are different from those permitted to the federal courts.[116]

The former difficulty has been ameliorated by a Supreme Court case, *United Mine Workers v. Gibbs*,[117] which was decided after Loss wrote his original critique. This case permits federal courts, in their discretion, to entertain pendent state claims at least (1) when they arise from a core of operative facts common to the federal claim and (2) where under the circumstances a plaintiff would be expected to join the claims in one lawsuit.[118] Assuming the narrowest view of pendent jurisdiction under *Gibbs*,[119] part of the efficiency costs of exclusive federal jurisdiction of

---

discussed later in this article. The second problem, the one described in the text, is the problem of plaintiffs' need to sue twice to vindicate all their rights, a need which results from a combination of (i) cooperative state-federal substantive regulation with (ii) exclusive federal jurisdiction over claims under federal law, and (iii) the inability of federal courts to grant all the relief under state law which is available in the state courts.

Given the fact that characteristics (i) and (iii) are currently features of our system of regulation, exclusive federal jurisdiction generates the costs described by Loss. Depending upon one's view of the magnitude of uniformity benefits of exclusive federal jurisdiction in the proxy area, it could be entirely proper to reject exclusive federal jurisdiction as not cost-justified.

The continued vitality of characteristic (iii) is at least somewhat in question. See notes 117–123 *infra* and accompanying text. To the extent that it is no longer a factor, one suit in federal court will suffice to vindicate all of a plaintiff's rights. Additionally, Congress may well be able to further cure the need for bifurcation. See notes 119 and 121 *infra* and accompanying text.

Beyond this, if state law were entirely preempted by a federal law regulating the shareholder voting process of national corporations, state-created rights would not exist and a federal court with exclusive jurisdiction could grant all the relief which could be obtained in any forum.

115. Hurn v. Oursler, 289 U.S. 238 (1933); see the description of *Hurn's* test in United Mine Workers v. Gibbs, 383 U.S. 715, 721–24 (1966).

116. Loss, *supra* note 114, at 1278–84.

117. 383 U.S. 715 (1966).

118. *Id.* at 724–25.

119. The question still open under *Gibbs* is whether both requirements (i) and (ii) described in the text above must be met in order for pendent jurisdiction to be available or whether either will suffice. See Baker, "Toward a Relaxed View of Federal Ancillary and Pendent Jurisdiction," 33 U. Pitt. L. Rev. 759, 764–65 (1972).

suits brought under any federal law will be that a plaintiff will have to bring a separate state-court suit where either (1) or (2) above is not satisfied. These efficiency costs would continue to be appreciable, as Professor Loss makes clear in his current supplement.[120] Such problems of multiplicity, however, are clearly not as severe as those which seemed possible when Loss first discussed the problems of exclusive federal jurisdiction: the simultaneous prosecution of a state and a federal lawsuit arising from identical or substantially overlapping facts. Additionally, Congress could expand the scope of pendent jurisdiction in cases arising under federal corporate law, permitting all theories to be joined in one suit at the expense of more federal courts' time spent on state-law claims.[121]

The other difficulty described above involves the power of federal courts to grant relief under state law which would not otherwise be available under federal law.[122] There may still be limitations upon the power of federal courts in diversity cases to grant a remedy novel to them but provided for by state law.[123] Such a limitation could result in duplicative judicial effort. Even with respect to wrongs arising out of the same factual transactions, some relief may be available only from state courts, while any relief under federal law generally would be available only from federal courts.[124] Even if one assumes the continued existence of such limitations, they, like the court-defined scope of pendent jurisdiction, would yield to congressional action. Congress could, for example, provide that with respect to any claim for relief under state corporate law properly before a federal district court as

---

120. L. Loss, *Securities Regulation* 2962–76 (vol. V 1969 Supp. to vol. II 1961).

121. While there might be legitimate debate about the constitutional limitation upon pendent jurisdiction, a strong argument can be made that, to the extent that lack of pendent jurisdiction would constitute a severe deterrent to the use of a federal forum for a federal claim, there is justification for such jurisdiction. See P. Bator, P. Mishkin, D. Shapiro, and H. Wechsler, *Hart & Wechsler's The Federal Courts and the Federal System* 922–23 (2d ed. 1973).

122. See Loss, *supra* note 114, at 1278–84.

123. There seems to have been some amelioration of this difficulty as well. There are suggestions that in a diversity case, federal courts can grant remedies provided by state law even where such remedies are not otherwise available in federal court. Susquehanna Corp. v. General Refractories Co., 250 F. Supp. 797 (E.D. Pa. 1966) (dictum), *aff'd in part per curiam*, 356 F.2d 985 (3d Cir. 1966). Loss' argument is itself a powerful authority favoring federal courts' power in diversity cases to use state remedies. At a minimum, federal courts seem capable of adapting clearly permissible federal remedies to approximate relief available under state law. See Stern v. South Chester Tube Co., 390 U.S. 606 (1968); *Susquehanna Corp.*, *supra* this note. See generally L. Loss, *Securities Regulation*, *supra* note 120, 2958–59.

124. Loss, *supra* note 114, at 1250. But it is arguable that the states might use federal duties as the basis of state-created causes of action. *Id.* at 1263–77.

pendent to a claim under federal corporate law, the federal court may order any remedy available to a court of the state whose substantive law governs the claim.[125] The resulting costs of such a statute would be the extra judicial costs of providing whatever relief would have been unavailable in federal court prior to the expansion of remedies.

Some Conclusions: A Trial Period of Exclusivity. There seem to be few arguments for exclusive federal jurisdiction over suits under any particular federal corporation law if (1) its directives provide little interpretive leeway or (2) its directives, while vague, require a court principally to determine mixed questions of law and fact. With respect to those federal standards which contemplate a great deal of judicial lawmaking, Congress should seriously consider exclusive federal jurisdiction.

Two sorts of costs which must be weighed against the benefits of exclusive federal jurisdiction are (1) the increased workload which results from sharing none of the burden with state courts[126] and (2) the possibility that exclusive jurisdiction would result in two suits—one state, one federal—in instances where one suit in either forum would have sufficed had jurisdiction been concurrent. Not only has the latter difficulty been ameliorated significantly by judicial decision, but it is likely that Congress could virtually eliminate it. The cost of such a solution would be an increase in the time the lower federal courts spend hearing state-law claims.

Ultimately it is such an increase in the workload of the lower federal courts along with that caused directly by the absence of alternative state forums which Congress must weigh against the uniformity benefits described above.

If these costs and benefits seem too difficult to weigh in the abstract, perhaps the best way to decide about federal exclusivity is to decide after having some experience with both the quantity of litigation and the kinds of legal issues generated by each new federal regulation. This seems workable in the case of the limited federal intrusion envisioned by Cary. Jurisdiction over all claims arising under the new federal corporate law could be made exclusively federal for a period of seven

---

125. It seems impossible to construct an argument that Congress could not, if it so desires, permit or even require the federal courts to grant a traditionally judicial remedy, available in the state courts, for state-law claims properly before those courts pursuant to diversity or pendent jurisdiction.

126. It could be argued that this cannot legitimately be considered a cost and that Congress should be willing to provide sufficient federal judicial resources to administer litigation under its substantive programs. From a congressional perspective, however, the possibility that some of the federal-question caseload will be absorbed by the state courts could naturally be viewed as a benefit. In any event such a sharing is frequently described as a legitimate end. See Redish & Muench, *supra* note 77, at 334.

years.[127] The expiration of the seven-year period would provide an occasion for considering the exclusivity issue on the basis of the data amassed.[128] Additionally, although seven years would surely not be long enough for the federal courts to have answered definitively all major questions under the new federal law, the lower federal courts would have at least begun to give it shape.

Under a scheme of federal regulation more comprehensive than Cary's, it seems important to attempt a jurisdictional solution at the outset. The problems peculiar to more comprehensive regulation are discussed in the next section.

SPECIAL PROBLEMS OF COMPREHENSIVE FEDERAL REGULATION

The discussion under the heading "Federalization and the Caseloads of the Lower Federal Courts Under Existing Jurisdictional Grants" above is for the most part germane to questions of allocation of jurisdiction under either partial or comprehensive federal regulation of national corporations. The material that follows in this section deals with issues which are peculiar to a program of federal chartering and comprehensive regulation. If the current system of state regulation of national corporations were modified by the very limited scheme suggested by Cary,[129] the respective chartering states would continue to provide almost all of the law governing such corporations' internal affairs and appropriate forums for hearing disputes under such law. Under a scheme of exclusive federal chartering and regulation of national corporations like that proposed by A. A. Sommer,[130] other problems arise.

Exclusive Federal Chartering—Choice-of-Forum Difficulties. Under a scheme of exclusive federal chartering and comprehensive regulation coupled with concurrent jurisdiction in the state courts, questions about appropriate state forums arise. There no longer would be a state of incorporation for each national corporation. Under these circumstances, and assuming a congressional desire to spare the federal courts some of the burdens of suits under federal law, which states may, or even must, open their courts to suits to enforce the charter rights of

---

127. Such self-terminating laws have been referred to as "sunset laws." See Adams, "Sunset: A Proposal for Accountable Government," 28 Ad. Law Rev. 511 (1976).

128. Of course it would be impossible at the end of such period to compare the effects of exclusive federal jurisdiction with those of concurrent jurisdiction, since the latter would not have been tried. It seems to me that the magnitude of the uniformity benefits is more predictable than that of the increase in pressure on the federal courts. A seven-year period of exclusivity would provide a better understanding of the latter.

129. For the substantive features of his proposal see note 57 *supra*.

130. See note 59 *supra*.

shareholders of such a corporation? For example, what would be an appropriate state forum to hear a suit to compel payment of dividends to preferred shareholders of a national corporation? No state has a truly unique interest in the controversy. A preponderance-of-the-shareholders test, or a principal-place-of-business test are not only arbitrary but would require determinations that may be too difficult to make and in any event result in a potential for a frequent change of appropriate state forum. The most workable method of providing concurrent state-federal jurisdiction mandatory upon the states would be for a statute to provide that each national corporation certify the identity of its headquarters state to a federal agency and to expressly provide that the courts of that state have mandatory concurrent jurisdiction over suits under federal corporate law involving that corporation. It is not clear that the federal government has the power to use state courts in this way.[131] Even if Congress could create such concurrent jurisdiction it seems unwise for it to do so under a federal chartering scheme. States are free to permit their courts to refuse on the grounds of forum non conveniens to consider questions involving the internal affairs of corporations chartered by other states. When courts so refuse, the effect is to force such litigation back to the chartering state, which alone can charge such a corporation taxes without regard to the amount of its business or property in the state.[132] Unless, under federal chartering, headquarters states were permitted to charge for the headquartering privilege as states can now charge for the expenses they bear as chartering states, the net result would be a redistribution of wealth to the federal government.

A. A. Sommer's proposal for exclusive federal chartering and total preemption of state law would structurally resemble the current state enabling model and would presumably create in shareholders of national corporations at least all of the individual rights now enjoyed by them under most state laws.[133] As discussed earlier, under 28 U.S.C. 1337 suits brought to enforce rights conferred by federal statute and most probably those to enforce rights granted by the federal corporate charters could be brought in federal court regardless of the amount in

---

131. To the extent that a state's courts refused on forum non conveniens grounds to hear suits involving the internal affairs of foreign-state-chartered corporations, its courts could perhaps invoke that doctrine as a valid excuse for refusing to hear cognate suits involving federally chartered corporations. See note 55 *supra* and accompanying text. Note that state-court refusals to entertain federal causes of action found to rest upon a valid excuse all involved congressional silence as to the duty of the states to hear them. It is, however, an open question whether Congress can override an otherwise valid excuse. See Missouri *ex rel.* Southern Ry. v. Mayfield, 340 U.S. 1, 4–5 (1950); Douglas v. New York, N.H. & H. R.R., 279 U.S. 377, 387–88 (1929).

132. See notes 23 and 24 *supra* and accompanying text.

133. See note 59 *supra*.

controversy.[134] Beyond the implication for individual plaintiffs with small claims, civil actions could proceed on behalf of classes of shareholders regardless of the fact that some members, indeed that all members, had claims not in excess of $10,000.[135]

A Congress considering preemption of state corporation laws with respect to national corporations would need to consider how to deal with such small claims. As we have seen, doing nothing would most likely result in federal original jurisdiction concurrent with state courts and unlimited by jurisdictional amount.

Frivolous shareholder suits against management to obtain coercive relief—e.g., to inspect books and records,[136] to enjoin ultra vires acts,[137] and to correct wrongs with respect to shareholder voting[138]—could be particularly vexatious.

Perhaps the best way of avoiding many of the difficulties described above would be to provide for a large measure of exclusive federal jurisdiction divided between a federal administrative agency and the federal courts. Federal chartering would necessarily entail the use if not the creation of an administrative agency to deal with such matters as recording charter amendments. Such an agency could also be given a judicial role. To avoid the familiar problem of agency coziness with those regulated, federal courts could entertain suits requesting large amounts of money damages or nonmonetary relief on behalf of those representing a reasonably large percentage of securities of any relevant class. Suits seeking shareholder lists and other suits for nonmonetary relief pressed against management by those representing a fairly small percentage of securities in any class would be decided initially by the agency. The appropriate U.S. court of appeals would review only determinations of law. Suits to recover small sums of money might be dealt with in the same fashion or farmed out to the states, provided the problem of the choice of the appropriate state forum described above had been dealt with. Depending upon the location of agency offices, a shareholder might indeed be forced to travel a great distance to obtain coercive relief against actions of management which violate charter rights. This would not involve a change for the worse. Today shareholders often must travel a great distance to obtain such relief under state law.

Exclusive Federal Chartering—Diversity Jurisdiction. If federal regulation of national corporations were to entail the substitution of a federal certificate of incorporation for the state certificate currently held by each

---

134. See note 47 *supra* and accompanying text.

135. See note 51 *supra* and accompanying text.

136. See, e.g., N.Y. Bus. Corp. Law § 624 (McKinney 1963).

137. See, e.g., N.Y. Bus. Corp. Law § 203 (McKinney 1963).

138. See, e.g., N.Y. Bus. Corp. Law § 619 (McKinney 1963).

corporation, the result under the existing diversity jurisdiction-conferring statute would most likely be the elimination of diversity jurisdiction over suits to which such corporations are parties.

A literal reading of 28 U.S.C., section 1332(c), hardly compels such a result: "For the purposes of this section and section 1441 of this title, a corporation shall be deemed a citizen of any State by which it has been incorporated and of the State where it has its principal place of business. . . ." From such text alone one could argue plausibly that national corporations would retain citizenship in the state of their principal place of business even though there would no longer be any state of incorporation. Courts which have grappled with virtually identical issues, however, have decided otherwise.[139] They have noted that the addition in 1958 of the possibility of a second citizenship in a corporation's principal place of business was designed to cut back on diversity jurisdiction by creating the possibility of identity of citizenship between a corporation and the citizens of an additional state in which parochial bias against the corporation is unlikely.[140] This purpose of creating additional domiciles is violated when instead of limiting the possibility of diversity jurisdiction against a true state-citizen corporation, the principal-place-of-business domicile is used as the only ground of the statute's applicability. If, as is likely, an exclusively federally chartered corporation would be treated as a citizen of no state under section 1332, then that section's complete diversity requirement would never be satisfied in an action where the corporation is a necessary party.[141]

---

139. See Federal Deposit Ins. Corp. v. National Surety Corp., 345 F. Supp. 885 (S.D. Iowa 1972), holding that the Disabled American Veterans, a federally chartered corporation, not domiciled by Congress in a particular state, is the citizen of no state for diversity purposes, not even the state where it has a principal place of business. See also Rice v. Disabled American Veterans, 295 F. Supp. 131, 132–34 (D.D.C. 1968).

If the United States Government had owned more than one-half of the stock of the federal corporation involved in either of the two cases described in the preceding paragraph, a special jurisdictional provision would have created federal jurisdiction regardless of diversity of citizenship or the presence of a federal question. 28 U.S.C. § 1349 (1976).

140. 345 F. Supp. at 887; 295 F. Supp. at 134.

141. The statement in the text refers to all suits by or against business corporations chartered exclusively by the federal government, not solely to suits under federal corporate law. Under existing statutes, a federal court can never have diversity jurisdiction with respect to that portion of a lawsuit involving a party who is neither a citizen of a particular state nor of a foreign nation. See Fahrner v. Gentzsch, 355 F. Supp. 349, 353 (E.D. Pa. 1972); see Wright, *supra* note 64, § 3621 at p. 756 n.5 and accompanying text. It is clear that the citizenship of such a party can never be used to create diversity. *Id.* Can such a stateless United States citizen be an additional party to a suit between other parties whose citizenship pattern otherwise satisfies the requirements of § 1332(a)(1) or (a)(2)? The *Fahrner* court

In the current climate, as evidenced by the legislative history of the 1958 amendments to section 1332,[142] by American Law Institute proposals to cut back diversity jurisdiction,[143] and by recently proposed legislation,[144] it is possible that Congress would be delighted with the contraction of diversity jurisdiction which would result from combining federal chartering with extant section 1332. Nevertheless, a Congress considering a federal chartering scheme should advert to the probable result of its inaction. To avoid otherwise inevitable litigation, Congress, if it desires such constriction of diversity jurisdiction, should include as a part of any federal chartering law a clear declaration that a federally chartered corporation is a citizen of no state for purposes of diversity jurisdiction. Congress' authority to do so is unquestionable.[145] If on the other hand Congress wishes to retain diversity jurisdiction over national corporations, it should so indicate expressly. While

---

permitted such a person to continue as a party plaintiff but only on the theory that his claim was pendent to claims asserted in a suit which otherwise met the requirements of § 1332(a)(2). 355 F. Supp. at 353–54.

It is, however, clear that pendent jurisdiction would at best only occasionally make available diversity jurisdiction over a suit involving a stateless national corporation holding only a federal charter. First, where such a corporation is the only possible plaintiff or defendant there can be no diversity, because (i) neither § 1332(a)(1) nor (2) is satisfied (see Kaufman and Broad, Inc. v. Gootrad, 397 F. Supp. 1054 (S.D.N.Y. 1975); *Fahrner* at 353), and (ii) there is no diversity action among other parties to which such a corporation's claim might be appended. Second, even where an action might continue among other parties who satisfy the requirements of § 1332, the availability of pendent jurisdiction in diversity cases is by no means settled. Cf. Seyler v. Steuben Motors, Inc., 462 F.2d 181 (3d Cir. 1972).

142. 2 U.S. Code Cong. and Admin. News 3101–03 (1958).

143. ALI, *supra* note 113, at 12–13, 125–30.

144. See H.R. 2202, 96th Cong., 1st Sess. (1979) currently pending before the House of Representatives and proposing the abolition of federal district court diversity jurisdiction. Recently the members of the Judicial Conference of the United States independently proposed the abolition of such jurisdiction. See release dated March 11, 1977, of the Public Information Office of the United States Courts.

145. Sheldon v. Sill, 49 U.S. (8 How.) 441 (1850), affirms great power in Congress to limit the jurisdiction of the lower federal courts to less than that which might be given under article III of the United States Constitution.

In 1809 the Supreme Court held that corporations are citizens of no state. Bank of United States v. Deveaux, 9 U.S. (5 Cranch) 61 (1809). In 1844 the Court began treating corporations as citizens of their chartering states. Louisville, C. & C. R. Co. v. Letson, 43 U.S. (2 How.) 497 (1844). Although the rationale for such treatment has shifted somewhat over the years, the net effect of the *Letson* case has remained constant. For an interesting discussion of judicial difficulties with the notions of the corporate person's state citizenship see C. Wright, *supra* note 37 at 101.

some may doubt Congress' power to make a federally chartered corporation a state citizen for diversity purposes, those doubts seem ill founded.[146] Perhaps, as in current American Law Institute proposals, the best solution would be for Congress to permit federal diversity jurisdiction over suits by or against national corporations in carefully defined situations where discrimination against such corporations seems plausible.[147]

FEDERAL CORPORATE LAW: PROBLEMS OF JUDICIAL EFFICIENCY ARISING FROM THE FIT BETWEEN FEDERAL AND STATE LAW

As discussed in the introduction, the structural inelegance of the current system of state regulation of national corporations is by itself an insufficient reason for change. From the perspective of various critics of the substance of state corporate law, however, the benefits of some federal intrusion are clear. Should one consider problems of federalism in determining the scope of any proposed federal intrusion?

From a federal perspective, the possible costs of any scheme of federal regulation are (1) the inevitable costs of designing and creating a new regulatory scheme, (2) the continuing costs of running such a scheme, and (3) the intangible injury to federalism caused by federal intrusion into an area formerly regulated by the states. In the case of regulation of national corporations, only potential costs (1) and (2) seem worth considering. There are good arguments that federalism often requires that Congress decline to exercise the legislative power it possesses under the commerce clause. Many local activities having national impact also have a particularly strong local impact as well. Given the vastness of commerce clause power, if the states are to be more than administrative arms of the federal government, some congressional restraint is necessary. Additionally, there is often an independent federal interest in permitting the states to serve as laboratories testing the results of different legislative approaches to similar problems.

---

146. The argument that there are limits upon Congress' power to expand diversity jurisdiction by redefining state citizenship is not entirely frivolous. Article III of the Constitution must impose some limitations. For example, it is unthinkable that the words "citizens of states" in article III are sufficiently broad to permit Congress to expand diversity jurisdiction by designating a person or a corporation a citizen of a state with which he or it has no contract. On the other hand it seems likely that article III would be read to permit Congress' designating an exclusively federally chartered corporation a citizen of the state where it is headquartered or where it has a principal place of business.

147. ALI, *supra* note 113, at 13, 125–30. Note that the current proposal prohibits a corporation from invoking diversity (either originally or by removal) in a state where it has certain substantial contacts. *Id.* Diversity could be further restricted by prohibiting the invocation of diversity jurisdiction against a corporation in such a jurisdiction.

Choosing federal restraint based upon federalism in the case of possible federal regulation of national corporations, however, is to apply deferential federalism where it is least justified.[148] The federal interest in regulating the internal affairs of such corporations is obviously great. With respect to a national corporation, no state has a special and legitimate interest in regulating the various relationships among its management and shareholders. As discussed above, the chartering state's only interest is in selling its local law to govern this most national of all contractual relationships. Such an interest is obviously entitled to no weight at all against the great federal interest described above. Finally, is a federal interest served by permitting the laboratory-states a few more experiments? From the perspective of greater management accountability—that of the proponents of federal incorporation—the experimentation would seem to have run a long and useful course. From that viewpoint, there seems to be no need to hold up federal legislation, otherwise quite justifiable by means of a state- and federal-interest calculus, solely on the ground that some good ideas might emerge from a further period of state regulation.

The remaining costs of comprehensive federal regulation which are of legitimate concern to a federal legislator are those of starting and running the regulatory program. It is difficult to estimate the costs in dollars of any particular regulatory program. Were figures available, each reader would still have to weigh them according to his own system of values against the benefits of increased fairness. Instead of attempting this impossible calculus, I want to assume that the difficult decision has been made in favor of a certain amount of federal regulation and discuss how the regulation can be made most efficient from a judicial perspective.

We have seen in an earlier portion of this article that chaos would have been the result if states had not practiced an informal, voluntary federalism by generally choosing to apply the law of the state of incorporation to govern the internal affairs of foreign corporations appearing in their courts.[149] The chaos would have resulted from the application of different but parallel laws to different portions of a transaction which could be regulated reasonably only by means of one set of coherent rules.

Partial federal preemption of the regulation of national corporations raises no such problems. To be sure, partial preemption involves the existence of two sets of laws—one state, one federal—both regulating conduct within a substantive area. The difference between multiple regulation by several states and joint state and federal regulation is that, with respect to the latter, there is truly only one set of laws. It is made up of an amalgam of state and federal law, but it is internally consis-

---

148. But see R. Nader, *supra* note 1, at 240.

149. See note 140 *supra* and accompanying text.

tent.[150] The existence of a conflict between the law of a state of incorporation and a federal regulation and the proper resolution of such a conflict would be determined by federal law.

While the relationship between state and federal law would get worked out in each case, the expenses of nonpreemption are precisely the judicial expenses of working out the relationship. Consequently, the costs are greatest where there are alternative plausible ways of viewing the relationship between state and federal law.

One good example explored by Professor Loss is the complex relationship between state law governing the shareholder franchise and the federal proxy rules.[151] Professor Loss has discussed in detail the difficult judicial decisions which have been and may be occasioned by the necessity of determining the proper fit between state and federal law in this complex area.[152]

A simpler example of such problems of fit can be found in Professor Cary's proposal to require by federal law that certain provisions be inserted in the state-issued charters of national corporations.[153] Is the breach of such a provision a violation of state or of federal law?[154] Regardless of which law is found to create the duties, is the remedy for a breach of such a duty to be determined by federal or by state law? Can a violation of such a provision be ratified by the shareholders? If so, will federal law or state law determine what is a valid ratification? Ultimately, without legislative guidance, the federal courts would answer such questions of fit between state and federal laws which clearly continue to operate together but in a way only vaguely if at all suggested by federal statute.

Congress could, however, save courts and litigants time and trouble by spelling out clearly and in advance the more important features of the contemplated relationship. In regulating the internal affairs of national corporations, because no strong state interest justifies deferential federalism, the simplest way to spell out the relationship is for Congress to preempt state law completely in a convenient area.

The same problems can arise in substantive areas other than those discussed immediately above. Should federal fiduciary standards be

---

150. The law which governs daily living in the United States is a single system of law; it speaks in relation to any particular question with only one ultimately authoritative voice, however difficult it may be on occasion to discern in advance which of two or more conflicting voices really carries authority. In the long run and in large, this must be so.

Hart, "The Relations Between State and Federal Law," 54 Colum. L. Rev. 489 (1954).

151. See Loss, *supra* note 114.

152. *Id.*

153. See note 57 *supra*.

154. Cf. Loss, *supra* note 114, at 1263–77.

minimum standards in the sense that more stringent state laws are not preempted?[155] This pattern works well where federal objectives are clear, limited, and quantifiable. In the area of pollution control, Congress requires of industries in all states a quantifiable level of cleanliness, but permits states to require even more.[156] A fiduciary standard, on the other hand, represents an attempt to vindicate not only vague but diverse substantive ends. Even if the question is how much care is required of a director, it is possible to harm the national shareholder constituency of a corporation by requiring either too much or too little from corporate managers. While it may not seem realistic to assume that states would impose more exacting standards, litigants will nevertheless so argue. Why should federal courts have to concern themselves with the relationship between state and federal law in the area of no legitimate localized interest? Again, the proper solution seems to be a thorough federal preemption of a conveniently isolable area of regulation.

One might, I suppose, attempt an argument that corporate regulation is such an interlocking system that total preemption is necessary because none of its parts is truly isolable. This seems untenable. The partial regulation described above—for example, Professor Cary's proposal—seems to involve substantive areas which are reasonably isolable from other corporate regulation. Occasional unforeseeable problems of fit may occur in any scheme of partial preemption; what is important is to avoid those which are foreseeable.

The suggested approach is for the legislature to think much more carefully about the potential interaction of state and federal law. Beyond this, the suggestion is that when Congress is partially regulating in an area of no legitimate state interest, it should clearly eliminate some of the most foreseeable and troublesome potential connections between its regulation and state laws. One device helping to accomplish this would be a provision to accompany any scheme of partial federal regulation. It might read as follows:

> Sections ____ through ____ of this title preempt state laws governing the same subject matter and are to be construed liberally to effectuate their purposes. The following determinations shall be made solely according to federal law determined by the courts in accordance with the purposes of this title:
>
> (1) the nature and scope of the rights and duties created by or recognized under such sections;

---

155. Professor Kaplan suggests such a minimum federal standard pattern. Kaplan, *supra* note 1, at 481.

156. See 33 U.S.C. § 1370 (1976) (Federal Water Pollution Control Act); 42 U.S.C § 1857d-1 (1976) (Clean Air Act of 1970); 42 U.S.C.A. § 6929 (1976) (Resource Conservation and Recovery Act of 1976).

(2) the identity of beneficiaries of rights, or the objects of duties, created by or recognized under such sections;
(3) the existence, nature and scope of any cause of action created by or recognized under such sections or of any defense thereto;
(4) the waiver of any rights created by or recognized under such sections; and
(5) the existence, nature, and scope of any remedy for the violation of any right or the breach of any duty created or recognized under such sections.

In determining the federal law contemplated by this section the laws of the several states may be considered but shall be without binding effect.

While such a provision would enlarge the area on the federal side of the inevitably blurred line which separates state and federal regulation, I believe it would also help bring that line into somewhat sharper focus.

CHAPTER SEVEN

Reweaving the Corporate Veil: Management Structure and the Control of Corporate Information

Deborah A. DeMott, *Associate Professor of Law, Duke University School of Law*

There is a striking similarity in much recent writing about the derelictions of large corporations. Corporations, it is asserted, often behave badly as a result of their internal organization and structure; the remedy for this disturbing proclivity is said to involve going behind the corporate veil, forcibly intruding on the corporation's private spheres, to reshape the process through which it makes decisions. Equally striking about this genre of corporate literature is its failure to describe actual experience behind the veil and to examine specific instances of the kinds of corporate decisions to be reached by its proposed reforms. Similarly, much of this writing tends to downgrade more traditional remedies for corporate wrongdoing—the shareholder's derivative suit, civil and criminal fines and penalties—in favor of changes in management structure.

The restructured corporation envisaged by these critics would feature an independent and knowledgeable board of directors vigilantly monitoring the performance of operating management, assessing that performance in terms of goals set by the board while detecting any crucial missteps in management's operation of the business. After describing these proposals for restructuring, this article examines some recent instances of corporate behavior which, in the author's view, bear heavily on the proposals' likelihood of success.

REWEAVING THE VEIL—PROPOSED CHANGES IN INTERNAL CORPORATE STRUCTURE

The recent style in critical writing about corporations has been to attribute a fair number of their misdeeds to the nature of their internal organization. Examples of socially disfavored behavior as various as polluting the environment,[1] marketing unsafe products,[2] and paying out corporate funds for sensitive purposes[3] have all been pointed to as the results of internal corporate structure. Not surprisingly, the proposed remedies accompanying such critiques of corporate behavior have changes in the corporation's internal structure as their focus, while often discounting substantially or disregarding entirely other kinds of remedies.

The most extensive exposition in this style, that of Christopher Stone,[4] argues that corporations are less responsive than other entities to traditional legal sanctions. The structure of large corporations diffuses the impact of those sanctions, as well as making it difficult to allocate responsibility for illegal acts to individuals and providing a climate in which individual managers may perceive the risks associated with illegal conduct as worth taking.[5] As a result, Stone asserts, the civil and criminal penalties with which the corporation and its employees are threatened ofttimes do not effectively deter illegal conduct.[6] Lacking as well, according to this analysis, is any effective internal check on corporate wrongdoing. The board of directors, mandated by statute to manage the corporation, is seen as having abdicated that task to the corporation's executives long ago, remaining as only an honorific vestige of a legal model that never matched business realities.[7] Further, the corporate structure itself provides incentives to employees to keep information about activities which may prove embarrassing or harmful to the corporation away from the board.[8]

To be sure, there are precedents for these critiques of boards of directors in earlier descriptions of directors' performance.[9] The persis-

---

1. See C. Stone, Where the Law Ends 116 (1975).
2. See *id.* at p. 135.
3. See Stevenson, *"The SEC and the New Disclosure,"* 62 Cornell L. Rev. 50, 91 (1976).
4. See C. Stone, *supra* note 1.
5. See *id.* at pp. 35–73.
6. See *id.*
7. See *id.* at pp. 125–30.
8. See *id.* at 61–62. The fact that directors' lack of actual knowldege of illegal acts by corporate employees may be an effective defense in shareholders' derivative litigation may itself create a desire to protect board members through the insulation of ignorance. Cf. Graham v. Allis-Chalmers Mfg. Co., 41 Del. Ch. 78, 84–85, 188 A.2d 125, 130 (Sup. Ct. 1963) (directors under no duty to suspect wrongdoing by corporate employees in the absence of specific grounds for suspicion). This defense has proved unsuccessful in prosecutions under the Federal Food and Drug Act, because that statute imposes liability on corporate managers who may not know of specific violations but nonetheless are authorized within the corporation to prevent or correct them. See United States v. Park, 421 U.S. 658, 670–71 (1975).
9. See, e.g., J. Bacon & Brown, *Corporate Directorship Practices* (1973); H. Koontz,

tent charge is that many corporate boards fail to monitor effectively the performance of the corporation's executives, with the result that the board, as well as observers outside the corporation, may be surprised and dismayed by the consequences of some of the executives' activities.[10] Consequently, these analyses of corporate behavior all include proposals which, while varying in their specifics, uniformly look toward increasing and improving the level of board performance. For example, Ralph Nader's proposal for federal incorporation,[11] which attributes the low quality of board performance to the heavy influence of the corporation's chief executive officer on the board,[12] would increase director independence by prohibiting a corporation's officers, employees, and providers of services from serving on its board.[13] To upgrade board performance, the board would be furnished with its own separate staff, and individual directors would be limited to serving on only one board at a time.[14] Another critic of contemporary boards, Melvin Eisenberg, although favoring the suggestion that boards ought to be composed solely of outsiders, argues that much the same advantages can be obtained by requiring only that a majority of the directors be outsiders.[15] On the other hand, Eisenberg rejects the proposal that boards be separately staffed as a change which would create an in-

---

The Board of Directors and Effective Management (1967); M. Mace, *Directors: Myth and Reality* (1971); S. Vance, *The Corporate Director* (1968).

10. See, e.g., M. Eisenberg, *The Structure of the Corporation*, pp. 140–48 (1976); H. Koontz, *supra* note 9, at pp. 220–22; M. Mace, *supra* note 9, at p. 187; C. Stone, *supra* note 1, at pp. 127–28. The SEC states similar criticisms of outside directors' performance in its report of its investigation into Stirling Homex Corp. See Report of Investigation in the Matter of Stirling Homex Corp. Relating to Activities of the Board of Directors of Stirling Homex Corp. [1975-76 Transfer Binder] Fed. Sec. L. Rep. (CCH) ¶ 80,219. The directors are criticized for failing to play "any significant role" in directing the company's affairs, and specifically for failing to gain a strong enough understanding of the company's accounting principles to enable them to make judgments about important business questions and the abilities of corporate officers. See *id.* at 85,462–63. The corporation had no internal system with which to furnish the board with important information; the directors apparently aggravated this deficiency by accepting superficial answers to the general inquiries they made to operating management. See generally Caplin, "Outside Directors and Their Responsibilities: A Program for the Exercise of Due Care," 1 J. Corp. L. 57 (1975).

11. See R. Nader, M. Green, and J. Seligman, *Taming the Giant Corporation* (1976) [hereinafter cited as R. Nader]; *Corporate Rights and Responsibilities: Hearings before the Senate Comm. on Commerce*, 94th Cong., 2d Sess. pp. 197–206 (1976) (testimony of Ralph Nader).

12. See R. Nader, *supra* note 11, at 97.

13. See *id.* at 126–27.

14. See *id.* at pp. 121, 126–27.

15. See M. Eisenberg, *supra* note 10, at 174–75.

efficient adversary relationship between the board's staff and the corporation's operating management.[16] Finally, Christopher Stone's analysis recommends, along with some changes in board composition discussed later, enactment of a legislative mandate to directors to review management's performance.[17]

What is most striking about these critiques is that they all recognize, at least implicitly, that boards of directors appear to have difficulty in obtaining information about their corporations and making meaningful use of it, and are thereby severely restricted in their capacity to monitor management. Whether this difficulty is entirely the consequence of corporate structure, or whether it may be attributable even in part to other factors, is not investigated by these critiques. They do, however, present a variety of proposed methods for strengthening the board's posture in the flow of corporate information.

Eisenberg analyzes the board's effective isolation from corporate information solely in terms of the present deficiencies of independent auditors;[18] he would have the auditors, rather than management, select the accounting principles appropriate to the corporation's financial statements, while placing the power to select and dismiss the auditors with board rather than with operating management[19] or with the shareholders.[20] Obviously, these changes, however desirable in themselves, would not improve the board's access to information which management keeps from or misrepresents to the auditors.[21]Although

---

16. See *id.* at 155–56.

17. See C. Stone, *supra* note 1, at pp. 143–44. It is not clear how this requirement could be made enforceable to exclude pro forma or rudimentary reviews. The existence of the mandate might, nonetheless, have a hortatory effect.

18. See M. Eisenberg, *supra* note 10, at 186–87.

19. See *id.* at 198–209.

20. See *id.* at 205–09. Eisenberg would require the board of each publicly held corporation to have an audit committee composed solely of independent directors to nominate and recommend dismissal of the outside auditor and to direct and set the terms of the auditor's engagement, on behalf of the entire board. *Id.* at 205. Eisenberg disagrees with Douglas Hawes' proposal that the power to appoint and dismiss outside auditors be placed solely in the corporation's shareholders, see Hawes, "Stockholder Appointment of Independent Auditors, A Proposal," 74 Colum. L. Rev. 1 (1974). Although Eisenberg argues that the shareholders' involvement resulting from Hawes' proposal would be too limited and would be unduly responsive to management's suggestions, his argument leaves open the possibility of shareholder ratification of the audit committee's recommendations. See *id.*, at 205–06. See also Lovdal, "Making the Audit Committee Work," 55 Harv. Bus. Rev. 108 (1977).

21. The auditors themselves may not be able to detect "false entries made by people in responsible positions," see Forbes, May 15, 1976, at p. 92, *reprinted in* Staff of Subcomm. on Reports, Accounting and Management, Senate Comm. on Gov't Operations, 95th Cong., 1st Sess., *Study on the Accounting Establishment* 663

Eisenberg suggests that the board might want to direct the auditors to undertake nonfinancial audits of management's performance to assist it in evaluating the quality of that performance,[22] the board may still be effectively precluded from learning of some of management's activities until the corporation has been harmed. In short, it may be desirable to increase the independence of outside auditors and limit management's choice of accounting principles; doing so will not necessarily give the board prompt information about all of management's actions which may prove harmful to the corporation.

In contrast to Eisenberg's emphasis on improving the performance of outside auditors, both the Nader and Stone proposals envisage more direct director access to information about the corporation through the appointment of directors with designated responsibilities. To assure that critical problems do not slip by the board's purview, Nader proposes assigning to each director a specific area of concern with its own identifiable constituency—employee welfare, consumer protection, compliance with law, environmental protection, finances—corresponding to each director's expertise.[23] Presumably, to be effective in scrutinizing the corporation's performance in each of these areas, the designated directors, with the board's separate staff,[24] would need to obtain access to internal corporate information, wholly apart from any they might receive from operating management or the corporation's outside auditors. This proposal is awkward in at least two respects. First, it presents some of the same problems as the proposed separate staff for the board: operating management may strongly resent the directors' efforts, leading to an unhealthy degree of adversariness, while some duplication of activities appears to be inevitable. Second, identifying each director with a separate constituency might vitiate the board's collegiality, thereby weakening its ability to deal vigorously with management.

Stone's method for assuring greater director access to corporate in-

---

(1977) [hereinafter cited as *Accounting Establishment Study*] (quoting William Gladstone, managing partner of the New York office of Arthur Young & Co.) Gladstone was of the view that management was more likely to heed the admonitions of an outside auditor who generally had a positive, can-do attitude than one who maintained a persistently adversary stance. *Id.*

22. See M. Eisenberg, *supra* note 10, at 210–11. Eisenberg does not, however, explore the magnitude of the cost of such audits.

23. See R. Nader, *supra* note 11, at p. 125. Short of the board level, Nader has also proposed that the board be required by statute to designate an internal SEC compliance officer to be responsible for assuring adherence to disclosure requirements. See *Foreign and Corporate Bribes: Hearings on S. 3133 Before the Senate Comm. on Banking, Housing and Urban Affairs,* 94th Cong., 2d Sess. 19 (1976) (testimony of Ralph Nader) [hereinafter cited as 1976 *Senate Hearings on Foreign and Corporate Bribes*].

24. See text accompanying note 14 *supra*.

formation turns on government appointment of designated "public" directors to the boards of large corporations whose duties would include, along with acting as the corporation's "superego" in reminding it of legal and ethical concerns,[25] reviewing the adequacy of the corporation's internal systems for handling critical information and serving as a receptive audience for employees who seek to bring pieces of information to the board's attention.[26] Since these directors would, under Stone's proposal, be nominated by a government agency,[27] their presence on the board would represent a marked increase in governmental intrusion into the private corporate sphere. In the absence of a convincing demonstration that the public directors would succeed,[28]

---

25. See C. Stone, *supra* note 1, at pp. 158–62.

26. See *id.* at pp. 165–70.

27. Stone proposes that such directors be appointed by a Federal Corporations Commission, if one comes into existence, or by the Securities and Exchange Commission. Appointment to a corporate board as a "general public director" would require a majority vote of the other board members. Ten percent of each board would be composed of such public directors, who would be removable only by unanimous board vote without a showing of cause, or by a two-thirds board vote with a showing of cause. Shareholders would not vote on the appointment or retention of such public directors. See *id.* at pp.158, 159.

Stone's reasons for thereby disenfranchising shareholders as to part of the board are not apparent from his discussion. To be sure, shareholders under his proposal would still elect the remaining members of the board, whose majority vote would be required to seat a public director, leaving shareholders with an indirect franchise as to the public directors. This in itself does not explain why shareholders ought to be denied the right to vote on the retention in office of public directors once they have served a term on the board. Equally unclear is whether Stone intends to divest shareholders of their judicially recognized inherent power to remove directors for cause, see Campbell v. Loew's, Inc., 36 Del. Ch. 563, 572–73, 134 A.2d 852, 858 (1957), a right presently recognized by statute in Delaware, see Del. Code Ann. tit. 8 § 141(k) (Michie Supp. 1976), which his proposal on its face surely appears to do. If shareholders cannot remove public directors for cause, Stone's proposal denies shareholders one remedy if the nonpublic members of the board are unwilling to act to remove errant public directors. Again, there appears to be no reason to so penalize shareholders.

28. The only historical experience proffered at any length by Stone to support his proposal is a discussion of the public directorships created by Congress in the nineteenth century on the board of the Union Pacific Railroad. By Stone's account, Union Pacific's public directors performed dismally, failing to protect the government's substantial financial interests in the efficient development of the railroad. C. Stone, *supra* note 1, at pp. 153–56. Stone concludes that the functions of the Union Pacific directors were insufficiently defined and that the directors themselves were not of the professional stature their jobs required. *Id.* at pp. 155–56.

it is difficult to regard this proposal seriously. One can only hypothesize that the response of the "id" directors and of operating management to their superego public directors might be one of hostility and evasion. Stone also proposes enactment of a legislative requirement that information falling into designated categories be brought to the board's attention.[29] However, the legislative designation of critical categories may lag somewhat behind current problems, and if corporate directors are as remote from crucial information about their corporations as these critiques suggest, they may have difficulty in determining whether they should request additional kinds of information, as well as whether management is obeying the legislative mandate.

Interestingly enough, some of the critiques also propose that the shareholders' derivative action be revived by prohibiting devices such as corporate indemnification of managers' expenses, which reduce the costs of such litigation to individual managers,[30] and by providing a variety of novel sanctions to be available against individual defendants who are found liable in such litigation.[31] None of the proposals, however, considers whether the posited need for extensive structural reform might thereby be reduced.[32]

What prompts Stone's belief that his public directors would perform more satisfactorily? First, presumably, the lessons of history, the assumption that by analyzing the reasons for past failures one avoids their future repetition. As it happens, public directors have failed in contexts other than that of the Union Pacific, see, e.g., *id.* at pp. 154–57 (discussion of government-appointed directors on the board of the Communications Satellite Corporation); S. Vance, *supra* note 9, at pp. 144–51 (conclusion that government-appointed boards at the General Analine and Film Corp. were "the epitome of ineffectiveness"). The inference that the difficulty lies with the institution of government-appointed directors, rather than with any particular strategy for appointing them, appears irresistible. Second, Stone argues that business attitudes have evolved to such an extent that his public directors would be able to perform their superego function effectively. This may be true – such a statement is impossible to disprove – but it may also be the case that such changes consist primarily of a stronger understanding of the benefits of good public relations. Finally, Stone maintains that if the other changes he recommends in boards of directors are made, the public directors are more likely to be effective. C. Stone, *supra* note 1, at p. 161. It is nonetheless possible that other directors, however independent and well motivated, might resent the presence of a government appointee in their midst. *Cf.* Schwartz, "Governmentally Appointed Directors in a Private Corporation—The Communications Satellite Act of 1962," 79 Harv. L. Rev. 350, 357, 359 (1965) (public directors of Union Pacific Railroad complained they were treated "as spies and antagonists" by remainder of board).

29. See C. Stone, *supra* note 1, at p. 151.

30. See R. Nader, *supra* note 11, at p. 251

31. See C. Stone, *supra* note 1, at pp. 148–149 (suspension of culpable directors from eligibility to serve on boards).

32. Although two of the critiques also refer reproachfully to the extensive substantive

As it happens, some aspects of these structure-oriented critiques of corporate behavior are reflected in several recent settlements of shareholders' derivative actions[33] and of injunctive actions brought by the Securities and Exchange Commission (SEC).[34] The settlements, as relief ancillary to the defendants' consent to an injunction barring the repetition of illegal conduct, typically change the composition of the corporation's board so that outsiders constitute a majority of the members;[35] in some cases the composition of the board's executive committee has been similarly altered.[36] Some of the mechanisms to restructure the board are more intrusive than others: in some cases the corporation simply consented to the appointment of directors to be approved by the court,[37] or selected through negotiations between incumbent management and the SEC,[38] while in other cases incumbent management

---

protection available to directors in derivative litigation through the "business judgment" defense—the defense that, although negligent, management's conduct fell somewhere within the very broad perimeters of the permissible exercise of business judgment—neither appears to recommend any changes in the defense. See R. Nader, *supra* note 11, at 102–05; C. Stone, *supra* note 1, at pp. 62–63.

33. See Springer v. Jones, Civil No. 74-1455 (C.D. Cal. 1975). Plaintiffs in *Springer* alleged that directors and officers of the Northrop Corp. violated the federal proxy rules by failing to disclose the corporation's involvement in illegal contributions to the 1972 campaign of President Nixon.

34. For a list of the SEC injunctive actions involved, see Mathews, "Recent Trends in SEC Requested Ancillary Relief in SEC Level Injunctive Actions," 31 Bus. Law 1323, 1334–35 (1976). See generally Levine & Herlihy, "SEC Enforcement Actions, 10 Rev. Sec. Reg. 951, 953–54 (1977); Treadway, "SEC Enforcement Techniques," 32 Wash. & Lee L. Rev. 637 (1975); Comment, "Court-Appointed Directors," 64 Geo. L.J. 737 (1976). See also Mathews, "SEC Civil Injunctive Actions—II," 5 Rev. Sec. Reg. 949 (1972); Pitt & Markham, "SEC Injunctive Actions," 6 Rev. Sec. Reg. 955 (1973).

35. See Second Amended Judgment at 4, SEC v. Mattel, Inc., Civil No. 74-2958 (C.D. Cal. 1974); Undertaking at 3–4, Springer v. Jones, Civil No. 74-1455 (C.D. Cal. 1975) (incorporated by reference into Final Judgment).

36. See Second Amended Judgment at 4, SEC v. Mattel, Inc., Civil No. 74-2958 (C.D. Cal. 1974); Undertaking at 4, Springer v. Jones, Civil No. 74-1455 (C.D. Cal. 1975) (incorporated by reference into Final Judgment).

37. See Undertaking at 3–4, Springer v. Jones, Civil No. 74-1455 (C.D. Cal. 1975) (incorporated by reference into Final Judgment). The corporation also agreed to solicit proxies for shareholder election of its new outside directors. *Id.* The Undertaking does not contain provisions which would be applicable if shareholders fail to abide by the board's recommendation that they vote in favor of the election of the court-approved outside directors. It is not clear from the Undertaking whether the shareholder vote was believed to be necessary to the election of the new directors; the Undertaking appears to contemplate that the new directors would assume office on the board prior to the next shareholders' meeting.

38. See Second Amended Judgment at 4, SEC v. Mattel, Inc., Civil No. 74-2958 (C.D.

agreed to nominate and propose new unaffiliated directors to the shareholders for their election to the board.[39] Since the corporation is ordered to maintain a majority of such directors on its board for a specified period of time, it is clear that if the corporation simply consents to the appointment of the new directors, without any shareholder involvement through an electoral process, the shareholders are being at least partially disenfranchised for a corresponding period of time.[40]

The legality of this kind of disenfranchisement has never been directly confronted by any court,[41] and indeed, incumbent management may have a strong incentive to consent to the structural changes rather than litigate the SEC's ability to obtain them otherwise.[42] At the least,

---

Cal. 1974). In *Mattel* the corporation agreed to "appoint to, and maintain on, its Board of Directors" the new outside directors. No shareholder participation in this process is mentioned.

39. See Judgment at 5–6, SEC v. Canadian Javelin, Ltd., 73 Civil 5074 (S.D.N.Y. 1974).

40. See Second Amended Judgment at 12, SEC v. Mattel, Inc., Civil No. 74-2958 (C.D. Cal. 1974) (five year term specified); Malley, "Far-Reaching Equitable Remedies Under the Securities Acts and the Growth of Federal Corporate Law," 17 Wm. & Mary L. Rev. 47, 57 (1975). Presumably, the shareholders retain the ability to elect the remaining directors.

41. The case closest to the point, Int'l Controls Corp. v. Vesco, 490 F.2d 1344, 1352 (2d Cir.), *cert. denied,* 417 U.S. 932 (1974), involved an attempt in state court by defendants to enjoin International Controls' new federal-court-appointed board from exercising its powers, on the argument that the old board had improperly abdicated its responsibility to shareholders when it consented to the federal court's appointment of new directors. The Second Circuit upheld the lower court's injunction restraining the defendants from prosecuting their state-court challenge to the new board, on the rationale that the federal court was thereby protecting its judgment from frustration by a state-court proceeding. The question of the legality of the remedy, especially in the absence of the defendants' consent, has proved a troublesome one to commentators, however. See, e.g., Stevenson, *supra* note 3, at 86.

More recently, however, the SEC was rebuffed in its efforts to obtain a court order removing the president of a real estate investment trust and appointing additional trustees to the trust's board, as relief ancillary to a permanent injunction enjoining defendants from future violations of the Securities and Exchange Act of 1934 and the Securities Act of 1933. The defendants did not consent to the injunction, and the court held that its power to order relief functionally equivalent to receivership ought to be reserved for "the most egregious cases." SEC v. American Realty Trust, 429 F. Supp. 1148, 1178 (E.D. Va. 1977), *rev'd on other grounds,* [1978 Transfer Binder] Fed. Sec. L. Rep. (CCH) ¶ 96,604 (4th Cir. 1978).

42. See Farrand, "Ancillary Remedies in SEC Enforcement Suits," 89 Harv. L. Rev. 1779, 1806 n. 143 (1976).

One motive for settling with the SEC is the possibility that, through litigation, the Commission may be able to persuade the court to appoint a receiver for the

however, shareholders in some of the settlements are being temporarily deprived of one of the incidents of stock ownership, the right to elect the members of the corporation's board of directors, without any showing that the stockholders' exercise of their voting rights had any connection with management's illegal conduct. Although an argument can

---

corporation, a prospect presumably more bothersome to operating management than court-appointed directors. Indeed, many of the analyses of the remedial propriety of court-appointed directors analogize the remedy to that of receivership. See, e.g., *id.* at 1790; Malley, *supra* note 40, at 50–52; Comment, "Equitable Remedies in SEC Enforcement Actions," 123 U. Pa. L. Rev. 1188, 1206–07 (1975); cf. SEC v. Beisinger Industries Corp., 552 F.2d 15 (1st Cir. 1977) (analogizes appointment of special agent to bring corporation into compliance with SEC reporting requirements to receivership).

Thus, it is ironic that in one of the injunctive actions discussed herein, that brought against Canadian Javelin, Ltd., the SEC initially sought the appointment of a special receiver to assure compliance with SEC regulations, for a Canadian corporation with apparently no assets in the United States. See Complaint at 2, 20, SEC v. Canadian Javelin, Ltd., 73 Civil 5074 (S.D.N.Y. 1974).

That Canadian Javelin's shares were listed on the American Stock Exchange sufficed, under the reasoning of Schoenbaum v. Firstbrook, 405 F.2d 200, 206–09 (2d Cir.), *rev'd en banc on other grounds,* 405 F.2d 215 (2d Cir. 1968), *cert. denied,* 395 U.S. 906 (1969), to give the court subject matter jurisdiction. Similarly, listing the shares on an American exchange, along with issuing press releases directed to American investors, as Canadian Javelin did, is enough of a purposive involvement with American commerce to support personal jurisdiction over the corporation. See Bersch v. Drexel Firestone, Inc., 389 F. Supp. 446, 459 (S.D.N.Y. 1974), *modified,* 519 F.2d 974 (2d Cir. 1975).

Although subject matter and personal jurisdiction are prerequisites to the appointment of a receiver, their presence alone is insufficient. The court must further be satisfied that only through receivership can the corporation's interests be protected. See 1 R. Clark, *Law of Receivers* §§ 59, 59(a) (3d ed. 1959). Moreover, although the appointment of a receiver is an equitable remedy premised on a suit in personam, a receivership is regarded as being in the nature of a proceeding in rem. Consequently, even when courts possess the jurisdictional requisites of appointment, they will generally not appoint a receiver when there are no corporate assets within their territorial jurisdiction. See *id.* at § 77(a). Although the court takes constructive possession of res in appointing a receiver, that constructive possession does not extend beyond the court's territorial jurisdiction. Thus, the receiver cannot go outside the territorial jurisdiction of the appointing court to exercise his official power. See *id.* at § 71(a). The court could, however, give binding instructions to the parties before it concerning the extrajurisdictional property, on penalty of contempt. See *id.*

Consequently, the court could have required Canadian Javelin to consent to the appointment of a receiver to handle its SEC compliance problems, on penalty of contempt or perhaps delisting or suspending trading of its stock. This is, nonetheless, not the simple receivership remedy sought by the SEC.

be made that shareholders are thereby being afforded protection of their interests which is more effective than the shareholder franchise,[43] all shareholders may not be persuaded. They may strongly prefer the shareholder franchise to other mechanisms for choosing the board of directors;[44] they may even prefer incumbent management over a restructured board with a different management style.[45] Further, identify-

---

43. See Comment, *supra* note 42, at 1206.

44. Cf. M. Eisenberg, *supra* note 10, at 65 n.1 (that many shareholders regularly execute and return proxies is some indication that they regard voting as meaningful). Divesting stock of some of its voting rights presumably lessens the possibility that an outsider might purchase shares with the objective of eventually achieving voting control. This possibility has been hypothesized to act as a check on management inefficiency, see Manne, "Some Theoretical Aspects of Share Voting," 64 Colum. L. Rev. 1427, 1431–32 (1964), by stimulating management efforts to prevent the price of the corporation's stock from becoming undervalued, see M. Eisenberg, *supra* note 10, at 66. Restructuring the corporation's board by disenfranchising shareholders denies existing shareholders any choice between the checks on management misconduct implicit in the market for corporate control and the checks provided by court-appointed directors. Prospective shareholders may choose simply not to purchase stock with truncated voting rights.

45. Of course, the quality of a corporation's management is one of the factors traditionally deemed material to investors in their decisions to purchase or retain stock, see *in re* Franchard Corp., 42 S.E.C. 163, 169–71 (1964), and shareholders may prefer to make their own assessments of the proper response to indicia of management quality.

One of the corporations involved in the injunctive actions discussed herein, Mattel, Inc., apparently underwent a substantial change in management style as a consequence of the proceeding. Prior to the SEC's injunctive action, Mattel was operated as a small company in which formal organizational lines were ignored and various functions were attributed to specific persons rather than to management positions. See Report of Special Counsel at 34, SEC v. Mattel, Inc., Civil No. 74-2958 (C.D. Cal. 1974). The company's management was in the habit of disseminating press releases which falsely overstated its business prospects, see Complaint at 2–5, SEC v. Mattel, Inc., Civil No. 74-2958 (C.D. Cal. 1974), and tended to increase the price of its stock. To settle the SEC action, the corporation agreed, among other things, to regularize its handling of the media by creating a board-level committee, with a majority of court-appointed directors, to review and approve or disapprove all information released to the media. See Second Amended Judgment at 4–6, SEC v. Mattel, Inc., Civil No. 74-2958 (C.D. Cal. 1974).

Another company against which the SEC obtained similar relief, Canadian Javelin, Ltd., see note 48 *infra*, also appears to have undergone changes in its management style, at least as to the dissemination of press releases. In sharp contrast to its prior practices of quickly issuing optimistic press releases about developments in its business, see Complaint at 8–12, SEC v. Canadian Javelin, Ltd., 73 Civil 5074 (S.D.N.Y. 1974), after institution of a board-level committee to review all such releases, the company went through seventeen drafts of one release prior to its issue. See Letter from Meyer Eisenberg, Esq. to Michael Drake,

ing the precise constiuency to be served by these directors may be difficult. They, like government-appointed directors and directors with designated areas of concern, may be representing constituencies other than the corporation's shareholders.

The settlements address the problem of improving the board's access to information about the corporation in a variety of ways. One, in a provision reminiscent of a very general New Year's resolution, simply commits the corporation to an undertaking to strengthen its management structure.[46] Some settlements mandate that certain kinds of transactions or activities—consultants' contracts,[47] press releases,[48] internal financial control systems[49]—be brought to the board's attention or submitted for its approval. Although one of the settlements required the appointment of an internal SEC compliance officer and the creation of a compliance committee of the board,[50] none appears to assign separate oversight responsibilities to individual directors, as the Nader proposal advocates,[51] or to specify the duties to be performed by the new directors.

Quite apart from the conceptual problems created by restructuring corporations as a remedy in litigation or through government intrusion into internal corporate structure, these proposals raise a number of questions, two of which will be addressed in the remainder of this article. First, are outside directors on all restructured boards likely to be significantly more successful in deterring or correcting questionable corporate conduct than directors have been in the past? More specifically, how will their mandate be defined and how will the directors themselves interpret it? Second, is it likely that outside directors will attain effective control over corporate information? If such control is achieved, is the accomplishment necessarily related to changes in managment structure?

Esq. (Jan. 9, 1975) (contains handwritten note that "There really were 17 drafts . . . [s]ometime I'll show you the first . . .") (copy obtained pursuant to 5 U.S.C. § 552 (1976) on file with author).

46. See Undertaking at 5, Springer v. Jones, Civil No. 74-1455 (C.D. Cal. 1975) (incorporated by reference into Final Judgment). The corporation also undertook to appoint a president within 18 months, separating that office from that of the chairman of the board and chief executive officer.

47. See *id.* at pp. 5–7.

48. See Judgment at pp. 6–7, SEC V. Canadian Javelin, Ltd., 73 Civil 5074 (S.D.N.Y. 1974); see note 45 *supra* (Mattel, Inc.).

49. See Second Amended Judgment at pp. 4–5, SEC v. Mattel, Inc., Civil No. 74-2958 (C.D. Cal. 1974).

50. See Judgment at pp. 6–7, SEC v. Canadian Javelin, Ltd., 73 Civil 5074 (S.D.N.Y. 1974).

51. See text accompanying note 23 *supra*.

PEERING OVER THE VEIL—THE EMERGENCY LOAN GUARANTEE BOARD AND THE LOCKHEED CORPORATION

Introduction

Central to all proposals to restructure corporations is the institution of an independent entity to scrutinize the performance of operating management,[52] although proposals vary in how they define the tasks to be performed by these outside monitors.[53] The proposals, as described above, appear to recognize, at least implicitly, that the outsiders' mandate to monitor management is difficult to pursue effectively without access to internal information about the corporation and the ability to make meaningful use of that information.[54] Nonetheless, strategies to restructure corporations do not resolve the problem of control of corporate information in any promising or even coherent fashion.[55]

The escapades of the Lockheed Aircraft Corporation over the past few years illustrate the tenuous nature of the connection between management structure and the control of corporate information. Lockheed revealed in 1975 that it, like a number of large American corporations, had made sizable commission payments to foreign agents to facilitate sales of its aircraft and that the ultimate recipients of some of these payments may have been officials of foreign governments.[56] Indeed, it soon became apparent that Lockheed itself had made direct payments to foreign government officials.[57] Apart from the general pother raised by all such revelations of "sensitive" payments,[58] Lockheed's behavior created special consternation in some quarters, for the federal government's credit had been pledged to guarantee bank loans to the company in 1971.[59] As part of the loan guarantee legislation enacted that

52. See text accompanying notes 7–10 *supra*.

53. See text accompanying notes 23, 25–26 *supra*.

54. See text accompanying notes 18–29 *supra*.

55. See *id.*

56. See, e.g., *Multinational Corporations and United States Foreign Policy: Hearings Before the Subcomm. on Multinational Corporations of the Senate Comm. on Foreign Relations,* 94th Cong., 1st Sess. 347 (1975) (testimony of Daniel J. Haughton, Chairman of the Board, Lockheed Corp.) [hereinafter cited as *1975 Senate Hearings on Multinational Corporations*].

57. See *id.*; cf. Kotchian, "Lockheed's 70-Day Mission to Tokyo," Saturday Rev., July 9, 1977, at p. 6 (personal account of making payments to foreign government officials).

58. See, e.g., Guzzardi, "An Unscandalized View of Those "Bribes" Abroad," Fortune, July 1976, at pp. 118–19.

59. See, e.g., *To Provide for the Termination of Any Loan Guarantee Made Under the Emergency Loan Guarantee Act: Hearing on H.R. 15295 Before the Subcomm. on Economic Stabilization of the House Comm. on Banking, Currency and Housing,* 94th

year,[60] a government board—the Emergency Loan Guarantee Board (ELGB)—composed of the Secretary of the Treasury and the Chairmen of the Board of Governors of the Federal Reserve System and the Securities and Exchange Commission, was created to administer the guarantees[61] and, significantly for our purposes, to attend to the quality of Lockheed's management.[62] That Lockheed's sensitive payments came as a complete surprise to the ELGB[63] was itself an unpleasant revelation to many observers.[64] The history of the creation and operation of the ELGB is an instructive one in the context of proposals to restructure corporations.

The "Financial Tonkin Gulf Resolution"[65]— The Tortured History of the Board's Mandate

In 1971, Lockheed was afflicted by a serious cash flow problem caused by a variety of factors. The corporation had recently settled, at substantial losses to itself, four contract performance disputes with the Department of Defense.[66] Further, Lockheed had begun to diversify its production, reentering the commercial airplane market with the goal of becoming less dependent on sales to the Department of Defense.[67] After it failed to obtain the government contract for development of the supersonic transport, Lockheed concentrated its commercial aviation efforts on a wide-bodied subsonic jet, the L-1011.[68] Lockheed reached a crisis point in its relationships with its bankers when Rolls Royce, the British manufacturer of the engine chosen for the L-1011, went into receivership.[69] The British government, which acquired the aeronautical engine operations of Rolls Royce, initially supplied substantial funding for the engine's continued development and eventually refused to

---

Cong., 2d Sess. 1–2 (1976) (remarks of Representative Moorhead) [hereinafter cited as *1976 House Hearings on Termination*].

60. Emergency Loan Guarantee Act of 1971, 15 U.S.C. §§ 1841–52 (Supp. V 1975).

61. *Id.*, 15 U.S.C. §§ 1841–42 (Supp. V 1975).

62. See *id.*; 15 U.S.C. § 1845(b) (Supp. V 1975).

63. See *Lockheed Bribery: Hearings Before the Senate Comm. on Banking, Housing and Urban Affairs*, 94th Cong., 1st Sess. 6–7 (1975) (testimony of William E. Simon, ELGB Chairman) [hereinafter cited as *1975 Senate Hearings on Lockheed Bribery*].

64. See, e.g., *1976 House Hearings on Termination, supra* note 59, at 10 (testimony of Representative Harrington).

65. 117 Cong. Rec. 26794 (1971) (remarks of Senator Taft) (referring to Pub. L. No. 88-408, 78 Stat. 384 (1964)).

66. See Emergency Loan Guarantee Board, *First Annual Report* 19-30 (1972) [hereinafter cited as *1972 ELGB Annual Report*].

67. *Id.*

68. *Id.*

69. *Id.*

proceed further with the L-1011 engine unless it received assurances of Lockheed's continued existence.[70] Lockheed's own financial condition worsened throughout 1971; by April 1971 the corporation was on the verge of bankruptcy, with $400 million in bank credit outstanding, and $350 million (including $100 million in prepayments from airline customers for the L-1011) in new credit needed to meet its cash requirements.[71]

The Nixon administration responded to its perception of the widespread economic dislocations that would follow a Lockheed bankruptcy[72] by introducing legislation to authorize federal loan guarantees of up to $250 million for Lockheed.[73] Although the administration's bill did not contain any provision going specifically to the quality of Lockheed's management, the bill authorized the Secretary of the Treasury to make guarantees "on such terms and conditions as he may determine,"[74] suggesting the possibility of conditioning the grant of the guarantee on reviewing and upgrading the quality of Lockheed's management.

The loan guarantee legislation passed by Congress in August 1971, in contrast to the administration bill, included a specific mandate to the ELGB to assess the quality of the corporation's management and the relationship between that management quality and the corporation's inability to obtain credit. Under section 6(b) of the Act, if the ELGB[75]

> determines that the inability of an enterprise to obtain credit without a guarantee under this chapter is the result of a failure on the part of management to exercise reasonable business prudence in the conduct of the affairs of the enterprise, the Board shall require before guaranteeing any loan to the enterprise that the enterprise make such management changes as the Board deems necessary to give the enterprise a sound managerial basis.

There appears to have been considerable confusion at the time the legislation was proposed about the scope and nature of the mandate thereby imposed on the ELGB—about its proper function prior to making the guarantee as well as its role once the guarantee was made—a confusion which persisted throughout congressional consideration of the measure.

---

70. *Id.*

71. *Id.*

72. See *Emergency Loan Guarantee Legislation: Hearings Before the Senate Comm. on Banking, Housing and Urban Affairs*, 92d Cong., 1st Sess. 5–9 (1971) (testimony of John B. Connally, Secretary of the Treasury) [hereinafter cited as *1971 Senate ELGA Hearings*].

73. S. 1891, 92d Cong., 1st Sess. (1971).

74. *Id.* § 3(a).

75. 15 U.S.C. § 1845(b) (Supp. V 1975).

That the provision appeared in the loan guarantee legislation is attributable to the attention given during the congressional deliberations to the quality of Lockheed's management.[76] Some supporters of the legislation were unequivocally complimentary to management's performance.[77] Other supporters of the legislation emphatically attributed part of the responsibility for Lockheed's plight to the procurement practices and dispute settlement techniques of the Department of Defense,[78] leaving one to infer that the remaining portion of responsibility might be allocated to Lockheed's internal management. Those of Lockheed's banker's[79] suppliers,[80] and customers[81] who testified before

---

76. Present section 6(b) became part of S. 2308 as a result of an amendment proposed by Senator Cranston. See 117 Cong. Rec. 26423 (1971) (remarks of Senator Cranston).

77. See, e.g., 1971 Senate ELGA Hearings, *supra* note 72, at 283 (testimony of Daniel J. Haughton, Chairman of the Board, Lockheed Aircraft Corp.)

78. See, e.g., *id.* at 162 (testimony of David Packard, Deputy Secretary of Defense). In Secretary Packard's later appearance before the House Banking and Currency Committee, his prepared statement expressly attributed fault for Lockheed's plight to the corporation's management and to the Department of Defense, claiming that the Department's procurement process encouraged contractors to take on projects they could not effectively control under the assumption that means of covering large cost overruns would be found. Secretary Packard refused to read this portion of his prepared statement—other aspects of it conflicted with the position taken by other administration witnesses—but Representative Patman read it into the record. See *To Authorize Emergency Loan Guarantees to Major Business Enterprises: Hearings on H.R. 8432 Before the House Comm. on Banking and Currency*, 92d Cong., 1st Sess. 292 (1971) (testimony of David Packard, Deputy Secretary of Defense) [hereinafter cited as *1971 House ELGA Hearings*].

79. See, e.g., *1971 Senate ELGA Hearings, supra* note 72, at p. 377 (testimony of William H. Moore, Chairman of the Board, Bankers Trust Co.); cf. *id.* at 404 (testimony of Chauncey J. Medberry III, Chairman of the Board, Bank of America) (major changes in management at that time would be academic because they would cause Lockheed's bankers and customers to reconsider their commitment to the L-1011 and Lockheed would run out of cash flow before the new management began to function). Mr. Medberry observed that at least one critic of the loan guarantee proposals, Professor Galbraith, see note 83 *infra,* did not understand the bankers' problems "in a guts way." *Id.* at 201.

Representatives of all 24 of Lockheed's creditor banks were present at the 1971 House Hearings and from time to time were asked questions as a group, to which they always responded with unanimity. All responded (by silence) in the negative when asked whether any of them would extend the $250 million in additional credit to Lockheed without the loan guarantee. See *1971 House ELGA Hearings, supra* note 78, at 191 (remarks of Representative Rousselot).

The banks' position in opposing changes in management appears to have been internally inconsistent. See *1971 Senate ELGA Hearings* at 713 (testimony of Vern Countryman, Professor, Harvard Law School):

> [W]hile everybody professes to prefer going along with the present Lock-

congressional committees appraised its management favorably, as did representatives of the Nixon administration, although some administration witnesses reserved judgment on management's quality.[82]

The rhetoric of opponents of the loan guarantee legislation typically asserted that Lockheed had been poorly managed,[83] ofttimes with the same degree of generality and hyperbole surrounding the claims that Lockheed's management had behaved admirably.[84] Most of the specific criticism of management performance centered on Lockheed's experience with four contracts awarded it by the Department of Defense, especially with its development and production of the C-5A troop and supply transport.[85] That Lockheed's costs in developing the C-5A exceeded its own internal cost forecasts and reports as well as cost estimates and reports submitted to the Department of Defense was singled out by critics of the loan guarantee program as an indication that management lacked sufficient control over operations.[86] Indeed, the Department of Defense recognized problems in the plant working on the C-5A[87] and expressed its concern with the management of some of Lockheed's subsidiaries.[88]

---

heed management rather than taking their chances on something else, somebody, and I am still mystified as to who, wants a $250 million Government guarantee before they will go along with the present management.

80. See *1971 Senate ELGA Hearings, supra* note 72, at 679 (testimony of Gerald J. Lynch, President and Chairman of the Board, Menasco Corp.) (manufacturer of L-1011 landing gear).

81. See, e.g., *id.* at 338 (testimony of Charles C. Tillinghast, Jr., Chairman of the Board, Trans World Airlines).

82. See *1971 House ELGA Hearings, supra* note 78, at 379 (testimony of John B. Connally, Secretary of the Treasury).

83. See, e.g., *1971 Senate ELGA Hearings, supra* note 72, at 853–54 (testimony of John K. Galbraith, Professor of Economics, Harvard University) ("[t]he corporation has established a reputation of spectacular mismanagement as a defense contractor."); 117 Cong. Rec. 26983 (1971) (remarks of Senator Weicker) ("the most incredible record of corporate mismanagement that we have witnessed within our free enterprise system within our lifetimes.").

84. See, e.g., *1971 Senate ELGA Hearings, supra* note 72, at 452 (testimony of Fred J. Borch, Chairman of the Board, General Electric Co.) (statement that Lockheed's management did not perform incompetently but merely took high risks).

85. See, e.g., *1971 Senate ELGA Hearings, supra* note 72, at 171 (testimony of David Packard, Deputy Secretary of Defense).

86. See *1971 Senate ELGA Hearings, supra* note 72, at 466–70 (statement of A. E. Fitzgerald).

87. See *1971 House ELGA Hearings, supra* note 78, at 309 (testimony of David Packard, Deputy Secretary of Defense).

88. See *1971 Senate ELGA Hearings, supra* note 72, at 167 (testimony of David Packard, Deputy Secretary of Defense).

Some of the specific doubts cast on the quality of Lockheed's management concerned the corporation's apparent inability to forecast its costs with sufficient accuracy when bidding on fixed-price government contracts.[89] Similarly, doubts about the validity of Lockheed's financial projections for its L-1011 project were viewed as reflecting on the adequacy of the corporation's internal planning and forecasting abilities.[90] Concern was also expressed over the disparity between Lockheed's internal projections of future sales of the L-1011 and the much lower projections available from other sources.[91] Finally, some critics of the loan guarantee pointed to Lockheed's choice for the L-1011 of an untested foreign-produced engine using novel technology[92] over an American-made engine which became certified by the Civil Aeronautics Board for actual use much more rapidly than did the engine chosen by Lockheed.[93]

Disenchantment with Lockheed's management was also reflected in some senators' suggestions of the appropriate remedial response for Congress to make to Lockheed's plight. One argument advanced in favor of doing nothing was that Lockheed would thereby plummet into a chapter X bankruptcy reorganization proceeding[94] in which its present management would be investigated by independent trustees[95] and then, if warranted, replaced by suitable new management personnel.[96] It was also suggested that, short of precipitating Lockheed's bankrupt-

---

89. See note 85 *supra*.

90. See 117 Cong. Rec. 24860–62 (1971) (remarks of Representative Moorhead).

91. See *id*.

92. See 117 Cong. Rec. 26426 (1971) (remarks of Senator Weicker) (characterization of the Rolls Royce engine chosen by Lockheed as a paper engine and of Lockheed's selection of it as "the substitute of a calculated gamble for sound business judgment").

93. See *1971 Senate ELGA Hearings, supra* note 72, at 447 (testimony of Fred J. Borch, Chairman of the Board, General Electric Co.).

94. 11 U.S.C. §§ 501–676 (1970).

95. See 117 Cong. Rec. 26815 (1971) (remarks of Senator Hart). The remarks of some of the supporters of loan guarantee legislation indicate that they regarded the prospect of bankruptcy as one having a punitive significance for Lockheed's management. See, e.g., 117 Cong. Rec. 26423 (remarks of Senator Cranston) (supports S. 2308 out of desire to help "innocent" Lockheed employees and subcontractors; but in general the free enterprise system "penalizes" inefficiency with financial failure).

96. See *1971 Senate ELGA Hearings, supra* note 72, at 240 (remarks of Senator Cranston). The professed support of Lockheed's bankers for its incumbent management, see note 79 *supra*, caused one Senator to query whether management would be ousted even in a Chapter X reorganization proceeding, because "the people who would be concerned" would elect the incumbents. See 117 Cong. Rec. 28014 (1971) (remarks of Senator Gambrell).

cy, Congress obtain for the corporation the therapeutic equivalent of chapter X by conditioning its grant of loan guarantee authorization on the ouster and replacement of Lockheed's incumbent management.[97]

None of these arguments prevailed; Congress passed the Emergency Loan Guarantee Act[98] with the view that it was thereby keeping Lockheed from certain bankruptcy, in an atmosphere characterized by high-pressure politics and intense lobbying efforts.[99] The legislation passed contained the present section 6(b) of the Act; to the extent that Congress' deliberations considered the meaning of the section, they demonstrate only confusion about its significance, along with unnoticed conflicts in its interpretation.

On its face, the section is susceptible of severable equally plausible interpretations of the mandate thereby conferred on the ELGB. Before guaranteeing any loans, it could be, on the one hand, that the ELGB is mandated to conduct an independent fact-finding review of management's performance in which it may not indulge any presumptions about the quality of that performance.[100] On the other hand, the ELGB's role prior to guaranteeing a loan may be limited to assessing the facts

---

97. See *1971 Senate ELGA Hearings, supra* note 72, at 67–68 (remarks of Senator Cranston). Senator Taft introduced a bill, S. 1892, which would have made federally guaranteed loans available only to corporations which had actually gone into involuntary bankruptcy and were in a bankruptcy reorganization. See 117 Cong. Rec. 15495–96 (text of S. 1892).

98. By its terms, the Act does not limit the availability of federal loan guarantee assistance only to Lockheed, although the maximum amount available for guarantees under the Act, $250 million, see 15 U.S.C. § 1847 (Supp. V 1975), was viewed as the amount necessary to meet the needs of Lockheed, see S. Rep. No. 92-270, 92d Cong., 1st Sess. 7 (1971). The bill reported out by the Senate Banking, Housing and Urban Affairs Committee, S. 2308, would have authorized a total of $2 billion in guarantees, with a limit of $250 million on loans to any one enterprise, to establish general federal standby authority to assist major business enterprises in dire financial condition. See *id.* at 5, 7. Some Senators objected that the implications of providing a general guarantee authority had not been sufficiently considered, since the hearings had been concerned specifically with Lockheed, see 117 Cong. Rec. 26408–11 (1971) (remarks of Senators Proxmire and Aiken), while others favored a general program of federal guarantees to distressed large businesses, see 117 Cong. Rec. 26971 (1971) (remarks of Senator Javits). The final version of the legislation, however, does not contain the additional amount authorized in the Senate committee bill for a wider guarantee program. *See* 15 U.S.C. § 1841–52 (Supp. V 1975).

99. See 117 Cong. Rec. 26411, 27471–75 (1971) (remarks of Senator Proxmire).

100. Some of the language in the Senate Committee Report explaining the bill reported out supports this interpretation: "The Committee contemplates that in assessing the need for assistance under this guarantee program, the Board will discover from the relevant records and persons both within and without the enterprise what management personnel or policy changes, if any, need to be made." S. Rep. No. 92-270, 92d Cong., 1st Sess. 11 (1971).

about management's performance developed by other sources, perhaps looking only for indications that management did not behave reasonably. The legislative history is not dispositive on this point. One senator expressed justifiable confusion about the nature of the review the Board would undertake.[101] The Secretary of the Treasury assured Congress that the Board's review would be a "careful" one of "the whole question of management's performance,"[102] but the starting point and initial assumptions of that review were never clarified. Likewise, views differed on the aggressiveness with which the ELGB was expected to carry out its review tasks: one senator who supported the legislation argued that the Board clearly had the capacity to make substantial changes in Lockheed's management, even to the extent of insisting that the corporation go into bankruptcy reorganization proceedings,[103] while another, an opponent of the legislation, emphasized that any such changes, because they were discretionary with the Board, were not likely to be made.[104] Statements made to Congress by two of the prospective members of the ELGB referred only to the Board's mandate to "look at"[105] and "review"[106] management's performance; they did not indicate what kind of review was contemplated, how it would be conducted, or what results might follow a negative assessment of management.

The Act is equally unclear as to any mandate the ELGB would have to continue reviewing management's performance once it guaranteed a loan. The language of section 6(b) may be construed such that the mandate expires once a loan is guaranteed, since section 6(b) refers to the review process as occurring only "before" a loan is guaranteed. This interpretation is supported by the testimony of one putative member of the ELGB that the legislation would not involve the Board in any "surveillance" of management.[107] Similarly, there is nothing in the Act to pre-

---

101. See 117 Cong. Rec. 26995 (1971) (remarks of Senator Mondale) ("[h]ow does the board determine whether the problem is management, changing demand for the product, or whatever?").

102. See 117 Cong. Rec. 28746 (1971) (letter from John Connally, Secretary of the Treasury, to Senator Javits) (July 30, 1971).

103. See 117 Cong. Rec. 27150 (1971) (remarks of Senator Javits).

104. See 117 Cong. Rec. 27141–42 (1971) (remarks of Senator Proxmire).

105. See *1971 House ELGA Hearings, supra* note 78, at 432 (testimony of Arthur F. Burns, Chairman, Board of Governors, Federal Reserve System).

106. See text accompanying note 102 *supra*.

107. See *1971 House ELGA Hearings, supra* note 78, at 432 (testimony of Arthur F. Burns, Chairman, Board of Governors, Federal Reserve System). One Representative stated that the Board ought "to take into account" Lockheed's important contributions to the nation's defense establishment. *Id.* at 417 (remarks of Reprepresentative Blackburn). It was also his view that any corporation, such as Lockheed, which could produce an airplane, like the L-1011, which was competitive

vent the Board from making long-term blanket guarantees rather than serial guarantees of relatively short durations, which even under a narrow interpretation of the section 6(b) mandate would require the Board to review management's performance more than once; namely, prior to making each guarantee commitment.[108]

Nonetheless, it is equally plausible that the statute contemplates a continuing review of management performance by the ELGB. Such an interpretation is clearly not expressly excluded by the Act, and the federal government's interest in the borrower's ability to make timely repayments of its loan—the basic rationale for the creation of any review capacity in the ELGB—is surely no less once a guarantee has been made than it is before. Finally, one senator, arguing in support of the legislation, asserted that, if the Board members were "worthy of their salt," they would "oversee the requirement that . . . there is not inefficient management."[109]

The scanty and inconsistent nature of the legislative history of section 6(b) leads to the conclusion that Congress' consideration of the management review function of the ELGB was neither extensive nor detailed enough to result in a clear definition of the Board's mandate. Thus, it is far from surprising that the Board apparently chose to define its responsibilities narrowly and that it failed to perceive Lockheed's practices of paying dubious foreign sales commissions.

The ELGB in Operation

Once the Emergency Loan Guarantee Act became effective, the ELGB met to consider the loan guarantee application of the Lockheed Corporation.[110] The Board reviewed documentation of the gravity of Lockheed's financial problems; it also considered, citing its statutory mandate, "whether [these problems] were the result of imprudent management," determined that they were not and that Lockheed would not be required to make any management changes as a condition of its loan guarantee.[111]

---

in price and in some of its operating characteristics was "obviously . . . not practicing bad management." *Id.*

108. An amendment, No. 234, to S. 1891 to prohibit blanket guarantees and require the Board to proceed on a 90-day serial guarantee system was introduced by Senator Stevenson. See 117 Cong. Rec. 22292–93 (1971) (remarks of Senator Stevenson). The amendment, never adopted, would also have required that the ELGB be furnished financial statements and all other pertinent documents which the borrower had provided to its banks before a guarantee could be made by the Board.

109. See 117 Cong. Rec. 27150 (1971) (remarks of Senator Javits).

110. See 1972 ELGB Annual Report, *supra* note 66, at 4.

111. See *id.* at 31. In addition, the statute provided that the Board could guarantee loans only if it found that

Before the ELGB made its decision, the chairman of Lockheed's board of directors announced that changes in Lockheed's management were planned.[112] The corporation's board was also realigned so that a majority of its membership was not otherwise affiliated with Lockheed.[113]

However, the Board's review of management, as described in its annual report, was something much less than a searching inquiry into management's performance. Far from requiring Lockheed's management to justify the results or techniques of its stewardship over the company's fate, the Board may have presumed management's competence and looked only cursorily for evidence to rebut that presumption.[114] The Board apparently gave heavy weight to the congressional committee testimony of Lockheed's bankers, suppliers and customers, which in the Board's view "indicated that the persons who had longstanding business relationships with the company would have been troubled by sudden changes in key management."[115] There is no indication that the Board pursued these statements[116] further with the wit-

---

(A) the loan is needed to enable the borrower to continue to furnish goods or services and the failure to meet this need would seriously affect the economy of or employment in the Nations or any region thereof,

(B) credit is not otherwise available to the borrower under reasonable terms or conditions, and

(C) the prospective earnings power of the borrower, together with the character and value of the security pledged, furnish reasonable assurance that it will be able to repay the loan within the time fixed, and afford reasonable protection to the United States. . . .

15 U.S.C. § 1843(a)(1) (Supp. V 1975). The certification of the guaranteed lender that it would not make the loan but for the guarantee was also required. 15 U.S.C. § 1843(a)(2) (Supp. V 1975).

Furthermore, the Board was prohibited from guaranteeing a loan unless it received an audited financial statement for the borrower and unless the borrower permitted the Board access to any of its records bearing on its ability to make timely repayment of the guaranteed loan, the interest of the United States in its property, and assurances of reasonable protection for the United States. 15 U.S.C. §§ 1845(c), 1846(a) (Supp. V 1975).

112. See *1972 ELGB Annual Report, supra* note 66, at 31–32.

113. See *id.*

114. The Board describes its conclusion as one that "on the basis of the record before it . . . it could not find the need for a guarantee was a result of the failure on the part of management to exercise reasonable business prudence . . . ." *Id.*, at 31. This, of course, suggests that such a failure may have occurred, but that the Board was unable to isolate it as the sole cause of the company's financial predicament, perhaps as a result of the kind of record on which it made its decision.

115. See *id.*

116. Although the testimony of all four witnesses mentioned in the Board's report, see *id.* at 31 n.21, is surely complimentary to Lockheed's management, it differs sharply in the witnesses' reaction to the suggestion of changes in Lockheed's

nesses, or made any other attempt to determine the causes, extent, or consequences of their opposition to management changes.

Thereafter, the Board apparently made no systematic effort to scrutinize the overall performance of Lockheed's management. It received financial data about Lockheed's operations[117] and met from time to time with Lockheed's bankers, outside auditors, and management to discuss the corporation's current financial results.[118] In particular, the ELGB became concerned about disparities between actual and projected costs on the L-1011 program, prompting it to meet many times with Lockheed's management to review the situation.[119] Although the ELGB consented to a request by the fiscal agent for the preparation of a report by Arthur Young & Company, Lockheed's outside auditors, describing its procedures for auditing Lockheed and describing and evaluating Lockheed's internal accounting and forecasting procedures,[120] it does not appear that the Board required any changes in Lockheed's internal systems based on the report, even as to management problems directly affecting the L-1011 program. Indeed, one critic of the Board's operations characterized it as having demonstrated "little interest in expediting such internal reforms."[121]

---

management. Three of the witnesses addressed this specific point. One witness, William H. Moore, Chairman of the Board, Bankers Trust Co., stated that "the continuity of this management at this time is vital to the future success of the company." *1971 Senate ELGA Hearings, supra* note 72, at 377. Another witness, Floyd D. Hall, Chairman of the Board and Chief Executive Officer, Eastern Airlines, responded that the question was a hypothetical one, unanswerable unless one knows "what moves are made, and who is being replaced by whom." *Id.* at 363. The third witness, Charles C. Tillinghast, Jr., Chairman, Trans World Airlines, states that he "hope[d] there are no management changes," because any shifts would result in delay on the L-1011 program. *Id.*

117. See note 128 *infra.*

118. See Emergency Loan Guarantee Board, *Second Annual Report* 7–9 (1973) [hereinafter cited as *1973 ELGB Annual Report*]; Emergency Loan Guarantee Board, *Third Annual Report* 7–9 (1974) [hereinafter cited as *1974 ELGB Annual Report*].

119. In 1972 and 1973, Lockheed's management met about 40 times with representatives of the ELGB, the General Accounting Office, surety companies, and its banks to discuss the problems related to its L-1011 program. See "Lockheed Aircraft Corporation: The Crisis Years 1969–1975," in Exhibits to the Report of the Special Review Committee of the Board of Directors, Lockheed Aircraft Corporation 41 (1977) (material prepared by Lockheed management at the Committee's request). Between meetings with ELGB, Lockheed submitted weekly data of its progress on the L-1011 and other programs to the fiscal agent, who notified the Board of any significant developments. See *1973 ELGB Annual Report, supra* note 118, at 9.

120. See *1973 ELGB Annual Report, supra* note 118, at 9.

121. See *1976 House Hearing on Termination, supra* note 59, at 10 (testimony of Representative Harrington).

Consequently, it is not surprising that the ELGB was apparently unaware prior to June 1975 of Lockheed's payments to foreign officials and political organizations.[122] On August 1, 1975, the company publicly announced that an estimated 15 percent of its $147 million in payments to foreign sales consultants and others was known or strongly suspected to have gone ultimately to government officials and political organizations in several foreign countries.[123] That the ELGB was remote from the decision-making structure at Lockheed on the foreign payments question is best demonstrated by the fact that the Board and its review and monitoring functions are nowhere mentioned in the Lockheed directors' report intensively scrutinizing the payments problem, although the report discusses other potential controls on management's actions.[124] Thus, whether one takes at face value the ELGB's claim that it was "intensive[ly] monitoring" Lockheed's activities.[125] or chooses instead to conclude that the Board interpreted its statutory mandates very narrowly,[126] the ELGB's review of Lockheed's management does not appear to have been an effective and fully informed one.[127]

In retrospect, some of the Board's ineffectiveness seems attributable to its apparent passivity with respect to internal Lockheed information. The Board rarely if ever initiated inquiries to which Lockheed would respond and never initially scrutinized internal Lockheed data itself.[128] Even in

---

122. See *Lockheed Bribery: Hearings Before the Senate Comm. on Banking, Housing and Urban Affairs,* 94th Cong., 1st Sess. 22 (1975) (testimony of William E. Simon, ELGB Chairman) [hereinafter cited as *1975 Senate Hearings on Lockheed Bribery*]. The ELGB became aware of Lockheed's sensitive payments after Arthur Young & Co., Lockheed's outside auditor, refused to certify the company's financial statements unless the company acknowledged that it had paid bribes to foreign officials and defined the extent of those payments. See *id.* at 6.

123. See Emergency Loan Guarantee Board, *Fourth Annual Report* 8 (1975) [hereinafter cited as *1975 ELGB Annual Report*].

124. See Special Review Committee of the Board of Directors, Lockheed Aircraft Corporation, Report (1977) [hereinafter cited as Lockheed Directors' Report].

125. See *1975 ELGB Annual Report, supra* note 118, at 9.

126. See *1976 House Hearings on Termination, supra* note 59, at 10 (remarks of Rep. Harrington).

127. The current chairman of Lockheed's board of directors, Robert W. Haack, has asserted that the company endeavors to keep the ELGB "as informed as we can." See *Oversight on the Lockheed Loan Guarantee: Hearings Before the Senate Comm. on Banking, Housing and Urban Affairs,* 94th Cong., 2d Sess. 118 (1976) [hereinafter cited as *1976 Senate Oversight Hearings*].

128. Lockheed regularly furnished the ELGB with unaudited and audited annual, monthly and quarterly financial statements, copies of reports to stockholders and the SEC, and "other data pertinent to continuous surveillance of its operations." See *1972 ELGB Annual Report, supra* note 66, at 60. Chairman Haack described the Board's operation as follows: "They have held our feet to the fire, there is no question about that. We met with them periodically, we review the

its "intensive monitoring" stages the Board was confined to a role of reviewing information presented by Lockheed. Perhaps the Board's passivity is understandable in light of its meager staff.[129] On the other hand. Lockheed had been persistently reticent about releasing internal information, both during congressional consideration of the loan guarantee legislation[130] and after the Board began its monitoring functions,[131] and its disclosure practices had earlier been criticized in a publicly available SEC staff report.[132]

---

finances, we show them our forecast, we endeavor to keep them as informed as we can." *1976 Senate Oversight Hearings, supra* note 127, at 118. This suggests that most of the actual initiative and direction for such "informing" came from Lockheed rather than the ELGB.

129. Initially, the Board's staff consisted of an Executive Director who was also General Counsel to the Treasury Department and a Secretary who was a Special Assistant to the Treasury's General Counsel. The Board used personnel on a when-needed basis from the Treasury Department, the Board of Governors of the Federal Reserve System and the Securities and Exchange Commission. In March 1972 the Board hired a financial analyst to provide continuing staff assistance. See *1972 ELGB Annual Report, supra* note 66, at 8–9. To advise it on the technical aspects of Lockheed's operations, the Board hired in April 1973 a technical analyst who went from full time to part time status in July 1974. See *1974 ELGB Annual Report, supra* note 118, at 3 n.3.

130. See, e.g., 117 Cong. Rec. 15450 (1971) (speech of Senator Proxmire) (Lockheed refused to furnish Congress with a cash flow statement); 117 Cong. Rec. 28367 (1971) (remarks of Representative Mitchell) (staff of the Banking and Currency Committee had an "almost impossible" time obtaining breakdowns of cash flow and profits by divisions); *1971 Senate ELGA Hearings, supra* note 72, at 656 (remarks of Senator Stevenson) (committee unable to get a copy of the recent Lockheed–Rolls Royce contract); *id.* at 768 (testimony of Ralph Nader) (General Accounting Office having difficulty in getting information about Lockheed).

131. Section 7(b) of the Act required the General Accounting Office (GAO), an investigative arm of Congress, to make a "detailed audit of all accounts, books, records and transactions of any borrower" applying under the Act, and to report the results to Congress and the ELGB, 15 U.S.C. § 1846(b) (Supp. V 1975). The GAO made a number of such reports. In August 1975, the GAO, complying with a request from Senator Proxmire, attempted to determine the amounts of payments made by Lockheed to foreign officials to consummate foreign sales. Lockheed refused to give the GAO access to any information other than records concerning the amount of payments that may have been charged to overhead allocable to U.S. Government contracts. See *1976 Senate Oversight Hearings, supra* note 127, at 41 (statement of Elmer B. Staats, Comptroller General). Although section 13 of Lockheed's Loan Guarantee Agreement of 1971 authorized the GAO, along with the ELGB and its staff, to inspect the corporation's records, Mr. Staats concluded that, since the GAO lacked subpoena power, there was no "ready and direct method" for it to obtain records despite the statutory and contractual assurances of access. *Id.* at 45. Those granted access by the 1971 Loan Guarantee Agreement could use it in their sole discretion, in making determinations related to the borrower's ability to repay its guaranteed loans, the interest of the United States in the borrower's property, assurances that reasonable protection was afforded to the government, and compliance with the Act. The GAO's inquiry, concerning Lockheed's past sales practices and thus to some extent its future sales prospects, seems clearly encompassed by these purposes, which it could determine in its sole discretion. But cf. *Abuses of Corporate Power: Hearings Before the Subcomm. on Priorities and Economy in Government of the Joint Economic Comm.*, 94th Cong., 1st & 2d Sess. 57 (1976) (testimony of Richard W. Gutmann, Director, Procurement and Systems Acquisition Division, GAO) (questions whether GAO needs the requested information to assess Lockheed's ability to repay its loans).

At any rate, the ELGB itself had an earlier skirmish with the GAO. In September 1971 representatives of the GAO met with representatives of the Board to arrange the GAO's audit of Lockheed. See *Defense Production Act Amendments—1972: Hearings on S. 669 and S. 1901 Before the Subcomm. on Production and Stabilization of the Senate Comm. on Banking, Housing and Urban Affairs,* 92nd Cong., 2d Sess. 34 (1972) (letter from Elmer B. Staats, Comptroller General to John B. Connally, ELGB Chairman) (Sept. 21, 1971) [hereinafter cited as *1972 Senate Hearings on Defense Production*]. At the same meeting, when the question of GAO review of ELGB decisions was raised, the Board's representatives questioned the GAO's authority to review Board decisions. The Board subsequently met, formally took the position that the GAO lacked authority to review its decisions, and refused to grant the GAO's request for records and documents incident to such decisions. See *id.* at 34–35 (letter from John B. Connally to Elmer B. Staats) (Dec. 9, 1971). The Board eventually granted access to the GAO, asserting that it was complying only to accede to the wishes of congressional committees. See *1972 ELGB Annual Report, supra* note 66, at 11.

As to the dispute over the GAO's authority, its position clearly appears to have been stronger than that of the ELGB. The GAO sought specifically to examine the data and analysis supporting the basic findings that the Board was required by statute to make prior to guaranteeing a loan, see note 111 *supra,* as well as whether the Board had received the required audited financial statement from the borrower. See *1972 Senate Hearings on Defense Production, supra* at 52 (GAO memorandum). In addition, the GAO was interested in how the Board made its determination that Lockheed's inability to obtain other credit was not the result of management failures. See *id.* The Board's initial argument, that Congress demonstrated its intent in the Emergency Loan Guarantee Act that the ELGB's decisions not be audited by the GAO, by failing to provide for such an audit, see *id.* at 34–35 (letter from John B. Connally to Elmer B. Staats) (Dec. 9, 1971), is unpersuasive if the GAO's basic statutory grants of authority are broad enough to extend access to the ELGB's records. See *id.* at 35 (letter from Elmer B. Staats to John B. Connally) (Feb. 10, 1972). The Board subsequently expanded its argument to one that the GAO lacked a statutory right of access to the internal records of executive agencies related to their decisionmaking processes. See Comptroller General of the United States, *Report to the Congress on Implementation of Emergency Loan Guarantee Act* 28 app. II (1972) [hereinafter cited as *GAO Loan Guarantee Report*]. This argument is undercut by the breadth of the GAO's statutory grants of audit authority. See, e.g., 31 U.S.C. § 53(a) (1970), authorizing the GAO to investigate "all matters relating to the receipt, disbursement, and application of public funds;" and 31 U.S.C. § 1154(a) (1970), authorizing the GAO to "review and analyze the results of Government programs and activities." Finally, although the Board initially stated a claim of

Although Lockheed's prior history might have served to put the ELGB on notice of the corporation's secretiveness, Lockheed came extremely close to making affirmative misrepresentations to both Congress and the Board. About one month before the ELGB learned of Lockheed's sensitive payments overseas, the Board's staff asked Lockheed's management whether it had used overseas subsidiaries as a mechanism for making illegal domestic political contributions, as other corporations were then alleged to have done. Lockheed responded that no such activity had occurred; the Chairman of the ELGB later concluded that "[i]n retrospect it would have been advantageous to inquire as to whether Lockheed had made any payments to foreign officals."[133] Further, in some instances, Lockheed appears to have structured foreign payments transactions while anticipating and planning around the reaction of its outside auditors.[134] Since these evasions were partially successful as to the much more aggressive inquiries of Lockheed's outside auditors,[135] one might

---

executive privilege as to the records of its decisionmaking process, see *GAO Loan Guarantee Report, supra* at 24, it did not rely on that claim and probably invalidated it in a letter from its Chairman to the Comptroller General stating that "[i]f Congress intends for the General Accounting Office to review the decisions of the Emergency Loan Guarantee Board, we believe amendatory legislation should be enacted making it clear that the GAO has this authority," see *1972 Senate Hearings on Defense Production, supra* at 34 (letter from John B. Connally to Elmer B. Staats) (Dec. 9, 1971). If Congress is able to pass appropriate amendatory legislation, that appears to rule out a constitutionally based claim of executive privilege.

132. See 1 Securities and Exchange Commission, *Staff Report of Investigation In Re Lockheed Aircraft Corporation* 4, 43, 57 (1970). The focus of the investigation was the quality of Lockheed's disclosure of its cost overrun problems on the C-5A program. The investigators discovered that Lockheed's outside auditor, Arthur Young & Co., had developed a cynicism about Lockheed's internal cost estimates and had concluded that no one at Lockheed had an "overall grasp" of the C-5A program. See *id.* at 63.

133. See *1975 Senate Hearings on Lockheed Bribery, supra* note 122, at 10 (testimony of William E. Simon, ELGB Chairman). Secretary Simon characterized Lockheed's behavior as not having been "forthright" with Congress and ELGB. *Id.* at 5.

134. See *1975 Senate Hearings on Multinational Corporations, supra* note 56, at 1034–35.

135. Arthur Young & Co., Lockheed's outside auditors since 1933, questioned two series of foreign currency payments in the late 1950's and 1960's and were told that such payments were necessary marketing expenses. In the early 1970's, Arthur Young learned of questionable bank transfers in Japan and of commissions paid to a third party by a Lockheed consultant, and discussed these with Lockheed officers.

During its 1972 audit, Arthur Young discovered substantial cash payments in Japan and insisted, over the objection of Lockheed's then chairman and then president, on notifying the corporation's audit committee. That committee, composed of three outsider board members, was told that the payments might well be used for political campaigns in the foreign country. It decided that the

doubt the ELGB's prospects for success even had it assumed a more assertive inquisitorial stance.

Once the Board learned of Lockheed's sensitive payments, it urged the corporation to take strong internal measures to assure that none would be made in the future, and it eventually procured an amendment to its 1971 Loan Guarantee Agreement with Lockheed making any additional such payment an event of default under the guarantee agreement.[136] In addition, Lockheed was required periodically to certify to the ELGB that no questionable payments were being made.[137] The Board also determined, soon after learning of the payments, that it "should obtain additional information about [them] so as itself to assess the potential impact of public disclosure of identifying details.[138] The Board's staff, at its request, determined that Lockheed could "survive" the consequences of disclosing its past practices to repay its guaranteed debt.[139]

Although the Board's report does not reveal whether it was successful in obtaining the additional information it sought, it is apparent from other sources that Lockheed never provided the Board with two kinds of pertinent data: specifically, names of the recipients of the payments and of the countries in which they were paid.[140] It is not clear from any source whether the ELGB ever requested that information. Moreover, in early 1976, the Board took the position that it did not need the kind of detail this information would supply "for it to perform its function of evaluating Lockheed's ability to repay its guaranteed borrowings."[141] If, however, Lockheed's financial strength and consequent ability to repay its guaranteed loans might be jeopardized by public disclosure of the payments' recipients—as Lockheed argued it would be[142]—then the Board

---

payments were "proper" sales costs and did not need to be reported to the entire board. See Lockheed Director's Report, *supra* note 124, at 18–20.

This version of Arthur Young's knowledge of Lockheed's questionable foreign payments may conflict with its 1975 assertion, stated by Secretary Simon, that it was "unaware of the fact that Lockheed had paid bribes." See *1975 Senate Hearings on Lockheed Bribery*, *supra* note 122, at 9. Apparently other questionable payments went undetected by Arthur Young. See A. Briloff, *More Debits Than Credits* 58 (1976).

136. See Emergency Loan Guarantee Board, *Fifth Annual Report* 10-11 (1976).

137. *Id.* at 11.

138. *Id.*

139. *Id.* at 11–12.

140. See *1976 Senate Oversight Hearings*, *supra* note 127, at 4, 9 (testimony of William E. Simon, ELGB Chairman). To the extent the Board knew the countries in which the payments had been made, it gleaned the information from newspaper reports. See *id.* at 9.

141. See *id.* at 4.

142. See *1976 Senate Oversight Hearings*, *supra* note 127, at 107 (testimony of Robert W. Haack, Chairman of the Board, Lockheed Aircraft Corp.); *1975 Senate Hear-*

needed the information to assess the magnitude and probability of the risk to which the government's credit as guarantor had been exposed.[143]

The Significance of the ELGB's Failure

To be sure, the ELGB is not identical to the restructured boards of directors advocated by corporate reformers—Lockheed's board of directors, with a majority of outside members,[144] coexisted with the ELGB. Thus, it may be argued that the ELGB's experience is irrelevant to proposals for corporate restructuring and that, in any event, the ELGB's failure is attributable to its position outside Lockheed's management structure, beyond the corporate veil. Neither of these arguments need long detain us. It is evident that the mandate given to the ELGB, unclear as it may appear in retrospect, was the same as that given by proposals for corporate reform to boards of directors—to monitor and assess the performance of operating management. Further, the resources available to the ELGB with which to pursue its mandate were similar to, if not greater than, those afforded boards of directors.[145] As to the ELGB's position outside the formal structure of corporate management, the ELGB had

---

ings on Multinational Corporations, supra note 56, at 348 (testimony of Daniel J. Haughton, Chairman of the Board, Lockheed Aircraft Corp.).

143. Secretary Simon may have rejected this argument in the following colloquy with Senator Proxmire, Chairman of the Senate Banking Committee:

> The Chairman: How can you adequately assess the prospect of repayment for the Lockheed loan unless you know the full facts about the bribe, the most devasting development that has hit Lockheed and Lockheed's future prospects in recent history?
>
> Secretary Simon: I would say that it's potentially devastating from the credit analysis and financial analysis point of view, yes, and no one can make a judgment as to what the future implication of these disclosures is going to have as far as future contracts and cancellations and indeed concern on the part of potential customers and existing customers as to whether Lockheed will still be in business. So knowing this uncertainty certainly helps, but knowing the specific names involved would not assist us as far as this financial analysis is concerned . . . .

1976 Senate Oversight Hearings, supra note 127, at 11. Nonetheless, had the Board reviewed the information it might have concluded, as its staff may well have concluded without reviewing the information, that Lockheed's assessment of the devastation to be wrought by disclosure was exaggerated. See text accompanying note 139 *supra*. The Board might also have been able to make an independent determination of the order of magnitude of devastation to Lockheed and increased risk to the guarantor.

144. See text accompanying note 113 *supra*.

145. See notes 111, 128, 129 *supra*.

substantial access to operating management personnel and may have met with them more frequently than would a board of directors.[146]

Some of the ELGB's infirmities may also come to afflict restructured corporate boards. If the board's mandate is not defined clearly and specifically, the board may interpret it narrowly, as did the ELGB. Defining the board's mandate may be especially troublesome for some of the restructured boards, since it is apparent that the goals advanced by some of their proponents are inconsistent. Although vigilance on behalf of shareholders, especially minority shareholders,[147] is imposed by the proposals on the board, some proposals also partially disenfranchise shareholders,[148] as well as identify individual directors with non-shareholder constituencies.[149] The inherent confusion in the board's mandate thereby created is not likely to prompt agressive board activity. Further, if the board's position with respect to internal corporate information is essentially a passive or receptive one, it, like the ELGB, may be unable to detect misrepresentations or deceptions by operating management as well as failures by the outside auditors. To enjoy a sustained and general success, restructured boards ought, at the least, to be premised on a realistic assessment of how corporations actually handle information. Without it, they may be compelled to monitor management from the same remote stance taken by the ELGB.

LIFTING THE VEIL—SELF/SCRUTINY IN THE WAKE OF SENSITIVE PAYMENTS

Origin of the Self-Scrutiny Reports

Over a period of almost four years, many American corporations have revealed that they used corporate funds improperly, creating slush funds to make illegal domestic political contributions and to make payments to officials of foreign governments and to dubious overseas sales consultants. The efforts by the SEC to prompt disclosure of the payments have provoked a large volume of commentary analyzing their propriety;[150]

---

146. See text accompanying notes 118 and 119 *supra*.

147. See M. Eisenberg, *supra* note 10, at pp. 159–60; R. Nader, *supra* note 11, at pp. 128–30; C. Stone, *supra* note 1, at p. 145.

148. See note 27 *supra*.

149. See text accompanying note 23 *supra*.

150. See e.g., Lowenfels, "Questionable Corporate Payments and the Federal Securities Laws," 51 N.Y.U. L. Rev. 1 (1976); Nehemkis, "Business Payoffs Abroad: Rhetoric and Reality," Cal. Management Rev., Winter 1975, at 5; Solomon & Linville,"Transnational Conduct of American Multinational Corporations: Questionable Payments Abroad," 17 B.C. Indus. & Com. Rev. 303 (1976); Stevenson, "The SEC and Foreign Bribery," 32 Bus. Law. 53 (1976); Note, "Disclosure of Corporate Payments and Practices: Conduct Regulation Through the Federal Securities Laws," 43 Brooklyn L. Rev. 681 (1977); Note, "Disclosure of Payments to Foreign Government Officials Under the Securities Acts," 89 Harv. L. Rev. 1848 (1976); Note, "Disclosure of Corporate Payments Abroad and the

more relevant to our purposes, however, are the descriptions of corporate decision-making processes stemming from the Commission's disclosure and enforcement programs. By describing corporations' treatment of ticklish internal information, they suggest that corporate officers' behavior while making decisions perceived to be questionable or illegal is not likely to be reached by purely structural attempts at corporate reform.

The SEC first turned its attention to sensitive payments practices as a result of revelations during the Special Prosecutor's investigation of the Watergate scandals, which the SEC believed were pertinent to public investors and perhaps subject to the disclosure requirements of the federal securities laws.[151] The Commission's staff, while examining matters initially investigated by the Special Prosecutor, discovered that secret corporate slush funds had been used for payments abroad, in some cases to officials of foreign governments, as well as for domestic political contributions.[152] After bringing several enforcement actions in response to these revelations,[153] the SEC concluded that a supplement to the enforcement actions was necessary due to the magnitude of the problem it perceived.[154] Accordingly, it announced a voluntary disclosure program, in which companies suspecting the existence of sensitive payments practices would investigate their problem under the auspices of someone not involved in the practices, typically outside members of the board of directors, and then consult with counsel and perhaps with the SEC staff to determine the disclosures that might be necessary.[155] Settle-

---

Concept of Materiality," 4 Hofstra L. Rev. 729 (1976); Note, "Foreign Bribes and the Securities Acts' Disclosure Requirements," 74 Mich. L. Rev. 1222 (1976); Comment, "Bribes, Kickbacks, and Political Contributions in Foreign Countries—The Nature and Scope of the Securities and Exchange Commission's Power to Regulate and Control American Corporate Behavior, 1976 Wis. L. Rev. 1231.

151. See Securities and Exchange Commission, *Report of the Securities and Exchange Commission on Questionable and Illegal Foreign Payments Submitted to the Senate Comm. on Banking, Housing and Urban Affairs,* 94th Cong., 2d Sess. 2 (P-H 1976) [hereinafter cited as *SEC Report on Questionable Payments*]; *The Activities of American Multinational Corporations Abroad: Hearings Before the Subcomm. on International Economic Policy of the House Comm. on International Relations,* 94th Cong., 1st Sess. 68 (1975) (testimony of Philip A. Loomis, Jr., Commissioner, Securities and Exchange Commission) [hereinafter cited as *1975 House Hearings on Multinational Corporations*]. Commissioner Loomis would not state whether he thought the SEC would otherwise have discovered the practices. *Id.*

152. See *1975 House Hearings on Multinational Corporations, supra* note 151, at 36–37 (statement of Philip A. Loomis, Jr., Commissioner, Securities and Exchange Commission).

153. See *SEC Report on Questionable Practices, supra* note 151, at 3–6.

154. See *id.* at 6–7.

155. See *1975 House Hearings on Multinational Corporations, supra* note 148, at 63–64 (testimony of Philip A. Loomis, Jr.).

ments of most of the enforcement actions, as well as the voluntary disclosure program, resulted in reports of internal corporate investigations of sensitive payments practices conducted under the direction of independent members of the board of directors.[156]

Critics of the SEC's role in the sensitive payments incident argued that the Commission's staff was importuning the disclosure of information that was not material to investors[157] and that the Commission lacked the requisite statutory authority to demand the extensive disclosures brought about by its voluntary program and settlements of enforcement actions.[158] Further, the SEC was accused of considerable obtuseness in its refusal to set guidelines specifying the kinds and amounts of payments that needed to be disclosed.[159] Without conceding that its present statutory base was lacking, the SEC proposed legislation which would have amended the Securities Exchange Act of 1934 to require that registered corporations keep records which accurately reflect their transactions and maintain an adequate system of internal accounting controls.[160] Falsifying accounting records and making false statements to accountants would have been made unlawful.[161] After Congress failed to pass its legislative package, the Commission restated the same provisions in rule-making proposals, asserting that the reporting requirements of the securities laws gave it authority to promulgate such a rule.[162] This assertion has been criticized as aggrandizing the SEC's authority.[163] Apart from the issues raised by the Commission's

---

156. The Internal Revenue Service embarked on its own contemporaneous investigation of sensitive payments, posing a set of eleven broad questions to large corporations. For an analysis of the IRS investigation, *see* Special Subcommittee of the Committee on Practice and Procedure of New York State Bar Association, "Report on the Internal Revenue Service "Slush Fund" Investigation," 32 Tax L. Rev. 161 (1977).

157. See, e.g., Lowenfels, *supra* note 150, at 24.

158. See, e.g., Note, "Disclosure of Payments to Foreign Government Officials Under the Securities Acts," 89 Harv. L. Rev. 1848, 1861 (1976).

159. See e.g., Lowenfels, *supra* note 150, at 23–24.

160. The SEC's proposals were introduced as S. 3418, 94th Cong., 2d Sess. (1976). See generally *Prohibiting Bribes to Foreign Officials: Hearing on S. 3133, 3379 and 3418 Before the Senate Comm. on Banking, Housing and Urban Affairs,* 94th Cong., 2d Sess. (1976) [hereinafter cited as *1976 Senate Hearing on Prohibiting Bribes.*].

161. See S. 3418, 94th Cong., 2d Sess. (1976).

162. See Exchange Act Release No. 13185, in [1976–77 Transfer Binder] Fed. Sec. L. Rep. ¶ 80,896 (CCH) (1977).

163. See Fed. Sec. L. Rep. (CCH) No. 693, at 9-10 (1977), describing the position of the American Bar Association's Committee on the Federal Regulation of Securities. The Committee argued that the SEC's authority to promulgate the rules was weak, and was made especially dubious by the emphasis placed in the Supreme Court's opinion in Santa Fe Industries, Inc. v. Green, 430 U.S. 462

attempt to use its rule-making authority, its self-scrutiny approach must assume that beneficial change will follow the discernment and disclosure of historical inadequacies, and presuppose the existence of some duty to maintain accurate accounting records and effective internal controls. If not, self-examination and disclosure are mere empty rituals. The Commission has also argued that investors' concern with the integrity of management makes information about management's falsification of accounting records or evasion of proper internal controls material, without regard to the amount of corporate funds thereby affected.[164] The risk thereby created that the funds might be used for noncorporate purposes,[165] along with the doubt inevitably cast on management's judgment, supports this assertion.[166] In any event, most questions about the legitimacy of the Commission's involvement became of merely historical interest in 1977 with Congressional enactment of the Foreign Corrupt Practices Act.[167] The Act makes illegal most sensitive payments to foreign officials or candidates for foreign political office,[168] and requires registered corporations to maintain accounting

---

(1977), on the desirability of not federalizing corporation law, in the absence of a strong showing of congressional intent to do so. Plaintiff's argument in *Green,* however—that defendants' plan to eliminate public shareholders in the corporation for no valid business purpose through a short-form merger legal under Delaware corporate law was a deceptive and manipulative device in violation of § 10(b) of the Securities Exchange Act of 1934 and rule 10b-5 promulgated thereunder—involved federalizing the regulation of conduct in which adequate disclosure was assumed to have been made to shareholders. Thus, at least initially, the SEC's stance in promulgating rules as to internal corporate accounting practices is stronger than the position of the plaintiff in *Green,* for the accounting rules are strongly related to disclosure concerns. Both the Securities Act of 1933 and the Securities and Exchange Act of 1934 give the Commission broad authority to establish accounting standards and compel compliance with them, by delaying or suspending the effectiveness of registration statements, and through investigations and injunctive actions. See *Accounting Establishment Study, supra* note 21, at 1451–56 (letter from Roderick M. Hills, Chairman, Securities and Exchange Commission, to Senator Metcalf). Since § 13(b) of the Securities Exchange Act of 1934, 15 U.S.C. § 78m(b) (1970), gives the Commission the authority to determine "the methods to be followed in the preparation of reports," it seems querulous to maintain that its authority over the methods of preparation extends only to financial statements filed with the Commission and not to the integrity of the internal systems behind those statements.

164. See *SEC Report on Questionable Payments, supra* note 151, at 13, 15.

165. See Taylor, "Preventing Improper Payments Through Internal Controls," 13 Conf. Board Rep. 17, 19 (1976).

166. See McCloy, "Corporations: The Problem of Political Contributions and Other Payments At Home and Overseas," 31 Rec. A.B. City N.Y. 306, 309–10 (1976).

167. Pub. L. No. 95-213, 91 Stat. 1494 (1977).

168. Section 30A of the Securities Exchange Act, 15 U.S.C.A. § 78dd-1 (Supp. 1979).

records which describe transactions accurately, along with a system of adequate internal accounting controls.[169]

How Corporations Make Decisions

The reports written by corporations describing their entanglements in sensitive foreign payments and illegal domestic political contributions provide some useful insights into how corporations make decisions which are internally perceived to be questionable. They suggest that such decisions may be made under a layer of secrecy so pervasive as to be impenetrable by the normal control and audit mechanisms available even to a restructured corporation.

It is apparent that corporations made illicit payments for a wide variety of reasons. Some large illegal domestic political contributions were made as the result of repeated solicitations by high campaign officials stressing that the size of the corporation made appropriate a contribution in a particular amount.[170] Payments to officials of foreign governments were made to procure business in the country, to prevent government interference in the conduct of the business, to reduce foreign tax liability, and to expedite low-level ministerial decisions, the so-called grease payments.[171]

Apart from the variety of reasons and motives for making the payments there is a striking similarity in some aspects of corporations' decisions to make them. Generally, the decisions were made by a small number of the corporation's officers, and knowledge of the practices was similarly narrowly confined.[172] Although in some cases top management did not know of the payments,[173] it is significant that the most notorious instances were initiated by high-level officers and kept secret among them, thereby reducing the degree of review likely to follow the decisions.[174] The decisions to make the payments were not submitted to the

---

169. Section 13(b)(2)–(3) of the Securities Exchange Act, 15 U.S.C.A. § 78m(b) (2)–(3) (Supp. 1979).

170. See Select Senate Comm. on Presidential Campaign Activities, 93d Cong., 2d Sess., *Final Report* 448, 451–52, 459, 489–90 (1974).

171. These categorizations of purposes are set forth in Herlihy and Levine, "Corporate Crisis: The Overseas Payment Problem," 8 Law & Pol. Int'l Bus. 547, 550 (1976).

172. See, e.g., J. McCloy, *The Great Oil Spill* 32, 68 (1976) (paperback edition of the *Report of the Special Review Committee of the Board of Directors of Gulf Oil Corporation* (1976)) [hereinafter cited as *Gulf Directors' Report*]; Ashland Oil, Inc., *Summary of Report of the Special Committee and the Action of the Board of Directors Thereon* 5–6 (1975) [hereinafter cited as *Ashland Directors' Report*]; *Lockheed Directors' Report, supra* note 124, at 16; Phillips Petroleum Company, Form 8-K Current Report to SEC 11–12 (Sept. 26, 1975) [hereinafter cited as Phillips 8-K].

173. See *SEC Report on Questionable Payments, supra* note 151, at 41.

174. In some cases officers initiating the payments created virtually a separate organization within the corporation, in which their subordinates learned not to

corporation's board of directors,[175] and were only rarely reviewed by corporate counsel.[176] In the few cases in which counsel became involved in the decisions and gave cautionary advice it appears to have been ignored.[177]

Ability to make the payments generally depended on the establishment of two separate mechanisms, one to generate a fund of off-the-books cash, another to disburse the cash to its designated recipients without leaving "tracks" apparent to the normal corporate control systems. Due, perhaps, to the corporate office and extent of discretion of the persons establishing them, a variety of such mechanisms were readily created. Funds with which to make illegal domestic political contributions were generated through several different methods: by paying "bonuses" to selected employees with the understanding that they would be used for contributions to candidates,[178] by diverting and returning to headquarters funds transferred overseas for the apparent benefit of foreign operations,[179] and by withdrawing funds from the overseas accounts of foreign subsidiaries resulting from various overseas transactions.[180] Similarly, the money used for sensitive foreign payments usually originated from transactions creating off-the-books funds,[181] through some of the same methods used for illegal domestic political contributions as well as through rebates from brokers and suppliers[182] and repayments on false invoices.[183] Some corporations made extremely large commission payments to foreign sales agents, and

---

question deviations from standard corporate procedures. See *Lockheed Directors' Report, supra* note 124, at 16.

175. See, e.g., Independent Outside Directors on the Board of Directors of Northrop Corporation, *Report to the Board of Directors of Northrop Corporation on the Special Investigation of the Executive Committee* 2 (1975) [hereinafter cited as *Northrop Directors' Report*].

176. See, e.g., *Gulf Directors' Report, supra* note 172, at 35.

177. See, e.g., *Northrop Directors' Report, supra* note 175, at 10.

178. See, e.g., American Shipbuilding Co., Form 10-K Annual Report to SEC 12 (Sept. 29, 1974) [hereinafter cited as American Shipbuilding 10-K].

179. See, e.g., *Ashland Directors' Report, supra* note 172, at 5; *Gulf Directors' Report, supra* note 172, at 37–38. The United States Customs Service is reported to be investigating possible violations of the Bank Secrecy Act in movements of cash into and out of the country, *see* New York Times, June 27, 1977, at p. 41, col. 6.

180. See Phillips 8-K, *supra* note 169, at pp. 33–41.

181. See, e.g., *Lockheed Directors' Report, supra* note 124, at 13; Exxon Special Committee on Litigation, *Determination and Report of the Special Committee on Litigation, Exxon Corp.* 56 (1976) [hereinafter cited as Exxon Directors' Report].

182. See, e.g., Cities Service Co., Form 8-K Current Report to SEC (September 1975), *reprinted in 1975 House Hearings on Multinational Corporations, supra* note 151, at 183 [hereinafter cited as Cities Service 8-K].

183. See *Exxon Directors' Report, supra* note 181, at 21.

failed to maintain much control over the agents' activities. As a result, some of the "commissions" were eventually paid to officials of foreign governments.[184] In any event, some of the funds thereby generated were simply kept in cash under the custody of a corporate officer,[185] some were maintained in foreign banks;[186] and disbursements, often in cash, were under control of a very small number of corporate officers.[187]

The most striking qualities of these schemes are the ease with which they were established, the success with which they eluded corporate checks and the degree of disparity in their founders' attitudes toward various potential controls. For example, although some mechanisms set up to generate off-the-books cash resulted in federal tax consequences which may not have been recognized at the time,[188] many corporations were scrupulous in the care with which they planned for the proper tax treatment of their payments practices.[189] In sharp contrast to the deference with which they regarded the Internal Revenue Service, some officers initiating off-the-books funds and questionable payments expressed hostility and resentment toward corporate lawyers—and in one case outside members of the corporation's board—who might unearth and question their activities.[190]

---

184. See, e.g., *Northrop Directors' Report, supra* note 175, at 6–9, 14–16, 20–25. Some corporations formed separate foreign corporations for the purpose of furthering their foreign sales interests. Very little, if any, actual control was retained over the foreign sales corporations' activities. See id. at 9–13.

185. See, e.g., *Gulf Directors' Report, supra* note 172, at 42–43.

186. See, e.g., Phillips 8-K, *supra* note 172, at 33. Several corporations favored Switzerland as the site for these bank accounts, probably sharing the view that "it does not excite anybody's curiosity if you walk in and ask for $100,000 out of a Swiss bank," *Presidential Campaign Activities of 1972: Hearings Before the Senate Select Comm. on Presidential Campaign Activities*, 93d Cong., 1st Sess., Bk. 13, at 5444 (1973) (testimony of Orin E. Atkins, Chairman of the Board, Ashland Oil Co.).

187. See, e.g., *Gulf Directors' Report, supra* note 172, at 64–66.

188. See Phillips 8-K, *supra* note 172, at 34–35. Phillips obtained cash for domestic political contributions from the Swiss bank accounts of two Swiss corporations. Funds in the accounts represented rebates on contracts of an overseas subsidiary of Phillips along with interest income and miscellanous receipts. *Id.* at 40–41.

189. See Herlihy & Levine, *supra* note 171, at 596–97. But see 1975 *House Hearings on Multinational Corporations, supra* note 148, at 57 (testimony of Donald C. Alexander, Commissioner, Internal Revenue Service) ("I am skeptical enough to be surprised if a majority of those making the illegal payments were so mindful of their tax obligations as to refrain from deducting them.")

190. When William F. Whiteford, Chairman of the Board and Chief Executive Officer of the Gulf Oil Corporation, established its off-the-books fund for political contributions, he emphasized to his associates his desire that knowledge of the arrangement be kept from the Mellon family, who at the time held the largest

Similarly, internal corporate auditors, and to almost as great an extent, outside auditors, were not viewed as significant obstacles to the payments. Although most of the reports do not discuss in any detail the failure of internal audit systems to detect sensitive payments practices, it is apparent that the internal auditors' function could easily be circumvented or evaded.[191] Within many corporations, the internal auditors apparently lacked independence and stature[192] and in some cases failed to pursue indications that corporate funds were being used for unaccountable, sensitive ends.[193]

On the other hand, most of the sensitive payments practices fell—through either coincidence or careful design—through the interstices of possible internal corporate checks. If the funds with which to make the payments were generated through a rebate scheme, they went off the books upon their receipt. Even as to funds produced through other mechanisms, ordinary corporate checks and controls were easily circumvented. The departmental budgeting process, resulting typically in annual budgets reviewed by a central corporate officer and later compared to actual expenditures, did not provide much control over the actual use of corporate funds, at least as long as the amounts expended did not exceed those budgeted.[194] Further, in the case of multinational corporations, control over current expenses may be left to the local foreign affiliate, with only capital expenditure items reviewed on the corporate level.[195] Corporate controls over expenditures and over intracorporate transfers likewise were easily evaded, ofttimes as a result of the high level of the officials involved.[196]

---

single block of Gulf stock and were represented on the board, as well as from other officers he characterized as "the Boy Scouts." See *Gulf Directors' Report, supra* note 172, at 33. Whiteford was also known by his close associates to dislike "bloodhound" lawyers who became involved in the corporation's business or policy questions. See id. at 231.

191. See Williams, *"Illegal Payments: The Legislative Outlook,"* 142 J. Accountancy 58, 60 (1977).

192. See, e.g., *Gulf Directors' Report, supra* note 172, at 209–12; *Lockheed Directors' Report, supra* note 124, at 18. Through coincidental budget cuts, the size of Lockheed's internal auditing force was drastically reduced during the period under review, changing the corporate perception of it "from a control concept to a trouble-shooting role." *Id.* One report states that the corporation's internal control procedures lagged behind the development of its overseas sales, although the cause of this lag is not explored. See *Ashland Directors, Report, supra* note 172, at 9.

193. See note 192 *supra.*

194. See *Gulf Directors' Report, supra* note 172, at 199–201.

195. See *Exxon Directors' Report, supra* note 181, at 48–49.

196. See *Gulf Directors' Report, supra* note 172 at 202–04. Gulf's corporate controller was himself a knowing participant in the payments practices.

Although in a few instances outside auditors discovered some aspects of the sensitive payments practices,[197] for the most part they did not unearth them.[198] This failure has led to considerable discussion of the scope which an outside audit can reasonably be expected to attain, along with some reformulations of the approach with which an outside auditor conducts an inquiry.[199] In addition, there has been some dispute about whether the outside auditors' failure to discover the practices was the result of a lack of diligence[200] or merely the unavoidable consequence of successful management attempts to make the practices undetectable.[201]

However, the secrecy with which some corporations surrounded their sensitive payments appears to have exceeded even that necessary to evade internal controls and outside auditors. It was common for domestic political contributions made from the funds to be disbursed in cash with no records kept of disbursements.[202] Likewise, in some cases few records were kept of payments to foreign agents.[203] This reluctance to record disbursements obviously reduced effective corporate control over the ultimate end to which funds were applied, and increased the possibility that they might be used for unforeseen ends which would prove embarrassing to the corporation, or even that they might be expended for noncorporate purposes.[204] Given these evident risks, it is surprising that

---

197. See note 135 *supra.*

198. See *SEC Report on Questionable Payments, supra* note 151, at 48–49; *Accounting Establishment Study, supra* note 21, at 7.

199. See Solomon and Muller, "Illegal Payments: Where the Auditor Stands." 142 J. Accountancy 51 (1977); cf. American Institute of Certified Public Accountants, *Statement on Auditing Standards* No. 1, §§ 327–28 (1977) ("The Independent Auditor's Responsibility for the Detection of Errors of Irregularities;" "Illegal Acts by Clients"). See generally Barrons, April 19, 1976, at p. 5 (interview with Abraham J. Briloff).

200. See *Ashland Directors' Report, supra* note 172, at 8 (conclusion that there was "some basis for suggesting that greater care might have been exercised" by the outside auditors).

201. See *Gulf Directors' Report, supra* note 172, at 207 ("In view of the elaborate measures taken by Gulf officials to conceal the facts it is doubtful that any outside auditors, performing normal audit procedures, would have detected the facts.").

202. See, e.g., *Ashland Directors' Report, supra* note 172, at 5.

203. See *Northrop Directors' supra* note 175 at 19, 24. In contrast to its meagre records of these transactions, Northrop kept relatively full records of government and military personages entertained at its duck hunting facility in eastern Maryland, appparently for the purpose of determining the number of dressed birds to be delivered to each person, as required by state law. See 1975 *Senate Hearings on Multinational Corporations, supra* note 56, at 187–88, 199–237.

204. See Taylor, *"Preventing Improper Payments Through Internal Controls."* 13 Conf. Board Rep. 17, 19 (1976) ("I suspect that more than one board is wondering

some of the payments made from the off-the-books funds were for entirely legal purposes. Some corporations apparently made contributions to candidates for state office in states where such contributions were legal, using the same off-the-books funds used for making illegal federal campaign contributions, with a similar reluctance to keep records of the contributions.[205] Similarly, some corporations made legal and unquestionably proper overseas payments—for legitimate attorneys' fees and other service fees—in the same furtive and unaccountable manner used to make payments to dubious agents and officials of foreign governments.[206]

Remarkably enough, none of the corporations' reports on sensitive payments practices explores or explains this curious use of furtive means to accomplish legal ends. It is not apparent from the reports whether the off-the-books mechanisms were established with the express notion of using them for legal as well as illegal purposes, or whether they were initially intended for illegal or dubious ends and came only later to be used for legal and unquestionable ends as well. Thus, one is left with mere conjecture to explain this phenomenon. It may well be that once a secret unaccountable mechanism is established within a corporate hierarchy, the temptations to increase its uses are strong and even irresistable. For one thing, decisions made through this mechanism are unassailable, at least at the time, and can only add to the unchecked discretion of the officer in charge of the secret fund. Once a secret mechanism is available, it may prove tempting to eliminate all questions about some kinds of payments by using it rather than going through any systematic process of checks, reviews, and audits. Use of a secret mechanism may also reflect the influence of some officers' expressed hostility toward outside monitors.[207]

This analysis of the factors behind some corporations' compulsive internal secrecy is analogous to the explanation of corporations' attempts to keep information secret from outsiders developed by the sociologist Max Weber in his classic essay on bureaucracy.[208] Weber postulates that the power of a bureaucratic organization resides in its mastery of quantities of detailed information, and that the bureaucracy increases its power to the extent it succeeds in keeping secret its knowledge and intentions.[209] Thus, in Weber's analysis, wherever a bureaucracy feels threatened by outside forces, it responds with secrecy. However, the

---

whether all funds presumed to have been used for unvouchered and improperly accounted for corporate purposes were so used.").

205. See Phillips 8-K Report, *supra* note 172, at 26–27, 52.

206. See *Northrop Directors' Report, supra* note 175, at 27, 34–35, 37, 40–41.

207. See note 190 *supra*

208. H. Gerth & C. Mills, From Max Weber: Essays in Sociology pp. 196–244 (1946).

209. *Id.* at p. 233.

bureaucracy's obsessive penchant for secrecy may extend beyond its rational self-interest:[210]

> The pure interest of the bureaucracy in power, however, is efficacious far beyond those areas where purely functional interests make for secrecy. The concept of the "official secret" is the specific invention of the bureaucracy, and nothing is so fanatically defended by the bureaucracy as this attitude, which cannot be substantially justified beyond these specifically qualified areas.

Although Weber's essay is concerned with bureaucratic secrecy as to outside inquiry,[211] the same analysis is applicable to secrecy within the corporate structure itself.

It is precisely this sort of dysfunctional, obsessive secrecy within the corporation which proposals to restructure corporations through rejuvenated boards of directors fail to take into account. The only aspect of Christopher Stone's proposal that comes close is an argument in favor of protecting the job rights of employees who blow the whistle and disclose what the corporation prefers be kept secret.[212] To be sure, the success of this remedy depends on the availability of a supply of whistle blowers; it is unlikely to be very effective in the absence of a more thoughtful examination of the reasons for corporations' obsessive internal secrecy.

The Literature of Corporate Self-Scrutiny

The corporations' reports on sensitive payments are interesting in themselves as a new genre of corporate literature: exercises in public self-examination and repentance. As such, they are useful background for assessing the prospects of some of the more optimistic proposals for reform. Perhaps the most striking characteristic of the reports is the wide variation in their quality. Although the former Chairman of the SEC expressed its satisfaction with the quality of the reports it had reviewed,[213] some of the reports are unclear and confusing at points, a fact recognized by the SEC staff in its analysis of the reports.[214] Contrasting

---

210. *Id.*

211. For a further elaboration of Weber's argument, see Nadel, "*Corporate Secrecy and Political Accountability,*" 35 Pub. Ad Rev. 14 (1975).

212. See C. Stone, *supra* note 1, at pp. 213–16.

213. See 1976 *Senate Hearings on Prohibiting Bribes, supra* note 160, at 27 (testimony of Roderick M. Hills, SEC Chairman).

214. See *SEC Report on Questionable Payments, supra* note 151, at 36, 40. The staff of the Subcommittee on Oversight and Investigations of the House Committee on Interstate and Foreign Commerce prepared a report criticizing the SEC for accepting disclosures about payments practices which omitted some identifying details. The Subcommittee report did not, however, comment on the occasional confusions in the corporate reports. See Staff of Subcomm. on Oversight and Investigations, House Comm. on Interstate and Foreign Commerce, 94th

with the evident care and thoroughness with which some reports have been prepared[215] is the sketchy and confusing quality of others.[216] Only a few reports contain discussions of the inadequacies of the internal corporate control and audit procedures which failed to check or detect sensitive payments.[217] Moreover, few of the reports consider in any detail the frustration of the role of the corporation's independent auditors.[218]

Not surprisingly, most of the reports conclude with a list of reforms to be implemented by the corporation, and a statement of optimism about the reforms' ability to prevent similar abuses in the future. More specifically, the assertion is made in many of the reports that the corporation's internal audit and control systems have been revised so that unaccountable applications of corporate funds cannot recur.[219] However, the lit-

---

Cong., 2d Sess., *Study on SEC Voluntary Compliance Program on Corporate Disclosure* (P-H 1976).

215. See *Gulf Directors' Report, supra* note 172; *1976 Senate Hearing on Prohibiting Bribes, supra* note 160, at 26.

216. It is unclear from the report of American Shipbuilding, *see* note 178 *supra,* who designated the political candidates as recipients of the largesse of the company's bonus program. The report also fails to discuss any potential federal income tax consequences to the corporation resulting from the bonus program. In cases in which corporations used their slush funds to make legal domestic political contributions, see text accompanying note 206 *supra,* the reasons for such usage are not discussed. Further, it is impossible to determine from some reports whether some of the state contributions specifically disclosed were legal or illegal. *See* Phillips 8-K, *supra* note 172, at 24–27, 52.

217. See American Shipbuilding 10-K, *supra* note 178 (no discussion of internal audit and control systems); *Ashland Directors' Report, supra* note 172 at 9 (no discussion of internal audit and control systems beyond a summary assertion that company's audit procedures failed to "keep pace" with its growing overseas involvement); *Northrop Directors' Report, supra* note 172 (very little discussion of internal audit procedures); Phillips 8-K, *supra* note 172 (no discussion of internal audit systems).

218. See Cities Service 8-K, *supra* note 182 (no discussion of independent auditor's performance); Phillips 8-K, *supra* note 172 (no discussion of independent auditor's activities).

219. For example, Ashland Oil adopted a policy, recommended by its investigating board committee, prohibiting "the maintenance of, or any disbursement from, funds created or maintained for purposes which are not disclosed or are not appropriately reflected in its books and records." See *Ashland Directors' Report, supra* note 172, at 13. Lockheed's committee recommended upgrading the corporation's internal audit function, along with requiring periodic representations by management members that they are abiding by the corporation's code of business conduct. See *Lockheed Directors' Report, supra* note 124, at 25. A monitoring system introduced by Lockheed was elsewhere described as being "as tight as anything could be as far as the central approval mechanism that's been set up for all payments for the corporation"; at Lockheed, "[n]o outside funds. It's all back in the budget. No ability for slush funds where improper

erature of the accounting profession recognizes explicitly, even though the reports do not, that no such internal procedure is tamper-proof or foolproof and that all potentially can be subverted by management.[220] The revelations of the reports also demonstrate that no particular corporate officer—controller,[221] corporate counsel[222]—or independent board or its audit committee[223] will always exercise sound judgment when questionable activities are proposed or discovered. Moreover, reforms directed to sensitive payments problems may not be effective deterrents against other kinds of corporate misconduct. Thus, it is not surprising that two of the reports expressly come to the conclusion that only the tone set by top management in its control of the company can assure that legal and ethical norms of conduct will be abided by.[224] It is, nonetheless, ironic that this final assurance stems from factors other than the structure of the corporation's management.

Repent and Be Saved—Defenses to Shareholders' Derivative Suits

One consequence of the corporate self-scrutiny process, perhaps unforeseen by some of its proponents, is that it has the effect of furnishing the corporation's officers and directors with an additional defense in any derivative shareholder litigation challenging the conduct in question.

---

payments had existed before," *1976 Senate Oversight Hearings, supra* note 127, at 24 (testimony of William E. Simon, ELGB Charirman).

220. See American Institute of Certified Public Accountants, *Statement on Auditing Standards* No. 1, § 320.32 (1972), which states that a system of internal control procedures should be regarded as "reasonable, but not absolute, assurance that the objectives expressed in it will be accomplished by the system." The assurance is less than absolute in part because

> [P]rocedures whose effectiveness depends on segregation of duties obviously can be circumvented by collusion. Similarly, procedures designed to assure the execution and recording of transactions in accordance with management's authorizations may be ineffective against either errors or irregularities perpetrated by management with respect to transactions or to the estimates and judgments required in the preparation of financial statements.

Id. § 320.34.

221. See note 196 *supra*.

222. Gulf Oil's investigation concluded that the company's former counsel was aware of the company's practice of making illegal domestic political contributions out of corporate funds. See *Gulf Directors' Report, supra* note 172, at 233–34.

223. See note 135 *supra*.

224. See *Gulf Directors' Report, supra* note 172, at p. 292; Preface to *Lockheed Directors' Report, supra* note 124.

Without the self-scrutiny ritual, defendants in a derivative suit would be in the position of arguing that their actions were good-faith exercises of their business judgment.[225] Specifically, operating management defendants would argue that they undertook the activities prompting the litigation in good faith,[226] and outside members of the board would argue that their failure to detect or prevent operating management's activities was within the permissible scope of business judgment.[227] Once the internal scrutiny process is undergone, however, the focus of the derivative litigation shifts, so that rather than litigating the business judgment attributes of the defendants' actual conduct, the plaintiff is forced to litigate the good faith and disinterestedness of those directing the self-scrutiny and deciding whether the corporation ought to assert claims against the defendants.[228] This shift in focus narrows the permissible scope of the representative shareholder's discovery, reduces the showing the defendants must make to support a motion for summary judgment, and in general makes it very unlikely that the representative shareholder will ever prevail on the merits in such litigation. The fact that the likelihood of success in such shareholders' litigation is so slim virtually eliminates one potential way of enforcing directors' and officers' duty of care to the corporation, by ensuring that their actual behavior will not even be litigated.

One recent case, *Gall v. Exxon Corp.*,[229] illustrates the effect of the self-scrutiny study in the context of a shareholder's derivative suit. Plaintiff in *Gall* sued derivatively, alleging that the corporation's directors and officers, by failing to prevent its Italian subsidiary's payment of $59 million in bribes and political contributions, had breached their fiduciary duties to Exxon, wasted its assets, and violated various provisions of the federal securities laws.[230] Defendants, apparently prior to any plaintiff's discovery, moved for summary judgment dismissing plaintiff's complaint on the grounds that a special committee of disinterested directors had investigated the payments problems and had determined that it was not in the corporation's interest to maintain suit against any of the defendants, thereby exercising their sound business

---

225. See H. Ballantine, *Corporations* § 63a, at pp. 160–61 (rev. ed. 1946); note 32 *supra*.

226. See *id.*

227. See Bates v. Dresser, 251 U.S. 524, 529–30 (1920); Barnes v. Andrews, 298 F. 614, 615, 618 (S.D.N.Y. 1924).

228. See H. Ballantine, *Corporations* § 147, at 349 (rev. ed. 1946); Lipton, "*Directors of Mutual Funds: Special Problems,*" 31 Bus. Law. 1259, 1263 (1976).

229. 418 F. Supp. 508 (S.D.N.Y. 1976), *complaint dismissed*, No. 75 Civ. 3682 (S.D.N.Y. Jan. 17, 1977).

230. See 418 F. Supp. at 509.

judgment.[231] After affording plaintiff the opportunity to conduct discovery as to the good faith and independence of members of the special committee, the court granted defendants' motion and dismissed the complaint.[232]

As a consequence of its procedural history, *Gall* does not raise directly the question of whether Exxon's directors performed properly on its board; rather, the issue posed is one step removed—whether the special committee's decision not to sue represented a good-faith exercise of business judgment. Nonetheless, some aspects of the special committee's report call into question both the quality of the directors' service and the efficacy of the self-scrutiny technique.

It is apparent from the report that Exxon delegated a great deal of authority to the chief executives of its subsidiaries.[233] The chief executive of its Italian subsidiary, Esso Italiana, was believed to need extensive authority in order to inspire sufficient confidence in the representatives of other companies and of the Italian government with whom he would be dealing.[234] In particular, the chief of Esso Italiana had the authority to open bank accounts and borrow money.[235] He used this authority to open secret bank accounts out of which he paid bribes and legal political contributions, generating the necessary funds through rebates and bank overdrafts.[236] Ordinarily, the existence of the secret bank accounts would have been revealed in annual audits of Esso Italiana by its outside auditors, who would contact its banks as a part of normal audit procedures for confirmation of the balances in its accounts. The chief of Esso Italiana successfully defeated this audit check by asking the banks not to reveal the existence of the accounts or the overdrafts in them to anyone; the banks complied.[237]

Although some members of Exxon's central management knew that Esso Italiana had been using rebates to make political contributions, they did not know of the secret bank accounts.[238] Further, at the time central management control was almost exclusively concerned with sub-

---

231. See *id.*

232. No. 75 Civ. 3682 (S.D.N.Y. Jan., 1977) (complaint dismissed). The propriety of granting the same authority to dismiss derivative litigation to the independent directors of a mutual fund is raised by Lasker v. Burks, 99 S. Ct. 1831 (1979), which holds that the Investment Company Act of 1940 does not absolutely prohibit director termination of nonfrivolous actions.

233. See *Exxon Directors' Report, supra* note 181, at 11–12.

234. See *id.* at 12–13.

235. See *id.*

236. See *id.* at 8–9.

237. See *id.* at 57.

238. See *id.* 41.

sidiaries' use of capital, while operating expense budgets were not examined in any detail.[239] The board's interest was the bottom line; no individual expense items were examined.

While classical statements of directors' duty of care to the corporation clearly envisage a more active and detailed review of operating management's performance,[240] Exxon's directors may not have behaved improperly. They may have had reason to believe that internal corporate check and audit systems and independent auditors' inquiries were sufficient to assure that corporate funds were being used for business purposes and were not being misapplied to other ends. Although it concludes with the assertion that internal audit and control procedures were inadequate in Italy until 1972,[241] the special committee's report does not discuss the extent or quality of such procedures at Exxon, a striking omission in light of its significance to the propriety of the directors' conduct. Indeed, it appears that at least some directors knew that some financial records were false and thus perhaps had good reason to suspect other improprieties in expense records.[242]

One interesting variation on the self-scrutiny defense, although not raised directly by the facts of *Gall*, is suggested by the practical implications of the case. Suppose the representative plaintiff in a similar litigation is able to demonstrate that information about the challenged activities was withheld from or misrepresented to the disinterested directors conducting the investigation and determining the corporation's position in the derivative litigation. Plaintiff's argument would then be that the defense otherwise afforded by the self-scrutiny exercise ought to be unavailable. If the sole permissible focus of the plaintiff's inquiry is the good faith and disinterestedness of those making the inquiry, then the defense is still available, for the plaintiff has shown only that the disinterested directors' decisions may have been mistaken, and has not shown that the decisions were not the result of a good faith exercise of business judgment. On the other hand, once the inquiry, albeit disinterested, has been tainted by withheld or misrepresented information, the integrity of the self-scrutiny process has been so seriously jeopardized that the defense ought not to be available. Especially if the information appears to be material to the decisions made by the disinterested directors, the self-scrutiny process has not fulfilled even its minimal role of enabling the corporation to have a fully informed stance in the derivative litigation. This argument is supported by cases decided after *Gall*

---

239. See *id.* at 16.

240. See M. Eisenberg, *supra* note 10, at 139. The classic statutory mandate is that the directors manage the corporation and set its business policy by exercising their good-faith business judgment. See *id.*

241. See *Exxon Directors' Report, supra* note 181, at 80.

242. See *id.* at 38–41. Some directors knew that political contributions had been improperly recorded on the books of Esso Italiana.

which emphasize the "depth and amplitude" of the independent directors' investigation as pertinent to whether a court should treat their decision as an exercise of bona fide business judgment.[243]

Thus, unless the defense it affords is somehow made unavailable, the self-scrutiny mechanism may not get much further into an analysis of the quality of directors' performance than does the derivative suit with its procedural peculiarities. In light of the wide protective swath cut by the business-judgment rule, it is difficult to specify the incentive to directors to reform their conduct posed by such a self-study. Again, the success of reform appears to be tied to the overall tone of management rather than to the specific review process.

CONCLUSION

Increasing the proportion of independent directors on boards of large corporations while exhorting those directors to be knowledgeable and aggressive is a widely supported reform. So widely supported, in fact, that one suspects opposition to it could be grounded in only quixotic folly or "an invincible repose upon the status quo."[244] Nonetheless, some of the predictions of universal success made for this reform by its proponents are exaggerated or unfounded.

Mere structural change is probably not sufficient to assure that large corporations will behave as law-abiding and ethical citizens. Effective reform requires an informed assessment of corporations' actual practices in handling and shaping information about the corporation; without such an assessment even an independent board may be denied effective control and use of corporate information. Moreover, without coherence and clarity in the goals to be achieved by these structural reforms, the independent directors' mandate may be unclear. Finally, strong emphasis on structural reform probably has the effect of distracting attention from other possible remedies for corporate problems—shareholders' derivative suits, civil and criminal penalties—and diffusing efforts to make the other remedies more effective.

---

243. Auerbach v. Bennett, — App. Div.2d ——, 408 N.Y.S.2d 83, 87 (2d Dept. 1978), quoted with approval in Rosengarten v. ITT, [Current] Fed. Sec. L. Rep. (CCH) ¶ 96,788, at 95,098 (S.D.N.Y. 1979).

244. Bates v. Dresser, 251 U.S. 524, 530 (1920).

CHAPTER EIGHT

Corporate Response to a New Environment

THE ENVIRONMENT AND THE DEVELOPMENT OF POLICY

Wm. van Dusen Wishard, *Consultant on corporate social and public policy; formerly special Advisor to the Secretary of Commerce for Public Policy*

In 1959 Edward S. Mason, then George F. Baker Professor of Economics at Harvard University, observed that "the business corporation is so much our most important economic institution and it is so thoroughly integrated into our business culture that to suggest a drastic change in the scope or character of corporate activity is to suggest a drastic alteration in the structure of society."[1] It is evident that in the intervening two decades the reverse of that process has been taking place: to wit, drastic alterations in the structure of society are causing fundamental changes in the scope and character of corporate activity.

To even the casual observer of the business scene, the corporate world appears to be at the barricades. As James Q. Wilson portrays it.[2]

> Public confidence in the corporation has fallen . . . the national media are increasingly critical, capital formation is inhibited by taxes and inflationary policies, the profit margins of corporations have declined, social and economic regulations proliferate almost faster than the Federal Register can print them, anti-trust prosecution . . . falls more heavily on firms here than elsewhere and the barriers to public control of traditionally private industries . . . are dropping rapidly.

Corporations counter these developments through economic education, advocacy advertising, and public relations. Yet behind the charge and countercharge lie fundamental changes in society that have moved many institutions of government, education, law, medicine, religion, and family—as well as business—to redefine their roles. The modern

---

1. *The Corporation in Modern Society* 1 (E. Mason ed. 1960).

2. Wilson, "Democracy and the Corporation," Wall St. J., Jan. 11, 1978, at p. 14.

American corporation has adapted its relationship to society before; but its original design as a private institution producing profit for a relative few has survived all social change—until now. Today the large corporation is being redefined as a public institution engaged in a wide range of activities some of which appear unrelated to short-term profitability.

This article examines the effects of these recent developments on the relationship between the corporation and public policy.[3] It considers the social environment in which a corporation must operate and suggests how corporations can interact with public policy to achieve an improved equilibrium between public and private enterprise.

THE NEW ENVIRONMENT

Today's social environment is changing with a rapidity unequaled in the history of the human experience. Such changes have been amply chronicled in numerous books and journals.

However, it is worth noting the new social environment in its historical context.

In A *Study of History* Arnold Toynbee defines a shift in emphasis that takes place at a certain stage of a civilization's growth. Toynbee observes.[4]

> [W]e may persist in the view that a given series of successful responses to successive challenges is to be interpreted as a manifestation of growth if, as the series proceeds, *the action tends to shift from the field of the external environment—whether physical or human—to the* for intérieur *of the growing personality of the growing civilization.* In so far as this grows and continues to grow, it has to reckon less and less with challenges delivered by alien adversaries and demanding responses on an outer battle-field, and more and more with challenges that are presented by itself to itself in an inner arena. [Emphasis added.]

Victorious responses, Toynbee suggests, "do not take the form of surmounting an external obstacle or of overcoming an external adversary but manifest themselves, instead, in *an inward self-articulation or self-determination.*"[5] (Emphasis added.) Toynbee then concludes, "Growth means that the growing personality or civilization tends to become its own environment and its own challenger and its own field of action. In other words, *the criterion of growth is progress towards self-determination* . . . ."[6] (Emphasis added.) Toynbee is suggesting that how a society re-

---

3. Throughout this discussion, unless otherwise specified, the term "corporate public policy" will refer to a corporation's relationship with all of its publics.
4. A. Toynbee, III *A Study of History,* p. 216 (1934).
5. *Id.* at p. 192.
6. *Id.* at p. 216.

sponds to the internalization of its growth determines whether or not the society moves to a higher stage of development.

Toynbee's observations offer a helpful perspective on the public issues of the present day. For over two centuries America has successfully responded to a long series of external challenges. We forged a nation, cleared the wilderness, preserved our union, established an industrial base, defended our freedom in history's two greatest wars, provided the necessities of life for the majority of our people, amassed the most gigantic concentration of wealth and power in the history of mankind, probed the heavens and landed on the moon, and we now seek to master the structure of matter and the process of life itself. Present-day international problems notwithstanding, we have thus far successfully responded to the external challenges of growth, and now the challenges of growth are being internalized.

Most of our economic and political institutions were conceived and developed in the eighteenth and nineteenth century context of social stability, modest per capita wealth, and unlimited room for expansion. We are now readjusting our economic and political institutions for a twenty-first century context of social flux and mobility, high per capita wealth, and limited room for expansion. This is forcing us, as Fritz Stern said of present-day Germany, "to wrestle not only with practical issues of economic well-being in a world of contracting opportunities, but with the more fundamental questions of moral purposes and national priorities."[7]

The change taking place is, according to Willis Harman, "a change involving all our social, political, and economic institutions; our social roles and expectations; and even the basic premises underlying modern culture and values."[8] Much that is traditional in thought and practice is being challenged, and the problem is to know what to discard and what to retain from the old order.

Public opinion polls daily confirm the search—to use Toynbee's term—for a new self-articulation. Daniel Yankelovich, for instance, talks of "the emergence . . . of . . . the self-fulfillment movement."[9] Sensitivity training, group therapy, an interest in Eastern religions, and the resurgence of Christian fundamentalist movements are all part of this search for a new self-articulation.

In a historical context, the process of internalization is what the entire public discussion for over a decade has been all about. The questions of income distribution, public spending on social services, equal opportunity, new lifestyles, resource use, the quality of life, institu-

---

7. Stern, "The Pressures of Liberalism and Terrorism in West Germany," N.Y. Times, Dec. 30, 1977, at p. A25.

8. W. Harman, *An Incomplete Guide to the Future,* p. 3 (1976).

9. Yankelovich, Emerging Ethical Norms in Public and Private Life, Seminar, Columbia University, at 10 (Apr. 20, 1977).

tional legitimacy, the role of women, corporate social responsibility and accountability—these are all part of the internalization of growth. Specific public discussion of the legitimate role of the corporation—exemplified in the work of Peter Drucker,[10] Milton Friedman,[11] and Robert Heilbroner[12]—continues to have priority in this national agenda. Many commentators point to specific changes in underlying values for an explanation.

George Lodge, for example, suggests that basic value shifts have extended to such areas as individualism, property rights, and the social concepts on which America's liberal democracy has been erected. Lodge sees individualism yielding to communitarianism and property rights replaced by community need.[13] Yet in some fundamental ways there has never been such an extension of individualism as there is today. Increased individualism is one of the results of affluence and greater access to information. Prosperity and knowledge multiply individual choice, which in turn leads to greater social diversity, witness the proliferation of life styles or the increasing tendency in politics to ignore the party line and follow one's own instincts and preferences.

Robert Heilbroner identifies a more specific effect of recent change on our economic values: dissatisfaction with the unbalanced pursuit of materialism. Writes Heilbroner, "Economic growth and technical achievement, the greatest triumphs of our epoch of history, have shown themselves to be inadequate sources for collective contentment and hope. Material advance, the most profoundly distinguishing attribute of industrial capitalism and socialism alike, has proved unable to satisfy the human spirit."[14] Louis Harris has detected this dissatisfaction, reporting that people feel it is time to learn to live on less of the material goods of life, but with better human relationships.[15]

The corporate world itself, of course, is the source of genuine concern over the apparent decline of the Protestant Ethic. Such a decline, however, may be one of the unintended consequences of our pursuit of affluence. What, for instance, did the credit card do to thrift and delayed gratification? What has the commercial pursuit of hedonism done to those transcendental intangibles which have historically been the cohesive element in our institutions of family, education, and church? What have advertising pressures done to make the seven deadly sins of a bygone age become propelling forces of our modern consumer economy?

---

10. See P. Drucker, *Management: Tasks, Responsibilities, Practices,* p. 40 (1974).

11. See M. Friedman, *Capitalism and Freedom* (1962).

12. See R. Heilbroner, *Business Civilization in Decline,* p. 20 (1976).

13. See G. Lodge, *The New American Ideology,* pp. 163–97 (1975).

14. Heilbroner, "Second Thoughts on The Human Prospect," 18 Challenge, May–June 1975, at 21, 26.

15. Harris, "Harris Survey," Washington Post, May 17, 1977, at p. D8.

If our traditional values have indeed declined, it has resulted, in part, from a distortion of the business method—a distortion which tends to hold technical efficiency and financial profit as life's primary measurement and reward, and to define progress and culture in econometric and commercial terms.

There are inevitable long-term effects on corporations of the fundamental quest for different values and the concomitant search for new levels of self-determination. Lodge's perception of the change in individualism is borne out in our corporate economic arrangements, where community ownership has been replacing individual ownership for decades. Berle and Means long ago highlighted the initial move away from the traditional concept of private property—the move to a "managerial capitalism."[16] The latest chapter in this trend was chronicled by Peter Drucker, who tells us that it is the American worker, through pension funds and other means of institutional investment, who now owns over one-third of the equity capital of American business, a control which will increase to two-thirds of equity capital before the turn of the century.[17]

Heilbroner's view of materialism also affects corporations. One major consumer-oriented firm recently published a forecast for the coming decade which predicts that "for society as a whole, materialism will become a weaker motivator."[18] Louis Harris reports that "in the late 1970s non-material values have become dominant to Americans,"[19] while Nelson Foote suggests that emerging aspirations of consumers "have successively reoriented them from seeking more to seeking better to seeking different to seeking less."[20] Others have predicted the rise of an anti-industrialism movement which will seek a role in deciding what goods and services will be made available to whom.[21] If such impulses are translated into reduced consumer purchases, it will have a profound impact on jobs, income, and the structure of our economy.

Tentative evidence suggests that value changes are beginning to affect work habits as well. Personnel officers are reporting a decline in employees' readiness to accept overtime or weekend work, even at double pay.[22]

---

16. See A. Berle & G. Means, *The Modern Corporation and Private Property* (1932).

17. P. Drucker, *The Unseen Revolution: How Pension Fund Socialism Came to America*, p. 1 (1976).

18. General Telephone & Electronics Corporation, *Towards the year 1990: A Scenario*, p. 23 (Aug. 1977).

19. Wash. Post, Nov. 23, 1978, at p. A19.

20. Foote, "From More to Better to Different to Less," 21 Cal. Management Rev., Fall 1978, at 5.

21. Bloom & Stern, "Emergence of Anti-Industrialism," 19 Bus. Horizons, Oct. 1976, at 87.

22. "How Men Are Changing," Newsweek, Jan. 16, 1978, at p. 53.

Executive recruiters find corporate executives less willing to uproot their families to transfer. One survey finds that the percentage of companies reporting that employees turn down transfers has doubled over the past four years.[23]

These effects are summed up by Daniel Bell, who suggests that the corporation is undergoing a shift from an "economizing" mode to a "sociologizing" mode in which increased numbers of people find the human needs of security, recognition, and new experiences and responses are satisfied.[24] "To think of the business corporation, then, simply as an economic instrument," says Bell, "is to fail totally to understand the meaning of the social changes of the last half century."[25] The more than $208 billion paid by private industry in 1976 for employee benefits beyond wages and salaries certainly supports this proposition.

In short, the corporation has evolved from a private facility under the control of a few people aiming for profit maximization into a "social unit also having, like other basic social entities . . . responsibilities that transcend economics."[26] A new legitimacy for the corporation as a public institution is in fact evolving. This is made manifest not by some neat logic but, as Ackerman and Bauer point out, in terms of "the future relationship of business to [its] constitutencies." The corporation's role, they suggest, is being "determined by the way in which these relationships are worked out."[27] This is evident as one surveys the interaction between the corporation and its stakeholders. Corporate response to consumer complaints, for instance,—horror stories notwithstanding—has never been so great. The awareness of the corporation of its responsibility to the communities in which it operates led IBM, for example, to contribute worldwide over $21 million in 1976 to community causes;[28] or Control Data to build new manufacturing plants in inner-city communities in Minneapolis–St. Paul, and in Washington, D.C.;[29] or Cummins Engine to provide economically disadvantaged employees with personalized training in such basic areas as reading, mathematics, shop skills, and work habits.[30] Thus also Polaroid Corporation has instituted a

---

23. *Id.* at p. 54 (reference to Atlas Van Lines).

24. See Bell, *The Coming of Post-Industrial Society,* pp. 269–98 (1973).

25. *Id.* at p. 295.

26. The American Assembly, *The Ethics of Corporate Conduct,* p. 4 (Report of the 52d American Assembly, April 14–17, 1977).

27. R. Ackerman and R. Bauer, *Corporate Social Responsiveness: The Modern Dilemma,* p. 15 (1976).

28. Kleinfield, "Corporate Charity: Running the Alms Race," N.Y. Times, Jan. 1, 1978, § 4, at p. 12.

29. C. Burger, *The Chief Executive,* p. 18 (1978).

30. "How Can We Employ the Hard-to-Employ?" Speech by Robert C. Holland, President, Committee for Economic Development, before the Detroit Economic Club (Apr. 3, 1978).

hearing procedure for employees who believe themselves to have been wronged by superiors,[31] and New England Telephone operates a hotline for employees who have questions or grievances.[32]

This is not to suggest that corporations are becoming charitable institutions bestowing largesse on the needy. It is to suggest, however, that as John Paluszek says, "Something is stirring in the corporation—in the way it relates to people, be they employees, shareholders, customers, or neighbors in the community or in society generally. In many corporations there is under consideration—and, in some, under development—a new ethic, a new way to do business."[33] New modes of conduct are being developed by corporations in response to the dynamics of social change and the new perspectives such change brings.

Nowhere is this more dramatically exemplified than in the Securities and Exchange Commission's consideration of corporate governance, and in Chairman Williams' proposal that boards of directors and audit and nominating committees be independent outsiders.[34] There is no doubt that the issue of corporate governance was dramatized by revelations of major corporate misdeeds during the Watergate affair. The corporate world was stunned at the ease with which government figures were able to pressure corporate executives for political contributions. Even more startling has been the incapacity of auditing procedures to reveal illegal payments, both at home and abroad. This has led to a fundamental reconsideration of the audit function as well as to public and governmental demands for more complete disclosure.

The basic impulse towards some type of reform of the board system, however, has its rationale in a deeper influence than the revelation of misconduct. Changes in technology and communications, increased global interdependence, and individual awareness and aspirations have all played a part in forcing a reevaluation of the board's function. Although there are legal complexities to the issue, the logic underlying such a reevaluation is simple and irrefutable: an institution that has such a dominant influence on the lives of so many citizens—in terms of jobs generated (directly and indirectly), prices, psychic satisfaction of workers, the environment, and the course of the economy—any institution with such widespread and fundamental effects is for all practical purposes a public institution and as such should be subject to some form of public accountability. And in fact such a trend is well under way.

A recent Business International study, for instance, notes that the United States has done more than any other nation in having outside

---

31. Ewing, "The Corporation as Public Enemy No. 1," Saturday Rev., Jan. 21, 1978, at pp. 12, 16.

32. *Id.* at p. 15.

33. J. Paluszek, *Will the Corporation Survive?* p. 4 (1977).

34. "The SEC: Going Too Far Too Fast?" Bus. Week, Nov. 27, 1978, at p. 86.

directors serve on corporate boards.[35] On average the present ratio of outside to inside directors of major U.S. companies is 2 to 1, with the exception of the oil and steel industries.[36] A recent Conference Board survey finds that in 1976 83 percent of the 300 companies surveyed had a majority of outside directors.[37] In the brokerage business all firms listed on the New York Stock Exchange were required by the SEC to have an audit committee composed entirely of outside directors by June 1978,[38] and the Business Roundtable recommends that all audit and compensation committees be composed entirely of nonmanagement directors.[39] A study further shows that women now serve on 28 percent of manufacturing company boards and on 41 percent of the boards of nonmanufacturing companies; black directors serve on 17 percent of manufacturing company boards and on 32 percent of nonmanufacturing company boards.[40]

The issue of control of corporate decision-making nonetheless will be a central political issue for the foreseeable future—simply because the evolutionary impulse in many areas of life is to move from representation to participation. This inevitably means more involvement of employees in decision-making, greater participation by stockholders in selection of directors, and greater participation of both the public and government in areas which affect the public welfare. Whether these developments will carry America to the point of Sweden's Democracy at Work Act, which gives Swedish labor a significant voice in all corporate decisions,[41] depends in part on how American executives respond to the participatory trend reshaping American institutions. The need is to make required adjustments without upsetting the balance of "the superior economic achievement of our private enterprise system and our unequalled political and personal freedom . . . ."[42]

Equally important to the legitimacy and purpose of an institution as its responsiveness to the external society is the question of internal authority: Who commands? A primary characteristic of the modern

---

35. See Business International, *New Trends in Directorships and Corporate Governance* (Dec. 1977).

36. *Id.* at p. 26.

37. The Conference Board, *The Board of Directors: Perspectives and Practices in Nine Countries* (1977).

38. Crittenden, "World's Companies Changed by Moves For Accountability," N.Y. Times, Jan. 4, 1978, at p. D7.

39. The Business Roundtable, "The Role and Composition of the Board of Directors of the Large Publicly Owned Corporation," 20 (Jan. 1978).

40. The Conference Board, *supra* note 32, at 85.

41. Business International, *supra* note 35, at p. 10.

42. Harold M. Williams, Speech on "Corporate Accountability," Fifth Annual Securities Regulation Institute (Jan. 18, 1978).

search for a new legitimacy is a reformulation of authority. When one looks at trade unions, families, universities, even the military, it is evident that the age-old mode of hierarchical authority is yielding to new forms. Nowhere is this fragmented authority more evident than in the political arena, where public interest groups have usurped much of the political authority of our traditional governmental institutions.

Equally evident is the changing character of authority within the corporation. The popular picture of the corporate state portrays the poor disenfranchised worker as a faceless digit in a massive computerized process. This view was perhaps valid during the period when Frederick Taylor's view reigned supreme: "In the past the man has been first; in the future the system must be first.[43] Taylor's methods of scientific management were developed during the height of Cartesian scientific rationalism as applied to the industrial process. It was called "functional rationalism" and was the underlying rationale of Alfred Sloan in the development of General Motors.[44]

But if we recall Toynbee's definition of growth as progress towards self-determination, we recognize that there is a definite trend in the American corporation towards the dispersal of authority, a tendency to be less "like the Prussian Army and more like a collection of colleagues,"[45] as Carl Madden describes it. Far from being simply a faceless digit, the employee is slowly becoming more of a participant in shaping the course of the corporation than at any point in the past century. According to Ted Mills, director of the American Center for the Quality of Work Life, there is a spreading notion in corporations that "the best work organization for all, employees and employer alike . . . is a structure in which individualism, liberty, life space, and dignity of every employee—from worker to senior manager—become critically important concerns and goals of the total organization."[46] This is a notion, Mills suggests, "which postulates that untapped, dormant and latent in our work organization lie major reserves of now-educated employee expertise, which if tapped through new decision-making decentralization could and would arrest the decline of productivity of American work organizations."[47]

Mills cites General Motors as one corporation which has "reversed its basic management practice"[48] and put "primary management emphasis

---

43. F. Taylor, quoted in Lodge, "Managerial Implications of Ideological Change," in *The Ethics of Corporate Conduct,* p. 79, at p. 88 (C. Walton ed. 1977).

44. See D. Bell, *supra* note 24, at p. 276.

45. Madden, "Richer Lives: Outlook for Americans Beyond '77," 81 U.S. News & World Rep., Jan. 3, 1977, at pp. 84–86.

46. Mills, "Europe's Industrial Democracy: An American Response," Harv. Bus. Rev., Nov.–Dec. 1978 at p. 150.

47. *Id.*

48. *Id.* at 151.

on human growth and dignity at work with an assumption that the secondary payoffs, or necessarily following results, is improved profitability, which is the organization's basic end."[49]

This practice was borne out with the GM plant in North Tarrytown, New York. Ten years ago this plant was a cauldron of union-management hostility, absenteeism, and consumer grievances. Through a series of steps that started with assembly-line employees helping to plan new work areas, employee involvement in plant decisions has substantially increased and employee morale is reportedly at an all-time high. And there has not been a strike or work stoppage in many years.[50]

A redefinition or sharing of authority is, of course, the whole basis of the Scanlon Plan,[52] of the concept of interlocking work teams, and of various other forms of employee participation which are in place throughout industry.The concept of matrix management which pushes decision-making down to more people and puts a premium on teamwork is but the latest example of the trend towards dispersed authority. David Ewing of the *Harvard Business Review* notes that in many companies "there is a growing rejection of the chain of command, a feeling that this age-old device of leadership is too military and, for all the comfort it gives the corporate poo-bahs, too likely to insulate them."[53] Ewing goes on to report "a new kind of innovation in industry—an innovation in the rights of a consitutional nature . . ." Ewing has in mind the renunciation of the traditional prerogative of corporations to suppress criticism and whistle blowing by firing employees who speak out. Several leading companies, such as General Electric, Dow Chemical, IBM, and American Airlines, have established communication mechanisms which allow an employee to remain anonymous while challenging management decisions and practices.[53] The National Center for Productivity and the Quality of Working Life recently published a study of 180 worker-management committees in such firms as U.S. Steel, TRW, and General Foods which deal with such issues as work methods, waste reduction, productivity, energy conservation, education and training, and health and safety.[54]

McCormick & Co., the specialty food company, is another organization that has successfully experimented with new structures of

---

49. *Id.* at 151.

50. Work in America Institute, Inc., 2 World of Work Report No. 12, at 133 (Dec. 1977).

51. See "Participative Management at Work," 55 Harv. Bus. Rev., Jan.–Feb. 1977, at 117, 126.

52. Ewing, *supra* note 31, at 15.

53. *Id.*

54. Batt and Weinberg, "Labor-Management Cooperation Today," 56 Harv. Bus. Rev., Jan.–Feb. 1978, at 96, 97.

decision-making. McCormick has developed "multiple management boards" which consist of supervisors and middle management of the various units.[55] These boards are elected by their peers and they make policy recommendations to the board of directors on substantive matters such as setting production goals, entering new markets, producing a particular product, or developing new employee benefits.

Although such new modes of operation so far only obtain in a small fraction of industry, it is fair to say that knowledge and competence are increasing in importance as the real basis of authority.

While corporations continue to internalize the process of growth they must adjust to the effects of the phenomenal external social and economic growth that has occurred, especially since 1950. Consider these examples:

— This year our economy passed the $2-trillion mark, double what it was seven years ago and four times the size of the economy when John Kennedy was elected President.[56] This constitutes an output approaching $10,000 for every American.
— In the U.S., even with a relatively stable population growth, the equivalent of a town of about 400,000 inhabitants is constructed every eight weeks.[57]
— In the past twenty-six years we Americans have consumed more raw materials than were consumed by the whole of mankind in all previous history prior to 1950.
— In 1903, when Henry Ford launched his enterprise, the Ford Motor Company had an authorized capital of $150,000. It employed 125 men. In 1976 Ford had assets of over $15 billion and employed nearly 450,000 people.[58]

One of the consequences of our gigantic growth is that the large corporation has become a uniquely integral component of our total economic system. Subsystems of finance, production, marketing, transportation, research, education, and communication combine to form what Eugene Loebl describes as a "single, incredibly complex and integrated system, which acts as one giant transformer [of natural resources to finished goods]."[59] Or as Jack Burnham has illustrated, "When we buy an automobile we no longer buy an object in the old sense of the word, but instead we purchase a three-to-five year lease for participation in the state-recognized private transportation system, a

---

55. C. Burger, *The Chief Executive*, p. 22 (1978).

56. See N.Y. Times, Jan. 8, 1978, § 12, at p. 1.

57. See Wellesley-Miller, "Towards a Symbiotic Architecture," in *Earth's Answer*, p. 79, pp. 79–80 (M. Katz, W. Marsh, and G. Thompson eds. 1977).

58. See A. Nevins, *Ford, The Times, The Man, The Company* (1954) and Fortune, May 1977, at p. 366–67.

59. E. Loebl, *Humanomics*, p. 26 (1976).

highway system, a traffic safety system, an industrial parts-replacement system, a costly insurance system . . . ."[60] An interesting political sidelight of Loebl's "integrated system" is that the historic economic question of ownership of the means of production as the decisive economic factor has been replaced by the presence of applied science as the decisive factor in the creation of wealth. This is recognized even in Russia where, according to Cyril E. Black, there is a "change in emphasis from the literal view of Marxism-Leninism that predominated in the Stalin era to a new and dynamic appreciation of the role of science and technology as the critical factor in economic and social development."[61]

The creation of such an integrated economic system means that economic problems cannot be dealt with in discrete parts but must now be seen as part of whole systems. We no longer talk about unemployment, for instance, solely in terms of jobs but must consider transportation systems, educational facilities, government spending patterns, housing patterns, crime prevention, and much more.

Nor has integration of our economic system stopped at the United States borders. With the relatively free international movement of technology, capital, goods, and services, the United States and other national economies now constitute one interlocking global system. U.S. corporations have played a primary role in this process, fostering world economic development and international trade and investment. Indeed, *Forbes* has identified "the multinationalization of industry" as the greatest single fact of world commerce in the late sixties.[62] Today many American companies are world corporations—with General Electric deriving one-fourth of its revenues from foreign operations, Xerox almost two-fifths, and Exxon almost two-thirds.[63]

The phenomenon of an integrated world economy has been even more evident since the oil crisis. The problems that define the economic environment of U.S. corporations are global in character:

- Third-world industrial capacity is growing at a rate which increasingly threatens Western industry.
- A $30-billion trade deficit continues to depress the dollar in world financial markets.
- Protectionism increases, raising the spectre of an all-out trade war.
- Mounting debt in the Eastern bloc countries raises questions as to their continued ability to pay for more Western goods.

---

60. L. Burnham, *Beyond Modern Sculpture* (1968), quoted in D. Bell, *supra* note 24, at p. 285.

61. Black, "New Soviet Thinking," N.Y. Times, Nov. 24, 1978, at p. 27.

62. "Sixty Years of American Business," Forbes, Sept. 15, 1977, at p. 90.

63. *Id.*

- Uneven growth rates among countries of the Organization for Economic Cooperation and Development make unified approaches to common economic interests difficult.

Furthermore, there may be limitations in resources and in environmental tolerance that will restrict the future rate of world expansion more than in the past. Adapting to this changing world economic situation poses several significant challenges for U.S. corporations.

First, private enterprise growth in the future may depend more heavily upon capturing a larger share of the market than upon overall market growth. Coupled with the increased international production of manufactured goods, slower economic growth implies intensified competition in domestic and international markets.

Second, the prospect of slower growth also suggests that national expectations generated by the exponential growth of the postwar period may not be met by available resources. Furthermore, U.S. corporations are likely to act as lightning rods in the future as they inevitably attract the tensions of interest groups with competing claims on output. The involvement of U.S. corporations in such issues as environmental protection, consumerism, and minority rights may inexorably increase and, as Neil Jacoby has suggested, "[t]he clamor for deeper governmental intervention into the internal affairs of business will continue. . . ."[64]

Finally, international frictions that already exist may also be exacerbated. The commonality of world economic problems may serve to circumscribe unilateral government action. Advanced nations, already struggling to preserve their sovereignty in a world of growing interdependence, may desire more effective national oversight of multinational corporations (MNC's) and act to strengthen national controls. In much the same vein, the less developed nations, struggling with rising population and food and energy shortages, may further press the MNC's to assume a larger social responsibility for establishing a new and just international economic order.

One factor contributing to the ambiguous social role of U.S. corporations is the lack of effective international institutions to deal with worldwide economic problems. The need, as Daniel Bell portrayed it, is "to design effective international instruments—in the monetary, commodity, trade, and technological areas—to effect the necessary transitions to a new international division of labor that can provide for economic and, perhaps, political stability."[65] Interestingly, a Delphi panel (whose members came from academia, industry, and government) believe that several supranational groups are likely to be formed in the coming years, such as oil consumer organizations, a world food bank,

---

64. Jacoby, "Six Challenges to Business Management," 19 Bus. Horizons, Aug. 1976, at 29, 30.

65. Bell, "The Future World Disorder: The Structural Context of Crises," Foreign Policy No. 27, Summer 1977, at 109, 134.

and ocean resources management organizations.[66] Whether such developments would serve to clarify the public responsibilities of corporations is not clear. One thing, however, is certain: to adapt to changing international economic conditions and restructure international economic relationships and institutions we will require a more explicit and open interchange among all the segments of our society.

THE CORPORATION, GOVERNMENT, AND PUBLIC POLICY

It is against the background of the preceding discussion that the relationship between large corporations and government in developing public policy can best be viewed. This relationship is continually evolving.

During the first sixty years of the republic, government was primarily a support for business expansion. Economic development required a base and infrastructure, and government taxation, education, and transportation policies were tailored to meet this need.

As corporations began to develop during the last quarter of the nineteenth century, government began regulating the conditions of the competitive process within the market. Such regulation was frequently aimed at promoting an industry that was of special concern to the public. This practice lives on in the form of the independent regulatory agencies.

With advent of the New Deal and, later, passage of the Full Employment Act of 1946,[67] government, through its fiscal policy and taxation powers, became committed to maintaining an acceptable level of economic growth and activity.

Since the 1950's at least two developments suggest we have entered a new phase of the business-government relationship. Over the past three decades the corporation has become one of the primary instruments by which government economic, social, and foreign policies are executed. In the area of foreign affairs, for instance, seven presidents for some thirty years have pursued policies which relied heavily on the involvement of thousands of corporations. This pattern has constituted the basis of America's strategic capacity during one of the most volatile and unstable periods of world history.

Government economic and social policies have generated many efforts since the early 1960's to use the corporation to fight urban decline, create job opportunities, enhance individual skills, attain social equality, and generally encourage expansion. Since passage in 1974 of the Employees Retirement Security Act[68] the corporation, through pension plans, has become a principal instrument of income security for America's retired workers.

---

66. See O'Toole & The University of Southern California Center for Future Research, *Energy and Social Change*, pp. 38, 68 (1976).

67. 15 U.S.C. § 1021 (1946).

68. Pub. L. No. 93-406, 88 Stat. 829 (1974).

Critics, of course, have warned of the dangers inherent in the development of the business-government relationship. John Kenneth Galbraith has persuasively analyzed the self-serving aspects of cooperation between "the planning system" and the "public bureaucracy," and he urges that government "be broken free from the control of the planning system."[69] Yet Peter Drucker sees this new phase as an era of the "mixed society" in which government is "a policy maker, a vision maker, a goal setter," while corporations and other nongovernmental institutions "carry out the doing work of needed programs."[70] Thus it would seem that use of the corporation as an instrument of government policies is here to stay and can only increase with time.

The other aspect of this relationship is the government's role in ensuring corporations' accountability as public institutions. In the past 15 years 150 major pieces of legislation have been enacted by Congress regulating or restricting business activities as they relate to various corporate constituencies. An industry such as the steel industry is subject to some 5,000 regulations administered by 27 agencies. A study by the Diebold Group reveals that four out of five major decisions made by large corporations are directly connected with government regulatory bodies at one level or another.[71]

The cost of such regulation is staggering. The Office of Management and Budget reports that government regulation cost the public $130 billion in 1976, involving 80 regulatory agencies or commissions employing over 100,000 people.[72] According to Paul Weaver, EPA alone will have required by the mid-1980's the direct investment of well over $100 billion plus an unknown amount in operating expenses, inflation, and other social costs.[73]

Eli Lilly & Company says that the cost of complying with Federal paperwork alone adds fifty cents to the price of every Lilly prescription.[74] Near-term price increases, as Robert Leone suggests, may result from regulation that changes an industry's cost structure, thus modifying its competitive structure and influencing its cyclical characteristics of performance.[75] And Murray Weidenbaum points out that one hidden cost of federal regulation is a reduced rate of introduction of new

---

69. J. Galbraith, *Economics and the Public Purpose*, p. 242 (1973).

70. P. Drucker, *supra* note 17, at pp. 172, 173.

71. See The Diebold Group, Inc., News of the Professional Practice of the Diebold Group (Summer 1976).

72. N.Y. Times, Dec. 23, 1977, § 3, at p. 7.

73. Weaver, "Regulation, Social Policy, and Class Conflict," 49 Public Interest, Winter 1978, at 45, 53.

74. See N.Y. Times, Jan. 9, 1977, § 3, at p. 15.

75. Leone, "The Real Costs of Regulation," 55 Harv. Bus. Rev., Nov.–Dec. 1977, at 57, 62.

products. Weidenbaum contends that a four-year delay in introducing some drugs has caused America to lose its leadership in medical science.[76]

So there is a solid basis for concern that "[t]he real problem before the country is not whether new standards of social performance for business are necessary. Rather, it is the terrible inefficiency of government attempts to achieve improved business performance."[77] What such a view fails to consider, however, is that much government regulation has been occasioned by the slowness of corporate leaders to respond to the genuine needs of their stakeholders. The Equal Employment Opportunity Commission, for instance, is clearly a legislative reaction to deliberate exclusion from the economic process. The Occupational Safety and Health Administration is a reaction (perhaps an overreaction) to neglect and lack of concern for the individual's working conditions. The Toxic Substance Control Act[78] is a reaction to insensitivity and gross mismanagement. The rapid expansion of federal regulation clearly has arisen, in part, from a lack of consensus within the business community about more constructive ways to achieve social purpose. As *Business Week* notes, "In a system where profit is the measure of performance, business does not respond to the demand for values that cannot be quantified and fed into the market mechanism."[79] Thus, the public uses the political machinery to make the economy respond to a demand which the economy ordinarily would have ignored.

Nevertheless, it is clear that the regulatory situation has become dangerous. Excessive or ill-conceived regulation is eroding productivity just when, with the prospect of slower growth rates and increased foreign competition, enhanced productivity and better management of resources are necessary.

Barry Bosworth, director of the Council on Wage and Price Stability, says that present regulation adds 3/4 of a percent to the annual inflation rate.[80] Willard Butcher, President of Chase Manhattan Bank, suggests that had we taken one half the 1977 $100 billion regulation bill and invested it in productive projects, "we could have created just about 1 million new jobs."[81]

Regulatory reform, of course, has become a staple of every good political speech, and at least three administrations have committed themselves to achieving regulatory reasonableness. The results of the

---

76. Weidenbaum, "Regulation or Over-Regulation," Wall St. J., Apr. 6, 1976, at p. 22.

77. W. Gruber and J. Niles, *The New Management*, p. 198 (1976).

78. Pub. L. No. 94-469 (1976).

79. "Government Intervention," Bus. Week, Apr. 4, 1977, at p. 43.

80. U.S. News & World Rep., Sept. 18, 1978, at p. 27.

81. Bus. Week, Nov. 6, 1978, at p. 22.

CAB in deregulating the airlines—lower air fares and record revenues—are encouraging similar attempts at deregulation of the trucking industry. Perhaps the greatest stimulus for regulatory reasonableness will come from President Carter's anti-inflation program which calls for the formation of a federal Regulatory Council. Comprised of all federal regulatory departments and agencies, the Council will develop a unified calendar of proposed regulations. Such a calendar will facilitate a comprehensive and consistent approach to the evaluation of costs and benefits of proposed regulations.

The regulatory quagmire, however, was not created by one section of society nor will it be eradicated by one section. Federal regulatory legislation is the product of (1) business activities which give rise to the need for order, justice, or restraint, (2) congressional legislation which, in an attempt to bring order, justice, or constraint, mandates all regulation, and (3) regulatory agencies which convert laws into operating rules. Any intelligent remedy to the current regulatory impasse must include both self-examination and self-restraint by all three of these sectors.

Beyond the question of existing regulation stands the issue of national economic planning. Few subjects have aroused deeper passions. Some people view this concept as the death of freedom for America, while others see the absence of such planning as chaos.

However, increasing numbers of people, including members of the business community, see some sort of increased national economic planning as likely. Resource scarcity, endemic inflation, economic externalities, and probable slower growth rates make such planning all but inevitable. As George Cabot Lodge observed, "The American state no longer seems to have any real choice between planning and not planning. It will either choose to plan well and comprehensively, or badly and haphazardly."[82] Or, as Herman Kahn points out, the "important issue is not planning versus chaos but rather who does the planning, at what level, from what perspectives, with what motivation, and how rigidly or flexibly."[83]

The business community by and large does not distinguish between a planned economy as exists in the Socialist countries and economic planning as proposed for America. Few proponents of economic planning would urge the establishment of rigid production targets and prescribed ways to achieve them. Admittedly, some advocates foresee extended government control over wages and prices and, eventually, over dividends and profits as well. But modern industrial economies are far too complex to permit details to be efficiently planned from the top down. Even the more sophisticated socialist economies are moving toward increasing use of market forces. Economic planning for most of its American adherents constitutes the kind of planning that uses government

---

82. G. Lodge, *supra* note 13, at p. 265.

83. H. Kahn, *World Economic Development,* p. 185 (1978).

taxation and spending powers to promote more even regional economic growth, more equitable distribution of income, and more stable international trade. This would simply move us along the road suggested by Keynes in *Democracy and Efficiency*, where he urged "... a system where we can act as an organized community for common purposes, and promote social and economic justice, while respecting and protecting the individual—his freedom of choice, his faith, his mind and its expression, his enterprise and his property."[84]

Three broad categories of consideration—corporations as an extension of government policy, the quality of federal regulation, and the degree and efficiency of economic planning—underline the centrality of the business-government relationship. Perhaps the state needs emancipation from the clutches of the corporate planning system as has been urged; it is certain that private enterprise feels it needs emancipation from the clutches of the state.

It is unlikely that major functional readjustment will be attained, however, in the present climate of antagonism. As Christopher Stone has so suitably observed:[85]

> [W]hat is most evidently missing in our corporate/social relations today, and needs to be restored is a measure of mutual trust and respect. As things stand, we are settling into a self-defeating cycle in which the anti-corporate sentiment is increasingly shrill and ill-informed, and the corporate response is too often self-defensive, unheeding, and unconstructive.

Stone speaks to the heart of the problem: the wide divergence of outlook and purpose between those who represent the corporate planning system on the one hand and the public bureaucracy on the other. This divergence, to some extent, is inherent in the differing roles of business and government. Business is basically innovative, active, and flexible; government is reactive and bureaucratic. Business is concerned with performance which can be measured in finite monetary terms; government addresses less finite issues of equitable solutions and social tradeoffs.

The public bureaucracy tends to be drawn from Irving Kristol's "New Class":[86] the intellectuals and policy professionals who populate government, academia, public interest groups, the press, and research institutes. Their world view has been shaped to a degree by their reaction to what they perceive as American inordinacy: inordinate corporate power, inordinate popular materialism, inordinate consumption of resources, inordinate use of American power overseas, etc. To them, such inordinacy is debasing and insensitive to human suffering and need. The

---

84. Keynes, "Democracy and Efficiency," 17 New Statesman and Nation 121 (1939).

85. Stone, "The Future of the Corporation: Pt. I Controlling Corporate Misconduct," 48 Public Interest, Summer 1977, at 55, 70.

86. See Kristol, "Business and the New Class," Wall St. J., May 19, 1975, at p. 8.

compulsion behind this New Class is the commitment to restraint of the inordinacy of American power and profligacy in all its forms.

The world view of those in the corporate planning system, on the other hand, tends to have been shaped by the traditional American adherence to progress, economic growth, individualism, and the belief that "both human liberty and economic efficiency depend heavily on limiting the power of the state. . . ."[87] They see the mass communications media and academia as claiming the sole right to define the public interest, and they fear the consequences of political factors replacing market factors in America's overall economic arrangements.

These two groups represent fundamental opposites in the American political process, and the consumer, who subsidizes both groups, is caught in the middle. It is a conflict of no small consequence. Neither group will willingly yield on policy. In true Hegelian terms, the thesis of the corporate planning system is confronted by the antithesis of the New Class. The outcome of the current national discussion on regulation and economic planning will determine the synthesis which will constitute America's socioeconomic structure at least until the turn of the centruy. A synthesis that combines social justice and private initiative will require a broad awareness of the forces America confronts in the world and a readiness to seek arrangements that satisfy unprecedented circumstances. To create the climate in which such a synthesis can evolve is surely one of the highest challenges which has faced the leadership of any generation.

The second development which suggests a new phase of the business-government relationship is the evolution of enhanced corporate capacity to evaluate the social impacts of its operations and to resolve any subsequent problems. Different aspects of this capacity have gone by various names: social responsibility, public affairs, corporate action, corporate public policy, etc.

The first sign of corporate awareness of obligations—other than economic ones—emerged in the latter part of the nineteenth century. Such corporate activity emanated from the social concern, and to a degree the Judeo-Christian paternalism, of individual entrepreneurs. Andrew Carnegie's "*Wealth*" in the *North American Review* of 1889 best expressed the underlying philosophy. "The problem of our age," Carnegie began, "is the proper administration of wealth, so that the ties of brotherhood may still bind together the rich and poor in harmonious relationship."[88] To Carnegie the successful businessman should be a trustee of the interests of the community at large.

Corporate social awareness further evolved in the mid-1920's when corporations, because of their increasing size, began to be perceived as social agents as well as economic instruments, and the phrase "social

---

87. The Business Roundtable, *supra* note 34, at p. 1.

88. Carnegie, "Wealth," 148 N. Am. Rev. 653 (1889).

responsibility" was first used. In one of the classic expressions of corporate social purpose, Wallace B. Donham, Dean of the Harvard Business School, wrote in the *Harvard Business Review* of 1927:[89]

> The development, strengthening, and multiplication of socially minded businessmen is the central problem of business. Moreover, it is one of the great problems of civilization, for such men can do more than any other type to rehabilitate the ethical and social forces of the community and to create the background which is essential to a more idealistic working philosophy in the community.

In a prophetic assessment Dean Donham warned:[90]

> Unless more of our business leaders learn to exercise their powers and responsibilities with a definitely increased sense of responsibility toward other groups in the community, unless without great lapse of time there is through the initiative of such men an important socializing of business, our civilization may well head for one of its periods of decline.

Though Donham's convictions were not shared by most of business leadership, a growing sense of social responsibility did begin to pervade the civic awareness of individual managers. The public-affairs profession was developed to assist the corporation in its relationships with its public, and the concept of the corporation as a good citizen took shape. It is significant that the emergence of such social awareness coincided with the rise of mass production and mass consumption which began to transform the life of middle-class America. Conceptually, however, this social responsibility was treated as an appendage to business. It did not share centrality with the concerns of finance, marketing, and production. Its implementation depended on the degree of development of the individual manager's social sensitivity.

The present phase began emerging at the time of the urban unrest of the 1960's and has received further impetus from public concern over the environment, consumer needs, illegal payments, and a host of other issues. The central characteristic of this phase is that social concern is no longer an appendage to corporate activity. It is now central to the whole process of production and distribution. Social concerns no longer depend on the charity of the individual manager but increasingly are on the policy agenda of the chief executive officer.

The conceptual basis of this phase was well defined by Hargreaves and Dauman in *Business Survival and Social Change*. "Any organisation," they point out, "has a responsibility for planning and managing its relationships with all those involved in or affected by its activities, or with those who, in turn, can affect the ability of the organisation to

---

89. Donham, "The Social Significance of Business," 5 Harv. Bus. Rev. 406 (1927).

90. *Id.*

operate effectively and achieve objectives." Essential to this capacity is "the anticipated, planned and managed response of an organization to social and political change."[91]

In the industrial sphere this development is naturally correlated with the growth that has occurred in the scientific sphere. Scientific reductionism is giving way to the concept of holism, or the awareness of the interrelatedness of all things. Further, with technological and social developments moving as rapidly as they are, the management of change, uncertainty, and an evolving future has become a principal function of the modern manager. Such management cannot be accomplished by considering only the discrete parts of the production process. It must include management of the total environment—technological, human, and social—in which the corporation functions.

The formal expression of this development came in a report issued by the Committee for Economic Development (CED). The CED report noted that the terms of the contract between society and business are changing in substantial ways and that the future of business enterprise "will depend on the quality of management's response to changing expectations of the public."[92] The report listed ten major areas where the corporation is responsible for its impacts on society.[93]

Thus, corporate public policy has come of age. Corporate public-policy activities have been outlined in many ways; one of the best outlines is offered by Hargreaves and Dauman.[94] One type of corporate activity, they suggest, should include traditional economic functions—those pursuits which are guided primarily by the dictates of the private market. The fundamental mission of any corporation clearly is to satisfy a customer need and, in doing so, to create wealth by providing jobs for the corporation's workers and an adequate return on investment for its shareholders. In this context profit becomes a measurement of the success of a corporation in fulfilling its mission. Inherent in fulfilling the corporation's economic function is the requirement to adhere to fundamental societal laws and customs in its dealings with customers, employees, suppliers, and investors. This includes an obligation to produce quality products at fair prices.

A second group of activities are described by Hargreaves and Dauman as "organizational responsibilities."[95] The objective of these actions is to increase individual capacity and fulfillment and to minimize the negative impacts of organizational activities. Such actions include the assurance of equal job opportunity and advancement, opti-

---

91. J. Hargreaves and J. Dauman, *Business Survival and Social Change*, p. 21 (1975).

92. Committee for Economic Development, *Social Responsibilities of Business Corporations*, p. 16 (1971).

93. *Id.* at pp. 37–40.

94. See J. Hargreaves and J. Dauman, *supra* note 91, at pp. 15–23.

95. *Id.* at pp. 15–23.

mal working conditions, and new patterns of corporate decision-making. They extend as well to concern for the environment and resources; to adequate consideration of the secondary impacts of products, evolving technology, advertising; and to general compliance with the spirit, rather than just the letter, of the law.

The third category in Hargreaves and Dauman's outline consists of societal responsibilities to contribute to a healthy external environment. This includes contributing towards those political, social, economic, and cultural needs which form the foundations on which the whole of society rests. Corporate philanthropy and participation in regional and economic development are but two examples of such contributions.

As we move from discussion of the outer boundaries of corporate public policy to assignment of responsibility to particular firms, we encounter broader practical and philosophical problems. Who, after all, determines the priority of society's needs or says how the corporation should respond to them?

The genius of America is that we employ a combination of the marketplace and the political process to determine what need or combination of needs deserves preference. Through the political process the public may decide that its common interest requires a cleaner environment, a safer workplace, or more jobs. To meet these objectives the public, through government, develops incentives and constraints.

Through the marketplace businessmen can implement their own individual judgments regarding public needs and what may legitimately be required from them. For any given company, therefore, public policy will be defined in part by government legislation and in part by the collective judgments of each of the corporation's participants.

Take for instance what might be described as corporate environmental ethics. Corporations must adhere to mumerous laws protecting the environment. A company could comply with the letter of environmental laws, thus assuming what might be described as a conservative stance. But a company could also take a progressive stance by going beyond the letter of the law to take a lead in implementing the underlying intent and spirit of environmental legislation. The heart of such a progressive stance would be a commitment to environmental quality through voluntary action. It might include adoption as an integral part of a corporate research and development program of a system of environmental or technological assessments of the impact of new products and production technologies on the community. It could mean promulgating an environmental code of ethics which goes beyond the narrow limits of the law.

The starting point for a corporation's public-policy initiative is top management's decision to act, to take the lead. Much pain and expense would be avoided if the public interest were to be consulted at the conception of a manufacturing process rather than, as so frequently happens, after problems have been thrust on management by accumulated public resentments.

Having decided to address public-policy concerns, the corporation must next commit staff and financial resources to the professional implementation of clearly defined objectives. To achieve this end, approximately six hundred companies currently direct some form of public-affairs program. Such programs range from crude image-building efforts to serious and effective attempts that anticipate the emergence of critical social and economic issues and formulate public-policy alternatives. Some of the larger corporations have established sophisticated mechanisms to track and manage the various stages of development of up to two hundred public-policy issues. The *Harvard Business Review* recently published a list of thirty-five major corporations which have public-policy or public-responsibility committees at the board level.[96] A company like Cummins Engine has a corporate action division, while the Bank of America maintains a social policy department directed by a senior vice-president. The Sun Company has established an Environmental Assessment group consisting of Sun's chief economist, a specialist in technological assessment, and a public-issues consultant—all reporting to the vice-president for Environmental Assessment. Other corporations are establishing periodic public-and social-policy objectives as an integral part of their long-range economic and growth goals. Such objectives are usually related to the economic functions of the company or to the particular problems of its residential communities. Thus Xerox Corporation provides employees one year's paid leave to engage in any socially significant activity of their own choosing,[97] and IBM lends experienced executives to municipalities to help solve problems, or to universities to teach for a year.[98] Thus also some 200 health and life insurance companies contributed over $35 million in 1977 to education, federated drives, urban and civic organizations, and to health, safety, and cultural projects. These same insurance companies contributed over 290,061 man-hours of employee service for volunteer work and community services.[99]

Such examples, however, are exceptions rather than the norm. The majority of major corporations in America are still unorganized to respond adequately to public-policy concerns.

The charge heard from some corporate executives that discharge of public-policy responsibilities reduces profits and antagonizes stockholders has thus far had little substantiation. Studies comparing economic performance and discharge of public-policy responsibilities lead to the conclusion that "there is evidence that, in general, the respon-

---

96. "Public Responsibility Committees of the Board," 55 Harv. Bus. Rev., May-June 1977, at 40, 60.

97. *The Handbook of Corporate Social Responsibility*, p. 229 (Human Resources Network 2d ed. 1975).

98. *Id.* at p. 221.

99. *1978 Social Report of the Life and Health Insurance Business.* Clearinghouse on Corporate Social Responsibility, Washington, D.C.

sively managed firm will enjoy better economic performance.[100] While undertaking public policy responsibilities is not a causal factor in better economic performance, it "is a signal of the presence of a style of management that extends broadly across the entire business function and leads to more profitable operation.[101] It is an indication of a forward-looking posture in dealing with a multivectored changing environment.

CONCLUSION

We have discussed a few of the responses of large corporations to the new social environment in which they operate. We have considered some—and only some—of the issues corporations are facing. We have talked of these issues in general terms and we have not offered definitive prescriptions.

A further question remains.

New stages of growth require new definitions of human or institutional relationships. One requirement of the internalization of growth is a greater consensus about the ultimate ends of social policy. When growth is predominantly external, growth itself is the primary purpose, and the public discussion focuses on the means or character of growth. When growth becomes internalized, it ceases to be the primary end by itself. Thus, a new consideration of what constitutes the desired ends of socila policy is required.

Yet one of the primary characteristics of the present-day social environment is the absence of any widely shared definition of the public good. While we confront common problems of unprecedented proportions, there is no commonly held social philosophy underpinning our approach to these problems. Since we have not defined the common good, since we have not agreed upon our mutual interests, we tend to concentrate on personal or sectional agendas.

Nor are our traditional political philosophies giving satisfactory aid and support. Conservatism suggests that our present social disarray is caused by a retreat from ultimate truths. While there is a growing fiscal conservatism in the country, conservatism itself appears to lack an informing philosophy or vision for the future.

Traditional liberalism seems unable to hold a cohesive conviction in the face of increasing political demands and cultural disintegration. Liberalism can only succeed where there is a measure of self-restraint, and the temper of the times, both culturally and politically, is towards unfettered self-expression and gain.

---

100. Sturdivant and Ginter, "Corporate Social Responsiveness," Cal. Management Rev., Spring 1977, at 38.

101. Bowman and Haire, "Strategic Posture Toward Corporate Social Responsibility," Cal. Management Rev., Winter 1975, at 49, 54.

Two of the most obvious results of this circumstance are the accelerating disinclination of the public to participate in the electoral process and the rise of organized sectional interest groups which have stepped in to pick up the slack left by political parties which have lost ideologocal clarity.

Clear political definition may be a problem for the political parties. A concept of the public good, however, is a problem for us all. For when there is no concept of the public good, no public philosophy which commands the adherence of a substantial portion of our people, then social arrangements disintegrate into a power struggle for material resources, and the idea of nationhood is tragically undercut.

Some in the corporate world claim it is the responsibility of the total society to define public philosophy. The majority of Americans, however, would agree with Clarence Walton, who expressed what one hopes is a growing business view in suggesting that "greater economic power is paralleled by greater moral responsibility."[102]

A renewed public philosophy might start with a fresh expression of the basic elements embodied in the heritage of Western experience. For regardless of the changes taking place, the future must be built on the best of the past. Such an expression should address the fundamental issues of the individual: his rights, responsibilities, and relationship to the community and the state. It should consider the rise of giant institutions and the relationship of these institutions to both government and the individual. It should further consider what ethical values must be commonly accepted if we are to advance towards more harmonious associations.

A renewed public philosophy must address the questions of a new balance between equality and liberty, private fulfillment and public need, equity and efficiency. Such an articulation would suggest "how to find common purposes, yet retain individual means of fulfilling them; and how to define individual (and group) needs and find common means of meeting them."[103] Above all, a new public philosophy must consider the evolutionary changes occurring worldwide; what America's world role should be in light of such developments; and what the government-business relationship ought to be in order to achieve new long-term goals.

Critics of corporate America might argue that to expect American business to attempt the expression of such a public philosophy is the triumph of hope over experience. Possibly. But to expect resolution of the seemingly intractable problems facing America in the next decades without a broad-based commitment to what the late Clinton Rossitor termed "the enduring interests of the whole community"[104] is a fatal

---

102. Walton, "Overview," in *The Ethics of Corporate Conduct*, p. 1, at p. 7 (C. Walton ed. 1977).

103. D. Bell, *The Cultural Contradiction of Capitalism*, p. 279 (1976).

104. C. Rossitor, *1787: The Grand Convention*, p. 69 (1966).

illusion. The delay and difficulty of formulating a national energy policy and in resolving the 1978 coal strike highlight only too painfully this point.

For decades American business has been on the leading edge of social advance. It has generated a wealth which, when taken as a whole, has satisfied the basic material needs of its people. When one views the centuries-old struggle of mankind for sufficiency, this achievement is one of history's greastest triumphs. It is now time for American business, building on this record of achievement, to exert even greater leadership—to articulate for America a new public philosophy as the foundation for the public-private enterprise of the future.

ANOTHER VIEW

Richard W. Duesenberg, *Vice-President, General Counsel and Secretary, Monsanto Company*

Large corporations are inviting targets for the strong, sometimes strident, antibusiness environment of the twilight years of the twentieth century. In his essay "Corporate Response to a New Environment,"[1] Wm. Van Dusen Wishard gives provocative and eloquently expressed views on the consequences likely to flow from the accusations and allegations that make up this current atmosphere.

The pages which follow are another perspective of the same phenomenon.[2] They are written with an attitude conditioned not so much by a career lived predominantly on the inside of a major corporation, as by a philosophy which, in the Lockean tradition, holds power suspect and evaluates political and other social action against an historical perspective conditioned by history's never-ending account of the malignancy of unrestrained authority.

The elevation of the individual spawned by eighteenth century English political theorists and played out by American political democracy is by all accounts the noblest of human experiments. But fate seems to have written a tragic counterplot: the creation of the welfare state. As centralized planning spreads its authoritarian control over more and more facets of human action, it is not surprising that the corporate entity should come under attack. Capitalism and liberty are closely, if not inseparably, connected.[3] With the emergence of the corporate form

1. Wishard, "Corporate Response to a New Environment," pp. 325–50 in this volume.
2. The writer hastens to add that the views expressed are his own, and not necessarily those of the corporation which employs him, its management, or his colleagues. Any attribution of his views to the corporation for which he is counsel is simply wrong.
3. See G. Dietze, *In Defense of Property* (1963).

as the paramount economic organization of the capitalist system, it is natural for its critics to take aim at this institution.

THE CORPORATION AND INDIVIDUALISM

A lament of a jurist over a century ago was that a corporation "has no pants to kick or soul to damn, and, by God, it ought to have both."[4] This earthy expression acknowledges a basic fact about the corporate form. No one has ever seen one or touched one. It is "invisible, intangible, and existing only in contemplation of law."[5] Of itself, it can do absolutely nothing, being incapable of either benefiting or injuring anyone or anything. Whatever it does can only happen by the participation of individuals, singly or in concert one with another.[6]

This fact would seem to be conveniently ignored by many contemporary critics of corporate America. A reading of much of what is allegedly wrong with corporations would leave one with the impression that corporations are beings, each with a volition of its own, created and let loose on society to do its own thing. Corporations pollute, corporations produce unsafe products, corporations ignore the humane aspirations of the humans that they employ. They also meet with each other to conspire to monopolize trades, to set prices illegally, and to establish national policy for everything from waging war to hoarding wealth to keep it from trickling to the masses. With all these ills laid at the doorsteps of corporations, there can be little wonder that the question is currently asked: Can the corporation survive?

Corporations, of course, do none of these things of which they are accused. Whatever is right or wrong in a corporation, and whatever it may rightly or wrongly be criticized for, is right or wrong in the actions of people who manage and carry out their collective economic purposes through this legal form. "Business," "corporation"—these are abstractions. Neither has any responsibility. Neither has any goal. People have

---

4. M. Ernst and A. Lindey, *Hold Your Tongue!* p. 259 (1932) attributes this description to an unnamed but "irascible" Western judge.

5. Chief Justice John Marshall in Trustees of Dartmouth College v. Woodward, 4 Wheat. 518, 636 (1819).

6. Bayless Manning, in his superb essay, "Thinking Straight about Corporate Law Reform," p. 11 in this volume, puts it well:

> A corporation is an organizational form. It is a particular legal way of organizing an ongoing operation, as a partnership is a particular legal way of doing so. . . . From being told that an object is a cube, one can infer nothing about its size, weight, color, smell, or value; from being told that an enterprise is a corporation one can infer nothing about its scale, character, bargaining power, strategic importance, functioning, or value. Thus, to inveigh against or applaud 'corporations' without specifying particular enterprises, or at a minimum a class of enterprises sharing common substantive attributes, is simply to make noise.

responsibilities. People have goals. When talking about "corporate social responsibility," what is referred to is the personal and collective responsibilities of the individuals who have pooled their resources for the pursuit of a business purpose. Critics who declare what the social responsibilities of corporations should be are prescribing for others their social responsibilities. Keeping this in mind can be helpful to the current struggle, for it brings into sharper focus who the real participants are. Knowing that the enemy could be a friend might reduce the level of belligerency and polemics.

But it can also be helpful for another and much more important reason. Recognizing that a corporation is an abstraction, evidenced at best by a piece of paper—called the charter—issued by a state official, helps to quicken its identification as a voluntary association of individuals joined for particular purposes. Group action is a natural response to the accomplishment of tasks and the attainment of objectives which are too difficult for solitary effort. It is obvious that most of what is considered materially beneficial and desirable would be unavailable without concerted effort and concentrated capital. But as group action the endeavor is no less private; nor do its assets thereby become public property.

Often unexpressed but yet a major assumption of corporate critics is that corporations as economic institutions evidence a shift in the "traditional concepts" of private property. It is assumed that if ownership is divided among many holders, what was previously private ownership is thereby translated to something variously denominated "communitarianism" or "managerial capitalism."[7] Usually the transmutation is reserved for only large, widely held corporations.[8] In any case, the words *private*, and even *property*, are lost, making the leap to public ownership a disingenuous intellectual tour de force. Nowhere has this been more aggressively advanced than in a recent speech by the current chairman of the Securities and Exchange Commission:

---

7. See Wishard, *supra* note 1, at p. 328.

8. It is incongruous to base this selection on the fact of public ownership, if the concerns of scarcity, environment, widespread need, and other factors are the proffered justification for imposing a "public interest" standard on ownership. A large corporation that is closely held has the same relationship to society's need for its services or products as does a widely held corporation. If being widely held creates a need for protection of those members of the public who exercise their private interests by investing in the enterprise, that need can be satisfied by libertarian principles which justify government action to prevent fraud. To take the step of calling such corporations public property because of widely dispersed private investors is a non sequitur. Rather, it reflects a different perception of the legitimate role of government. In simple terms, the phrase "public interest" or "public property" as used here represents an intellectual crutch for the exercise of power against those who disagree with an idea advanced by the one seeking government coercion.

> The fact of the breadth of the corporation's constituency is almost universally recognized today, but the consequences are seldom perceived. What I believe this expanded constituency *necessarily* means is that the large corporation *has ceased to be private property*—even though theoretically still owned by its shareholders—and has become, in essence, a quasi-public institution. As a society, we depend on private enterprise to serve as the instrument through which to accomplish a wide variety of goals—full employment, equal economic opportunity, environmental protection, energy independence, and others. When viewed in light of these social implications, corporations must be seen as, to a degree, more than purely private institutions, and corporate profits as not entirely an end in themselves, but also as one of the resources which corporations require in order to discharge their responsibilities. And, to the extent that business is perceived as failing to discharge those responsibilities, the argument is strengthened, not only for federal corporate governance legislation, but for federal taxation to transfer profits to the common weal.[9]

How profoundly ominous are the implications of this extract for a society under limited government. It reasons, essentially, that private individuals, by pooling their private property, lose it by the sheer weight of their numbers. From there, all other steps toward expropriation follow. If their joint activities are profitable, which presumably means they are successful, the profits belong to society, for by having become public property, there are no returns to which a claim of ownership can attach. The concept of ownership is vanquished, and with it all who aspire to its rewards. What returns to the "owners" is what is allowed them by government. With this view of corporate ownership, no limits constrict or restrain actions which government is empowered to take in the regulation and control of institutions created by private individuals to pursue privately chosen ends. The legitimacy of government then transcends the function of protecting the rights of one person or group from infringement by others; it goes ultimately to the extreme of being at war with the interests of society.[10]

---

9. Address of Harold M. Williams, Chairman, Securities and Exchange Commission, to the Fifth Annual Securities Regulation Institute, San Diego, California, Jan. 18, 1978.

10. The theory of unlimited legitimacy of government is not new, of course. Indeed, it probably is the oldest political concept known, though embraced by theorists to our own day. Hans Kelsen, the German jurisprudent so influential in Hitlerian Germany, developed the theme that a wrong of the state must under all circumstances be a contradiction in terms. See generally H. Kelsen, *General Theory of Law and State* (1945). It collides head-on, however, with the concept of a constitutional government, so fundamental to the American legal experiment. A fateful turn in that system evolved with the decision in Munn v. Illinois, 94 U.S. 113 (1876), predecessor to a long line of cases constructing a concept of being affected with a public interest. That case and its progeny, however, stand far off from the proposition that enterprises "affected with a public interest" are public property.

The battle line forming in the struggle over corporate governance is, in a very real way, one between the forces of individualism in the Hayekian sense[11] and collectivism in the central planning sense. In a recent article, Hayek argued that

> the very complexity which the structure of modern economic systems has assumed provides the strongest argument against central planning. It is becoming progressively less and less imaginable that any one mind or planning authority could picture or survey the millions of connections between the ever more numerous interlocking separate activities which have become indispensable for the efficient use of modern technology and even the maintenance of the standard of life Western man has achieved.[12]

In no manner is this a thesis for government nonaction. Rather, it sees its role as one fostering the fullest opportunities for human expression through the protection of private spheres of action. The antithesis between this orientation toward the legitimacy of government action and that expressed in the quotation above is sharp indeed.

To the extent that the critics of corporate America achieve their objectives by persuasion of others to modify their privately determined aims and conduct, they engage, of course, in a process consistent with traditional libertarian principles. But when these objectives are mandated through legislation which substitutes itself for the spontaneous interplay of private actions, an intrusion on liberty results. As philosophers have repeatedly warned, "be well assured that everything will then dwindle by degrees."[13]

In the final analysis corporations are nothing more than structures by which certain actions and objectives of individuals are carried out and achieved. Historically, these have aimed at the creation of wealth through individual investment to create production and employment.[14]

---

11. Individualism and freedom are nearly synonymous in Hayek's works. His preference for individualism over collectivism has always been impressive, particularly in view of the experiences of the twentieth century:

> The main merit of . . . individualism . . . is that it is a system under which bad men can do least harm. It is a social system which does not depend for its functioning on our finding good men for running it, or on all men becoming better than they now are, but which makes use of men in all their given variety and complexity, sometimes good and sometimes bad, sometimes intelligent and more often stupid.

F. Hayek, *Individualism and Economic Order,* p. 11 (1948).

12. Hayek, in *Morgan Guaranty Survey,* Jan. 1976, at 4, 7.

13. My files attribute the words to Edmund Burke but the reference eluded discovery.

14. But not exclusively. The corporate form is also used for charitable institutions and for other not-for-profit pursuits—schools, churches, foundations, and many others. Here, as with business organizations, two primary objectives are insulation from personal liability and continuity of existence.

Unless poverty is to be elevated to a virtue ordained for all to suffer, these are necessary activities of the citizenry of any society. The question then becomes, how will society be organized to perform them? Ultimately the choice is in one of two directions: either under a system authoritarian in nature in which individual liberty becomes increasingly difficult to protect and identify, or under a system which for the members of the community maximizes the opportunities for choice, a condition which Voltaire described as freedom.

THE CORPORATION AND ITS ASSAILANTS

Being the butt of social criticism is surely not new for corporate America. Cartoons at the turn of the century depicting President Roosevelt wielding the big stick are a testimony to how politically profitable it was then, as now, to dislike business. What is different at this end of the century is the very real prospect that the criticism levelled at capitalism may succeed in destroying it, as well as many of the liberties which allowed it to flourish. Corporate America has adapted to social change before, but whether it will any longer be given that chance is an issue which attends the current debate. For, to a large extent the current criticism is predicated on misperceptions of business which, if the criticism is believed, may well lead to fundamental alterations in the social structure as to how and by whom economic decisions are to be made.

In Mr. Wishard's essay are numerous observations and references which are open to serious challenge. He states early on that the design—by origin and practice—of the American corporation has been that of "a private institution producing profit for a relative few."[15] This makes good grist for the political mill, but as an interpretation of history it simply will not stand the test. The corporate form from the early years of the industrial era was a form available to anyone almost for the asking. However dark and satanic may have been some of the factories and mills of early industrialization, the millions who flocked to them did so for a reason, often to escape from a more abysmal rural poverty, and to find, as many did, the opportunity for new expression, new experiences, and new status.[16] No society in recorded history has forged so large a middle class or made so commonplace the status of nouveau riche as has America's capitalist-corporate society. By com-

---

15. See Wishard, *supra* note 1, at pp. 325–26, where he writes: "The modern American corporation has adapted its relationship to society before; but its original design as a private institution producing profit for a relative few has survived all social change—until now."

16. The factory system in England of the early nineteenth century is differently interpreted from the generally held view in an essay of W. H. Hutt, "The Factory System of the Early Nineteenth Century," in *Capitalism and the Historians*, p. 160 (F. Hayek ed. 1954).

parison to others, whether contemporary or of the past, America's huge middle class is extraordinarily affluent, the beneficiary of a system that has created and distributed wealth in proportions previously unrealized.

Repeated often enough, such and similar accusations linking corporations to the fortunes of the few can and do shape attitudes that are hostile. In part this may explain the decline of the public's respect for corporations, a decline which futurists cite as evidence of their unstable stature. One would have to have one's head in the sand, however, not to see that most institutions with authority over the lives of individuals are traversing a period of stress and declining respect. Charts which depict the drop in esteem for corporations and business show similar patterns for government, religious institutions, and even the family—a flattening of the American institutional landscape, as Professor Robert H. Bork of the Yale Law School describes the process.[17] Perhaps this phenomenon is a response to the increasing educational level of the population; a professionally trained society is not as likely to be unquestioningly subservient to institutions of authority. Ironically, in at least the case of economic interests, men who were once very free appear willing to surrender more and more of their freedom to the authority of central planners.[18]

Wishard relies heavily on three archcritics of the capitalist system: Robert Heilbroner, George Lodge, and Daniel Bell. Heilbroner is an opinion maker whose writings help sustain what Irving Kristol calls a preference of fantasy over reality.[19] In his *Beyond Boom and Crash*,[20] he predicts a crisis with not only American capitalism, but worldwide capitalism, whatever that is, and, true to the modern intellectual's

---

17. Bork, "Assault on the Corporation," Across the Board, Feb. 1978, at 50.

18. In a thoughtful and provocative lecture presented under the auspices of the Graduate School of Business and the Divinity School of the University of Chicago, lawyer Elmer W. Johnson made this observation on the opposing legal trends of contemporary America:

> The society that has seen the need to limit freedom of contract in the economic arena and protect us against our gullibility and our vulnerability to manipulation and fraud, the society that has recognized the inability of the market by itself to sustain an adequate business ethic—that same society, ironically, has also decided that poor frail man should be given nearly complete freedom of contract in the sexual arena, that the publishers and producers of film and literature should bear no fiduciary obligation to society to preserve minimal decency, that all varieties of sexual goods and services should be considered merely as additional items to be distributed in accordance with mass consumer demand operating within the exchange system, with full opportunity on the part of the suppliers to manipulate mass taste. Johnson, "Fiduciary Ethics and the Market," Oct. 1977, at 14 (unpublished).

19. Kristol, "Business and 'The New Class'," Wall St. J., May 19, 1975, at p. 8.

20. R. Heilbroner, *Beyond Boom and Crash* (1978).

penchant, chooses centralized governmental planning as his prescription to cure the ills of the capitalist economy. Heilbroner's doomsday rhetoric and dire forecasts in this and other writings are not all that convincing; in any event the prescience of those who purport to know what will be a quarter or a full century into the future has not in past times been so good as to command very serious attention. What is revealing is his commentary on the wealth-producing qualities of the capitalist society. His attitudes align well with those of other corporate assailants,[21] many of whom see a growing disparagement of things material.[22] To him, capitalist-generated wealth is a "plastic wealth," meaning, of course, the usual assets owned by most Americans—automobiles, houses, furniture, and appliances of all kinds—items used for recreation and the like. And capping this is a central theme of his message, namely, that capitalism has a tendency to create poverty alongside riches, a charge he adds to earlier denunciations of capitalism's failure to satisfy the spiritual side.[23]

Only a monastic conscript or a sheltered intellectual could really accept these evaluations as genuine. Obviously, capitalism does not create poverty; it creates wealth, and has done so better than any other institution ever happened upon. Capitalism's intellectual father prescribed a formula not for the creation of poverty, but of wealth.[24] Expositions such as Heilbroner's are more obscuring than enlightening and should not be uncritically accepted as valid judgments of the qualities of the system. But, unfortunately, they often are, and thus lend respectability to the clamor against capitalism by placing on the system a responsibility for shortcomings that it was not its objective to prevent. It is one thing to acknowledge that man is essentially a religious animal, and quite another to lay at the doorsteps of his economic institutions responsibility for whatever void he may be experiencing in that side of his nature.

Heilbroner's dissatisfaction with the "plastic wealth" of corporate America Wishard interprets as a societal change in attitude concerning materialism. He cites George Lodge's provocative *The New American Ideology*[25] to support the postulates that a new ideology of communitarianism is replacing individualism, that property rights are giving way to rights of membership in communities, and that the criterion of community need is replacing market forces in determining resource

---

21. See Wishard, *supra* note 1, at pp. 328–29.

22. E.g., H. Cleveland and T. Wilson, Jr., *Humangrowth, An Essay on Growth, Values and the Quality of Life* (Aspen Institute for Humanistic Studies 1978).

23. See Heilbroner, "Second Thoughts on the Human Prospect," 18 Challenge, May-June 1975, at 21, 26, quoted by Wishard, *supra* note 1, at p. 328 n. 14.

24. A. Smith, *An Inquiry into the Nature and Causes of The Wealth of Nations* (1776) (Modern Library ed. 1937).

25. G. Lodge, *The New American Ideology* (1975).

allocation and utilization. Convinced of these changes in value, Wishard attributes them in part to "a distortion of the business method—a distortion which tends to hold technical efficiency and financial profit as life's primary measurement and reward, and to define progress and culture in econometric and commercial terms."[26] He speculates—maybe even agrees—with a well-known national pollster "that people feel it is time to learn to live on less of the material goods of life, but with better human relationships."[27]

Clearly, if these premises of a "fundamental quest for different values and the concomitant search for new levels of self-determination" are correct, there will, as Wishard concludes, inevitably be long-term effects on corporations.[28] The premises, particularly when stated in some of their more extreme forms, are not necessarily self-evident, nor even necessarily discoverable on close investigation. Most Americans would undoubtedly prefer to retain their "plastic wealth," believing that much of the drudgery of ancestral lives has been relieved by it, and convinced that some of the pleasures formerly indulged in only by nobility have become commonplace experiences with their available use. If there is any doubt about this, ponder for a moment the most maligned of Heilbroner's plastic-wealth instruments, the automobile. It has made accessible to nearly every citizen an opportunity which in almost all of previous history was within reach of only the very, very wealthy or those sitting on the thrones of power.[29] This American is not one who is willing to surrender to central bureaucrats the power to determine what may or may not be enjoyed, nor does he believe that there is much of a public sentiment in that direction. As for countries which have yet to experience the deliverance from poverty and squalor, the deliverance that the capitalist system has been so effective in accomplishing, theirs is still a venture engaged in merchandising hope.

Nevertheless, there are stirrings throughout the country to which corporations and the capitalist system must pay attention. Employees, shareowners and the public in general do not look at corporations in the same way as did their forebears. But to say this is to repeat a truism of all of history—that things change from generation to generation. That they are changing faster today than in any other period of recorded history is another of those value judgments that need not be unquestionably accepted.[30] Barbara Tuchman's readable classic[31] draws many parallels

---

26. Wishard, *supra* note 1, at p. 329.

27. *Id.* at p. 328.

28. *Id.* at p. 329.

29. A refreshing view of the automobile and its social value is found in B. Bruce-Briggs, *The War Against the Automobile* (1977).

30. Wishard states: "Today's social environment is changing with a rapidity unequaled in the history of the human experience." Wishard, *supra* note 1, at p. 326. Maybe so, for certainly many rapid developments have been taking place in

between the present and a century of the past which is a half millenium removed. The present era is not unique in its experience of the rapid uprooting of what Russell Kirk has tagged "the permanent things."[32] Rather, what is done with change is what is meaningful.

Heilbroner, Lodge, Wishard, and others see change leading to increased centralized government authority. Wishard writes: "A new legitimacy for the corporation as a *public* institution is in fact evolving." (Emphasis added.) Again: "An institution that has such a dominant influence on the lives of so many citizens—in terms of jobs generated (directly and indirectly), prices, psychic satisfaction of workers, the environment, and the course of the economy—any institution with such widespread and fundamental effects is for all practical purposes a *public* institution and as such should be subject to some form of public accountability." (Emphasis added.) And finally:

> The issue of control of corporate decision-making nonetheless will be a central *political* issue for the foreseeable future—simply because the evolutionary impulse in many areas of life is to move from representation to participation. This *inevitably* means more involvement of employees in decision-making, greater participation by stockholders in selection of directors, and greater participation of both the public *and government* in areas which affect the public welfare.[33] [Emphasis added.]

Lodge sees the state emerging as the establisher of community objectives and the judge of community needs,[34] which in turn leads him to suggest,

---

recent years. But the same was true of many past eras. Think of the decline of institutional authority which the Reformation precipitated, the alteration of the American social landscape that the abolition of slavery led to, and the mobility generated in the middle two quarters of this century by the massive love affair with the automobile. I really don't know what significance is attached to the observation that current times are times of rapid change. To some, this indicates a need for centralized authority; to others it is a reason for just the opposite. What hasn't changed much is the character of humanity itself. Pride and prejudice, charity and greed, and the lust for power, all seem to be rather immutable and permanent attributes of the species. Change in social environment, at some times more rapid than at others, is a fact of all times. What is done about it in terms of the liberation of the individual from the grip of illegitimate authority is the question of importance.

31. B. Tuchman, *A Distant Mirror* (1978).

32. See R. Kirk, *Enemies of the Permanent Things* (1969).

33. Wishard, *supra* note 1, at p. 332.

34. Lodge, *supra* note 25. In chapter 9, titled "The State as Planner," Lodge writes:

> Multiple forces will unquestionably accelerate the transition of government from its old role to the new one—that of comprehensive planner. . . . State Planning can take two forms: the kind we have generally practiced, and the kind toward which we are inexorably tending. The first emanates from the

among other things, adoption of federal corporate chartering. To Heilbroner, the demise of the capitalist system is inevitable as is a necessary concomitant: the evolvement of a "high degree of political authority." This, he says

> augurs for the cultivation of nationalist, authoritarian attitudes, perhaps today foreshadowed by the kind of religious politicism we find in China. The deification of the state. . . seems therefore the most likely replacement for the deification of materialism that is the unacknowledged religion of our business culture.[35]

A manifestation of this deification which Heilbroner believes expectable if not inevitable is the assimilation into state communes, not unknown in today's China, or even Israel, of children of future generations. Given this vision of a future, perhaps he should prefer the improvement of what he presently has.

But sticking with what is is not the choice of many fueling the attack on corporations. They do not seem satisfied with persuasion, but insist on resorting to the sanctions of authoritarian decree to accomplish their objectives. Irving Kristol suggests that what he refers to as the New Class[36] has reached a stage of strength that puts it effectively into a struggle for the power possessed by those whose interests are business related or business derived. "This 'new class,' " he says, "is not easily defined but may be vaguely described." It includes[37]

> scientists, teachers and educational administrators, journalists and others in the communications industries, psychologists, social workers, those lawyers and doctors who make their careers in the expanding public sector, city planners, the staffs of the larger foundations, the upper levels of the government bureaucracy, etc., etc. It is, by now, a quite numerous class; it is an

---

> old conception of the state's role—planning that is largely the product of the interplay of interest groups. This can only be tactical, shortsighted, and short-lived at best, for it arises out of the conflicts of self-interested powerholders who merely seek relatively short-range profit or protection. . . . The second form of planning we have known only in time of war. . . . This form of planning is integral and holistic; it is long-range; it emanates from the leadership, initiative, and vision of the state itself.

Id. at pp. 266–67.

I wonder how many Americans would embrace this if the planners are the likes of Dean, Ehrlichmann, and Haldeman. In a century that has had Stalin, Hitler, Mao Tse-Tung, Chiang Kai-Shek, and how many others, it is an enigma how the hopes of centralized dominance over the lives of others still live on—unless, of course, one is captivated by the prospect of being the planner.

35. R. Heilbroner, *Business Civilization in Decline,* p. 119.

36. See Kristol, "Business and 'The New Class'," Wall St. J., May 19, 1975, at p. 8.

37. *Id.*

indispensable class for our kind of society; it is a disproportionately powerful class; it is also an ambitious and frustrated class.

This is the sector which he sees as substituting for the economic decision-making of business the political decision-making of government. They are, in Kristol's observation, a well-educated group which looks on the processes of the marketplace as being too bourgeois to be endured. Rather than working to "elevate" to the level of their preferences the preferences of the masses they look down on, their choice is to politicize economic decision-making through economic planning by government bureaucracies.

CORPORATIONS AND THEIR RESPONSES

If Kristol is right about the power and strength of his New Class, then surely corporations face a challenge never before met on the American scene. Change, contrary to popular myth, has been neither impossible nor unnatural for corporate America. Corporations are an experiment in individualism,[38] and social innovation and individualism are bosom allies.

Today, change is becoming more and more a response to the command, "Do it my way, or else." It is less and less the voluntary experimentation of individuals or groups of individuals seeking different and improved ways for doing things. Whether the continuance of this trend is as inevitable as collectivists profess to know is something which only the future will unfold. Nevertheless, the trite observation of the certainty of change raises the inquiry: What kinds for corporate America?

Traditionally, mutations in corporate or business practices have been largely motivated by the good business sense they made. Critics who want to believe in the myth of corporate immutability usually attribute "progress" in the business arena to a grudging capitulation of management to external and noneconomic pressures. Wishard, for example, cites the "more than $208 billion paid by private industry in 1976 for employee benefits beyond wages and salaries" as supportive of the proposition that corporations are undergoing a shift in their self-perception from one of "economizing" to one of "sociologizing,"[39] juxtaposing the two as though they were discordant one with the other. But a more credible explanation of such expenditures is that they do indeed add up economically to a positive bottom-line result. Sound economics, and not some nebulous shift in moral suasion, promoted the postwar explosion in these programs, considering their value to employer and employee alike under changing tax laws. This interpretation seems also borne out by the wholesale and unexpected abandonment and cancella-

38. Cf. F. Hayek, *The Constitution of Liberty* (1960), especially chapter 2.

39. Daniel Bell uses the "economizing" to "sociologizing" description in D. Bell, *The Coming of Post-Industrial Society*, Chapter 4 (1973).

tion of many such plans as a choice preferred to complying with innumerable and often senseless burdens of new federal legislation regulating them. Given the legislative factors involved, the growth of benefit plans beyond salaries and wages would doubtless have been no different under management a century or half century ago, than it has been more recently. Said another way, the dominant forces of the market were at work. To attribute them to a "new legitimacy" in the corporate psyche is, it seems, to claim more than is demonstrable,[40] and to give to opponents of the system a reason to proclaim they are right.

This is not to deny an input value or even catalytic quality to legislation or its threat in corporation decision-making. Societal shifts in value systems occasionally need the establishment of ground rules for market forces to deal adequately with them. Protection of the environment is probably an example. The norm today, however, is not for government to set ground rules but for its central planners to establish goals, and to prescribe in every minutia the steps toward their attainment. Example followed by example can be given, but a typical one is the Employee Retirement Income Security Act,[41] which had as its genesis the goal of making sure that the funds established behind pension promises would be there when the time for performance arrived. The result was a nearly incomprehensible statute followed by inconsistent and demonstrably incomprehensible regulations that prescribe every detail of pension planning and pension administration, along with a concomitant government bureaucracy to regulate them. Save for the decision to have such plans, the freedom of independent decision-making is nearly extinct in this area. ERISA is only one example. The facts are that individual choice in the accomplishment of the goals of people in the business arena—and elsewhere—has been seriously eroded in a short span of time. In view of the historic linkage of freedom in economic affairs with personal and political freedom, this is a concern of no mean proportion for advocates of a free society.

It is this attribute of central planning which, it seems, is of such concern to corporate America. Irving Kristol's New Class will undoubtedly not be satisfied with the goal of "corporate accountability," corporate "social responsibility" or whatever other tag is used. Unmindful of history's teaching that the greatest dangers to liberty lurk in insidious encroachment by men of good will, the New Class will aim to dictate precisely how those goals are achieved—in product quality, employee and plant environment, corporate governance—in short in the whole

---

40. Cf. the following from J. Paluszek, *Will the Corporation Survive?* 4 (1977): "In many corporations there is under consideration—and, in some, under development—a new ethic, a new way to do business." A new way of doing things, yes. But a new ethic? That smacks of a sanctimonious slandering of alleged trespasses of the past, which opponents of the market system are quick to agree with.

41. Pub. L. No. 93-406, 88 Stat. 829 (1974).

panoply of business activity. To draw on Kristol again, his New Class wants "its place in the sun."[42]

In the years just ahead, much of their effort will be directed to getting changes and ultimately, if successful, a measure of control over the structure of corporate governance in this country. Critics of the modern corporation reflect many views of what they regard as significant issues. Some focus primarily on the laws which regulate substantive decisions of a corporation, such as trade regulation and antimonopoly laws, or laws dealing with product quality, plant safety, or environmental pollution. Others have as their primary concern matters which are more traditionally regarded as within the sphere of corporate laws—shareholder democracy, management authority, and board of directors constituency. Still others have all of these matters and more on their list of grievances to be addressed.

As previously suggested in the reference to ERISA, government laws regulating specific substantive decision-making by business have proliferated alarmingly in the last decades.[43] Coming next, and indeed already with us, will be increasing debate over issues of corporate governance: board representation, voting rights, procedural standards within the corporate organization, disclosures to the public and between management and the board of directors, and federal chartering. These areas have already received considerable attention in recent years from corporate managers, lawyers, and accountants.[44] Much has been accomplished, some of it good and some not so good, but presumably few are of the opinion that conditions are perfect or that all has been done which needs be done. Control of the corporate decision-making process—restructuring its board—will be the central issue of all of these.

To some, including Mr. Wishard, this is "simply because the evolutionary impulse in many areas of life is to move from representation to

---

42. Kristol, *supra* note 36.

43. In an interesting issue dedicated to the corporation, the editors of *Dun's Review* in July, 1976 listed no less than sixteen major laws to regulate business enacted since the closing years of the 1800's. Dun's Review, July 1976, at 26–27. But these were only high watermarks; the laws enacted to modify and strengthen them are many, and the regulations promulgated pursuant to them now typically consume tens of thousands of pages annually in the Federal Register. To be in compliance with all federal laws and regulations governing business, let alone to avoid violations of state laws, is now a nearly human impossibility. Their own inconsistencies assure this. The "pollution of the law," as this might be described, has postured corporations for headlining of law violations, itself a factor in the nurturing of the antibusiness animus latent in today's public.

44. Witness the adoption of guidelines for corporate governance by the American Bar Association, "Corporate Directors Guidebook," 32 Bus. Law. 5 (1976), and the study issued on the same topic by the Business Roundtable, "The Role and Composition of the Board of Directors of the Large Publicly Owned Corporation," 33 Bus. Law. 2083 (1978). Both are products of considerable debate and reflection.

participation." Whether this will bring to this nation the extreme of labor control over all corporate decisions, whether it will bring split board representation between labor, management, and other groups, will, in his view depend "in part on how American executives respond to the participatory trend reshaping American institutions."[45]

Stated so generally, Mr. Wishard's premise for how extreme future rules might be is hard to argue with. If implicit in the premise is, however, that boards of the future will "voluntarily" be made up of various groups—labor, consumer, community, public interest (whatever that is), and others—lest their constituency along such lines be governmentally mandated, it is then less acceptable as a universal sentiment. Advocates of split or participatory boards have certainly not made their case to the public at large, at least not in this country. Not even from shareowners is there any clamor for split boards, or, for that matter, for more involvement in the decision-making process. Shareowner concerns with management have not changed from their predominant interest in the best possible bottom-line results, and their resolution with dissatisfaction continues primarily to be the election to get out, rather than to stay in and seek an expanded franchise.[46] Labor, too, is not enthusiastic about board membership, although a shift in this attitude seems possible. George Meany expressed labor's traditional view of board participation in this country when he offered that such a role might make it difficult to identify whether the employee is labor or management.[47] It is quite possible that Mr. Meany's view overlooks the impact of today's workers more and more becoming stockholders through company purchase plans and tax-incentive ownership plans. How this will affect the traditional labor-employee response to board participation in the future is open, but it is likely to cause an occasional reassessment.

The principal objection, it seems to me, of forcing boards to restructure for represented constituencies is very pragmatic. On the philosophical plain is the very valid objection that corporations belong to their owners, and they, rather than the government, should determine who is to direct their business. On the practical level, however, corporations are

---

45. Wishard, *supra* note 1, at p. 332.

46. The increasing number of shareholder proposals does not counter this proposition. In many instances—for example, efforts to affect corporate investments in South Africa—shareholder proposals are put forward by owners holding only one or two shares acquired to be able to raise the issue. In the overwhelming number of cases, shareowners vote heavily with management, a condition which the cynic—maybe correctly—attributes to blind following.

47. Mr. Meany is quoted in Nation's Business, "Workers on Boards of Directors," Feb. 1976, at 52, as saying "Who are you if you are a labor man on a board of directors? Whom do you represent? Labor does not want to run the shop. In the United States, participation is absolutely and completely out. It will not work." But another leader, from the United Auto Workers, in the same article suggested that at least a look at the opposite European experience is merited.

not minipolitical entities which should be run by quasi microlegislatures. Presumably, such representatives would be able to disregard shareowner interests in the interests—as they perceive them to be—of their constituencies. Decision-making would then be approached on the basis of potentially unlimited missions, rather than with economic evaluations being of primary concern. American business corporations rightfully claim as one of their finest accomplishments an organizational form that has operated with great efficiency in the creation of capital for the production of goods and services for society. Tampering with this by making small-town meetings out of directors meetings would almost certainly impair if not destroy this historic efficiency.[48]

Another fault with compulsory representative composition is that it ignores the heterogeneity of business enterprises. Corporations in every industry, even the largest of them, have unlike needs which alter from time to time as the scale and scope of each enterprise expand and shift. Movement into the international arena, increasing competitive pressures, a venture into retailing from manufacturing, the need for special services from professionals such as lawyers, accountants, financiers, engineers and scientists, all of these and more are considerations which any given business may have in greater or less degree at different stages of its existence. Why, then, is it sensible to decree that certain constituencies must always and forever be represented? If shareholders, or the management selected by them, judge that employees, the public, ethnic minorities, women, or another "interest" be included in board membership, that is a decision which they can make or later unmake. Certainly no evidence has yet been forthcoming to demonstrate that representative boards are an unmixed blessing. Some of the most ballyhooed examples have turned in dismal performances.[49]

---

48. Cf. the remarks of former SEC Commissioner Robert B. Smith:

> A debating society at the top of such an organization would make a business corporation about as efficient as the Congress. We don't look to our political institutions for business efficiency; and comparably, we should not look to our business institutions for essentially political representation. Also, there is still something to be said for making sure in the business world that the same people are not on both sides of the bargaining table, whether it's in labor-management negotiations or in purchaser-supplier negotiations, or in making a sale to a customer. Discipline in our system or making optimal use of capital, and it's easy to forget that capital is a scarcer resource than clean air, is for investors to have confidence that management is acting on their own behalf.

Proceedings, New York State Bar Ass'n 100th Annual Meeting, Section on Banking, Corporation & Business Law, Jan. 27, 1977, at p. 92.

49. See the discussion in Vance, "Director Diversity: New Dimensions in the Boardroom," Directors & Boards, Spring, 1977, at 40. Professor Vance makes this observation on the prospects of representative boards:

> While the representation issue generates considerable emotion, its pros-

Common shareowners have the greatest investment in keeping the decision-making process efficient. The corporate franchise should be lodged in them. Diluting it by assigning to others the power of representation for interests much less affected will surely politicize decision-making, inevitably with a detrimental effect for many more than just shareowners. Over time, it is hard to believe that decisions bearing on risk-taking, on the accumulation and employment of capital, on all the myriad of issues concerned with business growth, would not be affected by increasingly political considerations which reflect special interest groups rather than the interest of shareowners in an efficient and profitable operation. This could not be healthy for return on investment, and injury to return is an experience that is usually followed by slower growth and lower stock market value. Neither is good for employment opportunities or for the many investments of individuals and institutions in a given corporation's equities.

Special interest board representation is the darling of many who call for some form of federal chartering. Obviously, to win the battle for such representation in all fifty states, thus cutting off the escape route for those caught in a jurisdiction making such a move, would be an almost insurmountable undertaking. Consequently, the call for federal chartering arises. Though not the same from all corners, with a good deal of variance existing in the announced objectives of different federal chartering proponents, the movement must be attentively watched. In view of all the federal laws which already exist affecting corporate governance and economic decision-making, it is easy to relax and think benignly of federal chartering. But the push must be recognized to represent a scheme for fundamental redistribution of economic power. Centering authority for the chartering of corporations—most proponents limit their demand to only the giants—would present an opportunity which could not be resisted for gaining further control over economic planning and wealth distribution. To those who believe that the increasingly complex issues of society can better be decided by fewer and fewer persons,

---

pects are dim. For example, if it can be demonstrated that adding these representative groups to the board stimulates sales to these groups, or that it generates significant productivity improvement, then the . . . dimension has some merit. Even then, sustained effort for [representativeness] by organized groups is essential and this effort is difficult to maintain. And aside from the fact that many of these representatives may be ill-prepared to accept both the responsibilities and liabilities of a directorship, other serious obstacles are present. For instance, in its most desirable form, [representativeness] can be viewed as a vital aspect of industrial democracy, yet [it] also has some characteristics that . . . can lead to collusive action, factionalism, favoritism and endless bickering. If each vested group demands its 'fair share' and the demanded shares total up to three or four times the size of the production-pie, this version of industrial democracy will easily lead to industrial chaos.

Id. at 44–45.

namely by bureaucrats convinced that they incarnate public policy, federal chartering, of course, fits. But for those who think societally in terms of the maximization of choice, of the finiteness of individual intelligence and wisdom, and of "public policy" as the sum of all private interests, federal chartering is a substantial threat.[50]

It would be expected, therefore, that corporate America on the whole will resist with all its strength moves for federal chartering and compulsory representative boards. But there will likely be tinkering with board membership. The move toward outside board members will probably continue and even accelerate. Not something new on the corporate scene, this inside-outside tug-of-war has been going on for some time, even since before the New York Stock Exchange decided in the early 1960's to require such memberships as a condition of new listing,[51] and long before it got a substantial impetus from the Exchange's rule effective in the summer of 1978[52] that all members of a board's audit committee be outside and unaffiliated with management. That persuasive evidence is wanting to show that outside or outside and unaffiliated[53] directors are any better watchdogs of the shareowner's interests does not seem to have

---

50. Joseph Hinsey, an attorney with considerable experience on American Bar Association committees concerned with corporate governance, made the following remarks on corporate federal chartering at the hundredth anniversary meeting of the New York State Bar Association:

> Federal chartering is a bold and far-reaching proposal, and involves a question of basic philosophy regarding our business structures and our market economy. It presents the question of how our economic resources are to be administered, who will administer them, and for what purposes. Clothed in innocent raiment, the federal corporation movement represents a call for an important reordering of the distribution of economic power, and tremendous extension of government power over our economic system.

Proceedings, New York State Bar Ass'n 100th Annual Meeting, Banking, Corporation & Business Law Section, Jan. 27, 1977, at 77.

51. Adopted July 16, 1956, NYSE Company Manual at B-23.

52. Adopted Jan. 6, 1977, NYSE Company Manual at A-29.

53. Who constitutes an outside board member is not something on which there is universal agreement. An employee member obviously is an inside member, but being an "outsider" can mean many things to different viewers. Is an employee who remains on a board following retirement an outsider? Or a lawyer or banker whose firm or corporation does substantial business with the corporation? Or a director or employee of a supplier? Or of a customer? The SEC's attempt to toy with these distinctions in proposed proxy disclosure rules ran into substantial and heated criticism in the summer and fall of 1978, with the result that it found it politic to back down from its proposals. That debate illustrates the extremes and varieties of opinions which exist over these designations.

slowed the trend,[54] and it is likely to continue as a response to a consensus or even perceived need, however unsubstantiated may be its premise.[55] Beyond this trend, the prospects for a mandated board design are dim, and properly so. Against this intrusion into the management structure stands the formidable experience that no optimal design exists. Each corporate entity has its own peculiar needs, and the trial and error experience of corporate America has served it exceedingly well. The obloquies which the system has suffered can be better addressed through other responses.

In this observer's perception, self-interest of corporate directors, officers, and advisors will be a major motivating force for new experiments in corporate governance in the years just ahead. The people who occupy these chairs are very intelligent individuals, not in any way interested in having careers, or assets accumulated during careers, destroyed by liabilities imposed for malperformance of their responsibilities. The "coral reef of law," as Bayless Manning has descriptively labeled it,[56] built up over recent years in judicial decisions shaping director, officer, and advisor liability law[57] is a persuasive reason for

---

54. Cf. Vance, *supra* note 49, at 41:

> Interestingly, this fictionalized role of public director has been ballyhooed by many directorate analysts who invariably sit as outsiders on corporate boards. Undoubtedly, this self-adulation or self-defense should be seriously questioned because the facts show that outside directors are *not* the common stockholders' best friends. In every recent headlining corporate boardroom scandal, beginning with the classic Texas Gulf Sulphur Company case, there was a preponderance of outsiders on the board at the time of the scandal. For example, the inside/outside balance was 2 to 10 at Texas Gulf, 5 to 12 at Lockheed, 4 to 18 at Penn Central, 3 to 6 at Northrup and 3 to 9 at Gulf Oil. Even at W. T. Grant and Company, where the embarrassment was bankruptcy rather than illegal action, outsiders outnumbered insiders by 11 to 6.

55. In this connection, it is interesting to note that the Business Roundtable report issued in January of 1978, *see* note 44 *supra*, endorsed the position that in most instances the board should be composed of a majority of nonmanagement directors. Considering the blue-ribbon status of this committee, it is likely to have a catalytic effect on the continued swing toward outside boards. A similar view has been expressed by others, including members of the Securities and Exchange Commission and the American Assembly at its institute on Corporate Governance in America, April, 1978.

56. Manning, *supra* note 5, at p. 25.

57. In mind are such decisions as Escott v. Barchris Construction Corp., 283 F. Supp. 643 (S.D.N.Y. 1968), and the various proceedings involving the Securities and Exchange Commission against those who had a part in the National Student Marketing debacle, culminating thus far in SEC v. National Student Marketing Corp., 457 F. Supp. 682 (D.D.C. 1978). In *Escott,* severe warnings emerged on what it takes to discharge the duty of due diligence in the review of a registration statement, the court writing that a person "is presumed to know

continually reevaluating the processes in place within the corporate structure to insure that the standards of performance being called for in contemporary environment are satisfied. As the implications of these case-by-case tests of real-life situations are understood, there is a high likelihood that mechanisms adopted to protect against liability will intersect with the aims of many critics, including the SEC.

Out of this long line of judicial decisions comes the number one teaching: a need for an adequate flow of information to make intelligent and responsible decisions. Directors who direct cannot direct without needed information, and directors who do not direct are a risk to themselves and their enterprises.

The prestigious Business Roundtable adopted a position paper early in 1978[58] which emphasizes the need for information to flow first to board members to enable them to participate effectively in the management decision-making for which they are responsible. Four key areas for board responsibility were identified: succession planning, financial performance, social impact of corporate activity, and development of policy and implementing procedures to ensure acceptable ethical standards and law compliance at all levels of an enterprise.[59] The specific recommendations of the Roundtable for implementing the flow of information to discharge these duties are not as innovative as some would have liked. While articulating the desirability of audit, compensation, and nominating committees, the report stops short of embracing and indeed rejects the recommendations of those who, like Chairman Harold Williams of the SEC, oppose the inclusion of any board members from management other than the executive officer.[60] "Its value," one commentator has remarked,

---

his responsibility when he becomes a director," and "can escape liability only by using that reasonable care to investigate the facts which a prudent man would employ in the management of his own property," 283 F. Supp., at 688. *National Student Marketing* expressed some seminal thoughts in its attempt to balance a counsel's fiduciary duty to a client against disclosure obligations of securities laws. See 457 F. Supp. at 713–15. Decisions such as these make doing business as usual very unintelligent.

58. 33 Bus. Law. 2083 (1978).

59. *Id.* at 2097–2104.

60. See Williams, *supra* note 9:

> The ideal board, in my opinion, would be constructed as follows: First, since the board guards two thresholds—that between ownership and management and that separating the corporation from the larger society—it must be recognized that there are some people who do not belong on boards—members of management, outside counsel, investment bankers, commercial bankers, and others who might realistically be thought of as suppliers hired by management. Some of these, as individuals, can and do make excellent directors. Yet all must be excluded unless a mechanism can be designed whereby they can establish their ability to function on a basis independent of their management-related role.

is not so much substantive as catalytic. Its positive contribution will turn on what behavioral response it produces among the members of the Roundtable, all of whom have it in their power, if they would, to move their boards in the direction of the letter and spirit of these recommendations. . . . The Roundtable influence could thus radiate throughout our corporate structure.[61]

This report is reflective of the winds of change already touching corporate boardrooms. Not only have nominating and other committees become a standard feature of board organization, but at the leading edge of suggestions are some ideas which may in time come of age.

(1) Consultant/lawyer Victor H. Palmieri has posited the proposition that lawyers should be "officers of the board," in the same sense that trial lawyers have been considered as officers of the court. Three critical tasks to be performed by the corporate lawyer are to call attention to material inaccuracies or omissions in management's presentation on issues under discussion, to explain to the board the risks involved in proposed actions, and to make themselves available to discuss with board members their particular concerns.[62] Similar sentiments were expressed by SEC Chairman Harold Williams in a speech before the American Bar Association Section on Corporation, Banking and Business Law, where he said that "lawyers are, in their many diverse roles, architects . . . of the accountability mechanisms in our corporate structure." In commenting on their educative role, he added that in his view their most "fundamental task is to sensitize and inform management and directors regarding the implications of the public's expanded perception of corporate responsibilities."[63]

(2) In a speech to financial executives, the SEC Chairman made the suggestion that the internal auditing function of corporations not report to the

---

Second, ideally, management should not be represented on the board by other than the chief executive. Such a board environment would not preclude other members of management, counsel, and bankers from being present to contribute their expertise to the deliberations in an uncontentious context. Yet, when it comes to the discussion and vote, the independent director would not be faced with, and discouraged or worn down over time by, what is so often a stacked majority against him.

Third, I believe the chief executive should not be the chairman of the board. Control of the agenda process is a powerful tool, and the issues presented at board meetings should be determined by a chairman who is not a member of management.

61. Andrews, "The Roundtable Statement on Boards of Directors," Harv. Bus. Rev., Sept.–Oct. 1978, at 25, 30.

62. Palmieri, "The Lawyer's Role: An Argument for Change," Harv. Bus. Rev., Nov.–Dec. 1978, at 30, and Palmieri, "Officers of the Board?," Wall St. J., Aug. 14, 1978, at p. 12.

63. Speech by Harold M. Williams, Aug. 8, 1978, to the American Bar Association Annual Meeting, reprinted in BNA Sec. L. Rep. No. 465 (Aug. 9, 1978).

chief financial officer, or chief accounting officer, but to someone "high enough in top management to minimize the risk of pressure to prevent issuance of a critical report or to impede access to the audit committee or board."[64]

(3) In many companies the chairmanship of the board and the chief executive office are held by different occupants. Whatever the merits of this arrangement, and at least one prestigious organization has proposed it as a standard structure,[65] the thought recently surfaced of eliminating the title "chairman of the board," and substituting for it the office of "chief corporate governance officer." It would be the responsibility of the "Chairman-CGO" to lead the board in establishing policies and strategies which would serve the "best interests of shareholder," which presumably are seen as potentially distinct from what is good for current management of a company.[66]

(4) While establishment of nominating committees has become widespread, the scope of their specific functions and how they are executed are not universally the same. SEC Commissioner Roberta Karmel has opined that "This committee can be the single most effective force in improving corporate governance because of its impact over time on the composition of the board and, accordingly, the succession of management."[67] Companies differ on whether the chief executive officer should be a member of the committee, let alone whether he should chair its functions. The American Bar Association, the American Assembly, and the SEC all endorse the idea of nonmembership by the CEO, but the Business Roundtable, for not insignificant reasons, did not go along. Similarly, there is much debate over the scope of the committee activities, and of how and from whom solicitations of candidates should be made.[68]

(5) New approaches to disclosures of board activities and board membership have been advanced for the purpose of affecting corporate management, as distinguished from the traditional purpose of protecting stockholders from fraud and misleading financial reports. During late summer

---

64. Address of Harold M. Williams to the Financial Executives Institute, Los Angeles, Cal., Oct. 9, 1978, reprinted in Wall St. J., Oct. 11, 1978, at p. 8.

65. American Assembly, *Report of Meeting,* April 13–16, 1978, at p. 7.

66. Verity, "New Job at the Top: Chief Governance Officer," Financier, Nov. 1978, at 18. The specific tasks seen performed by this new officer would include structuring and managing the board, leading it in selecting candidates and in educating new members about the company, and leading the board in monitoring its scope and function. He would also be responsible for developing the board's means of gaining information, both within and outside the company.

67. See "The Men Who Pick the Board," Dun's Review, Dec. 1978, at 57.

68. The workings of the nominating committee of General Motors are described by Thomas A. Murphy in "The GM Nominating Committee: How Does it Accomplish its Function?," in Directorship, Nov. 1978, at 3.

and the fall of 1978, controversy raged over numerous disclosure proposals of the SEC, some of which seemed designed to test the waters as to how far they might go without risking challenge.[69] Most offensive was the proposal to label directors in accordance with their nexus to management, a proposal that many found to be pejorative in character and to constitute an implicit qualitative judgment beyond the Commission's jurisdiction. Another dealt with disclosure of the reasons for any director's resignation or failure to stand for reelection, and still others with board organization and functioning. An articulate proponent of this technique for affecting corporate governance gives this defense to the disclosure mechanism: "A properly designed set of disclosure requirements would force all corporations to analyze thoroughly how their boards should be constituted and what roles they should play. . . ."[70]

In these five areas, there is more than enough for all interested parties to keep occupied with for months and even years to come. They raise many questions that call for serious study and experimentation and which defy easy solutions. One is the lawyer's role vis-à-vis boards: Who is the lawyer's client? The American Bar Association guidelines state that the "entity," rather than the "management," "board" or "shareowners" is the client, a choice of words which obviously recognizes the fundamental difficulties involved in the inquiry.[71] Concerning disclosures, what are the legal rights of resigning directors, such as the protection the law gives to all citizens against self-incrimination? Concerning board committees, should board members be afforded assistance from employed staff of the company or from independently retained sources? Other questions involve nominating committees: How wide should their searches for independent directors be? Should they seek out members who will bring tension, and if so, how much? In the auditing function, what is the proper relation between the internal auditors and the audit committee, and what should the scope of the latter body's inquiry be? And what of

---

69. For a sampling of the articles which evidence the extreme reactions voiced against the recent actions of the SEC, see "What the Top 500 Corporations Think," Directorship, Nov. 1978, at 1; "The SEC: Going Too Far Too Fast?," Bus. Week, Nov. 27, 1978, at 86; Hills, "After Awesome Gains, Caution in Corporate Governance," Financier, June 1978, at 15; Kohlmeier, "SEC Seeks Governance Goals Far Beyond its Mandate," Financier, Aug. 1978, at 6; and Editorial, "The Adversarial Board," Wall St. J., Oct. 20, 1978, at 22.

70. Weiss and Schwartz, "Disclosure Approach for Directors," Harv. Bus. Rev., Jan.–Feb. 1978, 18, 19.

71. The American Bar Association Code of Professional Responsibility, Ethical Consideration 5-18, reads in part: "A lawyer employed by a corporation . . . owes his allegiance to the entity and not to a stockholder, director, officer . . . or other person connected with the entity." For a discussion of this topic, see "The Murky Divide: Professionalism and Professional Responsibility, Business Judgments and Legal Advice—What Is a Business Lawyer?," 31 Bus. Law. 457 (1975).

the imposition of a duty for lawyers/or accountants to report to government agencies any violations of law which are discovered? To most schooled in the Anglo-American principles of jurisprudence this is a profoundly troubling and offensive suggestion.[72] None of these are easy issues to resolve nor are they but a smattering of those which can be raised.

There is no reason to believe that all corporations will arrive at the same resolutions to all these questions. The important thing will be to keep these questions up front, so that incrementally the process of improvement which has taken place through the years can continue without massive interference from government, with its concommitant inefficiency and intrusion on private lives. It will be no easy task to resist the power which those seeking government involvement will exercise. The apparent growing awareness of the stultifying results of the regulatory process may be helpful. It is encouraging when a distinguished sociologist at one of the nation's leading universities can say:

> The regulatory power does not destroy, but it prevents existence. It does not tyrannize, but it compresses, enervates, extinguishes and stupifies till [individuals] are reduced to nothing better than a flock of timid and industrious sheep, of which the government is shepherd.[73]

CONCLUSION: WILL THE CORPORATION SURVIVE?

Will the corporation survive? I think so.

But the question is not the one of penultimate importance. Viewing, as these pages have done, a corporation as essentially a legal form for getting things accomplished, whether it continues with us is not the critical question, although it is significant. Not even is the inquiry, Will capitalism survive? But here the focus comes closer to the mark. Of transcending importance is whether American society will reserve for its citizenry the right to pursue privately discerned individual objectives, to experiment, to succeed and to fail—in short, whether it will preserve a condition for the maximization of choice. If it does this, capitalism has a future and the corporate form will probably be with us for some time to come.

Along the way, there will be many changes in the practices comprising "corporate governance." This is as it should be; few would presume a perfect state of affairs to exist today—nor at any other time. Among the threats to the "American Order," Russell Kirk has opined, have been excessive individualism and unbridled competition, practices which

---

72. For the view of Stanley Sporkin, Chief of the SEC's Enforcement Division, see "What the SEC Expects from Corporation Lawyers," Fortune, Oct. 23, 1978, at p. 143.

73. Robert Nisbet, quoted from a speech on the "Future of the University," in Wall St. J., Sept. 19, 1978, at p. 22.

are, in his judgment, insensitive to the demands of justice and oblivious to the need for a balance between authority and liberty.[74] Another has commented that contentment with ownership of stock in a corporate private enterprise system should not undermine the vital active interest in the philosophy of individual freedom as long as a majority of corporations retain an easily surveyable human scale enabling shareowner participation in free decision.[75]

Both of these are reflections on the ethics of responsibility to the market system. Together, they call to mind a preference even by Adam Smith for business organizations in which the management was also owner, because of the "anxious vigilance" that would be inspired by the commonality of interest in the stewardship of one's own property.[76] Maintaining an accountability standard of fiduciary responsibility is what the debate over corporate governance is all about. If that objective continues to be pursued, there should be reduced doubt about whether capitalism will probably "survive, because of its enormous intrinsic virtues as a system for generating wealth, and promoting freedom."[77] Or better still, and once again from Irving Kristol:[78]

---

74. R. Kirk, *The Roots of American Order* (1974).

75. Kohr, "Property and Freedom," in *Property in a Humane Economy,* p. 68 (S. Blumenfeld ed. 1974):

> What we have in the United States is essentially a corporate free-enterprise system, with most individuals being content with ownership of stock in private enterprise rather than of private enterprise itself. This does not in itself undermine the vital active interest in free enterprise and the philosophy of individual freedom as long as a majority of corporations retain an easily surveyable human scale, enabling the stockholders to participate, if not physically, at least emotionally in the exercise of free decision. But if an excessive part of the free-enterprise system becomes dominated by a relatively small number of nation-like large corporations, vying with the state itself not only in size but even in function, the boundaries between private and public purposes tend to become so blurred that the gate is opened to the insensible infiltration of collectivist patterns of thought, ending in veneration no longer of society of the free but of a free society.

76. Smith, *supra* note 24, Book V, chapter 1, at 700.

77. Johnson, "Has Capitalism a Future?," Wall St. J., Sept. 29, 1978, at p. 24. Mr. Johnson adds:

> But those who man and control it must stop apologizing and go onto the ideological offensive. They must show to ordinary people that both the Communist world, and the Third World, are parasitical upon industrial capitalism for their growth technology. That without capitalism, the 200 years of unprecedented growth which have created the modern world, would gradually come to an end. We would have slow growth, then nil growth, then minus growth; and then the Malthusian catastrophe.

78. Kristol, "When Virtue Loses all her Loveliness"—some reflections on capitalism and the "free society," Across the Board, June 1978, at 60, 66.

[I]f the situation of liberal capitalism today seems so precarious, it is likely nevertheless to survive for a long while, if only because the modern era has failed to come up with any plausible alternatives. Socialism, communism, and fascism have all turned out to be either utopian illusions or sordid frauds.

Index

Accountability:
  government's role, 339
  SEC settlements, 194–199
  (*See also* Accountability, management; Corporations; Corporations, national; Managers)
Accountability, management:
  adequacy of constraints on, 29–30, 33–35
  aspects of, 33
  reasons for attention to corporate governance, 3
  shareholder democracy as implementing, 29n.9
  (*See also* Accountability; Corporations; Corporations, national; Managers)
Accountants, as beneficiaries of disclosure, 68
Accounting practices:
  and corporate reform, 20
  methods used to achieve misrepresentation, 55–56, 96–98
  SEC's proposed rules, 207–208
  (*See also* American Institute of Certified Public Accountants; Audit committees; Auditors)
Administrative agency:
  federal chartering administered by, 271
  (*See also* Federal chartering)
Advertising, line-of-business reports, use of numbers criticized, 66
Airlines industry, special chartering, 14
American Assembly of Columbia University, 128
  outside directors recommended, 147
American Bar Association, Code of Professional Responsibility, 222
American Bar Association, Committee on Professional Ethics, 222
American Center for the Quality of Work Life, 333
American Institute of Certified Public Accountants, 47
  audit committees, 209
  internal control procedures, 320n.220
  (*See also* Accounting practices; Audit committees; Auditors)

American Law Institute:
  diversity jurisdiction, 273–274 (*See also* Diversity jurisdiction)
  Federal Securities Code, 265
American Stock Exchange, audit committees, 209 (*See also* Audit committees)
Amount-in-controversy rule, 247–248
Anderson, Allison, 113
Annual reports, SEC requirements, 41
Anti-inflation program, 341
Arab oil embargo, 17
Arrow, Kenneth J., 120, 129
Arthur Young & Company, Lockheed's auditors, 301, 305
Attendance, directors, 150–151
  (*See also* Directors)
Attorney-client privilege, corporate counsel's allegiance, 222–226
  (*See also* Corporate counsel)
Audit committees, 128–129
  AICPA mandates, 209
  basic concept of, 233n.47
  corporate counsel's advice to, 233 (*See also* Corporate counsel)
  Foreign Corrupt Practices Act as mandating, 209 (*See also* Foreign Corrupt Practices Act; Sensitive payments)
  outside directors to predominate, 211, 332 (*See also* Outside directors)
  reporting relationship, 371–372
  special duties, 198–199
  (*See also* Accounting practices; American Institute of Certified Public Accountants; Auditors)
Audited statements, publication of, 91
Auditors:
  change in, disclosure, 167–168, 170
Auditors (*Cont.*)
  liability, 42
  reform proposals, 282–283
  SEC's impact on, 90
  sensitive payments problem, 315–316 (*See also* Sensitive payments)
  (*See also* Accounting practices; American Institute of Certified Public Accountants; Audit committees)

Bank of America, 347
Bell, Daniel, 330, 337, 357
Bentham, Jeremy, 75
Berle, Adolf A., 1, 20, 22, 112–113
Black Americans, as directors, 332
Black, Cyril E., 336
Black, Eli, 202
Blue Chip Stamps v. Manor Drug Stores, 79n.37, 260–261
Boards of directors:
  audit committees, 128–129, 198–199, 209 (*See also* Audit committees)
  benefits of disclosure requirements, 140
  Business Roundtable position paper, 370–371
  committees on, 160–161
  constraints on new disclosure regulation, 140–142, 159
  corporate counsel:
    advice, 232–235
    officer of, 371
    responsibility to, 222–226
    (*See also* Corporate counsel)
  criticisms of contemporary boards, 280–289
  defining restructured board's mandate, 308
  elections, proposed requirements, 143–145
  Emergency Loan Guarantee Board's Lockheed experience compared, 307–308
  field investigation of, 130

Boards of directors (*Cont.*)
ideal board described, 121, 191, 214–215, 370n.60
inadequacies of, 129–131
independent monitoring boards, SEC's support, 125–127, 134
information flow to, 161–163 (*See also* Information)
management's interaction with, 230–231
Model Business Corporation Act's provisions, 122–123
monitoring:
function stressed, 122–129
systems, 163–165
1977–1978 disclosure rules, 135–137
nominating committees, 372
proxy review by, 159 (*See also* Proxies)
quality as element in investment decisions, 131–132
roles, 118–120
rules re composition and operation, 4, 6–7
SEC's Advisory Committee proposals, 205
separate staffs, 281–282
split-board concept, 26–27, 365–367
staff assistance, 165–166
unusual corporate payments, 130 (*See also* Sensitive payments)
(*See also* Directors; Disclosure; Golberg, Arthur; Outside directors)
Bock, Betty, 63
Boilerplate, 141–142, 165
Bork, Robert H., 357
Bosworth, Barry, 340
Brandeis, Louis D., sunlight aphorism, 37, 74, 113, 181–182
Bribery:
corporate reform, 17–18
expediting payments contrasted, 18n.3
(*See also* Sensitive payments)
Bright-line solution, 240
Brokerage firms, 20
Burden of proof, 74–75
Bureaucracy:
corporate world view contrasted, 342–343
Max Weber on, 317–318
Burlington Northern, 169n.221
Burnham, Jack, 335–336
Business and Society, 184
Business-government relationship, 338–339
categories of consideration, 338–342
Business-judgment rule, 118, 124, 286n.32, 321–322
Business Roundtable, 128
boards, position paper, 370–371
Business Week, 340
Butcher, Willard, 340

California, corporate law revision, 24
Canadian Javelin, 195n.73, n.75, 196n.76, 197n.78, 288n.42
Capital markets, corporate conduct controlled by, 117
Capitalism, critics of, 357–362
Carnegie, Andrew, 343
Cary, William L., 115n.20
federal minimum corporate standards, 22–26, 237, 250n.57, 251–253
"race to the bottom," 22, 24, 243
Caseloads, federal corporate law's effect on federal courts, 244–249, 251
Cash flow, information to predict and discount, 92–93
Cash flow accounting, SEC's opposition to, 53–54
Chandler, Marvin, 149
Charters:
Madison's (James) proposals, 180n.18
monopoly grants distinguished, 13–14

Charters (*Cont.*)
origins, 13–14
special charters, 14–15
(*See also* Federal chartering)
Choice-of-forum, federal chartering of national corporations, 269–271
Civil Aeronautics Board, 14
Class actions, 247
Clayton Act, 19
"Co-determination," 26
Code of Professional Responsibility, 231–232
Collins, Daniel W., 59
Commerce clause, and congressional restraint, 274
Committee for Economic Development, corporate impact on society, 345
Common stock, shareholder democrats, 20–21
Compensation, directors, 149–150
(*See also* Compensation, management)
Compensation, management
disclosure of, 4, 6–7, 33
as proof of unaccountability, 35
Confidentiality, boards of directors, need for, 140–141
(*See also* Boards of directors)
Conflict of interest, chief executive officer and director selection, 152–156
Conflict of laws:
bright-line solution, 240
law of the state of incorporation, 240–241
Connecticut:
corporate activity, 11n.1
special chartering for insurance companies, 14
Consumers:
corporate decision-making, 2
corporate reform, 17
as financers of disclosure,69
Control Data, inner-city manufacturing plants, 330
Controlling person, 185–186
Cook, G. Bradford, 187–189
Corporate counsel:
attorney-client privilege, 222–226
counseling areas, 228–232
counseling directors, basic principles, 232–235
dilemma, 226–228
groups to whom responsible, 221–222
identification problems, 219
officer of the board, 371
outside and in-house, 219–220
proper role, 226
SEC position on, 220
staff function of, 221
Corporate democracy, 182
Corporate Director's Guidebook, 123
Corporate governance:
individualism and collectivism in struggle for, 355
Investment Company Act of 1940, 202
patterns of legal response to, 4–5
SEC's impact summarized, 213–215
SEC's settlements, 194–199
strong-executive model, conditions, 34
Corporate investors, and corporate reform, 19–20
Corporate law, scope defined, 5–6
Corporate manager (*See* Managers)
Corporations:
bureaucracy's world views contrasted, 342–343
Committee for Economic Development, report, 345
costs of regulation, 339–340
critical inquiries, 1–2
external/internal condition requisite to efficiency of, 33–34
federal incorporation proposed, 180n.18 (*See also* Federal chartering)

Corporations (*Cont.*)
global character of economic environment, 336–337
historical background, 179–180
instruments of government policies, 338–339
internal controls, disclosure, 208–209
locus of decision-making power, 221–222
models for reform, 243–244
profit maximization, 117n.26
public policy activities, 345–346
public's negative image, reasons, 10
quasi-public institution, 354
secret payments, 3, 5 (*See also* Sensitive payments)
self-scrutiny:
program, 199–202, 308–312
reports, 318–320
social awareness of, 343–345
social questions resolution, 219n.6
social responsibility, 2, 343–344
"sociologizing" mode, 330–331
state and federal laws, conflicts, 2
state law as governing, 210, 238, 242
(*See also* Boards of directors; Corporate governance; Corporations, national; Directors; Diclosure)
Corporations, national:
Cary's (William L.) proposal, 250n.57, 251–253
choice of forums in federal chartering scheme, 269–271
costs of exclusive federal regulation, 265–268, 274
federal corporate laws effect on caseloads, 244–249
federal preemption of state law, 277–278
models to reform, 243–244
Sommer's (A.A.) proposal, 250n.59
Corporations, national (*Cont.*)
(*See also* Boards of directors; Corporations; Directors; Disclosure)
Cort v. Ash, 210
Cost allocation, line-of-business program's use of criticized, 65–66
Cost-benefit analyses, measurement problems, 83–84
Cost-benefit disclosure model, weaknesses, 81–82
"Creative judicial lawmaking," 259
10b-5 rule development, 260–261n.102
Cummins Engine, 330, 347

Debt security issues, 47
Defense Department, Lockheed contracts, 292, 295
Delaware:
assets for corporate enterprise, 24–25
corporation act criticized, 22–26
Derivative suits, 285–286
and diversity jurisdiction, 245–246
self-scrutiny as defense to, 320–324 (*See also* Self-scrutiny program)
venues of, 247n.42
Dewing, Arthur, 50
Diebold Group, 339
Directors:
affiliations with corporate management, 145–149
attendance disclosure, 150–151
black Americans as, 332
classified boards, 21
compensation, 149–150 (*See also* Compensation, management)
considerations in selection, 157n.182
"controlling person," 185–186
corporate counsel's advice,

Directors (*Cont.*)
232–235 (*See also* Corporate counsel)
designated responsibilities proposed, 283
Douglas (William O.) on, 185
elections, proposed disclosure requirements, 143–145
firings, survey, 171n.229
government appointed "public directors," 284–285
In the Matter of Franchard Corporation, 131, 186
independent and nonmanagement, 128
"independent," objections to terminology, 148
labeling of, 136–137, 147–148, 206, 373
legislative history concerning, 111
liability for disclosure errors, 42
mutual funds, 123–124
negligent conduct defined, 188
nominating procedures, 152–156, 372
disclosure of, 156–158
other directorships, 151, 372–373
proxy soliciting material, shareholder access to, 205
reciprocal directorship relationships, 148–149
renomination, disclosure of criteria for, 158–159
resignation or retirement:
disclosure, 167–170
problems arising from disclosure, 171–173
SEC's rule, 173–174
responsibility under Investment Company Act of 1940, 202–203
SEC Chairmen's comments on, 188–191
SEC's guidelines abandoned, 188

Directors (*Cont.*)
Securities Act's provisions, 184–187
women as, 332
(*See also* Boards of directors; Disclosure; Outside directors)

Disclosure:
beneficiaries of, 67–69
benefits delineated, 48–49
board activities and membership, 372–373
boards of directors:
benefits, 140
constraints on new regulation, 140–142
proposed election requirements, 143–145
SEC's Advisory Committee on Corporate Discipline, 135
SEC's 1977–1978 rules, 135–137
(*See also* Outside directors)
Brandeis' comment on, 37, 74, 113, 181–182
Cary's (William L.) comments, 115n.20
corollaries in re value of, 51–54, 92–93
corporate counsel's counseling duties, 230 (*See also* Corporate counsel)
corporate internal controls, 208–209
and corporate reform, 20
director's failure to exercise responsibility, 187
economic disincentives to, 73
effect on management, 32–33
existing shareholders harmed by, 92
fair corporate suffrage as goal, 111
FTC and SEC programs differentiated, 47–48

Disclosure (*Cont.*)
legal response to corporate governance, 4–5
literature of the 1930's on, 111–114
1934 Act requirements, 37–38
(*See also* Securities Exchange Act of 1934)
opportunity costs of mandated disclosure, 45–46
product-line disclosure, usefulness, 59
regulated industries, 38
SEC requirements, 40–42
SEC's voluntary program, 199–202, 308–312, 318–320
securities laws:
antifraud provisions as essential, 78
direct costs, 88
dual nature, 77–80
dynamism of system, 86–87
fraud-minimizing benefits, 94–96
indirect costs, 89–90
replacement cost of fixed assets, 38, 41, 88
weaknesses of cost-benefit model, 81–82
securities market's efficiency, effect of, 60
social objectives achieved by, 115
"soft" information, 86–87, 142
timeliness of, 54, 93
utilitarianism and economic analysis compared, 104–108
value when required, 52–53
voice as enhanced by, 133
Wheat report, 103, 114–115
(*See also* Boards of directors; Corporations; Directors; Line-of-business reports; Securities and Exchange Commission)
Diversity jurisdiction:
ALI proposals, 273–274
Diversity jurisdiction (*Cont.*)
Congress' power to expand, 273–274n.146
derivative suits, 245–246
federal chartering as abolishing, 238, 271–274
(*See also* Federal jurisdiction; Federal question jurisdiction; Jurisdiction; Pendent jurisdiction; State court jurisdiction)
Donham, Wallace B., 344
Douglas, William O., 114
on directors, 185
Drucker, Peter, 128, 163, 328, 329, 339

Ecology, and corporate reform, 17
Economic analyses:
divisibility problems, 84–85
predicting the universe's future, 85–86
utilitarianism:
compared, 104–108
related, 77
Economists, as beneficiaries of disclosure, 68–69
Efficiency, defined, 72n.9
Eisenberg, Melvin Aron, 122
board of director's reform, 281–283
Eisenberg, Theodore, 257
Elections, illegal payments to candidates, 3, 6
(*See also* Sensitive payments)
Emergency Loan Guarantee Act, legislative history of Sec. 6(b) 297–299
Emergency Loan Guarantee Board, 6
composition, 292
Lockheed oversight critiqued, 299–307
mandate re Lockheed's management, 293–295, 298–299
staffing deficiencies, 303

Employees Retirement Security Act, 338, 363
Entrepreneurial margin, 27
Environment, corporate reform, 17
Environmental ethics, corporate progressive stance urged, 346–347
Environmentalists, corporate decision-making, 2
Equal Employment Opportunity Commission, 340
Equity Funding, 20, 55
Ernst & Ernst v. Hochfelder, 78n.30, 79n.37, 99n.122, 173n.234, 290n.130
Estes, Robert M., 153, 166
Ethical system, criteria for rejection, 106–108
Ewing, David, 334
Executives (*See* Managers)
Exit and voice, Hirschman's theories on, 132–134
Expediting payments, bribery contrasted, 18n.3
  (*See also* Sensitive payments)
Externalities, defined, 72n.10
Exxon Corp., sensitive payments, 321–324
  (*See also* Sensitive payments)

Fair corporate suffrage, 111, 132, 133
Fairness, to non-insiders, 99–101
Fannie Mae, 11
Federal chartering:
  administrative agency to accompany, 271
  choice-of-form difficulties, 269–271
  critiqued, 367–368
  diversity jurisdiction abolished, 238, 271–274
  Sommer's (A. A.) proposal, 270–271
  (*See also* Charters)
Federal jurisdiction (exclusive):
  benefits, 259–265
  costs, 265–268, 274
  superiority of, 262
  trial period suggested, 268–269
  (*See also* Federal-question jurisdiction; Jurisdiction; Pendent jurisdiction; State court jurisdiction)
Federal-question jurisdiction, 252–253
Federal Rule of Civil Procedure 23, 247
Federal Trade Commission:
  line-of-business program (*See* Line-of business reports)
  SEC reporting rules contrasted, 47–48
Federalism, 2, 7
  state court jurisdiction of federal corporate law, 251–258
  state/federal regulation of national corporations, 247–248
"Fictitious person," 12
Fiduciary standards:
  federal minimum standards law to set, 22–26
  quantification problems, 277
  vagueness in, benefits, 261n.102
  (*See also* Directors)
FIFO/LIFO accounting, 55–56, 96–97
Financial Accounting Standards Board, 20, 43, 47, 85
  price-indexed data recommended, 88–89
Financial analysts:
  as beneficiaries of disclosure, 68, 93
  effect on accountability, 31
Financial statements:
  certification as frustrating fraud, 50
  fraud in, 54–55, 94–96
  misrepresentation in, 55–56, 96–98

Fixed assets, replacement cost disclosure, 38, 41, 88
Fixed Income Analysts Society, 68
Forbes, 336
Foreign Corrupt Practices Act of 1977, 18n.3, 80n.39, 129, 178n.8, 208–209, 228, 311
  provisions, 5
  (*See also* Sensitive payments)
Forum non conveniens, 270
Franchard Corporation, 131, 186
Franchise taxes, as state revenue, 22, 24
Frankfurter, Felix, 113–114
Fraud:
  common law actions suggested, 78
  disclosure as frustrating, 49–51, 94–96
  financial statements, 54–55, 94–96
  objectives to achieve a law of, 79n.38
  regulation's benefit as discloser of, 90–91
  Securities Act's effect, 54–55
  U.S. Supreme Court's refashioning of, 79
  (*See also* Misrepresentation)
Free-market economy, socialism contrasted, 16
Friedman, Milton, 328
Full Employment Act of 1946, 338
Functional rationalism, 333

Galbraith, John Kenneth, 339
Gall. v. Exxon Corp., 204n.108, 321–324
Garner v. Wolfinbarger, 222–224, 226
Garnett, Ray, Jr., guidelines re directors, 188, 189, 190
General Motors:
  management practices reversed, 333–334
  staff assistance to board, 166
Germany, co-determination, 26
"Going private" transactions, SEC's proposals, 204–205
Goldberg, Arthur J., TWA directorship resigned, 165, 169 n.221, 184, 233
Goodwill, SEC mandated write-off, 46
Gould, Inc., 213
Government agencies, as beneficiaries of disclosure, 67–68
Grease payments, 312
  (*See also* Sensitive payments)
Great Britain, co-determination, 26
Great Southwest Corporation, 169
Griffin, Paul, 59–60
Growth:
  examples, 335
  Toynbee's definition, 326–327, 373
Gulf Oil Corporation, 227

Harmon, Willis, 327
Harris, Louis, 328, 329
Hart, Henry, 75–76, 105
Harvard Business Review, 149, 334, 344, 347
Hayek, F., 355
Heilbroner, Robert, 328, 329
  critiqued, 357–358, 361
Hills, Roderick M., 125, 128, 149
Hirschman, Albert O., 132–134
Historical cost accounting, 47, 89
  SEC's use of, 66

IBM, 347
  community cause contributions, 330
Illegal payments (*See* Sensitive payments)
In personam jurisdiction, and multiple presence concept, 239

Industrial Revolution, chartering, 13–14
Information:
  boards of directors:
    access to, 161–163
    proposals to improve, 282–285
  Securities Acts as beneficial to production of, 58–60, 101–102
  timeliness of disclosure, 54, 93
  usefulness criterion, 92–93
  value of, in mandated disclosure, 51–53, 101–102
  (*See also* Boards of directors)
Injunctions, SEC settlements, 286–287
Insider trading:
  market efficiency promoted by? 91
  unfairness of, 99–101
Institutional investors, growth after 1933, 103–104
Insurance companies, Connecticut's special charter, 14
Internalization of growth, U.S. examples, 327–328
Intracompany transfers, distortion of reported data, 64–65
Investment bankers, reputation as guard against fraud, 50
Investment Company Act of 1940, 123–124
  director's responsibility under, 202–203
  sec. 42(e), 192n.67
  Securities Act contrasted, 182–183
  (*See also* Securities Acts)
Investment decisions, board's quality as element, 131–132
Investor Responsibility Research Center, 133n.94
Investors:
  common stock holders, 20–21
  and corporate reform, 19–20
Jacksonian democracy, corporate charters, 14
Jacoby, Neil, 337
Jawboning, 188, 214
Jurisdiction:
  shared state-federal and exclusive federal, 259
  (*See also* Diversity jurisdiction; Federal jurisdiction; Federal question jurisdiction; In personam jurisdiction; Pendent jurisdiction; State court jurisdiction)

Kahn, Herman, 341
Karmel, Roberta A., 191
Keynes, J. M., 342
Kirk, Russell, 360, 374
Koreagate, 218
Kripke, Homer, 60, 102
Kristol, Irving, "New Class," 342–343, 363–364, 375–376
  described, 361–362

Labor unions:
  corporate decision-making, 2
  representation on corporate boards, 26–27, 365–367
Lasker v. Burks, 203
Lawyers, as beneficiaries of disclosure, 68
Leech, Noyes E., 123
Legislative history:
  "creative judicial lawmaking" as alternative, 259
  directors in Securities Acts, 184–185
  Emergency Loan Guarantee Act Sec. 6(b), 297–299
  securities acts, 111, 181–182, 206n.118
Legislatures, charter grants, 13–14
  (*See also* Charters; Federal chartering)

Leone, Robert, 339
Lewis, Ralph, M., 149
LIFO/FIFO accounting, 55–56, 96–97
Line-of-business reports:
  benefits listed, 61–62
  compliance costs, 43–45
  cost allocations, 65–66
  described, 39
  In re FTC Line-of-Business Report Litigation, 45n.17, 62n.56
  intracompany transfers, 64–65
Lockheed Aircraft Corporation, 6, 227
  history of financial problems, 292–299
  loan guarantee legislation, 291–292
Lockheed C-5A troop transport, 295
Lockheed L-1011, 292–293
Lodge, George, 328, 329, 341
  critiqued, 358–359, 360–361
Loebl, Eugene, 335
Loomis, Philip A., 189, 191, 200
Loss, Louis, 265–267, 276
Lower federal courts, caseloads, federal corporate law's effect, 244–249

Mace, Miles, 130, 154
Madden, Carl, 333
Madison, James, 180n.18
Managed income practices, 96–98
Management accountability (*See* Accountability, management)
Management compensation (*See* Compensation, management)
Managers:
  board of directors interaction with, 230–231
  business-judgment rule, 118, 124, 286n.32, 321–322
  corporate counsel/director relationships, 232–235
  corporate counsel's role with, 228–232 (*See also* Corporate counsel)
  daily concerns listed, 30–31
  Emergency Loan Guarantee Board's review of Lockheed, 300–307
  images of, 32–33
  liability for disclosure errors, 42
  Lockheed Aircraft Corporation management, 293–299
  skills needed, 32
  (*See also* Accountability; Accountability, management)
Manipulation, disclosure as frustrating, 49–51, 98–99
Manning, Bayless, 3
Marris, Robin, 119
Mason, Edward S., 120, 325
Materiality, 230
Matrix management, 334
McCormick & Co., 334–335
Means, Gardiner, 1, 20, 22, 112–113
Measurability, difficulty of, 83–84
Michigan Supreme Court, 184
Mills, Ted, 333–334
Minority shareholders, federal minimum standards to protect, 22–26
Misrepresentation:
  disclosure as frustrating, 49–51, 96–98
  financial statements, 96–98
  methods to achieve, 55
  (*See also* Fraud)
Model Business Corporation Act:
  board committees, 160
  board provisions, 122–123
Model Corporation Act, 24–25
Monopolies, charters distinguished, 13–14
Moody's Investors Service, 57, 99
Moody's Manuals, 60, 99
Multinationalization of industry, 336

Multiple presence concept, 239
Mundheim, Robert H., 123
Mutual funds, directors of, requirements, 123–124

Nader, Ralph, 250
  federal incorporation proposal, 281, 283
National Association of Securities Dealers, audit committees, 209
  (*See also* Audit committees)
National Center for Productivity and the Quality of Working Life, 334
National economic planning, 341–342
National securities market, 20
National Student Marketing Corp., 55, 187, 221n.14, 225–226, 369n.57
Negligence actions, fact-finding and law-declaring process related, 264n.107
New Deal, disclosure efforts, 38–39
New Deal Brain Trust, 112
New England Telephone, 331
New Mexico Supreme Court, state court's jurisdiction to enforce federal law, 253–255, 258
New York Stock Exchange, 93
  audit committee rule, 128–129, 130, 209, 332
    composition, 4, 211 (*See also* Audit committee)
New York Times, 184
Nixon administration, Lockheed problem, 293
  (*See also* Lockheed Aircraft Corporation)
Noninsiders, fairness to, 57, 99–101
Northrup Corporation, 202

Occupational Safety and Health Act, 340
Odell, Robert, 169–170, 173
One-person, one-vote, 21
Opportunity costs, 66, 93
Optimal quantity, defined, 51
Outside directors:
  American Assembly recommendations, 147
  assertiveness, 153–154
  audit committee makeup, 211
  conflicts of interest in selection, 152–156
  definitional problems, 368n.53
  independence of, 34–35
  monitoring as central function, 123
  nominating committee recommended, 155–156
  nominating procedures, 152–156
  Penn Central collapse, 212–213
  reelection conflicts, 154
  SEC v. Shiell, 212, 214
  SEC's convictions re responsibility, 203
  SEC's impact upon, 90
  staff assistance, 165–166
  statistics, U.S., 331–332
  Stirling Homex Corp., 150n.52, 162n.191, 211–212
  (*See also* Boards of directors; Directors)

Payments (*See* Sensitive payments)
Pendent jurisdiction, 245n.35, 266–268
  (*See also* Federal jurisdiction; Federal question jurisdiction; Jurisdiction; In personam jurisdiction; Pendent jurisdiction; State court jurisdiction)
Penn Central Company, 169–170, 212–213
Political contributions (*See* Sensitive payments)

Polaroid Corporation, hearing procedures, 330–331
Populism, corporate reform, 16–17
Preemption language, federal regulation of national corporations, 277–278
Preponderance-of-the-shareholders test, 270
Prescriptive drugs, regulation's cost, 339
Price-indexed data, FASB's recommendations, 88, 89
Principal-place-of-business test, 270, 272
Privity rule, 54, 94–95
Product-line disclosure, usefulness of, 59
Product markets, corporate conduct controlled by, 117–118
Profit maximizers, corporations as, 117n.26
Prospectuses:
- financial data in prior to 1933 Act, 55
- length and contents, 41–42

Protestant Ethic, 328
Proxies:
- board of director's disclosure rules, 137
- board's review of, 159
- corporate control mechanism, 117–118
- director's elections, disclosure proposals, 143–145
- Exchange Act jurisdiction, problems, 265–266
- federal regulation, 1–2, 6–7
- legislative history concerning, 111
- 1934 Act, 182
- original rules, 134
- SEC releases concerning, 205–206
- (*See also* Boards of directors)

Proxy statements, expansion of, 20
Public affairs programs:
- corporation's use of, 347
- identified, 345–346

Public-interest law firms, corporate reform, 17
Public opinion polls, 327
Public Utility Holding Company Act of 1935, 183
Pygmalion syndrome, 80–81, 87

Racial minorities, corporate decision-making, 2
"Race to the bottom," 22, 24, 243
Random walk, successive share price changes, 57
Reciprocal directorship relationships, 148–149
Reform of Regulation Act of 1979, 74
Registration statement, contents described, 41–42
Regulated industries:
- disclosure requirements, 38
- organizational avenues, 14

Regulation:
- costs, 339–340
- as response to corporate slowness, 340–341

Relativity, 80n.40
Research and development, Line-of-business's use of numbers criticized, 66
Ripley, William, 112–113
Robinson-Patman Act, 19, 218, 228
Roche, James, 166
Rolls-Royce, bankruptcy, 292–293
Roosevelt, Franklin D., 1933 Act support, 37
Roosevelt, Theodore, 180n.18
Rossitor, Clinton, 349
Russia, changes, 336

Sacks, Albert, 75–76, 105
Safe-harbor provision, 41

Sales, nondisclosure prior to 1934 Act, 58–59
Santa Fe Industries, Inc. v. Green, 79n.37, 80n.39, 99n.122, 128n.71, 138n.110, 218n.5
Scanlon Plan, 334
SEC v. Nat'l Student Marketing Corp., 55, 187, 221n.14, 225–226, 369n.57
SEC v. Penn Central, 212–213
SEC v. Shiell, 212, 214
Securities:
  ALI's Federal Securities Code, 265
  defined, 71n.5
Securities Act of 1933, 181–182
  Douglas's (William O.) comments, 114
  Frankfurter's (Felix) comments, 113–114
  legislative history, 111
  Roosevelt's support for, 37
  Schedule A, 183
  section 12(1), 185
  (*See also* Disclosure; Securities; Securities acts; Securities and Exchange Commission; Securities Exchange Act of 1934)
Securities acts:
  benefits of corporate disclosure, 48–49
  directors, references to, 184–187
  independence of share price changes, effect of, 58
  Investment Company Act contrasted, 182–183
  legislative history, 111, 181–182, 206n.118
  Supreme Court's curtailment of, 209–210
Securities analysts, as beneficiaries of disclosure, 68, 93
Securities and Exchange Commission:
Securities and Exchange Commission (*Cont.*)
  Advisory Committee on Corporate Disclosure, 68, 70–71, 108, 205
  Disclosure Policy Study (Wheat report), 103, 114–115
  disclosure requirements, 40–42
  FTC reporting rules contrasted, 47–48
  going private rules, 204–205
  rule 10b-5, 20, 25, 34, 173, 209–210
    limitations, 261n.102
    origins, 73
    unfair insider trading diminished, 100–101
  rule 14a-8, 187
  rule 14a-9, 173
  rule 14A, 134, 148–149
  rules re boards of directors, 4
  settlements in corporate governance and accountability, 194–199
  voluntary disclosure program, 199–202, 308–312, 318–320
Securities Exchange Act of 1934, 181–182
  disclosure requirements of, 37–38
  jurisdiction under, 265
  legislative history, 111
  records and internal accounting controls amendments proposed, 310
  Sec. 9, 185
  Sec. 12, 207
  Sec. 13(e), 204
  Sec. 14(a), 1–2
  Sec. 14(d), 204
  Sec. 15(d), 207
  Sec. 16(a), 100–101
  Sec. 18, 173
  Sec. 21(a), 213
Securities markets, public confidence in, 61, 103–104

Security investments, disclosure as enhancing efficiency, 102–103
Self-determination, growth as progress towards, 326–327, 333
Self-scrutiny reports, 318–320
  as defense to derivative suits, 320–324
Sensitive payments, 116, 191–192, 194
  congressional response to, 207
  corporate reform, 17–18
  effects on:
    management, 32–33
    share prices, 59–60
  Exxon Corp., 321–324
  Foreign Corrupt Practices Act, 5, 18n.3, 80n.39, 129, 178n.8, 208–209, 228, 311
  Gulf Oil, 227
  how corporations make them, 312–318
  Lockheed Aircraft Corporation, 6, 227, 291, 302, 305–306
  methods by which made, 313–314
  reasons for, 312
  SEC's voluntary disclosure program, 199–202, 308–312
Shareholder democracy, 1, 111–112
  corporate reform successes, 20–21
  management accountability, 29 n.9
Shareholder proposal rule, 134 n.98, 135
Shareholders:
  corporate counsel's attorney-client privilege with? 224
  proxy soliciting material, access to, 205
Sherman Act, 19
Shutdowns, 28–29
Simon, Norton, 169n.221
Sloan, Alfred, 333
Small Business Administration, 19
Smith, Adam, 375
Smith, Richard B., manager's daily concerns, 30–31
Social objectives, disclosure as tool to achieve, 115
Social questions, shareholder resolutions on, 219n.6
Social responsibility, 343–344
  corporation's duty, 2
Socialism, corporate reform, 16
"Soft" information, 142
  disclosure of, 86–87
  SEC's prohibition on publication of, 46
Sommer, A. A., 99, 190–191
  federal corporation law proposal, 250n.59, 270–271
  10b-5's limitations, 261n.102
South Africa, investment in 218, 219n.6
Split-board concept, 26–27, 365–367
Standard and Poors, 60
Standard Industrial Code:
  FTC's use of criticized, 63
  line-of-business reports, 39, 43 (*See also* Line-of-business reports)
State court jurisdiction, federal corporate law, 251–258
Stern, Fritz, 327
Stigler, George, 74
Stirling Homex Corporation, 126, 150n.152, 162n.191
Stock market crash of 1929, 180
Stock price manipulation, 56–57, 98–99
Stone, Christopher, 318, 342
  reform of internal corporate structures, 280, 282–285
Sunset laws, 269n.127
Sweden, Democracy at Work Act, 332
Synge, H., 80n.40,81

Taft, William Howard, 180n.18
Takeover bid, corporate control mechanism, 117–118
Taylor, Frederick, 333
10b-5 rule (*See* Securities And Exchange Commission)
10K's, shareholder's lack of interest in, 60
Toxic Substance Control Act, 340
Toynbee, Arnold, 326–327, 333
Tuchman, Barbara , 359–360
TWA, and Arthur Goldberg, 165, 169n.221, 184, 233
Twentieth-century utilitarianism, 75–77, 104
Type I and II errors, meaning of, 89n.69

Underwriters, SEC's impact upon, 90
Unfair competition, corporate reform, 19
Unfairness, disclosure as frustrating, 49–51, 99–101
Union Pacific Railroad, public directorships, 284n.28
United Brands, 202
United Mine Workers v. Gibbs, 266
United States Supreme Court:
  fraud law development, 79n.38
  Securities Acts, curtailment of, 209–210
  10b-5 action, 20, 34 (*See also* Securities and Exchange Commission)
United States v. Simon, 97, 98
Utilitarianism:
  economic analysis
    compared, 104–108
    related, 77
  twentieth century, 75–77, 104

Valid excuse doctrine, 270n.131
  state court's refusal to hear federal claims, 253, 256n.78
Voice and exit, Hirschman's theories on, 132–134
Voting republics, 1

Wall Street Journal, 184
Wall Street rule, 133
Walton, Clarence, 349
Watergate, 199, 218, 309, 331
Weaver, Paul, 339
Weber, Max, on bureaucracy, 317–318
Weidenbaum, Murray, 339–340
Wheat Report, 103, 114–115
Whistle blowers, 318, 334
Williams, Harold M., 175, 191, 198
  corporation as quasi-public institution, 354
  ideal board of directors, 214–215, 370n.60
Wilson, James Q., 325
Wishard, van Dusen, 351
Women, as directors, 332

Xerox Corporation, 347

Yale Express, 55
Yankelovich, Daniel, 327